The MAN in the ARENA

An Aviator's Turbulent Roller Coaster Ride to the Clouds.......

and Back

Captain Thomas L. Cooper

© 2018 Thomas L. Cooper
All Rights Reserved.

First Edition

No part of this publication may be reproduced, stored in a retrieval system, or transmitted, in any form or by any means, electronic, mechanical, photocopying, recording, or otherwise, without the written permission of the author.

First published by Dog Ear Publishing
Published by CTC Press, 2020

ISBN: 978-0-578-68654-7 (Hardcover)
ISBN: 978-0-578-68656-1 (Paperback)

Printed in the United States of America

Dedication

This book is dedicated to:

My two children and their spouses:

Cathryn Mary Brunk and Stephen

And

Thomas Paul Cooper and Melissa

And

Their lovely children

Bridgette, Bradley and Christopher Brunk

And

Jacob, Madilyn and Ryan Cooper

And finally to my lovely wife, Jerrie Ann Cooper

Without whose encouragement this book
would never have been written.

Table of Contents

"THE MAN IN THE ARENA" Theodore Roosevelt ix
Preface. xi

PART I
THE HIGH POINT YEARS
"Cranking Up and Taxiing Out"

Chapter   Page

1. Growing up in High Point, *A Simple life* 3
2. Fraley Field, *Gateway to the Sky*.. 17
3. American Legion Baseball, *Learning the game from a pro*. 23
4. Solo Flight and First Cross Country, *Ace of the Base* 25
5. Romantically Crushed. . . . . *But wait* 31
6. First "real job", Or, *Work is the curse of the young playboy pilot* 35
7. Private pilot license, *The adventures of a 'know-it-all'* 39
8. UNC, Chapel Hill, *Here I come, ready or not*. 47
9. Baseball and life at UNC, *Settling down* 56
10. Working the Air Show Circuit, *Melvin was the consummate Showman* 64
11. UNC. *The second year*. 67
12. The "Secret Plan". . . . .*Shhhhhh*. 69
13. Baseball vs Flying, *A tough decision* 70
14. An Act of Faith, *Melvin, I trust you* 74
15. The "Wind Sock" Saga, *Mom comes through* 78
16. Finalizing my "Secret Plan", *A career in aviation was almost in my grasp*. 80
17. Good-bye High Point, *Hello future*. 86

PART II
MAELSTROM
"A large and Violent Whirlpool, an Agitated State of Affairs"
Webster's Dictionary
"Climbing Out"

Chapter	Page
18 Southbound in a Buick	103
19 Busted in New Smyrna Beach	105
20 Hello Miami	107
21 First Job in Aviation....Kendall flying School	112
22 A Taylorcraft to Havana, *Automatic 'rough' over the ocean*	123
23 The Instructing Routine at 'Mary's Flight School'	128
24 "There are no small parts, only small Actors", *Stanislavski*	132
25 Piper Cub, Miami to Buenos Aires	138
26 The United States Air Force, *But not as a pilot*	158
27 Air Force surplus T-28 to Havana.....*almost !*	167
28 Flying Business picks up....., *To Havana!*	173
29 "If the Phone don't ring.....it's the Airlines," *To paraphrase an old hill-billy song"*	178
30 My First Airline job, *almost!*	184
31 Finally, my First airline job, *And the beginning of the Airline Merry-go-round*	194
32 Out of Gas, Daylight and Ideas, *Over the Jungles of Ecuador*	211
33 Continental Airlines, *The Flight Engineer's strike and the FAA Inspector's secret agenda*	224
34 Continental Airlines, *Good news, Bad news*	235
35 Back to the "Non-skeds"	242
36 Bay of Pigs, *Unwitting Accomplice*	246
37 The Airline Merry-go-round Continues	254
38 My Short Career as "Paramedic"	256
39 Same old......Same old	258
40 Engine Failure. *Mid Pacific*	265
41 Merry-go-round Continues, *Will I ever get off?*	273
42 Bound for Vientiane *With the CIA*	278
43 Saved by Eastern Airlines	281

PART III
THE EASTERN AIRLINES YEARS
"Cruising"

Chapter	Page
44 Hello Miami, Again!	297
45 Flying the "Shuttle"	303
46 Adventures on "Shuttle Standby"	310
47 A Visit by the Easter Bunny, Really!	317
48 Good bye New York......, Hello Douglas DC-7	318
49 Bob Jones and Jack Shaw, *Entrepreneurs Extraordinaire*	320
50 Soloing a Lockheed Constellation, *and other 'Jack Shaw' adventures*	324
51 Entrepreneurial "Juices" discovered	339
52 Boeing 727 school, *The party's over and a new era begins*	342
53 My short career as an ophthalmologist	348
54 Airline Owner, *This Airline Management stuff is easy*	350
55 Back to College, *Embry Riddle Aeronautical University at thirty-four years of age*	367
56 Another Airline venture, *I'm a slow learner*	369
57 Remembering the Bahamas, *Bimini and Chub Cay*	371
58 CUBA! *Rekindling a love for Cuba after seventeen years*	379
59 Boeing 727 engine failure, *Training pays off*	394
60 Storm Clouds at Eastern, *Labor strife "ramp" up*	400
61 STRIKE!	410
62 Revolution in Guatemala, *You've just won the airport.... Now let's use it*	420
63 Flying through the strike	426
64 From number one "SCAB" to union Boss..	432
65 Eastern Airlines ceases operations	444

PART IV
GULFSTREAM INTERNATIONAL AIRLINES
"Approach and Landing"

66 Beginning All Over, *with Nothing*	463
67 Cape Haitian.....*first route*	468
68 Resurrecting Aerial Transit Airlines, *My EAL pals to the rescue*	472
69 SABOTAGE!	479
70 Expansion, *Routes awarded into the Bahamas but no aircraft*	483
71 Secretary Vs. Receptionist? *An angel interviews*	492

Chapter	Page
72 Undercapitalized and Understaffed, *Full Speed Ahead*	496
73 Hurricane Andrew	503
74 Faith, Hope and Beechcraft	508
75 Frank Lorenzo Called, *Will the Eastern wound never heal ?*	514
76 Expansion to Key West, *WOW, I've always wanted one of these Coconut heads.*	518
77 Further expansion and capital from an unlikely source	521
78 Senator George McGovern, *Fellow aviator, gentleman and pal*	527
79 Cayman Brac, *Well, it looked good on paper*	529
80 Aviation Insurance, *Simply Complex!*	534
81 Five Years, *The company has survived and so has the Union grudge*	541
82 "Tea with Tom," *And the Florida Panthers Rat Mascot Saga*	545
83 The Highs and Lows continue, *Our Chief Pilot goes with Sir Freddy*	548
84 Continental Connection, *But the highs and lows continue*	551
85 DISASTER, *The 9-11 survival story*	566
86 Lunch with Fidel	572
87 Winding down, *Unwinding the Continental Airlines arrangement, saying good-bye to an old friend and health issues.*	577
88 To retire or not to retire?	583
89 Retired......almost	588
90 With George McGovern and Wayne Smith in Havana	590
91 The Cuban Operation, *Labor of Love*	595
92 Good bye Senator McGovern	601
93 Sadly, It was time to sell the Cuban Operation	603
94 The Last Aviation Enterprise....... *Gone!*	607
Epilogue	609
Acknowledgements	627

Photographs and Illustrations

		AFTER PAGE
PART I,	The High Point Years	87
PART II,	Maelstrom	281
PART III,	The Eastern Airlines Years	447
PART IV,	Gulfstream International Airlines	610

The Man in The Arena

It is not the critic who counts, not the man who points out how the strong man stumbled or where the doer of deeds could have done better.

The credit belongs to the man who is actually in the arena; whose face is marred by dust and sweat and blood, who strives valiantly; who errs and comes short again and again; who knows the great enthusiasms, the great devotions, and spends himself in a worthy cause; who, at the best, knows in the end the triumph of high achievement; and who, at the worst, if he fails, at least fails while daring greatly, so that his place shall never be with those cold and timid souls who know neither victory nor defeat.

Theodore Roosevelt

Preface

I suppose that if I had any great regret in my life, it would be that I didn't spend enough time with my grandparents. It wasn't that I didn't enjoy my time with them; on the contrary, I considered it precious, and the stories they told, especially the ones told by my mother's father, Fred Franklin, were wonderful.

The regret that I have is simply that I didn't insist on more stories about their parents and ancestors and that I didn't keep some record of the stories that they did tell.

As I was growing up in a small community just south of High Point, North Carolina, I was privileged to know all four of my grandparents. My mother's parents lived nearby, and I spent much more time with them than I did with my father's parents. Dad's parents still lived in his hometown of Albemarle, North Carolina, fifty miles southeast of High Point.

It is with that guilty admission that I have decided to record, for my grandchildren, my remembrances of those early days with my parents and grandparents and also to share some moments of my life that they might find interesting.

I begin my story, not at the beginning, but strangely enough at the end. Well, not at the final end, but at the ripe old age of eighty, close enough.

I wedged myself into the copilot's seat next to Stephen Fisher, the captain of his Piper Cherokee, for a short forty-minute flight from Sebastian, Florida, to my home in Wellington, Florida…

Stephen had just bought a small aviation company that I had owned for the past five years at the airport at Sebastian, Florida. He had picked me up in his airplane earlier in the morning. We had closed the transaction with the usual paperwork, he gave me a cashier's check, and now he generously offered to fly me back to my home in Wellington, Florida.

He went through the usual preflight checks, started the engine, and taxied to the active runway. The small airport had no tower, so the normal procedure was to announce your intentions over the aircraft's radio in the "blind," and wait for an answer. If no other aircraft were in the traffic pattern, you would simply take off.

No other aircraft answered, so Stephen looked at me and asked, through the intercom radio, "Ready?" I nodded "Okay" and he proceeded with the takeoff roll. The aircraft sped down the runway and he gently raised the nose and lifted it off.

We were on our way to Wellington.

As we climbed southward, I began to realize that, after sixty continuous years, the final chapter of my aviation career had ended. I no longer had any commercial aviation interest at all and I was effectively…retired.

Stephen was climbing toward our cruising altitude of 6,500 feet. It was a beautiful day, and I allowed my mind to wander back to how it all began.

PART I
The High Point Years

Cranking up and taxiing out

CHAPTER 1
Growing Up in High Point

A simple life

I CAN'T REMEMBER A TIME when I didn't have a love affair with airplanes. I'm not sure where or when the aviation bug bit me but as I think back, I have vivid memories of the airplanes of World War II. I was born on May 26, 1936 and was almost six years old when the war started. I remember that I was infatuated by the vast array of airplanes that I would see in the newspapers and in newsreels at my infrequent visits to the movies. I also had two relatives—Ed Franklin, my uncle, and A. B. Salley, a cousin, both about twelve to fourteen years older than I was—who were aviation enthusiasts, and they had a great influence on me.

I spent my early years cutting out cardboard airplanes, and as I grew older, I began to build model airplanes. In the beginning they were powered by rubber bands and later, in my early teens, small gasoline engines. I even made some tiny airplanes and powered them with June bugs. That was a tedious project, consisting of first catching the bugs, placing them in the refrigerator until they were numb, and then, at the exact time, removing them and gluing their hind legs to the airplane before they woke up. As I remember, the fascination with that grew thin: first because Mother didn't appreciate my use of the fridge, but mostly, when the June bugs woke up, they flew off with the airplane in tow and the recovery was never successful.

As I look back on my early years in High Point, the odds of me becoming an airline pilot and later an aviation entrepreneur were highly unlikely. No one in my immediate family had any interest in aviation at all. My father had witnessed an air crash at Myrtle Beach, South Carolina, and was adamant that I should not enter aviation. He believed that the ideal career field was in professional baseball, and with his encouragement, that became my early goal in life…to become a baseball player.

My father was a grocer. My earliest memories are of being at his grocery store, sitting by a big potbellied stove while he waited on his customers and of Mother ringing up the cash register.

Dad was raised in Albemarle, North Carolina, and in his early twenties, he moved to High Point and worked in the hosiery mills for a while.

Dad's father, Thomas Lee Cooper, was the owner of Carolina Printing Company and one of Albemarle's most prominent citizens. He married Mary Ella Craven in 1898. Ma Cooper, as I called her, was raised in Randolph County. One of her relatives, Mr. Braxton Craven, was a co-founder of Trinity College, serving for forty years as its president. It was then located in Trinity, North Carolina, but was later renamed Duke University and moved to near Durham, North Carolina.

Ma Cooper was very political and religious as evidenced by the name she gave my father. She told me that she gave Dad the name of Paul Washington because she wanted him to be either a preacher or a president.

My mother, Pearl Francis Franklin, was born in High Point. Her father was Fred McCoy Franklin and her mother was Bertha Ann Newton.

Grandpa Franklin was a carpenter and woodworker by trade. To say he was a woodworker is a gross understatement. He was a gifted master at his craft and was highly respected in our community for the making of musical instruments, cross-hatching shotgun stocks by hand, and cabinetmaking. He was a wonderful five-string banjo player and won many musical contests throughout the state.

Grandma Franklin was a hardworking woman. Even after Grandpa Franklin retired, she continued to work as a seamstress at one of the commercial factories in High Point, and she remained there until Grandpa Franklin became ill with a stroke.

Dad went into business for himself about the time I was born. He borrowed fifty dollars from Grandpa Franklin and, with my uncle Robert, opened up a grocery store. The partnership lasted about a month, when Dad took over sole ownership of the venture. He never borrowed a dollar from anyone after that and he never got involved in any partnership for the rest of his life.

Dad's store was located about a mile south of the High Point city limits on South Main Street Extension. It was small, consisting of two aisles, with a meat market in the rear and a checkout counter in the front. About halfway back on the right was a potbellied stove that was used to heat the building during the winter. Outside, in the front, was an overhang roof on which were two Coca-Cola signs and a large, round sign advertising Gulf gasoline. Under the overhang was a Coca-Cola machine and two gasoline pumps. The gasoline pumps were the gravity-feed types. If someone purchased ten gallons of gas, Dad would hand pump that quantity up into the glass bowl at the top of the tank, and with the spout of the hose in the fuel receptacle of the car, gravity would dispense the fuel.

There was a sign hung prominently from the overhang, "CLOSED ON SUNDAY."

In the afternoon, the old men of the neighborhood would gather out there under the roof and discuss the current topics or just gossip. They would sit there, on Coke crates, drinking their favorite soft drinks. Usually they would pour salted peanuts into the drink while expounding on the progress of the war or the pros and cons of the proposed church extension or the latest baseball scores.

Until I was about four years old, we lived next to the store in a rented house that was separated from the store by a narrow alley.

Mother would walk over to the store at around three o'clock daily to help Dad as that was when the mills in town let out and his regular customers would come by to buy groceries for their evening meals. She would handle the checking out and the cash register. Since Dad was known locally as the best meat cutter in the area, he enjoyed a large clientele based on the quality of his meat products, so in the afternoons he was always busy back in the meat department.

Dad had to manage by himself on Saturdays since Mother was a Seventh Day Adventist. From time to time he would hire a neighborhood teenager to help out, but he didn't like that much. Most of the time he just worked it alone.

The alley by the store is where I learned to ride a bicycle. I was about four years old and Dad bought me a half-size bike. When no customers were inside he would take me to the alley and push me along, as this was before training wheels. I can distinctly remember the day he "soloed" me. He was pushing me along when suddenly he turned me loose, stepped back, and there I was, riding all by myself. It was euphoric! I recall thinking that not only was this easy, it was fun. Then, unfortunately, I came to the end of the alley, and I learned the hard way that riding a bike might be easy but stopping is more difficult. Dad helped me up, surveyed any damage, and declared that with a few more lessons, I'd be okay to ride by myself. It wasn't long before I had the whole thing solved.

Somewhere around 1940, Dad and Mom had our own home built. It was on Moore Avenue, about three blocks from Dad's store. The street was graveled, not paved, and Mother always had a fit about the dust. Our home was a nice little two-bedroom brick structure and Dad bought the two adjoining lots to ensure privacy. When we moved in there were only four homes on the street, and there was plenty of room to grow up in.

Dad had a small barn built at the back end of the lots as his hobby was horseback riding, and I used the corner lot for the neighborhood baseball field. There were only about four or five local boys in the neighborhood as I was growing up. But closer to town there were a few more boys, and we would get together for a game from time to time on the weekends.

The only downer that I can remember about that period was that Mom decided that I should become a violinist. To further complicate things, there was a Mrs. Crowson who lived about two blocks away and she was a violin teacher. Mother took me to town to the music store and purchased a half-size violin and hired Mrs. Crowson to teach me to play the instrument. My heart wasn't really in it… I liked Dad's idea best about me being a professional baseball player, but Mother prevailed and for some time I took lessons. It was bad enough having to lug the violin down to Mrs. Crowson's house in front of the neighborhood kids, but practicing was just too much to expect of a five-year-old. I learned the basics of the instrument, but a tragic event caused my violin career to come to an abrupt end. Mrs. Crowson's husband was killed in a bus accident and she moved away.

I never resumed lessons after that, but I did play with Grandpa Franklin a lot and instead of becoming a violinist I became somewhat of a fiddler. After he fell ill I never picked up the violin again.

It wasn't long, thereafter, that my first great adventure happened…I started grade school. It is as clear as if it were yesterday. Mom watched the store and Dad drove me to Allen Jay High School. Allen Jay was located out in the middle of the farm country about five miles from our home. It was a low, single-story building built in the shape of an "H." The "H" housed all of twelve grades beginning from first grade up through the twelfth, and in the middle of the "H" was the auditorium and principal's office.

There was an athletic field at the back of the schoolhouse with not one blade of grass. Finally, there was a gymnasium at the east side. My fellow first graders numbered about twenty-five, and my first-grade teacher's name was Mrs. Inghram. She was an older lady, really old—I suppose, at the time, she had to have been up around forty-five or fifty years old!

After the first couple of days of being shepherded by my parents to school, it became apparent that I should learn to catch the school bus. That was another great adventure. I learned a lot about life riding that school bus. I learned about timeliness and, oddly enough, I learned about discrimination.

The bus made numerous stops along its route and the nearest stop to our house was down on South Main Extension in front of Ellington's Bar and Grill. So far so good, except that if you didn't get to the bus stop on time, the bus driver would leave you. Then you would have to scurry home and explain to your mother as to how you were late and that she would have to drive you to school. This, to Mom, got old very quickly, and sometimes Dad would get involved—and that's the last thing that you would want to happen. It was just a lot better to be at the bus stop on time.

With regards to discrimination, the seat layout of the bus consisted of, not forward-facing seats, but benches running from the front to the back of the bus. There were side benches on each side and one long bench running down the center. The side benches were higher and they were designated for the upper classmen. The center bench was for us "lower" classmen and we hated it. To make it worse, if the school bus driver caught you slipping over to the side bench, he would stop the bus and rap on the ceiling, making such a racket that it could be quite embarrassing. Supposedly, if you were a continuous pest, you could be banned from the bus, and that would take some explaining to your parents. There was no recourse; no sit-ins, no protest marches, and any complaints to our parents fell on deaf ears. This issue would be settled with time only. One would have to tolerate the "injustice" until one was in the sixth grade or the school busses were replaced. I forget which happened first.

First grade was a fairly easy transition for me. In our area, we didn't have a kindergarten program, and being an only child, I had not enjoyed a lot of camaraderie with other kids other than at church, Additionally I had no preschool training with regards to reading, writing, and arithmetic, so I looked forward to this adventure with some trepidation. However, since my fellow classmates all came from similar backgrounds, we all started from a level playing field, so I don't recall a great deal of inter-class competition as we all tackled the great issues of learning numbers and the alphabet with equal energy and wonderment. I have fond memories of my early grade school years.

I do recall one incident that led to me being "most popular" in my class. It had nothing to do with my personality. My father showed up one day with a large box of cherry red lollypops for everyone. At the time the class loved it. At that moment I was "big man on campus" but later, and for many years, my classmates wouldn't forget that, and I took a lot of good-natured ribbing.

On reflecting on my time at Allen Jay, I don't think, at the time, that I really appreciated the atmosphere of "family" that existed there. Of the twenty-five fellow students in first grade, I graduated from the twelfth grade with twenty-two of them. We matured from first graders into grown-up adults and I don't think we ever stopped to notice.

World War II started, for the United States, in 1941, just before I started grade school. Although I was only five years old when the war started, I still have vivid memories of it. There were convoys of trucks filled with army material and troops traveling down South Main Street toward Fort Bragg; U.S. War Bond drives were promoted everywhere; furniture factories in High Point were converted to the manufacturing of aircraft parts; fuel was rationed, and the sky was filled with wonderful airplanes. I remember that everyone, not just the soldiers, was at war.

My mother was a strong woman. I only saw her cry once; when my uncle Ed Franklin, her baby brother, went off to war. He stopped by our house on Moore Avenue to say good-bye. He brought me a model airplane that he had just completed and he spent some time with Mother. When he left, he told her not to worry as he wiped a tear from her eye. I remember that moment well; it wasn't the last tear she would shed that day.

Uncle Ed went off to war and came back three years later. My cousin A. B. Salley wasn't so lucky. He wanted to be an Air Force pilot but his eyesight wasn't good enough, so he enlisted in the Army. He was wounded on D-Day but rejoined his group and was killed in France shortly thereafter. His remains, today, lie buried in France with his fallen buddies.

My elementary school years were relatively easy for me. I enjoyed school and the life in our neighborhood was simple. Dad would go to work every day except Sundays, and Mom would help me dress for school on school days. She and Grandma Franklin would attend the Seventh Day Adventist Church in town on Saturdays, and Dad would attend the Springfield Quaker Church in our neighborhood on Sundays. I don't think Dad was that religious; he just attended that church because most of his customers at the grocery store attended and it was, commercially, the smart thing to do. I attended church on both Saturday and Sunday until I was about sixteen years old. I always thought that I was getting cheated out of one play day each week. I made the most of it though by sitting in the back of the church with a pencil and pad drawing airplanes.

Being exposed to two different religious denominations simultaneously can be quite confusing to a small child, and such was the case with me. I remember once, after an exceptionally emotional sermon at the Adventist church, asking Mother why there was more than one church. Her answer was wise and simple, and I understood the answer perfectly. "Well, Tommy, there is a heaven and to get there, there are several different roads. The Quakers have one road and the Adventists have another but they all lead to the same place." That simple explanation has remained with me and it has come to my mind more than once since.

Our family recreation consisted of a Sunday afternoon drive, either up to the mountains or down to Albemarle to visit my grandparents. Ma and Pa Cooper lived in a large, two-storied, wood-frame house built in 1910 on a very large corner lot. It had a front porch that extended from the front of the house around both the sides, and the house was cooled by a number of giant oak trees. Across from the house, on the side street was a giant cylindrical water tower that could be seen for miles. The house was elegant but quite old as evidenced by an abandoned "privy" in the rear of the backyard. A regular bathroom was added by partitioning off part of the back porch, and that modernized the house quite nicely.

Pa Cooper's hobby was gardening and he kept a garden in a large back lot at the rear of their home. I can remember always having fresh tomatoes, corn, okra, and anything else that might be in season when we visited.

I don't recall going upstairs at the Cooper home ever. My dad's younger brother, Bobby, was killed by a neighborhood friend while playing with a loaded gun at the neighbor's house, and from then on, his bedroom just wasn't used much. Although Dad kept a 22-caliber rifle at our house, I was never allowed anything that resembled a firearm, not even a BB rifle as I was growing up.

Pa Cooper was a tall, thin man who was very quiet. He was raised on a farm in the area but later in life he took up printing as a livelihood. His company was very successful and his customers were located throughout the state. He would travel around the state and take orders for his print shop, return to Albemarle, produce the printed materials, and on his next trip, deliver the order. As a businessman, he traveled a lot and, as was his custom, he would tip a waiter if the service was good. I used to love to travel with him and Ma Cooper. When we would stop to eat, Pa Cooper would leave a tip of twenty-five cents. Ma Cooper would scoop it up as we left the table and give it to me. That endeared her to me tremendously.

I have always had a keen interest in my ancestry and I suppose that Ma Cooper is the reason for that. She was very active in researching her family's background, and I can remember listening to her talk for hours about her forefathers. Her mother was an Albright and she owned a book outlining that family's ancestry as far back as the House of Hapsburg, 662 A.D. As a youngster, I took such an interest in that book when I would visit her that she willed it to me at her passing. It, with Ma Cooper's copious margin notes, is now one of my prized possessions.

I recall, on several occasions, she would come up from Albemarle, pick me up, and we would go exploring graveyards in and around Guilford County. She would equip us with pencil and paper for the recording of names and dates. There were some gravestones that were so old, she would have me hold the paper over the eroded inscriptions while she rubbed the pencil over the paper to create a negative inscription so that we could accurately record the data.

Pa Cooper was a fixture in Albemarle. He could be seen every Sunday afternoon, after church, sitting on the front porch in his favorite rocking chair enjoying the cool shade of the large oak trees that surrounded the house.

Our only other family outing was an annual Fourth of July trip to Myrtle Beach. Dad would hire one of Mother's brothers to watch the store on a Saturday and we would leave Friday evening for the beach. We always stayed at a small inn called Rambler's Rest. It was a block from the ocean; Dad could walk over and "surf" fish. By noon on Sunday we would pack up and head back home so Dad could open the store on Monday.

Once, we heard of a special fishing spot south of Myrtle Beach called Murrell's Inlet. There was a pier that reached out past some marshland that was occasionally used by the navy for maneuvers. The fishing was good but the thing that I remember most about Murrell's Inlet was that the road between Myrtle Beach and the pier went by a World War II German prisoner-of-war camp. As we drove by, just a few feet from the wire fence, we could see the German prisoners up close. It was somewhat confusing to me. They looked absolutely normal, not as I imagined a German soldier to look,

They could have been my uncles, my dad's customers, or even my dad. It was later in life that I began to understand the politics of war and the effectiveness of mass hypnosis. Actually, I have never figured it out completely.

Sometimes small things stay with you. I was six or seven years old and we were on our annual three-day vacation to Myrtle Beach when one such instance happened.

Dad had gone fishing at the beach across from our small motel. We were to join him later after Mom had straightened up the room. I was helping her make up the bed and I was in a hurry because I wanted to get to the beach quickly. Disregarding a rumpled sheet, I pulled the bedspread up over it and reached for the pillows to finish the job. Mom stopped me at that point and instructed me to smooth out the rumpled sheets under the bedspread. "What's the use? Nobody will know that the sheets are not smoothed out," I said.

"I will," she replied quietly as she smoothed out the sheets and finished making up the bed. "I will."

Mom and Dad taught me, not by lectures, but by example. This was one such example; do the right thing, even if nobody's watching.

The beach trip always seemed like a forced march, but I loved the water and looked forward to that part of the year.

World War II came to an end in 1945 during my third year of school. Dad had moved his grocery business a few blocks up the street to a larger location, and my grandparents, Mother's parents, built a home on Moore Avenue next to ours and moved there.

It was during that time that I really bonded with Grandpa Franklin. He was a big, barrel-chested, handsome man with a full head of wavy white hair. He had built a workshop next to his new house on Moore Avenue, and he and I wiled away many happy hours there. People came from miles around to have him do special woodworking projects for them. He was very painstaking with his work and took no shortcuts. I can remember him taking days to hand crosshatch rifle stocks for some of his clients. He was kept busy by repairing musical instruments for the local folks in High Point.

He was an absolutely wonderful banjo picker. He would play his five-string banjo with such clarity and ease that the music would flow effortlessly from the instrument. Saturday night was a special night for me as Grandpa Franklin and several of his buddies would get together and "make music". There was a fiddler, a guitar picker, and Grandpa on the banjo. *Such music they would produce*! And they did it for their own entertainment, as there was usually no one there to listen except me. Grandma Franklin would go to another room and read her Bible and I would just sit and enjoy the music.

There was an interesting old man, a vagrant, who used to stop by several times a year. His name was Danner Johnson and he was probably the best musician I have ever seen or heard. He dressed in old ragged bib overalls and his shoes were practically worn out. His hair was uncut and scraggly and his long white beard was permanently stained with tobacco juice. He claimed to have been a trumpet player for the famous John Philip Sousa of marching band fame, but now his teeth were in such bad shape that he couldn't play that instrument anymore. But if an instrument had strings, he could play it. He played the violin so softly and sweetly that you would have to lean toward him to hear it. The guitar he played wonderfully well and he approached my granddad's skill level on the banjo. Heaven only knows what else he could play.

He would come walking up unceremoniously. Grandpa Franklin would welcome him graciously, as he loved the old man's music, but Grandma Franklin didn't share Grandpa's enthusiasm for Danner's visits. As a matter of fact, she wouldn't allow him in the house, unless he needed a bathroom break, and so his impromptu concerts were always on the front porch on Moore Avenue. She would fix him something to eat, but it was served on the front porch. She would also pack him a lunch, just to make sure he didn't stay for dinner.

He would stay a while, play some music with Grandpa, and just as stealthily depart down the street, brown bag in hand. We never knew where he stayed.

The last time I saw Danner was in Randleman, North Carolina. Grandpa Franklin got word that he was living in a barn about ten miles south of our house, so we decided to go visit him. Mother watched the store and Dad, Grandpa, and I took off for Randleman. We found Danner just where we were told, living in a barn. He seemed pleased to see us and we had a grand ole time with him. I brought my violin, Grandpa his banjo, and we took a guitar also. Danner entertained us royally with a repertoire of wonderful music on each of the instruments, and I have precious memories of him and Grandpa Franklin taking turns dancing a sort of soft shoe on the straw-covered floor of that old barn in Randleman.

In 1948, Mom and Dad built a larger house across the street at 206 Moore Avenue. It was brick and had three bedrooms. It was built on a slight elevation, and with the windows open, a nice breeze was always present.

I had my own room, paneled with knotty pine, and the walls were decorated with pictures of airplanes. I was extremely conscious about my height as to become a professional baseball player I would need to be at least six feet tall. I tracked my height regularly by pencil marks on the edge of my bedroom door.

At about that time, eleven or twelve years of age, my main interest was baseball. I outgrew the small field next to our old house and joined a baseball league called the Red Shield League. The league was organized by the Salvation Army and each team was sponsored by a civic organization such at the Lions Club, Rotary Club, Optimist Club, etc. It was great! Each team had uniforms, the bats weren't taped, and the baseballs weren't unraveling. I could catch the city bus for ten cents in front of Dad's grocery store and it would drop me off near the ball field. I played for three summers and it was a wonderful stepping-stone in preparation for playing for Allen Jay's high school varsity baseball team.

Grade school was fast coming to an end. There wasn't much fanfare at Allen Jay when you were promoted from eighth grade to ninth. There had been an additional classroom building built recently out back of the original schoolhouse, and that's where the high school classes were held. We simply went home after the last day of eighth grade and came back three months later and were in high school. It was a bit different from grade school in that although we had a homeroom teacher, each teacher specialized in a particular subject and we would change rooms for each subject to accommodate the teacher's schedule and specialty.

High school at Allen Jay was a meaningful experience. Most of my fellow classmates had begun school with me eight years earlier, our teachers were dedicated in their responsibilities to us, and there were few issues that required harsh discipline. In our senior year our class went to Washington, DC, on a field trip, and our football team visited the University of North Carolina.

Those trips have faded into vague memories, but one event has stayed with me to this day. Mr. O. E. Moye was the history specialist during my high school years and he was also the mentor for a boy's organization called the "Hi Y" Club, an affiliate of the YMCA. We would meet regularly in the evenings, and the discussions would center generally on current events and other subjects that would not come up in the classroom.

One night, Mr. Moye announced that, based on his request, we had been invited to visit a Jewish synagogue in High Point. Although I had no idea just what the Jewish religion was, I was happy to attend, and I think, on purpose, Mr. Moye didn't brief us.

We arrived at the appointed time and the rabbi greeted us graciously. The meeting went well and the rabbi gave us a wonderful lecture on the history of the Jewish people and their beliefs. Somewhere toward the end of the talk, he explained that the Jewish people did not believe that Jesus Christ was the Son of God but that he was a particularly good man who was a good teacher.

Once we returned to Allen Jay, Mr. Moye reviewed the visit with us and reiterated what the rabbi had explained. I was still somewhat confused as I was still attending church on Saturday *and* Sunday and the preaching that I had heard in those classes were quite contrary. It was only when I combined my mother's explanation about more than one road leading to heaven with Mr. Moye's "debriefing," which was almost the same as Mom's, that I felt that I understood the complex issue. That evening was a very meaningful experience and lives with me today. I wonder if Mr. Moye knew of the influence that he had on me and how a simple act, a visit to a Jewish synagogue, could mold a youngster's conscience for a lifetime.

In the summer of 1952 a greatly anticipated event took place. I turned sixteen and was eligible for my driver's license. We didn't have a driver's education class at Allen Jay, so the responsibility to teach me to drive fell on Dad's shoulders. I remembered Dad teaching me to ride a bicycle thirteen years earlier. What could possibly go wrong?

We went down to the courthouse for the driving instruction pamphlet so that I could learn the rules of the road. The training vehicle of choice was Dad's Chevrolet pickup truck.

So far so good, except that the truck was a stick shift. I was sure that I would never learn to do three things at one time. You had to simultaneously let off the gas, push in the clutch—"Let's see, which pedal is the clutch and which is the brake?"—While moving a lever attached to the steering wheel to some imaginary position while trying to stay on your side of the road. To further complicate the issue, you had to release the clutch pedal at a proper rate so as not to stall the engine.

Well, like the bicycle episode, I figured it out pretty quickly and the big day came when I took the driving test. It went fine. Well, the parallel parking part wasn't something to write home about, but I managed and I was issued a driver's license.

I soon convinced Dad I needed a car. We shopped around and finally settled on a 1948 two-door Chevrolet. It was black with lots of chrome and in general, a nice-looking car. The only deal was that I had to pay for all gas, oil, tires, and maintenance. Dad would pay the insurance. And, oh yes, I could go anywhere I wanted to go in the new-used car except the local community airport, Fraley Field. I'll talk about that later.

Along with the advent of the driver's license and the car came other issues. In addition to all the safety items, which Dad covered nicely—Don't follow too closely; mind the speed limit; and you should drive as if the other driver is crazy—there were two other decisions that had to be made. The first one was centered around the grocery store. At sixteen years of age, I was old enough to help Dad at the store on weekends, and that also sprung me from having to go to church, at least on Saturdays. I welcomed the new responsibility as it gave me some spending money, but I never really warmed up to the grocery business. I did, however, like it better than going to church.

It was the summer of '52 and I began my working career at Dad's grocery store. I usually got stuck with pricing and replacing the canned goods on the shelves, sorting out the soda bottles that the customers redeemed for deposit money, and delivering grocery orders that the customers called in.

The bottle sorting was the absolute worst job I ever had. The returns were stored in a small side room adjacent to the store, and the temperature in there was always either too hot or too cold. Additionally, it seemed that every bottle housed at least one cockroach. I hated that job.

The second decision that had to be addressed was that upon getting a driver's license and a car, tradition had it that you must have a "steady."

All the older boys in my class and the upper classmen had cars, and they all had steady girlfriends. With all the eligible girls taken, and since many young ladies weren't allowed to "court" at an early age, the selection was slim.

Fate stepped in and bailed me out. The Tuttle family became customers of our grocery store and when Mrs. Tuttle ordered her groceries over the phone, we would deliver to her. On my first delivery I discovered to my delight that she had two lovely teenage daughters, Bobbie Leigh and Donnie. Wonderful!

I looked forward with great anticipation to Mrs. Tuttle's call and order. "Dad," I would ask, "has Mrs. Tuttle called in yet?" "No, son," he would answer and I would return to the cave of "bottle hell" and continue sorting.

When that glorious moment came—"Son, Mrs. Tuttle just called and she needs some groceries"—I would spring into action: shirt tail tucked in, hands washed, and hair slicked down, I was ready for the delivery. Dad would collect the groceries, add up the bill, sack up the groceries, and off I would go.

The Tuttles lived three or four miles away, over beyond Springfield Church. I would pull up in the driveway, grab the groceries, knock on the front door, and pray that Bobbie Leigh, who was becoming my favorite, would answer. More often than not she would, and I would smartly deliver the groceries to the kitchen, trying to say something clever like "Nice weather" and she would come back with just as clever a response, "Yes, it is."

As the summer wore on, I finally got up my nerve to ask Bobbie Leigh out. There was a popular movie coming to town, and during a grocery delivery I blurted out, "Do you want to go to the movies Saturday night?" To my surprise she answered, "Yes, I would, but I have to ask my mother first. Can I call you later?" What a relief. She didn't say no. I was so afraid of rejection. "Yes, I'll be at the store." "Okay," she said, and I left.

Bobbie Leigh's parents said yes and we went out. The date went okay. We went to the movie and later stopped by the White House Barbecue, a popular drive-in on South Main Street for a sandwich and Coke. I also wanted to show off my date. Since Bobbie Leigh was on a strict curfew, we went home early and I saw her to the door. Incidentally, I was on a strict curfew also. I said that I had a good time and she said that she had had a good time too, and as I turned to leave, she reached up and gave me a peck on the cheek. I almost fainted. Bobbie Leigh disappeared through the door and I staggered back to my car. Wow, this Bobbie Leigh was some great girl. She obviously knew more about this dating stuff than I did, and I decided then and there that my "steady" problem, issue number two, had been solved.

Solved at least from my end.

When Dad bought me the '48 Chevy in the summer of '52, the only caveat that came with the deal was that I shouldn't go near the local airport, Fraley Field. I'd been there a few times before, but I had never visited at length or struck up a conversation with anyone there.

The next day I was at Fraley Field.

CHAPTER 2

Fraley Field

Gateway to the sky

FRALEY FIELD. IT WAS WONDERFUL. It really didn't match up to any airport that you might compare it to by today's standards. It wouldn't even match up to a good cornfield. The runways were short and rough. The main runway ran up a slight incline and, on takeoff, as you crested the top, you must make a small right turn as you lifted off in order to miss an apple tree and a service station.

There were two large wooden hangars that were of early World War II construction and both were in a terrible state of repair. Attached to one was a small room that was used as the business office. Some homemade benches surrounded a wood burning stove and a dilapidated showcase served as a counter for the meager amount of business that was conducted there. Across the field there were two small hangars built in the form of the letter "T" which held one aircraft each. Up on the hill, near where the runways crossed, stood the frame of what used to be a windsock. It was useless now because the cloth "sock" part had long since rotted away and had not been replaced. There was a dilapidated World War II biplane trainer, a Stearman, parked outside, next to one of the hangars with "Civil Air Patrol" faded and barely recognizable painted on its tail. A reminder of earlier times, on which the weather had taken its toll, she would never fly again.

The usual "hangar flyers" would congregate around the office in the afternoons and on weekends to share "war" stories. There was Dwight Lohr, a flying traveling salesman, Melvin Robinson, an airshow entrepreneur, and Pete Dickens, who was my absolute hero. Pete was an airline pilot for

Piedmont Airlines and flew DC-3s. A small fellow, he could have been Eddie Fisher's twin brother. A few others might be loosely considered in the group, but these were the stars.

The unofficial "uniform" of this group consisted of Levi's or khakis, an old army surplus zipper jacket, and one final item. This was almost mandatory; leather flying boots. The boots were the slip-on kind that pulled up over your ankles for about eight inches, and if you were really "cool," you could make one pant leg stay out while the other would hang up over the rear of the boot top.

Mr. and Mrs. John Spencer ran the airport. Mr. Spencer was a lumber salesman by trade who spent his afternoons and weekends at the airport giving flight instruction and pumping gas. Mrs. Spencer—the older fellows called her Rosie, but I always called her Mrs. Spencer—ran the operation Monday through Friday.

The business consisted of a few airplane tie-down rentals, fuel sales, and some flight training. Mr. spencer did the flight instructing and most of the local pilots would pump their own gas and just report the amount to Mrs. Spencer.

That's the picture I saw as I drove up to the airport that summer's day of '52.

It was a Sunday. I got out of my car with no apparent intention except to look around, and I ran into Mr. Spencer. He was not large in stature, of medium build with a full head of white hair. He introduced himself and asked if he could help me. I allowed that I had always had a keen interest in flying and was an avid model plane builder and someday I might like to be a pilot. He said that he was a flight instructor and he asked me if I'd ever been up in a plane. I explained that I had never been up before, but I wanted to someday. "Well," he said, "why not today?" He explained that a full hour of training would cost nine dollars, but a thirty-minute demonstration flight was only five.

Since Dad had paid me Saturday night, I was practically rich. I did some quick budgetary calculations considering my new social obligations, and before I knew it I was walking with Mr. Spencer toward his two-seater, Taylorcraft airplane. He explained to me that a Taylorcraft airplane is almost the same as a Piper Cub except the seats are side-by-side instead of front and back and that they both use the same type of engine.

I watched as Mr. Spencer did a quick "walk-around" as he called it and after checking the oil quantity in the engine he motioned for me to get into the right-hand seat. He called over to one of the hangar flyers for a prop. This totally confused me, as I was sure that there was a propeller on the airplane when I got in and I wondered why we would need another one. I was to learn quickly that these airplanes had no electric starters and must be cranked by hand. This was called "propping the airplane," and Mr. Spencer was simply asking one of the hangar flyers to spin the propeller for starting.

He slid into the seat next to me and I could hardly breathe I was filled with such anticipation.

This was, by far, the most exciting thing that had ever happened to me. The aircraft smelled faintly of gas, an aroma that still excites me today. The interior was musty and a bit threadbare. The instrument panel was very plain with only a few instruments. There were two steering wheels protruding from the instrument panel, and a push/pull throttle between them. The seat belts were worn and, yet, I felt as if I were in a spaceship with Buck Rogers preparing for a space launch.

Mr. Spencer helped me with my seat belt, gave a nod to one of the hangar flyers, and after a loud command, "switches off" the helper pulled the propeller through several times. Mr. Spencer explained that this was to prime the engine. He continued to give me a good explanation of what he was doing during the preflight and engine starting procedures. I'm not sure if it was because he noticed that I was scared to death or whether he was selling me on future flight lessons.

"Brakes set," he called out of the window, "and switches on." That was the signal for the helper to pull the propeller through with some force and to exercise caution, because with the switches on, the engine was hot and ready to fire up. This, Mr. Spencer explained to me as he went along with his procedures.

The helper gave the prop a robust pull and the engine came to life with a pop and a belch of smoke that drifted by my window. I was sure that we were on fire and here I sat, all tied to the airplane with a seat belt, but when I looked at Mr. Spencer he didn't seem alarmed, so I assumed all was okay. I had the utmost faith in him.

Until we started taxiing.

He explained that the wind direction dictated that we taxi to the far end of the field, up past the dilapidated windsock, by the apple tree, and next to the service station for our takeoff run. Well, Mr. Spencer was taxiing all over the place. Left and then right, he would taxi, and I was sure that he was drunk. Again, he saw my concern and explained that when taxiing a tail wheel airplane, the nose is higher and hampers the view straight ahead, so the pilot must zigzag to make sure that the taxiway is clear up ahead. With my faith restored in Mr. Spencer, I tried to relax as he prepared for takeoff.

I watched him as he did some "mystical" things in the cockpit, I assumed, in preparation for takeoff. With his heels depressing two brake pedals down between the rudder pedals, he brought the aircraft to a stop, pulled the steering wheels back in our collective laps for some reason or another, and revved up the engine. He then did something with the engine switch. He explained over the noise of the engine, "I'm checking the mags." I nodded knowingly, having no idea what a mag was. My brain was spinning wildly and I hadn't taken a breath in minutes, knowing that in seconds I would be airborne.

The next maneuver that Mr. Spencer did completely destroyed any confidence that I might have had in him. He turned the aircraft away from the runway directly toward the rear of the service station and I was sure that he was going to attempt to take off from its parking lot. Again, he saw my concern and explained that he was looking for "traffic." Again I nodded knowingly, thinking, *why is he looking for cars out here at the service station?* It wasn't too long afterward that I learned in aviation jargon, "traffic" means "other aircraft." He was checking to see if there were any other aircraft on final approach for the runway.

Much to my relief, he turned the aircraft around, aligned it with the runway, inquired if I was ready, and pushed the throttle full in.

The engine roared and the aircraft began to move, slowly at first, and then it accelerated. I could feel every bump and rut that we ran over. The tail lifted and I could see the far end of the runway approaching just as Mr. Spencer lifted her off the ground.

Of all the experiences of my life, this was the most memorable. As we lifted off, the roughness of that crude runway transitioned into a serene and magical emanation, and we climbed as if in a dream.

The runway dropped rapidly below, the airplane hangars disappeared behind me, and I looked ahead and saw my hometown, High Point. We were already above the tallest buildings. I looked down and saw the baseball field that I used to play on.

And then, we were barely off the ground, perhaps five or six hundred feet, I felt compelled to fly the airplane. It wasn't that I was completely ignorant of the principles of flight. I knew, from my model airplane building, what the ailerons, the rudder, and the elevators did. I knew that they would cause the aircraft to turn, climb, and descend, and so, almost subconsciously, I reached up and took the controls. To my surprise, Mr. Spencer removed his hands from the wheel, nodded to me to continue, and to my amazement, I was actually flying the airplane!

After takeoff, he reduced the power, as was the procedure, and with the noise level reduced, we could communicate easily. He said, "Let's try a turn; it's almost like driving a car." He motioned to the left and I turned the wheel to the left. The airplane turned nicely but in the turn I lost altitude and he explained that in an aircraft, when you turn, you must use a little bit of back pressure on the wheel as the wings lose some of their lift. I tried a turn to the right and it went better. And I had actually begun to breathe again.

We did a few more turns, and he explained how it was necessary to advance the throttle if we wanted to climb and to reduce power to descend, and soon, much too soon, he indicated that it was time to return to the field and land. Much to my relief, he took over control of the aircraft and turned back toward the airport.

I had one more shock on that flight. It was when we returned to the field and entered the traffic pattern in preparation to land. I didn't realize it but all small aircraft, in order to actually descend for a landing, must have the throttle completely retarded to idle and so the airplane becomes, effectively, a glider. When Mr. Spencer pulled the throttle back, the engine noise stopped and I almost fainted. I thought that the engine had quit. Again, upon checking his expression, I was relieved and he glided in, over the service station, to a perfect three-point landing and the wheels, bouncing over the ruts, announced our arrival.

What an adventure!

As I walked across the dirt ramp toward the office with Mr. Spencer, I was Orville and Wilbur Wright, Charles Lindbergh, and Jimmy Doolittle all rolled into one.

Mrs. Spencer was in the office and asked how it went. Mr. Spencer put his arm around my shoulder and told her that the "sightseeing" trip actually turned into a flight training session, and as a reward for me doing so well, he would like to offer, as a gift, a pilot logbook. She pulled a logbook out of the showcase and presented it to me. It was the typical small black logbook with gold writing on the cover that every student pilot begins with, but to me, it was absolutely the finest gift anyone had ever given me. When Mr. Spencer recorded my thirty minutes of flight training—turns, left and right, climbs and descents—and signed his name and instructor's number, my chest was out to here and a wide grin covered my whole face.

Later, I learned that he gave a lot of logbooks to prospective students. Mr. Spencer not only was a legend around those parts as a flight instructor, but he was also a pretty good salesman.

As I drove away from the airport that day, I knew that I would soon return, but my main concern was where to hide my pilot's logbook so Dad wouldn't find out about the flight.

I told Mom. She could keep a secret.

The summer of '52 was enchanting. There were flying lessons, when I could afford them. Yes, Dad found out about my new hobby. "Son," he conceded, "you can go out to the airport, and you can ride in one of those confounded things, but don't ever go up in one by yourself." *We'll see about that*, I thought with my fingers crossed behind my back.

The "steady" girl thing was going okay. Bobbie Leigh seemed to go along with the program, with Saturday night movies, a sandwich and Coke at the White House Barbecue, and an occasional ride on Sunday afternoon.

As baseball was of prime importance to me, I collected my nerve and set my sights on playing for the High Point American Legion baseball team.

CHAPTER 3
American Legion Baseball

Learning the game from a pro

I HAD ENJOYED A GOOD sophomore baseball season at Allen Jay earlier that spring and I looked forward to playing baseball in the summer. I was too old for the Red Shield league, so with some reservations, I showed up for the first practice of the American Legion team at the High Point High School athletic field.

Generally, the High Point team was made up of baseball players from the high school in High Point. The High Point team had many more boys to choose from and in addition, the high school players from the outlying rural schools were mostly from the farming areas and were required to work during the summer.

A former Major Leaguer, Dick Culler, coached the team. He had been an outstanding baseball player at High Point College, and had played in the Major Leagues for such managers as Connie Mack and Leo Durocher. He brought such a degree of professionalism to the program that you felt as if you were actually playing for a Major League team. The practices were intense, no fooling around, and the utmost detail was given to even the most routine play. I was extremely fortunate and I made the team.

I think that Coach Culler took a particular liking to me. He was a small man; only five feet and nine inches tall and he weighed about 155 pounds. He was never known for his hitting, only his quickness and his ability with the glove. I suppose that's about where I was. I wasn't known as a power hitter, but I made up for it with enthusiasm. He took me under his wing and taught me everything possible about playing first base. All of the acumen that he had accumulated over his career was imparted to me.

"Cooper," I think he was the first person to call me Cooper, "Cooper," he would say, "playing first base is like dancing in a ballet. You don't just stand there with one foot on the base and wait until an infielder throws a ball to you. Play away from the base during the pitch. Over here." He would mark an X about ten feet behind and toward second base. "Stand here, in case the batter hits one between first base and second. Bend over from the waist, balancing yourself on the balls of your feet. Like this," he would say, "and then, if the ball is hit away from you, you can move quickly to the base. Don't favor one foot or the other, straddle the bag, and when the infielder throws the ball to you, you are in a position to adjust your stance to the left or right, depending on where the ball is thrown, and if it's in the dirt, you can block it." He would make me practice that maneuver time after time, with no ball, just getting in position, dashing toward the first base, setting up in front of the base, and on his command, left or right, I was required to hop accordingly. It was a sort of a dance step and the intense training would bode well for me later in college.

He taught the other boys their positions as well. I would see him teaching the finer points of playing second base and shortstop for hours on end. And base running was his specialty. "Cooper," he would instruct, "when you're a base runner, be ready to run at the crack of the bat. Don't pick up your right foot to start running; cross over with your left foot. It'll save you a half a step. Look," he would say, "like this." And he would demonstrate the value of quickness.

Playing baseball for Dick Culler was extremely gratifying. He would push you, where you were strong; to do better and he would identify your weaknesses and work to help you improve. The intensity of training and the attention to detail that Coach Culler instilled in me remains with me today and I am grateful for having had the opportunity to play for him.

We had a fairly good season, competing against other American Legion teams around the state, and before I knew it, my junior year at Allen Jay High School had begun.

CHAPTER 4

Solo Flight & First Cross Country

The Ace of the Base

BASEBALL SEASON WAS OVER AND although it was football season, Dad had put his foot down and I wasn't allowed to play that sport. "Courting" was going along pretty well, and with the exception of having to focus on schoolwork, my attention was almost entirely on flying.

I had scraped up enough money to continue my flying lessons and in the fall I soloed. John Spencer had trained me well. I had been accepted into the inner circle of "hangar flyers" that gathered around the office and I had bought a pair of those high-top boots like all the other "aces" wore. I hadn't mastered the one pant leg in, one pant leg out, but I was pretty cool anyhow.

My aviation career was soaring. Mr. Spencer was my guru of aviation and I hung onto every word he spoke. I collected all the magazines and periodicals that I could find about flying and I spent every available minute at the airport listening to the war stories from the regulars.

On the day that I soloed, the gang met me on the ramp as I deplaned and, as was the custom, they cut off my shirttail, and all of them signed it as a reminder of that accomplishment. The only problem was that I was wearing one of my dad's favorite shirts.

Dad mustn't know, but I told Mom. She could be trusted.

Dad found out soon and we had another discussion concerning those "confounded" airplanes. Dad gave in a little and allowed, "Son, you can go up by yourself but you can't leave the airport area."

I was beginning to think that Mom was the "leak" but I had no evidence and since some of Dad's grocery store customers would occasionally visit the airport, and since I was becoming well known there, I assumed that Dad followed my progress through them.

I began to accumulate the flying time that was required in order to apply for a private license—a permit issued by the CAA, now the FAA, that allowed you to carry passengers. To qualify for that license, one must accumulate forty hours of flying time; a combination of instruction time and solo time. There was some cross-country flying time and some nighttime required also. The final exam consisted of a written exam and a flight test administered by a representative of the CAA.

Throughout the fall of '52 and the spring of '53 I flew as much as I could. Each minute of each hour was logged meticulously in my pilot's logbook. As I approached the required forty hours, I scheduled my dual cross-country. Since Mr. Spencer was out of town, I booked the flight with the Piedmont Airlines Captain Pete Dickens. As a new member of the hangar flyers bunch, I had made friends with Captain Dickens and he had been very helpful with flying tips concerning my fledgling career.

Captain Dickens advised me of the route that we were to follow: Fraley Field to Hickory, North Carolina, where we would land. From there we would fly to Charlotte, circle the field, and then fly directly back to Fraley Field. For days in advance I prepared for the flight. I bought maps from Mrs. Spencer, drew lines on them, and figured the courses to take and just how much time between legs. I reviewed the altitude required for the flight and I studied the intended airports in great detail.

I was ready.

The much-anticipated day came. I was ready. This should be easy. After all, the aviation maps looked exactly like the terrain; the land was green, rivers were blue, and roads were gray, just like they actually were. To make it easier, there were power lines that looked like power lines and railroads that looked like railroads drawn on the maps. Lakes were big blue blotches. I was ready.

We had a preflight briefing. Captain Dickens reminded me that Hickory was toward the west about eighty miles away and if we flew due west we could pick up a highway, follow it for about forty-five minutes, and we could see Hickory and land there. Once on the ground in Hickory we would prep for the rest of the flight.

I did a preflight of the airplane and checked the fuel and oil. Captain Dickens spun the prop, got in, we taxied away from the dusty ramp, and we were off. It was the first time I had been out of the traffic pattern of Fraley Field and suddenly everything looked different.

The buildings of High Point disappeared behind me and nothing looked the same. I reached the instructed altitude of twenty-five hundred feet, leveled off and looked at the compass. I wasn't heading west. *Let's see, which way to turn? I must concentrate on the heading more.* Oops, Captain Dickens was tapping on the altimeter. I was at three thousand feet. I had to concentrate on the altitude. Back at twenty-five hundred feet I checked the compass. It wasn't cooperating one bit. Nor was the altimeter. I had been flying for twenty minutes and I had not mastered the heading or the altitude necessary for a successful cross-country flight. Finally, I managed to identify the highway that cut between Winston Salem and Hickory and by watching it, and glancing at the altimeter, I gradually got under control. Somewhat.

Captain Dickens asked over the noise of the engine, "What is your ETA for Hickory Airport?" I gave him a blank look as I didn't know what an ETA was. "When do you estimate reaching Hickory?" again he asked.

I remembered the briefing. "Forty-five minutes after we took off," I said.

"When is that?" he asked.

Oh, Lord, I thought, *in the excitement of the takeoff, I didn't record the time. Was it 8:30 or 8:45...or 9:00?* He saw my puzzled look and gave me a hint. He pointed to a scribbled note at the top of the map...T. O. Fraley, 8:45. Boy, I thought, those airline pilots think of everything. "Nine thirty," I proudly exclaimed, and I noticed a hint of a smile.

The airport was near a lake and I found it relatively easily. Captain Dickens pointed out the windsock and we determined the wind direction and decided which runway to land on. Now, I knew all about traffic patterns, about entering the downwind leg at a 45-degree angle, about turning on base leg and then final approach for the landing. The only issue here at Hickory was that there was no Model Dairy Farm barn over which I would cut my engine to begin my pattern descent. At Fraley Field, there was a barn conveniently located on the downwind leg that we all used as a mark to cut the engine. From over that spot one could, with small adjustments, plan a normal approach and landing.

This cross-country stuff was harder than I had anticipated.

Captain Dickens talked me through the approach and landing and, alongside the taxiway, with the engine idling, he taught me not only how to figure out how to land at a strange airport, but a valuable lesson in life. "You'll approach a lot of different airports in your career, and the winds will always be different. Pick an arbitrary spot to cut your engine and simply glide as best as you can for the runway. If you are too low, add power. If you are too high, simply go around for another attempt. *Don't just give up.*" That advice was very useful then and I have referred to it many times, in everyday experiences, since.

The takeoff was uneventful, although it was my first experience on a paved airport, and we headed toward Charlotte. The flight to Charlotte was only about thirty minutes and it went rather smoothly. The noon updrafts had not yet begun and the cruising altitude of thirty-five hundred feet was still relatively smooth. I identified the Charlotte airport easily and, after circling it, began my last leg to Fraley Field. The plan was to turn northeast to intercept the newly constructed highway that passed through Charlotte up north to High Point, follow that road, and land at Fraley Field.

Easy enough.

As I circumnavigated around Charlotte, the smooth airway suddenly became a bumpy road, the compass refused to obey me, and the altimeter had a mind of its own. While fighting the compass, trying to maintain my altitude over this "new" bumpy road, the highway that would lead me back to High Point passed beneath me unnoticed.

Captain Dickens had explained in his preflight briefing that he might help me through the first two legs, but on the leg from Charlotte to High Point I would be on my own.

I began to sense that I should have seen the highway by now. Not to worry, out of the window highways look just like they look on the map and soon it would come into view. Minutes passed. From the corner of my eye I could see that Captain Dickens' fingers were drumming an impatient beat on his knees.

Should I give up? Certainly if I did he would fail me on my cross country and it would be weeks before I could muster up enough money to afford another… Not to mention the embarrassment with my new friends, the hangar flyers. I would be laughed out of the group, excommunicated. More time passed.

Finally, he could take it no longer. Over the roar of the engine he appealed, "Do you have any idea just where you are?"

In my many years of flying, I have been in some tight jams, mostly of my own doing.

This was the first of many. My career and reputation were at stake and just as I was about to give up, probably in tears, a miracle happened...

I must digress here momentarily. Later in life, as an Eastern Airlines pilot, I was summoned to the chief pilot's office. I remember that on his wall was a plaque, which read, "Not only do I believe in miracles, I rely on them."

This moment in my young career was the first of many miracles that "bailed" me out.

One second before giving up I took one last look out of the window and, miracle of miracles, I saw the large cylindrical water tank that stood next to my grandparents' home in Albemarle.

"Yes sir," I replied proudly, "we're over Albemarle, North Carolina."

"How in the devil do you know that?" he asked in amazement.

I nodded down. "That water tower down there sits across the street from my grandma's house, and High Point is up that way." I pointed.

Captain Dickens turned away, looked out of his window, and I'm sure that I heard him stifle a chuckle as I confidently turned the aircraft north along the familiar highway that I had traveled for years when my parents would visit my grandparents. In about twenty-five minutes that beautiful, wonderful Fraley Field came into view.

I circled the field, chopped the power over Model Dairy Farm barn, and glided in for a perfect three-point landing.

Lindbergh had just landed at Le Bourget!

My junior year went pretty well. Classes were good, especially English under Mrs. Purvis, history under Mr. Moye, and math under Mrs. Hussey. French under Miss Chilton was a different story. I didn't like French and French didn't like me. I just didn't have an ear for a foreign language and I dreaded every class.

Spring came and with it came baseball. I couldn't wait. Some of us would begin early in March when the weather was still cold, and a hard-hit ball would really sting your hands to high heavens. By the end of March, the high school baseball coach would call for tryouts, and all of the boys who wanted to play would muster up at the baseball field. We didn't have many boys in high school, so almost anyone who showed up made the team. For those who didn't make the team the coach would try to give them something to do, such as equipment manager or first or third base coach.

I had made the team, last year, as a sophomore, as second-string first baseman, and I was looking forward to this year. With a season with the High Point American Legion team under my belt and with Dick Culler's training I made the first team quite easily. I had a good year with the high school team and at season's end I looked forward to another summer with the High Point American Legion baseball team.

CHAPTER 5
Romantically Crushed

But, wait…

MY BASEBALL CAREER WAS GOING along well, my flying was improving as I built up flying time for my private license, but, I'm sad to say, in the spring, my "steady" Bobbie Leigh, strayed. I'm not sure how it happened. I suppose she just got tired of playing third fiddle behind baseball and airplanes and she began seeing an upperclassman.

Well, rejection is a hard pill to swallow and so it was with me. I moped around the house and I moped around the store and was, in general, a pain in the neck. I suppose Mom and Dad knew just what was going on, as they were pretty good at things like that. Dad, especially, suspected something when I stopped asking if Mrs. Tuttle had called in her order. When I did have to deliver groceries to Mrs. Tuttle, Bobbie Leigh would be scarce.

I was crushed.

But, at seventeen, one's resiliency is boundless. Just when I thought I was sentenced to a forsaken life of loneliness…Mrs. Owens called for groceries.

Dad and I sacked up the groceries and with little enthusiasm, I loaded them into the truck and headed for Mrs. Owens' house. Now, I had delivered to her house lots of times before, but today would be different. It was summer and High Point High School was out and, unbeknownst to me, Mrs. Owens' granddaughter was staying with her for the summer. I knocked on the screen door expecting Mrs. Owens to answer.

Geraldine Fitzgerald was her name. She was sixteen, dressed in shorts and a T-shirt.

She was the prettiest girl I had ever seen in the world.

I couldn't speak.

I just stood there. Finally she said, "Are you the grocery boy?"

"Yes," I managed to stammer.

She grinned and directed me to the kitchen. "My name is Jerri," she said.

"I'm Tommy," I muttered, depositing the groceries and floundering back toward the kitchen door. I couldn't think of anything clever to say as I left the kitchen for the front door.

"I'll see you later," she offered cheerily. "I'm here all summer with my grandma."

"Good," I mumbled. "I'll see you next trip." It was all I could think to say as I went out toward my delivery truck.

"I'll watch for you." She smiled as she waved good-bye.

Back at the store I was whistling and humming and I even volunteered to work in the "bottle Hell," where I sorted pop bottles with a smile.

Dad knew something was up when, next day, the first thing I asked was "Has Mrs. Owens called in her order yet?"

In the summer of '53 a strange thing happened to me. I couldn't explain it then and I can't explain it now but it really happened.

I developed a small growth on the ball of my right foot. I didn't pay much attention at first, but then as it began to grow and cause some discomfort, I pointed it out to Mom and she took me to a chiropodist. He identified it as a seed wart and removed it surgically.

I assumed that I was finished with the wart, but to my disappointment it reappeared several weeks later and had grown even larger. By now it was the size of a dime and very painful.

We returned to the doctor and he repeated the procedure with assurances that we had seen the last of the wart. Again, after about two weeks, it appeared again. This time it was the size of a quarter and the pain was intense!

During all of this I had been playing baseball with the American Legion team. I didn't want to jeopardize my chances of playing, so with the exception of my parents, I didn't disclose this affliction to anyone. In order to continue playing I would wrap a bandage around my foot at the instep as tight as I could stand it. This would cut off the circulation and ease the pain. Between innings, when it was not my turn to bat, I would loosen the bandage, allow the blood to flow, and in anticipation of my return to the field, I would rebind my foot.

By now, Mom and Dad were seriously concerned as this thing was getting out of control. In discussing the issue, my grandpa Franklin mentioned that he knew an old farmer down near Trinity, about five miles south of our house, and that he could take off warts.

Dad jumped at the idea and Grandpa Franklin agreed to take us down. I was ready for any remedy to ease the pain of this thing. The three of us jumped into the car and off we went to Trinity. After some inquiries we found the old farmer out in a field plowing with his mule. Grandpa approached him and after politely passing the time of day explained why we were there.

"My grandson has a wart," he explained, "and we heard that you could remove them."

"Yes, I can," the old man replied, quite confidently. "Is this your grandson?"

My grandfather replied, "Yes."

The old farmer looked at me and asked, "What is your name?"

"Tommy Cooper."

"No," he said, "I want your whole name."

"Thomas Lindsay Cooper," I replied.

"Okay," the old man said, "that's all I need."

"Do you want to see the wart?" I asked.

"No, I don't need to see it. It will go away now," he replied matter-of-factly.

Dad asked, "Okay, what do we owe you?"

"Nothing," the old man said. "If I take money, it won't work." With that he bade us good day, slapped the reins on the rump of his mule, and continued his plowing.

There we stood, two men and a boy, believing that an old farmer in the middle of a field could cure something that a medically trained foot doctor with all the tools of modern medicine could not do.

We returned home and I discounted the visit as a waste of time…well, maybe not a complete waste of time, as in the back of my mind I sincerely wanted this thing cured, and I hoped that the visit might prove to be successful. I wasn't a complete cynic yet at the tender age of seventeen.

My thoughts turned to other things and it wasn't until about four days later when I was dressing for baseball and preparing to wrap my foot for the afternoon game that I noticed there was no pain in my foot. Upon visually checking the bottom of my foot, to my absolute amazement, I saw that the quarter-sized seed wart had disappeared completely. There was only a tender pink spot where the wart had previously been. Within two or three days all evidence of the wart had disappeared completely.

The visit with the old man lasted less than five minutes. The conversation above is almost verbatim. I didn't understand it then and I don't understand it now.

Summer vacation was going pretty well. Baseball with the American Legion team, especially with my foot cured, was going well enough. My hitting was suspect but my fielding was outstanding. When I was benched for lack of batting production, my replacement made so many errors at first base that I was always quickly reinstated.

Jerri Fitzgerald filled the social void left by Bobbie Leigh's departure as her grandmother allowed her to date me, although she kept a tight rein on her. Dates were limited and curfews were strictly enforced and exceptions were nonexistent.

The summer of '53 promised no major events. Dad sold the big grocery store on South Main Street and purchased a smaller one on Taylor Street closer to downtown High Point. It was in a section of town commonly referred to as "Colored" town and since the store was quite small, I was not required to work there full time, only on Saturdays. The loss of my full-time job with Dad resulted in my first real-life experience.

CHAPTER 6
First "Real" Job

Or "Work is the curse of the young 'playboy' pilot"

BASED ON MY SOCIAL AND flying budget I now had to go out into the workplace and look for a real job. What an eye-opener that was. My first summer job was at a paper box company called Carolina Container. It was a dingy little factory that produced small paper cartons for the hosiery mill industry. The boxes were about twelve to fourteen inches long and about four inches deep. A large roll of cardboard was fed into a giant machine that made the boxes. My job was to sit at the outgoing side of the machine and, as the boxes came out, stack them. Once you got a stack of boxes about five feet high, you would cut the machine off and carry the stack across the room for the final shipping process. The worst thing about the job...well, there wasn't just one worst thing... Everything about the job was the worst.

To begin with, they expected you to be on time every day. Management had a punch clock that I hated. If you were on time in the morning, the clock would print your time card in black ink. If you were late, even one minute late, the card would show red ink. My card began to look like a Hawaiian sunset. I hated that clock.

To add to the aggravation, a horn would sound when you were supposed to begin work, and it would sound when you were expected to take a break. I hated that horn.

And finally, the very worst thing about the job was the machine itself. It was big and black and oily and it smelled bad. It smelled of burnt oil mixed with hot glue. And it made a horrible, intimidating noise...ker thump, ker thump, ker thump. At each ker thump, a new box would squirt out and I would have to grab it and stack it. The only pleasure I got from that job was when my stack of boxes got to five feet high, I could step on the emergency-stop floor switch that would stop the machine so I could deliver the stack of boxes to the shipping area. The machine had a personality of its own. I'm sure that it knew I took great pleasure in killing it. I would step on the stop-switch, the machine would groan, slow down slowly, belch some burnt oil and glue fumes at me, and die a slow death.

Great.

Carrying the stack of boxes was another story entirely. For the first few weeks, I was the entertainment source for the whole factory. When my stack grew to the point where I must carry the boxes across the room, the other workers would nudge each other in preparation for the juggling show. To my chagrin, I accommodated them with some pretty awesome crashes. These were met with great spasms of laughter and I was the source of much amusement for all concerned…except my immediate supervisor. We had more than a few conversations concerning my performance, and the only thing that saved me from being fired was that…mercifully…school started.

Years later I would watch Lucile Ball on TV standing in front of the chocolate drop candy machine, placing candy in boxes, getting further behind, and experiencing the same frustrations that I had felt, stuffing the excess candy in her blouse. Only, I couldn't stuff the excess boxes in my shirt.

My senior year started and Mrs. Purvis was my senior class homeroom teacher. Her specialty was English and we had enjoyed her English classes for the past three years. She was a large, elegant lady with bluish white hair. She stood erect before the class and just her presence commanded respect. Over the past three years she had taught us to conjugate verbs, compose words into organized thoughts, and diagram sentences. This year she would expose us to the great literary giants such as Chaucer and Shakespeare, and more contemporary authors like Hemingway, Steinbeck, and Cronin.

Her classes were always extremely interesting. I can remember her standing before the class for the whole period, reading from Shakespeare and acting out the parts. She made the plays come alive and she planted seeds of literature in some, if not most of us, that would continue to grow for years to come.

Just as Allen Jay commenced the school year in the fall of 1953, alas, so did High Point High. And with that, Jerri Fitzgerald returned to her mom's home in High Point. It wasn't that her home was so far from south

High Point where I lived; she was just so popular at High Point High that I couldn't compete. We would go out occasionally, her mother liked me, but as a steady, no way.

I had been courting for the most part of two years now and I was getting pretty good at it. Mom had given me some tips. "Don't settle on one girl, son," she would advise. "There are always more fish in the pond." She had also taught me dating manners and I was about the only boy in my class who would actually, when calling on a young girl, go up to her door, knock, and chat with the parents. Mom also taught me how to dress correctly. "No plaid shirts with striped pants and vice versa and when in doubt, go solid," she would instruct, "and always keep your shoes shined."

The politics of courting, as it related to parents versus their daughters, was a science which, in my case, took some understanding. As a young man with impeccable manners, I was always a favorite with the parents. "Tommy Cooper is such a nice boy," they would say to their daughters.

This was the kiss of death.

It seemed that most daughters had a tendency to rebel against their parents, and my type wasn't always cool with them.

On the other hand, when the parents learned that I was a pilot, they cooled somewhat and were not quite as "bullish" on their daughters going out with me. The fear of flying was still prevalent in High Point. Perfect! That gave me just enough mystique to counter the "Tommy Cooper is such a nice boy" attitude of the girl's parents and it satisfied their daughter's rebel tendencies.

That worked out pretty well, and with my limited budget, as I was only working on Saturdays with Dad, I did okay socially and I had a few bucks left over for flying.

I tried out and made the football team in the fall. Dad had given up on his objections to my playing football. I suppose he figured that nothing could be worse than "flying those fool airplanes." Being the second-string quarterback, I really didn't play in the regular games that much. I'd get in the games when we were far ahead or far behind. I did get a lot of playing time at practice as I headed up the second team, and during scrimmage I got my fill of getting my head bashed in by the first team. I was happy when basketball season started. Not because I was a basketball player, I was not, but because I could turn in my football uniform and forever retire from that sport. Dad was right!

Winter came and went. The year 1954 began uneventfully and soon it would be baseball season. My schoolwork was going okay and, with added senior activities and my limited budget, my flying tapered off. I still would visit the airport and hangar-fly with the regulars, and sometimes one of the airplane owners would invite me for a spin. I had almost completed all the requirements for my private license and I was preparing for the written exam, which I anticipated taking in the summer.

Baseball was set to begin in the first week of April and final exams for graduation would be coming soon after, toward the end of May.

Baseball, that season, went very well. Physically, I had matured, reaching my height goal of six feet. My hitting had improved considerably. The Allen Jay baseball team had a good season, winning the county championship in our class, and we advanced to the state semifinals where we played Mt. Holly down near Charlotte.

We got clobbered.

The season wasn't a complete disaster, however, as I made All State in our school category.

We had the senior prom, final exams were administered, and the graduation ceremony was scheduled. Tradition had it that each senior class would hold a picnic at High Point City Lake park and so we did.

We all gathered there under the giant oak trees next to the lake. We brought covered dishes and shared our meals on blankets spread upon the grass. One of the teachers, who was acting as chaperone, got somewhat emotional and in an impromptu speech allowed that this might be the last time we would be together ever again and that after twelve years we should take one last look at each other and remember the times we had enjoyed growing up together.

I listened to that, but it didn't register until years later. She was right. With the exception of one class reunion, about thirty years later, my family of twelve years split and I never met them again.

Graduation came and went. We received our diplomas and went our separate ways.

I went looking for a job in High Point and my thoughts turned to my aborted career in aviation.

CHAPTER 7
Private Pilot's License

The adventures of a know-it-all

WITH THE SUCCESSFUL COMPLETION LAST summer of the dual portion of the cross-country, I had to then complete a solo cross-country to finally comply with the requirements of a private pilot license. As I had learned on my dual cross-country flight, it was easier if you planned your trip along familiar highways. So that's exactly what I did. The solo cross-country was uneventful and with that completed, I had accumulated all the prerequisites for the private license. Now, all that was required was to successfully pass the written exam and, finally, pass a check ride administered by the CAA.

Mr. Spencer explained that I must take the written exam in Charlotte at the CAA office located at the Charlotte Municipal Airport in the terminal building. He briefed me on landing at a controlled airport that had a control tower. Since I didn't have a two-way communications radio in the airplane, I would have to receive light signals from the tower; green to land and red to go around. Simple enough. I had studied that for my written exam. Further, he explained, that the practical flight test portion could be taken in Salisbury, about forty miles south of High Point, at a later date.

I prepared for the written by studying everything I could get my hands on and I pestered Mr. Spencer and Captain Dickens to the limits of their patience.

Finally, I felt ready for the written exam. I was so anxious to take the test that I didn't spend much time planning my flight down to Charlotte. It looked easy enough on the map—just pick up U.S. 85, which ran next to

Fraley Field, fly south until I saw Charlotte, and the airport would be about five miles west of town. Easy.

It was easy. The flight was smooth. I could hold altitude and heading fairly well now, and after about forty-five minutes Charlotte came into view. As I flew closer to the city I visually found the municipal airport and began my preparation for landing.

Let's see, the windsock said the wind was coming from over there; that made this runway, most directly into the wind, my desired runway. I entered the downwind leg and looked for the tower. I located it and a green light magically appeared and I chopped the power for the landing. I glided in comfortably, and the tires squeaked, telling me that I was down. I rolled out and turned off the runway and looked for a place to park.

Trouble.

This wasn't like Fraley Field at all. There was no dirt ramp with an occasional small airplane tied down where a student pilot could park. This airport was all concrete with very large buildings and giant airplanes everywhere. I looked over to the side of the taxiway where I had stopped. There was a large hangar with SOUTHERN FLIGHT EXECUTIVE TERMINAL written on the front. *Well*, I thought, *that's not for me. I'm no executive.* So I taxied further down the taxiway. Not seeing anything that looked like Fraley Field, I simply pulled off the taxiway onto some grass, cut the engine, found some stones to chock the wheels, and headed on foot toward the terminal building. I knew it was the terminal building because it had CHARLOTTE emblazoned across the roof and there were a number of Eastern and Piedmont airliners parked there.

The route from my parking place to the terminal took me directly across an active runway. Carefully, after waiting for an airliner to land, I proceeded to walk across the runway to the terminal, casually strolling under the wing of an Eastern Airlines plane, into the terminal. Once there, I found a directory, looked up "Civil Aeronautics Administration," and proceeded up the stairs to the CAA office to present myself for the written test.

The secretary was nice. She looked at my logbook very knowingly, pulled out a blank written exam, showed me to the testing room, explained the procedure to me, and left me to complete the exam.

The test was pretty easy. It took me less than thirty minutes to complete. As I was preparing to turn it in I heard a commotion in the reception room just outside. It sounded as if two men were arguing. I got up to turn in my test and the door opened. There was a tall, gray-haired gentleman, very distinguished looking, and a shorter man with a pronounced red face.

The gray-haired man asked, "Who are you?"

"Tommy Cooper."

"What are you doing here?"

"Well, sir, I came to take my private pilot's written exam."

"How did you get here?"

"Sir, I flew down from High Point, Fraley Field."

I was beginning to get a little nervous and the small red-faced man's face got redder.

The gray-haired man's lips were pursed as if to stifle an expression that I couldn't make out, and the secretary, head down, was trying to look busy.

"And," the gray-haired man queried after a long pause, "just where did you park?"

"Well, sir, I parked over there, across the field, out of the way," I explained. "After landing, the only place that I saw to park said it was for executives, and not being an executive I found some grass and parked there."

The gray-haired man took a deep breath, the secretary buried her head in her arms, and the small red-faced man began to clench his fists over and over again.

"Bill, why don't you go back up to the tower and let me handle this down here," the grey-haired man suggested.

The red-faced man rolled his eyes, spun around, and left. I was happy to see him leave.

"Well, Mr. Cooper," he said, with a relieved smile, "you caused quite a stir here at the airport. We've been looking all over the field for you. The main office of the CAA is the last place that we would have thought to look. Why don't you come into my office and we'll get better acquainted?"

I was beginning to feel a lot better.

Until I saw the inscription on his door.

Odell Garrison, Chief
Aviation Safety District Offices
CIVIL AERONAUTICS ADMINISTRATION

My heart sank!

I was dead. My career was destroyed before it got off the ground. He offered me a seat with a nod and as I sat down I was prepared for the worst. How could I face the hangar-flyers back at Fraley Field?

But he couldn't have been nicer. He reminisced about Fraley Field. He said that he had been in there a number of times, as part of his job was to travel around the state in a government-sponsored Piper Super Cub to inspect certain aviation facilities.

I was still holding my completed test and he asked to see it. "Good," he said, "looks like you passed with flying colors. You did miss a few questions though." He marked up my test. He went over the ones that I missed, explained my errors, and with that he called in the secretary and issued a receipt to me indicating that I had successfully passed the test.

"Okay," he said, "let's get you out of here before dark. I've got a car downstairs and I will drive you around to your airplane and give you a crank and get you on your way."

On the ride to the airplane, he explained how private aircraft operated at large commercial airports and that you didn't have to be an executive to park at the executive terminal.

He parked his car at the SOUTHERN FLIGHT EXECUTIVE TERMINAL parking lot, borrowed a tug, and took me to my airplane. I did the preflight inspection, got in, and he pulled the prop through for the engine start. He walked around to the side of the cockpit for a final good-bye. "Taxi down this taxiway to the end of the runway," he directed over the noise of the engine. "And after you check the mags, turn the airplane toward the tower and look for the green light from your friend," he said with a smile. "After takeoff, your runway heading will take you north toward Fraley Field. Oh yes," he added, "tell John Spencer that I said hello." He backed away, gave me a quick salute, and pointed down the taxiway as I spun around to taxi.

As I flew north along U.S. 85, I thought of the lessons that I had learned that day. I learned a lot about matters related to flying, but I think that the most important thing I learned was that no matter how important your position might be, it doesn't hurt to be nice to people and give a hand to those who might be under you. You will be rewarded, if only by a chuckle… or a belly laugh.

Fraley Field looked awfully good coming up over the horizon, and I knew that the hangar-flyers would be waiting…for my "war story."

The Man in The Arena...

Jobs were scarce in the summer of '54 in High Point. I refused to return to the box factory, even if they would rehire me, so I applied to, and was hired by, Merita Bakery.

The only thing I knew about Merita Bakery was that it sponsored the *Lone Ranger Show* on the radio every Monday, Wednesday, and Friday afternoon. At a younger age, I would listen to the radio show with Grandpa Franklin all the time. Any company that sponsored the Lone Ranger—a man who rode through the West fighting injustice and destroying evil—must be a nice place to work.

I was wrong.

I thought that nothing could be worse than the box factory, with its cruel *ker-thump* machine, but I was mistaken. The first thing was that my work shift was from 10:00 at night until 6:30 in the morning. And they had one of those infernal clocks that would spit out red ink on your time card if you checked in late.

Also, there was another machine, more sinister than Mr. ker-thump at the box factory. This machine gave out a loud whirring noise and smelled like fried grease. It squirted out half-baked brown-and-serve rolls at a fierce pace onto a turntable. Three or four workers sat there, placing the rolls into paper cartons, twelve to a box, and, in turn, placing the boxes on a conveyer belt for cellophane wrap and labeling. There was no stopping this machine until break time. The whirring of the machine during the midnight hours could put you to sleep, except that the odor of the fried grease made you want to throw up, and that would keep you awake.

I don't know how I did it, but I lasted out the summer there.

To this day, when I pass a bakery and smell what some people refer to as a "wonderful smell," I gag.

I lasted the summer at the bakery but not with Jerri. Her dance card was just too full for either of us to handle and she dumped me...again.

With the terrible bakery job on my back and my social life in shambles I turned back to aviation for my sanity. I scraped up every available dollar that I could and rented Mr. Spencer's old T-craft and practiced the maneuvers that I might be expected to demonstrate for the final flight check ride. There was a CAA flight examiner located in Salisbury, North Carolina, about forty miles south of Fraley Field. I booked with him and on July 23rd I flew down and passed the check ride.

I was about the proudest person on earth as I fired up the ole T-craft and headed back toward Fraley Field. The one thing that I wasn't too happy about was that it was tradition that when one went for his private license and was successful, one had to do a loop over the field, sort of a victory roll.

The closer I got to Fraley Field, the more nervous I became. I had never performed a loop before… Heck, I'd never even ridden through one. Fraley Field loomed up on the horizon…much too fast.

I could just land and go to my car, I thought. *No, I couldn't do that…the hangar-flyers would never let me live it down… Let's see. How do you do a loop? I know that you need some speed.* I'd heard someone say that it was like swinging a pail of water with a rope over your head. That was not such a confidence-building picture, I surmised. *I'm not even sure how much altitude I need. I'll climb to about three thousand feet and that should be enough*, I guessed.

Peer pressure was winning out over common sense. I was at three thousand feet and the field was under me now; there was no one in the traffic pattern. I had no further excuse if I was going to do this thing. Speed—that was important, so I pushed the nose down and pushed the throttle full in. The speed was building much too fast and it was time now to pull the yoke back… *Here goes…* I closed my eyes and pulled the yoke back as hard as I could. It's a wonder the wings didn't come off. I felt heavy on the seat, the skin on my face sagged to my belly button, and up and over I went.

Except, I didn't stop with one. The hangar-flyers down below swear to this day that I did two loops in succession with a hammerhead stall at the end, coupled with a full spin to end the maneuver. I can't swear to that as I had my eyes closed during the whole thing.

I regrouped, got myself back under control, entered the traffic pattern, and landed to a rousing round of applause from the hangar-flyers. I was really one of the gang now.

I couldn't wait to get home to tell my parents. Mom was pleased but Dad, always cautious, warned me to never even think of getting him up in "one of them confounded things."

"How about you, Mom?" I asked.

"I suppose so," she answered cautiously. "When do you want to go?" We agreed to go up on Sunday and as I wanted Mom to be my first passenger, I grounded myself for a couple of days.

On the appointed day Dad wouldn't even go to the airport to watch, but Mom bravely showed up and just as bravely crawled into the cramped cockpit of the old Taylorcraft and off we went. Thank goodness all went well. As we flew around the area, Mom relaxed and began to point out some landmarks that she recognized, including our house, and I think she enjoyed the ride. I'm not sure that she wanted to make a habit of it, but she knew how important it was to me, so she mustered up her courage and took her first airplane ride…and I flew my first passenger.

I had graduated from high school with honors, having won the English and Mathematics awards. I was eighteen years old and working the graveyard shift in a bakery for a dollar an hour. Although I had never done much actual planning for college, I assumed that I would attend somewhere, and after two summers of toiling for a buck an hour, higher education seemed like the only way to escape.

My social life was stagnant. Entertaining young ladies and trying to build a flying career was a financial juggling act that I was having trouble mastering. I had a few dates, here and there, but nothing serious. It seems that all the eligible girls were going steady and the only dates I could muster up were "rebounds"—that would last for about two dates and they would end up back with their steady boyfriends.

It was in the late summer of '54 that I met Billy Garner. Billy's sister, Von Ella, was a classmate and I knew of Billy, as he had been an upperclassman at Allen Jay.

I had joined a flying club of ten members and the club owned a Taylorcraft. It was cheap flying and I spent a lot of time tinkering with it when it was not being flown.

I was working on the T-craft one day when Billy came up and introduced himself. He said that he had taken a few flight lessons at Fraley Field and he thought we ought to get to know each other. I was okay with that, as Billy's reputation had preceded him. He was quite a scholar at Allen Jay and I knew that he was attending the University of North Carolina.

He wanted to talk about flying and I wanted to talk about college. He said that if I wanted to go to UNC, I'd have to get moving. Classes would be starting soon. He gave me a date and said to look him up if I came, and, being a senior officer in the Air Force ROTC, he could get me in that program.

Wow! Air Force ROTC, Reserve Officers Training Corps, Airplanes, Air Force uniforms, aeronautical studies, marching. That sounded great, so I made up my mind that UNC was for me. Besides, its very name was "The University of North Carolina" and since I lived in North Carolina, that's probably where I was supposed to go anyway. With my mind made up, I sold my one-tenth interest in the Taylorcraft club, pocketed the money for college, and began to prepare for my departure from High Point.

Now, at Allen Jay, you just showed up on the first day of class. You would be told where to go and classes would begin then and there. With that in mind, I set a date to arrive at Chapel Hill one day before classes would start. I didn't want to be late on my first day of college.

I told Mom and Dad of my decision to attend UNC. Mom seemed pleased but Dad, who was by nature very cautious, wasn't entirely convinced that UNC was the place to attend. "Where is it located," he asked, "and how much does it cost?"

I explained that it was near Raleigh, the state capital, in a small town called Chapel Hill, but I didn't know how much it cost. I supposed that there were some costs—books, rooming, food, and such—and I promised that once I got there I would let him know. We agreed tentatively on an allowance of twenty dollars per week. On the appointed day of departure, Mom helped me pack, I loaded the black Chevy, and I was off.

CHAPTER 8
UNC, Chapel Hill

Here I come, ready or not.

CHAPEL HILL WAS ONLY ABOUT fifty miles away, and I arrived just after noon. Mom had packed a lunch for me that I ate on the way, so I wasn't hungry when I got there. Anyway, I was anxious to sign up and start college. I located a parking place and, equipped with my high school diploma, I started looking for some place to sign up.

I asked a few people for directions for the sign-up place, and before long I found myself in front of an old brick building with a sign on the door, Enrollments.

So far, so good, I thought.

The door was ajar, so I walked in. The room was filled with desks and chairs and it was in an extremely disheveled state. There were only three or four people there and papers were strewn all over the floor.

A woman seated behind a desk looked up at me quizzically and asked, "Can I help you?"

"Yes, ma'am," I said. "I'm here to sign up for college."

"What?" she asked as she straightened up at her desk.

"I'm here to sign up for college," I repeated. "Is this the right place?"

"Yes, it is," she confirmed. "What's your name?"

"Tommy Cooper."

"No, your full name, please," she corrected me.

"Thomas L. Cooper."

She began to shuffle through several pages of names and said, "I can't find your name anywhere."

"No, ma'am, I just got here."

"You just got here to enroll for the *fall semester?*" she asked with a quizzical look.

"I'm not sure what that means," I explained, "but I'm here for the classes that begin tomorrow. I wanted to come a day early so that I wouldn't be late."

She turned to a man seated next to her, put her hand aside her mouth, and through a chuckle whispered to him, "Hey, Charlie, get a load of this one."

Well, we had a nice chat. She explained that normally people signed up for UNC weeks, if not months, in advance. They must forward their credentials and select their courses well in advance and, normally, they show up several days early to move into their dorms to prepare for the semester. She also told me what a semester was.

I didn't know what to do at that point. I suppose she saw the disappointed look on my face and took pity on me. "Look," she said, "let me see what I can do. We have some classes that are open due to cancellations. They are not very popular, but I can perhaps fit you in. Just sit there," she offered, "and I'll be right back."

She came back directly with a list of classes that, as a freshman, I could take. There was English 1, a math course, Social Science, Hygiene, and my old *favorite*, French. She explained that to enroll in ROTC I would have to go to another area and she gave me directions. She explained that Physical Education was mandatory and with the ROTC drill periods I would have a full plate. She reviewed the schedule with me and reminded me that my first class was English, the next day at 8:00 a.m. in Bingham Hall, Room 203. She gave me a map and pointed out all the buildings where I would be studying.

I filled out some forms; she looked at my diploma and enrolled me into the University of North Carolina. I was quite proud.

She asked where I was staying and I told her that I didn't have a place to stay yet and I would be much obliged if she could direct me to the office where I could sign up for a dorm room. She identified that office on the map she had given me and wished me good luck. Charlie, at the next desk, had long since turned his chair toward the window and, as I left, I could see his head shaking.

The building with the office for the dorm sign-up wasn't far and I found it easily.

I entered a room with a sign on the door that said Dormitory Confirmation. There was a long counter in that room and before long a young lady came over and inquired if she could help me. I explained, proudly, that I had just enrolled in college and that now I needed a dorm room.

She asked, "What's your name?"

"Tommy Co—" I trailed off there and corrected myself quickly. "Thomas L. Cooper," I asserted. I had been in college only half a day and I was beginning to get this college stuff pretty good.

"Let's see," she was shuffling through a stack of papers. "I don't see your name anywhere."

"No, ma'am," I explained for the second time that day, "I just got here."

"You haven't requested a dorm before today?"

"No, ma'am, I just signed up, er, enrolled today," I stammered.

"I'm sorry to say, Mr. Cooper, but we have no dorm rooms at all and we've had no cancellations," she explained.

I was beginning to have visions of sleeping in the ole Chevy for the first semester when she offered, "We do have some cots over in the basement at Cobb Dorm. It's newly constructed, but we have put some other classmen there and it works out pretty good on a temporary basis. You will have to share a bathroom but that's all that I can offer right now."

I thanked the lady, she gave me a set of keys to the basement and a list of the other roomies I would be sharing with, and I departed to look for the ROTC place.

ROTC headquarters was located fairly central to the campus and housed in a series of what looked to be temporary structures left over from the second world war.

I was made to feel welcome there by an officer in full Air Force uniform and before long I had signed up and was enrolled in the U. S. Air Force Reserve Officers Training Corp.

Would miracles never cease?

I located Cobb Dorm, over past the tennis courts, found the door to get into the basement, met some of my new roommates, and moved in. Each boy had a cot and a small desk with a chair and that was about all, with no walls for privacy. Sharing the bath was the understatement of the year. There were ten of us and only one bathroom. This was going to take some scheduling. It was a long way from Moore Avenue.

It was late afternoon, Mom's box lunch was wearing thin, and I was hungry. A couple of my new friends took me under their wing and escorted me to the cafeteria. It was a large building, just beyond the right field fence from the baseball field. The food was good and the price was cheap.

We ate and walked back to Cobb Dorm in the dark. Passing the baseball field, I remembered that I hadn't given one thought, that day, to baseball or flying. The excitement of coming to the university, enrolling there, and signing up for the ROTC program was just sinking in. A lot had transpired since I pulled out of the driveway back at Moore Avenue that morning and I wondered just where this adventure would take me.

I slept soundly.

Some rustling about and muffled voices awakened me. I wasn't sure where I was. I had slept so soundly that I wasn't sure if I had been dreaming or had actually enrolled in UNC. I opened my eyes and the truth suddenly sank in. There were pipes overhead, a few dim lightbulbs hung above, and some boys were moving about quietly in the dim light. I was definitely in college.

It was early, barely 6:30, so I had plenty of time for my first class. My turn for the bathroom came fairly quickly. I showered and dressed and, with notebook in hand, was off to the cafeteria and to my first class.

Bingham Hall was a stately brick three-story building and quite intimidating. The classrooms on the first two floors were brightened by tall windows extending from about two feet off the floor up to the ceiling. They remained open during the warm season and closed when the weather dictated. Bingham stood adjacent to a broad open area called Polk Place that was surrounded by giant oak trees. Just off to the left was the library and to the right stood several other similar buildings along Polk Place.

I found my classroom and took a seat and settled in. I looked around and discovered that I didn't know a soul. This wasn't Allen Jay. I was used to seeing classmates I had grown up with. Not here, and strangely enough, I discovered that they were all men. I learned soon that UNC had been, up till recently, an almost all-male, white school and only recently had women been allowed to enroll. Blacks were admitted during my second year.

Our teacher, Miss Putzel, arrived right on time, introduced herself, and immediately asked each student to stand, say his name, and tell the class where they came from. That went okay. When my turn came, I stood up, managed to remember my name, and said that I was from Allen Jay High School and sat back down. Miss Putzel asked quickly, "Where's that?"

I jumped back up and said, "High Point…High Point, North Carolina."

"Thank you," she said, "and you may be seated." I would have probably still been standing had she not invited me to sit down. I was frozen stiff.

I took down every word that Miss Putzel said that day and before I knew it the class was over and I was on my way to Math class at Phillips Hall.

French at Murphy Hall followed and that was followed by Social Science at Sanders Hall. They were all the same, but somehow different. My new classmates were all the same, the buildings were all similar, but the teachers were all surprisingly different. Miss Putzel, English, was all business. Mr. Brown, the math professor, was very old and apparently recovering from a stroke. He was almost immobile and his speech was halting at best. The French and Social Science teachers were obviously graduate students and not very enthused at being there.

The first day of classes were taken up by routine stuff. Each of the professors advised us as to their individual rules for their course, the reference books that would be required, and a preliminary test schedule. Some professors scheduled individual interviews and some did not. It was noon and since I had no further classes for the day I stopped by the cafeteria for lunch and retreated to Cobb basement to digest the day's adventures.

A day and a half had passed since I had pulled out of the driveway back home at Moore Avenue and my head was spinning. I hadn't conjugated the first French verb yet and still I had learned so much. I knew now just why one should arrive more than one day before classes were to start. In reviewing my patchwork schedule, I discovered that in having to settle for the "leftover" classes, my schedule spanned six days. This would not give me any time to return to High Point to maintain my weekend flying or any semblance of a social schedule. Plus, there was a good chance that I would run out of clean laundry as I was counting on a weekly visit home for Mom to do that.

I was beginning to recognize the importance of the locations of the classrooms also. My schedule had me zigzagging all over the campus when, with careful scheduling, one could transit from one class to another one nearby quite casually.

Books! I needed books. One of my roommates suggested that I go over to the book exchange near Old South Hall where I could find the necessary textbooks. Also, if I was lucky, I could find some used books, recently turned in by upperclassmen, that would be considerably cheaper. I found the book exchange, located the required books, and luckily, found all of the books that I needed. Some were pretty well used—marked up along the margins and dog-eared—but at the prices that I paid, I was pretty happy.

With the day almost over, I stopped by the cafeteria, had dinner, and returned to home sweet home, my basement. Wednesday would introduce me to the rest of my classes: Physical Education at Woollen Gymnasium at 9:00, followed by Air Science at 11:00 at the ROTC area, and finally, Hygiene back at Woollen Gym at noon.

Sleep came quickly and I slept hard through the night.

I awoke with a great deal of anticipation. Phys. Ed. could be fun and since I had somewhat of an athletic background it should be easy. I was really excited about the ROTC class at 11:00, and Hygiene would finish the day.

I rushed through breakfast and hurried over to Woollen Gym. The physical education instructor was young and extremely nice. The program proved to be educational to me as it introduced me to a number of sports that I was not familiar with. In our neighborhood in Allen Jay we only focused on football, basketball, and baseball, and this program would expose me to many more.

I almost ran over to the ROTC class. It was in building three, room three. I found the building and classroom and broke my lifetime tradition of always sitting at the back of the class. I found a seat up front and sat down. Being up front felt strange.

After being totally immersed in aviation for the past two years, and possessing a private pilot license, this would be the first time that I had ever sat in a formal class and studied from a fixed curriculum. My notepad was open, my pencil was in hand, and I was ready when the instructor entered the room.

His name was Captain Joseph Gerrity. He was dressed in class A blues and was most impressive. He went right to work; reviewing class protocol, passing out our research books, and explaining just what the ROTC was. He reviewed our immediate schedule, which included two drill periods and two classroom periods weekly. When he got to the part where, upon graduation from UNC, we would go immediately to active service and that would include flight training, I almost swooned.

Next came the best part; the issuance of uniforms. We got a lecture on the care of the uniforms and appearance of the cadet while in public view. Uniforms would be distributed at the next drill period, and mine was scheduled for tomorrow.

Hygiene was next, but it was anti-climactic. Nothing could top the U.S. Air Force show featuring Captain Joseph Gerrity. My body was in Hygiene class, but my mind was somewhere in the clouds, soaring with Captain Gerrity as his wingman.

Back at the basement I relaxed, reviewed my schedule, and with the exception of a Library Acquaintance lecture, I had completed one round of classes. Tomorrow it all started again with English, Math, French, and Social Studies…and…ROTC drill and the distribution of *uniforms*. What could be better than that?

On looking at my schedule, I found that I could leave Chapel Hill at noon on Saturday, spend Sunday at home, and be back on Monday for my 9:00 Phys Ed class. Perfect. I dropped a postcard to Mom, reviewed what I had to do for the remainder of the week, and fell asleep.

The remainder of the week was uneventful. I bonded with a couple of my roommates, made all of my classes on time, received my Air Force uniform, and began to study in earnest. I was driven not so much by a quest for knowledge, but out of a fear of failure. I rededicated myself to the mastering of the French language and set a personal goal of being the best student cadet in the Air Science classes.

Saturday noon came, my car was packed, and when Social Science class let out, I was on my way to High Point.

A couple of hours later, I pulled into the driveway at 206 Moore Avenue. Mom was waiting and seemed genuinely interested in the events surrounding my first week of college. We sat on the back porch as I related all my recent adventures. I dropped off my dirty laundry and headed down to the grocery store to see Dad. He announced to all the old men sitting around that his son had just started college at the "North Carolina University." He was proud and they appeared to be very impressed. After some small talk, I headed directly to Fraley Field.

All the hangar-flyers were there and I caught up on all the gossip. Everyone asked about the university and Mr. and Mrs. Spencer were happy that I had enrolled. Mr. Spencer was especially pleased that I had enrolled in ROTC and he said that he knew that I would make a good Air Force officer. Mrs. Spencer reminded me to "bear down" and study.

It was getting late so I headed home. I checked my finances and allowed that I had enough cash for a movie and a couple of hamburgers at the ole White House Barbeque and Grill, so I decided to call up an old girlfriend for a date.

Gail was the last girl I had dated last summer. She would be nice to see again and I was sure she'd like to see me. I decided to call her.

"Hello, Gail?" I asked.

"Yes," she said. "Who is this?"

"Tommy Cooper."

"Oh," she sounded surprised, "I thought you were at Carolina."

"Yes, I am enrolled there," I explained, "but I'm home for the weekend. Would you like to go to a movie tonight?"

"Oh, I'm so sorry," she said, "but I have plans tonight."

"That's okay," I said, acting nonchalant, "maybe some other time."

"Yeah, sure," she said as she hung up.

Well, fine, I thought. *Let's see, who can I call next?*

I went through about five phone numbers of girls I had dated over the summer and it was like a recording. "Sorry, but I have plans," they would all say. "Call me later?"

I gave up.

Sunday morning with my parents was nice. Mom supplied me with clean clothes, bedding, and a box lunch, and Dad gave me my allowance for the week, plus some additional money for books. I stopped by Fraley Field to say good-bye to my hangar-flying buddies and headed back to Chapel Hill.

It had been exactly six days since I had last traveled this road to Chapel Hill. How different it felt today. Last week my mind was filled with doubt and misgivings and today, well, I felt a calmness and a feeling of self-confidence brought about by the progress that I had made this last week. The apprehensions that I had felt just six days ago were replaced with feelings of confidence to face whatever might present itself in the future.

I wasn't that happy about striking out with all the ladies back in High Point though. Someone back at the basement had said, jokingly, "Absence makes the heart grow fonder...of somebody else." Boy, was that true. I decided to work on that situation.

But not now. My thoughts were on school, and especially ROTC.

On arriving back at the basement. I found a note from Billy Garner. He asked me to meet him at Winston dorm when I returned from High Point as he had something important for me. I found Billy and he advised me that he had gotten approval for me to join the prestigious Air Force Drill Squadron. He explained that the group was made up of a select group of cadets who performed complex marching maneuvers at football games and other events. I would be issued additional uniform items including a white scarf, spats, and gloves, and on special events, I would be issued a white rifle.

"Billy," I protested, "I haven't had my first drill session yet and I don't know my right foot from my left."

"Don't worry," he said confidently, "I'll give you a quick lesson and you'll be just as good as the rest of us. Meet me tomorrow at the field next to Woollen gym and we'll go through the basic drill. The advanced stuff will come later."

I was a sucker for anything to do with the ROTC so I agreed.

I met Billy there at the agreed time. He went through all the elementary moves; which foot to start on, how to stand at attention and parade rest. He taught me how to salute, how to turn ninety degrees, and how to do an "about-face." He reviewed the basic commands that I might expect and then we practiced. We must have made quite a spectacle out there on that enormous field, all alone, just two men; one barking orders and the other stumbling around as if drunk.

My first drill at ROTC was Tuesday, so I imposed on Billy to give me another private lesson Monday afternoon. I was doing pretty good after that one and I was looking forward to my first drill.

It went okay. Luckily, there were a couple of guys there who had issues with the commands and who required special attention, but with Billy's training I did okay. Any rookie mistakes went unnoticed and after the first session, Billy and I had a "debriefing," an Air Force word Billy taught me, and we reviewed any questions that I had. It went pretty good after that.

Being a member of the drill team was a valuable experience and I was a proud member for the next two years. We performed at a number of football games and at special events throughout the state, including the Azalea Festival down at Wilmington. We also performed at an Air Force base in West Palm Beach, Florida, which, incidentally, led to my first flight in a large aircraft, a twin boom C-119. I let the captain know that I was a private pilot and he allowed me into the cockpit. I had never seen so many gauges and switches in my life. *How*, I thought, *can anyone ever remember what all those things are for?*

My second week was going well. The classes were demanding but not too difficult and I was really getting into the ROTC Air Science classes. I decided on a routine of going home every other week and to use my off days at Chapel Hill to catch up on my studies.

To my surprise, toward the end of September, I noticed in the newspaper that there was to be a fall baseball practice session lasting for two weeks. This was something that I wasn't used to. Back at Allen Jay we would only play baseball in the spring. I checked the date for the first training period and made a note to be there.

CHAPTER 9
Baseball and Life at UNC

Settling down

I SHOWED UP AT THE baseball park, Old Emerson Field, at the appointed time, fully equipped with my first baseman's mitt and my spikes. I was dressed in Levi's and a T-shirt and I looked like anything but a baseball player.

There were two stern-looking coaches dressed smartly in UNC baseball uniforms, and about a hundred players dressed in an assortment of uniforms, practice garb, and…Levi's. We were all a motley bunch.

That is, until one of the coaches introduced himself and instructed the players to split into two groups; the returning players from last year were instructed to assemble over along the third base line and all others were to go to the first base line. It was then I noticed that all of the returning players were dressed in smart practice uniforms. They looked spiffy and the rest of us looked like a bunch of clowns.

The regulars took to the field right away, warming up, and were looking like real baseball players.

One of the coaches came over and addressed us. He introduced himself and explained that under the college rules, only sophomores, juniors, and seniors could be on the Varsity team and the first-year students would comprise the freshman team. There were fifty or sixty of us freshmen, and the coach instructed us to separate in order of our desired position and he would interview us personally, one at a time, over at the far end of the bench.

The pitchers were first, then the catchers, and then the first basemen. There were five or six first basemen and soon my turn for the interview came.

I was pretty nervous.

"I see you're a first baseman," he said, looking at my mitt. "What's your name?"

"Thomas L. Cooper," I said, with as much confidence as I could muster.

He had a clipboard with lots of names and information. He frowned down at the clipboard. "I don't see your name here," he said, looking back up at me.

"No, sir," I explained. "I just got here about three weeks ago." I had a flashback to the enrollment interview.

He explained that the boys listed on his clipboard has been scouted during the last year or so while playing for their high school teams and had been *invited* to participate in fall training. He explained that it wasn't necessary to be scouted to participate in fall training or to play and he wished me luck. He took some more information down and, with a nod, indicated that the interview was over. I went back to the others and awaited further instructions.

After the interviews were complete, we moved to the freshmen practice area and began to perform for the coach. On the second day, we were issued gray colored practice uniforms and blue caps. Now we looked like a baseball team! The drills were pretty simple at first, but, as the days progressed, they became more intense. We were tested at our individual positions with a litany of situations created by the coach. Ground balls would be hit our way, erroneous throws were made to check our reaction and skills, and batting practice was conducted with the coach taking copious notes.

Thanks to Dick Culler and my American Legion training, I did pretty well. My play around the first base bag brought favorable comments from the coach and my hitting at batting practice was passable. Since the right field fence was about 450 feet from home plate, it was impossible for me to hit a ball over it, so I just concentrated on meeting the ball solidly and it worked.

I began to notice that the group of initial applicants slowly began to be reduced. As it turned out, the coach would quietly, if a player wasn't making it, take him aside and inform him, "Better luck next time." By the end of the fall training session there were two players for each position and eight pitchers remaining. The coach had a final team meeting, congratulated those of us remaining, and informed us that we would be invited to spring training next year as we had made the team.

I was delighted. This was a giant step toward a career in organized baseball. UNC was a highly credited baseball school and to make the team as a walk-on was nothing short of miraculous. I was happy for myself, but I was happier for Dad.

I got another nice surprise later that week. I received a note from the Housing Officer to stop by New East Annex as I had been assigned a real room in a real dormitory. I went over, signed some documents, and walked directly to see my new home.

Winston Dorm was located directly across the street from Woollen Gymnasium. It was of brick construction and had four floors. From the rear it overlooked a large open yard that was bordered by two other dorms: Conner and Alexander. I walked up to the second floor, found my new room, number 206, and knocked.

My roommate to be was a breezy type of character. His name was George Artope and he was about my size. He had curly blond hair and wore horn-rimmed glasses. He welcomed me in and said that he was glad to see me. He indicated that he didn't care for his previous roommate, as he was a slob. He didn't keep his side of the room tidy and refused to study. I quietly made up my mind to remember to keep my side tidy and to study. The studying was a necessity and would come easy but the tidy part might need a little work. I remembered Mom's lesson back at Myrtle Beach and that reinforced my conscience.

I said good-bye to my friends at Cobb basement and moved into Winston Dorm right away. George and I gossiped a bit about our high school days, reviewed our new experiences at UNC, and became instant friends. He was a preppie sort of guy and highly intelligent. He leaned toward the fraternity life at school, but I didn't really get into that. I suppose we were different there and that made us compatible somewhat. He joined a fraternity his sophomore year and moved there. However, we remained friends throughout our college days and corresponded for several years afterward.

I was anxious to get home and break the good news to Mom and Dad. They were happy; Mom was happy about the dorm room and Dad was happy about me making the baseball team.

After my last socially disastrous visit home I had developed a plan that I thought might improve things somewhat. It was pretty simple. I called it "operation touch base." I would drop a note weekly to the eligible ladies back at High Point just to show some interest in them. If a young lady answered, it was an indication that she was available and somewhat interested, and if she didn't, well, I knew that I shouldn't waste my time.

It was Saturday afternoon and time to test my theory. On my second call…bingo! I was set for the evening and now I could visit my friends at Fraley Field and catch up on all the aviation gossip.

The chatter was always the same. Dwight Lohr was holding court with some funny salesman stories, Pete Dickens was relating a true-life story about a recent flight as a pilot on Piedmont Airlines, and Melvin Robinson was keeping everyone spellbound with stories about his experiences as an air show performer.

There was another topic that popped up that day though. It seems that one of the mechanics who came around infrequently had rebuilt an aircraft for resale and he needed the money immediately. He would let the airplane go real cheap for a quick sale, so we all went over to the "T" hangars to take a look.

The airplane was a J-5 Piper Cub. The only difference between a J-3 Cub and this Cub was that this one had a more powerful engine and it could carry two passengers in the backseat, and a Cub would only carry one. The seller said that it was worth about $1,000, but he would let it go for $700 if it were a quick sale. Since there were no takers, we all paraded back to the office and continued our afternoon of hangar flying. I really liked the airplane but I knew that I couldn't afford it and Dad wouldn't even think of it.

Later that afternoon, I got a phone call from the seller. He said that he would lower the sale price to $500 for the airplane if he could get the money before Wednesday. I said that I would think about it and get back to him.

I went out on a date that night, but my mind wasn't on the young lady. It was on the J-5 Cub and how I could present the argument to Dad to purchase it. My parents weren't rich by any stretch of the imagination, but they were comfortable—primarily because they were frugal and they didn't spend money foolishly. Their only luxury was to purchase a new car every three or four years and that was it. The odds of me convincing my dad to fork over $500 for an airplane was simply overwhelming, but I thought I'd give it a try. *Let's see, how can I approach this argument?* I thought.

I decided on the safety angle. By flying to college, I would not have to travel over those dangerous country roads between High Point and Chapel Hill. And then I would counter punch with economics. The purchase price was 50 percent of the value and it was just as cheap as driving. Plus, there were several fellows I had met at college who would help with expenses in order to fly back and forth to High Point. I didn't dare tell him that by flying back and forth I could accelerate my flying time toward a commercial flying license and reach my goal as a commercial pilot much sooner.

It was Sunday morning. I tried my argument out on Mom while Dad was at church. It fell on deaf ears. Mom's only comment was that Dad probably wouldn't agree to such a plan because he was afraid of planes and, anyway, she thought that I had enough to do, what with college and all, without worrying about an airplane too.

Dad came home and we sat down to dinner. In High Point in 1954, dinner was the noon meal and supper was the evening meal. I got up my nerve and blurted out my petition to Dad. The words came gushing out in no particular order but he got the idea. Dad was a man of few words.

"No," he said.

There was no rebuttal on my part. It was useless. I had made my case, albeit not very well, and Dad had made his decision known quite well.

That was that. I really didn't think that Dad would acquiesce to such a scheme, but I had to give it a try. I went through the usual drill; picked up my clean laundry, Mom packed a lunch, Dad gave me the allowance, and I said good-bye and went to Fraley Field. I gave the mechanic the bad news and was on my way to Chapel Hill.

After two months at college, the program was fairly routine. Classes were going well, except for French, and I was getting along very well with my new roommate, George. Tuesday came, the Piper J-5 was completely out of my mind, and I attended all classes plus ROTC drill. After lunch, I returned to my dorm for my self-imposed study period.

There was a Western Union telegram under my door.

"AIRPLANE WILL BE READY THURSDAY," it read. "P W COOPER."

I don't recall much after that. I know that I sat on the edge of my bed for a long time trying to digest the news. I wrote a quick note to Mom and Dad, thanking them and saying that I would be home, as usual, on Saturday afternoon.

The week passed very slowly. Finally, Saturday came and I drove home to see my prized possession. After a quick stop at home to see Mom, I stopped by the store to thank Dad. He just said to be careful and that the airplane would be at the airport ready for me.

Mr. Spencer had pulled the airplane to the front of the hangar for my arrival. I drove up and there she sat, glistening in the sun—freshly painted beige with an orange stripe extending from around the nose to the tail. The hangar-flyers were all gathered around and congratulated me loudly as I walked up. Mr. Spencer allowed that I would need a checkout before I could solo it as I had never flown a tandem seated aircraft. My only flying time was in the T-Craft that had side-by-side seating and the J-5 had front and back seats.

We went up right away. After three or four landings, Mr. Spencer declared me safe to fly the J-5 alone, and back at the hangar he endorsed my pilot logbook accordingly.

As I look back on my career, this day was a major turning point. Heretofore, my career field and my future had been directed toward baseball. Now, although I didn't realize it then, the direction took a turn toward professional aviation. Instead of logging a few hours of flying per month, I could now, by flying back and forth to college regularly, log around ten hours monthly. Since one only needed 200 hours to qualify for a commercial pilot's license, it was clear to see that I would amass those required hours in about a year and a half. I mentally set a goal to be ready for those tests in the summer of 1956.

With an airplane at college my schedule took on a new dimension. There was a large grass airport with multiple wide runways near Chapel Hill. It was used during the Second World War as a navy training base and there were a few buildings from that era remaining. There was little, if any, activity there with the exception of football weekends, and for my commuting it was ideal. I would leave the Chevy there on weekends, fly home, and use my parents' car for social activities in High Point. Billy Garner would occasionally fly home with me, as would several others when there was room.

After the novelty of owning my own airplane and commuting to college wore off, I settled back into my new routine.

Winter came; the first semester was finished with final tests to be administered in January of '55. I registered for the second semester timely and enrolled in the classes that were better suited to my schedule. If I had learned anything in the first semester it was to register early.

Winter passed uneventfully. Classes were going okay. ROTC Air Science class was exciting and so was working out with the Drill Team. Commuting in the J-5 worked out well also. If the weather was questionable, I just drove the Chevy home. Billy Garner and I flew a lot together and I met another graduate from High Point High School, Jim Sink, who would hop a ride now and then.

Spring came to Chapel Hill and with it came baseball. Baseball at UNC was a big thing, even for the freshman team. The freshman team traveled around the state and played most of the other college freshman teams. I was first team, first baseman, and played full time. As usual, my fielding was good but my hitting was somewhat lacking. At the end of the season, May 26, I, along with the other freshmen players, was awarded an athletic sweater for participation in the program. The sweater was cardigan style, navy blue, with the UNC logo emblazoned on the front pocket.

Neat.

The second semester tests were administered and summer was here. I packed up the car, having left the airplane at home earlier, said good-bye to my roommate George, and headed home. All in all, my first year in college had gone pretty well. Most of the classes were interesting and I did okay in all with the exception of my old nemesis, French. ROTC Air Science was terrific and I eagerly looked forward to those class periods. The Drill Team was exciting also, especially performing at the football games at Kenan Stadium with thousands of fans watching.

Summer vacation brought relief to the demands of the scholastic life of a college freshman, but it also brought something else. Something worse… The necessity of a summer job.

I reviewed my options… Let's see…paper box company…NO! Merita Bread Bakery…NO! I had learned my lessons well at those two companies.

I was hanging out with Grandpa Franklin, bemoaning my circumstances, when he suggested that I might apply with the Perley A. Thomas Car Works, a school bus manufacturing company in High Point. It seems that he had worked there in the woodworking department in the late '20s and '30s and had known Mr. Thomas personally. He told me that Mr. Perley Thomas had retired but he thought he remembered the daughter, Mrs. Melva Price, and that I should ask for her.

Grandma Franklin told me later that Grandpa had been working there before the Great Depression and when it hit, most of the employees left. Grandpa was only one of approximately ten people left with the company, and often he would go for months without pay to help Mr. Thomas and the family out. The earlier school buses were made almost entirely of wood during that time, but in the late '30s there was a transition to metal, and Grandpa retired from the company soon after.

I didn't know much about building school buses. My only experience with school buses was the bad memory of having to ride on that demeaning center bench seat back in grade school. I had qualified as a school bus driver in my senior year and drove one all that year.

I mustered up my nerve and visited the employment office of Thomas Car Works. It was a pretty big company located on the outskirts of town. I asked about a job and a woman gave me an application to fill out while offering a comment: "We're not hiring now but if we do, I'll call you in." I thanked her and filled out the application. As I turned it back to her I told her that my grandpa Franklin said to say hello to a Mrs. Price.

"You're Fred Franklin's grandson?" she exclaimed.

"Yes, ma'am," I replied.

"Well, I'm Melva Price." She smiled. "Wait right here and I'll be right back." She returned quickly and with a firm handshake she said, "You've got a job; when can you start?"

I'm sure that she created a job for me to, in some way, pay back my grandfather for the kindness he showed to them back in the '30s. My job was to manage the receiving lot out next to the railway siding. The completed chasses would arrive by rail complete with engines, transmissions, and wheels installed. I would receive them, drive them off the flatbed train cars, and position them, in a predetermined line-up, so as to have them ready to feed into the assembly line for completion. As chasses were needed, I would position them at the beginning of the assembly line. As they were completed I would drive the finished bus to the final prep area for checkout prior to delivery. The job was outdoors and from time to time, when the wind was right, the airliners would come over on their approach to the Greensboro airport and I would catch myself daydreaming about being up there some day.

That turned out to be the best summer job I ever had.

Summer vacation also brought something else. It brought Jerri Fitzgerald back to her grandmother's house for the summer.

Inevitably, the flame was rekindled. Well, it wasn't a real flame…more like a dying ember. However, Operation Touch Base was working pretty well during the spring and I had been seeing several young ladies. I continued those loose relationships, and once in a while Jerri would condescend to see me. The summer was working out better than expected. Anyway, since I had set a goal of attaining my commercial license next summer, it was necessary to fly as much as I could in order to build up my flying time. That caused severe issues with my social budget and it limited my courting opportunities, so I wasn't too upset with limited dating.

CHAPTER 10
Working the Air Show Circuit

Melvin was the ultimate showman.

IT WAS IN THAT SUMMER that I bonded with Melvin Robinson. Melvin was a free spirit in the truest sense of the word. He was small in stature, but he was a tough little man and he was the spitting image of Audie Murphy. He had built a small aerobatic airplane from scrap parts and would perform at weekend air shows around the state. He was quite a performer in his midget airplane and he would end every show with a parachute jump from a locally rented airplane.

I was hanging out with the other hangar-flyers at Ellington's Grill on South Main Street one Saturday afternoon. The usual gang was there: Dwight, Pete, and some others, and Melvin was talking about the air show business. One of his problems was that he would have to hire a local pilot at the airport where he was performing to fly him up over the airport for his parachute drop. He had experienced some problems with the pickup pilots, and especially with their airplanes, and he just wasn't comfortable with that system.

As we were leaving, he looked at me and asked, "How would you like to be in the air show business?"

"I don't think I'm that good of a pilot," I confessed. I had a quick vision of me performing aerobatics before a crowd.

"No, no." He laughed. "I need someone I trust to travel with me to fly me on my parachute jumps and do other odd jobs," he explained. "You might want to take your Cub and I'll pay for the gas, plus a few bucks for your time."

I couldn't wait until the next air show. It worked out perfectly. Melvin would fly his midget to the shows, his girlfriend, Betty, would take his Thunderbird, and I would fly the J-5. We would take the door off the J-5 at Fraley Field and, with its wide backseat and extra horsepower engine, it made an ideal jump plane.

We made quite a team. Betty, in Melvin's T-bird and dressed provocatively, me in the J-5 Cub, and Melvin in his midget home-built airplane.

Barnum and Bailey had come to town!

Betty would show up early, meet the airport managers, and review the financial arrangements that Melvin had made earlier. Melvin always got a fixed fee plus a cut of the ticket sales. Betty made sure that the customer count was accurate. I would land about an hour before show time and brief the announcer who operated the airport public announcement system on the schedule that Melvin would fly. Soon after that, Melvin would show up overhead.

Melvin was the consummate showman. Although the air show had been advertised weeks before in the local newspapers, Melvin would come across the field, do a slow roll with the smoke exhaust bellowing, and continue over the town at a reasonably low altitude just to remind the locals that an air show was about to begin.

After the show, Betty would squeeze every last penny out of the sponsors, I would carefully fold up Melvin's used parachute and store it in the trunk of the T-bird, and Melvin would take his bows and mix with the adoring crowd. He loved them and they loved him too.

But the best part of the deal was practicing with Melvin. Occasionally, he would want to try a new series of maneuvers and he would grab me and the J-5 and off we would go. At a safe altitude, he would practice the exercise until he felt comfortable enough to perform it in his midget at low altitude. He would always save a little time to instruct me in basic aerobatics, and it wasn't long until spins, loops, barrel rolls, and snap rolls were second nature to me.

Traveling with the air show that summer and the next was simply enchanting. Melvin was larger than life and the skills he taught me lived on with me throughout my career. More than once did I call on those skills to bail me out of situations that my ego had gotten me into.

There was a car salesman Dad used to deal with exclusively who worked for Neill Pontiac, the Pontiac dealership in High Point, and he would show up about every two years to begin to soften Dad up for a new car. Mom was wise to him and he knew it. If he came by the grocery store when she was there he would just have a Coke and keep going. If Dad were alone, well, it was open season and if Dad hadn't traded cars for two years, the salesman would usually win.

When I began to drive, Dad had called him, and he was the dealer who sold us the '48 Chevy. This opened the door for him to come more often and to push Dad to upgrade my car. It was an off year for Dad to buy a car but the salesman reckoned that he could persuade him to buy a new one for me.

He showed up one Saturday in July, with a beautiful tomato red 1954 Mercury convertible. He explained that he took it in on a new Pontiac and that it had low miles and was in perfect condition. He said that the first person he thought of was my dad and he was right. I think Dad liked the car better than I did. The salesman gave Dad an offer on the Chevy that he couldn't resist, and before the day was over, I had a shiny, tomato red Mercury convertible.

The summer was fast coming to an end and my thoughts were quickly turning to UNC and the fall semester. It was to be my second year and, with no job to support my aviation and social habits, I decided to sell the J-5. A friend made me an offer and since I had accumulated almost enough flying time to qualify for my commercial pilot license, I reluctantly let it go just before school started.

This September at UNC would be a lot different than last year. My classes were already selected and my room was reserved. All that was left was to load up the tomato red Mercury convertible and head east.

CHAPTER 11
UNC

The second year

THE DAY CAME TO LEAVE. Mom gave me some last-minute instructions. "Be careful with your damp towels; you were getting rust stains on them last year. Wipe the towel rack before you hang them up," she instructed. Dad said, "You be careful driving."

With Mom's box lunch on the front seat and the top down I was off for my second year of college.

My old roommate, George Artope, had succumbed to the pleasures of fraternity life and had moved to his frat house. My new roommate was a far cry from George. He was a messy sort and wasn't too interested in studying. I made up my mind to try to get along as best I could and hope that he would move on quickly. He didn't.

In the fall, baseball practice began. I remembered last year when I had to line up with all the new freshmen in our various uniforms and outfits while the varsity team began to practice in fresh UNC uniforms. This year I was invited to practice with the varsity team and was given a complete uniform including a new first baseman's mitt and new shoes.

Practice went well, and at the end of the session I was playing as second-string first baseman on the varsity team. I looked forward to the spring baseball season with great anticipation.

Sometime in the fall I took a job at the local hotel, the Carolina Inn. It was a prestigious facility as it was extremely popular with the parents visiting their children attending UNC and for fans attending the local sports events. The job wasn't that great. I was assigned to kitchen duty and was given the great responsibility of cleaning and stacking plates while my coworker loaded them into the dishwasher. I had frightening flashbacks of working in the paper box factory and the bakery. I think it caused me to rededicate myself to studying so as to avoid hard labor later in life.

I'm not sure just what prompted me to take a part-time job. Did my conscience trouble me because Dad was funding my whole budget or was it simply that I needed more money to feed my vices of courting and flying? I fear that it was the latter.

Classes were going well and I felt that I was especially excelling in ROTC Air Science. I was in my third semester and the ROTC subjects were becoming more technical. The class topics included the theory of flight and the operational aspects of specific aircraft, along with the background of United States policies with regard to both defense and strategic air operations.

The one "downer" this year, especially in ROTC, was that my old buddy, Billy Garner, had graduated in May and was already in USAF cadet training at Lackland Air Force Base in Texas. I really missed him, especially on the drill team. We had bonded in my senior year at Allen Jay and I suppose it was because of him that I decided to attend UNC. Being a senior, he had mentored me in my first year at college with the ROTC program and especially with the precision drill team.

We had spent many hours flying between Chapel Hill and High Point. On one occasion, after landing at Chapel Hill I hopped out and let him go solo. Although I wasn't an instructor, I had let him fly so much, and he showed so much aptitude for flying, that I knew he could do it. He did fine. With just a couple of bounces, he made a successful landing and we both were pleased. As we both remember, the airport manager watched the whole spectacle and did not share our pleasure in the least.

CHAPTER 12
The Secret Plan

"Shhhh."

BILLY'S LETTERS TO ME RELATING his progress at Lackland were a great incentive to work hard and prepare for my entrance into the ROTC cadet program when I graduated from UNC. I must admit that I was a little envious of him because, after all, didn't I teach him to fly and didn't I already have a private license? And here he was, about to leapfrog me in my aviation career. I still had two and a half years to go before I could be admitted to the ROTC Cadet program. I began to weigh my options.

A plan was beginning to evolve in the back of my mind. I wouldn't divulge it to anyone, but a part of the plan was to work as hard as I could, score as high as I could in Air Science, and successfully complete two years of college. Then I could enlist in the Air Force and go directly into cadet flight school, bypassing my last two years of college at UNC.

CHAPTER 13
Baseball vs. Flying

A tough decision

WINTER CAME AND SPRING WAS just around the corner. Baseball spring practice began in late February and I was on the varsity team. Baseball took up a lot of time, so I had to make the decision between it and the Carolina Inn. The decision was easy. With my studies, baseball, and the drill team taking up so much time, I didn't have much spare time and even my visits to High Point suffered, as did my social life. Even Operation Touch Base with the ladies wasn't working very well.

Playing baseball for UNC was like playing for a professional team. We had a team of coaches along with trainers and equipment managers. In the locker room we had our own locker, and fresh T-shirts were laid out before each practice or game. The baseball bat manufacturing company came by and provided the team with personalized bats with each player's name imprinted on it. To see your autograph etched on your own personal baseball bat was an ego trip that was hard to dismiss.

We traveled all over the East Coast from Maryland to Florida and played all the colleges in those areas. In March we traveled to Tallahassee, Florida, to a tournament sponsored by the Florida State University. As a second team player I didn't play very much, but just to make the squad and travel with the team was exciting, and the pregame warm-ups were fun.

We were in Tallahassee, warming up for one of the tournament games, and an interesting thing happened, especially to a player like me who was not known for his hitting. In our practice routine each player would get five swings in batting practice. The first team would go first and then the second team would get their swings. My turn came up and I took my place in the batting cage. The right field fence looked inviting and, being a left-hand hitter, I decided to go for it. I dug in and, lo and behold, I connected and sent the first pitch over the fence. Out of five pitches, I sent three over the fence, flipped my bat nonchalantly toward the bat rack, and trotted to my position at first base to complete my practice session.

After I finished the infield drill at first base I headed toward the dugout. I had forgotten about my previous batting display and was ready to take my place on the bench for the game.

An older gentleman called me over to the retainer fence next to the dugout and asked my name and what year I was in at UNC. I gave him my name and told him that I was a sophomore. He handed me his card and said, "I'll be watching you for the next two years," and with that he turned and walked away. I looked at his card. It read, LEON HAMILTON, Scout, Brooklyn Baseball Club, and it gave his address as Jacksonville Beach, Florida.

I didn't know it then but that would be as close as I would ever get to realizing my early childhood ambition of being a professional baseball player.

My fourth semester was rapidly coming to an end. We played our last baseball game on May 11, classes ended on May 21, and all my tests were done by May 28. I loaded the Mercury and said good-bye to Winston Dorm and the University of North Carolina. If my secret plan worked, it would be forever.

I had barely settled in back in High Point when one of my flying buddies from Fraley Field stopped me at the airport and asked if I had a job for the summer yet. I told him that I probably would try to get back on with Thomas Car Works, but I would listen to any suggestions he might have.

He was a draftsman at Tomlinson Furniture Company in downtown High Point and he said that he was leaving town. He wondered if I might be interested in his position. "Jim," I said, "I've never had any draftsman training and I think that it might be a stretch."

"There's nothing to it," he assured me. "Let's get together tomorrow and I'll teach you all you have to know."

Now Tomlinson Furniture Company was one of the most prestigious furniture manufacturing establishments in the world. It was established in 1901 and was second to none in the quality of its products. To land a job in High Point, the Furniture Capital of the World, with Tomlinson Furniture was quite a coup. I didn't know if I could do it, but I agreed to give it a try.

Jim explained the job to me at our training session the next day. This was before computers were even thought of, and all art design and manufacturing plans were done by hand. The art department at Tomlinson's would draw a piece of furniture from three views: front, side, and top. Those drawings would then be sent to the department where Jim worked and he and his fellow draftsmen would dissect the drawings to create individual parts of the original conceptual artwork. Each piece would be drawn carefully to include specific dimensions of the parts in three dimensions and would include the placement of dowels, wooden pins that gave the piece strength when glued together. Those plans would then be distributed to the factory, where the woodworkers would cut to the plan's dimensions and somewhere down the assembly line the parts would be assembled and hopefully the finished product would look exactly like the original artwork that had been supplied to his drafting department.

"Simple enough," he said, having taken drafting courses in school. I hadn't any formal training in drafting, but I did have somewhat of a talent for drawing and it looked like something that I would enjoy.

Jim brought some files with him and we began the task of making me a draftsman in one day. He shared his tools with me: rulers, compasses, dividers, T-squares, and those dainty little lead pencils that draftsmen use.

Jim was a patient teacher and he worked to educate and drill me on the specific jobs that I would be expected to accomplish. I caught on pretty quickly and by the day's end I felt as if I might be able to fill his shoes at the furniture company.

Monday came and Jim and I showed up together at his department to attempt a seamless swap of personnel. He was leaving and I would take his place. Luckily, the job was at such an entry level that his immediate supervisor could approve the transaction, so there wasn't such a big interview process. Charley was the supervisor and he had worked there forever. We talked for a while and then the moment came for me to exhibit my drafting skills. He gave me a simple problem and I breezed through it. Jim had taught me well. After a few more, slightly more difficult problems, Charley approved the swap, sent me to personnel, and I was a junior draftsman for Tomlinson Furniture Company.

At last, a white collar job in the summer. Well, at least white-ish. As new man on the block, I not only was a draftsman, I was the official go-fer. I was given the simple jobs of running errands and delivering the finished plans to production. I settled in nicely, got to know Charlie well, and we became best friends. He took me under his wing and covered my mistakes. He taught me a lot and I was grateful for the interest he took in me. In addition to being the department's head, he was the department's clown. He could keep you laughing for hours. It was a pleasure to work with him.

Summer had started nicely. I had a good job and although I had sold my treasured Piper J-5, I was still helping Melvin and Betty with the occasional air show. Betty and I would leave early in Melvin's T-bird to drive to the location of the next air show. She would do her financial thing with the sponsors and I would busy myself in renting a local airplane and removing the door for Melvin's grand finale, the parachute jump. My social life was just ho hum, so the stage was set for me to activate my secret plan.

The plan was two-pronged but simple. I would continue to work toward attaining my commercial pilot's license along with an instructor's rating, while simultaneously applying to the U S Air Force for direct entry into the aviation cadet program. College was conspicuously absent from my plan. I was ready to take the test for the commercial license, and the flight instructor's test wouldn't be far behind.

It was early June when I visited the Air Force recruiter at the post office building in High Point and signed up for the cadet program.

Operation Secret Plan was activated. A career in flying had just won out.

The recruiting officer filled out some papers and said I would be hearing from Cadet Headquarters in Waco, Texas, shortly. He was correct. Within about two weeks I received notification for a date to take my acceptance medical examination. It was set for July 24 at Shaw Air Force Base in South Carolina.

While waiting for that date I could concentrate on the commercial license and the flight instructor's rating.

CHAPTER 14

An Act of Faith

"Melvin, I trust you."

IT WAS EARLY SUMMER AND all of us hangar-flyers—note that I included myself in that sacred group now—were hanging around the hangar at Fraley Field. Pete was lamenting the fact that he was still a copilot, Dwight was trying to make a flight to Gastonia sound exciting, and Melvin was just listening and grinning.

There was a break in the conversation and Melvin spoke up. "I want ten of you guys to put up twenty bucks each for an act of faith."

"What's it for?" we all asked.

"If I tell you in advance, it won't be an act of faith," he answered coyly.

We prodded him but he wouldn't acquiesce. There was lots of laughing, speculating, and pawing the dirt while Melvin waited to see who would be the first sucker.

He pulled a twenty out of his pocket and threw it on the ground. "Okay," he challenged. "Who's next?" Well, that did it. Not to be outdone, Dwight, with much bravado, pulled out a twenty and threw it down. A few others followed and pretty soon Melvin had seven takers.

"Don't let this opportunity slip by," he chided the group like a county fair barker. "There's only three slots left and after those spots are gone, there will be no more forever."

I couldn't stand it any longer. "Here's a ten and my IOU for the rest," I said. There was some friendly grumbling, but Melvin said that he would cover me and I was in.

Finally, the pot was filled. We all waited for Melvin to tell us what we had bought for our twenty-dollar bills. He counted out the proceeds slowly and deliberately. "Okay," he said, "its all here—one hundred and ninety dollars and an IOU for ten dollars." He was making us sweat.

"Okay," he dragged it out, "you lucky fellows are the proud owners of a PT-26."

Nobody knew what a PT-26 was. All the members of this new club were asking the usual questions, all at one time. What is a PT-26? Where is it located? When will it arrive?

Melvin just grinned and pulled out a photograph. It was a picture of a barn! "That's where your airplane is." He laughed.

Another round of questions and finally Melvin, who was enjoying this charade far too much, explained, "The airplane is in a barn in Lexington about twenty-five miles south of here." He went on to tell us that the airplane was practically new with only forty hours' flying time on it. The owner had bought it from the Canadian Air Force five years ago, flew it to Lexington, North Carolina, and soon thereafter was killed in a car crash. The family took the wings off it and stored it in a barn. Melvin had bought it for $125 and planned to use the balance of the money to put it back together.

Melvin didn't have an air show the next week, so we all decided to set Saturday as the day that we would go down to Lexington and retrieve our prize.

The airplane was in a barn, but other than being extremely dirty, it looked to be in pretty good shape. Whoever stored it earlier did a good job and there were no dings or damage that we could see. Melvin had acquired the use of a flatbed truck and we carefully loaded the wings on it using the old quilts that Mother had supplied. We pulled the wingless airplane out of the barn, raised the tail onto a sling that Melvin had constructed on the rear end of the truck, hung a red flag on the prop, and off we went, pulling the airplane backward along the back roads to Fraley Field.

We borrowed the smaller of the two hangars at Fraley Field and went to work reassembling the PT. Melvin did most of the work with the rest of us relegated to cleaning parts, washing and waxing the airplane, and running errands for him.

He took a lot of time on the engine. I watched him change the spark plugs, put some "magic" potion in the cylinders to make sure that any accumulated rust would not damage the engine once it started, blow out fuel lines, and clean the carburetor. New bolts to secure the wings were purchased and soon the airplane was back together.

I don't think, in the history of aviation, there has been a more anticipated or glorious airplane roll out. It was Saturday noon when we pushed her out of the small hangar and over to the front of the larger hangar—a fitting place of honor.

There she stood, a proud military war bird in all her glory. Her wings were mounted low and her landing gears were placed wide apart. She had two cockpits, in tandem, with a sliding canopy that allowed you to fly with it either open or closed. The yellow paint, highlighted by the Canadian insignia, was waxed and shone like a diamond in the noon sun.

Marcel Dassault, the famous French aircraft designer, once wrote, "For a plane to fly, it must be beautiful." He must have had this PT-26 in mind.

If the PT was the star, then surely Melvin was the co-star. He walked around her, while we all watched in rapture. He checked the fuel, drained the sumps, moved all the control surfaces up and down knowingly, and finally hopped into the cockpit.

Dwight volunteered to pull the prop through. On the PT, even though it had an electric starter, one must pull the prop through manually about eight turns to ensure that the cylinders were free of any oil buildup that would cause damage when the engine started.

Finally, the big moment came. You could see Melvin pumping the throttle to prime the carburetor as he leaned his head out of the cockpit and yelled, "Clear!"

The prop began to turn. One turn, then two and then she caught. A belch of smoke emitted from the smokestack and the engine came to life. A roar came up from the assembled crowd as the engine smoothed out and purred at idle. Melvin checked a few more gauges and, with a confident wave and a cloud of dust, taxied toward the runway.

There was a lot of laughing and backslapping on the ramp while we waited on Melvin to do the normal preflight check. He would take extra time today since the aircraft hadn't been flown in about five years.

When Melvin was satisfied with the engine run-up and with a short burst from the engine he turned onto the runway, pushed the throttle full open, and the PT-26 began its takeoff roll. Slowly at first, then she accelerated, bouncing along the uneven runway and finally lifting off to great cheers from the admiring crowd.

The Man in The Arena...

The test flight went well. Melvin was complimentary in his analysis of the flight and allowed that members of the group could now check out and fly her when they wanted to. He had no takers today but eventually we all went up with him and he designated three of us as check captains: Pete Dickens, Dwight Lohr, and me.

We adjourned to Ellington's Bar and Grill to celebrate the wonderful events of the day with hamburgers and Cokes and to listen to Melvin expound on the qualities of the PT 26.

It was a wonderful summer. The PT-26 was about the safest airplane ever designed. Its landing characteristics were very docile and it handled wonderfully well in flight. We all got a lot of use out of it and Melvin even worked it in some of his air shows as a "high-powered," complex war bird. It was my job to buzz the field and circle the local town in the PT before the air shows.

CHAPTER 15
The Windsock Saga

Mom comes through.

WORKING NINE TO FIVE, HANGING out at the airport on weekends, and studying for the commercial written exam kept me busy, but once in a while the hangar-flyers at Fraley Field would try to get into some project out of sheer boredom.

We were sitting around one Saturday afternoon when, for some reason, the subject of the old rusty, neglected windsock on the hill in the middle of the airport came up. No one could remember when the metal frame had last been covered, not even the old guys. As we sat there, staring at this old derelict skeleton, a sacred cause began to develop.

It became the most important thing in the world for us to do. We *must* recover the old windsock and bring it back to life. After all, hadn't it stood sentinel over this old airport since its inception and wasn't it the last vestige of the noble history of Fraley Field?

Yes!

It deserved more than to just sit out there and rust away, so we decided to recover it; to restore it, to bring it back to life! Dwight volunteered that we could purchase a new cover through an aviation mail order house. Good. Let's do that and restore the old windsock to its original splendor, we decided. Mr. Spencer could steer us in the right direction. We went to him and asked for his opinion. He thought that it was a splendid idea. As a matter of fact, he had recently seen a new windsock cover advertised and he could direct us to the proper address for ordering.

"By the way," he said, "the cost would be $150 plus shipping."

That was a sobering revelation. We regrouped to come up with a second solution. It didn't have to be too sophisticated. We just wanted to be able to tell the old windsock that we cared and also it would be helpful if we knew the wind direction from time to time. Surely we could come up with a cheaper idea. We agreed to return the next day with some practical suggestions.

That night, without an idea, I went to Mom and posed the problem to her. I gave her the approximate dimensions of the frame and she said that she had an idea. She disappeared for a few minutes and returned with a wonderful red full-length dress. It was an old party dress she hadn't worn for years. She probably would never wear it again and it was mine for the taking. I thought that was the best idea ever and what a way to honor the old windsock than to adorn the rusty skeleton with Mom's old party dress?

We all met the next day at Fraley Field and when no one had any suggestions I presented them with the idea of using Mom's red party dress. The idea was met with a rousing vote of approval and riotous peals of laughter. What a way to honor the old windsock and to reward it for standing thankless guard for all these many years.

Dwight ran home for a ladder, Pete scrounged some cup grease for lubricating the turning mechanism, and I found some coat hangers to use for securing the dress to the frame. We were a motley but dedicated crew trudging through the knee-high grass to the middle of the airport on our self-proclaimed noble mission.

The ladder went in place. Dwight went up first and lubricated the ball bearings that let the windsock rotate. He proudly heralded that the lube job was a success as he spun the frame around deftly. I next climbed up the ladder, equipped with the red dress and some coat hangers. I slipped the dress up over the frame, pulled it all the way up, and fastened it with pieces of wire cut from the coat hangers. It fit perfectly. *This is going to work*, I thought confidently. The job was finished and I descended the ladder, and with my two other worthy crusaders, we admired our job.

As if on cue, as we stood there looking up at our masterpiece, a gust of wind came along. Mom's red party dress billowed out full and the windsock miraculously turned into the wind. With the arms of the dress gyrating to the syncopation of the wind, it seemed as if the old windsock was beckoning to the wayward pilot, "Look, see the wind's direction. I'm back."

CHAPTER 16
Finalizing My "Secret Plan"

A career in aviation was almost in my grasp.

ALONG WITH THE FRIVOLITY OF restoring the wind sock and the seriousness of breathing new life into the PT-26, I didn't lose track of my secret plan. While waiting for the assignment of my cadet physical, I prepared for the commercial pilot test in earnest. The day came to take the written exam. The flight to Charlotte and the landing at the airport were a lot less eventful than the time I was there two years earlier. I taxied up to the SOUTHERN FLIGHT EXECUTIVE TERMINAL, a lineman came out, chocked the wheels and took me over to the terminal, and I climbed the stairs to the CAA office.

The secretary looked up and right away recognized me. She chuckled and reminded me of the "adventurous" visit two years ago. We laughed, I presented my logbook to prove that I had accumulated enough flying time to take the written, and she pulled a blank test from her desk and motioned toward the testing room. I was proceeding with the test when the door opened.

It was Mr. Garrison, the head of the CAA there. "I just wanted to say hello. You must have made it in okay this time. I haven't had a call from the tower," he said jokingly.

"Yes, sir," I replied, "and I parked at the fixed base operation just as you suggested when I was last here."

He made some more small talk; I told him of my plans to finish my commercial pilot's license and instructor's rating before going into the cadet program and he offered any assistance that his office could give. He mentioned that after completing the commercial written, there was a CAA examiner in Salisbury who could administer the commercial flight check, but for the instructor's flight check I would have to ride with him.

I told him that I knew Inspector Brown at Salisbury and that he had administered my private pilot check ride and I would be happy to ride with him again.

As Mr. Garrison said good-bye, he allowed that he would look forward to riding with me for my instructor's rating. I said that I would call him and I went back to finishing the written exam.

The results of the commercial written exam came back positive. I had passed all parts and now I had to concentrate on the flight portion of the commercial test. But first, I had the Air Force Cadet physical exam to contend with.

I was instructed to present myself at 9:00 a.m. to the FSO 4453D USAF Hospital, Shaw AFB, South Carolina. Shaw AFB was about forty miles east of Columbia, South Carolina, so I decided to drive down a day early, find a cheap motel, and be ready and fresh in the morning.

The physical exam went great. I passed all tests with flying colors, and the results of the psychological portion, which I would read later, read "highly motivated and should make a good officer and pilot in the Air Force."

I felt extremely good about my chances of passing the physical exam and since I had been approved conditionally, I felt confident that I would be accepted in the cadet program.

Back at Fraley Field I began to work on the flight test portion of my commercial license in earnest.

Mr. Spencer flew with me a couple of times to demonstrate the maneuvers that I would have to perfect before taking the flight test, but I spent most of my time flying solo as it was cheaper. I would take a booklet published by the CAA that described all of the required maneuvers and the tolerances allowed and, in flight, I would review each one and then practice it.

The flight check was scheduled for August 13th. I showed up, Inspector Brown gave me a detailed oral exam, and we went up for the ride. The flight check went well and after the required number of maneuvers was completed, Mr. Brown gave me a thumbs-up and nodded to return to the field. We landed and he gave me a post-flight debriefing and issued the coveted commercial license.

I was sky high. At twenty years old, I had my commercial pilot license. I was a red-hot pilot and Operation Secret Plan was well on its way.

I thanked him, jumped in the airplane, took off, and visually found the highway that would take me north to High Point. Being the sharpest pilot in the world, I needn't look at the compass or the map. By simply following the highway, soon Lexington would come into view and then Fraley Field. I was twenty minutes into the flight and...

Something just didn't look right!

Lexington was not coming up on the horizon and the sun was setting on the wrong side of the airplane! The sun should be setting on the left, which was west, but now it was setting on the right side, which was... How embarrassing! My first flight as a commercial pilot, the ink wasn't even dry on my certificate yet, and I got lost! I had picked up the correct highway, but I had turned south instead of north and was following it stupidly in the wrong direction.

What would Inspector Brown think? What would he do? My mind imagined terrible things. What if he had watched me take off and turn the wrong way? Would he cancel my commercial license and maybe even revoke my private license if he saw me turn north now?

I mustn't let him see me turn and fly north. The answer was simple. Just descend to treetop level, turn east, and pass by the Salisbury airport so low that the inspector couldn't see me. My guilt at making such a bone-headed error had excited my imagination to such an extent that common sense would not prevail.

I did just that, even though, now, I realize that Inspector Brown was probably home having supper by the time I discovered my mistake. I descended and gave Salisbury a wide berth as I corrected my course and headed, finally, at treetop level toward Fraley Field.

Back at Fraley Field, there was much celebration and Dwight even bought a round of Cokes for the assembled in honor of my success. I didn't dare tell them of the wrong-way Corrigan act that I had just bumbled through.

On August 15, I received the confirmation that I had passed the physical examination for entry into the United States Air Force Cadet training program and that I should stand by for the official reporting date. Operation Secret Plan was moving along nicely except that it wasn't much of a secret anymore. I had shared my success stories with all who would listen, and all that remained was to wait on the assignment to cadet training. While waiting, I would concentrate on the flight instructor's rating and I should be finished before the year's end.

September was fast coming and with it a decision that must be made concerning UNC. I had made up my mind long before, but qualifying for cadets just sealed my decision.

I would not return to UNC.

Dad was okay with it, but Mom was not happy. She was quite proud of me attending a big school and was looking forward to my graduation. She had attended a Seventh Day Adventist College for one year in Tennessee in the '20s but was stricken with diphtheria and had to withdraw. She was disappointed in not finishing and was happy that I would be able to graduate. I promised her that when I finished the Air Force Cadet program and was flying with a major airline that I would re-enroll and finish.

I wrote a letter to the admissions department and the housing division at UNC and cancelled all of my previous arrangements for classes and lodging. With that I put college out of my mind.

Well, almost out of my mind. I felt somewhat guilty, as it was the first time I had quit anything before finishing. And to add to my guilt, September came and it was the first September in fourteen years that I wasn't attending a school. I rationalized the whole thing by telling myself that soon the Air Force would call and I would be back in a classroom with the same routine of regimented study.

My social life was dragging somewhat. I suppose that my first choice for female companionship might have been Jerri Fitzgerald, but she stayed all booked up, so I didn't push it. As Mom said, "There's always more fish in the pond." I managed to go out as much as my limited budget would allow, and with the cadet assignment looming and my determination to finish my flight instructor's rating, I stayed pretty busy.

Winter was fast approaching, and I wanted to complete the instructor's rating before Christmas. I spent a lot of time studying for the written exam and did all the flying that I could afford in practicing for the flight portion. Mr. Spencer said that he thought I was ready, so I scheduled November 7th for the date to fly to Charlotte to take the written examination.

The trip had begun to be old hat. I flew down to Charlotte, took the test, said hello to Mr. Garrison, and told him that I would look forward to seeing him soon to take the flight portion of the test. I cranked up the T-craft and headed back home to Fraley Field.

I received a telegram from the CAA on November the 9th advising me that I had passed all sections. All that remained to do now on my "Operation Not So Secret" was to schedule the flight test…and pass it.

I called and scheduled the flight check with Mr. Garrison. His next available time slot was January 11; he suggested that we meet at a small airport north of Charlotte called Brockenbrough Airport and do the check ride there. He explained that since we would be doing a lot of local airport work, takeoffs and landings, that the big Charlotte airport would not be able to accommodate us.

Christmas and New Year's came and went and no news from the Air Force.

I met Mr. Garrison at the appointed time and place and we commenced with the check ride. It went pretty well. He showed me a few things that he thought I should know as an instructor, and after we landed he offered some helpful suggestions that he felt would make me a better flight instructor. It was not necessarily flying stuff, but the psychological end of instructing and the responsibilities that went with the flight instructor rating. He shook hands with me, wished me good luck, and handed me the newly endorsed commercial license with the rating "flight instructor" typed across the front. I watched as he crawled into his Piper Super Cub and taxied away. I considered him a friend and I owed him a lot, I thought as he took off and disappeared over the horizon. Our friendship had extended, the last two and a half years, over my entire, although short, aviation career from a green corn field teenage novice student pilot to a fully licensed commercial pilot certified as a flight instructor.

As I methodically checked my aircraft for the flight back to Fraley Field, I was overwhelmed with a feeling of gratitude for the help that Mr. Garrison had given me. First, for not busting me when I had invaded the sacred Charlotte airspace on my first visit, totally unprepared, and second, for his encouragement as I advanced in my aviation career, even up through this day. He had played a major part in my young career.

I would never see him again.

Operation Not So Secret Plan was complete now. The only thing missing was that letter from the Air Force assigning a starting date for cadet training.

Lackland Air Force Base, here I come!

Over the last year or so I had made friends with another High Point boy. His name was Jim Sink and he had been enrolled at UNC during the same time that I was. We had carpooled and airplane-pooled a few times and, like me, he had dropped out this past year. We would double date from time to time in High Point and we seemed to get along quite well. He was a handsome young man with a keen sense of humor and I suppose we bonded because we were both dropouts.

We had just dropped our dates off and had decided to stop by the White House Barbecue restaurant for a Coke. After Jim dropped out of college, he took a menial job and was getting pretty tired of it. I was getting bored with the drafting job also.

As we talked, a plan evolved.

CHAPTER 17
Good-Bye, High Point

Hello, future

WE AGREED THAT WHILE I was waiting on the Air Force to call me that we would pack up, drive to Miami, and seek our fortunes there. If it didn't work out, it would be a good vacation. It was Saturday night. We agreed to resign from our respective jobs on Monday and pack. Tuesday, Jan 15th would be our departure day.

In anticipation of passing my flight instructor test I had corresponded with a very large flight school in Miami, Florida, called Embry Riddle. Although they did not promise me a job, they indicated that they kept an active list of prospective instructors and that when I completed my license to advise them. I had just written them a note upon passing my test, so to drive down there and show up in person might seal the deal. It was worth a try and besides, Miami was a "hot bed" of aviation activity; surely, with my credentials, I could land a job as an instructor.

On Sunday, I explained to Mom and Dad my plan. They had been prepared for me to go away to the Air Force, so to leave a few weeks earlier didn't seem to bother them that much. Besides, they expected us to return home in a couple of weeks after we tired of living alone in a strange town.

I went by Fraley Field and said good-bye to all the hangar-flyers and to Mr. and Mrs. Spencer. I offered my share of the PT-26 for sale for $20.00 with a notice on the bulletin board and I left. I couldn't help but to notice, as I drove away, that the wind sock, sporting Mom's red dress, was still proudly billowing out...perhaps waving good-bye.

Monday came and I stopped by Tomlinson Furniture and gave Charlie the bad news. He seemed genuinely saddened, but he wished me well and said that he would send my last paycheck to my parents' address when it was issued. I got a call from someone at Fraley Field who saw the notice and indicated that he would like to purchase the interest in the PT-26. I met him at Ellington's Grill with a receipt and we consummated the deal. Jim Sink called and reconfirmed our schedule and we agreed that he would pick me up at seven on Tuesday morning.

Mom and Dad were up early to see me off and the conversation around the breakfast table was somewhat constrained. Dad had little to say. He asked how much money I had for the trip and I told him about sixty dollars, counting the twenty that I got yesterday for the PT-26. He gave me another twenty and asked me if I needed any more. "No," I answered confidently, "once I get to Miami I should get some work soon." Mom suggested that I hide the last twenty in my underwear in case I got "stuck up." "Stuck up" was Mom's phrase for being the victim of an armed robbery by a criminal. I laughed and agreed. I would learn later that it was to be a fortuitous move. Moms are always right.

Jim came right on time. We loaded his big Buick, I gave Mom and Dad a round of good-bye hugs, and we were off.

Good-bye, Mom and Dad, good-bye, grandparents, good-bye, Allen Jay, good-bye, Fraley Field, and good-bye to all the young ladies who had tolerated a boring young man who had nothing on his mind but airplanes. Good-bye, High Point…hello, Miami!

Jim turned south on the highway that led toward Charlotte.

Other than a few short visits I would never return.

MA AND PA COOPER

Thomas Lee and Mary Ella Cooper, Dad's parents

Dad's father, Tom at his desk at his print shop.

GRANDMA AND GRANDPA FRANKLIN

Fred and Bertha Franklin, Mom's parents.

Me and my best pal growing up, Grandpa Franklin

SWEET SIXTEEN

Grandma Franklin, Bertha at sweet sixteen, 1906.

Pearl Francis Cooper, my mom

SCENES FROM HIGH POINT

Dad in front of grocery store on South Main Street, High Point, N. C.

Mom and Dad at our home

Dad at Bank.

GROWING UP IN HIGH POINT
1936/1956

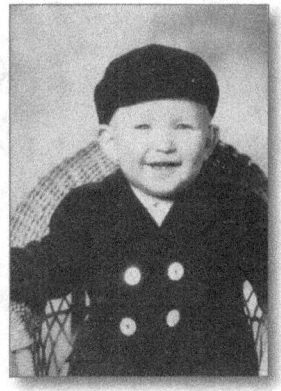

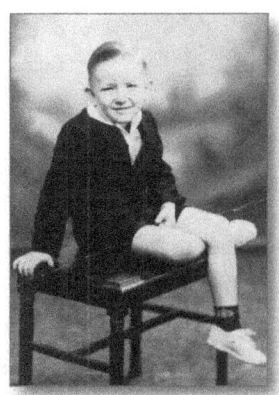

PUPPY LOVE

Bobbie Leigh Tuttle, "First love"

Jerri Fitzgrald, "Second love"

Tomato-red Mercury Convertible, "True love"

THE MAN IN THE ARENA...

FRALEY FIELD, LOVE AT FIRST SIGHT

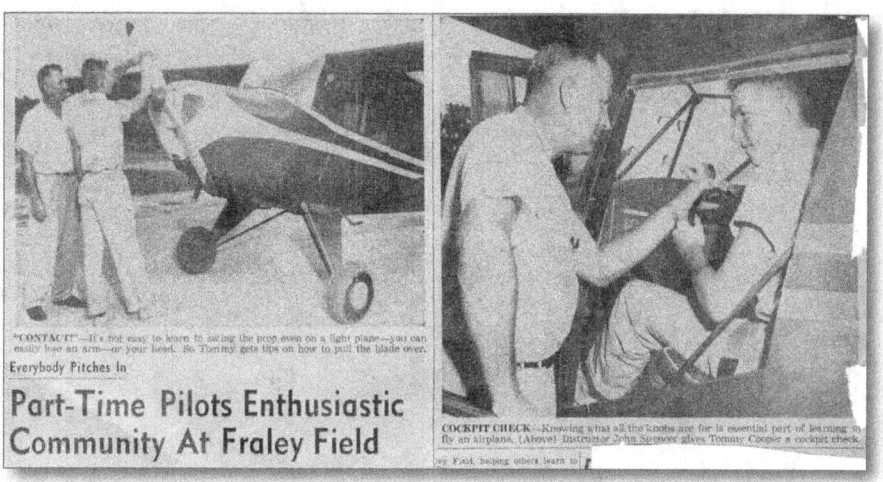

The beginnings of a lifetime love affair with aviation

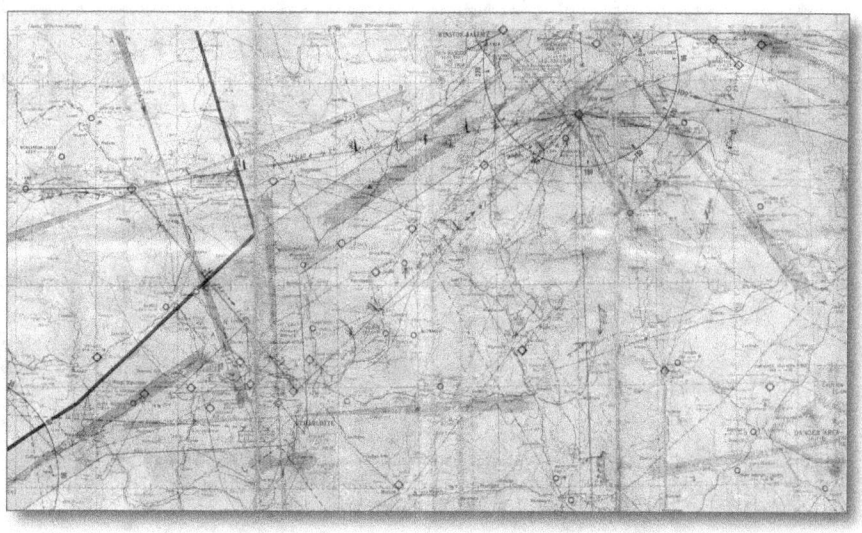

Map used on my first cross-country; High Point, Hickory, Charlotte and back home.

UNIVERSITY OF NORTH CAROLINA

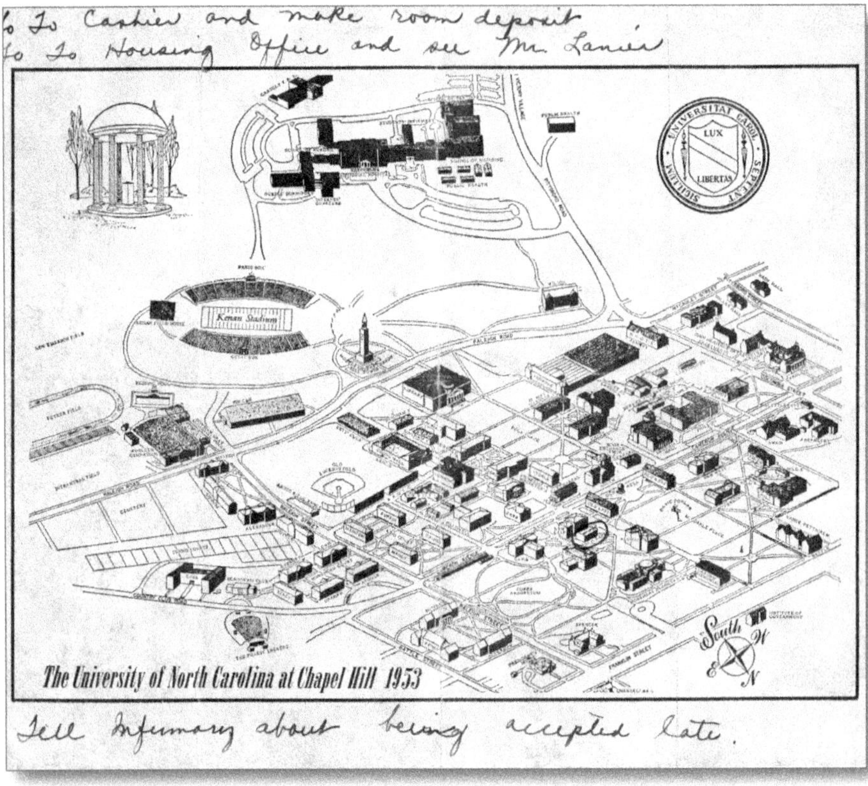

Map of UNC campus, 1956. (See note at bottom, "accepted late")

Baseball at UNC, 1956...Me, menacing with a bat.

THE MAN IN THE ARENA...

ALWAYS A WELCOME SIGHT

It wasn't LaGuardia, but it was to me.

Mom's letter allerting me to "rust on my clothes"

CAPTAIN THOMAS L. COOPER

A SHOCKER!

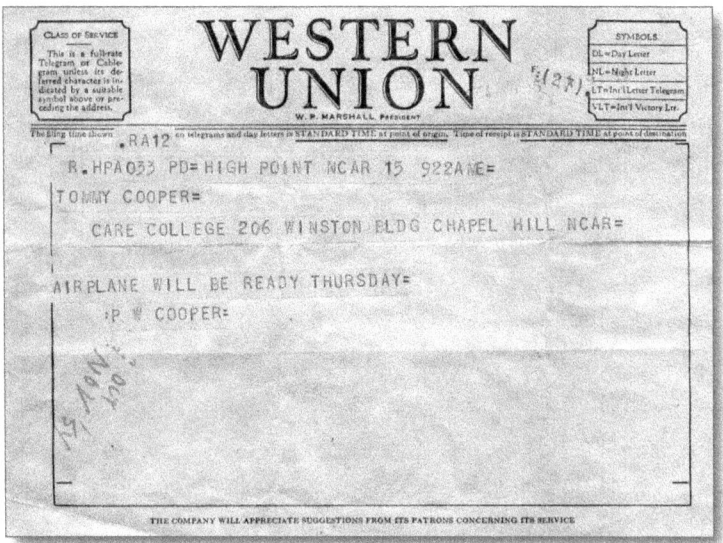

Dad bought an airplane but he never flew in one.

Comimg home from college in my own Piper Cub. Terrific!

TRAVELING THE AIRSHOW CIRCUIT

Melvin preparing for a parachute jump with me at the Piper controls.

A sketch of my beloved J-5 Piper Cub found in my French study material.
I should have been studying, not day dreaming.

PART II
Maelstrom

"A large and violent whirlpool, an agitated state of affairs." Webster's Dictionary

"Climbing out

CHAPTER 18
Southbound in a Buick

STEPHEN HAD LEVELED OFF AT 6,500 feet and was talking to Orlando Air Route Traffic Control. They had cleared him direct to Wellington Aero Park, pointed out some other aircraft in the area, and now all was quiet on the radio.

Stephen looked over and asked, "How are you doing?"

"Fine," I answered, "I'm doing just fine."

We were just passing Vero Beach and I looked down and visually picked up U.S. 1, the paved roadway that slices through the city as it meanders alongside the Intracoastal Waterway on its way, southbound, toward Miami. How long had it been since Jim Sink and I traveled that road, I asked myself? Sixty years? Yes, sixty years, almost to the day.

We had left High Point at around 8:00 on the morning of January 15, 1957 and were headed toward Charlotte. We didn't have much to say for a long time. We were both deep in our own thoughts, having just left our familiar surroundings for a place that neither of us had ever visited. We had agreed that we would divide the driving and that we would not stop but drive straight through. We wanted to conserve our financial resources as much as possible, and motels were not in our budget.

We passed Charlotte and I took over the driving. After a while, as High Point was left well behind us and Miami was ahead of us and was to be our future home, our conversation picked up. We began to work out a plan to activate upon arriving there.

We reviewed our finances and between us, we had $135. That wouldn't go very far in Miami, so we began to work out a budget as we drove. With the expense of fuel being our biggest financial drain, we should arrive in

Miami with about $110. With that we should be able to rent a room while we looked for work.

Passing Columbia, we stopped at a filling station, filled up, visited the men's room, bought a couple of Cokes, and with Jim now driving, we continued our trip. Our parents' lunches were coming in handy now, and we dined lavishly as we drove southbound.

As we approached the Florida state line, we were in good spirits. We were looking forward to a great Miami adventure and our conversation became almost giddy. We intercepted U.S. 1 north of Jacksonville and crossed the Florida state line just after dark. "Welcome to Florida," it read, "the Sunshine State."

I took over the driving and Jim stretched out for a nap. We passed Jacksonville and I was estimating Daytona Beach at around 10:00 p.m. I pulled into a gas station there, woke Jim, and I filled the gas tank. He washed his face and took his turn at the wheel.

CHAPTER 19

Busted in New Smyrna Beach

JIM'S BIG BUICK WAS COMFORTABLE and I had no trouble falling asleep.

I was awakened by a siren and a flashing red light! I sat up, trying to figure out where I was when a very large police officer came up to the window. We were petrified.

"You boys were doing forty in a thirty-five-mile zone," he drawled in his best southern accent, placing a long emphasis on "boys" as if it were a dirty word.

Jim protested as politely as he could, but it was to no avail.

"We don't like strangers to come into New Smyrna Beach and break the law," he said. "I have no recourse but to run you boys in until we can put you on trial," he added.

It was the middle of the night, we were in a strange town, we were being arrested, and with a police record, our futures were doomed. We were absolutely scared stiff.

The officer ordered Jim out of our car and motioned for me to get in the driver's seat. "I'm taking this boy with me and I want you to follow," he directed. "Do you understand?"

"Yes, sir," I replied.

We only drove about six blocks when we pulled up in front of a residence. The officer had Jim in tow and came over and directed me to follow them. We went up to the door of the house, and the officer knocked. Shortly an elderly man appeared, dressed in a robe and bedroom slippers, wiping the sleep from his eyes.

"Good evening, Judge," he said, "sorry to bother you at this late hour, but I caught these boys breaking the law."

The judge directed us to an adjoining room that obviously was some kind of private office and ordered us to sit down.

"What'd you catch these boys doing?" he asked the officer, in an even thicker southern accent.

The officer explained that we were speeding; making forty in a thirty-five-mile zone.

"Well," the judge said, "we can either put them in jail or they can pay the fine."

Jim finally got up enough nerve to speak. "How much is the fine, sir?"

The officer interrupted and said, "Let's just see how much money you boys have."

We emptied our pockets and laid $118 on the table.

"The fine is $113," the judge said. "Give 'em five dollars to buy gas with and see to it that they leave town tonight! Case dismissed," he said as he slapped his hand on the table and scooped up our last dollars before leaving the room.

The officer escorted us out to our car and with a very convincing command. "U.S. 1 is two blocks over there," he pointed, "and don't ever let me see you in this town again."

Well, that was all right with me. I never wanted to see New Smyrna Beach again either…and Jim shared my sentiments exactly. We drove, slowly, to U.S. 1, turned south, and once again headed toward Miami.

Once we were outside of the city limits of New Smyrna Beach, I reached inside my underwear and pulled out my hidden twenty-dollar bill and slapped it on the dashboard.

"Thank you, Mom!" I exclaimed.

"We're rich," Jim shouted with glee. "Let's go to Miami and get richer."

So far the Sunshine State hadn't been very sunny to us.

CHAPTER 20

Hello, Miami

IT WAS DAYLIGHT WHEN WE passed through West Palm Beach and pulled into downtown Miami at around ten o'clock Wednesday morning. We had less than twenty dollars between the two of us.

The city didn't seem very warm to us. People were bustling around and there were a lot of tall, ominous buildings. There was a Sears store that was bigger than any store that we had in High Point, and off the left was a large hotel that read across the top, Columbus Hotel.

We found a park near the water, parked the car, found a park bench, and while finishing off the remainder of our box lunches from home, took stock of our situation.

We couldn't spend any money on anything. Fuel for the car would be the only luxury that we could spend money on, and when we were hungry, well, we'd cross that bridge when we came to it. Jim would find a job doing anything while I located Embry Riddle flight school and applied for a flight instructor's job.

Jim took a walk around the park and came back with a newspaper. We immediately turned to the classified "help wanted" section. We found two or three positions that showed some promise, all in the downtown area, and off we went. Jim would go into the place of business and interview while I would stay outside with the car.

It was the same everywhere he went. "Sorry, but the position has been filled," they would say. We were getting pretty discouraged, but we weren't beaten. We looked further in the classifieds and there were some openings in a supermarket in Coconut Grove. We didn't have a clue as to where

Coconut Grove was, so we went to our map. We located it south of Miami just off U.S. 1, so off we went.

The town was wonderful. It was small and quiet. It was snuggled alongside Biscayne Bay and it had a welcoming air about it. We were praying that the job would be open. Jim stopped at a gas station and freshened up, put on a clean shirt, and while I waited in the parking lot with my fingers crossed, he went in to apply.

Ten minutes went by. Then twenty, and then Jim came out with a big grin on his face with his thumb stuck high in the air. "I got the job," he said. "It's not much, seventy- five cents an hour, but they pay every Friday and I start tomorrow."

We were set. Jim had made friends with the service station manager and got permission for us to park the car there overnight. He went shopping in the supermarket and splurged. We blew two dollars on a loaf of bread, two cans of Vienna sausages, and two cartons of milk. We dined royally in the old black Buick and prepared for the next day. The Buick was fairly comfortable, and we went to sleep eagerly looking forward to an uncertain future in Miami.

Jim got dressed and walked next door to his new job. The service station manager gave me directions for the Tamiami Airport, home of Embry Riddle, and I was off.

I found the airport and I found Embry Riddle, but I didn't have as much luck as Jim had. The personnel department advised me that they had no openings, but if I would leave them my phone number, they would call me for an interview if a position came available. I explained that I didn't have a phone but that I would drop by from time to time.

As I left, I noticed another small flight school adjacent to Embry Riddle. The name on the roof of the hangar said Blue Star Aviation.

I pulled into the parking lot, found the office, and introduced myself to the woman behind the counter. The place reminded me of the office at Fraley Field as it was a bit shabby and the counter was an old broken-down showcase filled with maps and logbooks. The chairs in the setting area were worn and old; outdated aviation magazines were strewn everywhere. The lady was nice and I felt comfortable talking to her and she listened to my story with interest.

Although she didn't have anything for me at that minute, she did give me a lead for an instructor job in Ft. Lauderdale. The company's name was Broward Aviation, the owner's name was Ben Bradley, and the airfield was named Bradley Field. I wouldn't find out until later that Ben Bradley was a legend in South Florida aviation circles.

It was still early and Jim wouldn't be off until around six o'clock, so I struck off for Ft. Lauderdale. I found Bradley Field easily enough and after inquiring around, I found Ben Bradley. His company did everything there. If it had anything to do with aviation, he did it: instructing, charter flights, seaplanes, banner towing, photography, skywriting, and airplane maintenance.

As busy as he probably was, he took some time with me. He showed me around his hangar and shops and invited me into his office for a Coke. He seemed sincerely disappointed that he had nothing for me, but he offered a suggestion. It seems that he routinely did work for a woman by the name of Mary Gaffaney, owner of a flight school in South Miami. He overhauled the engines for all of her J-3 Cubs. "As a matter of fact," he said, "her husband, Charley, was just up here yesterday and in the conversation, he asked if there were any flight instructors available to come to work down there."

Mr. Bradley wrote her name on a piece of paper: "Mary Gaffaney, Kendall Flying School, Brown's Airport, South Miami." I thanked him and headed for Coconut Grove with bubbling confidence that tomorrow I would visit Mrs. Gaffaney and come back with a job.

I picked Jim up at the supermarket with the news of a prospective job. He had some good news also. It seems that his main job at the market was bag boy. That didn't sound too red hot to me at the time, but he explained that when he helped the women to their cars with their bags of groceries, they would often tip him. From his first day's take, it looked like he was making more from tips than from salary, and it was ready cash! He proudly pulled out a wad of small bills totaling over ten dollars, and we did a quick calculation as to when we might be able to rent a room.

Reality set in about that time as the first hunger pains hit, and we had to settle on another night of Vienna sausages in the dining room of the black-and-white Buick.

We took turns sleeping in the backseat of the Buick, which wasn't too bad, but the front seat was tough. The first one to wake up usually woke the other and we would have breakfast. Breakfast was simple. We had bought a small ice chest where we kept our milk and the small individual packages of cereal and some plastic utensils worked just fine.

Jim was soon off to his job as bag boy and I headed south on U.S. 1 for Brown's Airport with the specific address supplied by our new friend, the service station manager.

I found it easily. A left turn off U.S. 1 and a right turn about two blocks later, and I ran right into the west end of the airport. The airport was bounded on the north side by the narrow street on which I had turned and along that street, on the right side, was where all of the related airport businesses were located.

The first buildings that I saw were two small hangars with "Tursair" written on the side. That wasn't the company that I was looking for, so I continued slowly down the dusty road. There was a small tie-down area where several planes were parked and the next building that I saw advertised, Howe Aviation, Piper Aircraft Dealer. No luck there. I looked to the left and there, on a small, long-shaped, one-story building, I read, "Kendall Flying School."

I was already in love with Brown's Airport. I had been there for only about two minutes and it had captivated me. It was like a toy airport. Everything was small, clean, and inviting. The grass runway ran east and west and was well maintained. The small buildings that lined the north side of the runway were neat, and all were painted white. A low white coral wall separated the buildings from the flight line, and four small J-3 Piper Cubs with "Kendall Flying School" painted on them were tied down in a perfect row.

I parked, took a deep breath, and headed for the door.

The woman behind the counter greeted me. "Hello, I'm Joan; may I help you?"

"Yes," I said, "I'm Tommy Cooper, and I would like to talk to someone about flight instruction."

"Fine," she said, "Mr. Hudson is right here, and he'll be able to talk to you." She waved a tall, skinny man over and introduced me to him. "Chuck, this is Mr. Tommy Cooper and he would like to talk to you about flight instruction."

With a handshake, the tall man asked me if I had ever flown before. "No, no," I explained, "I don't want to *receive* flight instruction, I want to *give* flight instruction. I'm looking for a job as a flight instructor."

The tall Mr. Hudson immediately lost interest in me as he turned and introduced me to a nice-looking woman who looked to be about ten years my senior. "Mary, this is Mr. Tommy Cooper and he is looking for a job as a flight instructor. Mr. Cooper, this is Mary Gaffaney. She owns the school."

We shook hands and I explained that a Mr. Bradley from Ft. Lauderdale had told me that she might be hiring flight instructors and so I came right away.

"We had one of our instructors get hired by Delta Airlines just last week, and we were looking all over for a replacement," she explained apologetically, "but just yesterday I hired a fellow by the name of O'Mara as his replacement." She offered the usual, "If you leave your phone number, I can call you if something opens up."

"No, ma'am," I replied dejectedly, "I don't have a phone, but I can stop by every week to check if anything is available," and I turned to leave.

At that instant, at that VERY instant, a person burst through the door and exclaimed, "Dick O'Mara is in the hospital with appendicitis!"

Mary stopped me. "Tommy," she asked, "when can you start?"

CHAPTER 21
First Job in Aviation

Kendall Flying School

THE PROCESSING FOR EMPLOYMENT AT Kendall Flying School was easy. There was no interview and no flight check. I simply gave my social security number to the woman at the front counter and we reviewed the flight schedule together.

"It looks like Mr. O'Mara had several students booked for tomorrow, and the first one, a Mr. Nelson, is booked for 9 a.m., and one more in the afternoon," she said. "Is that okay?"

"I'll be here bright and early," I replied as I headed for the front door, "and thank you very much."

"Your permanently assigned aircraft is Piper Cub number 3," she said as I left.

I'm not sure just how I made it home. I had a job, I had an assigned airplane of my very own, and I had a student. I could barely concentrate on my driving, but somehow I managed to make it home, or rather, make it to the service station.

I was waiting on Jim when he got off work. I told him the good news and he was delighted. He also had a good day in tips and our bankroll was growing. The cost of fuel was taking its toll on our finances, but we now had over thirty dollars and the pot was growing.

We had our routine down pretty well. We were still eating at the "Buick Diner" as we called it, and Jim discovered a term at the market called shelf life, which spiced up our menu somewhat. It seems that when a supplier packages a product, they put a date on it by which it must be sold. If not sold by that date, the product must be taken off the shelves and disposed of. Jim made good use of that information and improved our selection considerably by becoming good friends with the clerk in charge of "disposing."

We had a good dinner that night and slept well knowing that our nights in the Buick were numbered.

Saturday was a big day for me. I was up early and on my way to Brown's Airport at the crack of dawn.

While waiting for my student to arrive, I chatted with Joan, the scheduler. She gave me some background on my first student. It seems that he had recently attended Embry Riddle Flight School and was disappointed with his training there. He had received about thirty hours of dual instruction and still hadn't soloed.

That was a situation I hadn't considered as I prepared for my instructor's rating. Questions arose in my mind. Was the student untrainable? Were the instructors who had been assigned to him inferior? I had to answer those questions quickly on our first ride. Additionally, as a green instructor, I hadn't really developed a system for instructing, as I had no experience at all. I would have to draw on the training that I had received from Mr. Spencer back at Fraley Field some three years earlier and the short lecture by Mr. Garrison, the CAA inspector.

Bill Nelson was his name. He showed up right on time. Joan introduced us, we shook hands, and I invited him outside to discuss the program in private.

He looked to be about my age. We agreed to call each other by our first names and I asked him about his previous experience. He gave me the Embry Riddle story and during his discourse, a plan for him, and me, became clear.

"Bill," I said, "let's find out just where you are in your flight training progress. I would like to see you go through all the preflight preparation on this airplane and tell me exactly what you are doing, and why. After that," I added, "we'll go up and review your high work and, if we have time, we'll come back and do some landings."

Based on Bill having had thirty hours of instruction and still not being able to solo, I was expecting a bumbling display of amateurish airmanship.

"Okay," he said. "I will start in the cockpit. First I make sure that the ignition switch is off and then I check the position of the trim tab indicator. Then we'll move around the aircraft, starting at the engine. We'll move in a counterclockwise direction as we check the aircraft, finishing up where we began, at the engine.

"The engine is a sixty-five horsepower Continental engine. Its oil capacity is four quarts, but it can operate down to one-half pint in emergency. We'll check the oil now. Good, three and one-half quarts. One must add oil if the oil quantity is less than three quarts. Now, we check the engine for oil leaks, frayed spark plug lines and cowl fasteners. They all look okay," he asserted. He then kneeled down to view under the engine. "This is the fuel quick drain," he explained. "Any condensation collected in the tank or fuel lines will accumulate here, so we must drain it and inspect for water. Water will separate from fuel in the form of droplets and can be easily recognizable."

I was shocked. I had never been exposed to such detail on a preflight before, and *HE* was the student. He continued around the airplane touching things, pulling things, pushing things, moving controls while droning on as to why he was doing it.

When he finished the preflight, ending back at the engine where he had started, I commented, trying to act unimpressed and nonchalant, "Good job. Now let's see how you fly." Secretly, I was awestruck.

His flying was just as good. His takeoff was fine and his traffic pattern was excellent. We climbed up to two thousand feet and he did some turns for me and they were good. After a few other maneuvers, I motioned to return to the airport with a thumbs-up sign, and over the engine noise I shouted, "Let's go back and do some landings."

He entered the traffic pattern nicely, properly reduced the engine power on the downwind leg abeam the landing spot on the runway, and glided around for his final approach. All was good until…

Instead of landing, he practically flew the airplane into the ground. I grabbed the controls quickly as we bounced, pushed the throttles forward to full power, and recovered in a climb. Once we got to a safe altitude, I asked him to try it again.

He repeated the same mistake. His flying was good; he just couldn't land the airplane. I was ready this time and I took the controls earlier and landed the airplane further down the runway.

I taxied the airplane off the side of the runway and parked on the taxiway away from any other landing traffic.

I might have been shy of sophisticated book learning, but I could flat-out fly an airplane. Mr. Spencer, Pete Dickens, and Melvin Robinson had seen to that. I knew exactly what Bill needed. He needed someone to show him how to land. His problem was that he was trying to *land* the airplane. The proper procedure is to hold the airplane off the ground inches above the runway, power off, with the nose elevated, until it stalls and quits flying. Then the airplane will land itself in a perfect three-point attitude.

We discussed that method and I told the student to observe as I demonstrated a proper three-point landing.

I took the airplane around, made the landing, and performed a touch and go—a maneuver whereby the pilot, after the landing is accomplished and during the roll-out, can apply full power and take off again without taxiing back to the end of the runway.

Bill took the controls and set up for his landing. I reminded him, as we glided in on final approach, to round out just a few feet above the runway, keep the nose just above the horizon, and try to keep the airplane from landing by applying back pressure on the stick.

He made a perfect landing.

"That was excellent. Do you want to do one more?" I asked as we rolled out.

"You bet," he said proudly. He made one more landing, just as good as the first one, and we taxied back for debriefing.

As we walked toward the office, he was ecstatic. "You know," he said, "no one ever showed me how to make a landing like that before. The irony of the whole thing is that you don't try to *land* the airplane; you try to hold the airplane off until it's ready to land itself. Amazing."

I signed his logbook; he rescheduled for the next week and left smiling.

Mary came over and said, "We all saw the air show. Do you think he'll ever be able to solo?"

"He'll be fine," I said confidently. "He just needed a few pointers."

I pulled out my brown bag, a sandwich from the "Buick Diner," bought a Coke from a nearby vending machine, sat on the wall next to the flight line under a palm tree, and was convinced that I had died and gone to heaven.

I had a moment to reflect as I waited for my second student to arrive. A lot had happened in the last week. Last Saturday, at this time, I was hanging out at Fraley Field in High Point waiting on the Air Force to assign a cadet training class to me. One week later I was in Miami, Florida, with a job as a certified flight instructor. Mary Gaffaney had assigned an airplane to me and someone was paying me to fly it. It suddenly occurred to me that I didn't know exactly how much they were paying me to fly. Oh well, it really didn't matter. I wasn't about to march in and ask, anyway. I would find out when my first paycheck came.

I thought back on this morning's first instructional period. The flying part was easy. My old buddies back at Fraley Field saw to that. The other stuff, the psychological stuff that Mr. Garrison had talked about, was becoming important. And the professional instruction that was demanded of me, I realized, would take some attention. The morning session pointed that out graphically. I was sure that I had made great strides with my first student in identifying and fixing his landing problems, but he had given me much more. Unwittingly, he had pointed out an area that I must fix and fix soon. That flying period taught me a lesson that has stayed with me throughout my flying career: "Watch other pilots closely and learn from them. Emulate the good qualities and use their bad traits as examples of what not to do."

I walked into the office and Joan introduced me to my next student. She explained that he was a brand-new student taking his first lesson. We shook hands and I invited him to the flight line to begin his lessons.

"Okay," I said very professionally, "I will start in the cockpit. First I make sure that the ignition switch is off and then I check the position of the trim tab indicator. Then we'll move around the aircraft, starting at the engine. We'll move in a counterclockwise direction as we check the aircraft, finishing up where we began, at the engine.

"The engine is a sixty-five horsepower Continental engine. Its oil capacity is four quarts but it can operate down to one-half pint in emergency," I instructed masterfully.

Little did the unsuspecting student know that the polished words coming out of my mouth were almost the exact words that my student taught me two hours earlier.

We took off. I was at the controls and climbing out when I suddenly had a flashback to the day that Mr. Spencer took me on my first ride. I remembered my emotions and feelings as I tried to understand the new student's excitement. Did he possess the same passion that I had when I took my first ride? Was his goal to be an airline pilot or did he just want to be a weekend flyer? It didn't matter. I would teach him to fly safely and professionally. I didn't want to scare him with any crazy aerobatics on his first flight. We would go nice and easy.

We did some turns, climbs, and glides, and then it was time to return to the field. We checked in at the counter, and Joan sold him a logbook. It was the same type that Mr. Spencer had given me four years earlier. I signed the log and he said that he enjoyed the lesson and would be back next week. Joan scheduled him and he left.

My first day of flight instructing was finished. I felt good about the day's results. As I looked around the room that served as a scheduling department and a classroom, several of the other veteran flight instructors came up and introduced themselves. I didn't remember any names, but I would soon, and although I didn't realize it then, we would all become a sort of family and remain friends for years.

Joan reviewed my flight schedule for the next day and I left for Coconut Grove.

Back at the service station, at a pay phone, I finally got up the nerve to call Mom...collect. It was Saturday, so I knew she would be home. She accepted the call and was excited to hear from me. I gave her the good news about my flight instructing job and she sounded genuinely happy. She wanted to know if I was eating well and I said yes. She couldn't see my fingers crossed. Then she asked where we were staying. Truthfully, I said, "Coconut Grove, it's a small town about five miles south of Miami." I didn't mention that we were still sleeping in the car at a service station. In closing she mentioned that a letter came from the Air Force. I gave her the address of Kendall Flying School and asked her to forward the letter to me, C/O Tommy Cooper, Flight Instructor. That sounded so grand! We said good-bye and hung up with the usual salutations.

Jim had another good day with tips and we were accumulating funds at such a rate that we began to think of looking for an apartment. He was off all day Sunday and I didn't fly until the afternoon, so we decided to scout the neighborhood for a suitable, and cheap, apartment.

There wasn't much to choose from in the town of Coconut Grove, and we didn't want to move to an apartment too far from Jim's work. After looking around near the bay, to no avail, we worked our way inland, west of town, and happened upon a small house with a For Rent sign in the front yard. Actually, it was one of four small weatherboard houses on a lot located on McDonald Street, about four blocks from Jim's job.

Although we weren't financially prepared to rent just yet, we stopped in anyhow to inquire as to the rent rate.

The woman in charge lived in a large house next door and she greeted us warmly. She showed us the house. It was ideal, one bedroom with bath, a living room, and a kitchen. The rent was fifty dollars a month plus utilities.

We explained our situation and that we were both gainfully employed and that we loved the house and would like to rent it when we accumulated enough money, if it was still available. We estimated that we would have the funds in about a week, as I got paid on Friday and Jim's tips were averaging eight dollars a day. We asked her if we could put down a twenty-dollar deposit and move in later in about one week when we had the full amount.

She asked where we were staying and we told her, "In Jim's car at the service station down at the corner."

I suppose she felt sorry for us. She took the twenty, gave us the keys, and allowed us to move in immediately. It was wonderful. The little house was fully furnished, including pots, pans, dishes, and silverware. The only things that we needed to supply were the bedsheets and towels, and our mothers had packed that stuff for us before we left High Point.

We were home, 3318 McDonald Street, Coconut Grove, Florida.

We moved in immediately. We decided that one of us would sleep in the bedroom and the other would sleep on the couch. We would swap every month. Jim was a jazz aficionado and he had brought a small record player with him. He had a nice selection of LPs and I learned to enjoy that style of music right away.

Since I needed to go to the airport for my afternoon student, Jim rode with me, as he was anxious to see what I was talking about with such enthusiasm.

We stopped back by the service station on the way to Brown's, thanked the manager for allowing us to homestead on his back lot, and pledged everlasting loyalty to his station for fuel and oil.

While I flew with my student, Jim took a walk around the airport and got the lay of the land. It didn't take him long to discover that I was correct in my assessment of the airport. As he surveyed the property he discovered that there were several jobs he could apply for when they came open, such as driving the fuel truck and mowing the runway. He would apply for those jobs later, after we got settled in.

Jim showed up that evening with our meager supply of groceries.

"Tommy," he said, "to celebrate our first week in Miami, I have broken our pledge of 'no luxuries' and I have brought home a six-pack. Let's celebrate!"

I had never had a beer before. Jim was a frat boy at UNC and it was my understanding that beer was common, almost mandatory, at the frat houses. That was not the case in the dorms.

It was apparent that Jim was more of a man of the world than I was, so I succumbed to peer pressure and agreed. *What the heck,* I thought, *twenty years old, a flight instructor, I can handle it.*

With the jazz greats J. J. Johnson and Kai Winding on the record player, Jim pulled two cans of beer out of the refrigerator, grabbed the church key, and with much bravado, served me a beer.

We toasted each other's success and I took a big swig.

Ugh! I had never tasted anything so ugly in my life. I could barely get it down. I made a face and slid my full can over to Jim. "You can have mine," I offered. "How can anyone drink that stuff?" That was the last alcohol I had in my mouth for a long time.

We settled into our respective routines. Jim would walk to work, and I would take the Buick to Brown's Airport. We both received our first paychecks, so we split the existing pot and began handling our own expenses. I would pay for the fuel in the Buick since I was using it the most, and we would split the food bill.

The long-awaited letter came from the Air Force. It had arrived about three days after I left High Point and Mom had forwarded it to the flight school.

It stated, "Your cadet class has been scheduled for March 7, 1957 and you must confirm that you will attend no later than February 7, 1957." There was a form with a place to check off that you accepted or didn't accept along with a self-addressed envelope to HEADQUARTERS, AIR FORCE FLYING TRAINING, WACO, TEXAS. I only had about two weeks to decide what to do.

I stared at the letter for a long time and then I folded it back up and put it away. I gave myself a deadline of February 3rd as a personal decision date. I would pull that letter out often over the next two weeks and ponder my future.

Should I stay in Florida at Kendall Flying School and continue to build flying time and hope to get hired by an airline at the risk of being drafted in the Army, or should I take the Air Force offer?

If I refused the assignment to the cadet program, the Air Force would advise my draft board and I would return to draft eligibility. That would mean a commitment of two years. If I stayed in Florida, I'd need to pass an instrument and multi-engine rating to be qualified for the major airlines. That would not be too hard as I could do those ratings at Kendall Flying School on my days off and at a reduced rate.

If I agreed to cadet training I would be committed to the Air Force for four years. Once out of the Air Force, the path to the major airlines would be relatively simple.

It was a tough decision and I mulled all the options over and over again.

As I became more comfortable with my job as a flight instructor and as I became friends with the other instructors, my decision was becoming clearer.

The basic instructors were Chuck Hudson—he was the tall, skinny man I met when I first walked in the door; Carroll Kern, maybe the funniest guy in the world and an excellent pilot; and Sandy Forbes, a handsome New Englander, somewhat reserved and slightly older. Jim Dillard was the only one married. He was the old man of the bunch, about thirty years old and he handled all the instrument instruction in a Piper tri-pacer.

Just after Mary hired me we lost another instructor to an airline up north, so when Dick O'Mara got out of the hospital, he was hired.

With the exception of Dick, all the others had been in the army and were older with more flight time than we had. Dick was only one year older, and we became instant friends.

Kendall Flying School was a busy place. We had a lot of students. I suppose it was because we were located on a small field away from the hustle and bustle of the busy airports around Miami. Also, the students felt more relaxed in the friendly atmosphere that Mrs. Gaffaney presented.

It looked like I would fly between fifteen and twenty hours a week and at that rate I would achieve the thousand hours required by most airlines in less than a year. The veteran flight instructors had accepted me into their club and I was beginning to put some cash away for the instrument and multi-engine ratings.

February 3rd came and I made my decision. I checked the box that said, "Do not accept," sealed the envelope, and deposited it in the mailbox at the post office in Coconut Grove.

The instant that I dropped the letter in the slot at the post office, I knew that I had made the correct decision. I felt relieved and a euphoric feeling came over me as if an enormous weight had been lifted from my shoulders.

Instructing at Kendall Flying School was wonderful. The schedules were good and we could take a day off when we wanted to. The new students kept coming through the front door, and there was plenty of flying for all of us.

The students came from all sorts of backgrounds and for a number of reasons. Most seemed to come directly out of the military after doing their two years. Those students all were working toward their commercial licenses so they could eventually work for the airlines. A few students just wanted to learn to fly because they thought it would be fun. Some were housewives and salesmen. We even had two women who worked at a local beauty parlor, Darlene and Colleen. They were a lot of fun, as you never knew what color their hair would be when they showed up. Dick O'Mara fell in love with one right away; I think it was the green hair. Uncle Sam fixed that pretty quick as Dick was drafted in February and was off to the army for two years.

I suppose that Mom and Dad had given up on me. They were reconciled to the fact that I was happy in South Florida, so they volunteered to bring my Mercury down. They came in late February with Mom driving the family Pontiac and Dad the Mercury. They stayed a few days, met our friends at the school, and visited our house in Coconut Grove. When they left I think that they were comfortable with my decision to work for Mary Gaffaney and stay in Florida until I was drafted or got on with a major airline.

Life was perfect; getting paid to fly airplanes, having a red Mercury convertible, and living in South Florida.

Jim and I were still in the frugal stage with our money, so there wasn't much socializing for either of us. About the only thing we did for fun was to get a group of our instructors and student friends and hang out at Crandon Beach on Sundays.

Upon being accepted into the veterans' instructor club, I was regularly invited to join the other instructors for lunch at a small restaurant called The Luncheonette, located in nearby Sunland Shopping Center. This was quite an honor and additionally, I got to hear the stories that the older instructors told. The cost wasn't that much more than brown bagging, and listening to their experiences with students was extremely helpful.

It was at one of the earlier lunches when one of the instructors commented on the fact that a Piper Cub just couldn't do aerobatics. They all agreed that it could do spins as that was a full stall maneuver, and maybe a loop, but snap rolls and barrel rolls would be impossible. I listened and I knew that they were misinformed. I didn't say anything, being the new kid on the block, but I remembered the discussion.

A few days later, Charley, Mary's husband and chief mechanic, asked me to take one of the airplanes up for a test flight. On the way to the airplane

I grabbed Carroll Kern and asked if he would like to go with me. "Sure," he said as he jumped in and off we went.

I flew out over the tomato fields where we would practice with the students and at a safe altitude I turned and asked Carroll if he remembered the discussions that we had at lunch a few days ago. He nodded yes. I told him to hold on for a snap roll.

I eased the nose up, pulled the stick back abruptly, while simultaneously applying full power and full left rudder. The aircraft hesitated for a split second and then paid off with the nicest snap roll you could ever see. "Hold on again, for a barrel roll," I said. I did a nice barrel roll with positive G-force all the way around, looked back at Carroll, and headed back to the airport.

Back on the ground, he was laughing and asked me, "Where in the world did you learn to do that stuff?"

"I used to travel with an air show in the summers," I said casually as I walked away.

Word got around about the aerobatic guy and I enjoyed a bit more respect after that. I never told them that I wasn't an air show performer, but just a go-fer.

Pete Dickens borrowed a Super Cub and, with his girlfriend, came down in the spring for a quick visit. I caught up with all the gossip at Fraley Field. Nothing much had changed. One of the local pilots had built a strip down at Randleman, and Dwight was hanging around there a lot of the time. Melvin had bought a Stearman and was working on it most of the time, getting it ready to add to his air show. Mr. Spencer was still instructing and sent his best to me.

Shortly after that a gentleman came in for a refresher course. He was a pilot but hadn't flown in five years. He was an architect and had just moved to Miami from Havana, Cuba. The dispatcher assigned him to me and we began his refresher course immediately. I reviewed the basic items and he did quite well. After about two hours, I soloed him. Later, he would come out, from time to time, and fly just for fun.

One day he asked me to walk down to the tie-down area toward the east side of the field. There he proudly showed me a new "toy" he had just purchased. It was a used Taylorcraft, and he asked me to check him out. We got Mary's approval and I did the checkout. He was a quick learner and before long he was flying by himself.

CHAPTER 22
A Taylorcraft to Havana

Automatic "rough" over the ocean

A COUPLE OF WEEKS LATER, the Cuban gentleman approached me with a suggestion. He wanted to visit some friends in Havana and asked if I would fly him down in the T-craft. Well, I didn't know that much about Cuba except that it was a sort of playground for wealthy folks who liked to gamble. And, oh yes, there was someone out in the eastern part of Cuba, in the mountains, who was stirring up trouble. I think his name was Castro, or something like that.

Mary agreed to four days off, Joan rescheduled my students, and before we knew it, we were on our way to Key West to clear customs for our trip to Havana! We cleared customs, rented two life jackets, and we were off. The trip to Key West was nice. We simply followed U.S. 1 and landed when it came to an end. Upon taking off, I turned southbound and picked up the compass heading for Havana. The coastline of the Florida Keys slowly faded in the distance behind me. The water turned from a greenish hue over the shallow banks to the deep blue of the Gulf Stream.

And there was nothing but water as far as I could see…nothing but water…and more water.

I had heard the older pilots talk about the engines running rough when you get over water. Now I believed it. I had flown this airplane before for about twenty hours and it purred like a kitten, but now…"automatic rough."

It was my imagination, of course, but out there in a single-engine airplane, your mind does strange things to you. Oh well, it was only about a hundred miles, and that would only take an hour, so I decided to sit back and enjoy the ride. That didn't work and I spent the whole flight staring through the windshield, anxiously, for the first glimpse of Havana.

Thankfully, the Cuban coastline came in view right on schedule. The haze on the horizon slowly turned into a dark green, lush countryside. I breathed a sigh of relief, flew past the Havana downtown area to a point southwest of the city, and located Jose Martí International Airport. I circled the airport, saw the green light from the tower, and landed.

We found the private aircraft parking area, cleared customs, hailed a taxi, and soon we were on our way to Mariel, my student's former hometown.

The relief that I felt upon landing was short-lived. I was only in the taxi about one minute when I questioned my odds of surviving this trip—not from an air accident, but from the antics of this taxi driver.

It appeared that the cab only had two speeds; wide open or a violently braked stop. There were no traffic lights and the intersections were only for the brave-hearted and the cab with the loudest horn. Passing did not require an open lane ahead, but the driver relied on the oncoming cars to pull over to avoid a head-on collision. These near misses were always accompanied by a raised fist and a string of expletives that only a Cuban could understand.

My friend saw my concern. Calmly, he advised me that this method of driving was not unique with this driver but was the accepted practice in Cuba by all taxi drivers, and all other drivers too. It was not only accepted but expected.

We survived the ride and his family welcomed us graciously. They opened their house to us and I learned my first Spanish phrase: "Mi casa es su casa."

We stayed with this family, in Mariel, for two days. A visit to Havana was another death-defying taxi journey, but the tour of the city was exciting, and we visited some of the buildings that he had designed.

Good-byes were said as we packed up the cab for our departure. I believe that his family hated to see us leave. They were genuine people. They had made me feel so welcome that I felt sad to leave also.

With that trip began a love affair with the Cuban people and their country that would last my whole life.

The flight home was equally uneventful. Once over the Gulf Stream, the engine, again, went into automatic rough, but I was prepared for it. My nerves were already shot from the taxi rides in Havana, and the return flight to Miami was somewhat easier this time. Flying over water in a single-engine airplane takes a certain amount of courage, or daring, and one never gets used to the feeling of impending doom. I never did anyway.

Back at Brown's Airport my trip caused quite a stir. I was the first in our group to make such a daring flight, and my stories at the Luncheonette became more exciting with each rendition.

Spring came and in addition to nurturing my regular students, new students enrolled, and I was scheduled with my fair share. One such student was a middle-aged housewife by the name of Dee Dee Stout. She and her husband, Darwin, showed up one day and both enrolled. She was assigned to me.

I had learned over the past three months that each student was different, not only in their personality, but in their learning ability. I had learned that even the slowest learners would eventually attain their goal of becoming a good, safe pilot. Their learning curve was just shallower. That knowledge was about to come in handy.

In talking with Dee Dee, I felt that she was really nervous about this venture. So I decided to go slow and careful in my instructions with her. I wanted to make sure that the required maneuvers would not frighten her during the initial stages of her training.

I explained the preflight to her and when we were ready to depart, I took the controls for takeoff and climb. We took off and headed for the practice area. Once at altitude I reviewed how the airplane turned. I asked if she understood, and she nodded.

"Okay," I said, "let's make a turn to the left." I turned my attention back to the front of the airplane. Nothing happened. I touched the control stick. It was frozen solid. I put more pressure but nothing happened. Did we have a mechanical malfunction? I looked back at Dee Dee and immediately knew what the problem was.

She was petrified! Her legs were extended against the rudder pedals with her knees locked and she had a death grip on the control stick. Her eyes were big as saucers and she, in her mind, was personally holding that airplane in the air all by herself.

As calmly as I could, I said, "I've got it," and pointed to the control stick up front. She relinquished control and for the remainder of the flight I flew and she was just a passenger. This would take some patience, I thought, from both of us.

After a few sessions Dee Dee got the hang of the small airplane and began to progress at a normal pace. She and Darwin became great friends of Jim and me and they became our surrogate family in Miami. Dee Dee continued with her training, but Darwin wasn't interested and dropped out.

My bankroll had grown to a sufficient size that I could afford to rent one of the school's airplanes and finish my instrument rating. The rating required a written examination and a flight test to be passed. Kendall Flying School recommended a ground school company, Sheffield's School of Aeronautics, located at Miami International Airport for any students needing ground instruction.

I enrolled. It was a strange experience, as, with the exception of the ROTC courses at UNC, I had never sat in a formal classroom in preparation for a CAA written exam. In preparation for previous written exams, I simply ordered the CAA pamphlets and studied privately until I felt that I could pass the test. This was different. The class was very organized and at the end of the week we were given several sample tests for practice.

With that preparation, I aced the written, scoring a 100 percent. I was happy with that score, but my roommate Jim was happier. It seems that when any Sheffield's student scores a 100 percent on any CAA written test, the school awards the student a case of beer. I would have preferred Cokes.

For the flight portion, I teamed up with Carroll Kern, who was working on his instrument rating also, and we rented Kendall's instrument trainer, the Piper Tri-pacer. Jim Dillard was the instructor. When Carroll flew, I sat in the back and took notes, and when I flew the reverse was true. We worked with that system and when Jim felt that we were ready, he set us up with Mr. Conrad, a CAA designated flight examiner, at the Ft. Lauderdale airport for our check ride.

The check rides went fine and an instrument rating was added to our commercial license.

Career-wise, I was almost there. I had two years of college and a commercial license with an instrument rating. The only thing that was left to meet the airline's qualifications was the thousand hours of flight time. I had over eight hundred hours now, so the thousand-hour mark wouldn't be far off.

It was late in May and I had a surprise visit from my old friend from Fraley Field, Dwight Lohr. He had driven down to see if there were any opportunities in his field as a salesman in the South Florida area. He was only there for a couple of days when he discovered that my twenty-first birthday was coming soon.

He, along with Jim, decided on a birthday celebration. They took me out to dinner at the King's Inn, a posh restaurant in Miami Springs. The dinner and conversation lasted quite late and as it neared midnight it was decided that there was nothing to do but visit a local nightclub: Helen Polka's Jungle Club. The Jungle Club was a renowned watering hole near Miami International Airport, just off 36th Street, near the Jai Alai fronton.

As we entered the front door we were all asked for our identification cards to prove that we were twenty-one years old. Everyone passed except…me. The birthday boy.

I, a non-drinker, had the distinction of having to wait outside a nightclub of questionable reputation, fifteen minutes, until midnight, until I turned twenty-one.

What an honor! Mother would have been so proud.

Dwight left a few days later, not finding any opportunities that suited his liking.

Life at the Tom and Jim house returned to normal.

CHAPTER 23

The Instructing Routine at Mary's Flight School

SUMMER CAME AND MARY'S SCHOOL was booming. She purchased another J-3 Cub, bought uniform shirts for the instructors, and hired a second scheduler. Her name was Janet Guthrie.

Janet was a tall, pretty girl with an infectious smile. She had a wonderful sense of humor and a personality that propelled her into the Kendall Flying School family instantly. She had a bit of tomboy about her while still maintaining an air of femininity.

She was between semesters at the University of Michigan and was a welcome addition to our group. Whether it was lunch at the Luncheonette or a Sunday at the beach, Janet always added to the fun.

She arrived with some notoriety. As we found out later, in 1954, she coerced her father, an Eastern Airline captain, into taking her up in one of Mary's Piper Cubs for a parachute jump. After learning of that feat, we all looked upon her with a certain amount of awe, or curiosity.

She later became a renowned racecar driver, having been the first woman to race in the Indianapolis 500 and the Daytona 500. Her racing suit and her helmet would later be placed on display in the Smithsonian Institution.

With summer, my life became a routine of flight instructing and of building flying time toward a career with a major airline. There were lunches at the Luncheonette, the occasional Sunday at the beach at Crandon Park, and for a special treat we would go to Shorties Barbecue on nearby U.S. 1.

Almost every weekend Dee Dee and Darwin would invite Jim and me over for dinner. The bill of fare was always white beans and onions. It was our favorite. They also introduced us to our first social cocktail, CC and 7—Canadian Club and 7-Up.

That summer Jim got a job as line boy at Brown's Airport and we moved from our quaint cottage in Coconut Grove to a house nearer Brown's airport. Mary's business was growing, so she hired an additional instructor and I moved up a notch on the seniority list. Janet went back to college and fall was here.

It was about that time that I met Bob Jones. Bob was larger than life itself. He was a handsome man and looked exactly like the movie star Cliff Robertson. He was just out of the army and was a man of the world. He was always the life of the party and he was right up there with Carroll Kern at being entertaining. He could do card tricks, and at a cocktail lounge, he could get up and sing as well as the entertainers. He was a "must invite" for any parties that we held.

He also was a lovable bunko artist. If you went out with Bob, you knew that you would get stuck with the tab. But he was so entertaining that it was worth the expense.

He worked at Tamiami Airport at Blue Star Aviation as an instructor, and once in a while he would drop in to Brown's for a visit. We became good friends, and still are. Our paths would cross time and time again in the future.

Bill Nelson, my first student, had soloed months ago and was almost ready to take his private pilot's exam. Dee Dee was doing just fine. She had soloed and was progressing nicely. I had developed quite a number of students whom I had taught to fly. They all required nurturing and progress monitoring and my days were filled with responsibilities surrounding my flight instructor's rating.

Among my many students, there was another middle-aged woman, Mrs. Averman, who was scheduled to fly with me. She seemed to have some knowledge of aviation and, as I got to know her better, she admitted that her husband, Bud Averman, was a pilot for Mackey Airlines, a Ft. Lauderdale-based regional airline company, flying throughout Florida and the Caribbean. In addition, he also owned a non-scheduled airline called Regina. That company, it turned out, operated two large transport aircraft, Curtiss C-46s, that they chartered out to the government for transporting military personnel around the U.S.

Although I didn't proposition her directly for a job with Regina, I knew that if I did a professional job with her, my chances of becoming a pilot with her husband's airline would be very good. It wouldn't be a part of my long-range career plans, but the heavy flight time in a large airplane would be a great resume enhancement.

In our small circle of friends at Brown's Airport, it was inevitable that Dee Dee and Mrs. Averman would become acquainted. They did and Dee Dee became a source of information regarding Regina Airlines. Later, it would be Dee Dee who would tell me that I was the next in line to be hired there.

In late summer, the airline hiring rumor mill began to churn. Word on the street was that Eastern was about to hire a new class, but nobody had any concrete evidence. I had reached the thousand-hour minimum that Eastern required and, like the rest of my friends, had submitted my application and was ready for the call.

Jim Dillard, our instrument instructor, was the first to go. Carroll Kern was the second, and in September, Chuck Hudson was hired.

I was ready but no call came.

As the senior instructor at Kendall Flying School, I became the de facto instrument instructor. Instrument instructing is quite a bit different from basic instruction. It entails a lot of preparation on the student's part and a lot of blackboard work by the instructor before the flight. Once the day's instructional plan is explained by the instructor, the student takes off in visual conditions. At a safe altitude, he dons a device on his head called a hood that restricts his vision outside the aircraft. The instructor maintains a safety watch and assumes the role of the air traffic controller. Using the actual navigational radio signals from the ground, the student complies with the directions from the instructor and operates the airplane solely with reference to the instruments inside the aircraft.

As I learned from my first basic student, so did I learn from my instrument students. I have always maintained that the best way to learn is to *give* instruction. To watch a student work through the assigned directions—to observe his errors and corrective actions—was very helpful and I felt that, as an instrument instructor, I better prepared myself for my future career as an airline pilot.

By October I had saved enough money to rent a twin-engine airplane for my multi-engine rating. The instructional periods went well and I was set up for a check ride with the CAA. The inspector's name was John Paul Revere. The ride went well and he endorsed my commercial license to include a multi-engine rating. While at Brown's that day, he accidently met one of our extremely attractive lady students. It was love at first sight and we saw a lot of Mr. Revere that fall. He was an extremely serious man, ex Air Force, and he almost never smiled. We all kept a polite distance from him.

CHAPTER 24

"There are No Small Parts, Only Small Actors."

—Constantin Stanislavski

IT WAS IN LATE FALL that a lesson taught to me by my mother showed its value. She would always quote George Washington: "It is a fixed principle with me that whatever is done should be well done." I suppose she put an exclamation mark on that quote with the example she displayed with the bedspread episode at Myrtle Beach years before.

After ten months at the flight school, I was becoming a veteran. Mary had hired a few instructors, junior under me, so my flight schedule stayed filled up with regular students. If someone came in with previous flying time for a check-out, that person was generally assigned to a junior instructor who might have some spare time on the schedule.

One such person showed up. I had a cancellation that day and Mary called me over. She was talking with an older man and she asked if I would give him a Piper Cub check-out. "He's flown before, but not recently in a Cub," she explained. "His name is Steve Wedge," she said as she introduced him to me.

Although a paltry check-out for an aged gentleman was now beneath me, I agreed.

"Sure," I said. "Can you go now?"

He replied that he could and I invited him to go with me to the flight line to get started. Walking out, I asked, "When was the last time you flew a Cub?"

"Oh," he thought a minute, "about fifteen or twenty years ago."

I surmised that this could take some time as I began the preflight. My preflight was quite professional now, as I had polished it over the last nine months. "First, we start in the cockpit," I began. I continued with the memorized spiel as Mr. Wedge followed along attentively.

After a detailed preflight, we cranked the engine and taxied out for takeoff. I asked him if he felt okay for the takeoff and he responded that he did. It was passable. He was a bit heavy on the controls but safe.

We flew out to the practice area and I asked him to do a few turns. "Not too steep," I warned, as I didn't wish to alarm him this early in the flight. Again, he did okay, but again, he was somewhat heavy on the controls. After I demonstrated a stall to him, he did a couple and we headed back to the field for some takeoffs and landings.

"Let me do the first landing," I suggested, "so you can get an idea of the aircraft attitude when we get close to the ground." He nodded his understanding.

I landed, taxied back, and gave him the controls of the aircraft. His takeoff was better and his landing was pretty good, not perfect. He was still heavy on the controls.

"Let's do one more," I said, and "try to be more careful on your pattern work. Your altitude was off and your downwind leg was sloppy."

"I saw that," he admitted. "I'll try to do better this time."

This landing was better and the pattern work was perfect. I complimented him on the improvement and suggested, almost apologetically, that I would like to do one more landing with him, "just to make sure you're ready."

He nodded and smiled and off we went for one more takeoff and landing. He did fine and as we taxied past the office, I stopped the airplane and got out with a word of caution. "There are some thunderstorms in the area. Be sure to check the wind sock when you return before you land."

"Okay, and thanks," he said as he taxied away.

I stood by the side of the runway while he took off, and once he had disappeared, I walked back into the office, knowing that I had administered a thorough and professional check-out in the Piper Cub.

Mary asked, "How did he do?"

I replied, "He's okay, he's safe, but a little heavy on the controls."

"Yes," Mary replied, "you might expect that. He's a vice president for National Airlines, one of their senior pilots and a DC 7 captain. And he's been involved in a project with Pan Am. He'll be one of the first pilots in the U.S. to fly the Boeing 707."

"Holy crap!"

I was dumbfounded. How stupid I felt. I had just humiliated the chief pilot of National Airlines and that was one of my favorite airlines. I anguished while I wondered what to do. I could just get in my car and disappear until he left and hope that he would forget my name if it came up on an application, or I could simply kill myself.

Or I could stay and face the music.

I decided to face the music. I went out beside the flight line, sat on the rock wall, and waited for Captain Wedge.

What could I say? I practiced a few speeches, but none seemed to be adequate. Just when I was beginning to feel pretty good about my career, this came along and destroyed my confidence altogether.

I saw the Cub round the corner of the flight pattern and line up on the runway for landing. My mind was still racing for something clever to say to abate what must have been a humiliating experience for him. He parked the airplane and headed for the office. I intercepted him and blurted out, "Captain Wedge, Mary just told me…"

He interrupted me. "Cooper," he said, "that was the finest, most thorough check-out I have ever had. You are one of the most professional instructors I have ever met, and when we hire the next pilot class, you'll be in it."

I almost passed out. My knees actually buckled as we shook hands. He went in and passed the compliment on to Mary, who gave me a wink and a smile. I was ten feet tall and sitting on top of the world.

Mom's advice and example had paid off. No matter how small the job, "whatever is done should be done well."

Winter was fast coming and Jim got a better job up at Miami International Airport with an aircraft supply company by the name of Air Associates. It required him to travel around South Florida to make sales calls, and when he wasn't traveling, he needed to be in the office. Since his new job location was quite a drive from Brown's Airport, we decided to split the difference and move to a spot about halfway. We found a house in South Miami. It was west of U.S. 1 and across from Holsum Bakery. With two other roommates, we moved in.

It had been almost a year since Jim and I traveled down U.S. 1 to seek our fortunes in Miami. He was progressing nicely in his chosen profession as salesman, and I was becoming a very good flight instructor. We were saving a little money and by all outward appearances we were successful.

I loved working for Mary and we had a "love-hate" relationship. She ran a tight ship, but at times she would join the gang if we were doing anything interesting. One such Sunday we decided that we *must* have a spot-landing contest. That's where the pilot chops the power of his airplane on the downwind leg, opposite the marked landing spot, and by extending or shortening his or her pattern, without adding power, tries to land on the spot. There is usually some money involved.

On this day, there was forty dollars involved, and it came down to Mary and me. We were tied and after much bravado, Mary went up first and made her spot landing. It was pretty good but not exactly on the money. I felt like I could beat her effort, and just to make sure that no one could say I had goosed the throttle on approach, I decided on a unique solution. In hindsight it was stupid, but instead of pulling the throttle back on the downwind leg, I pulled the nose up, switched off the engine, and did a "dead stick" landing, with the prop not turning.

To say that Mary was upset would be the understatement of the year—no, not the year, the century. She was screaming something about me possibly tearing up her airplane, safety, bad example before the students, and on, and on, and on.

She stormed into the office, tore up the two twenties, threw them in the wastebasket behind the counter, and at the top of her voice...fired me.

I went home and thought about it. We all knew that Mary could be a bit high strung at times, so I made up my mind to show up early next morning and apologize and maybe she would have cooled down. I also wanted to get there early to grab the remains of the two twenties and tape them back together.

I was the first one there next morning. I looked in the wastebasket and there were no giblets of twenty-dollar bills.

Just then Mary walked in the door. Before I could apologize she grinned and said, "I saw that you have some students this morning, so I came in early to clean up so you could make a good impression."

I never mentioned the two twenties and she never mentioned firing me.

There was another situation, when Mary and I were on the same side and she became my unwitting accomplice.

We got a call that one of our Piper Cubs had made a forced landing in a nearby field just west of Brown's Airport. We got the address, Mary grabbed me, and off we went, expecting the worst. When we found the plane, we were surprised that it was in perfect shape. And then we saw the problem. In the cockpit of a J-3, on the left side of the cockpit near the pilot's left knee, there are two pull knobs. One is the carburetor heat located on the left-hand side of the instrument panel, and the other is the fuel shutoff located just beneath it on the side of the cockpit. The carburetor heat knob is pulled before every landing to prevent ice buildup in the carburetor, and the fuel shutoff knob is never pulled.

We saw that the student, while practicing forced landings, had pulled the wrong knob by mistake, causing the engine to stop due to lack of fuel. We pushed the fuel shutoff knob back in and started the engine. It ran perfectly. Mary was eager to get the airplane out of there as it would be bad publicity if the news media found out, so I suggested that I fly it out. The field looked long enough. It wasn't a smooth runway by any stretch of the imagination. There was some tall grass and at the far end of the field there was a country road with power lines running alongside, but the field looked passable.

The takeoff run would be diagonally across the field to give me more room, and Mary was to position herself at the opposite end, next to a road, to ensure that no cars were coming as I took off.

She gave me the all-clear signal, and I revved the engine up to full power and released the brakes. I went bounding down the uneven, make-believe runway.

I was too far down the field to stop when I realized that I had underestimated the field capabilities and had overestimated mine. The field was rougher than I had thought and the grass too high to allow me to accelerate to proper flying speed as quickly as need be. The airplane was bouncing along, trying to gain enough speed to allow me to pull up and miss the power lines, but it just couldn't do it. I made a quick decision to snatch the aircraft off the ground, fly under the power lines, and level off over the next field until I could gain sufficient speed to begin my climb. I was barely off the ground and rapidly approaching the end of the field when a second issue presented itself.

Out of the corner of my eye, I saw an unsuspecting bus approaching from the right.

I had enough speed to get off the ground, but not enough altitude to clear the power lines at the end of the field—and certainly not enough altitude to clear the bus.

My situation was desperate, if not hopeless.

And just then, I was saved by an angel of mercy. Mary jumped the ditch, ran on to the road in front of the bus, and with arms flailing away caused the startled bus driver to stop.

I flashed past the front of the bus, under the power lines, and across the next field, gaining speed and altitude. When I gathered my wits, I flew back to Brown's Airport to await Mary.

I met her in the parking lot just outside the office. She didn't stop. "I didn't see what just happened, did you?" she asked. It wasn't really a question but a statement.

"No ma'am," I answered.

She kept walking and we never spoke of it again.

Working for Mary was fun, gratifying, and educational, but being a flight instructor for life wasn't exactly what I had envisioned as a career. Besides, I was getting a bit bored with instructing. It was always the same…you would meet a new student, interview him or her, and go to the airplane… "Up there, make sure the switch is off and…" It was the same thing, over and over.

And to make things worse, neither Eastern nor any other airline was calling. I was beginning to get an inferiority complex. Hudson, Kern, and Dillard had all been hired and were flying large aircraft, and there I sat, flying Piper Cubs. A few letters from Chuck was about as close as I came to a flying a large aircraft.

CHAPTER 25

Piper Cub, Miami to Buenos Aires

AND THEN I GOT A call from John Paul Revere, the CAA inspector who had administered my multi-engine rating. He inquired as to whether I wanted to take a trip to South America, and if I did, and if Mary would give me a couple of weeks off, I should call a Mr. Bob Iba. I found out later that he recommended me for the job based on the check ride that he had given me in the twin; he had also heard that I had "over-water" experience gained on the trip to Havana.

I called Mr. Iba. It turned out that he owned a company called Hialeah Aircraft Ferry, Co. The company's mission was to fly aircraft all over the world for various aircraft sales organizations. His primary source of business was with companies that had bought new airplanes from Piper Aircraft and needed them delivered to their customers. His pilots would fly commercially to Lockhaven, Pennsylvania, to the Piper factory, pick up a new airplane, fly it to Miami where it would be outfitted for extended flying, and off they would go to the contracted destination.

It seems that he had five Piper PA-18 Super Cubs contracted to be delivered to Buenos Aires, Argentina. His pilots had flown up to Lockhaven to pick up the aircraft for a departure on December 5th. The plan was for his five pilots to arrive back at Tamiami Airport on December 1st so as to have time to rig the aircraft for the extended over-water flight.

Four of the five arrived on schedule, but the fifth showed up two days later and submitted an expense account that was, according to Mr. Iba, outrageous. The pilot was fired immediately.

The Man in The Arena...

His name was Bob Jones.

Bob had flown down the East Coast, leaving a trail of broken hearts in every small town where he stopped and lost track of time. He entertained lavishly at the expense of Hialeah Aircraft Ferry, and Mr. Iba would have none of that.

Mary, suspecting that I was in need of a vacation, gave me the time off. I met Mr. Iba at the offices at 1545 Flamingo Way in Hialeah, where he briefed me on the trip. He then issued me maps, a life preserver, a small inflatable lifeboat, a ream of official documents for landing in foreign countries, and a six-hundred-dollar expense advance. It was only after reviewing the maps that I realized just how far Buenos Aires was from Miami. I made a quick calculation and was shocked. It is the same distance from Miami to Buenos Aires as it is from Miami to London, England.

The aircraft that we were flying down were Piper PA-18 Super Cubs with a Lycoming engine that produced 150 horsepower. It would be different from flying the Piper J-3 that I was used to, and I looked forward to the more powerful engine.

The route of flight took us from Tamiami Airport over the Caribbean Sea, over Cuba, and then on to Montego Bay, Jamaica. From Montego Bay, we flew directly to Panama City, Panama; Talara, Peru; Pisco, Peru; Antofagasta, Chile; Santiago, Chile; and finally, Buenos Aires, Argentina.

My fellow pilots were John Paul Revere, the CAA man on vacation; Ray Davidson, an ex-purser for Eastern Airlines; Bill Penn, a local south Florida pilot; and Bill Shergalis, a local pilot who ran a waterski school on 79th Street Causeway. Ray Davidson was named the flight leader.

Time was running out for rigging the aircraft for the flight. Ray Davidson met me at Tamiami Airport and taught me the rigging process. Since the aircraft were built for spraying crops, there was a large tank called a "hopper" just behind the captain's seat where the passenger seat is normally located. This could hold a hundred gallons of the spray solution for the crop dusters.

The tanks were new and clean, so the ferry pilots used them for the long-range fuel tanks. You simply dropped a neoprene hose down through a breather hole in the top of the tank with something heavy to keep it at the bottom. After sealing that opening, you ran the hose forward past the pilot's seat where an auxiliary portable fuel pump was connected inline. Then you ran that hose out of the pilot's left window to the bottom of the left-wing tank where it connected into the threaded receptacle where the quick drain was normally located. The fuel pump was electrically powered by a connection to the battery. A switch taped to the left side of the cockpit next to the pilot's left elbow would activate the pump when needed to replenish the fuel in the left wing tank.

The airplane carried, fully rigged, one hundred and forty gallons of gas. There were a hundred gallons in the hopper and twenty gallons each in the two wing tanks. The fuel procedure was to only use fuel out of the left-wing tank. When its quantity read about a quarter full, the pilot would turn on the aux fuel pump and replenish the wing tank from the reserve supply in the hopper. Since the Super Cub used only about ten gallons per hour you could expect to remain aloft, if necessary, for about fourteen hours.

I was at Tamiami Airport bright and early on Thursday the 5th of December. As per Mr. Iba's instructions I had stopped by a market on the night before and packed some fruit, snacks, and a soda for my inflight lunch.

When all the pilots showed up, Davidson called a quick meeting and gave us our final briefing. "We'll fly in a loose left echelon," he explained. "Cooper, you'll fly to my left and slightly lower. Make sure that you can see my head. If you can't see me, then I can't see you. Don't fly too close," he added to the group, "and, Penn, you're next; Shergalis, you guide on Penn; and Revere, you bring up the rear." And he added, "After takeoff we'll fly south, parallel to Le Jeune Road for a few miles to calibrate our compasses. It runs directly one hundred and eighty degrees south."

"Any questions?" he asked. "Okay, fly safe. Be especially careful on your takeoffs and landings, and remember, you are just flying a big gas tank." And with that he turned to his aircraft and announced, "Let's go." We all climbed into our Super Cubs, started the engines, and taxied out.

It was a surreal picture—the sun, just above the horizon, radiating a sparkling glow from the reflection off the dew-covered wings. Five tiny Piper Cubs, white and red, all in a glistening line, taxiing out for an adventure I could only have dreamed of a year earlier sitting at my desk at the furniture company in High Point.

We had arrived at the designated run-up area at the takeoff end of the runway and I mentally returned to the cockpit to attend to the matters at hand.

My engine checked out okay and Davidson gave me thumbs-up. I answered him the same as he lined up for takeoff. In a second, he was lumbering down the runway with his full load of fuel and I watched as he lifted off.

My takeoff was the same. With Davidson's last-minute warning in my ear, I was extra careful. The airplane *was* a flying fuel tank and it took much longer than I was accustomed to for the airplane to become airborne. I was concentrating so much on the takeoff that once I was off and out of the pattern, I had lost sight of Davidson.

Two minutes into a flight that was scheduled to last six days and I was already lost. I headed southeast and pretty soon I found him, slightly above and ahead. Soon I was tucked under his left side and the other three were following in order. We were climbing south toward Cuba and on our way to Montego Bay.

The flight path took us almost directly over Brown's Airport. I looked down and I could see Mary's Piper Cubs, all in a row, and I must admit that I had mixed emotions. I was looking forward to this adventure, but I wasn't looking forward to all the over-water flying, and I certainly wasn't looking forward to flying through the Andes in a Piper Cub. Brown's Airport, and the practice area out by the tomato fields, suddenly looked awfully nice.

While my mind drifted back to Brown's Airport, I had let my airplane drift away from Davidson a bit. *I must keep my mind on what I'm doing,* I thought. I judged my distance from him by looking back and estimating how far the other planes were from each other. This formation was loose, and that was okay with me.

We departed the coastline of Florida in the vicinity of a small resort called Ocean Reef, and the mainland disappeared quickly behind us. I was estimating the north coast of Cuba in about two hours and Montego Bay in about four and a half hours. I remembered the flight to Havana earlier in the year. During this past year there had been a lot of turmoil in Cuba. I had read that the Cubans were fed up with their president, Batista, and that a revolutionary fellow by the name of Fidel Castro was creating havoc in the eastern part of the country and was holed up in the Sierra Maestra mountains. *I'll be on the lookout for those mountains,* I thought when I fly over Cuba.

We crossed the north coast of Cuba near an island called Cayo Coco. We were right on schedule. As we continued over Cuba, I had a great view of the countryside. It was a patchwork pattern of small farms and little cities. Every city had a church, a plaza, and a baseball field. The plowed fields gave off a reddish hue, and the grazing pastures were a brilliant green.

We passed over a fairly large town called Ciego de Ávila, and soon we were paralleling the coastline over a large bay called Golfo de Ana María. As

I watched the farmlands pass under my wings, I remembered the friendly hospitality that was shown to me earlier this year in Havana. I wondered if it would be the same out here in the country. I quickly satisfied myself that it would.

Another hour and the Cuba coastline passed beneath me. I looked to my left and saw some mountains far off to the east and checked my map.

Sierra Maestra.

An hour later and the mountains of Jamaica came into view, and soon we were circling the airport awaiting the green light signal to land.

Five small red Piper Cubs taxiing up to the customs ramp in Montego Bay was quite a sight. I was proud to be a part of this team and I was looking forward to the flight tomorrow.

We cleared customs, fueled the airplanes, and hired two taxis to take us to the hotel in Montego Bay. We had made arrangements to overnight at a hotel called The Hacton House. It was centrally located, on a hillside, high overlooking a popular area by the name of Doctor's Cave Beach.

We lined up to check in at the front desk. The desk clerk was a properly British-trained receptionist and was all business.

"Your name, sir," he asked the first of us.

"John Paul Revere" came the answer, and the clerk very officially completed the form.

"Next," he requested.

"William Penn" was the response. The clerk looked up briefly, hesitated, and finished completing the form.

I was next in line.

He took a deep breath, looked at me over his glasses, exhaled, and prompted me with "Ben Franklin, I presume?"

We all had a good laugh at the desk clerk's dry British humor, and the joke was repeated nightly throughout the flight.

The Hacton House was a beautiful inn. The rooms were decorated in a tropical motif, and the dining room overlooked Doctor's Cave Beach. I made a mental note that if I ever made another one of these trips, I would depart Miami earlier and bring my swimsuit.

Dinner with the veterans of these trips was educational. The conversation inevitably would come around to close calls that they had experienced and how to, first, avoid them and, second, survive if you got yourself into one.

It was during these dinners that the personalities of my new compatriots began to manifest themselves. Ray Davidson had a dry sense of humor. Bill Penn was a large man with a friendly and quick, jolly laugh. John Paul Revere was stoic and never came out of his shell, and Bill Shergalis was a large blond, happy-go-lucky guy who I instantly liked.

Tomorrow would be a long day. We ordered box lunches for the next day's flight and turned in early.

The distance from Montego Bay to Panama's Tocumen Airport was about six hundred and fifty miles. With the exception of about thirty miles over Jamaica and the same distance over Panama, the whole trip was over water with no landmarks by which to correct our course.

Ray Davidson briefed us on the heading. One hundred and eighty-six degrees was our compass heading, and the flying time would be six hours and thirty minutes. We started the engines, taxied out, and were off.

This leg of the trip was pretty simple. I was beginning to realize that the leader of the flight did all the work. He had to watch his heading the whole time, and if a thunderstorm interfered with the intended course, it was he who decided which side to fly on and what the corrected course to destination would be. All we had to do was to sit back, eat our box lunches, and follow.

We passed the mountains south of Montego Bay, and with nothing but water ahead for six hundred miles, we flew on.

Six hours over water is a long time, especially in a single-engine Piper Cub with no navigational instruments, no communications radios, and no autopilot. It gives you time to reflect on your past life and to ponder the future. You soon tire of being afraid. Being afraid is exhausting.

The drone of the engine begins to wear on you. Fatigue begins to set in and the cockpit gets smaller. Luckily you can open the sliding window on your left and the rush of fresh air will clear the cobwebs for a while. The Piper Cub is constructed in such a manner that there are two braces that extend from the forward corners of the instrument panel up toward the top of the cockpit connecting to the wing spars overhead. These come in handy as an exercise apparatus for pull-ups.

We were cruising at eighty-five hundred feet and the weather was no problem. After about five hours, we saw the cloud formations up ahead signaling that Panama would soon be in view. We finally saw land, and now the leader must decide whether we were east or west of course.

We had discussed that last night over dinner and, with no navigational devices on the airplanes, the answer lies in the average angle of the coastline. By looking on the chart you can see that the Isthmus of Panama is bowed to the north in the middle of the country. If you make landfall and you can't determine a landmark that will positively identify where you are, you simply fly along the coast for a few miles. Your average heading will quickly tell you which side of the canal you are on and you can adjust accordingly and select a heading for Tocumen Airport.

Ray's navigation was perfect and we readily identified a peninsula called San Blas on the north coast of Panama. With a new course to the southwest, we crossed some rough jungle terrain and some surprisingly high mountains as we descended toward the airfield.

I was amazed that by following nothing but a compass for six hours, you could come out within five miles of your intended point of destination.

We landed and performed the same routine. Clear customs, purchase fuel, and hire taxis to town.

Panama was a bustling town. It was nothing like Montego Bay. I would compare it with Havana as I noticed a similarity between the taxi drivers in Panama and those in Havana.

We stayed at a large hotel in downtown Panama called the Hotel International. I had time to pen a letter to Mom and Dad. They had voiced their objections to my taking this trip and I hoped that the letter would alleviate some of their concerns, if not mine. I even drew a map so Mom could follow my route. She would use my old Compton Encyclopedias for her references as she had in the past with the Havana trip.

I had splurged at a clothes sale in South Miami just before I left, and so I brought my finest wardrobe with me on this trip. This hotel was so nice that I thought I would dress up for dinner. The outfit is still my favorite summer uniform. It consists of navy blue trousers, white button-down shirt, red-and-blue striped tie, and a seersucker sport coat.

I was a dude at dinner.

After the friendly lampoonery at dinner over my attire, the conversation turned to tomorrow's flight.

The discussion centered around a term or phrase I had never heard—the Intertropical Convergence Zone, or as the seasoned pilots called it, the ITC. It was a weather phenomenon and they spoke of it in almost reverent tones. I got the firm idea that this was something to be respected.

I learned that the ITC consisted of a band of weather stretching around the globe in the vicinity of the equator. The actual location varied with the seasons, and the severity varied with the time of day. It was comprised of a band of clouds interspersed with thunderstorms. I listened intently and reaffirmed my determination to stay close to Davidson.

The ITC can be predictable with a reasonable degree of accuracy. When we arrived at the airport, we checked the weather as we filed our flight plans. The weather report would show the estimated latitude location of the ITC, but the severity was anyone's guess. The deal was, take off as early as possible and fly south and start climbing. The ITC was generally mild in the early morning, but when the sun was high in the sky, the temperature rose and so did the ITC. When flying into the ITC area in an airplane with no instruments, you have only three choices: fly over it, fly under it, or stay home.

After reviewing the weather forecast, Davidson decided to fly over the ITC as we were getting an early start and the temperature was not forecast to be unusually hot.

When you are flying with no communication radios, the control tower operators in Central and South America will not let you take off until daylight. That was fifteen to twenty minutes before sunrise, so in the dark of early morning we cranked up, and with Davidson leading the way, we taxied out.

I mentally reviewed the day's flight.

It would be about a thousand miles or ten hours nonstop. The first four hours took us from Panama across a corner of the Pacific Ocean direct to the northwest coast of Ecuador over a town called Esmeraldas. From there, depending on the weather, we would either follow the coastline south or fly direct to the Gulf of Guayaquil, pass about fifty miles west of the large port city of Guayaquil and, in around an hour and a half, we should arrive in the Peruvian city of Talara. We would clear customs there and hop down to the small city of Piura, Peru, where we would overnight.

A slight ray of pink began to show in the east, and Davidson flashed his position lights to the tower indicating that he was ready for takeoff. Shortly he received the green light and he was off. I was next. I pulled into position, advanced the throttle, and sped down the runway. I was off and the rest of the aircraft followed. We all caught up about ten miles south of Panama as the eastern sky lightened. We formed another loose "left echelon" and headed south, climbing so as to beat the ITC to ten thousand feet.

After three hours, the ITC began to form below us. First it was just a few transparent wisps of clouds. Another hour went by and the wisps became a solid under cast. We were estimating Esmeraldas by now, but the clouds were solid for as far as I could see, and to navigate by visual reference to the coastline was impossible.

Davidson wiggled his wings, which was the signal to come up close for a hand sign. I pulled up as close as I dared and saw him gesture with his hand to fly straight ahead. We were on a direct course for Talara, Peru, about six hours in front of us.

I looked at the map and saw that the equator should be passing just below us now. That was another first for me, and since I had no one with whom to celebrate, I pulled out a sandwich and a bottle of orange juice, gave a mock toast to no one in particular, and lunched alone. It was peaceful up there. It was just me and the Andes far off to the left and the drone of the little Lycoming engine to keep me company.

The ITC was rising up below us. In an airplane with no instruments, it is impossible to fly more than a few seconds without reference to either the horizon or an artificial one in the cockpit. The result of accidently penetrating a cloud layer with no instruments was always fatal.

I watched Davidson carefully select headings that would provide the most separation between the tops of the clouds and us. At this altitude, we could see for hundreds of miles, and in the distance some of the thunderstorms were topping thirty thousand feet or more.

Davidson stayed at our altitude and with cautious maneuvering we reached the southernmost critical area of the ITC, and the cloud level below us began to lower.

I breathed a sigh of relief and looked at my watch. We had been airborne for eight hours. Although I hadn't seen the ground in over four hours, I felt comfortable that we were reasonably on course and were passing Guayaquil. I was beginning to use the Andes, far off to the east, as a navigational aid by cross-referencing the tallest peaks. I had just identified one such peak—about 120 miles northeast of Guayaquil—that rose to an altitude of over twenty thousand feet. Just east of Guayaquil, about eighty miles away, there were several peaks that rose to between twelve thousand to fifteen thousand feet, and I could use them also as an indication as to our progress.

Another hour and the clouds beneath us began to break up. I could see the coastline. If my estimate was accurate, we should be crossing the border of Ecuador and Peru.

Davidson began a slow descent, and soon we were circling the airport at Talara, Peru.

I was ready to land. Ten hours in a small airplane is enough. My lunch was finished, my butt had given out, and my comfort cup was full. I suppose that I haven't mentioned that yet. One of the items in my Miami briefing was to bring a receptacle for relief on these long flights. It was a necessity.

We cleared customs in Talara and flew down to a small town called Piura, Peru, only thirty minutes away.

We fueled the aircraft and went to our hotel in town. I was not expecting what I saw. The town was small, neat, and looked like a movie set. The people were extremely nice, and the hotel was more than I expected. The personnel were very hospitable, and over dinner I read about the history of the town in some information supplied by the hotel.

Piura was a classic Spanish town. The Spanish explorer Francisco Pizarro settled it in 1532. It was the third Spanish settlement in South America. The city has a lovely river, the Piura, running through it, and the main attraction is the church, the Catedral de Piura, which was built in 1588. It is a landmark and its twin towers stand tall next to the central park, the Plaza de Armis.

Over dinner we talked about the next day's flight. Ray Davidson said that it was an easy one. We simply fly down the coast of Peru for about six hours and land at Pisco, Peru. He reminded us that we had something to look forward to, as Pisco was the home of the world-renowned cocktail, the Pisco Sour.

I had no idea what he was referring to, but the thought of an easy flight intrigued me, so I went to bed and slept soundly with no nightmares of any ITCs.

The morning routine was the same. Check the weather, file a flight plan, and take off.

As I walked to the airplane, I noticed that there was an overcast of about a thousand feet. We talked about it and Davidson decided that we should take off and stay below the overcast until we saw some blue sky and then climb on top and continue the flight to Pisco.

We all agreed and Davidson took off and headed south at about a thousand feet. I was second; I took the runway and shortly I was off and climbing. I headed south in the direction that I had last seen Davidson go.

Once airborne, I couldn't locate him, so I continued south at eight hundred feet altitude. I noticed, off to the left, a patch of sunlight on the ground indicating a hole in the overcast. I headed for it and when I saw blue sky, I climbed for it, and soon I was on top of a nice cloud level. I continued to climb southbound as I looked for Davidson. None of my other three buddies were to be seen either. I was on top of the cloud layer alone with nothing to do but to continue southbound until I could make ground contact and descend to look for them.

I held the last heading that Davidson had assigned on the briefing the night before, and with my new friends, the Andes, to my left, I continued toward Pisco and the famous Pisco Sour.

Three hours went by and no break in the overcast. Then four and then five. I was beginning to be concerned as I was estimating Pisco in another hour and a half. By looking at the mountains to the east and looking at my watch, I surmised that I had just passed Lima and was about one hour and a half from Pisco.

There were no breaks in the clouds beneath me. I had more concern. I had plenty of gas and the sun was still high in the western sky, but, just the same, I knew the consequences of being caught above the clouds with no instruments to guide me down. I looked harder for breaks in the cloud layer below me.

Nothing!

My watch told me that I had been in the air for six hours and thirty minutes. The mountains to my left told me that I was near or over Pisco. I throttled back, began a large slow circle, and reviewed my options. It looked like the tops of the cloud layer below me was only about two thousand feet high. My guess was, based on the forecasted temperature and the cloud formations back at Piura when we left, that there should be at least one thousand feet of clearance below the cloud level and the water, or ground, depending on how good my navigational expertise was. I had to figure out where I was without the use of navigational radios. Impossible?

Maybe not!

Ah ha. My friends the Andes. As I circled, I observed the highest peaks of certain mountains and began to work out a triangulation that would let me know approximately where I was.

In looking at the map, I saw, to my east, three mountains; the two most north and south were about a hundred miles away and were listed as approximately seventeen thousand feet high. The one in the middle was about sixty-five miles away and smaller and listed on the map at fifteen thousand feet. I identified those three mountains easily.

Closer, only about twenty-five miles to the east of Pisco, was a much smaller mountain that was only thirty-two hundred feet. I could see it sticking up through the clouds. On the map, it aligned perfectly with the smaller, middle mountain, and that gave me a perfect east-west line over Pisco.

Now, I only had to determine how far out Pisco was on that perfect line. Luckily, a hundred miles east of Lima, there's a giant mountain listed on the map as being 18,900 feet high. I had watched it as I flew southbound, and we had become friends, as I had no one else to talk to. Now he, or she, would do me a great favor.

By lining up the nose of the airplane on that mountain and flying north on a compass heading of ten degrees, I could tell exactly where Pisco Bay was when I crossed the east-west mountain chain line that I had established seconds ago, and I could ascertain that I was exactly off the shore near Pisco. I felt comfortable that I had established my location with a certain degree of accuracy.

Now the hard part. *How do I descend through a level of clouds with no instruments?*

I remembered a trick that an old barnstormer had talked about in one of my hangar-flying sessions back at Fraley Field. It dealt with the only instrument that I had in the aircraft, the whisky compass. Now that doesn't mean that it's filled with whisky. That's just a name left over from the barnstorming days. The compass is really filled with alcohol to keep it from freezing, and its only purpose is to tell the pilot the direction of flight.

The alcohol floats a small cylinder that rotates and points toward the north and tells you the direction of flight that you're heading. Accordingly, the old barnstormer allowed that on a perfectly calm day, by carefully watching the floating cylinder in the compass window, one can *possibly* keep the wings level for a short period of time. You are effectively using the compass as an artificial horizon. Additionally, the whisky compass is more accurate when flying west or east when you are attempting to keep the aircraft on a straight course. Was I about to put this harebrained, unproven idea to the test?

Yes! I had no choice.

After reviewing all the options, and with the sun sinking lower in the west, I decided to attempt the maneuver.

I was going to make an instrument approach into an area that I was unfamiliar with, in an airplane that was not, in any remote way, equipped for instrument flying.

Perfect!

I circled a few times to confirm my general location. Okay, the mountains lined up. I picked up a westerly heading so my compass would be of some help directionally, and I descended to fifty feet above the cloud level. My altimeter read two thousand feet. *So far so good*, I thought.

I set up a gradual rate of descent with idle power. My eyes were glued to the compass, not for the heading, the reason that it was placed in the aircraft, but for the slightest, ever so slight, indication that a wing was dipping or rising. The slightest overcorrection would send the airplane into a "graveyard" spiral, which would surely, at this low altitude, be fatal.

The airplane sank quietly into the cloud layer without a trace of turbulence. The cockpit darkened.

"Focus," I told myself out loud, "focus!"

I forced myself to trust any small indications that the homemade horizon in the window of the floating compass would give me. It was the only thing I had. The seat of my pants told me to make corrections, but my eyes told me NO! I must trust the little floating instrument in front of me. *Is that a slight wing drop?* Instantly I made a small adjustment with the aileron. "Not too much," I cautioned myself. "Don't change the rate of descent." *I murmured.*

"How thick is this damn cloud layer? I screamed in my mind.

It seemed as if I had been in the cloud layer forever.

"Concentrate," I mumbled out loud.

And then, at eight hundred feet, I broke out. I had managed to keep the wings level with the improbable help of the whisky compass.

I could see the dark gray ocean beneath me. Perspiration was dripping off my chin, and my hands were soaked with sweat. I looked around to see where I had ended up, and to my surprise I found myself over the Bay of Pisco, five miles from the Pisco airport.

The other four pilots were already there when I landed. I taxied up to the fuel pumps, and Ray Davidson sauntered over. "Did you get lost?" he asked.

"No," I answered nonchalantly, "I just came down over the top."

The conversation at the hotel that night was about the other four pilots' flight. They had remained under the cloud layer for the whole flight, passing off shore at Lima, Peru, and then following the coastline at about a thousand feet into Pisco.

We all ordered the mandatory beverage at the restaurant, the Pisco Sour. I can attest; it was sour.

Again, we anticipated a long but not too difficult flight the next day, so we went to bed early in anticipation of an early wake-up call.

The flight was easy. The weather was improved around Pisco, and after about a hundred miles, it cleared up completely. We climbed to a comfortable altitude and enjoyed, for nine hours, the sights along the Peruvian and Chilean coastline to the city of Antofagasta, Chile.

It was a short night in Antofagasta, as we had another long day planned for the next day. The briefing was easy, as Davidson said in his now familiar dry humor, "Just fly west until you hit the first Pacific Ocean, turn left, follow the coast until you see Santiago, and land." The flight was planned for a little over nine hours.

Again, the flight was uneventful. The weather was good, and the scenery was exquisite, with the high cliffs along the Chilean coastline highlighted by the white droppings of the local seafowl. The snowcapped mountains of the Andes, a hundred miles to the east, kept me company for the whole flight.

After about eight hours of sightseeing, we neared the large city of Valparaiso, Chile. Santiago lies about sixty miles to the southeast of Valparaiso at the foothills of the Andes. We turned inland toward Santiago and began our descent. Only then, as we neared the Andes, did I realize just how tall and ominous they were. In two days I would discover just how treacherous they really were!

We landed, checked in with the airport authorities, as we had already cleared into the country at Antofagasta the day before. We had a meeting at the gas pumps with regard to how much fuel to put on the aircraft. The issue was, as Davidson explained, we must be able to clear the mountain pass through a valley that was 14,400 feet high. *Did he say valley, I asked myself, at 14,400 feet high?*

"The mountains around here go up to as high as twenty-three thousand feet, so we must be able to climb to at least 14,500 feet. Our flight plan to Buenos Aires calls for a flying time of eight hours and thirty minutes, so at around ten gallons per hour fuel burn and with an hour reserve, you'll need a minimum of a hundred gallons of fuel. Any more and you won't be able to clear the mountain pass."

I had sixty gallons on board when we landed, so I ordered forty more and carefully watched the fueling personnel load my ship.

At the hotel that night, the conversation took on a more serious note. Davidson reviewed the issues with the terrain. This was the only time since we started the trip that he brought a map with him to dinner.

"As you saw," he said, "coming into Santiago, the mountains rise rapidly just east of town. The pass that we will use is only about forty miles east of the airport, so we must climb as rapidly as we can to reach our necessary altitude of 14,500 feet. We won't be able to make it by flying a straight line directly to the pass. We'll have to climb in a circle once we arrive at the rendezvous point. We'll meet over a lake by the name of Laguna Negra—it's here on your map—and this lake is about thirty miles from the airport on a heading of a hundred degrees. You'll see two mountains; the one to the north, Tupungato, rises to twenty-two thousand feet, and the one to the south, Marmolejo, goes up to twenty thousand feet. Our valley is between the two peaks at fourteen thousand four hundred feet. The average height of the terrain along this ridge of the Andes is approximately sixteen thousand feet."

He went on. "Over the lake, we'll climb in a left or counterclockwise circle in a trail formation. Cooper, you stay behind me, and the rest of you file in at your usual slots.

"And finally," he stated, "nobody goes through until everyone is at altitude and until I say the word. I'll pat myself on the head when we're all at altitude and I'll go first, Cooper, you follow me, and so on.

"Remember," he added, "and this is probably the most important item to remember. You don't have portable oxygen on this trip, and at 14,500 feet you will be gasping for air. Remember to force yourselves to breathe, and to breathe hard. Asphyxia can creep up on you, and you won't even recognize it. As you approach your altitude, you must continue to say to yourselves, 'Breathe! Breathe! Breathe!' You'll only be at this altitude for about ten minutes, so it is important that you maintain your senses while there.

"One last word of caution," he warned, "the prevailing winds are from the west at speeds in excess of one hundred miles per hour. Don't approach the valley until you are sure that you have sufficient altitude to clear the terrain. With tailwinds like that, once you commit, there's no turning back.

"We'll rendezvous east of the pass down at the small town of San Carlos, thirty miles east of the valley, and continue on to Buenos Aires." Then in his deadpan demeanor, he added, "Now, everyone sit back and enjoy your dinner."

Well, that was a sobering meeting, I thought.

We had to remain in Santiago for an extra day to secure our airline tickets home, so I took that day to do some real sightseeing.

The Man in The Arena...

Santiago was an interesting city with lots to do. After handling our airline ticket business, we all stayed together and took in the sights. We visited a hill next to the city that offered a panoramic view of the city. It was called Cerro San Cristóbal, and on the crest of that hill was a large statue of Christ.

I learned my second Spanish word, helados, which means ice cream. Santiago has the best ice cream in the world and I ate so much that I began to wonder if I could get the airplane high enough to make the pass the next day.

As nice as Santiago was, my mind kept returning to Tupungato and Marmolejo and I must admit, I looked at the upcoming flight with much trepidation.

The morning came, we assembled at the airplanes, and Davidson gave us a last-minute briefing ending with "Don't forget to breathe."

We cranked up and, in turn, took off. I stayed close to Davidson and we began to climb at a maximum rate almost immediately. We flew southeast for about twenty miles, following a railroad track and a river as planned. We left the railroad tracks with a left turn at the small village of San Gabriel and followed the valley northward toward the lake, Laguna Negra, the designated rendezvous point.

The countryside was beautiful, but the valley was climbing almost as fast as we were. Climbing we followed a river northeast with two nine-thousand-foot mountains on either side of us. We were about eight thousand feet high when we saw the lake. I could see the two large mountains off to the east as we began our circle over the lake and continued our climb. The upper limits of the vegetation had been reached, and the land off to the east was barren and the mountains were snowcapped.

Up until this trip, I didn't think that a Cub could fly as high as 14,500 feet. There are two things that make it almost impossible: one is the airflow over the wings and the second is the air going into the fuel carburetor system. The fuel/air ratio is important in the operation of the engine's efficiency. The higher you fly, the thinner the air gets, so to maintain the proper fuel/air ratio, one must reduce the amount of fuel going into the carburetor. This is called "leaning the engine," and there is a small pull knob in the cockpit that controls this operation.

As we climbed higher and higher, it was necessary to continuously lean the engine. The result of the proper leaning of the engine is that the engine will run smoother and maintain maximum power as you climb into thinner air. At this altitude it required constant attention and adjustments.

Also, as I gained altitude, I knew that the airspeed would continue to drop off. I knew that at the weight I was carrying and the altitude to which I was going, the airspeed would be reduced to near stall speed—the speed at which the airflow over the wings would not support the weight of the aircraft. In that case, the aircraft would quit flying and descend out of control until proper speed could be established to maintain flight. I must avoid that.

So we climbed. I was watching Davidson, the RPM gauge, and the airspeed gauge all at the same time. As the RPMs would fall off at the higher altitudes, I would have to re-lean the engine. The airspeed continued to drop as we climbed.

I glanced out of the cockpit for a second. The other three airplanes were slightly below us and in trail, and it looked as if they were climbing along nicely with us. Over to the east were the two tallest peaks, between which was the valley of fourteen thousand four hundred feet.

The sky was crystal clear.

We reached twelve thousand feet and I remembered that I must "force breathe." The remaining twenty-five hundred feet would be difficult. The engine fuel must be monitored, both by watching the RPM gauge and by listening to the engine.

"Breathe," I told myself.

The airspeed had to be monitored, second by second. The airspeed gauge must be watched constantly and, just as the ear is necessary to listen to any engine issues, the seat of the pants is a good gauge to an impending wing stall.

"Don't forget to breathe," I kept reminding myself.

The rate of climb had dropped to three hundred feet per minute; the airspeed had dropped to about ten miles per hour above stall speed. I was guessing that we would be at the crossing altitude in about eight minutes, and giving the other three pilots a couple of minutes to arrive at our altitude, we should be ready to fly across the valley in ten minutes.

I knew that I was getting light-headed, as I was having trouble adding ten minutes to the present time while watching Davidson, the RPMs, and the airspeed.

"Breathe, dammit," I scolded myself.

To the east I could see the valley clearly. We were almost high enough. I glanced at the altimeter, which read fourteen thousand feet.

The control stick got "light," indicating an impending stall, and I eased it forward, ever so delicately. "Lean the engine slightly," I reminded myself, as I could feel a scant loss of power in the engine. "And breathe," I chided myself. "Take deep, long breaths." Gasping, my chest was rising and falling deeply as I labored for air.

And then it was time.

Davidson gave me the signal; he tapped his head and slowly turned his aircraft toward the northeast and headed for the valley.

I followed.

"Don't stop breathing," I kept reminding myself.

There was a tall mountain to our left that went up to about 15,500 feet. That gave me confidence that my altimeter was correctly showing 14,500 feet. I followed safely behind Davidson. Off to the right was Marmolejo, the south bank of the valley, and in front and to the left of the valley was the giant Tupungato rising to over 23,000 feet.

The landscape below was rising almost vertically as it rushed up beneath my wings. The predicted tailwind was whisking me along at a breakneck speed for a Cub, although the airspeed indicator showed a bare sixty miles per hour. It was too late to turn back now. Things were happening fast.

Suddenly the terrain was less than a hundred feet beneath me. I was gasping for air while marveling at the sights around me. The landscape looked like the moon. There was no foliage whatsoever, only barren rocks and snow and mountains rising even higher on either side of me.

Although I was moving across the barren surface at more than 150 miles per hour, my airspeed was only showing about sixty miles per hour as I was being pushed along by the west wind prevalent through this valley. *I must continue to concentrate on the critical airspeed*, I thought, as I was actually only a few miles per hour over the stalling speed of the aircraft. I remembered. "*Don't be fooled by the speed of the aircraft passing over the rocks*—which were a scant fifty feet beneath my wheels. *Only a few more miles, only a few more minutes to go. Breathe, and watch the airspeed.*

And then, just as soon as it started, it ended.

The land fell suddenly, almost frighteningly, away from under me and, startled, I relaxed pressure on the control stick and let the airplane descend slowly to a safe altitude.

I made a slow right turn toward the southeast, passed abeam Mount Marmolejo, said good-bye to the Andes, visually picked up a small river that we had been briefed to follow, and continued on to San Carlos to meet up with the others in our flight.

Davidson made one circle, accounted for all the airplanes, and headed toward Buenos Aires. It was all downhill from here.

Buenos Aires was a big town. It made Miami seem small.

Apparently, they had a revolution a few years before and some of the buildings showed signs of bullet holes. The former president, Juan Peron, was ousted by a coup in 1955, and it must have been quite a show. His wife Evita was a favorite of the people, but she had died in 1952.

We stayed for two days and it was almost a vacation. The food was excellent and I was sorry to leave.

There was an interesting personal postscript to this trip.

When I boarded the airliner to Santiago heading back to Miami, it was the first commercial flight that I had ever taken. I was seated next to the window, and when the airplane began its takeoff roll, the wings began to flex up and down, as is normal. I didn't expect this and I surely thought that the wings would come off and, after flying a Piper Cub from Miami to Buenos Aires, I would die on my first airline flight. It scared the life out of me, but Davidson had a big laugh out of it.

Later, the stewardess told the captain that there were some small-plane pilots on board and he invited us up for a visit. I was in the cockpit when we passed my old friends, Mount Tupungato and Mount Marmolejo. The passage looked so easy from thirty thousand feet.

It was on that visit to the cockpit that I learned my third Spanish phrase. When the captain learned that I had flown a Piper Cub from Miami to Buenos Aires, he referred to me from then on as that *piloto loco*, crazy pilot.

We stopped in Santiago, Lima, and Panama on the way to Miami.

It was December 16, 1957, and I was glad to be home.

The pay for that trip was three hundred dollars.

Christmas came and it was my first away from home. Fred Bost, one of my students, and a local boy invited me to his parents' home for their holiday party. They had a gift for me and it was nice of them, but it wasn't home.

The year came to a close with no letter from Eastern. I was a senior flight instructor for Kendall Flying School, but my crushed heart was somewhere else, flying big airplanes.

January of 1958 began the same way that '57 had ended.

I was still instructing with Kendall Flying School. From time to time Bob Iba would call me for a quick ferry trip, and if my schedule permitted I would take it. I took an airplane to Chicago, another one to Cleveland, all the while instructing for Mary.

My enthusiasm for instructing was wearing thin; Mary knew this, so she was lenient with my schedule. I had some regular students who were working toward a career in aviation, and their schedule was pretty flexible. If I needed time off for a ferry trip, they would just schedule solo time and wait until I returned for the dual portion of the curriculum.

I anxiously checked the mail each day for the letter from any airline.

None came.

In reviewing the credentials and flying experience that the airlines advertised, it was becoming apparent that the only thing the fellows who were getting hired possessed that I didn't have was a discharge from the military.

On every application, hidden down in the corner, was a box to check that read, military status? I would write "none." Although it was discriminatory, it made perfect sense. Why would an airline want to train a pilot and then have him leave for two years or more?

CHAPTER 26
The United States Air Force

But not as a pilot…

IT WAS EARLY FEBRUARY. ONE of my students was an Air Force recruiter based in Miami. He flew often with me and we became good friends. After one of our training sessions, we decided to lunch at the Luncheonette. During the conversation over lunch, I was lamenting my plight. I was almost ready to enlist in the Army to get my two years out of the way rather than wait for the draft.

His eyes lit up. "Cooper," he said, "I've got just the thing for you. The Air Force has just initiated a new plan. You enlist for six years, put in only six months of active duty, and then you fulfill the balance of the six years as a reservist. You will do basic training at Lackland Air Force Base for two and a half months, and I can get you based in Miami at the Miami International Airport for the rest of your six months."

It took me about half a second to decide. The next day I was in his office in Miami, right hand raised, and I was sworn into the U.S. Air Force.

My orders came in a week; I was to show up at Lackland Air Force Base, two months later, on April 25th.

Chuck Hudson had been a pilot with Eastern for about six months. He had completed his training and was flying out of Miami. Although he had graduated from the ranks of a flight instructor up to the rarified air of that of an airline pilot, he still hung out with the old group.

There were Jim and me, Fred Bost, one of our senior students, Cal Cushman, an aircraft mechanic, Bob Jones, and Bud Dixon, another senior flight student at Kendall Flying School who made up the core of our motley crew. If we were the crew, then Dee Dee was the Den Mother, and we all spent many weekends at the Stouts' house.

Chuck was living in Miami Springs, the center of the social world of all airline personnel in South Florida. Eastern, Pan Am, National, and a slew of South American airlines all maintained their flight attendant schools there. It was the place to hang out.

Chuck was our connection with the ladies in that area. Often, he would invite us to parties that were attended by almost all airline people. It was mid-February, and he invited us to a party on Swan Avenue in Miami Springs. Jim and I accepted, and that's where I met Diane.

Her name was Diane Jacobs; she was an Eastern Airlines flight attendant and she was pretty—really pretty. She had just graduated from the Eastern Flight Attendant Academy and was already flying the line.

She wasn't seeing anyone and neither was I, so we began a friendship that evolved rather quickly into a steady arrangement. Since I was already sworn into the military and was due to report to the Air Force in a couple of months, neither of us thought that it would turn into anything serious. She was flying a lot and I was keeping busy with instructing and ferrying airplanes around the country, so we didn't see that much of each other.

Spring came and with the exception of a few ferry trips up north, I spent most of my time at Brown's Airport instructing.

Dee Dee worked hard at her flying and earned her private pilot's license. Her husband, Darwin, was her first passenger. My other students were progressing rapidly toward their personal goals, and as my time neared for basic training, I transferred them, over time, to other instructors at the school. This allowed me to work until the day that I was to leave for camp, and the money would come in handy.

I had flown quite a bit with Bill Shergalis over the past six months since we flew the long flight to Buenos Aires, and we had bonded. We would meet occasionally to discuss our respective futures, and generally we would meet at a cafe on 79th Street Causeway, the road that connects Miami with Miami Beach. The cafe was near the trailer that served as the office for his waterski school.

It was the first week of April and we both had gotten a furlough notice from Hialeah Aircraft Ferry Company. The letter was from Mr. Iba and was very apologetic but complimentary. It simply said that there just wasn't enough flying for all the pilots and that he could only keep five. He offered that if the business improved, or one of the five quit, he would call us back.

We talked for a while and I felt that Bill had something weighing on his mind. It wasn't long before the real reason for this meeting became apparent. Bill had a deal that would make him a lot of money, and fairly quickly. He offered me the opportunity to join him. He said he liked my flying skills, and since this opportunity would require a high degree of those skills, he thought that he would like to give me a shot at it. I was curious. I only had a few weeks before I had to report for Air Force duty, so a quick ferry flight might fit in just fine.

"Tell me more about the job," I queried him.

He called the waitress over and paid the check. "Let's go outside," he suggested, "where we can talk."

I followed him out and as we sat on the curb he told me what the deal was.

It wasn't a single ferry flight as I had surmised. It was more of a clandestine, ongoing operation. As he explained it to me, I became less and less interested.

"You've heard of this guy Castro, down in Cuba," he whispered quietly as he looked suspiciously around.

"I suppose so," I answered.

"I've been contacted by agents of his group in Miami," he explained, "and they've offered me a job flying cargo into the mountains where he's holed up. The planes are small Piper Apaches in a cargo configuration, and it pays between $2,000 and $3,000 per trip depending on where you leave from."

"I don't think so, Bill," I said, shaking my head. "This looks too political for me and, besides, if you get caught by either the U.S. Government or the Batista bunch, your odds of getting out alive are nil."

"I don't know," he argued, "I just read that the U.S. Government has suspended all arms shipments to the Batista Government, and that makes Castro's odds of success much better."

"I think," I added, "that I'll just stay around here and instruct until the time comes for me to go to the Air Force. When I get out in October, I'll look you up, and maybe Iba will have some work for both of us then."

When we got up to leave, he took off his watch and handed it to me. It was a chronograph stopwatch with all sorts of dials and a calendar. I had admired it on the trip to Buenos Aires and had mentioned that when I got rich, I was going to purchase one just like it.

"You take it," he offered. "I have another like it and you always liked this one. When we both get back next fall, you can put it to good use while we fly over the jungles of Ecuador," he added as he got in his car to leave.

"Can I give you something for it?" I asked as he pulled away.

"Nah," he said. "The pawn shop only offered me five bucks for it anyhow. It's yours." He laughed and sped away.

I didn't know whether he really had a second watch or not.

The next two weeks went by too fast. On April 25, I checked in at the Air Force Base at Miami International Airport for processing. I left my car at Diane's house in Miami Springs, and early the next day I was on my way to San Antonio, Texas, looking for an Air Force bus to Lackland Air Force Base.

I landed at San Antonio Airport and located the "mustering-up" point in the terminal. The room was set up to receive new recruits as they arrived from different locations around the U.S. It wasn't long before the room was practically filled with about forty boys.

Soon, a very large sergeant arrived and rudely introduced us to the U.S. Air Force.

"Okay, you men, line up two abreast and follow me," he ordered. "I said TWO abreast—can't you men count?" he chastised us as we fumbled around trying to get in line.

We finally got in some sort of semi-organized line and, behind the sergeant, stumbled toward the front of the terminal and into the Air Force bus that awaited us.

Lackland Air Force Base is not very far from the commercial airport, only about twenty miles, so we arrived quickly and were soon disembarking from the bus.

After aligning us up in a sort of squad, we were marched to what was to be our home for the next two and a half months. We were an assorted group, outfitted in our civilian clothes, and we looked like a kaleidoscope of various colors, styles, and sizes. As we marched by several barracks, we were berated by the seasoned airmen with catcalls of "rainbows, rainbows, rainbows." Apparently, that was traditional. It was somewhat demeaning, but within two weeks, we were yelling the same words to the next class of new recruits.

We processed into camp life with the usual procedures. We were issued our uniforms and had a visit to the barbershop. I came with a crew cut, so it wasn't too much of a shock to me to get the buzz cut. For the fellows with the "duck tails," it was another story. It was a horrifying experience for them, but a source of much entertainment to the rest of us.

Our first day consisted of getting used to the barracks and to barrack life. Making up the bed was a big deal and took a lot of training for some of my barrack mates. It was apparent that some had never made up a bed before.

I remembered Mom's lesson at Myrtle Beach and it came in handy.

We each had a foot locker, and the placement of our standard issue of clothes was exact; three T-shirts went here, three handkerchiefs went there, and over there, placed neatly, were three pairs of shorts. Everything else had its place, and you were inspected daily to ensure that each item was exactly placed as instructed.

We had show-and-tell with our new uniforms. We were asked to don the newly issued khakis for inspection. This was duck soup for me as I had been in the Air Force ROTC at UNC for two years and we had gone through this drill ad nauseam.

Our training instructor, the TI, came through and with a look of disgust exclaimed, "Don't any of you greenhorns know what a gig line is?"

I did, and timidly answered, "Yes, sir."

I learned later that in the military, one should never volunteer for anything.

He walked over slowly, looked me up and down, and with an air of approval exclaimed, "Okay, mister, suppose you tell your bunk mates just what a gig line is."

Nervously I stumbled through the explanation.

First, in the military when one errs, one is given a sort of a demerit. This is called a gig. When you amass a certain number of gigs, you will receive some form of punishment.

Second, in the proper wearing of the uniform, it is mandatory that the line formed by the vertical seams along where the shirt is buttoned aligns with the belt buckle and the fly seam. If an airman is caught with those three things out of alignment, he is given a demerit or gig. Thus the term "gig line."

Without further comment he spun around and left the barracks.

I didn't know if I would be marked as a wise guy, but after the TI left, the others came up and asked me how I knew about the dress code. When I explained that I had two years in the ROTC, I then became the expert on all things military. I enjoyed that notoriety amongst my bunkmates. I wasn't sure how it registered with my TI.

The routine set in. There were meal periods, classes, drills, and physical education.

The Man in The Arena...

With my previous experience in the ROTC, it all seemed easy. I acclimated to the formal studies consisting of military discipline, Air Force core values, and the history of the Air Force. The marching was second nature to me based on my two years with the UNC ROTC drill team, and the physical education was easy as I was still in pretty good shape from my baseball days at college.

I suppose the TI reviewed my application, as he began to single me out to head up the physical education classes, and I ended up as the guidon bearer for the drill ceremonies.

Although I was counting the days until I would return to Miami, the Air Force basic training went pretty well. Diane kept me up to date on the goings-on back in Miami Springs; Sandy Forbes went with Northeast Airlines, Fred got a job with Jim's old company at Air Associates, and the newspapers were full of that Cuban revolutionary fellow up in the mountains, Fidel Castro.

Mom kept me informed as to the family in High Point.

I turned twenty-two in May and some of my new buddies and I celebrated with a trip to San Antonio. We visited the Alamo and took a river cruise down the little river that bisects the city. The shoreline was dotted with small Mexican restaurants, and lunch there was a welcome relief from the Air Force cooking.

I was learning the Air Force system. Occasionally we were assigned to the Post Exchange, the PX, for work duty. We were the slave laborers at the giant market that supplied the local Air Force base families with their daily food supplies. I found that if I would dress smartly, find a clipboard, and walk the aisles, looking very official and knowledgeable, I could avoid the heavy lifting out back.

This went well until one day I decided to venture to the back loading dock to see how my buddies were faring with the loading and unloading of the never-ending food supplies.

They were all there, toiling and sweating. They needed to be entertained, I surmised. I spied a new mop head nearby and with a broom I decided to be the one-man local USO entertainment committee using the loading dock as my stage. I put the mop on my head, grabbed the broom as a guitar, and did my best imitation of Elvis Presley singing "Blue Suede Shoes."

The performance was met with frolicking peals of laughter, coupled with boisterous dancing about and a rousing round of applause. I was a great success!

And then I noticed that I was all alone out there on the loading dock stage. My fans had abandoned me suddenly, and I sensed another presence behind me.

It had to have been the biggest sergeant at Lackland Air Base.

"Well," he drawled, "what have we here? Is this Mis'tah Elvis Presley or is this a lowly airman about to go to the brig?"

"No, sir," I stammered as I quickly took off the mop head and tossed the broom to the side. "No, sir, just having a little fun with the troops, and now I must get back to work inside."

I grabbed my clipboard and rushed past him to my soft position back in the air-conditioned market while staying on the lookout for him for the rest of the day.

That was as close as I came to getting into trouble during basic training.

The rest of my stay at Lackland was uneventful, and soon my transfer date of July 10 came, and I was assigned to the 435th Troop Carrier Wing at Miami International Airport.

Diane and I picked up where we left off and began seeing each other regularly.

I rented a room out west of the airport at 535 S.W. 79th Court near a little development called Sweetwater, settled in, and prepared for my new job with the Air Force. I still had three months to put in at the U.S. Air Base at Miami International Airport.

I had an easy job. Based on the fact that I had two years of college, and more importantly, that I could type, I was assigned as clerk typist for the commander of the 435th Troop Carrier Wing, a division within the base. His name was Colonel John Pountnay, and he was a former Delta Airlines pilot before being called up to active duty.

I had a desk job with a nice window overlooking "9 right," the southernmost runway at Miami International Airport. It was difficult to concentrate as the large transport aircraft passed by my window only seconds away from touching down for their landings. In my new job, although the high-level secret stuff wasn't shared with me, I heard a lot of water cooler gossip, and the main conversation centered on the activities of Fidel Castro in eastern Cuba. I found it intriguing and I thought about my friend Bill Shergalis.

During my "active" time at Miami International Airport, Mom and Dad came down for a visit. I believe they were happy that I was not flying, and they were encouraged that once I finished my military obligation, I would be hired by a regular airline.

Dad, being the consummate car trader, decided that I should have a new car. I think that he just liked to trade cars for a hobby, and I went along with the deal. We visited Potamkin Chevrolet on Miami Beach and came away with a wonderful Chevy. It was a black, two-door Impala, and although it had the nicest lines of any car in the market, it was just a plain Jane. It had no power windows or power seats, no air-conditioning, and a small six-cylinder engine. It was ideal for me and for the next six years it served me faithfully as I crisscrossed the United States searching for the elusive airline job.

My artistic ability caught the eye of the office manager, and I was kept busy, when I wasn't typing correspondence, by producing pamphlets and promotional brochures for the base. My office manager would load me up with brochures, notices, and other projects that required artwork. He endeared himself to the commander and all the other organizations around the base at my expense.

It had been three months since I had flown and I was eager to get back into the air. Although I still had three months to go before I was to be released from active duty, I began to touch base with my old employers to see what was out there for a freelance pilot.

I called Mary at Kendall Flying School and she was agreeable to re-employ me when I was discharged. There was Allen Burnett, the manager of Howe Aviation, whom I had gotten to know at Brown's Airport. He was moving his operation up to Tamiami Airport soon and indicated that he might start up a flight school at the new location. He said to come by any time and maybe we could work something out. And of course, there was Bob Iba at Hialeah Aircraft Ferry Company.

I always enjoyed talking with Bob. It was like talking to a chapter of history. According to stories around the ferry company, he had been a Marine fighter pilot in the Second World War and had flown wingman for Pappy Boyington of *Baa Baa Black Sheep* notoriety and TV fame.

In one conversation, he said that he wished I were available now. He had lost two of his pilots and he had a contract coming up and could use me. "Great news," I said. "I'll stay in touch and maybe I can get a few days off for a quick trip."

As an afterthought as I was hanging up, I asked, "What about Shergalis, is he available?"

"Bad news there, Cooper," he said. "I don't have any proof, but word on the street is that he was flying cargo for that guy Castro, was double-crossed by a Batista sympathizer, and was ambushed while landing somewhere in the eastern part of Cuba. From what I hear, it was pretty ugly. There wasn't much left."

We exchanged condolences and hung up. It had been barely three months since Bill and I had lunched together on the 79th Street Causeway. The picture of him was still clear in my mind as I looked at the watch he had given me. "I guess we won't be flying with Bill over the jungles of Ecuador after all," I said to myself…and to the watch.

I stopped by his old waterski school on 79th Street later that week, and there was nothing to indicate that a school had ever been there. His trailer was gone and the area was swept clean. It was as if he had never existed.

July passed and I settled into the daily routine. Actually, it was quite pleasant. The pay was steady and the benefits of being a regular airman were very good. There was an Airman's Mess hall, a barbershop, snack bar, and laundry. The charges were much lower than on the outside, and every month some entertainers from Miami Beach would visit for a live show.

CHAPTER 27

Air Force Surplus T-28 Aircraft to Havana...

almost!

IT WAS MID-SEPTEMBER AND I had just about reconciled myself to the fact that I wouldn't see an airplane again, except from out of my window, when Bob Iba called.

"Cooper, how much time do you have left in your tour of duty?" he asked.

"I get out October 23rd," I answered. "What do you need?"

"We just got a contract to pick up six T-28s in Phoenix, Arizona, and they have to all be here by the end of September," he explained. "Davidson and Penn are doing two each; can you do two?"

I calculated the flight time quickly. It would take a day to get out there and two days to return, if the weather cooperated. "If we can commercial out on a Thursday evening and get out of there on a Friday, I might just be able to make it with only one day off," I offered.

"Let me check the commercial airline's schedules, and you check and see if you can get a Friday off," he said. "Let's talk later in the afternoon," he added and hung up.

My immediate supervisor was pretty easy to get along with, and when I offered to finish the brochures that we were producing over the next weekend, he agreed.

It was Wednesday. I called Iba up with the good news from my end, and he had good news also. He said that there was a red-eye flight on Thursday night that would get us into Phoenix around eight o'clock, Friday morning.

"I'll stop by tonight and pick up the charts and expense money," I offered, "and one more thing… What's a T-28?"

"A military trainer," he said, "and after you get them all here, and after some modifications are done to them, you're taking them to Havana!"

I met Ray and Bill at the airline counter the next night. They had the tickets and more importantly they had a T-28 flight manual. We boarded the flight, our seats were together, and we pored over the manual for practically the whole night.

A T-28 was an Air Force trainer designed in the early '50s and it was very popular. So popular in fact that the original 800-horsepower engine was replaced with a more powerful engine, thus making many of the older T-28s surplus to the U.S. military needs. These surplus aircraft were the ones that we were flying down to Havana.

All night we took turns napping and studying as the airliner droned on westward. We stopped in Houston and El Paso, and as the sun was coming up we were circling the airport at Phoenix for our landing.

The representative for the company that handled surplus aircraft sales met us and drove us from the main terminal across the airfield to his maintenance facility. The six T-28s, recently ferried from the Air Force storage facility at Davis-Monthan Air Base in Tucson, were all lined up for delivery.

That made them even more ominous.

In his office, the sales rep asked, "How much flying time in the T-28 do you men have?" He was accustomed to handing over military surplus aircraft to experienced Air Force veterans.

"None," we said, almost in unison.

"None?" He laughed.

"None," Davidson answered, "but we've read the manual and we're ready to go. We want to make Dallas by nightfall."

With a shake of the head, almost in fatal resolve, he pointed to the phone so that we could get a weather briefing and file a flight plan. Davidson handled all of that and soon we were walking across the tarmac toward our aircraft.

The rep gave us a quick preflight, we checked the gas and oil, and we were ready to go.

The Man in The Arena...

I strapped myself into the cockpit and looked around. Some of the instruments looked familiar and some did not. I had forgotten one important item in my self-study as we flew over last night.

I called the representative over with a wave of the hand. He hopped up on the wing and stuck his head in the cockpit. "What do you need?" he asked.

"How do you start this damn thing?" I asked.

We finally got all the airplanes started, made radio contact with each other on a prearranged radio frequency, switched back over to ground control for clearance, and taxied out.

It was quite cumbersome in the cockpit. I had my maps opened to the local area, and the aircraft manual was spread on my lap and opened to the section that read, "Before Takeoff Checklist."

I looked over at Ray and Bill and I could see that they were having the same difficulties.

I finally satisfied myself that the engine checked out okay for takeoff, stowed the aircraft manual, and waited for Davidson to give the signal that he was ready. It was less than a year ago that we had gone through the same routine as we left Miami for Buenos Aires in the Piper Cubs.

Bill gave Ray the thumbs-up signal that he was ready, and Ray, as flight leader, called the tower. "Phoenix tower, November 7286 Charley, flight of three, ready for takeoff."

The tower cleared us for takeoff and at about three-second intervals we were airborne and headed eastbound for El Paso.

We had decided on an altitude of 9,500 feet. That gave us ample clearance over the terrain, and since the weather was good, we simply followed the valley southeast toward El Paso.

I followed a safe distance behind Davidson, and Penn trailed behind me. It was a smooth day and I took the opportunity to pull out the flight manual and further familiarize myself with the cockpit. Davidson could do all the navigating.

By the time El Paso came into view, two hours later, I had fully briefed myself on the landing procedures and the speeds required for the flaps and landing gear. Most importantly, I knew what the stall speed was.

Davidson called the tower and they responded and cleared the "T-28s, flight of three," to land.

Taxiing in, I felt pretty good. We hopped out, ordered the fuel topped off and the oil serviced, and headed to the airport restaurant for a quick lunch.

We were back in the air in less than an hour and landed in Dallas, Texas, in three hours.

We overnighted in Dallas and in the morning we were on our way to Miami with fuel stops at Shreveport, Louisiana; Montgomery, Alabama; and our last stop before Miami—Orlando, Florida.

The weather was excellent throughout the whole flight and the airplane performed wonderfully. It was a stable platform and I could see why it was a favorite trainer for the Air Force. I knew that I would have flown this type of aircraft had I elected to go into the cadet program but, I guessed, with more preparation.

I was at my Air Force desk on Monday morning, but I didn't speak about the fact that I had just flown an Air Force trainer to Miami in preparation for delivery to Batista in Havana.

Bob Iba wanted the same team to fly to Phoenix and bring the last three T-28s back to Miami. I worked extra hard, and late, to catch up on any work that I might have missed by being off the preceding Friday, and on Wednesday I popped the question. "Can I get off on Friday?"

I was all set with my Air Force job, and the three of us—Bill Penn, Ray Davidson, and I—joined in the same routine, except for the overnight T-28 study hall on the airliner, and off we flew westward to Phoenix.

The same representative met us at the terminal. He almost seemed surprised to see us, as if he didn't believe we could have made it. We went through the same drill, except that he didn't need to show me how to start the airplane, and we were off.

The trip went smoothly, and once again the airplane performed nicely. We landed on schedule in Miami, and I was at my desk Monday morning.

The aircraft were parked at a maintenance facility on the north side of Miami International Airport. They were aligned alongside 36th Street awaiting the contracted modifications. Bill, Ray, and I were on standby to ferry them down to Havana's military airport, Campo Columbia, when ready. Bob Iba estimated that it would take about three weeks for the mods to be complete.

With the Cuba flights scheduled in the immediate future and with the Bill Shergalis rumor still vivid in my mind, I began to take a more active interest in the Cuban situation. There were daily articles about the advances of the insurgency in eastern Cuba, and there were many Cubans migrating to Miami. *Oh well*, I thought, *we're separated by the Gulf Stream, so it shouldn't concern us much over here.*

I was wrong!

About a week later I showed up at work and the place was all abuzz. The office manager told me that there had been an invasion of Castro sympathizers and that they had blown up a bunch of airplanes here at the airport. He shared his morning newspaper with me and… there they were. Our beautiful T-28s, all in a row…with their engines blown completely away.

For the next several weeks, in my department, there were numerous high-level meetings behind closed doors, and one can only presume that they dealt with issues pertaining to Cuba.

Needless to say, I kept my ears open and my mouth shut for the remainder of my active service there.

October 23 came and I was released from active service. It was an unceremonious event. The office manager came in at around three o'clock in the afternoon, handed me an envelope filled with papers, thanked me for the good work that I had done, and wished me well. I checked the papers and verified that they contained the treasured DD 214 form—evidence of completing my active service—duly signed. I picked up my personal stuff and left.

I walked out to my black Chevy Impala, got in, and didn't know where to go.

In late September, knowing that my Air Force days were numbered, and with no definite income on the horizon, I reverted to my conservative mode. I took a motel room with Fred Bost at the Royal Poinciana Motel in Miami Springs. He was traveling most of the time, it was cheap, and it worked out well.

That's where I went that day.

I sat on the patio overlooking the dark waters of the Miami Canal, an extension of the Miami River that flowed between Miami Springs and Hialeah. I sat for a long time, pondering my situation.

It had been almost two years since Jim Sink and I had driven down U.S. 1 to "seek our fortunes." My ultimate goal had been to be an airline pilot. I had never strayed from that objective. I had improved my resume to meet all the requirements that the airlines required, including the fulfillment of my military obligation. Now, all that I had to do was to be patient and wait until an airline, preferably Eastern, called.

I made the usual calls. Bob Iba at Hialeah Aircraft Ferry said that he would call me as soon as something came up. Al Burnett had moved Howe

Aviation over to Tamiami Airport and since he had a multi-engine aircraft in inventory, he indicated that he might open up a multi-engine training school and that he would hire me as his instructor when he made the final decision. I didn't call Mary at Kendall Flying School because I didn't think that I could look another primary student in the eye. Mary was great and I owed her a lot for giving me my first job in aviation, but I just didn't think that I could do her justice with my tainted attitude toward flight students.

    I had been seeing Diane regularly since I got back from Lackland, and that courtship took up a lot of time when she wasn't flying. Her house on Swan Avenue was constantly filled with her three roommates and their parade of suitors. So to get away we would frequently go to the beach or visit Dee Dee and Darwin. I had saved a few dollars, so I hadn't panicked yet.

CHAPTER 28

Flying Business Picks Up

To Havana!

TOWARD THE END OF OCTOBER, about a week after I was released from active duty, Bob Iba called and said he had a trip for me.

It was a rush job and since all the rest of his regulars were on trips, he needed me ASAP. He had the airline tickets ready, and I should come directly to his office, pick up the tickets, expense money, and maps, and head to the airport for a 7:00 p.m. departure on Eastern Airlines. As usual, the drill was to fly to Philadelphia, spend the night in the terminal, catch an Alleghany Airlines flight the next morning to Williamsport and then a bus to Lockhaven.

I arrived at the Piper factory at the Lockhaven airport in the afternoon, and the airplane was already on the ramp when I arrived. It was a Piper Tri-Pacer, and was fueled and ready to go. I noticed the registration number. It was CU-663. The "CU" told me that it was going to Cuba.

I'd think about that later. Right now I was hurrying to get off the ground so as to arrive at High Point before dark. On these pickup flights from Lockhaven, I always tried to overnight in High Point and visit Mom and Dad. I called and gave them my estimate for Fraley Field and off I went.

I arrived right on time and they picked me up. There were all the questions about the Air Force and my would-be career with the airlines. The visits were always fun and I was sad to leave. Mom always gave me a box lunch and Dad always offered money. I never took the money. I always took the box lunch.

Bob Iba met me at the designated parking spot at Miami International Airport. It was at the same business establishment where we had parked the T-28s except, this time, we parked in the hangar. As I taxied up, Bob approached me with two guards and a tow truck. I was towed into the hangar and the guards took up a position at the airplane. There would be no repeat of last month's problems.

Bob gave me the documents for the next day's flight. He explained that this airplane was to be delivered to Campo Columbia, a military airport located about five miles west of the downtown area of Havana. Since the area immediately over Havana was restricted, I had to fly over a small airport five miles west of Campo Columbia called Santa Fe, and circle there until I was cleared to proceed to the airport. I would approach the military airport from the west and land straight in.

"Here's a letter for the guards in the morning," he said. "They'll need this to release the aircraft to you. There will be a new set of guards and they won't recognize you. Use your passport for identification.

"If you have any trouble with the landing clearance in Havana," he handed me a slip of paper, "have the Campo Columbia tower call this number and you'll be cleared. Once on the ground," he added, "someone will drive you over to the José Martí International Airport for your flight home."

That night the *Miami Herald* newspaper headlines read, "Castro forces moving toward Santa Clara."

All went according to plan the next morning. I was to depart Miami International Airport at exactly 9:45 a.m. to arrive at Campo Columbia at exactly 11:00 p.m. I was off on time, and when Miami Air Route Control turned me over to Havana control, I was seventy miles north of Havana.

I began to see the haze of the city of Havana. I veered off to the west toward the small airport of Santa Fe as Havana Control transferred me over to Campo Columbia tower. I advised them that I was holding visually over Santa Fe airport west of their airport at 3,500 feet. They advised me to circle there until I could be identified. I pulled the paper with the phone number out of my pocket just as they cleared me to land, straight in.

A military truck met me as I turned off the runway and escorted me to a hangar at the south end of the field where they graciously received me with *medianoches*, the typical Cuban sandwich, and sodas.

The airport was teeming with activity. I had never seen such a display of various types of aircraft, mostly ex-U.S. military surplus. I thought of the

T-28s we flew from Phoenix to Miami that would never join their relatives here.

There were T-33 jets and British Sea Furies. There were B-26s, C-47s, and C-46s along with T-6 trainers. I even saw a Piper Super Cub and a P-51.

Trucks were bustling around feverishly and it seemed as if everything that could move was moving. It was clear that this was unusual activity, but I didn't ask, and nobody offered an explanation.

I was hastily cleared into the country by what looked like my personal customs official, and soon I was in a government vehicle headed toward José Martí International Airport. My commercial flight was on time, and within a couple of hours I was back at the Royal Poinciana Motel in Miami Springs, sitting on the back patio, staring at the black water of the Miami River and reflecting on what I had just witnessed in Havana—and what the future held for me.

Around the first of November, Al Burnett called and said that he had a multi-engine student and if I wanted to instruct him, the job was mine.

Multi-engine instructing was different from basic instructing. The students usually had extensive experience in single-engine aircraft, and the instructor wasn't required to teach them to fly—only how to operate a more complex aircraft. I enjoyed that end of instructing and I agreed to take on the project.

The student was an older man who acclimated to the twin nicely. We were almost finished with his training when I ran into my old friend, Bob Jones. He was doing the same thing at the neighboring flight school, Blue Star Aviation.

He came up with the grand plan of taking two aircraft, one with his student and the second one with mine, to Havana. His argument to the students was "Why spend all that money on domestic flying when you can gain international experience for the same amount of money?"

Both students bought in to the scheme, and around the middle of December, two small twin-engine Piper Apaches departed Tamiami Airport for Havana. The flights went well and before we knew it, we were in a taxi headed for a hotel in downtown Havana. We only intended to remain there for one night, so after settling in, we bought tickets to the famous nightclub, Tropicana.

I had never seen anything like the Tropicana. There was a fine restaurant, an elegant casino, and a show! What a show it was. The production was called "Under the Stars." It was held outside in a sort of amphitheater bordered by tall palm trees. There were three or four stages located all around the primary stage. The main stage would rise for the show and lower for dancing afterward. The ladies, the color, and the music were spellbinding and I fell in love with the Tropicana.

When we were seated, as was the custom, the waiter brought an ice bucket, some colas, and a bottle of rum. I wasn't much of a drinker. About the only time that I would partake would be at Dee Dee's house, and that would be a watered-down CC and Seven, just to be social.

We poured drinks all around and settled in to watch the show. I was so enthralled with the show that I failed to keep a good accounting of the drinks that Jones was pouring.

And then it hit me. Toward the end of the show, I managed to excuse myself and make it to the men's room. In the second toilet stall from the left, I ingloriously returned all the alcohol that I had consumed and was assisted out of the club; carried might be a better term, by our taxi driver.

We made it to the cab and were safely on our way toward the hotel. We thought!

Suddenly we were abruptly stopped and surrounded by several police cars. As the cab driver pulled over, he became very serious and turned to us. "Say nothing," he cautioned. There was much discussion in Spanish. The voices grew louder and to our absolute shock, we were herded out of the cab and forced to lie on the street while the police prodded us with their rifles and searched us thoroughly. After another round of discussions with the driver, we were allowed back in the cab and soon were on our way, thankfully, to the hotel.

The driver excused the "interruption" with a shrug of his shoulders by saying, in broken English, "problems out east, no problems here."

It was December 22, 1958. In exactly ten days, Fidel Castro would victoriously enter the city of Havana and set up headquarters in the Hotel Nacional.

The flight home was uneventful; the student received his multi-engine rating soon after and had a story to tell forever.

Bob Iba called on December 23rd for an aircraft pickup in Lockhaven, and I was on an Eastern flight to Philadelphia two days later.

Diane was on a flight on Christmas Eve; I spent my second yuletide holiday away from my family in a bar in Miami Springs.

Bryson's Bar was located near the corner of 36th Street and Curtiss Parkway in Miami Springs, and it was said, jokingly, that you must have a pilot's license to get in. That wasn't really the case, but it was a dive that was frequented by a cross-section of aviation people. There were mechanics, airline pilots, non-sked pilots, and pilots who claimed to be soldiers of fortune. It was a colorful joint and that's where I found myself on Christmas Eve, 1958. How was I to know that some thoughtless human being would put a quarter in the jukebox and play "Carolina Moon"?

CHAPTER 29

"If the Phone Don't Ring...... It's the Airlines." —

To paraphrase an old hillbilly song

I WAS IN LOCKHAVEN ON the morning of December 26th. I picked up a Christmas gift for my parents, a set of small stackable end tables, which fit nicely in the Cub, and I was quickly off for High Point.

After a belated Christmas dinner and a nice visit, I found myself in my old bed in High Point. As I dozed off I realized that this was not exactly the way I had planned my career. Four days ago I was lying spread-eagle on the sidewalks of Havana, Cuba, being accosted by the police, and in three days from now, I would be in a single-engine Piper Cub flying over the jungles of Ecuador. *When will the airlines call?* I thought as I fell asleep.

I got socked in by some bad weather in Brunswick, Georgia, and I didn't arrive in Miami until the afternoon of December 28th. Ray Davidson was waiting for me at Tamiami airport with a proposal that if we left early enough the next day, we could make Panama nonstop. That would let us fly from Panama to Guayaquil on the 30th and we could "commercial" home in time for a New Year's party that his wife was giving.

Miami to Panama is a long way. By flying directly over Cuba it's about 1,200 miles, and at the speeds that we were estimating, we would be airborne for over eleven hours. I agreed and soon he was helping me rig my Piper Cub for the extended overwater flight.

He had done all the paperwork, filed the flight plans over Cuba, and all that was left to do was show up the next day at daybreak and leave.

The Man in The Arena...

We met early the morning of December the 29th with our box lunches, maps, life-saving paraphernalia, and comfort cups. It was to be a long flight.

Davidson had checked the weather and said that it was okay. The thunderstorm buildups were expected in the afternoon, but nothing unusual. He briefed me on the route. "We'll just fly directly to Panama," he said. "We'll cross Cuba in the vicinity of Santa Clara and continue south of Cuba until we cross the Cayman Islands. If we are on course, we should cross directly over Little Cayman. From that point, there's nothing but water. We might see some reefs called the Serranilla Bank after about six hours. I'm estimating Panama around eleven hours after takeoff. When we see land, it's the same drill; we'll fly parallel to the coastline until we figure out just where we are and head toward Panama. Okay?"

"Okay," I answered, and we were off at dawn. It was 6:25.

An hour and a half later, we were passing the north coast of Cuba and I recognized the large city of Santa Clara. Havana was eighty miles to the west of us, and I remembered the frightening scene there just a week earlier. As I looked down at the peaceful city, I wondered if this placid scene could ever provide a backdrop for such violent behavior.

We passed the historic city of Trinidad, Cuba, in thirty minutes, and soon we were over the Caribbean headed for, hopefully, Little Cayman.

Little Cayman came into view right on schedule, and we set our course directly for Panama. I had seven more hours to go with nothing but water beneath my wings.

When you're sitting in a cramped Piper Cub for eleven hours, you have to do something to entertain yourself, to keep your sanity. You sing, but I didn't know that many songs. You quote poetry. That took me about ten seconds. You mentally calculate how many times the spark plugs will have to fire before you arrive at your destination. That's fun and it takes a lot of time. *Oh, no,* you remind yourself, *don't cheat, don't use your pencil...it must be mental. And the braces up in front of you. Don't forget them. The exercise will keep your heart pumping and relieve your aching posterior for a while.*

Clouds. The white, puffy, ever-changing clouds provide entertainment if you allow your imagination some slack. They can resemble a familiar face; they can bring back an old memory by stirring up a vision from your past. They are fun but just when they form something that you recognize, like a good dream, they slowly morph and change into something else. Clouds are fun to make friends with, if they are in the distance and not in the direction that you are heading.

That often happens when you are flying long distances at reasonably low altitudes. The ferry pilots talk about this often. Every pilot who navigates through the high castles of the cumulus clouds has his own unique theory as to how to handle the issues associated with dead reckoning.

Dead reckoning is the method of navigation used when a pilot has no navigational radios on board. He must navigate based on the compass heading beginning from a known point and adjusted by a number of things, the most important of which is the estimated winds that he may encounter en route.

On that day's flight, flight leader Davidson had landmarks—Cuba and Little Cayman—by which to make minor corrections to his course. From Little Cayman to Panama there are no landmarks, so he must trust his compass and watch the waves on the ocean for any telltale signs that would lead him to believe that the wind direction and velocity given to him by the weather forecasters had changed appreciably. Should a large buildup rise in front of him, he must make a course correction to circumnavigate that cloud.

Once a decision is made to circumnavigate, in order to maintain a general idea as to where you are, the pilot must note the new heading, note the time when he adapted the new course, and, once abeam the cloud that caused the deviation from the original course, make adjustments accordingly to place him back on course toward his destination.

Davidson had devised a method to implement when a deviation might be necessary. He simply made all corrections to the east of course. He did the usual mental calculations with regard to new headings, but he rationalized that when he arrived at his supposed destination, if he didn't recognize any landmarks, he would be east of course. It worked fine and his rationale was "If you make helter-skelter adjustments, left and then right, you are effectively becoming lost in the woods, and when you arrive at the estimated time of your intended landfall, you have no idea of your location."

None of those calculations mattered to me that day as I was just following him, looking at the clouds, and daydreaming. When it came time for lunch, my mind turned to my favorite pastime when flying a Piper Cub hundreds of miles from land and not having a clue as to where you were… food.

As I continued my "part-time" employment with Hialeah Aircraft Ferry Company, I began to develop a system for dining in-flight. Instead of simply grabbing a cold sandwich and can of Coke from the local deli before takeoff, I shopped at the local neighborhood market for my delicacies.

I had developed a program whereby I could enjoy a salad before lunch, a nice fruit cup for dessert, and for the main course…a hot meal.

The salad was easy, as I simply prepared that before I left home and saved it in an "oyster" cup. The fruit cup was also simple; it came in a convenient can easily opened with the attached key.

The hot meal was of my own inventing.

The Piper Cubs we flew had a method of heating the cockpit. There was a hole located forward, in the firewall, the panel that separated the engine compartment from the cockpit, between the rudder pedals. The hole was connected by a tube to a shroud that surrounded the exhaust stack. That allowed hot air to be accessible to the cockpit by a simple flapper valve that was controlled by a push-pull knob on the instrument panel.

When lunchtime came, I would open a can of Spam, Vienna sausages, or any one of the many selections I might have supplied myself with, place the open can on the floor up between the rudder pedals, crack the cockpit window for ventilation, and open the cockpit heat valve.

With a napkin tucked neatly in my collar, silverware of the finest plastic, I enjoyed a nice salad, with the dressing of my choice, I might add. The main course would be warmed nicely by the time I had finished my salad, and I would dine royally on Vienna sausages and crackers to my heart's content. The dessert came last and all that I needed when I finished was a nice nap. That's where I drew the line.

Davidson was doing a fine job of navigation, I guessed, and after about ten hours of flying, we began to see the cloud buildups that indicated land up ahead. We had been at 9,500 feet for the whole flight, and at thirty minutes out we began our descent toward Panama.

He did it again. Davidson hit the estimated fix, San Blas Point, on the nose and right on schedule. We headed toward Tocumen Airport and landed eleven hours after taking off from Tamiami Airport.

We taxied up to the custom's ramp and presented our passports to the officer in charge for entrance into the country.

"Where was your point of embarkation?" the customs officer asked.

Davidson replied, "Miami, Florida."

"No, no," the customs officer protested. "I mean, today!"

Davidson, deadpan, replied, "Miami, Florida."

The customs officer pulled himself up erect and pointed out of the window toward our two Piper Cubs. "It is impossible; where did you stop for fuel in transit?"

Davidson was beginning to have some fun at the expense of the customs official. "Nonstop," he said seriously, "we came nonstop from Miami."

The customs official beckoned for his supervisor to come over. They spoke in Spanish briefly, and the supervisor asked for any customs paperwork that Ray might have to prove that we had flown nonstop from Miami to Panama in such a small airplane.

Ray had our General Declarations stamped in Miami before we left, and that seemed to be sufficient. The supervisor let out a boisterous laugh and called over some more associates who also enjoyed the scene. They came around the desk, shook hands, slapped us on the back, and for an instant, Ray and I were aviation heroes.

They stamped our passports, and we ordered fuel and hired a taxi into town for the overnight stay.

We checked into the Hotel International in Panama and I picked up an English language newspaper in the lobby. The headlines read:

"CHE GUEVARA CAPTURES SANTA CLARA"

The next day's flight was only eight hours and was uneventful. We arrived at Guayaquil right on schedule, stayed overnight at the Humboldt Hotel, and were off for Miami, and Ray's New Year's party, the next day.

I wasn't invited.

I spent New Year's just as I had spent Christmas, at Bryson's Bar.

Only, thankfully, nobody played "Carolina Moon" on the jukebox.

The sun came up on January 1st, 1959, and nothing seemed different. I awoke, rubbed the sleep out of my eyes, and tried to put '58 out of my mind. But it just didn't work for me. About the only positive thing that came out of '58 was the completion of my military obligation. At least I was out of the Royal Poinciana Motel. Fred Bost, Calvin Cushman, and I rented a house on Westward Drive in Miami Springs. Fred was doing well with Air Associates as a traveling aircraft parts salesman. Cal was still a mechanic for Mary Gaffaney at Kendall Flying School. And I...I was waiting on an airline to call and scoop me up out of the doldrums that I found myself in.

But for the time being, I had to eat and pay the rent. The multi-engine instruction job with Allen Burnett was working out better than I expected.

He had added a Piper Cub to his fleet, and before he knew it, he had a pretty good flight school going. It was enough to keep me busy, and I found myself spending a lot of time at Tamiami Airport at Howe Aviation.

Diane had been flying for Eastern for almost a year and, as a former nurse, she felt that she wasn't living up to her potential. She became more and more disillusioned with the life of a flight attendant and continuously shared her disappointment with me. I, too, was unhappy with my current plight, and we became closer as we cried on one another's shoulders. The last thing either of us wanted was to give up and return home. We just toughed it out together and waited to see what was going to happen next.

CHAPTER 30
My First Airline Job…

almost!

AND THEN IT HAPPENED. OUT of a clear blue sky, Dee Dee called and said that the wife of the owner of Regina Airlines had called her and that they were ready to hire me. All I had to do was call them, make an appointment, show up, and I was in!

I called immediately and the appointment was set for the next day at 11:00.

I had my best outfit on—my *only* outfit—and I headed for their offices. I could not contain my excitement as I parked and entered the building that housed their offices. They were located at Miami International Airport in an old World War II building on 20th Street that was shared by a number of other non-scheduled airlines. The offices weren't well marked and as I wandered around the sprawling facility I happened to run into my old friend Bob Jones.

"Hey, Cooper," he called out. "What are you doing around here?" He always pronounced my name "Coo-pah." I knew immediately that it was Jones calling out.

I couldn't wait to tell him. "I'm looking for Regina's offices," I proudly exclaimed. "They're going to hire me as a copilot."

He pawed at the ground, and then he looked at me with a pained expression and said, "I just left the offices and they hired me. They said that if I saw you to tell you that they would call you for the next opening."

I was crushed. From the high that I was experiencing this morning to the lowest of lows now. I couldn't believe it. I turned and went home too depressed to return to Howe Aviation for my students that afternoon.

I called Dee Dee to cry on her shoulder.

She immediately called Mrs. Averman and got back to me immediately.

It turned out that Bob, when I told him of the opening that I was to fill, quickly diverted me from the interview. He then walked down to the Regina offices and calmly, with a straight face, told the chief pilot that he had seen me and I had turned down the opportunity and that he would gladly fill the position.

I had been given my first lesson in the non-sked airline business and I had passed with flying colors.

Dee Dee allowed that I was to get the next slot as soon as it came available. The company never said anything to Jones. I was soon to learn that acts of deviousness in the non-sked business not only were tolerated but encouraged.

Around the end of January, the ferrying business began to pick up. Bob Iba called and assigned a couple of pickups in Lockhaven. I would probably have to take one of them south around the first of February.

Both Bill Penn and Ray Davidson had been interviewed by Northeast Airlines and it looked as if they would be hired. The good news was that I would get more flying. The bad news was, it was all single engine, over water and jungle.

Bill, Ray, and I were assigned three Piper Cubs for delivery to Guayaquil, departing on February 9th. At the airport, Ray advised me that he had been asked by Bob Iba to let me be the flight leader, to watch how I handled it, as there was a good chance this would be his last flight. If Ray and Bill were hired by Northeast, I would be the senior pilot for Aircraft Ferry Company, and the responsibility for leading flights would rest on my shoulders.

I, of course, protested, as I rather liked following along behind Ray, daydreaming, eating, and watching clouds while he constantly watched the compass and circumnavigated the cumulus clouds that somehow got in our way.

He agreed to lead until we got to Panama, but I would have to work the last leg between Panama and Guayaquil so he could sign me off as flight leader for the company.

"Okay," I said, and we were off to Kingston.

The flight to Kingston went well. We spent the night there and the next day we had an uneventful flight to Panama. Ray reminded me, over dinner, that I must lead the flight the next day to Guayaquil. I agreed grudgingly and began to mentally prepare for the morning's flight.

The flight wasn't that hard. From Panama, we would fly directly south over the Pacific Ocean for about five hundred miles to a point called Esmeraldas on the north coast of Ecuador. From there we flew overland, or should I say, over jungle, direct to Guayaquil. About halfway between Esmeraldas and Guayaquil, we could pick up the river Daule, which would lead us directly to Guayaquil.

"Okay," I warned my two fellow pilots, "I'll lead, but you guys must follow closely. I won't tolerate any tomfoolery back there, and what I say goes. I do not expect any mutinous actions." I laughed.

We arrived at the airport, as usual, about an hour before sunup. We checked the weather; the ITC was not forecast to be very active, so that didn't pose a problem. We filed our flight plans, headed for our airplanes, taxied out, and, as leader, I waited for the tower to give us the green light at dawn.

As the eastern sky began to show a slight hint of pink, the tower gave us the green light for takeoff. I rolled into position, and as the other two pilots taxied behind me, I gave the Cub full power and took off to the east. After takeoff I turned south on a heading of 180 degrees and began a shallow climb toward my proposed cruising altitude of 8,500 feet. Looking back, I saw the wing lights of the others following at a safe distance.

Along the southern shoreline of Panama, the depth of the water is very shallow. It was low tide and odiferous. As the sky lightened I could see the mud flats extending south for over five miles. The damp, heavy, sweet smell of the marshland surrounding the airport had permeated the air, and as I climbed I cracked the sliding window to freshen the cockpit.

We soon passed my last landmark, the island of San Jose, ten miles to my left. I was on course and I continued directly toward Esmeraldas, four hours away.

The slow climb put me at 8,500 feet in thirty minutes. I set up cruise RPMs, leaned the mixture slightly, relaxed, and watched the compass settle in at a heading of 180 degrees. No sweat!

The procedure for extended flying with the auxiliary fuel tank in the backseat is to simply use the fuel from the left-wing tank until it shows about one-quarter remaining. Then activate the small pump next to the pilot's seat and pump fuel into the left-wing tank until full.

We had been flying for about two hours, and the left-wing fuel gauge indicated that it was time to refill.

I hit the toggle switch that should activate the aux fuel pump to start the fuel pumping.

Nothing happened.

I juggled the switch but still nothing. I could hear the whirring of the pump on the floor next to me, but no fuel was flowing through the clear neoprene hose that ran from the aux tank to the left-wing tank.

Okay, don't panic, you're the leader, I reminded myself. *Watch the compass and hold your heading while you figure this out.*

"Let's see," I began to compute, "I only have a few minutes of fuel remaining in the left-wing tank, and the right-wing tank has about two hours left. That's not enough fuel to reach Esmeraldas. I must figure out the problem and fix it up here or I'll be swimming in less than three hours."

And hold your heading, I remembered.

The neoprene hose that ran from the aux tank to the small fuel pump and then out the sliding window to the bottom of the left-wing tank was transparent. In examining the problem I saw immediately that there was fuel in the line to the pump. It just wasn't getting from the pump to the left-wing tank.

Something must have clogged the fuel filter in the small pump. *That should be easy to fix*, I surmised. I could simply disconnect the neoprene fuel lines from each side of the pump, open it up, clean out the foreign matter, reassemble, and, hopefully, I'd be on my way.

While doing this I kept telling myself, *hold your heading!*

My ego wouldn't let me slow down, give Davidson a signal to take over and give up the leadership role. My vanity wouldn't allow me to put up with the laughter all the way home. I would just hold the heading, fix the problem, and land in Guayaquil.

We always carried a few tools on these trips to use to disassemble the fuel pump and related paraphernalia for return to the office back in Miami. I also carried a large scout knife in my pocket along with a small toolkit that contained a wrench, some duct tape, and a few other items.

I swapped tanks so the engine was being fed by the right-hand wing tank. That would give me two hours to deal with this issue and I went to work, all the time holding the heading of 180 degrees.

I pulled the scout knife out of my pocket, spread a map over my lap as a workbench, and holding the control stick between my legs, went to work. I unscrewed the clamps holding the hoses onto the aux fuel pump. Then I folded the lines over to crimp them, taping them tight so that no residual fuel would escape.

One hundred and eighty degrees, I remembered.

With the pump now free of the fuel hoses, I could dissemble it to check the problem. It was relatively easy to dissemble. It had a twist-off type of cap covering the filter and with my wrench I opened the suspected fuel filter.

I immediately saw the problem. The aux tank was made of fiberglass. Upon assembly of the unit into the aircraft, there was some residue fiberglass left in the tank and, after three days of flying, the accumulation caused the fuel blockage across the fuel pump filter.

Easy enough. I cleaned the filter, reassembled the pump, connected it back up to the fuel hoses, hit the fuel pump switch, and, voila, the fuel pumped perfectly into the left-wing tank.

I cleaned up the mess, folded the map, and hung the scout knife on the altimeter stem on the instrument panel in case I needed it again and looked at my heading.

In concentrating on my in-flight repair, I had ignored my heading. I was off about thirty degrees. I corrected my course to the right, the compass settled down, and I proudly congratulated myself on the remarkable repair job.

I had been aloft for three hours, and Esmeraldas should be coming in view in another hour and a half.

Thirty minutes passed. *Esmeraldas should be coming into view within the next hour*, I estimated, *and we're right on 180 degrees course.*

About that time, Davidson flew up beside me and made a hand motion to turn left. I responded with a violent negative shaking of my head and signaled to him to continue to fly straight ahead and follow me. He fell back behind me in trail.

That lasted about fifteen minutes and soon he flew back up next to me and signaled to me, in no uncertain terms, to turn left.

I stubbornly refused his directions again and even more assertively, pointing to my chest and holding up one finger to indicate that I was the number one leader, and that we should continue on my heading.

Davidson dropped back near Bill Penn, and after a second or two, they both turned left.

I rechecked my heading. It was a perfect 180 degrees.

As their aircraft disappeared to the east, my ego began a debate with my brain. I knew my heading had been correct at 180 degrees for the whole trip, but yet, we had been up for four and a half hours and still no Esmeraldas! I would hold the heading for a few more minutes and surely I would see Esmeraldas. The joke would be on them.

Another thirty minutes. No flying buddies, and no Esmeraldas!

I noticed a hint of a fuel smell and I looked down and saw that a small drop of fuel was forming on the inlet side of the aux fuel pump. *I must tighten the clamp on the hose at the fuel pump*, I thought.

I reached up for my scout knife hanging on the instrument panel. "What's that?" I said out loud. The compass swung wildly to the left about thirty degrees. I hung the knife back up. The compass swung the other direction.

And then it hit me. The knife was magnetized and when I hung it on the instrument panel, next to the compass, the compass would read thirty degrees off course toward the west. I was hundreds of miles out, apparently, in the middle of the Pacific Ocean. And I was supposed to be a leader.

I swallowed my pride, pulled out my fuel-stained map, and set a new course for Guayaquil. In an hour and a half, I crossed the west coastline of Ecuador slightly north of the small town of Santa Elena, and in thirty minutes I was circling the airport at Guayaquil looking for the green light.

Humiliation! How could I face Davidson? What would he say? He was a pretty droll guy, but this would really upset him. *What CAN I say?*

I taxied up to the ramp where he and Bill were already busying themselves dissembling the auxillary fuel apparatus. I wanted to delay the inevitable chewing-out for as long as possible.

I popped out of the cockpit, tool kit in hand, and slid under the aircraft to begin the dissembling process.

Out of the corner of my eye, I saw Davidson approaching. *Here it comes*, I thought. *Get ready.*

He stood there for a whole minute. I could only see his boots. And then he spoke with mock disgust as he kicked my tire.

"Cooper," he said, "the fourth largest continent on Earth…and you missed it!"

No one at Hialeah Aircraft Ferry Company ever let me forget that.

Once back home I checked the mail. No luck. Not one answer to my many applications with the airlines.

Ray Davidson and Bill Penn were hired by Northeast Airlines and were gone to Boston for ground school. That left me as a senior pilot with the ferry company, and I was flying with them as much as I wanted to. I wasn't too much in love with the overwater stuff, but it provided enough money to live on, so I took every trip that came my way.

At the end of February, I took a single Cub to Bogota. Flying with no wingman is no fun, but the weather was good and I made the trip okay. I was growing weary of this ferrying business though.

In the first week of March Bob Iba called me for another trip to Bogota. He asked if I knew anyone who wanted to go with me as he had two planes and no available pilots. Almost as a joke I mentioned it to Chuck Hudson. Surprisingly he said yes. He had a week off from Eastern Airlines and agreed to go. I gave him a briefing, expense money and the usual equipment, and on March 3rd we were on our way to Bogota.

The first leg was easy. The flight over Cuba was always fun, and we got to see the countryside and small villages with parks, churches, and baseball fields.

Over dinner that night at the Myrtle Bank Hotel in Kingston, I briefed Chuck on the next leg. "As easy as the first leg was, the second leg to Bogota could be difficult," I explained. "The first half of the trip will be easy if the weather is good. We pick up a heading of 173 degrees out of Kingston and we should cross Barranquilla, Colombia, in about four and a half hours.

"There is a tall mountain just east of the city that you will see when we are about seventy-five miles out. It's called Santa Maria. The sky over the country is usually hazy, so you will see the outflow of the Magdalena River long before you see the shoreline. It discharges an enormous amount of water into the Caribbean and it's all muddy. You can see it at fifty to sixty miles out. At that point, just follow the Magdalena River for about four hundred miles until you reach a city called Palenquero. There are two airports there—old German airfields located on either side of the river.

"From there we leave the river," I continued. "We follow a railroad track that winds up along the side of the Andes. The elevation rises quite rapidly along here, so keep your distance from the mountains as you climb, but don't lose sight of them visually. Usually, this time of year, the farmers are burning their fields and it's hazy and the horizon is difficult to see."

Finally, I added, "The mountains around there go up to around twelve to thirteen thousand feet, but we can clear the pass at nine thousand feet, and it's downhill to Bogota from there. We'll land at the airport called Techo. Its altitude is 8,260 feet above sea level and its runway is plenty long."

The next day's departure was normal. The weather was forecast to be good and our takeoff was uneventful. The overwater portion of the trip went well. The mountain of Santa Maria showed up as advertised, the muddy outflow of the Magdalena heralded the arrival of Barranquilla, and we flew over the city right on schedule.

We followed the Magdalena River for four hundred miles and crossed the two airports at Palenquero as flight planned. We had flown quite low from Barranquilla as the weather was hazy, as expected, and to fly at a higher altitude would jeopardize our ability to see and follow the river. The field elevation of the airports at Palenquero was around five hundred feet, and we needed to reach nine thousand feet to transit the valley. As we began our climb, following the railroad track, the haze was thicker than I had expected and became problematic.

We snaked up the side of the Andes, following the railroad track, criss-crossing it first north and then south, trying to maintain a safe distance from the ever-rising mountains while keeping the railroad track in sight. To further compound the situation, as I flew higher, I noticed a cloud layer that appeared to be lying just across the mountain pass. This was not good. I looked back and Chuck was tucked in tight, slightly to the left behind and under me. I knew that he could follow me, so I redirected my attention to the mountain pass.

We reached nine thousand feet. The haze was lessening at this altitude, but the cloud layer now had my full attention. I could see the pass to the east. The valley was V-shaped with a layer of clouds lying across the top. The mountains disappeared up on either side of the valley into the cloud layer. It was now impossible to descend through the thick haze without instruments. The opening at the bottom of the V was slowly closing. I had no choice.

I had to go for it.

I headed for the bottom of the V, the bottom of the valley between the mountains

The clouds were lowering faster than I could fly. The mountain terrain was rising rapidly below me. The cloud layer was settling down onto the pass. I could still see a small sliver of clear blue sky outlining the valley just ahead.

This was a race that I couldn't lose. I pushed the throttles up to gain as much forward speed so as to get through the pass before the clouds settled down and blocked my path.

I was losing the race.

I was barely yards from the pass when the lowering cloud base ahead snuffed out the last glimpse of clear sky. I pushed the nose of the Cub down to but a few feet above the railroad, straining to see anything that could give me orientation. I could literally see the railroad crossties streaking a few feet beneath my wheels. Clouds engulfed my airplane. *Hold on for one second more*, I thought.

"Hold on, hold on, hold on," I repeated for what seemed like an eternity.

And just then…I broke out above the descending terrain. Up ahead there was a patch of blue and I saw the sun shining on the skyline of Bogota in the distance.

My thoughts turned to Chuck. I hoped that he had stayed on the other side of the pass and didn't attempt to follow me. He would have had a better chance descending, even in the heavy haze. I imagined the worst.

A movement to my left, just outside of my cockpit window, startled me. I looked quickly and there was Chuck, flying barely ten feet away from me, his wing just behind and under mine. I could see directly into his cockpit, and there he sat, with a broad grin!

We cleared customs, said hello to the customer, Mr. James Leaver, caught a taxi, and headed for the Taquendama Hotel in town.

Our adventure wasn't over yet.

Halfway into town, a bus drove through a stop sign, broadsided us, and down an embankment we went. We rolled once, landed on our side, and slid to a stop with a car full of mud.

I looked at Chuck. With the exception of a face full of mud, he looked okay. At the same time, we started laughing like two fools. We had just cheated death in an airplane an hour earlier, only to be killed by a crazed bus driver on the streets of Bogota. The bystanders thought that we were crazy.

I wiped the mud off Chuck's face.

As the crowd gathered, we got our belongings and decided to depart the scene before the authorities came.

An English-speaking Colombian saw the whole thing and offered us a ride to the hotel. It turned out that he owned a chain of ladies' clothing stores. He gave us his card and generously offered us carte blanche to shop for anything we wanted as a gift for our lady friends back in Miami.

Early the next morning we visited the ticket offices of Avianca Airlines to purchase our tickets for the return to Miami. There we saw the airline's advertising logo—an Avianca flight attendant wearing the traditional attire of a Colombian woman, a *ruana*. The ruana is similar to a parka. It's woven from wool with a slit that fits over the head and hangs loosely around the shoulders. The slogan of Avianca Airlines was "The Route of the Red Ruana."

With that image still in our minds, we stopped by the good Samaritan's shop later that next day and came away with two beautiful ruanas, one for Chuck's girl du jour, and one for Diane.

CHAPTER 31
Finally! First Airline Job

And the beginning of the airline merry-go-round

MARCH WAS ALMOST GONE WHEN Regina called. This time, when I went for my appointment, I didn't tell anyone, and I was hired. I was to meet on the 27th of March at their offices at the 20th Street terminal. A pilot would pick me up, along with some other pilots, and fly us up to Charleston, South Carolina, for a crew swap. From there we would pick up a series of charter flights throughout the U.S. for the military.

There were no words to describe my excitement. I dashed down to Talley Ho, the Tailor, a local uniform shop on 36th Street, and ordered my uniform. They put in a rush order and it came on time. I was fitted, and finally I was ready for the big airline experience when the morning of the 27th came.

Diane dropped me off at the curb at the Regina offices with a peck on the cheek and the usual "fly safe, be good, and write," and she was off. I watched my black Chevy Impala disappear around the corner as I turned to enter the office and begin my new career as a real airline pilot.

This is going to be great, I thought. *A real airline pilot flying a wonderfully maintained large airplane and with professional training.* My enthusiasm was exceeded only by my expectations of the promise of the grandeur of this airline experience.

The secretary motioned me toward an adjoining room. "You'll find the other pilots in there," she said, hardly looking up. I walked in and the first person I saw was my old friend Bob Jones.

"Hi Coo-pah," he said cheerfully. "It's great to see you." And then he whispered in my ear, "I pulled a lot of strings to get you in."

Right, I thought, but I didn't let on that I was friends with the owner's wife, *THE* Mrs. Bud Averman. "It's good to see you too, Bob," I lied. "What's the deal?"

"We're waiting on two more crew members, and when they get here we'll shove off to Charleston," he explained.

The other pilots showed up and we headed out to a Twin Beechcraft, a small twin-engine airplane, and with Jones flying and me in the right seat, we headed up the East Coast to Charleston, South Carolina.

In preparing for the morning's flight, I had dressed nicely to make a good first impression. I wore a pressed shirt and trousers, and Jones was dressed decently too. But the other two. That was a different story. They looked like they had just come in from sleeping under a bridge. Their clothes were wrinkled, they reeked of alcohol, and both had at least a two-day stubble.

We weren't two minutes into the flight before they were sprawled out in the back of the airplane, fast asleep.

The flight was easy, up the East Coast for a little over two hours and we were circling the airport at Charleston to land. As we taxied in I could see the giant C-46 parked on the ramp with Regina painted on the side.

Wonderful, I thought. For a second I forgot about the other two unsightly pilots in the back. *Surely, when they fly that beautiful airplane they will spiffy up.*

Jones checked us in at the general aviation ramp where the C-46 was parked, spoke with a couple of other Regina pilots who were going to fly the Twin Beechcraft back to Miami, and we were off to the hotel in downtown Charleston.

The rest of the crew was at the hotel. I was scheduled to fly my first flight as copilot in two days, and my captain, Captain Bob Lee, was already at the hotel. Jones was flying out the next day on a second airplane with another crew.

We checked into the hotel, and the other two pilots went immediately up to their rooms, but Jones, I assumed out of remorse for stealing my job earlier, immediately took me under his wing.

"Coo-pah," he said, putting his arm around my shoulders, "I'm going to show you the ropes here in this airline business. Let's you and I meet down here in an hour, have some dinner, and I'll explain just how this works."

I thought that was extremely nice and I showed up right on time.

We met in the lobby and Jones escorted me down the street to a rather nice steak house. We found a booth and sat down. Jones ordered a cocktail and I ordered a Coke.

We chatted over the drinks for a while, and after some small talk, Jones leaned over and began his "familiarization" course on flying with the airlines.

"The good thing about this airline business is that no matter what you spend on the layovers, you will be reimbursed by the captain when you check out of the hotel before every flight," he explained. "It's called per diem. That's French for *by the day*."

Wow, I thought, *this Jones fellow knows a foreign language; he's smarter than I gave him credit for.*

"And," he added, "the captains always carry cash; that's called captain's funds, and they pay everything from that. You just keep track of everything you spend, keep the receipts, and Captain Lee will be glad to give you cash when you check out."

The waitress came and we gave her our order. I had a hamburger and Jones ordered a T-bone steak and another cocktail. I still had some Coke left, so I didn't order anything else.

Jones continued to give me some more tips about this new venture, and when we got up to leave he casually said, "Cooper, you pick up this tab, keep track, and Captain Lee will reimburse you day after tomorrow when you check out of the hotel."

This Jones is an okay guy, I thought. *Spending all this time with me, filling me in on how this non-sked airline works.*

He had a few more cocktails as I finished my Coke. I was careful to keep the receipts for the per diem record for Captain Lee. Jones had to fly early the next day, so we returned to the hotel, said our good-byes in the lobby, and I went to my room, happy with the evening, and with a warm feeling of renewed friendship for my old buddy Bob Jones.

I got a call the next morning from Captain Lee. "Cooper," he said, "I need you to come with me to the airport for your checkout this morning. I have to check out a new captain and you can go along and get checked out too."

"Yes, sir," I said. "What time?"

"Let's make it ten," he said, "and no uniform."

"Yes, sir," I eagerly replied.

I was at the lobby early and met Captain Lee for the first time. He was tall, about six feet and three or four inches. He was thin with blond hair.

The Man in The Arena...

His skin had a pallor that looked like he'd never been in the sun before. He introduced himself along with the new captain, Mike Jackson, who was going to take the captain's check ride, and soon we were on our way to the Charleston airport.

At the airport I tagged along, watching the preflight and not drawing any attention or getting any either. The new captain seemed to be doing okay, and it was apparent that he had experience on the C-46 with an earlier airline.

We worked our way into the cockpit, and Captain Lee showed me the jump seat, a spare observer seat in the cockpit, and invited me to sit down and buckle my seat belt. I watched in absolute awe as Captain Lee and the new captain went through their paces. There were more dials and switches than I had ever seen before in one cockpit. They rushed through the checklist quickly, and soon the engines rumbled to life with a burst of smoke. We taxied out and were off.

Captain Lee put the new guy through the paces. He did all the normal stuff and then he did the emergencies. We did engine-out approaches with a missed approach go around and then a full stop landing. Although I was just watching, I was exhausted.

Captain Lee gave the new pilot a thumbs-up approval on the last landing and we taxied in. I assumed it would be my time for some remedial training before I had to perform some kind of copilot check ride. We got out at the ramp and I asked Captain Lee when I would get my check ride.

He smiled. "You just had it!"

So much for the professional training, I thought.

We returned to the hotel. I ate alone, keeping my receipt, and was ready in the morning for the 6:00 show at the hotel checkout desk.

I was all decked out in my new uniform and airline pilot's cap. I had three stripes on my jacket and I was ready to conquer the world. I had prepared my per diem report with all receipts neatly clipped to the corner. Captain Lee was in charge of checking all the pilots out and was paying the hotel bills in cash as each one checked out.

"Cooper," he said, "you're next, I believe you had two nights." I said yes and the desk clerk agreed, and Captain Lee peeled off the amount for two nights and paid for my room in cash.

"Captain Lee," I asked quietly, "is this the time when you pay me the per diem," and I handed him the neatly packaged report with receipts totaling $53.47.

"What the hell is this?"

"It's my per diem report," I answered. "Bob Jones explained to me how it works, and he said to keep all the receipts and that you would pay me in cash for all that he and I spent on the layover."

He howled so loud that he startled the desk clerk. "Cooper," he laughed, "you've fallen for one of Jones' favorite tricks. Here's your per diem," he said as he handed me sixteen dollars. "That represents eight dollars per day. I hope you enjoyed your party with your buddy Jones!"

He was still laughing all the way to the airport.

I wasn't.

A C-46 requires a crew of only two pilots. In order to fly almost continuously, Regina would staff the aircraft with double crews. In addition, there was one mechanic who rode along to service the aircraft and to take care of any minor mechanical discrepancies that might crop up. He also doubled as a steward and served any snacks or beverages that were made available to the passengers.

We were scheduled to fly to North Carolina, pick up some sailors, and transport them to San Diego, California. The flight plan showed that we would stop for fuel at Jackson, Mississippi, and Midland, Texas.

The new Captain Jackson and Captain Lee were fairly friendly, but the other copilot, Eddie Byers, was extremely quiet and wasn't at all friendly. He was scheduled to fly the first two legs, up to North Carolina and on to Jackson, where I would take over in the right seat and complete the trip to San Diego. I sat in the jump seat and took copious notes for the entire time that First Officer Byers was flying, and by the time I got in the copilot's seat in Jackson, I felt pretty comfortable.

We got out of Jackson just before dark, and as the sun set in the west, we were well on our way to Midland. Out of Midland, and at cruise, I was beginning to feel at home in the old lumbering C-46. As noisy as the airplane was on takeoff, it quieted down at cruise and the large cockpit was rather comfortable. The Bob Jones party was a distant memory now, and I was beginning to feel pretty good about the job.

Captain Jackson and I flew the last leg into San Diego, landed, and we all went to the hotel exhausted.

The type of flying we were doing was called CAM flying. There was a clearinghouse in Washington operated by the government that scheduled various non-scheduled airlines, such as Regina, to transport servicemen throughout the United States. The schedules were awarded without much notice, generally one or two days, so when a crew arrived at the East Coast or the West Coast, they had no idea when they would be required to fly next. That was the case here. We simply waited at the hotel until called by the captain.

It seemed to me that during these wait times, everyone stayed to themselves. The mechanic would spend some time at the airplane, and the others went their separate ways.

It was getting on in the evening of the second day of waiting when Captain Jackson called my room and asked if I would like to join him for a beer down at a bar near the hotel. I agreed and we met in the lobby and walked next door and sat down. It was rather dark in the bar. He had a beer and I ordered a CC and Seven.

We were chatting about our respective careers. His was on the decline, having flown in the war and later, with several, now defunct non-skeds, and mine, hopefully was on the rise, simply based on my age.

I wasn't paying much attention to the other patrons in the bar when I sensed someone behind me. I turned partially around on the bar stool and was met with a terrific fist to the side of my head. It wasn't a friendly tap on the shoulder but a full haymaker that caught me off guard. It floored me.

I found myself on the floor with a maniac standing over me yelling, "Cooper, you son of a bitch, you're taking money out of my pocket, you're taking food out of my baby's mouth." The tirade continued and I began to gather myself and prepare for a full-scale brawl. I got up on one knee and charged the assailant. The voice sounded familiar, and as we crashed to the floor, I saw that it was copilot Eddie Byers, and he was drunk.

By then, the bartender and Captain Jackson got us separated and Jackson wrestled the drunken copilot out of the door and to the hotel. I waited a few minutes and, at the bartender's suggestion and before the police came, I also left for the hotel and an ice pack.

Jackson took Byers up to Captain Lee's room and they had it out. It seems, according to Captain Jackson, that just before he and I were assigned to the crew, Byers was the only flying copilot in a supposedly heavy crew, and he was collecting the pay for a pseudo crewmember. He had the check sent to his house, thus effectively getting the salary for two pilots. Byers had rationalized that with my showing up, I was stealing one-half of his salary, regardless of the fact that the crew and airline had been operating illegally for weeks.

Captain Lee hushed that up real quick, and luckily, the second C-46 owned by Regina was scheduled through San Diego the next day. He had Byers swapped out for another copilot, and he was on his way eastbound by dark.

I had another couple of days to think about this line of work. I needed the job and the heavy aircraft time would be good for my resume, but so far I wasn't too enthralled by the prospects of making a career of the airlines, especially this one.

Looking at the four walls of a third-rate hotel in San Diego for five days was beginning to lose its appeal. I had no money, and eight dollars a day for basic expenses didn't go that far.

On April 3, we got an assignment. We were scheduled to go to Newark, New Jersey, on April 5, with fuel stops in Kansas City and Chicago. I was ready.

I was in for another non-sked lesson.

Captain Lee called a crew meeting in his room the day before the flight. I asked the other copilot what to expect. He, in a matter-of-fact tone, said that this was the usual "catering" meeting. I assumed that we were going to discuss the anticipated passenger load, the times of the flight, the meal service required by the military, and the particulars of the catering company that we were hiring to supply the meals for the flight.

I couldn't have been more wrong.

Captain Lee announced that we were all going down to the local market, purchase the foodstuffs necessary for sandwiches for the whole passenger load, return to his room, make the sandwiches, and package them in paper bags for serving to the troops. We would add a cookie and various drinks and juices to complete the meal.

I was shocked. I was shocked at the catering idea, but I was more shocked at the attitude of the rest of the crew. They acted like this was normal, and I was to learn later that it was.

The company would allocate a certain amount of money to be spent from the captain's funds per passenger. By having the crew fix the meals, the captain could shave three dollars per passenger and net around 150 dollars per trip. The captain would then, generously, give the crew fifty dollars to split up between themselves.

When there was time to do this, usually after a long layover, the practice was commonplace.

I was in a fog. I didn't wish to complicate my life by taking a moral stand where obviously there were no morals, so I stumbled along with them down to the local market.

Captain Lee assigned the crew to purchase the items necessary and to meet back at the checkout counter; he would pay the bill.

"Cooper," he ordered, "you go pick up enough bread for fifty-five sandwiches and the cookies." He went down the list and assigned the mayonnaise to one, the brown bags to another, the beverages to another, and the wax wrapping paper to another. "I'll go to the meat department and get the baloney," he volunteered, and off we all went on our assignments as instructed.

It was a bizarre scene back in Captain Lee's room. Someone dealt the bread out across the bed, over a desk, and placed the few remaining slices on the chair. Another came along with the industrial-size jar of mayonnaise and ladled globs of it on the bread. Next came the baloney, and finally, a crewmember finished the sordid affair by capping the sandwiches with the remaining slices of bread.

Captain Lee instructed me on the proper method of wrapping the final product, and we all joined in forming an assembly line to wrap and to pack them in the brown paper bags and stow the total production in a nice cardboard box.

The beverages were boxed in another carton, and we were ready for tomorrow.

Ugh!

I had been with this company for less than two weeks, and I was ready to catch the next bus home.

My expectations of professionalism were dashed. I was beginning to wonder if I had chosen the wrong field of endeavor when Pete Dickens, the Piedmont pilot back at Fraley Field, was my knight in shining armor.

The flying was great. As sorry as the situation was, the old surplus C-46 lumbered on, in spite of the operators. And just when I felt that it could get no worse, it would.

Captain Lee once "sold" the jump seat to a sailor who was desperate to return home when his scheduled commercial flight cancelled. "Cooper, you and the other copilot will have to take turns standing until we get this poor sailor back home to his parents," he lamented in his most compassionate tone of voice, as he pocketed a hundred dollars.

We crisscrossed the United States for a month with no hope of returning home. I would be on the verge of exhaustion after five or six days of constant flying and then we would get stuck in some fleabag hotel for three or four days.

The crewmembers, while convivial, were literally at the farthest end of the aviation spectrum. But they could fly! Boy, could they fly, but any other redeeming values were lost somewhere way back when in an earlier life. My developing disdain for this end of the business was matched by my feelings of pity for the crewmembers. This was all they had, and they were making the most of it. But that would not be the case with me.

We landed in Wilmington, Delaware, on April 25, and I jumped ship. Both of the Regina airplanes were there, so there were plenty of crewmembers to maintain the immediate schedule. I grabbed a bus up to Philadelphia and caught an Eastern flight to Miami. Diane picked me up and we headed for Westward Drive. I hung up my new Regina Airline uniform in the closet, retired it permanently, and sat down to reevaluate my situation.

Within two days I was on my way to Lockhaven, Pennsylvania, to pick up a Piper Cub for Hialeah Aircraft Ferry Company.

I was staying busy with the ferrying company and instructing with Allen Burnett when, on June 5, it came. It was the long-awaited letter from Northeast Airlines inviting me up to Boston for an interview.

A pass to Boston was waiting for me at the ticket counter at Miami International Airport. I boarded a shiny four-engine DC-6, and before I knew it, I was on my way to Boston and to an interview with Northeast.

The pilots were impeccably dressed in light blue uniforms, and the flight attendants served hot meals from dishes, not out of brown paper bags. I almost prayed out loud that I would pass the interview and be hired.

I was!

I said good-bye to Diane and drove my Chevy Impala to Boston. Ground school for DC-3 started on June 15, 1959, and I was in it.

There were three of us from Miami, and we rented an upstairs floor from an elderly woman on Belcher Street in Winthrop, near Boston's Logan Airport. Working for Northeast was everything that working for Regina was not. The training was excellent and thorough, and the professionalism displayed by the entire staff was impressive.

I checked out on the DC-3 with flying colors, thanks to the C-46 experience, and began flying the line on July 2, 1959.

The flying was exciting. It was everything that I had expected when I set my sights on becoming an airline pilot. The captains were excellent pilots and were very helpful to a fledgling airman like me. The trips were fun. Northeast only operated the DC-3 flights around New England, so the legs were relatively short. The weather was less than ideal, giving a Florida pilot like me valuable experience. I loved the airline and I loved the job.

The downside was that, as Diane and I had been going steady for about a year, my being based in Boston and her being based in Miami was making courting somewhat difficult. On several occasions we even discussed the "M" word—marriage. My job was not that secure as I was near the bottom of the seniority list, and the chance of furlough always loomed in the future.

We simply put any plans aside until I could be based in Miami with Northeast, and we continued to fly and see each other when we could.

Ray Davidson and Bill Penn, my old ferry pilot buddies, were senior to me and they had been promoted to the DC-6. We got together from time to time to remember the old times in South America, and I was comfortable that I soon would be promoted to the DC-6 when Northeast hired more pilots. They did continue to hire more pilots, and I began to see a few pilots beneath me on the seniority list.

I was promoted in early August and was assigned to the DC-6 flight engineer class.

A flight engineer's position in the cockpit came about during the Second World War to provide for a mechanic to ride on the airplane in order to handle any mechanical difficulties that might arise during the flight. The position jelled with the advent of the larger, four-engine piston aircraft, and the engineer became a part of the crew, handling certain chores in the cockpit dealing with technical matters. The engineer would conduct the preflight, start the engines, monitor the engine perimeters during flight, attend to certain fuel issues such as cross feeding the engines from the various fuel tanks, along with other things relative to the mechanical aspects of the flight, all under the directions of the captain.

This all seemed to make good sense. However, somewhere along the way the engineers formed their own union, and before long, arbitrary lines of responsibility were drawn within the cockpit; arguments became prevalent to the extent that the airlines, in order to keep peace in the cockpit, began to train the junior pilots as engineers. Most airlines offered the flight engineers an opportunity to become pilots, and a position was created called "pilot engineer" or "second officer."

Such was the case here. I found myself in a flight engineer's class studying engineering stuff, and it looked like I was to be stuck there for a long time. I reconciled my fate by rationalizing that in working on the DC-6, I would be flying to Miami, Northeast's long-haul route, and I would get to reunite with Diane and my old buddies.

The engineer class was moving along as well as could be expected when I got a call from Mary Gaffaney, the owner of Kendall Flying School, the woman who gave me my first job in aviation.

"Tommy," she said, "do you remember that National pilot, Steve Wedge, that you checked out in a Cub about two years ago? Well, he promised you a job with National when they hired the next pilot class, and he just called me and said to have you call him for a job."

Life is not easy, I thought. *Just when you think that you are stable, something comes up requiring you to make a life-changing decision.*

I hadn't had to make such a decision since I got the letter from the Air Force approving me for cadet training.

Again, time was not on my side. I had to make a decision quickly. I pondered all options. Did I want to be a flight engineer for an undetermined time or should I move back to Miami and be a copilot on a Convair 440 for National Airlines, my second favorite airline in the world? I labored with that question.

I agonized, I deliberated, and I weighed all options and came to a conclusion.

I walked into the chief pilot's office at Northeast Airlines headquarters and resigned. I was almost tearful as I handed him the letter. He was understanding and wished me well. I turned in all company material, packed my meager belongings in the trunk of the Chevy, and parked it in the National Airlines employee parking lot at the Boston Logan Airport and headed to Miami on a National DC-7.

Convair 440 ground school started, and I was assigned to the base in Miami upon completion.

It was finally coming together now. A good job, living in the place of choice, and a pretty girlfriend. I couldn't be more pleased with my lot in life.

After two years of barnstorming around the hemisphere, I was ready to settle down. Diane was eager to quit flying, so we decided to marry at the earliest time available. We had a window of opportunity between the end of ground school and the beginning of the flight training portion, so we set the date, invited family and guests, and scheduled the service to be held at Blessed Trinity Catholic Church in Miami Springs.

We were married in early October, 1959. Allen Burnett gave us the use of one of his Piper twins, and we honeymooned in Marathon, Florida, at the Jack Tar Resort.

We returned to Miami within the week and began to look for an apartment in Miami Springs.

Two of Diane's roommates had moved out, so we set up temporary housekeeping in one of the available bedrooms while we decided on an apartment. We visited a number of nice apartments in the area and were just about to decide when I got a call from "crew planning" at National.

"First Officer Cooper," the scheduler began quite officially, "we have had a change in base staffing, and you are now to be based in New York City. You are to report there on next Monday for your first officer check ride at Idlewild Airport."

Welcome to the airline business, I thought.

Diane and I decided not to panic. She could continue to fly, and I would go up to New York and bunk in with some of my fellow classmates who were in the same fix. Things could be worse, we surmised. I could still be flying to South America or flying with Regina. Once we examined the alternatives, we counted our blessings and decided to tough it out with smiles on our faces.

I flew to Boston and retrieved my car from the National Airlines employee parking lot at the airport. I drove to Kew Gardens in Queens, a borough just east of downtown New York City, where I met up with three other pilots from my class. We found an apartment near the corner of Lefferts and Metropolitan Avenue and moved in. It was handy to all three airports serving New York City and roomy enough for the four of us, if one slept on the couch. We devised a scheme whereby when one of us went on a trip, he would fold up his bed sheets and make his bed available to one of the other roommates. That worked pretty well, as at least two of us were out on a trip most of the time.

I passed the check ride and flew my first trip for National Airlines on October 22, 1959.

Juggling flight schedules is something that airline people learn to do early on in their careers, and Diane and I were no exception. She would try to fly to New York City, and I would try to schedule my trips so as to visit with her on her layovers. When I could work out three or four days off, I would fly to Miami.

That was working out as well as could be expected. We had fun on her New York layovers, and my visits to Miami gave me a chance to catch up on the gossip and visit with my old friends in Miami Springs.

We had perfected a pretty good routine and November went well. Diane had enough seniority to hold a schedule, but as junior pilot, I had to fly reserve but we managed to work it out. My roommates would juggle their days off to help me with commuting to Miami, and I would do the same for them.

December was here; Christmas was just around the corner. I was flying a lot out of Idlewild and enjoying the Convair 440. It was a terrific airplane that performed nicely. It was easy to fly and I was becoming quite proficient at it.

Diane and I were looking ahead at the schedules to try to have Christmas together. I had just returned from a trip to Norfolk when a crew scheduler called me. "First Officer Cooper? We have you going to Jacksonville."

"Fine," I answered. "What time does the trip leave?"

"No, it's not a trip," he answered. "You're being based there."

The airline business is a strange animal. This scheduler just, as casually as you would take a drink of water, moved me from my apartment in New York City to Jacksonville, Florida, with a phone call.

"You need to be there and ready to fly on December 20th," he said and hung up.

Oh well, I rationalized, *it's closer to Miami, so maybe it's a good thing.*

I called Diane and shared the news with her, then packed up the Chevy Impala and headed south to Jacksonville, Florida. It was December 15th.

I arrived at Jacksonville on December 20, found a cheap apartment, reported in to the National Airlines operations office at Imeson Airport, and settled in for a long stay in Jacksonville.

The apartment was on the second floor, over a bar just south of Trout River, about three miles south of the airport on State Road 17. It was close to the airport and it would make commuting to Miami easy.

I was assigned a trip to lay over in New Orleans on Christmas Eve. The trip offered a diversion from spending Christmas Eve in a dingy apartment over a bar in Jacksonville.

I arrived back in Jacksonville at a little after noon on Christmas Day and headed back to my apartment to await my next flight assignment. Upon arriving, I saw several police cars, and after I parked and got out of my car, I was arrested by a couple of policemen.

"Where were you last night?" one asked, quite rudely.

Since I had taken off my airline jacket and hat, I did not have the appearance of an airline pilot. I said, "New Orleans."

They didn't buy that as a viable alibi. I began to have visions of my last trip through north Florida and the New Smyrna Beach episode three years earlier.

It seems that in the early morning hours, after the bar had closed, someone broke into my apartment, cut a hole in the floor, and helped themselves to whatever of value they could find in the bar below. The owner, in his police questioning, identified me as a new tenant and could not account for my whereabouts on the previous early morning. That made me a prime suspect in the case.

I explained that I was an airline pilot, and after examining my uniform, my logbook, and a call to National Airlines at the local airport, I was released.

Merry Christmas!

I called Diane, shared the funny story with her, and guessed that I would be home just after New Year's when the January schedule was posted.

I was placed on reserve for the month of January, so I settled down to wait to be called for a flight. New Year's Eve came and no flight assignment. I spent the holiday downstairs with the owner and his wife and, once again, brought in the New Year in a bar. Diane was on a layover in New York, so it didn't matter that much.

On January 2nd, I received a call from the National office at the airport informing me that there was a letter there for me. I drove out and picked it up. On the front of the envelope was a nice red stamp that read, "Season's Greetings," accentuated by a picture of Santa Claus, in a sleigh, being pulled by a team of reindeer.

How thoughtful, I mused. *A company this large, taking the time to send a letter to its employees, remembering the holidays, and thanking us for our service.*

I opened the envelope. The letter read: "Our schedules are being reduced the early part of January, 1960, which necessitates placing you on furlough effective January 6, 1960."

Back at the apartment, at a pay phone in the bar, I gave Diane the bad news. "Diane, I have a New Year's present for you," I said, as casually as possible. "I just got furloughed from National."

She laughed and replied, "I've got a present for you too… I'm pregnant!"

Once again, I packed up the Chevy Impala and headed off for a new adventure, making sure not to speed while going through New Smyrna Beach.

I had asked Diane to call Bob Iba and give him the news that I was back in the job market.

When I arrived at Swan Avenue, there was a ticket on Eastern for a trip to Lockhaven for the next day. Before I knew what was happening, I found myself back in a Piper Cub heading toward Kingston and South America.

I wrote my parents a postcard from Bogota, Colombia, upon arriving. "Feel like a king in Bogota. Last night, supper by candlelight with violins…this beats the airlines." I wasn't a very good liar.

Bob Iba subcontracted me out to Libby Owens of Illinois' forestry division to fly as copilot on a DC-3 for two weeks out of Grand Bahamas Island, Bahamas. That was pretty interesting. The company operated their Bahamas division out of a large barge that served as offices, hotel, and clinic. They only used airports some of the time. The rest of the time the captain would just land on the best road nearest to where the barge was moored.

At the end of that two-week job, I was back in the Piper Cubs between Lockhaven and points south.

Dick O'Mara, my old buddy from Kendall Flying School, returned from his two years in the army and was busy building up his flying time to put him in position for a job with the airlines. He, like me, tired quickly of instructing, and when he asked if I could get him on with Hialeah Aircraft Ferry Company, I recommended that Bob Iba hire him and he did. Dick and I began to fly together as much as possible and became best friends.

Diane had resigned from Eastern. It was beginning to get a little crowded at Swan Avenue, and with a family on the way, we began, again, to look for a place to settle into. Toward the end of January, we put a down payment on a house in Hollywood, Florida, and moved in. It was a nice house with a pool, but small. We visited every used furniture establishment, and for very little expense, we found ourselves comfortably furnished.

When I flew, Dee Dee insisted that Diane, in her "family" condition, stay with them. The ferry company was doing well, and I was getting an average of three flights per month. The pay was good enough—better than the four hundred per month that the airlines were paying, but the flying was more demanding. We would make 160 dollars for a flight to Bogota or Guayaquil, and the trip from Lockhaven paid sixty. We were making ends meet, but I was away from home a lot.

Dick and I were assigned to ferry two Piper Cubs to Guayaquil on March 9th. Diane dropped me off at Tamiami Airport, and as we headed south to Kingston and Guayaquil, she headed over to stay with Dee Dee and Darwin. She knew the commercial flight schedule that we were scheduled to return on, and we agreed to meet back at customs in Miami on March 12th.

The flight went okay and we arrived back in Miami on schedule. We cleared customs and proceeded to the curbside outside the terminal to meet Diane.

Dee Dee and Darwin were there; I could tell by their expressions that something was wrong.

"Diane is doing fine," Dee Dee blurted out, "but the baby is not expected to live!" Before I could speak, she kept rambling on. "She was born almost four months premature and only weighed one pound and thirteen ounces, and she's in an incubator now."

With Dick and Darwin in the backseat, Dee Dee gave me the story about Diane's awakening in the middle of the night and the trip to the hospital. "So far," she added, "the doctors say that the baby girl is a miracle child."

Three days later I took Diane home. She was under doctor's orders to rest, but before long she was insisting on going to the hospital in Miami with me to visit Cathy. We had named her Cathryn Mary after two of Diane's roommates.

But the strain of moving, driving, and standing in front of the incubator window for an hour at a visit was too much for Diane. At home in Hollywood, she began to hemorrhage. I didn't know what to do. She wouldn't let me take her to the hospital, and it kept getting worse. Around midnight I called Dick O'Mara. He had just started going out with a nurse, and they rushed up to our house immediately.

His girlfriend took one look and exclaimed, "To the hospital, now!"

We literally wrapped Diane up in the bed sheets she was sleeping on and rushed her to the nearest hospital. Dick's girlfriend knew the ropes, and in record time Diane was in a room and a doctor was attending to her.

His orders were immediate transfusions, and later he confided to me, "You got her here just in time."

I have a wonderful memory of later in the week, seeing all of my buddies lined up at the hospital to donate blood.

I spent the night at the hospital. When the doctor advised that Diane was out of immediate trouble, I went home and collapsed on the couch. The bed was a mess.

The phone awakened me; it was Bob Iba. "Tom," he said, "Dick told me about your situation, so I'm just calling to see if there's anything that I can do."

"I guess I'll need some time off," I muttered. "I'm not sure just how long Diane will be in the hospital, but I do know that Cathy will be in the incubator for a long time."

"Take as much time as you need," he volunteered, "and let me know when you're ready to come back to work."

It was three days before Diane could return to the house in Hollywood. She was under strict doctor's orders to remain in bed, and she had to see him before she could be up and around and visit Cathy. Absolutely no housework was allowed until he approved it.

Diane had to wait ten days to visit Cathy and then, only if someone else would drive. With the hospital bills and living expenses piling up, money became an issue that I would have to address. I couldn't fly until Diane was able to drive, and the doctor said that she might not be released to do so until around April first.

Diane's doctor released her for light housework and driving effective April 1st, and I put myself back on standby with the ferry company.

I was back in the air on April first with a pickup in Lockhaven.

With Diane's health back to normal, we began to live like normal people. Cathy was putting on some weight, she needed to weigh five pounds before they could release her, and we were eager to have her home. She was the nurse's pet and they laughed and said that they might not let her go even though her weight got up to the minimum five pounds. When she was born you could hold her in your hand. Now she was growing larger and was perfectly healthy in every respect. We were elated at her progress. In anticipation or her arrival home in a couple of months, we visited the used furniture shop and bought a crib.

CHAPTER 32
Out of Gas, Daylight, and Ideas...

Over the jungles of Ecuador!

I GOT A CALL AROUND the middle of April for a trip to Guayaquil. It was for two aircraft. One was a Stearman, a World War II biplane popular for crop dusting that Dick O'Mara was flying to Barranquilla, Colombia, and the other was a Piper Cub that I was assigned to fly to Guayaquil, Ecuador.

The trip started off about the same as any other. Dick and I went to Tamiami Airport a day earlier and rigged the aircraft for extended overwater flight. The Cub was easy, but the Stearman required an extra tank to be installed in the aft cockpit. We strapped it in, rigged the fuel lines up through the struts to the wing tank on the upper wing, tested it, and went home to rest for the next day's flights.

The first leg of the flight to Kingston was normal. We had begun to use for our overnight stay a motel called Morgan's Harbour near Palisadoes Airport, the airport serving Kingston. It was located near a small village called Port Royal made famous during the pirate days. About two-thirds of the city sank after an earthquake in 1692, and the motel was always filled with interesting archaeologists willing to spin their yarns about undersea discoveries in exchange for our tall tales of the sky.

We were at the airport early, as usual, to check the weather and file our flight plans. The meteorological report stated that there were considerable buildups ranging from twelve to eighteen thousand feet along with forecasted showers along the route and at our destination at Barranquilla.

The Piper Cub that I was flying was capable of topping the twelve-thousand-foot clouds, but Dick's airplane, the Stearman, could not. We decided to head out toward Barranquilla and take a look at the weather firsthand. If we couldn't navigate, we would turn back.

After an hour and a half of climbing and circumnavigating cloud buildups, we gave up. I flew up next to Dick, who signaled that he wanted to return. I agreed and we returned to Palisadoes Airport.

I began to have a bad feeling about this flight.

We refueled and returned to the hotel to wait for the weather to improve.

The next morning the forecast was better; we left early and arrived at Barranquilla right on schedule. My bad feeling was dispelled, and we headed for the downtown hotel. This was the final destination for Dick's airplane; the plan was for me to fly on to Guayaquil the next morning, and Dick would catch a commercial airline back to Miami later that day.

The next day's flight would be extremely long, a little over one thousand miles, and I was flight planning it for eleven hours en route.

The weather wasn't very promising and the ITC was forecasted to be active, but the course was simple with a lot of options along the way. I would go as far as I could, and if the weather dictated, I would land and overnight.

I planned to fly down the coast of the Caribbean Sea, past Cartagena and on to a small town called Turbo, on the northwest corner of Colombia just southeast of Panama. From there it was only seventy miles over the jungles to the Pacific Ocean, where I could easily follow the coastline to Esmeraldas and, depending on the weather, go directly to Guayaquil or follow the coast down to the Gulf of Guayaquil and approach the city from the south.

I took off at the crack of dawn and was at a cruising altitude of five thousand feet as I passed Cartagena. The weather was holding up on the Caribbean side, and soon I was passing Turbo. Over the jungles I began to notice some scud below me. The thin wisps of clouds began to thicken, and I lowered the nose and descended to a lower altitude. With the ITC active, I decided to remain low, stay under the overcast, and follow the coastline to my destination.

I cleared a small hill and the gray Pacific Ocean spread before me. I was at a thousand feet, plenty of altitude, and I continued on down the coastline. I had been flying for three hours, and the weather was not improving. Actually, the ceiling kept lowering and I was trapped. I had no recourse but to continue south and continue to fly lower. I had managed, fairly comfortably, at five hundred feet to stay under the overcast, plus keep the irregular beach in sight on my left. The five hundred feet that I had enjoyed had gradually lowered to a hundred feet, and with no instruments there was no way to climb through the overcast now. I had to work hard to concentrate on looking ahead for small upcroppings of rocks protruding from the ocean, stay under the clouds, and keep the main coastline in view only yards to my left.

Minutes ran into hours. I had been flying for over five hours, and now my altitude was less than a hundred feet. Small rocky buildups would vaguely appear ahead and at my altitude I couldn't bank, so in order to miss them I had to push as hard as I could on the rudder pedals and force the airplane to make a flat skidding turn. The rocks would pass by and I would have to repeat the same maneuver in the other direction in order to stay away from the shore. I repeated this over and over. There was no time to eat, no time to read a map. There was only time to fly, concentrate, and survive.

Seven hours into the flight, the ceiling rose to a ragged five hundred feet, allowing me some relief. I guessed that I was south of Buenaventura, as the heading required to follow the coastline was toward the southwest. I realized that I had been flying at less than one hundred feet for more than four hours. I was exhausted.

I recognized the small coastal town of Tumaco, with its large bay to the north, and I knew that Esmeraldas was only a hundred miles ahead, barely an hour. The ceiling was lifting and I had climbed up to a thousand feet and was relaxed enough to finally have lunch. I didn't have enough altitude to allow me to enjoy my typical hot meal, but the cold Vienna sausages went well with crackers and a Coke.

I was approaching Esmeraldas. The cloud layer allowed me to climb higher and to relax somewhat. I began to plan my route of flight from Esmeraldas, and for the first time I began to consider my fuel. The weather had not improved enough for me to fly directly to Guayaquil from overhead Esmeraldas, so I would have to fly further down the coast before I made the turn into Guayaquil. That would require almost one additional hour of flight time.

In flying down the coastline, my concentration was totally on the problems created by the low ceilings. I could only allot a second to look out to the fuel gauge under the left wing to check the fuel quantity. When I needed to replenish my fuel, I would hit the aux fuel switch and return to the business at hand….. surviving.

I had been flying for nine hours when I passed Esmeraldas. I still had a little over three hours to go. My auxiliary fuel was used and there were only the two wing tanks remaining; the left one had about thirty minutes used up. I had three hours of fuel remaining.

I continued to fly south for another two hours along the coast but with my added flying time I decided to land at the small coastal town of Manta for fuel. I landed with twenty gallons on board. I quickly computed that my fuel burn was around thirteen gallons per hour, about three gallons per hour more than I usually planed on. The increase, I realized, was due to the fact that I had flown approximately eleven hours at treetop level. At the higher altitudes that we normally fly, the pilot leans out the fuel flow and can expect to burn much less.

I cleared customs, closed my old flight plan, filed a new one for a direct route to Guayaquil, and ordered ten gallons of gas. The local coastline cloud level that I had battled all day long had dissipated, and the weather was forecasted to be good with the exception of local thunderstorms on the west side of the Andes. Thirty gallons would be plenty for the short hundred-mile flight to reach Guayaquil.

I took off at 5:30 and headed southeast for Guayaquil. The flight would take only an hour and there was about one hour and a half of daylight left. From past flights, I knew that there were three large rivers that flowed from north to south into the Gulf of Guayaquil passing the city. I relaxed and expected to see the first one, Rio Daule, in about forty-five minutes after takeoff. I would intercept it, turn slightly right, and follow it on to Guayaquil.

Up ahead, the sky was beginning to darken. The weather report did say that there were thunderstorms in the area around Guayaquil. I expected them, so I would just locate the river, drop down, and fly south to Guayaquil at a lower altitude. The sky got darker and I began to see lightning far up ahead. *It's up at the western slopes of the Andes and shouldn't bother me*, I thought.

The sun was sinking lower in the west, behind me. I had been flying for about thirty minutes and the Rio Daule should be coming into view any minute now. It appeared that there was a line of thunderstorms moving westbound from the Andes, blocking my direct route to Guayaquil. It looked lighter to the north, so I turned to the northeast, approaching as near as I dared to the storm, and flew for ten minutes. No luck, the storm was intensifying. I flew to the south for ten minutes, skirting the edge of the fast-moving storm. It was useless; I had to give up and fly back toward Manta and overnight there.

It was sunset.

I turned northwest to take up a course toward Manta. To my absolute horror, the storm had moved northwest around my position and was now blocking my direct course to Manta. I turned to a west heading, toward the last minutes of dusk, and surmised that I had about fifteen minutes of daylight remaining to find a place to land.

Fuel was becoming an issue. The fuel gauge in the left-wing tank showed empty and I had switched to the right-wing tank. At my increased fuel consumption, that tank would last, maybe, for another thirty minutes.

I was in a predicament. It would be dark in fifteen minutes, I had thirty minutes of fuel remaining, the storm had blocked my path to the nearest airport, and there wasn't a light in sight. If I were to survive this, I only had one option. Fly westbound and hope that I could reach the Pacific coast, ditch the airplane, inflate the small one-man life raft, and pray that someone would pick me up.

I was at three thousand feet and headed toward the last glimmer of daylight on the western horizon. In ten minutes it would be dark. I rechecked my fuel. *I may have a few drops in the aux tank.* I quickly hit the aux fuel pump switch. Only air bubbles were visible going through the neoprene hose. There was no fuel remaining in the aux tank.

There may be a few drops left in the left-wing tank, I thought. *When the right tank runs out I will switch to the left and see how long it lasts.*

It was dark. The sun had set thirty minutes earlier and there wasn't a light in sight. Suddenly, my only thoughts were of my parents, Diane, and baby Cathy, still in the hospital. *She'll never know me*, I thought.

"I must find just one light," I prayed, "so at least they can find my body."

I swore at myself for quitting Northeast Airlines, and I swore at National Airlines for hiring and then furloughing me. But all the time I knew down deep, the fault was all mine. "I should have put on more fuel in Manta," I lamented.

There was a small red instrument light in the cockpit. I could cut it off intermittently so as to give me more visibility outside. My only thoughts now were to see a light.

A light to crash by.

There was nothing.

I had been flying an hour and forty-five minutes when the engine quit.

It startled me, although I had anticipated it. Fuel starvation! Quickly, I swapped to the left-wing tank. Its gauge had read empty when I switched over to the right-wing tank earlier. There would be some fuel there but not much.

The engine coughed, sputtered, picked up RPMs, and I was flying again.

The next time it quits, I thought, *it will be for good.*

I thought about crashing in the Ecuadorian jungle. Would I survive? Surely someone would come when I didn't close my flight plan in Guayaquil.

It was 7:20.

I hadn't much time left now. Five minutes? Maybe ten at the most!

How would I control the crash? I could control my speed in the powerless glide. I could slow to fifty or sixty miles an hour.

My mind was racing.

What are the odd of surviving a crash out here in the jungle, hundreds of miles from nowhere? And if I am lucky enough to live through a crash landing, how long can I expect to survive in this hostile environment?

My heart was pounding.

I covered the red lens again with my hand and peered ahead.

Nothing!

And then, up ahead.

"What's that?" I said out loud. Was my mind playing tricks on me? Was that a light far up ahead? "Yes!" I exclaimed. A small light! It was close enough that, if the engine quit now, I could almost glide there. As I flew closer I made out what looked like a small village.

My first thoughts were *I've found a place to crash. They'll be able to send my body home to my family!*

Was there joy in dying? No! I had to concentrate on surviving now!

I eased the nose over and pulled the power back slightly to maximize my fuel. I wanted to save every drop.

I was straining to determine just what the makeup of the land surrounding the village might be. I knew that almost all of the small villages in this area were situated near a river or on the coast.

My mind raced. *I should be near the ocean by now. If this village is on the ocean, then I can land offshore and surely someone will come and pick me up.*

My thought process had gone from a recovery mission to a rescue mission.

I was approaching the village when I saw the surf. I could see a line of waves just beyond the few lights of the village, which told me that it was located next to the ocean.

I knew what I had to do. I had the altitude to spare now, so I'd put the airplane in a shallow dive, build up my speed, cross the village at a low altitude so they'd know I was there, pull up, glide straight ahead to the ocean, and…ditch.

I was elated. I wasn't going to die in the jungle, and if I didn't drown in the ditching exercise, I'd survive.

I reached over my head and moved the lifeboat slightly to ensure that it was loose and available for use. I didn't have time to put on my life preserver, so I forgot about it. It would probably be in the way, I rationalized. I opened the cockpit door. It was constructed in two sections; the top half was hinged at the top and the lower half hinged at the bottom. I cinched up the seat belt and shoulder harness one more time and I was ready to ditch.

The village was coming up quickly, as in the dive I had built up a great deal of excess speed. I zoomed low over the village, pulled the nose up as I crossed the beach toward the west, and observed that the waves were evenly paralleled, indicating a sandy beach.

Just as I pulled up the engine quit cold. The last drop of fuel in the airplane had been used. With the excess speed, I soared upward into a left turn. My initial idea was to use the speed to make a left turn around to the north, line up just on the outside of the whitecaps, ditch the airplane in shallow water, and swim ashore.

My speed was depleting fast. I continued the left turn to a north heading and lined up on the ocean side of the whitecaps.

I had spent many hours looking at the surf at the beach back in Miami. These waves were telling me that this was a smooth beach where I might just be able to land. I had only a split second to make a decision. If I made the decision to land on the beach side of the waves and the shore was rocky, then I would surely destroy the aircraft and would, most likely, not survive the crash.

It was pitch dark. Only the reflection of the whitecaps was visible less than a hundred feet under me to my right.

I went with my barnstorming instincts.

At the last second, barely fifty feet high, I hit right rudder, made a quick maneuver to the right, aligned the airplane on the right-hand side—the land side of the waves—and pulled the stick back into my lap. The airplane stalled out about a foot above the beach. I bounced and the airplane settled in with a perfect three-point landing! The waves were barely ten feet to my left.

The airplane rolled to a stop.

I sat for a long time. I couldn't move. The red instrument light gave an eerie glow to the whole scene—a Piper Cub, coming out of the sky, landing on a beach in Ecuador in total darkness.

After a while, I don't know how long, I sensed some movement to my immediate right. I turned my head and was shocked to be looking down the barrel of a rifle. It was pointed right at my head. *Oh no*, I thought. *This is just not my day.*

I slowly collected my thoughts, had presence of mind to not make any quick movements, slowly raised my left hand, and pulled the red lens from off the instrument light. I wanted the "protector of the beach" to see everything that I was doing.

And, slowly, ever so slowly, I moved my right hand up to the rifle and redirected it slightly forward, away from my forehead.

With the red light suddenly turned to white, and the scene illuminated, I was surprised to see probably the whole village in a semicircle around the airplane.

With me in the cockpit, the "protector of the beach" standing with a rusty rifle in his hand and a pistol in his belt, and both of us trying to communicate, well, it was about as funny a scene as you could imagine, under the circumstances.

I knew no Spanish words except "ice cream" and "my house is your house," and he didn't even know that much English. I pulled out my paperwork and a map and began to draw pictures. I showed him a line between Manta and Guayaquil and drew a large thundercloud with lightning and rain coming from the bottom. He understood that.

He pointed to a spot on the map and began to laugh. He called over, I suppose, the assistant protector of the beach, and he, too, had a laugh. He pointed to a small town on the coast and said excitedly, "Puerto Cayo, Puerto Cayo, aqui."

I finally figured out that this was where I had landed. Puerto Cayo.

I was still in the cockpit when I noticed that the tide was coming in and would soon engulf the airplane if I didn't do something.

I drew an airplane being pulled out of the water by several men. The man understood perfectly. He made a few commands in Spanish, I got out of the airplane, and twenty men picked up the Piper Cub and carried it to higher ground, about fifty feet from the threatening surf.

The artistic ability that I had honed back home in the back row at church in High Point was coming in handy. I then drew an airplane with three guards standing at the wingtips and tail, and he immediately positioned his men there. They would guard the airplane the entire night.

We communicated by drawing pictures for the remaining time that I was a guest in Puerto Cayo.

As near as I could make out, the protector of the beach was really the mayor or senior elected official there. He took me to a centralized building—all the buildings in the village were primitive huts with thatched roofs—and called a meeting. One man who showed up spoke limited, broken English.

"I," he said proudly while pointing to his chest, "gummit man ah hippy hoppa."

I had no idea what he was saying. I shook my head and held my palms upward to show that I didn't understand.

Again he said, more emphatically, "I gummit man ah hippy hoppa!"

The "mayor" came over and asked for my map. He pointed to a town about fifteen miles to the northeast of Puerto Cayo. "Jipijapa."

And then I knew. The new man was somewhat of an official, a "government man" from the district capital of Jipijapa.

The "gummit man" called a meeting made up of some of the important townspeople that went on for some time. The mayor took my papers, the "gummit man" looked at them, and then they passed the whole bundle around—flight plans, weather forecasts, customs declarations, and maps—and everyone looked at them. They examined, frowned, talked among themselves, and finally the "gummit man" spoke.

"It cost benty dollars to land Puerto Cayo."

Again I turned my palms upward and shrugged my shoulders as if to say, "I don't know what a 'benty' is."

By now the mayor and I had bonded, we being the best two artists in Puerto Cayo, so he came over and took some paper. He drew a picture about the size of a dollar bill and wrote a dollar sign with the numeral 20 next to it.

Then I knew. Politics had reared its ugly head. The "gummit man" wanted a landing fee and he knew that I had some funds. I carefully reached into my pocket, and pulled out a "benty" and handed it over to the smiling, and quite satisfied with himself, "gummit man" from hippy hoppa.

I now knew three Spanish phrases.

I drew a picture of a phone, but they had no communication system whereby I could close my flight plan. I had visions of not only the Ecuadoran Air Force but also the U.S. Coast Guard out looking for me all night. It was imperative that I get out of there as soon as possible the next morning.

I needed two things: fuel and a long enough beach.

As luck would have it, there was a sort of community truck, and the mayor had access to a fifty-gallon gas drum. I bargained for twenty-five gallons of gas for eight dollars and, if the beach were long enough, I would be off the next morning and would be able to call the search off early.

The locals tried their best to entertain me that night. I was invited to the mayor's home, where, I'm sure, they fed me the best that they had to offer. The lady of the house fixed chicken with rice and I ate well. The main product in the kitchen for cooking was vegetable or olive oil, and everything was floating in the stuff.

As evening wore on I was ready to sleep, and I made that known to my new friend, the mayor, by putting two hands by my head and closing my eyes in mock sleep.

I was given the executive suite of the village. It was a lumpy bed, but it had a mosquito net covering the whole thing and it was very accommodating. After the day I'd had, I could sleep standing up.

Morning came. I tried to remember where I was and I sat up in bed. There were at least twenty kids all standing around me, just staring. When I sat up, they headed for the doors, windows, and anywhere else that would let them exit. I was a rock star.

They had coffee and bread for breakfast, and soon I was off to fuel the airplane and check the "runway."

As I walked down the hill toward the beach, I saw hundreds of people gathered around the airplane and the immediate area. It was like a carnival. People were selling local food from carts and sodas from coolers, and there were strolling musicians.

I found the guards still on duty and gave them two dollars each. I walked down to the beach and was surprised at the landing spot. I had luckily passed over some boulders about a hundred feet before touchdown, and up ahead, there was a stream that would have caused havoc if I had landed too far down the beach.

The mayor brought the fuel down to the airplane in five-gallon cans, and we fueled the airplane. I used a handkerchief as a filter to make sure that the fuel wasn't contaminated, and soon I was ready to depart.

I had a camera and I asked the mayor if I could take one picture of the people standing in front of the airplane. He happily agreed and stood with about fifty of the men, women, and children of the village.

I snapped the picture and I was ready to leave.

But the mayor wanted more pictures. I couldn't explain that I only had one film left on the only roll in my camera. So I took copious pictures. Of the mayor and his wife, of the mayor and his children, of the mayor and the "city council," and anyone else that the mayor wished to impress. All with no film.

Finally, we had the good-bye embrace and I was ready to go.

The runway was barely long enough, so I showed the guards how to hold the tail of the airplane until I had the engine revved up enough for takeoff, and we were set.

The men moved the airplane down to the farthest end of the beach, next to the rocks, and I started the engine. I could see and hear the crowd cheering.

I motioned for the men to grab the tail while I checked the engine. It ran a bit rough with the auto fuel, but soon I felt comfortable.

I pushed the throttle up slowly and then faster as I signaled the men to release the tail. Off I went, bouncing down the beach with hundreds of villagers waving and cheering. I managed to pull the aircraft off the beach just before I came to the stream and I flew northward.

I kept the airplane intentionally low as I made a turn out over the ocean so as to turn back and give my newfound friends a buzz job.

As I flew directly toward the beach, I could see the people in front of me scatter, but the others were waving good-bye as I streaked by barely fifty feet high. I flew up the hill over the village and continued on toward Guayaquil knowing that the Air Force and the Coast Guard would be out in full force looking for me.

The weather was good, and Guayaquil came into view right on schedule. I received the green light from the tower and landed. I taxied directly to the air traffic control building and ran inside to the desk.

I dashed in and exclaimed, "Call off the search, call off the search! I'm the lost pilot missing from the flight last night coming from Manta!"

The all looked up quizzically, shrugged their shoulders, and said "*Que?*" They had never heard of me.

Manta had failed to register my flight plan.

I had flown my last flight for Hialeah Aircraft Ferry Co. I had a long talk with Diane and we revisited our finances and I agreed to flight instruct if need be to avoid the excitement of the South America flights in single-engine aircraft with no navigational instruments.

On May 1st, I took a job with an air charter company at the Miami International Airport by the name of American Air Taxi. It had gone bankrupt recently and an attorney, Sanford Swerdlin, the trustee, advertised for a pilot. The company only operated one aircraft, a twin-engine Piper Apache, and with my experience, I got the job.

It paid next to nothing and I got paid only when I flew, but at least I wasn't flying to South America and I was home every night. The company was based in the Miami terminal and rented a counter there. The lone aircraft was parked at a gate just outside. I was the only employee, so I had to sit at the counter all day and be ready to fly at a moment's notice. Since the air taxi was the only business of that kind at Miami airport, the business could be brisk at times.

A customer would walk up, a result of a flight cancellation, and contract with me to fly them to a destination. I would take their money, write them a receipt, send them down to our gate, call Swerdlin, and advise him as to my destination.

I would rush back to the office behind the counter, grab my airline cap, put on a shirt sporting airline epaulets, and dash to the gate. At the gate I would reintroduce myself to the often amused customer, and off we would go.

The flying was interesting. One day I might go to the Bahamas and the next day to north Florida. Key West was a popular spot, as was Naples, Florida. I even had one flight to Central America. To fly over the jungles with an airplane that had two engines and navigational equipment was a new experience, and that trip reconfirmed my decision to never ferry a Cub to South America again.

Diane's health had returned, and with only one car, we set up a schedule so we could visit Cathy at the hospital every other day. Diane would drop me off at the airport, drive over to visit Cathy, come back to Miami Springs, and visit her former flight attendant roommates. After she caught up on all the gossip, she would pick me up in the afternoon. We began to establish somewhat of a home life, but with our limited finances our only recreation was an occasional day at the beach or dinner with the Stouts.

Dick O'Mara continued to fly for the ferry company, and when he had some time off, he would spell me at the air taxi company. Dick had built up his flying time and met all the airline's qualifications. We spent every waking hour filling out applications for flying jobs with legitimate airlines. As our flying time increased, we would send out newly revised applications so as to keep our names at the top of the list. The slightest rumor that an airline might be preparing to hire pilots would prompt another round of revised applications from us.

It was early June when Diane and I got the good news that Cathy could come home. She only needed a few pounds more, and she was scheduled to leave the hospital around the middle of the month.

The crib was in place at the house, but we needed to set up her wardrobe. We went to the department stores, to the baby departments, but she only weighed five pounds and there was nothing that would fit her. We finally went to the five-and-dime stores, to their toy counters, and young Cathy was fitted out royally with baby doll clothes.

We checked Cathy out of the hospital, the nurses all cried, I signed a promissory note for the bill, and the three of us went happily to our home in Hollywood, Florida.

CHAPTER 33
Continental Airlines

The flight engineers' strike and the FAA inspector's secret agenda

A WEEK LATER A SPECIAL delivery letter came from Continental Airlines. I was set up for an interview in Denver on June 20th. The phone rang. It was O'Mara. He had received the same letter.

We were authorized passes on TWA to St. Louis, and on a Continental interchange flight on to Denver. We arrived in Denver on Sunday evening and prepared for our interview, scheduled for the next day.

The Continental offices were in a large World War II hangar. The steps up to the interview office took us to a balcony overlooking a hangar floor. It was exciting to see the big four-engine DC-7s down below us being worked on. I let my imagination run away for a second and visualized myself in the cockpit of one of those aircraft. But first, I had to pass the interview.

There were a number of interviewees in the reception room as we waited to be called. My name was called and I entered the room. The chief pilot's name was Jack Weiler. He was an old codger, but likable. His looks were anything but that of a typical chief pilot. His complexion was of a reddish blue hue, and he had enormous cauliflower ears. I found out later that before he hired on with Continental, he worked in a circus as a bear wrestler; thus the ears. We got along fine, talking about the good old days. He related a few stories and marveled at some of my South American escapades. The interview went well. It was more of a hangar-flying session than an airline interview.

At the end of the interview he looked again at my application and pronounced, "Well, Cooper, you claim to have some DC-3 time. Let's see if you can really fly one." And with that he picked up the phone and called the hangar and asked a supervisor, "Hey, do you have a DC-3 that I can borrow for an hour?"

He smiled and asked me to wait outside until he interviewed the last guy.

The last "guy" was O'Mara and he, too, was invited to go fly. As we waited, Dick was nervous, as he had never been in the cockpit of a DC-3 before. I told him that since I had lots of time in one that I should go first. He could just watch what I did and hope for the best. "Do as good as you can," I told him, "and if you run out of ideas, just ask for the checklist." I added, "The hardest part of flying copilot on a DC-3 is retracting the landing gear." I gave him a quick lesson on the proper sequence of the two levers that worked the landing gear, and before we knew it, we were on our way to the hangar floor and a Continental DC-3.

We were the only two selected to go for an interview ride. I think it was because we were the only two applicants who had passed the flight engineer's written exam.

I had about four hundred hours in the DC-3 with Northeast Airlines so the ride was quite easy. After twenty minutes in the right seat, Captain Weiler gave me a slap on the back and motioned for Dick to get in. We swapped seats and Dick took over the duties of copilot. He did pretty well. He mastered the art of retracting and extending the landing gear, and when the captain reduced power on one engine to simulate engine failure, Dick just held the airplane straight and called out, "Engine failure checklist."

Captain Weiler laughed and said, "Good job, let's go back and process you boys in."

We were hired on the spot and assigned a DC-7, first officer class for June 28th, the next Tuesday.

Back in Hollywood, Florida, at the Cooper house, Diane and I held a family meeting. Cathy was there, but at six pounds she added little. She was, however, the prime topic of discussion. We discussed the choices, which were few. After running all of our options to their logical conclusions, we decided to take the Continental job. However, while I was in flight school, Diane would remain in Florida with Cathy and wait until I successfully completed the school and was permanently based.

When, and if, I passed, we would close the house in Hollywood, and she would move to the new base. In the back of our minds, we remembered the

National Airlines episode, and neither of us was anxious to make a permanent move too soon.

Dick and I landed back at Stapleton Airport, Denver, on Monday, found a cheap motel room, and prepared for the DC-7 first officer's class the next day.

We found our seats. There were about twelve other new hires there, and we were ready for class. Two men came in; one, a tall, lanky, younger man and another shorter man. "Hello, I'm Bob Woodhams," the taller one said. "I'm your instructor, and this is Mr. Bill Cody. He's the director of training and he's my boss. He'd like to say a few things to you before we begin class."

Mr. Cody was a no-nonsense type of a guy. He had no personality at all and addressed the class in a monotone voice that emphasized his seriousness.

It seems that the Continental's flight engineers had gone on strike, and instead of pilot school, we were about to embark on "flight engineer" school. He apologized for the inconvenience and offered that if anyone wished to leave they could do so now with no prejudice, and there would be no record of their being there.

No one took him up on his offer, and he turned and left. Bob Woodhams began the class with an explanation of the rules that he expected us to adhere to and gave out the usual handouts, manuals, graphs, etc.

Bob Woodhams had an unusual style of teaching. He was highly knowledgeable with the material, but during his lectures he would spice every statement with an unprintable adjective.

"This blankety blank switch makes this blankety blank pump go on, and that feeds this blankety blank tank," and on and on and on. It was a strange way of teaching, but it was highly effective, and I think that we remembered the material better with the spice sprinkled throughout the lectures. Privately, we had some good laughs at Bob's expense, but we remembered the stuff.

We were told that we would be based in Denver, so Dick and I took an apartment on Moline Street, east of town just off Colfax. It was furnished, so all we had to do was buy some plastic utensils and a coffeepot, and we were in business. This engineer stuff was a new experience for both of us, so we dedicated ourselves to total immersion in the task that lie ahead and set up a serious schedule of study.

Continental had no simulators at that time, so if we were to get any hands-on experience in the cockpit, we had to schedule time in the hangar while an actual DC-7 was being worked on.

The Man in The Arena...

We set the alarm clock for five o'clock in the morning and would be at the hangar at six o'clock just to sit in the cockpit and touch switches and levers and memorize what the gauges gauged. By eight o'clock we were in class, and with an hour for lunch, we were released from class at five o'clock. If there happened to be an aircraft in the hangar, we would spend an hour there reviewing any items mentioned in class. If no aircraft was available, we would return to our apartment, visit a local restaurant for a light dinner, and return to the apartment for study until ten or eleven o'clock.

We felt good with our study program, and we did well on the daily test that the company administered. One week turned into two weeks, and as we approached the end of the scheduled ground school, we were ready for the oral test.

On the last day of class, Mr. Cody came by for a visit. In his usual no-nonsense manner, he gave us a pep talk. He relayed Continental's president, Mr. Bob Six's, confidence that we would do well and that, due to the labor issues with the flight engineers, the company's success was directly related to our success. Mr. Cody said that he looked forward to seeing us "on the line" soon. With no small talk, as was his nature, he turned and left.

Bob Woodhams then gave us another talk entirely. He briefed us on the upcoming oral test scheduled for the next week and he didn't paint such a pretty picture. He had some inside information that the two FAA inspectors assigned to administer the orals were former flight engineers for C & S Airlines. A few years earlier C & S Airlines had merged with Delta Airlines, and as a result the flight engineers were fired. These two men were in the group that was fired, and they subsequently joined the FAA as inspectors.

Whether or not these two inspectors brought their personal politics to the FAA and thus to this class remained to be seen, but Bob felt that he had to warn us.

"As usual," he said, "when you finish your oral, stop by my office for a debriefing, and I will begin to compile a list of favorite questions that the examiners asked. That makes it easier for the next students."

The oral exams were scheduled for the next Monday—two in the morning and two in the afternoon—and the list of *victims* was posted. Dick and I were scheduled for Tuesday afternoon.

The entire class assembled in a designated study room to give the first two applicants some encouragement and to see just how difficult the two FAA examiners might be.

It didn't take long. The two students were back within twenty minutes, each with the same tale of woe.

"We were given an incomplete and told to return to class and study more," they each said.

The inspectors, after asking a few normal questions concerning weights, power settings, pressures, and temps, got into areas that were totally foreign to the class.

It appeared that they had set the class up to look bad, if not to fail, and the outlook for the whole class looked dim.

Woodhams came in and went over the few questions that the students remembered and was astounded that the inspectors would delve into the engineering aspects of the DC-7 as deeply as they did. The questions dealt with how to overhaul a magneto. How can you determine cracks in the propeller? How many vanes in a power recovery turbine?

The questions had little or nothing to do with in-flight operation of the DC-7 and were clearly being used for ulterior motives.

We had no choice. Woodhams dutifully copied down the few questions that the applicants could remember and sent the next two students in for the scheduled afternoon oral exams.

Disappointingly, the results were the same. A few operational questions were asked and then came the killer questions. It was always the same. The inspectors used a notebook with the questions written down, and they just went down the list. By the time they got to the second page, the questions began to reflect areas dealing with maintenance repair and overhaul of components rather than normal and emergency operations that one would expect to experience in-flight.

Bob Woodhams had no answer. There was nothing he could give us to study that would prepare us for this charade. He could only send the lambs to slaughter and hope for the best. Dick and I were set for the next day, and we had the same results. We lasted about twenty minutes each and were given the incomplete and told to return to class and to study.

Dejected, we returned to our apartment to plan for the inevitable. Surely the company would fire us if we couldn't pass the oral, and the outlook was grim. Neither of us wanted to return to the ferrying world, and there was no way we could prepare for the questions that these inspectors were coming up with.

We drove down to the local dimly lit hamburger joint to continue to review our options. We ordered the usual, a hamburger and a beer, found our favorite booth and began plotting for the future without Continental Airlines.

It was early and the place was quiet except for the booth next to ours. There were a couple of guys who obviously had been served their limit and appeared to be celebrating something.

Dick went up to the bar to freshen our beers. He came back and looked as if he had seen a ghost. He bent over, pointed over his shoulder, and whispered, "The guys in the next booth are the two FAA inspectors."

We listened intently. It was easy to make out what they were talking about. They were literally crowing about the last two days of orals that they had administered. They knew exactly what they were doing. They were delaying the passing of our test until Continental gave in to the demands of the flight engineers who were on strike. They knew that Continental desperately needed us to fly the line, and they surmised that the longer it took for us to pass, the better it would be for favorable negotiations for the engineers. And besides, they didn't have any love lost for our class that they referred to as "scabs."

"We'll just keep giving them incompletes until Continental gives up on them," they agreed. "It would look bad if we failed the whole class, and this way we don't have to fail any of them."

And then one of them brought up the name of the only classmate who already had an engineer license. "What about this fellow Peter Cox?" one asked. "We can't fail him as he is one of us." He laughed.

"Let's pass him and it'll give us credibility." The other laughed.

Dick and I listened to the whole conversation. They were still upset with Delta for firing them after the last Lockheed Constellation was grounded, and this was their way of striking one last blow for the dying flight engineer union.

We sat in the booth until they left and then we went back to the apartment to review these new developments.

We had no solutions, even with the new information about the politics involved. If we went to the company, with no evidence other than hearsay over a beer in a bar, Continental would have nothing to go on. And, we feared, even if we did go public with the information, it would blackball us for life with the FAA for any future licenses or tests. We pledged to each other not to reveal the conversation that we had been privileged to overhear and went to bed.

I had a fitful night, with nightmares of returning to Hollywood, Florida, empty-handed and finding myself, again, over the jungles of Ecuador in a

Piper Cub. I had no ideas as to how to combat this predicament that I found myself in. The whole industry was changing as the airlines were converting from the mechanic/flight engineer position in the cockpit to a pilot/flight engineer position. I was clearly and unwittingly in the middle.

The next morning Dick and I drove to the Continental hangar, trudged up the steps to the study room, and waited for the two sacrificial lambs to go into the oral room next door and take their medicine. There were six or eight of us in the room peering at any manual we could get our hands on to glean any obscure bit of information which might provide some ray of hope to pass these un-passable oral tests. It was deathly quiet. Except…

I was seated near the wall and I could make out, faintly, through the air vent, voices from the oral room next door. I leaned down nearer the vent, but it was of no use. I couldn't make out enough of the conversation to make sense. I motioned for Dick to come over and see if he could make out what the conversation was. It obviously was the oral exam in progress in the adjoining room, but we couldn't make out enough of the conversation to construct a sentence. Then the conversation stopped altogether, the student had been issued an incomplete, and they were done until after lunch.

Peter Cox, our classmate who was a licensed flight engineer, was scheduled for the one o'clock oral in the room next door.

I looked at Dick. He looked at me. We both knew what we needed to do unless we wanted to find ourselves back in the front seat of a Piper Cub headed for Bogota.

We needed to take the air vent off. One of us had to climb into the crawlspace in the wall separating the oral room from the study room and record Peter Cox's predetermined oral exam. The examiners had promised each other that he would pass.

Once again we weighed the moral and ethical issues versus the political situation in which the two rogue FAA inspectors had put us, and the whole class. We rationalized that we had to fight fire with fire, and so we set the scene.

We had less than an hour to organize.

First, the furniture in the oral room must be situated so as to provide the best position for maximum audio. We took all the desks out and placed the lone table next to the air vent. Finally we placed the only two chairs remaining on either side of the table. I went into the study room, removed the air vent, and slid into the air duct. Dick sat at the oral table and we tested the reception. "Loud and clear," I reported through the vent.

Secondly, since I lost the toss, I prepared for a long afternoon in the air passage chamber inside the wall. I collected several flashlights and some cushions and set up a rather comfortable alley in the wall. I equipped myself with ample notebooks and ballpoint pens, and I was all set.

We made a sign for our door. "No Admittance. Studying in Progress." We locked the door and posted a guard just to be safe. No one was to be admitted; not Woodhams and especially not Cody.

I crawled into the air passageway at about five minutes until one o'clock and waited. The air vent I crawled in through was now at my feet, so I had some light and it was not too claustrophobic. I had a flashlight in the crook between my neck and shoulder, one knee was pulled up, and a writing pad was resting on my thigh. I was ready.

Before long I heard the door open, some shuffling of chairs, and the usual introductions. I could hear as clear as day. The FAA examiner acknowledged that he knew that Pete had his flight engineer license and then put him at ease with a few easy questions. Then the zingers came. Pete knew enough to keep the conversation going, and the examiner worked with him through the oral. Question after question came, and Pete, obviously with extreme help from the examiner, did well enough to keep the oral moving along

As I filled up a page with questions, I would slip it down along my leg to the vent to Dick. He handed it over to one of the other students who, having made friends with one of the secretaries down the hall, ran the sheet down to her. She would type it on mimeograph paper and run off eleven copies.

This went on almost all the afternoon. Finally, the FAA examiner ran through his entire book of questions, closed the book, called the quiz to an end, congratulated Pete, and exclaimed that he had successfully passed his oral. Pete and the examiner had no sooner said their good-byes when the last page of questions was copied and each of our fellow classmates had a freshly mimeographed copy of the 'killer' questions that were originally meant to destroy us.

The whole class had a private meeting that afternoon as we handed out the study material. No one was to ever tell anyone of the events of the day. We nearly drew blood to solidify the vow as we went our separate ways to study and prepare for the second round of orals beginning the next day.

One of our classmates was a pretty good con man. He reminded us not to answer the hard questions too quickly. "When the tough questions are asked," he cautioned, "frown, hesitate, make some marks on a scrap paper, and pretend to dig far back into your memory before you come up with the answer."

The re-takes were scheduled for two days hence, and amazingly, all the class passed with flying colors. One of the FAA examiners complimented O'Mara on his performance, and Dick casually remarked, "Yes, sir, my father rebuilds aircraft magnetos, as a hobby, in our basement back home."

We were all scheduled to fly to Los Angeles in two days for the flight portion of our flight engineer training. We were to "muster" on the ground floor of the hangar at a given time, and a bus would take us across the ramp to the flight to LAX.

We met at the canteen area of the hangar, and while the remaining few showed up, Dick and I entertained ourselves with a game of Ping-Pong. While playing I noticed, out of the corner of my eye, Mr. Cody standing by the Coke machine, watching us intently.

This was no laughing matter. We never saw him unless there was something extremely important, and he was *never* in a good mood.

I was playing and watching him out of the corner of my eye. He was watching me. He was not smiling. I was so nervous that I couldn't hit the ping-pong ball anymore, so I gave up the paddle to another classmate and moved away from Cody.

He walked around the Ping-Pong table and came up to me.

This is not good, I thought. *This is not good.*

He came right up to me. He was about four or five inches shorter than I was, but he looked like a giant at that moment. "Cooper," he said, unsmiling, "Mr. Six wants me to tell you to relay to all the class just how proud we are of all of you and the way you turned this oral situation around."

"Yes, sir," I stammered, "we worked hard and burned the midnight oil, especially over the past several days."

"Please pass on my personal compliments to all the men in your class," he finished as he turned to leave.

I was backing away and finally breathing again when he turned and came back in front of me, about six inches from my face; he looked up at me straight in the eyes and whispered, "Cooper, if you get out of Denver without me giving me a copy of that study guide, I'll personally fire your ass on the spot."

By the time I had reached into my flight kit for my copy, he was gone. I dashed up to his office, got an envelope from his secretary, and sealed it with a note on the front, "STUDY GUIDE, private, Mr. Cody."

In an hour, I was on the flight to LAX and I was glad to be getting out of Denver alive.

I called Diane and based on the good news that I had passed the oral examination, we decided to begin to plan our move to Denver. She returned the house in Hollywood back to the sales company and had a garage sale of the furniture that we had accumulated. She piled the rest of our meager belongings, along with Cathy, into the Chevy and headed to High Point, North Carolina, to spend a few weeks with Mom and Dad as we made our final arrangements for the move.

There was a flurry of activity in Los Angeles with our group. We were scheduled for a series of observer flights, followed by a few hours of training, and then a final check ride in the airplane for our flight engineer license.

It all went smoothly. Our class was well prepared, and without the politics interjected by the last examiners, all passed with flying colors. Within six days we were on our way back to Denver for our final test, the observer flights. Those are real passenger flights with the newly licensed engineers in the F/E seat with a certified check engineer watching over his shoulder to ensure that the new pilot/engineer is competent.

Diane had left the Chevy in High Point and flew, with Cathy, to Youngstown to stay a few weeks with her mother while I finished the training and found a furnished house to rent in Denver.

I began to fly scheduled flights regularly until the end of August when Continental gave me two weeks off. I used that time to fly to High Point, pick up the car, drive to Denver and prepare the small house that I had rented for the arrival of Diane and Cathy.

They flew in from Chicago and on September 1st and set up housekeeping in a small house just off Colfax Avenue in Aurora, Colorado.

The small house was nice and adequately furnished. It sat back off a quiet street with two large trees in the front yard. We were only a few miles from Stapleton Airfield and the Continental operations office, and there was fine shopping nearby. It was the first time in three years that I could relax, and I almost felt uncomfortable. It had been almost three years since I left High Point, and during that time there were always mountains to climb and goals to strive for. There were oceans to fly over and mountain passes to fly through. And now, I only had to sit and wait for Continental crew scheduling to call and assign me a trip on a modern DC7 aircraft.

This relaxing stuff was foreign to me, and I was having trouble adjusting.

Diane did her best. She could see that I was fidgety and she tried to keep me occupied mentally. She would occasionally fix dinner for Dick and some of my fellow classmates. There were parks nearby, and she would plan picnics for Cathy and me, and it was working. I was just beginning to wind down and enjoy home life when a registered letter came from Continental Airlines.

Those official letters frightened me. I had a flashback to January when I received the same type of envelope from National Airlines.

In my paranoia, it took a while for me to get up my nerve to open it.

CHAPTER 34

Continental Airlines

Good news...bad news

"SECOND OFFICER COOPER," THE LETTER from Continental read, "you are to report to Continental Airlines Training Center at Stapleton Airfield on September 12, 1960, for Boeing 707 Second Officer training at 9:00 a.m."

So much for the unwinding.

Continental had been operating the Boeing 707 for about a year, and as a new hire of twenty-four years old, it was the farthest thing in my mind to become a jet crewmember. It was exciting and I thought my fortunes had finally turned around for the good.

Dick O'Mara and a few of our previous classmates were in class on the 12th. Bob Six came by to wish us well and remind us of our responsibility to the public and the company and so did Mr. Cody. Bob Woodhams began his teaching with his usual "This blankety blank switch causes this blankety blank valve to..." Bob's spicy jargon had not abated with the advent of the sophisticated B-707, and we all welcomed his informal method of instruction again.

The class went as would be expected. We all studied hard and applied ourselves to the maximum. Continental had no simulators for the B-707, so if we wanted to get some hands-on training we had to run to the airport gate, request permission from the captain to visit the cockpit, and with only minutes available, practice accomplishing the checklist and work through mock emergency procedures.

Someone had built a static training device in the training area. It was constructed of plywood and cardboard with paper instruments cut and pasted from a flight manual. The crew's chairs were typical cane wicker-back porch type, and the throttles were sawed-off broom handles. It worked pretty well for practicing checklist procedures.

Given the absence of a simulator, the main hands-on training came from OJT, or on-the-job training. After ground school was completed, we were assigned to ride the jump seat, the extra seat in the cockpit, and observe the regular second officer perform the duties of the flight engineer. We were scheduled for fifty hours of OJT, and upon finishing that, we had an actual check ride in the Boeing. Upon the successful completion of that, we were assigned a series of flights with a company check airman to observe us until he felt comfortable that we were competent.

I finished my final route check on October 11th and was signed off to fly the line on regular commercial flights. Continental claimed that I was the youngest commercial jet pilot flying in the U. S.

I returned home, elated that I was finally a jet pilot, only to find another registered letter.

"Second Officer Cooper, you are now transferred to the Los Angeles crew base as second officer on Boeing 707, effective October 20th, 1960."

Diane took it better than I did. I was happy to be a jet pilot, but this moving was getting a little bit old. I had one week to talk to the lessor and try to retrieve some of my deposit, cancel the electric, phone, and water service and worry about those deposits. Once in Los Angeles we needed to find a furnished place to stay and set up the water, phone, and electricity.

Diane sprang into action. Luckily, her sister, Roberta, lived in Van Nuys and her husband, Dick Tarantino, was the tower chief at the Santa Monica Airport. He had a friend, Gene Reich, who was a captain for American Airlines and a real-estate developer. Gene had an apartment house on Jefferson Boulevard very near the airport, and one unit was available. By the time I returned from cancelling all of our utilities and negotiating the refund of most of the rental security, Diane had us all set up in Los Angeles.

We were packed and on our way by morning with a planned stop in Las Vegas en route. The trunk was full and the linens and towels made a fine pallet in the backseat for Cathy.

We drove west from Denver toward Grand Junction and then toward Utah. The views were scenic as it was too early for the mountain passes to be snowed in.

To entertain us as we drove—to entertain me anyway—we listened to the last game of the 1960 World Series. It was the New York Yankees versus the Pittsburg Pirates, and it happened to be the game sporting the most famous homerun in the history of the game. Bill Mazeroski hit a homerun in the bottom of the ninth of the seventh game to win the World Series for the Pirates.

We spent the night in Las Vegas, and being low on funds we only enjoyed the food at the cheap motel where we stayed.

We arrived at Los Angeles the next morning and, following Roberta's instructions, found our new home with the door key under the mat. Captain Reich had arranged for the water and electricity to be on, and all we needed was a phone. The apartment was perfect. It was a quiet street across from the Hughes factory airport, a seldom-used strip for test flights, and about two miles from Playa Del Rey, a beautiful beach.

Exquisite. I was flying a jet out of a major airport and living two miles from the beach. We had a healthy baby daughter, and Diane's sister lived twenty minutes away.

Perfect.

We'd been married for a year and, with the exception of a couple of weeks, we had spent no time together. Diane loved the beach and it gave us a recreational area to enjoy at minimum expense. She could visit her sister when I flew, and we would have Dick O'Mara over for dinner often as he was transferred to LAX also.

I drove over to the Los Angeles International Airport to report in to the Continental operations and was assigned a trip for October the 20th. It was my first flight as second officer on the Boeing 707 and I couldn't wait.

In previous trips to the Los Angeles Airport, I had noticed the flight engineers picketing. Their picket line was small, only about two or three picketers, but it had been a drain on the flight engineer manpower of the company. Without the success of our class, there would have been major interruptions in schedules. With the success of our class, in October, the flight engineers union settled on the company terms and two-thirds of the old flight engineers joined the pilots union and the strike was over.

I noted this but didn't mention it to Diane. With the returning flight engineers, it was totally possible that some of the second officers on the bottom of the list would be furloughed. I was fourteen numbers from the bottom of the seniority list.

It was useless to worry about being furloughed, but just to be on the safe side, I compiled a list of airlines, wrote for their pilot applications, and filled each one out, ready to mail if I received the dreaded certified letter. I called it "Operation Furlough."

My first flight, on the 20th, went okay and I settled into the routine of a set flight schedule. Diane was enjoying seeing her sister occasionally, and with the beach nearby, she was content. Cathy was growing and healthy. I was doing some part-time flight instructing at the Santa Monica airport to subsidize my income, and we had settled down to enjoy a normal life.

Since I was a part-time instructor, Mr. Miller, the owner of the school, only gave me one or two special students. One such student was Mr. Wally Hunt. He was in his sixties, a wonderful gentleman who had his own airplane and was having trouble with progressing in his flight training to the point where he could fly by himself, solo.

It was an ideal project for me. Wally was a successful businessman, still active in his company, Asphalt Industries, Inc., so we could schedule around my flight schedule.

In our initial conversation, it was apparent that his previous instructors had spent very little time on the ground explaining the basics. I started off there. We spent a lot of time studying on the ground in skull sessions, and once we returned to the flying part of his training, he progressed normally. Soon he was flying solo.

We became great friends. He would invite me over to his home on Rodeo Drive for ground school, and when he needed to visit one of his plants—he had about forty plants in California—he would ask me to fly with him as safety pilot.

I met his family, his sons and his daughter, and he became quite an influence on me. He was a gentleman in every respect and he taught me that the very wealthy need not be abusive or crass, as was usually depicted on TV and the movies. He was a good example and a role model a young man could well emulate.

November came and went uneventfully with the exception of one flight around mid-month.

We were flying from Denver to O'Hare and were at cruising altitude when suddenly the aircraft pitched downward. The captain grabbed the yoke and leveled the airplane manually. He tried to re-engage the autopilot but to no avail. To fly without an autopilot wasn't a life-or-death situation, but frankly, the autopilot flew the B-707 better at altitude than a pilot, and without the use of an autopilot, we would have to descend to a lower altitude, use more gas, and perhaps have to land at an alternate airport for fuel.

I quickly checked all the circuit breakers on my panel and found nothing out of order. Then I remembered a procedure that Bob Woodhams had shown me on a walk-around instructional session back in Denver. There was a trapdoor in the rear of the cockpit floor that opened into a compartment called the lower forty-one. That was a cramped space where all of the electronics gear was stored. If I remembered correctly, Bob had showed me where the number one and number two gyros were located and how to cross utilize one for the other.

"Captain," I said, "do you mind if I go down into the lower forty-one compartment and look at the gyros? I may be able to correct the autopilot problem."

"Go ahead," he said, "but don't take too much time. I have to begin to descend pretty soon or we'll have some sick passengers in the back of this airplane."

I opened the trapdoor and let myself down into the hole. I found the light switch and sure enough, just like Bob Woodhams had explained, there were the two "blankety blank" gyros. To transfer from the failed "blankety blank" gyro to the other one would allow the captain to reconnect the "blankety blank" autopilot.

I disconnected the failed gyro and hooked the connectors up to the alternate gyro and hoped for the best. I stuck my head up through the door in the floor and asked the captain, "Try the autopilot now."

Miracle of miracles. The "blankety blank" autopilot connected and worked perfectly. Bob Woodhams would be "blankety blank" proud as we continued on our way to Chicago for an on-time arrival.

We arrived at O'Hare Airport and were met, as usual, by the ground mechanics to correct any discrepancies the crew might have noticed in flight. When the captain told them that we needed the number two gyro replaced, they questioned, "How do you know it's the number two gyro that failed?"

"The second officer went down into lower forty-one and swapped the autopilot over to the number two gyro and then it worked fine," the captain explained.

The new second officers were still suspect as we were not licensed mechanics, and the seasoned mechanics were not comfortable with that explanation from the captain. "We'll order a new one from the parts department, and while we wait we'll drop down and confirm the failure," the lead mechanic said.

He was gone about two minutes and popped back up with a grin on his face. "You're absolutely right, you've got a failed number two gyro." And again he questioned, "You swapped those two gyros in flight?"

"I sure did," I replied and then, remembering Dick O'Mara's reply to the FAA examiner's compliment, added, "My father used to overhaul gyros in the basement of our house for a hobby."

November turned into December and Christmas was rapidly approaching. Diane and I were preparing for the holidays, as it would be our first one as a family. The Christmas tree was up, presents were wrapped, and we looked forward to the Yuletide season with much anticipation.

It had been a year since the furlough letter came from National Airlines. A year since I found myself in a Piper Cub over the jungles of Colombia and Ecuador. I was now flying a jet for arguably the most progressive airline in the U.S., or even the world. Continental, led by one of the most innovative CEOs in the aviation business, Bob Six, was setting records in load factors, profits, and creative maintenance procedures that were the envy of the aviation community. The Golden Jet service was setting on-time performance records, and employee morale was at an all-time high.

In the back of my mind, I still remembered that the returning engineers might pose an excess pilot problem for Continental. However, no certified letter came as we celebrated Christmas with family and December came to an end. As 1961 came in, I was beginning to think that we'd dodged a bullet…

And then it came.

The letter was dated January 16th, and the furlough was effective as of January 31, 1961.

Diane was crushed. We'd been married for fifteen months, and during that time we'd been in four different residences, plus she'd stayed with our parents for over four months. In the past, when my job dictated a change in location, she was the strong one, but to pick up and leave this location was too much for her. The beach, her sister, and a regular job for me was about all that we could have wished for, and now, once again, it was taken away from us with the stroke of a chief pilot's pen. For the first time I could see that she was discouraged with the uncertainty of the industry that I had chosen and the sacrifices needed to succeed. I was beginning to question my judgment also.

Again, we had a much too often family meeting. The options were: one, go back to Miami and ferry Piper Clubs to South America. That was not an option! Two, stay in Los Angeles, work as a flight instructor, and wait until either National or Continental recalled. That was an option that would receive some serious consideration. Or three, apply to every other airline and see if anyone else was hiring, and if so, look at the possibilities of flying for a new airline.

We decided on option three, and if no other airline called, we would revert back to option two and instruct until something broke in the airline business.

Now it was I who had to put up a good face—and get a job.

That day I immediately activated Operation Furlough, fired off the pre-completed applications to about ten airlines, and waited. I still had a job with Continental Airlines to do, and I continued to fly the line with a smile on my face. But I was too discouraged inside to face the end of the month.

CHAPTER 35

Back to The Non-Skeds

AND THEN ON JANUARY 20TH a telegram arrived. "HAVE IMMEDIATE OPENING PILOT FLIGHT ENGINEER, CONTACT CHIEF PILOT RIDDLE AIRLINES IF INTERESTED. H W DAVIS SYSTEM CHIEF PILOT RIDDLE AIRLINES, INC."

Riddle Airlines was a cargo airline based in Miami. I had read in the aviation periodicals that they had purchased a fleet of DC-7CFs and that they intended to bid on some international charter routes. This might be just the place to sit until Continental recalled.

I checked my remaining schedule and immediately called Captain Davis for an interview. After flying all over the United States, I was finally returning to Miami for an interview with a Florida-based airline. He set me up with a pass on a Riddle Airlines cargo flight from Chicago to Miami, and I picked up a pass on Continental for Los Angeles to Chicago. I was on my way to Miami on January 22nd.

When I spoke with Captain Davis over the phone, he indicated that if there were any more pilot/engineers being furloughed, he would be extremely interested in talking to them. I advised him that I knew of about twenty and I would contact all of them with that information.

Now, seniority is a sacred thing with an airline pilot. It is said that the most important thing in an airline pilot's life is seniority. Generally being the youngest pilot in my class, I was always placed at the bottom of the seniority list. I couldn't do much about my age, but in this case, I could manipulate the hiring date.

I had kept the Riddle interview a guarded secret until I reached Chicago. Then I called Dick O'Mara and advised him of the opportunity in Miami.

"Great," he exclaimed, "I'll meet you at LAX and we'll fly down together."

"I can't do that," I explained, laughing. "I'm already in Chicago, and one day ahead of you. I'll be in Miami in the morning, and if I get hired I'll have one-day seniority on you and I'll finally be senior in the class."

He laughed out loud, swore using some of Bob Woodhams favorite expletives, and allowed, "I'll call the rest of the furloughed pilots and tell them about the Riddle opportunity."

"Not so fast, Dick," I cautioned. "Remember, you're the next youngest and they'll be ahead of you. Come to Chicago and call them from here, and you'll be senior to them if we get hired."

He did just that and there was a stream of furloughed pilots from Los Angeles to Chicago to Miami for the next week.

I made the interview on time, was hired, and Captain Davis mentioned that our date of hire would be on the class date. I petitioned him to show my hire date as of that day, my actual date of hire, and when I explained the reason, he laughed, shook his head in disbelief, and agreed.

I warned him, "There's another pilot coming through here tomorrow by the name of O'Mara, and he'll have the same story for you."

I was back in Los Angeles the next day and, again, Diane and I closed down an apartment. Dick and Roberta were gracious and offered to let Diane and Cathy stay with them until Riddle decided where I would be based. Dick and I headed to Miami for another ground school.

We arrived in Miami on Tuesday, January 31st, checked into the Green Mansions Motel, and prepared for another class. DC-7CF ground school started the next day on Wednesday, February 1st, and we seated ourselves in the rear of the class to observe the other twenty students.

The instructor laid out the training plan, which included two weeks of ground school, a week of observation flights, some actual flight training, and a check ride. It looked like we would be in Miami for at least a month. We settled in for a long stay.

The next day, around midday, the chief pilot, Captain Davis, came into the classroom and introduced himself. He announced that the company had just received a contract for additional flying in the Pacific, and they needed two volunteers to deadhead immediately to Oakland, California. When about ten students raised their hands, he said the selection would be based on experience on DC-7 type aircraft.

He started at the front of the class and pointed to the first student who raised his hand. "One hundred hours, sir," he said.

Davis pointed to the next student who had raised his hand.

I looked at Dick and he looked at me. The pay rate for ground school barely covered the motel expenses, but the flight pay more than doubled our income. We wanted to get to flight status as soon as possible, so we just waited until we were called. Being the last two students, we would have the last bid.

"Five hundred and fifty-six," Dick lied and then Captain Davis looked at me.

"Six hundred and twelve," I chimed in.

We were pulled out of ground school, sent immediately on a check ride to Idlewild Airport in New York, and were on a commercial jet bound for Los Angeles and Oakland, California, on Saturday.

We stopped by the Tarantinos' for a short visit with Diane and Cathy, grabbed the Chevy, and headed up to Oakland. The plan was to immediately secure an apartment and bring Diane and Cathy up.

We arrived at Oakland, rented an apartment in San Leandro, checked in with the Riddle Airlines operations department, and were immediately assigned a flight on Tuesday.

The company was desperately short of flight engineers, so we all were flying the maximum legal flight time. The trips went all over the Pacific. We would be routed over the North Pacific to Tokyo with stops in either Anchorage, Cold Bay, or Shemya in Alaska, for rest and change of crews. The routes to Tokyo via the mid-Pacific routes were through Hawaii and Wake Island.

I finally got a few days off at the end of the month and was preparing to move Diane and Cathy to San Leandro when I got a note in my box at the Oakland operations. "You are being transferred to Miami."

We were used to it by now. I promised Diane that I would drive down to Van Nuys, pick her up, and we would fly to Miami and find a place there. Her patience was wearing thin, understandably.

My last flight out of Oakland was on March 7th and my first flight out of Miami was on March 10th. Diane, Cathy, and I flew to Miami and arrived on the 9th and found the cheapest apartment in the area until I could get some time off to locate an adequately furnished place.

Our critical funds forced us to a place in Hialeah near the racetrack called Wayley's Motel. Dick took a room there also and we settled in. It was extremely sparse, so we had to do the usual shopping: plastic plates and silverware and a $1.29 coffeepot. We couldn't afford a phone, so we used the pay phone just outside the entrance.

I was on reserve flight status, so I awaited my next flight assignment while Diane visited her old friends in Miami Springs.

CHAPTER 36

Bay of Pigs

Unwitting accomplice

IT WAS LATE IN THE afternoon when the pay phone outside our apartment rang. It was Riddle crew schedule with a flight assignment.

"Be at National Airlines ticket counter at eleven o'clock tomorrow morning," he explained. "You are deadheading to Washington, DC, on the eight thirty National flight. Captain Sklenka is your captain, and he will have your tickets and expense money."

I pulled out a notebook and pencil. "Where do we go from there?" I asked.

There was a long silence. "We're not sure" was his answer. "Plan on five or six days…and don't wear your uniform."

"I never wear my uniform when deadheading," I said.

"No, I don't mean the deadheading on National leg," he quickly added. "I mean on the Riddle flight. And one more thing—is O'Mara there? This is shown as his contact number."

"He's next door," I volunteered.

"Can you tell him to be there too?"

"Yes, we'll both be there," I said as I hung up.

I stood in the evening light and thought about the conversation that I had just had with the Riddle scheduler. It was a long time before I went back inside. I was sure that the scheduler was truthful when he said he didn't know where we would eventually fly. I also knew that Riddle flew some strange flights from time to time. Some conversations I had held with Riddle crewmembers since I had joined the company alerted me to this fact.

With the Vietnam police action heating up, Riddle's flight concentration was in the Pacific arena, so why the secretive flight out of Washington, DC? I shook my head and walked down to O'Mara's room.

He asked the same questions and we had no answers. We had done weird flights before, so this wasn't that much of a departure from earlier assignments. We agreed to leave Wayley's Motel the next day at seven o'clock, head for the National Airlines ticket counter, and see what the future held for us.

Diane took the news in stride. By now she was used to the irregularity of an airline pilot's schedule. She would visit her old girlfriends and spend some time with Dee Dee and Darwin and wait until she heard back from me, when I knew what I would be doing. Dick and I pooled our money, kept ten dollars apiece, and gave the rest to Diane just in case we were gone for an extended period of time.

Seven o'clock came and an old roommate picked us up for the ride to the airport. I left Diane at that third-rate motel with Cathy, one year old that month, with less than thirty dollars in her pocket, our car in California, and not knowing when I would return.

We met Captain George Sklenka at the National ticket counter. He had two other crewmembers with him, and that constituted a heavy crew—a crew that could fly trips requiring extended flight time. He didn't have any more information than we had.

We landed at Washington National Airport, were picked up by an unmarked vehicle with an armed guard, and went directly to the Burlington Hotel on Vermont Avenue, NW. We were instructed to wait for further instructions. Captain Sklenka had been given instructions that none of us should leave the hotel as we must be ready to depart at a moment's notice.

The hotel wasn't that bad. It was centrally located, had a great café/lounge called the Sombrero Room, and rooms were only five dollars per night.

The crew hung out together that night, making good use of the Sombrero Room, and speculated on when and where we would be flying.

We got the call at noon the next day. "Be at Washington National Airport at two o'clock and the meeting place will be determined," the caller said. "You will be picked up by a private car at one o'clock."

We were picked up right on time by the same small government bus driven by a uniformed driver and the guard riding shotgun. The driver had a few words with Captain Sklenka and off we went toward Washington National Airport.

We were let in through a guarded gate and ended up on the northwest side of the airport in front of a row of large hangars, where a Riddle aircraft was parked. We were driven up to the airplane and dropped off. After another short conversation with the driver and his sidekick, Captain Sklenka asked us to remain with the airplane and do a preflight inspection. He was escorted over to the hangar and disappeared inside.

Dick and I began our preflight inspection and inspected the cargo on board for tie-down security. The load consisted of a number of barrels, crates, and small aluminum boats with outboard motors. We checked the weight and balance forms; all looked properly loaded and secure.

Captain Sklenka was back shortly and announced to the crew that we were flying to Miami just as soon as we finished the preflight inspection. All that remained to be checked was the fuel load, so Dick took the left set of wing tanks and I took the other side, and within about thirty minutes we were ready to fly.

I looked at my watch. It was two thirty, and I estimated that we would be in Miami in about three and a half hours. I had no way of calling Diane since we weren't allowed to leave the airplane, so I had no recourse but to wait until we landed. I would be home in five hours at any rate.

I was the engineer for the takeoff and for the first half of the flight, and Dick took the engineer's seat for the second half. We had a short conversation during the switchover, and neither of us could figure why we had a heavy crew for such a simple and short flight. As I pondered the events surrounding this flight, I began to sense that there was more to this than was advertised; no itinerary, no uniforms, heavy crew for such a short flight, sequestered in a DC hotel, and an unmarked bus with a guard for transportation in Washington.

We landed at six o'clock. I should be at Wayley's Motel within the hour.

As we began to taxi after landing, I moved up to the cockpit behind Dick, who was at the flight engineer's seat between the two pilots. Instead of heading toward the Riddle hangars, we were directed to follow an airport vehicle to the center of the airfield.

Dick looked back over his shoulder at me and shrugged his shoulders as if to say, "I have no idea what is happening."

We shut the engines down just as several cars and a fuel truck drove up.

Some rickety stairs were pushed up to the forward cargo door and the crew deplaned. We were ordered to remain with the airplane while Captain Sklenka was escorted to a van parked nearby. After about twenty minutes, he returned with a handful of papers, maps, and documents.

"Gentlemen," he began rather officially, "we are to fly this cargo to Managua, Nicaragua, just as soon as we can fuel up."

The questions began to fly fast and furious.

Captain Sklenka shut off the questions with "We are delivering these boats, engines and farm equipment to the poor people of Nicaragua," and he ended, "no more questions!"

The crew was upset, especially since we couldn't leave the airplane and call home, but that was the deal and we went to work. The attitude was "The sooner we do this trip, the sooner we'll get home."

It was my turn to work the flight engineer panel, so I assumed the seat between the two pilots, ran the checklist, and when Captain Sklenka gave the signal, I started the engines. As the fuel truck and other vehicles pulled away, we taxied from our position in the center of Miami International Airport. The copilot received the clearance for Managua as we reached the takeoff end of the runway. The engines checked out okay, and I nodded to Captain Sklenka that I was ready when he was.

He asked for the final items on the checklist to be accomplished, pushed the throttles up to take off power, and we roared down the runway. It was 7:00; the sun had set and it was almost dark.

The route of flight from Miami to Managua went from Miami to Key West, then a slight turn to the south directly over Havana. From overhead Havana, the route turned south for about three hundred thirty miles to a small island called Swan Island, and from there a turn southwest would head us directly toward Managua. Captain Sklenka had flight-planned the trip to take four hours.

After takeoff, the captain turned toward Key West and we climbed to our cruising altitude of ten thousand feet. I set up cruise power setting, leaned the engines, set the cowls and oil cooler flaps for cruise, and sat back to enjoy the flight. We had passed Key West and were headed directly for Havana.

We approached the Havana controlled airspace and, as normal, the copilot called Havana and gave them the estimate for entering their controlled area. Havana responded loud and clear, "Riddle 201, you are cleared to Havana radio beacon. What is your estimate?"

"Riddle 201 estimating Havana beacon at 7:43," the copilot responded.

"Roger, Riddle 201, estimating Havana at 7:43."

The copilot then signed off with Miami Center and went back to Havana Control as we crossed into the Cuban airspace.

Since Cuba did not have civilian radar, all position reports were made with precise estimates by the flight crews, and the progress of the flights were followed on the ground manually by the air traffic controllers.

The lights of Havana began to glow on the horizon, and soon we could make out the outline of the city with Morro Castle just east across the harbor from the city. It was a beautiful night, and we were enjoying the smooth ride. It was 7:40; we were just north of the coast of Havana when Havana Control came back on the air.

"Riddle 201, request you hold northwest of the Havana beacon, ten thousand feet, two-minute legs, right turns."

This was not too unusual, especially with the manual type of control system that Havana Control was using. It was possible that there could be another aircraft in our approximate area. So to create separation the controllers might place one aircraft in a holding pattern. A holding pattern is a sort of racetrack oval flight track crossing a radio beacon established to delay one flight and ensure separation from the other.

We crossed the Havana beacon, and Captain Sklenka entered a right turn to commence our holding pattern over Havana.

We flew outbound the prescribed two minutes and turned inbound, expecting to be cleared on course.

There was no clearance to proceed on course, so we continued over the Havana beacon and turned outbound for a second time. We had used up six or seven minutes in the holding pattern.

Captain Sklenka began to express some concern in the cockpit. He asked the copilot to ask Havana Control when we could expect further clearance, which he did.

Havana control came back. "Delay indefinite. We're confirming your destination and cargo on board!"

That got our attention.

Captain Sklenka turned to me. "Cooper, get O'Mara and go back and see just what the hell is in those barrels and crates!"

O'Mara was standing behind me and heard the order. We grabbed the fire ax and squeezed into the cargo area and began prying lids off crates and covers off drums.

To our absolute shock, we saw almost every kind of small- to medium-size arms. There were pistols, machine guns, and what appeared to be grenade shoulder launchers, among other war paraphernalia. There was ammunition of every size and shape, and even one crate of first aid supplies.

We had only looked at five or six crates and barrels before it sank in where we were and what was going on.

I rushed to the cockpit and relayed what we had discovered to the captain. We were still in the holding pattern and had just turned south toward the Havana beacon about two minutes up ahead.

We were in the third holding pattern; with each one taking about six minutes, we had been over Havana for approximately fifteen minutes.

We were in trouble, and Captain Sklenka knew it. We were flying contraband over the country that it was intended to be used against. We were in civilian clothes, and if we were forced to land here, we would be treated as spies and probably executed on the spot. Those executions really happened and were well documented in the Miami newspapers.

Dick whispered in my ear, "It was just five weeks ago that we were flying Boeing 707s out of Los Angeles."

The captain held a quick conference with the copilot and me. "Here's the deal, guys," he figured, "we know that they don't have civilian radar, but it's a safe bet that the military has some form of rudimentary radar system. We can either sit up here and wait till they come up and escort us down, or we can make a run for it."

I remembered that it wasn't too long ago that I was just ten thousand feet below us at the military air base of Campo Colombia and had observed the rows of jet aircraft on standby for just this sort of thing.

The copilot appeared to be frozen and offered no help.

"Captain," I said, "I think that when we cross the Havana beacon next time and begin our right turn toward the north for the next holding pattern, we should pick up a direct course for Boca Chica Naval Air Base at Key West. It's only about a hundred miles away. The copilot can get on the radio and ask the Navy for an escort back toward the U.S., and hopefully we can outrun the Cubans. I'll push the power up to maximum, watch the engine temperatures, and give you max cruise speed. You can push the nose over, we'll cut off the position lights and rotating beacon, and hope that they can't see us."

"That's my plan exactly," the captain agreed. "Get the radio frequencies for Boca Chica ready," he ordered the copilot, "and on my command, start screaming for help."

We were estimating the Havana radio beacon in one minute.

We approached the Havana beacon, and the captain had just begun the right turn outbound to the north. We were barely seconds from implementing operation escape when the radio crackled. "Riddle 201, you are cleared on course."

The captain looked at me. We were both thinking the same thing. *Is this a trick? Do the Cubans just want to get us over the Caribbean, south of the Isle of Pines, and destroy us with no evidence?*

The clock was ticking.

We had just crossed the Havana beacon and the captain had the airplane in a right bank when he said, "Cooper, what do you think?"

Whether we went south, on course toward Nicaragua, or north toward Key West was the question. It was a gamble either way. If the Cubans were planning any interdiction, a turn north would trigger it if they were watching us on military radar.

"Well?" the captain asked.

"My vote is southbound on course to Managua," I voiced.

O'Mara echoed over my shoulder, "Me too."

The captain took a deep breath, exhaled, nodded in agreement, and put the airplane into a left-hand bank and set the course south for Managua.

It was a beautiful cloudless night.

The few lights on the Isle of Pines became visible up ahead, and to our left the southern coastline of Cuba was outlined by the lights of the dozens of small fishing villages that dot the water's edge.

About seventy-five miles to the east of our position was an inlet with a quiet, sleepy village snuggled alongside its tranquil waters. The village was Girón and the inlet was Bahia de Cochinos—the Bay of Pigs.

Another thirty minutes and we were clear of Cuban airspace. We began to breathe again.

We landed in Managua just before midnight and were driven to the local downtown hotel by some form of military transportation. There was no formal customs entry procedure, and eight hours later we were rustled out of bed for an immediate departure. By nine o'clock we were airborne for Miami. This time the route we filed did not take us over Havana but west of Cuba airspace over Mexico, and then northeast toward Key West and on in to Miami.

We landed in Miami at 1:00 p.m., and ground control gave us taxi instructions direct to the Riddle hangar. There was no formal customs or immigration protocol. We grabbed our bags, deplaned, and walked to the parking lot. One of the crewmembers dropped Dick and me off at Wayley's Motel.

There was no official record of us leaving or arriving at Miami International Airport or Managua, Nicaragua.

CHAPTER 37

The Airline "Merry-Go-Round" Continues

DIANE HAD BEEN BUSY WHILE I was gone. One of her airline roommates had married a former flight student of mine, Fred Bost, and they invited us to stay for a while with them until Riddle decided what to do with me.

Fred and Fray Bost were very generous with their new home, and since Fred was an aircraft parts salesman, he was gone much of the time. That worked out well because it looked as if Riddle was going to use me on both the east and west coasts.

There were a few more trips to Nicaragua, with short trips between Managua and the small village of Puerto Cabezas on the Caribbean side of the country. It became common knowledge in Miami that there was something being planned to attempt to overthrow the new government of Fidel Castro. The question was…when?

At the end of March, I was sent back to Oakland to fly the Tokyo route. Diane stayed with Fray and Fred while we figured out where we might settle.

I returned from Tokyo on April 14th to find a telegram from Continental waiting for me. It read, "FURLOUGH TERMINATED AND YOU ARE HEREBY RECALLED TO DUTY EFFECTIVE MAY 1, 1961." My new assignment was first officer on the DC-3, and my base was to be El Paso, Texas. I was scheduled for one week of DC-3 school on May 1st.

Regretfully, I had to tell the Riddle chief pilot of my planned departure. It went well. He even complimented me on the good work and indicated that if it didn't work out with Continental, he would entertain rehiring me. I had one more trip scheduled, a round trip to Tokyo via Cold Bay, Alaska, on the 20th of the month.

It was April 18th and I was packing for the Tokyo trip and preparing for the move to El Paso when I picked up the local Oakland newspaper.

"CUBA INVADED BY COUNTER REVOLUTIONARIES. Invasion forces embarked from Nicaragua. Battle Rages. Suspect CIA involvement."

In two days, I would be carrying a load of *military advisors* to Tokyo on their way to Saigon.

I returned to Oakland on April 27th, turned in my maps and manuals to Riddle Airlines, caught a bus to Van Nuys, picked up the Chevy Impala, and drove to Denver.

Diane said good-bye to Fred and Fray and flew on to High Point to stay with Mom and Dad until I could get through another ground school and get settled in El Paso.

Dick and I breezed through the DC-3 class and were on our way to El Paso in the black Chevy Impala by May 6th.

Dick rented an apartment at the Cielo Vista apartments in El Paso, near the airport, and I inherited the couch until I could rent a house and bring Diane and Cathy out.

We were flying DC-6s and 7s from El Paso to Houston as flight engineers until we could finish the DC-3 flight portion of the checkout.

I rented a house on the outskirts of El Paso, and in June, Diane and Cathy came out. By then I was flying as copilot on the DC-3 between El Paso and Kansas City. It was a grueling run with about ten stops, but it was good to return to the right seat.

The house was nice. It was fully furnished, on a quiet tree-lined street and convenient to shopping and the airport. Once again the family was together. We settled down, and with the exception of one incident with Cathy, all was well.

CHAPTER 38

My Short Career as A Paramedic

It seemed that Cathy had mastered the art of walking. And she exercised that skill to the utmost. She was into everything. One day she pushed through the back-door screen and, before we could catch her, fell down the steps. She took quite a fall and cut a sizable gash in her cheek. She was bleeding profusely and I panicked. I was rushing around with no idea at all as to what to do. Luckily, Diane's nursing instincts kicked in and she quickly packed the wound with an ice pack and directed me to find the keys and get the car started.

I had just renewed my FAA physical examination with a local doctor. He operated out of his house nearby, and so off we went to see him.

He examined the wound and proclaimed that she would need stitches. Diane explained that she was a nurse and she would be glad to help. He thanked her and said that she could hold Cathy while he stitched her up, and the three of them moved into an office equipped for such an operation.

I proudly proclaimed, "I will hold my injured daughter while you sew her up." It was a father's duty to attend to his offspring at a critical time such as this.

They looked at each other, the doctor shrugged his shoulders, and while I held Cathy's head, he prepared the needle and began to sew.

The needle penetrated one side of the cut.

That's the last thing I remember.

I fainted dead away, hit the floor, and according to Diane's version, both she and the doctor had to drag me back to the living room, lift me onto the couch, and administer smelling salts while little Cathy lay, unattended, on the operating table.

The sutures in Cathy's cheek were a success and no sign of a scar remained, but the injury to my ego, to the ego of the world-traveled soldier of fortune macho pilot, left a scar that would be slow to heal. My fellow pilots did not hasten the process.

Life in El Paso was easy. The flying was good, the weather was outstanding, a pay check was regular, and we could hop over to Juarez, Mexico, every weekend for a jug of Oso Negro, the local Mexican vodka, and a supply of inexpensive beef steaks for the week.

CHAPTER 39

Same Old...Same Old!

IT WAS JULY 21ST AND I was on reserve status at home when Dick called from the airport. He was so upset that he couldn't speak; he indicated that he'd be right over. In ten minutes he bounded through the front door and exclaimed, "Those bastards did it to us again!" His face was red and his voice was shrill.

"Calm down, Dick," I said. I had no idea what could upset him so much. "The bastards did what?"

"Continental," he screamed, "they just furloughed us again!"

Diane heard the commotion and came into the living room. We had been in the house for less than a month. There were absolutely no flying jobs in El Paso, and we knew exactly what the news meant.

Pack up and move again...if I could find a flying job.

I had returned applications to all the major airlines just last January, and none responded other than with the stock answers: "We'll keep your application on file."

The effective date of furlough was August 6th. That was only two weeks away.

The three of us sat there in the living room, in the newly rented house, on the quiet, tree-lined street in El Paso, a year-old baby in the next room, completely engulfed in self-pity with only one thing for sure in our future: a Lone Star beer.

Dick always said, "A man in crisis can think better after a few beers."

It was Friday. I swallowed my pride and called the chief pilot for Riddle. It had been less than three months since we shook hands and he had showered me with compliments on a job well done.

I gave him my tale of woe; he sympathized with me and took down my phone number, just in case something came up.

We sat in the living room, drank beer, and cursed Continental…and drank more Lone Star.

The weekend came and went, and we still had no ideas. About the only thing left might be to drive to Miami, set up a household, and flight instruct until National or, heaven forbid, Continental recalled. August the 6th would soon be here, so we began to put together a plan to pull up stakes and move again.

The only bright spot in our lives at this time was Cathy. She was healthy and she loved the house, except the back screen door. She always had a smile for everyone, and people would stop us on the street to say hello to her. She had grown so much that she had graduated from the doll department in the five-and-dime stores for her clothes to the regular baby section in the department stores.

Monday morning came and the phone rang. I answered it halfheartedly, thinking it was Continental crew schedule assigning me a trip on the DC-3.

"Mr. Cooper, can you hold for Captain Davis?" the secretary on the other end asked.

"Yes, ma'am," I answered.

"Cooper, if you can be in Oakland by Thursday the 27th, you're hired…again."

"Yes, sir. How about O'Mara?"

"Him too" was his short answer.

"I'll tell him right now," but I added jokingly, "remember, you hired me thirty seconds before him, so I'm senior."

"Oakland, now," he laughed, and hung up!

I had two and a half days to get to Oakland. I had to clean the house and return the keys and try to retrieve the deposits. It was a drill that I had done many times over the past two years. The only other thing to do was to go to Continental, that day, and apply for a leave of absence for the last two weeks so that I could make the Thursday deadline for Riddle.

The chief pilot in El Paso was very accommodating and gave both Dick and me a leave of absence letter immediately.

While Diane was feverishly packing our few belongings, I made the rounds to collect deposits and shut off phones, water, and electricity. I rented a U-Haul trailer, stopped by Dick's apartment to collect his stuff, and we returned to the house for the final loading of the trailer.

The plan was, just like in January, to stop by Dick and Roberta's home in Van Nuys, drop Diane and Cathy off, drive to Oakland, establish another house or apartment, and bring them up as soon as possible.

We pulled out of El Paso at 10:00 p.m. I drove first as we headed west. Dick was in the backseat with an ice chest full of his new favorite beer, Lone Star. Diane was in the front seat, and Cathy was standing between us.

The weather was good, the sun had gone down, and the temperature was cool. As we passed the small western towns, the local country and western music stations kept up a steady musical beat in time with the hum of the tires as we drove toward a new job.

The Lone Star kicked in, and Dick was the first to fall asleep. Soon, Diane dug a pillow from the backseat and, resting against the door, she, too, fell asleep.

It was a peaceful scene. Just me and Cathy; she standing in the seat beside me, with the country and western music keeping us company as we drove through the night.

I stopped for gas once—no one woke up, so I continued on through until daybreak. Dick took over and drove us the rest of the way to Dick and Roberta's house in Van Nuys.

We arrived at noon on Tuesday.

Our intention was to drive on through to Oakland, but Dick Tarantino insisted that we stay one night with them, and since we were exhausted, we took them up on the offer.

I gave Diane all the money I had, except twenty dollars for fuel, and Dick and I left at six on Wednesday morning. We arrived in Oakland at around 2 p.m.

We checked in with the Riddle operations person, who welcomed us with open arms. We found out soon why he was so glad to see us. The police action in Asia was heating up, and Riddle had been asked to increase their flights almost overnight by the government.

"You fellas have a flight at seven tonight," he said, "heavy crew to Tokyo."

"We can't possibly make that," we chimed in together. "We haven't even unpacked our trailer yet."

"Then you're fired," he commented, casually.

"We can make it," we hurriedly agreed.

The next scene was a comedy. I parked the car with the U-Haul trailer in the Riddle crew parking lot, and we began to pack for a trip to Tokyo. Two grown men with suitcases spread out on the pavement, sorting out underwear, folding shirts, taking off the Continental emblems and wings from our uniforms, looking for passports, and, in general, trying to pack for a weeklong international flight out of a trailer.

We tidied up in the men's room at operations, put on our Continental blue uniforms with the Riddle wings and hat badges, combed our hair, and checked in, ready to go to Tokyo.

I made one last call to Diane before we left. Since it was a heavy crew, we would probably fly straight through, have a normal two-day layover in Tokyo, and be home in about a week. "We should be able to move you up here in about two weeks," I guessed as I hung up.

It was a routine trip. We hopped over to Travis Air Base to load the soldiers and advisors, and from there we flew eight hours to Anchorage, Alaska. From Anchorage we flew directly to Tokyo, a flight of fourteen hours.

There was a surprise waiting for me at the Tokyo airport. The station manager met me in the cockpit and handed me a company telex. "PLEASE ADVISE FLIGHT ENGINEERS COOPER AND O'MARA. TEMPORARILY BASED IN TOKYO."

I suppose that by then I was used to it…or maybe I was numb from airline abuse…or maybe I was just exhausted from twenty-two hours of being in an airplane. I simply shrugged and followed the captain and crew through customs.

We had transportation waiting and soon we were checking in at the Tokyu Ginza hotel, my home for the next six weeks.

My last conscious thoughts as I stretched out on the bed in my room were that exactly one week earlier, I was trimming the hedges in front of my house in El Paso, Texas, my wife was tending to our baby, and my only worry was when Continental would call me for a DC-3 flight.

Now, I was in Tokyo with less than five dollars in my pocket, my wife and child were with relatives in Van Nuys, California, with less than fifty dollars, and my car was in a parking lot in Oakland, with a trailer hooked onto it and all our worldly possessions inside.

The Asahi beer that we bought on the ride to the hotel did its job and I slept soundly.

The phone rang. It was O'Mara. I had slept for ten hours. We decided to make the best of our stay, so we met in the restaurant to plan for the unknown.

We had no idea how long we would be assigned to the Tokyo base. From what we read in the newspaper, the action in Vietnam was heating up.

The politicians kept telling the public that it would be over in a short time, and except for a few advisors, U.S. involvement would be minimal.

Our biggest concern now was to find a Riddle captain, hit him up for a per diem advance, and figure how to get some of it to Diane back in California.

That opportunity came soon. I was assigned an Anchorage flight. At least that would place me where I could wire some money to Diane and let her know what my status was.

Captain Jack Luss was the captain on that flight. He was very understanding and helpful. Although I was assigned to return to Tokyo after an overnight in Anchorage, he was flying on to Oakland. He advanced a hundred dollars per diem expense money to me. I wrote Diane a long letter for him to mail when he got to Oakland. He agreed to wire seventy-five dollars to her also. I included a note for the Oakland station manager to purchase a lock for the trailer and to call the U-Haul folks and extend the rental for a month.

The next morning I was on the way back to Tokyo, and I felt somewhat better about the situation. At least I was working and not sitting in El Paso with nothing to do.

The month of August was a flurry of activity. I was primarily flying a shuttle between Tokyo and Okinawa, with a few trips to Manila, Saigon, and Bangkok.

It was September 6th before I returned to Oakland. I turned in the trailer and drove to Van Nuys, picked up Diane and Cathy, and drove to Miami. We had decided to settle down in the Miami area, fly for Riddle as long as they had use for me, and wait for National Airlines to recall.

We moved into a furnished apartment in Virginia Gardens, a small incorporated town next to Miami Springs near the airport.

Riddle was a struggling airline. Their business plan was threefold. First, they hauled cargo over scheduled routes along the East Coast and San Juan. Second, they had government contracts in the Pacific, and third, they had ad hoc government contracts on the East Coast.

Being extremely junior, I was subject to fill in wherever I was needed. During the remainder of 1961, I spent some time in each of those areas. It wasn't very conducive to a normal home life, but I got home from time to time, and there was always that National Airline carrot hanging in front of my nose.

During the month of September, I flew primarily out of McGuire Air Force Base in New Jersey to Europe, mainly Ireland and Madrid, Spain.

October found me back in Oakland flying the Tokyo run. On the first of November, I was assigned to ferry a DC-7 from Tokyo to Miami with a stop in Oakland. I was coming home!

I ended up flying out of Miami for the balance of the year.

The year of 1961 was ending up pretty good. Diane and I were settled in, and Cathy was growing like a weed. We weren't getting rich but we did have a few bucks in the bank, and it was beginning to look like Riddle was going to keep me on the East Coast. Some of Diane's friends were still in the area and she seemed happy. We had a nice Christmas and, with guarded optimism, we were looking forward to the next year.

Since the nature of approximately two-thirds of Riddle's business came from government contracts, the pilot's future depended on those contracts being renewed. Most were renewed on a monthly basis, and so Riddle had to bid every month on the proposed trips published by the government. This placed Riddle management in a predicament as far as crews were concerned. If the government didn't renew the contracts, then Riddle would have surplus crews and would have to furlough accordingly. If they furloughed at month's end, at the end of the existing contract the company would have to pay the furloughed pilots for two weeks of non-productivity.

To avoid this expense, Riddle simply issued furlough notices on the 15th of each month; if the government renewed the contracts, Riddle would recall the pilots at the month's end.

This was commonplace and, although the pilots would be concerned about receiving a furlough notice, they were used to it, they understood why, and they lived with it. Not so the wives. Our wives were constantly concerned that there would not be a paycheck the next month, and it strained the relationships.

I received one such furlough notice on the 15th of January 1962. Along with that came a temporary assignment back to Oakland for a flight on January 26th. Diane was nervous and I could see why. Here she was in Miami, and I was assigned to the Pacific division with a furlough notice in my pocket effective on January 31st.

We talked it out and tried to see the bright side. We had established ourselves back where we wanted to live, the job was reasonably steady, and we had reunited with the Chevy Impala. I assured her that I would be back to Miami shortly, and off I went to Oakland.

I guessed wrong.

With the exception of two weeks in March, I flew out of Oakland until April 16th.

The Pacific flying was interesting. I wasn't in Oakland long enough to rent an apartment, so I just located the cheapest hotel near the airport and checked in when I was in town.

In Tokyo, the company paid for the room, so I stayed at their official crew hotel: usually the Dai Ichi or the Tokyu Ginza in the middle of town.

We were flying military advisors to Tokyo from Travis Air Force Base in California. From Tokyo, we took them to Okinawa, Saigon, or Bangkok. The Okinawa and Bangkok flights were easy, but the Saigon flights were getting a bit sticky.

The flight crews had to attend a special meeting prior to each flight for a briefing. It seems that the North Vietnamese would duplicate the radio frequency that led us to the airport serving Saigon, Tan Son Nhut, in hopes of redirecting the route of our flight for nefarious purposes. The U.S. military would change frequencies from time to time, so the frequencies listed on the maps did not necessarily represent the actual frequency at the airport.

The approaches were different also. We were not allowed to make long, straight-in approaches. We flew over the field at altitude and spiraled down in a circular pattern so as not to stray too far from the actual airport area. There was evidence that some of the local population was in sympathy with the North, and there had been small arms fire directed at aircraft landing there occasionally.

CHAPTER 40

Engine Failure

Mid Pacific

REMARKABLY, THE DC-7CS OPERATED BY Riddle crews were very reliable even though the airplanes came with a reputation that was suspect. The DC-7 was designed around the DC-6 with a few exceptions. It was intended to carry more weight and fly higher and farther than the DC-6. The design engineers had replaced the R-2800 engines used on the DC-6 with a new version, the R-3350.

Since an engine is nothing more than an air pump, the more air you can push into it, the more power it will produce. To push more air through the engine, the manufacturers added blowers, which were activated by the flight engineer when flying over ten thousand feet. This jammed more air into the engine. Then they coupled the eighteen exhaust stacks at the rear of the engine in groups of six, passed that exhaust gas through a turbine—there were three to an engine—and those spinning power recovery turbines, or PRTs, created additional power, which, in turn, gave the engine more power.

This was all well and good and looked good on paper. The only issue was that the engines were extremely sensitive to heat. At altitude, with the blowers in high position, the engine temperatures had a tendency to run hot. When the temperatures ran hot, the operational life of the PRTs was cut short and they had a tendency to fail. A failed PRT required instant shutdown of the engine to avoid total failure.

The Riddle engineering team decided that to avoid the constant high engine temperatures, they would simply order us to fly the aircraft at ten thousand feet or lower and not use the high blower feature. The engine temperatures stayed cooler and the PRTs life was extended.

In my total career with Riddle I only had one PRT failure, and we shut the engine down promptly to avoid total engine failure.

The ten-thousand-foot solution to the engine problem worked fine… except for one small issue, trans ocean navigation. In the 1950s, long-range navigation systems had not been perfected, so each aircraft required a navigator in the cockpit. The cockpit was designed with a small "bubble" window in the overhead ceiling behind the flight engineer and a desk off to the side. The navigator would use a sextant to "shoot" the stars, attain the aircraft position relative to the position of the stars, and then return to his desk to draw lines and compute degrees of heading that he would relay to the captain to keep the flight on course. The relay method was simply to write the new heading down on a scrap piece of paper and hand it to the flight engineer, who would hand it to the captain. The captain would then make the adjustments to the heading, and we would proceed merrily on our way, hopefully on course toward our destination.

This worked fine as long as you were flying in clear skies and the navigator could see the stars. When flying at ten thousand feet, you were not always guaranteed to be in the clear. When the navigator couldn't see the stars due to clouds, he reverted to dead-reckoning navigation, the same method we used when flying Piper Cubs to South America. Out here in the Pacific you simply estimated the wind along the route, set your course, and hoped that your estimate was relatively accurate until you were close enough to your destination to pick up a radio signal—or the sky cleared and the navigator could determine your position by the stars.

Such was the case on the night of January 29, 1962. We were scheduled to fly from Hawaii to Travis Air Force Base near Oakland, California, and the weather wasn't cooperating. We got a weather briefing from the dispatcher; the captain and the navigator discussed the weather anticipated en route. There was a major weather system between Hawaii and California, and the captain, along with the advice of the navigator, decided to deviate south of course for several hundred miles before heading directly to Travis.

Now, navigators in the fifties were a strange breed. They seemed to be a nomadic group, dwindling in size, left over from the Second World War, and their usefulness was waning as technology was rapidly replacing them. As the government contracts moved from one non-scheduled airline to another, sometimes on a monthly basis, they would simply sign on with the latest airline that got the contract, introduce themselves to the captain, and they were part of the crew. They might be outfitted in the uniform of an airline that had folded three or four years earlier. They were professionals, but they also were a breed apart.

They were characters, but I grew attached to them. They reminded me of the pilots I had flown with at Regina Airline. They were good at their job, but by necessity, they were drifters. One taught me to ride a surfboard at Waikiki. The training simulator was the coffee table in his room at the Waikiki Biltmore Hotel, and the actual training was on a rented surfboard at the beach.

Another kept me spellbound with stories about flying in the Second World War, and another mesmerized me with tales of flying in the same cockpit with Ernest Gann. Ernie would spend his time taking notes and keeping a ledger of the events as they happened, apparently planning on a career as a novelist after his airline career was finished.

The navigator tonight was a wise old bird outfitted in the uniform of a long since vanished airline, but still carrying himself with the cocky confidence of someone sure of his stature.

While the captain finished the flight planning, I completed the preflight, and soon we were airborne. The weather, as predicted, was miserable. We climbed eastbound, reached our cruising altitude of nine thousand feet, set the engines for cruise, and picked up the heading southeast to avoid the forecasted bad weather along the direct course.

The captain was glued to the radar, trying to avoid the numerous thunderstorms along our route, and I continued to tune the engines to ensure that they were running as cool as possible.

There was an instrument located in the radio rack at my left ear that I relied on for engine monitoring. It was called an engine analyzer, and it gave me a picture of each spark plug as they fired. Given four engines, each with sixteen cylinders with two spark plugs per cylinder, the total picture was of 128 spark plugs firing in sequence. I could select any one of them with a rotary dial, and I routinely checked each one every fifteen minutes. If there was any peculiar indication of an engine irregularity on the gauges on the instrument panel in the cockpit, I could refer to the engine analyzer and determine if there was a particular problem in any of the sixteen cylinders on any of the four engines.

We were four hours out of Hawaii. The captain was struggling to provide a smooth ride; we were in the clouds, and the navigator had not given us an adjusted heading since taking off from Hawaii. We had another hour before we were to turn toward California.

As was my habit, I took a walk through the cabin to check with the flight attendants, check on the soldiers, and visually check the engines through the side windows.

The soldiers were returning from duty in the Far East, some from routine duty in Tokyo, Korea, and other bases in Asia, but some were coming from that new police action in Vietnam. Almost all were my age or younger. They were different from the troops on our flights going westbound, toward their new assignments in the Far East. Those seemed so much younger as they went toward the west. It was as if they were teenagers going for summer camp. They joked with the flight attendants and told us pilots all the old pilot jokes that we had heard a million times before, which we enjoyed with them as if we had never heard them.

It was a different story with the troops headed east toward the U.S. They were much quieter, more mature, and many were very withdrawn. There were fewer jokes, and some just stared ahead as we flew eastward.

They left as boys and came home as men.

It was that way tonight. The flight attendants worked up and down the aisle, but there was little for them to do. The soldiers were almost all asleep; those awake just sat and looked straight ahead.

As I returned toward the cockpit, as usual I visually checked the engines. The PRTs gave off an eerie orange glow at night that was normal. I took one last glance out of the left window to check the number one and number two engines.

As I was turning away I was alarmed to see a shower of sparks come from the number one PRT on the number two engine.

I dashed back to the cockpit, checked the BMEP gauges on the forward panel, and noted a small drop in power on the number two engine. Quickly I checked the engine analyzer, number two engine, spun the selector knob, and noted a double-shorted secondary on the spark plugs on number eight cylinder. This indicated that something bad was happening inside that cylinder, and soon the whole engine would fail catastrophically.

"Captain," I called out, "we have an impending failure on number two engine, and we need to feather it now."

"Are you sure?"

"I'm sure," I said as I readied my finger on the feather button.

To "feather" an engine means to shut it down and move the propeller into a streamline position so that it will not windmill after the engine is shut off. A windmilling propeller will cause such drag on the airplane that prolonged flight will be jeopardized and life-threatening events will occur internally in the engine.

"You'd better be sure," he said as he looked at me in the dimly lit cockpit.

"I'm sure," I said with urgency, as to hesitate too long with the problem that I had diagnosed would certainly lead to a catastrophic failure and a possible engine fire compounding our situation.

He nodded. "Feather number two, and run the engine shutdown checklist."

We shut the engine down, feathered the propeller, and accomplished the engine shutdown checklist.

Since we had not passed the point of no return, we had no alternative but to return to Hawaii. The captain asked the navigator for a heading.

"Give me a second, skipper," he called out over my shoulder. He called every pilot "skipper." I surmised that he had been with so many airlines and flown with so many different pilots that it was impossible for him to remember new names. "Meanwhile," he added, "pick up a heading of 290 degrees until I can figure something out."

The captain turned the aircraft around toward the northwest, and I busied myself with watching the remaining three engines while figuring out how to balance the fuel load now that I was running three engines out of eight fuel tanks.

"Skipper," the navigator addressed the captain, "I think we'd better pick up a more westerly direction. We've been solid since we left, and I haven't been able to take a celestial fix. I'm figuring that a westerly heading will take us out of this weather in about one hour, and I can get a decent fix for an accurate heading for Hawaii."

"Cooper," the captain asked, "how does the fuel look for that zigzag? I figure it'll add thirty minutes."

"I'm just finishing up my fuel 'how goes it' sheet," I answered. "And I'm checking the three engine cruise chart for estimated fuel consumption per hour. We've taken a hit on airspeed since we shut down number two. I'll be with you in a second." I sensed that the captain was beginning to get a little anxious.

"We've got four hours and fifty minutes plus reserves, sir," I informed him.

The captain called the navigator forward and asked, "What's your best guess for Hawaii, if you're correct in your estimate for some clear skies?"

"Well," the navigator drawled, "if we can believe the winds aloft report that we got back in Hawaii, around four hours and change."

The captain was getting a bit flustered. "Dammit," he exclaimed, "I've shut an engine down with little indication of a malfunction, I've got a planeload of soldiers back there, and a navigator who can only guess at where we are and where we're going!"

I busied myself with watching the instruments of the three remaining good engines.

The navigator wasn't affected at all. "Well, skipper," he said, "that's the best I can do given the fact that I can't see the stars. We'll just have to wait an hour and see."

The captain spun back around, adjusted his heading, noted the time, and fumed.

It was a long hour. I began to question my decision to feather the engine. Did I really see sparks flying out of the number two engine? Did I really see a drop in the BMEP gauge? Was there really a double-shorted secondary in the number eight cylinder?

And worse, I began to question the navigator. This guy was a pickup crewmember. A drifter. He would have fit well in the cockpit of a Regina non-sched airplane.

I knew the captain was thinking the same thing.

We limped on westward on three engines.

Twenty minutes crept by, and then thirty, forty-five, and just before the hour was up we broke out of the clouds into clear skies.

The navigator climbed on his stool, pulled out his sextant, and began to "commune" with the stars. Back at his desk he made some hurried calculations, jotted down a note for the captain, and handed it to me.

Hawaii, 307 degrees. Three hours and forty-two minutes.

The captain turned northwest to the new heading, noted the time, and said nothing.

In two and a half hours the non-directional radio beacon receiver on the instrument panel came to life pointing directly ahead for Hawaii, and in thirty minutes we saw the dim glow of the island lights. Twenty minutes later we were entering the traffic pattern.

We landed and taxied in on three engines. The buses that we had called for the troops were waiting, and as the first officer completed the logbook, the captain packed up his bags and remarked that we could now go to the hotel.

"No, sir," I said, "I'm going to stay with the airplane until I confirm the problem with the number two engine. I'll be in later."

Our mechanics had been alerted that we were a "return" and had been rustled out of bed to meet us and survey the damage.

There were two of them, and they weren't happy to be called out this late at night. They were half serious as they needled me. "Hey, engineer, you better be right." "All those soldiers are being put up at a hotel; the airplane is out of sequence." "This is an expensive little turn back." "Headquarters will fry you if there's nothing wrong with this engine."

I failed to see the humor, and the question mark was still in my mind. Was there something really wrong with the engine?

They rolled a large stand up to the engine and crawled up. I was with them. They began a cursory inspection without removing the cowling. A mechanic could tell if there was an impending engine failure by reaching his hand into the PRT exhaust stack and spinning the turbine. If it spun freely, there was no damage; if it was seized, there was a problem.

They didn't ask my opinion and I didn't offer. I knew which PRT should be the problem. They checked the number three PRT, which spun smoothly. They chuckled. Then they spun number two, and it spun smoothly also. By now they were laughing out loud and having a good time with me, speculating on whether I would get fired in Hawaii or if management would wait until I was back in California. There were peals of laughter resounding across the dark ramp. And I was down to my last PRT.

The loudest comedian reached in to spin the number one PRT. It was frozen solid.

"Okay, wise guys," I laughed, "take the cowling off and check the number eight cylinder. You'll find two peened spark plugs there, and some loose metal too."

The laughter stopped as they removed the engine cowling and pulled the spark plugs on the engine that I had suggested.

The gaps on the plugs were welded closed, and there was a lot of loose metal in the cylinder indicating an internal failure. The cylinder was trash and the engine was seconds away from a disastrous failure.

"No apologies necessary," I said over my shoulder as I walked across the ramp toward the hangar.

I was feeling pretty good.

As I walked through the dark hangar toward the dimly lit operations office, someone called out, "Hey, skipper."

It was the navigator.

"I thought you might need some company. Are we celebrating or crying in our beer tonight?"

"We're celebrating. The number eight cylinder on the number two engine is junk. What are you still doing out here?"

"I've been doing this for a long time, and I can tell when someone needs some support. That was a real gutsy move you made up there. Could've saved our lives. Sometimes decision making is difficult, and you're not always guaranteed to be correct…but whether you're right or wrong, you can always use a friend," he said as we walked out of operations for the cab that he had called.

We went straight to the Waikiki Biltmore Hotel, left our uniform jackets and hat at the desk, hit the bar, and bonded over a couple of beers…or maybe more.

This guy, I thought, was a real class act. He would *never* have fit in with Regina Airlines.

Two weeks later I received a nice letter from the chief engineer of Riddle complimenting me on the prompt shutdown of the engine. He confirmed the problem—upper land failure in the number eight cylinder of the number two engine—and outlined how much money I saved the company by the timely engine shutdown.

On April 16th I was sent back to Miami and was assigned the East Coast scheduled cargo runs to Idlewild, Philadelphia, and San Juan.

On May 1st, I received my monthly furlough notice and thought nothing of it. I was conditioned to that game and expected the normal recall at month's end. On May 3rd, I was sent to Oakland to fly the Pacific again, and on May 14th, I was deadheaded back to Miami.

It was nearing the end of the month and I was relaxing in Virginia Gardens, expecting the routine furlough cancellation notice, when a strange thing happened.

It didn't come.

CHAPTER 41

The Merry-Go-Round Continues

Will I ever get off?

I CALLED RIDDLE AND WAS told that the furlough was real this time, as the government gave the contract to Overseas National Airlines, a competitor company.

Diane and I held another family meeting. There were more options this time. Western Airlines in Los Angeles and Piedmont Airlines in Winston Salem, North Carolina, had responded to the earlier applications and were offering positions as pilot.

Western paid more than Piedmont and the flights were in larger aircraft over longer routes. I was leaning toward the Western offer, which would take us back to Los Angeles, when Diane gave me the news.

"By the way," she said, "I'm pregnant."

It was time to give up my dreams of flying for a major airline flying international routes, and settle for the small regional airline and fly locally in the area that I grew up in. We would live in High Point, raise a family, and live a normal life.

Diane packed up, flew to Youngstown to visit her mother, while I closed up the apartment in Virginia Gardens and drove to High Point to prepare for yet another ground school.

Dick O'Mara and the other furloughed Riddle pilots signed on with Western and left for Los Angeles.

I moved back in with my parents in High Point and was in Piedmont's Martin 404 ground school on June 4th.

The school went okay. The Martin 404 was an easy aircraft to learn, especially with my recent engineer experience, but something just wasn't right.

I'm not sure what it was. Perhaps it was a combination of things. The pay was low for my experience, the route structure was not to my liking, and High Point didn't seem the same. I ploughed on through the first week of school.

And then, on Friday evening, the personnel department from Western called me. They were desperate for second officers to fly their DC-6s as they were expanding. The hiring person told of Western receiving the California to Hawaii route award from the CAB, and it was likely that I would be a captain within two years. They were hiring large numbers of pilots and I should get on board now to ensure a good seniority number. He said that based on the quality of the other Riddle pilots, I could consider myself hired over the phone. If I hurried I could make the DC-6 class on June 18th.

I called Diane and with the enticement of being with her sister again, she agreed that the Western Airline route was the one to take.

The next day I resigned from Piedmont and, with the passes that Western had sent to the Greensboro airport, I flew west to Los Angeles. I was in class on Monday morning with all of my old Riddle buddies and I felt very good about the decision.

The DC-6 class was easy and I passed the final written exam with flying colors.

Interestingly enough, as we prepared for our oral and flight test, the instructor passed out some highly confidential study materials. He spoke in hushed tones. "These questions and answers are extremely sensitive; after you study them they must be returned to me personally. They have been used extensively by other airlines and will be very beneficial to you in preparing for your oral examination."

We were pretty excited to be receiving such high-level secret stuff. When I opened up the folder, to my surprise I saw...

The questions and answers that I had copied while lying in the air vents in the Continental hangar two years earlier!

On June 28th, I passed all tests and was a certified Western Airlines DC-6 second officer.

I was based in Los Angeles. The American captain who had previously rented an apartment to us had another apartment available, even closer to the beach at Playa del Rey, so I rented it immediately. I made arrangements to fly to High Point, get the car, drive to St. Louis, meet Diane and Cathy there, and the three of us would drive to Los Angeles and move in.

We moved in during the second week of July, and I awaited my first flight assignment from Western Airlines.

It came, but it was not what I expected. I had been transferred to Salt Lake City. The word on the street was that there was a delay in the awarding of the Hawaii route, so Western was readjusting their domestic schedule while they awaited Washington to settle the issues.

Quietly I mailed out another round of applications.

After the initial shock of being transferred to Salt Lake City, we considered everything and decided to make the best of it until I could be transferred back to Los Angeles. The new apartment was very nice. It was on the second floor overlooking the Pacific Ocean on Vista del Mar across the street from Playa del Rey beach. It was literally across the street, a few steps, from the beach. Diane loved the beach, and with her sister nearby, she was reasonably happy.

About half of the flight schedules from Salt Lake City had layovers in Los Angeles, so I could be home a lot of the time. On the long days off, I could commute.

I packed my suitcase, flew to Salt Lake City, and checked into a small motel near the airport. There was a used car advertised on the bulletin board at the motel, and I purchased it for sixty dollars. It was a 1951 Ford. It wasn't much but it was transportation.

And then I really learned about segregation.

I was looking for a small furnished room, driving around the outskirts of Salt Lake City looking for a for rent sign, when I noticed one in a nice neighborhood. It read, "FOR RENT, ONE BEDROOM APT. LDS ONLY."

This was a quiet area and it would suit me perfectly.

I knocked on the door and a nice-looking middle-aged woman appeared. "Yes?" she said.

"Ma'am," I said, "I saw your sign and I am interested in renting your room."

"What's your religion, young man?"

I thought that to be a funny question, but I answered, "My mother is a Seventh Day Adventist and my father is a Quaker."

Her eyes looked like saucers and she slammed the door, just inches in front of my nose, and I heard the door latch violently on the inside.

I went back to my flophouse motel and asked the desk clerk, "What is an LDS?"

He explained about the Mormon religion and that LDS meant "Latter Day Saint." Since I expected to be transferred soon, I settled down to live in the motel. There was a cheap six-stool bar and small restaurant, and it worked out fine.

I settled into the flying routine of the Salt Lake City base and quickly learned that the corporate attitude of Western was not the same as it was at Riddle or even at Continental. The attitude was "take it or leave it." There was no swapping of trips so that one pilot could take another's trip to give both more time on their scheduled days off, even in an emergency.

My flying was either to Minneapolis or Los Angeles, so with the usual three days off each week plus layovers in LAX, I was home a lot.

Diane was due at the end of September and I was eager to get back to Los Angeles. Earlier, when I was assigned to Salt Lake City, the chief pilot indicated that it would be temporary, so I expected a transfer at any time.

August came and went and still no transfer notice.

I asked for an appointment to visit the Western chief pilot in Salt Lake City. I explained that my wife was pregnant and was living in Los Angeles alone with a two-year-old baby. I requested that I be allowed to change flights with another Western pilot based in Salt Lake City, which would give me about seven days off around the time that she was to deliver.

His answer was a curt, "No!"

My attitude toward Western, and Salt Lake City, had soured somewhat and I had no idea what to do.

My sister-in-law, Roberta, came to the rescue. She invited Diane to stay with them during this critical time.

I was on reserve flight status and sitting in the motel in Salt Lake City when Roberta called. It was September 11th and they had just taken Diane to the hospital.

I was due to have three days off beginning at midnight. I was at the airport early the next morning to catch the first flight to Los Angeles.

Dick O'Mara was there to meet me; he rushed me to the hospital in time for the blessed event. Young Tommy was born on September 12th. He was healthy and Diane was all smiles.

On the 14th of September, I received a telegram from Civil Air Transport from Washington, D.C., asking me to call a Mr. G. Wilmer. I knew that Civil Air Transport was a front for Air America and was a CIA operation. I had run into some of their pilots in Bangkok. I folded the telegram neatly, put it in my pocket, and said nothing to anyone.

We brought Diane and Tommy home, and Roberta stayed with her until she was up and around. I was back and forth between Salt Lake City and Los Angeles as Diane regained her strength and was able to handle light housekeeping by herself.

And then, right on schedule, Western furloughed me. They didn't receive the Los Angeles to Hawaii route award.

The furlough was effective October 1st.

CHAPTER 42

Bound for Vientiane

With the CIA

I FINISHED MY FLIGHT RESPONSIBILITIES with Western through September 29th. I had three layovers in Los Angeles during that time, and by the end of the month, I had sold the Ford in Salt Lake City and moved back to Playa del Rey. I made all the calls to all the airlines that might be hiring, but to no avail.

All I had going for me was that telegram from Civil Air Transport hidden in my back pocket.

Wally Hunt and I had maintained our friendship through the Western months, and I had flown with him several times. He knew of the furlough and called me on Monday, October 1st, and asked me to meet him at the Santa Monica airport.

We met and he generously offered me a job with his company at a very substantial salary. The only caveat was that I would tear up my commercial pilot licenses and give up flying as a career. He outlined a career path to include formal business courses and an executive job with one of his companies.

"Flying is not a career," he explained, "it's a disease. You're still a young man, and you have plenty of time to change your career."

I was humbled that he would take such an interest in me. We talked a while. I thanked him profusely and said that I would let him know shortly.

It was a tough decision to make. I knew Wally was right. Here I was in Los Angeles, with two babies, and out of work although listed on three major airlines' seniority lists. It didn't make sense to continue flying. The practical thing to do was to accept Wally's offer, have a commercial pilot license "burning party," and get out of this crazy business.

On Wednesday, October 3rd, I succumbed to the disease and called Civil Air Transport and told them that I would take the job in Indochina.

The training would be in Taipei and the base was in Vientiane, Laos, about three hundred miles north of Bangkok. The base salary was twice what I was making at Western, with additional pay for hazardous flying. I would be flying as copilot on C-46s and C-47s, and I could count on upgrade to captain within a year. For each six months of flying, I could return to the U.S. for a one-month vacation.

My plan was to keep the apartment in Playa del Rey, send money home to Diane, build up a bank account, and wait until National recalled. I wasn't too sure whether I would accept a Continental recall, but I was sure that I would never fly for Western again.

I had not shared this with Diane. I couldn't get my nerve up. Tommy was three weeks old, Cathy was two years old, Diane and I had been married for three years, and here I was, leaving for Indochina for a six-month stay.

It was crazy.

On Saturday October 6th, I received my confirmation letter from Civil Air Transport, only the letterhead read, "Air Asia Company Limited."

It included a ticket on Pan Am for Tokyo, instructions as to whom I was to meet for transportation arrangements to Taipei, Formosa, passport stamps, and a fifty-dollar expense advance.

My Pan Am flight was scheduled to depart Los Angeles on Thursday the 11th, just five days hence.

It was Saturday and I had to tell Diane.

She didn't scream or yell. She just walked over to the window overlooking the Pacific and began to cry.

She cried for a long time. She cried until the sun sank into the Pacific and then, I think she gave up.

She washed her face and began working in the kitchen and taking care of the babies.

There was no further discussion concerning the job in Asia. She had resigned herself to taking care of the children while I "killed" myself in Indochina.

I think that was the lowest point of my life.

O'Mara came over Monday. Diane excused herself and walked the children down to the beach while Dick and I talked. I told him of the opportunities in Asia. He wasn't interested as he was heading back to Miami to wait until Continental recalled. We had lunch and a few beers and the afternoon newspaper came.

As was always my habit, I checked the classified section, "help wanted," just in case someone was hiring pilots.

And there it was…

"EASTERN AIRLINES, HIRING PILOTS." There was an address—a cheap motel in the hills near Los Angeles where applicants would show up, fill out an application, and be interviewed on the spot.

We were at the motel at exactly 9:00 Tuesday morning. There were some of the furloughed Western pilots there along with some of our old Continental classmates. My turn came for the interview. The interviewer was an "old time" captain for Eastern by the name of O. B. Bivens. He explained that Eastern was experiencing a flight engineer strike, and the airline was intent on converting from having flight engineers in the cockpit to the second officer program whereby the flight engineers were also pilots.

I gave him a short history of my career and that I was well aware of the flight engineer issue. We had, what I believed, was a meaningful interview, and he indicated that he would like to send me to Miami for a final meeting with the hiring personnel; if I passed, classes were set to begin the next Monday, October 15th.

I explained that I was headed for Formosa on Thursday, two days away, and that I didn't have time to fly to Miami and still make my scheduled flight from Los Angeles to Tokyo. For me to commit to Eastern, I would need to know immediately.

He understood but he indicated that he would have to clear it with Miami headquarters, which would take some time. We agreed that if it took more than one day, I would be on my way to Formosa. He said he would do all that he could.

Dick O'Mara had his interview next, and as we passed in the hallway, I briefed him on my conversations with Captain Bivens.

When he walked in, he said, "Whatever Cooper said goes for me." The interview was short, and Dick and I drove back to Playa del Rey with mixed emotions. We had no idea whether we would get hired or not.

Diane was going through the motions of caring for the children. That was a full-time job and, except for a few questions about the interview, she kept to herself.

I spent the morning of Wednesday October 10th packing for the Asian trip. Diane was as helpful as she could be, but the enthusiasm wasn't there. We had lunch, and the opportunity with Eastern was slipping away. My mind was set for leaving the next day when the phone rang.

CHAPTER 43
Saved by Eastern Airlines

CAPTAIN O. B. BIVENS WAS on the phone. "Cooper, Miami signed off on the deal, you're hired. Can you make the Monday class?"

"Yes, sir," I exclaimed. "How about O'Mara?"

"Him too," he affirmed. "Can you two come down to this motel and get your introduction letters for the class?"

"Yes, sir, I'll be there within the hour."

Captain Bivens met us with the letters of introduction to the director of training and the invite to the class beginning on Monday the 15th.

Back at the apartment in Playa del Rey, the packing took on a different atmosphere. I was unpacking for six months with the CIA in Indochina and packing for a month in Miami, for my dream job.

Diane would stay in the apartment until I completed Eastern's school, and upon assignment of a base, she would join me.

At 6:00 a.m. the next day, O'Mara and I were in the Chevy heading eastbound to Miami and Eastern Airlines. I had finally reached the goal that I had set for myself five years earlier when I left High Point, North Carolina.

That day a Pan Am flight took off from Los Angeles International Airport for Tokyo with an empty seat.

BROWN'S AIRPORT, 1957....HEAVEN!

JIM SINK AND I

The Man in The Arena...

FIRST PIPER CUB TO SOUTH AMERICA

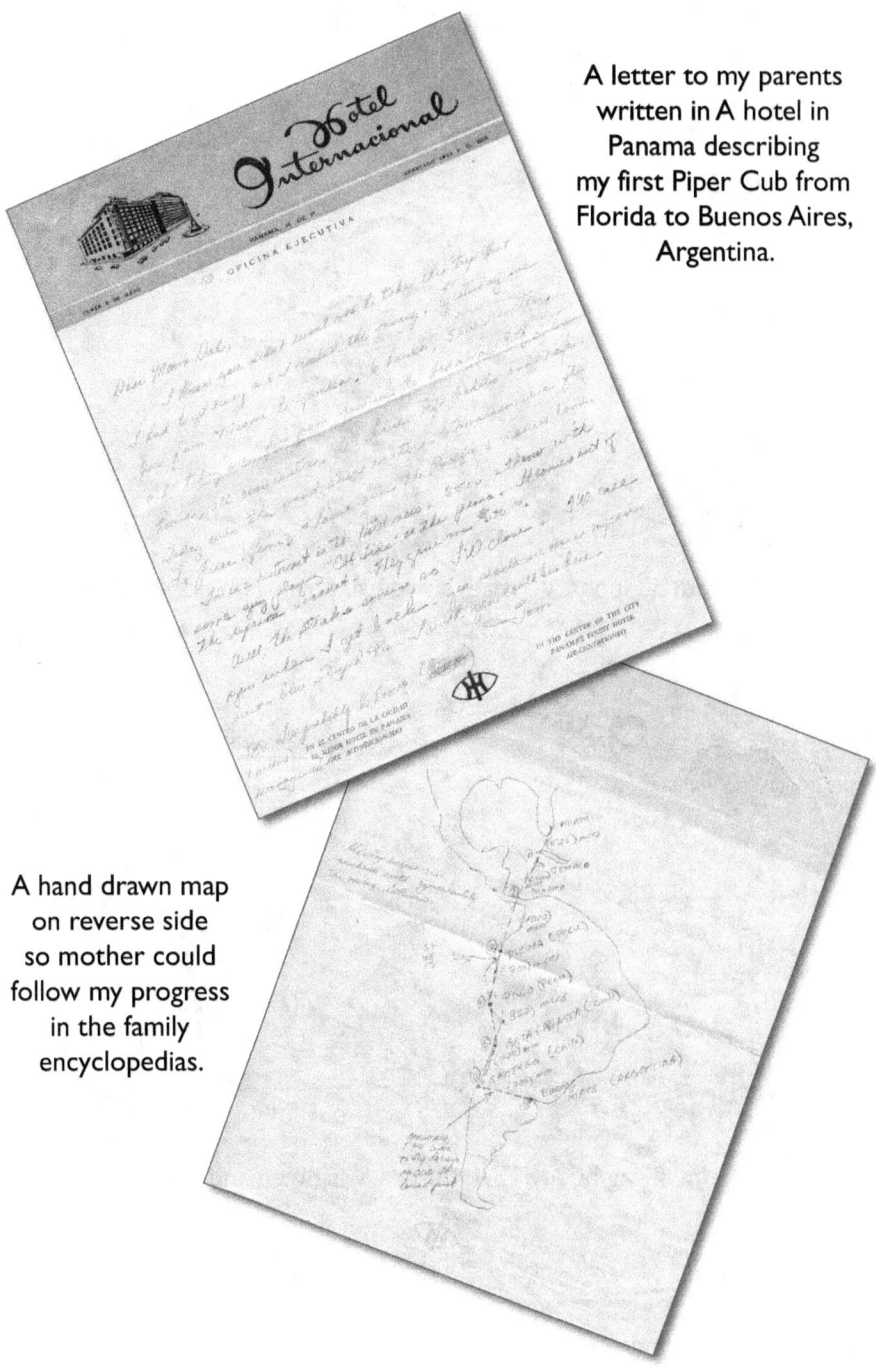

A letter to my parents written in A hotel in Panama describing my first Piper Cub from Florida to Buenos Aires, Argentina.

A hand drawn map on reverse side so mother could follow my progress in the family encyclopedias.

PREPARING FOR A FERRY TRIP TO SOUTH AMERICA

Me with a Piper Cub ready for departure to points south

My flying buddy, Dick Omara, wing man and pal.

PIPER CUB FROM LOCKHAVEN PA. TO BOGOTA, COLOMBIA

Skud running down the coast of Georgia

Over south coast of Cuba

Somewhere over the Carribean north of Colombia

ART IN THE US AIR FORCE

The ability to sketch brochures made me a favorite of the commanding officer, which gave me some time off for odd flying jobs.

USAF BROCHURES

TUCSON TO HAVANA (ALMOST)

Somewhere over Texas in a T-28

Arriving into Miami in a T-28. Proposed next stop…Havana

IN HAVANA WITH BOB JONES, 1958

Bob Jones and I at the Tropicana night club in Havana...1958

Tropicana Night Club in 1958. It looks the same today.

Havana 1958. Me and Jones by a street side artist.

Jones "teaching" my friend Al Burnett to play poker.

Preparing for a trip to Tokyo. Oakland, California

On the beach at Wake Island. It wasn't all bad,
flying for the "non-sked" airlines

UNOFFICIAL "WARS" WITH THE NON-SCHED AIRLINES

Visiting an "old friend," A P-51 in Managua

In support of some secret war somewhere in Central America.

"RIDING HIGH IN APRIL, SHOT DOWN IN MAY"

Flying a Boeing 707 across the U. S. one day and, furloughed, flying across the jungles of South America the next week.

THE END OF THE MAELSTROM

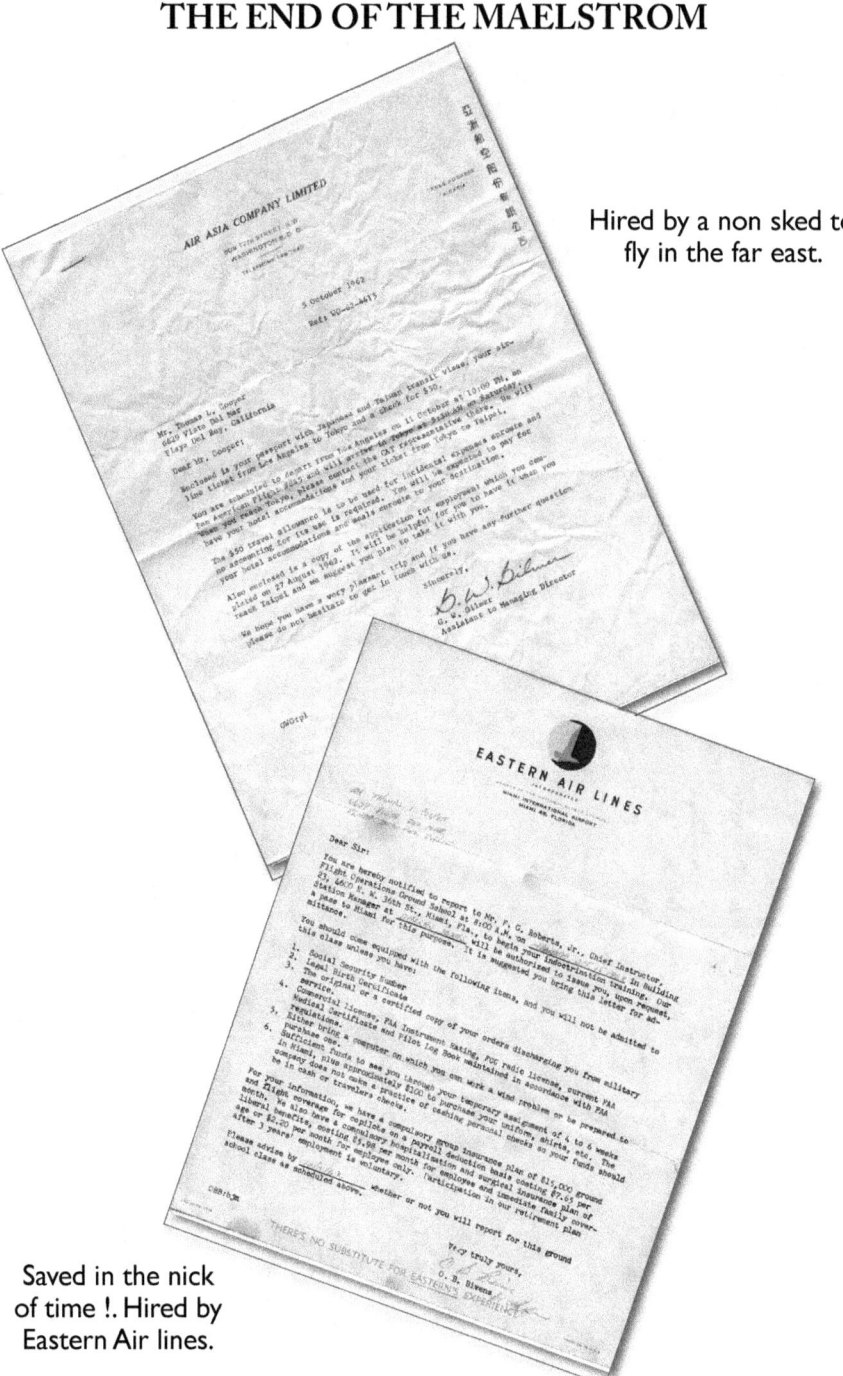

Hired by a non sked to fly in the far east.

Saved in the nick of time !. Hired by Eastern Air lines.

PART III
The Eastern Airline Years

Cruising

CHAPTER 44

Hello, Miami

Again!

OFF TO THE RIGHT I could see Lake Okeechobee on the horizon, and just west I could see U.S. Route 27 winding southward toward Miami.

Stephen chuckled over the intercom. "Hey, Cooper, I thought you were asleep."

"No," I replied, "you're such a smooth pilot that I'm just enjoying the flight."

"Good," he said. "We'll be there in about twenty minutes."

"Good," I replied.

Seeing the road to Miami brought back pleasant memories of that weekend in 1962 when Dick O'Mara and I drove from Los Angeles to Miami to accept a job with Eastern Airlines. We were upbeat as we left Los Angeles heading east toward Miami.

We planned to spend Thursday night with my old friend Bob Jones, in Las Vegas. He had stayed with Regina Airlines and checked out as captain. A run-in with the FAA caused him to resign, and he decided to become a professional gambler and move to Las Vegas.

We spent the night in Las Vegas with Bob and I wired the fifty-dollar advance back to Civil Air Transport and dropped the ticket to Tokyo in the mail to them also.

We were back on the road early for the twelve-hour drive to El Paso, where we visited some old Continental Airline friends. The plan was to spend the night with them and then drive straight through to Miami as money was short and we were in a hurry to get there to prepare for the ground school on Monday.

We pulled out of El Paso at six on Saturday morning for the thirty-hour drive to Miami. We made pretty good time crossing Texas. We crossed the Texas and Louisiana state border twelve hours later and headed toward Mississippi.

Night fell as we crossed Louisiana, and the country and western music on the radio that had entertained us as we drove across Texas was gradually being interrupted by news bulletins describing some sort of riots in Mississippi.

It seemed that a black man, an army veteran, James Meredith, had attempted to enroll in the University of Mississippi in Oxford, and was turned away. The radio reported that even though the U.S. Supreme Court had ruled that the university must admit black students, the Governor, Ross Barnett, had sent the state troopers to prevent that from happening.

I found that interesting as I remembered, back at University of North Carolina, black students enrolled during my stay there with no issues. Growing up in the middle south in a household where discrimination was never practiced, and with my father running a colored grocery store, I was never exposed to segregation. Dad never discussed the issue and Mom always taught me that all men were to be treated equally.

Dick and I discussed the news as we drove east, and I shared my segregation experience in Salt Lake City when the surprised woman, with saucer-like eyes, slammed the door in my face when she heard that I was raised as a Quaker AND a Seventh Day Adventist.

We had both seen segregation in the airlines. When we were hired by Continental Airlines, we were required to sign a release to the company that if the courts ruled in favor of a colored pilot who had been previously turned down by them, he would be inserted into the seniority list and we would agree to accept one seniority number higher. The rejected pilot would be given a hiring date as of the time of his rejection.

I had witnessed segregation in the Air Force also. At my base in Miami, where one of my jobs was creating the artwork for base brochures, I was astounded when I was given the following verbiage for a brochure welcoming new recruits. "There are no on-base swimming pools. This organization maintains contract facilities at two local hotels. The Miami Airways Hotel in Miami Springs and similar facilities for colored personnel at the Sir John

Hotel in Miami." The Miami Airways Hotel was only blocks away and the Sir John Hotel was near downtown Miami, miles away.

The segregation issue was beginning to boil, but that was not what was on our minds at this moment. We were only set on driving to Miami, passing the Eastern flight test, and commencing our career with the airline that we had worked to join for so long.

I was driving when we came to the bridge that spanned the Mississippi River connecting Louisiana with Mississippi. I mentally noted that we had crossed one more state, and there was only one more to go before we reached Florida.

I was halfway across the bridge when I noticed a commotion up ahead on the Mississippi side of the river. There were numerous flashing lights of red and blue, and when I cleared the bridge, I came upon a roadblock. I assumed that there had been an accident as the road was filled with Mississippi State Troopers.

I was waved over to the side of the road and forced to stop by a trooper. The next thing I knew, there was a very large shotgun resting on the windowsill about six inches from my chest and an enormous state trooper was glaring at me.

I kept both hands on the steering wheel and whispered to Dick, "Don't move or say anything."

"Where are you boys going?" he drawled.

I had a flashback of the same scene five years earlier in New Smyrna Beach, Florida, when Jim Sink and I were welcomed to Florida. The dialect was the same but the gun here was much larger.

"We're going to Miami, Florida," I said without moving my hands from the wheel.

"Let's see some evidence that you're going to Miami," he said in his thick southern twang. "You're not going to Oxford, are you?"

The gun was still on the windowsill, my hands were still on the steering wheel, and I answered, "I don't know where Oxford is, and we ARE going to Miami. We're airline pilots for Eastern Airlines, and if you move that gun we'll give you a letter to that effect," I offered, still not moving.

He slid the gun forward, still not moving it from the window, as I asked Dick, "Do you have the letter from Eastern handy?"

He did and we showed it to the trooper.

"I'm letting you boys go on through," he said, "but before you go I want you to sign this 'voluntary' petition to the President of the United States."

It read something to the effect of *"Dear President Kennedy, I, the undersigned, do hereby protest and object to the illegal invasion of Federal Troops into the sovereign and independent state of Mississippi."*

We couldn't sign it quick enough.

We weaved our way through the traffic jam as other travelers were "voluntarily" signing the petition and we hightailed it through Mississippi.

We found out later that Oxford was the location of the University of Mississippi and there had been a number of riots within the past week resulting in several deaths as a result of the integration problems at the school.

We continued eastward toward Florida and soon we were headed south to Miami. We arrived there around noon, checked into the Green Mansions Motel, went over to Ken's Lounge restaurant, just off the circle in Miami Springs, had lunch, and prepared for our first day at Eastern Airlines.

We felt as if we were conquering heroes as we returned to our "old stomping grounds" as Eastern pilots.

We checked in on Monday morning, October 15th, and were quickly enrolled in the indoctrination class that was to last for one week. We were issued ID cards, told how we were supposed to behave during our tenure at Eastern, and were educated on the culture, philosophy, history, and future of Eastern. The week went fast, and on Friday we got our aircraft class assignment for Monday.

Lockheed Constellation.

If the DC-7s were workhorse airplanes, the Constellations were sexy flying machines. The DC-7s were built around a tube fuselage with a standard tail at the rear. The wings were fastened mid-body with four engines mounted on them. It was made to do a job and it did it well. The Connie was constructed around a fuselage that was curved like an airfoil; it had three tails, and the four engines were fastened on the wings. Just parked at the ramp, it looked as if it could be flying. It did the same job as the DC-7 but it did it with grace and style.

To check out on the Connie meant that I would be assigned to New York and the newly established shuttle. It also meant that I was assigned to an aircraft that I had never flown before. The Connie, as it was affectionately known, was a complicated aircraft, and I knew that I had to rededicate myself to concentrate and study seriously. On my last three airlines, I was flying the DC-6 and the DC-7, both of which were familiar to me. The Connie was a different animal.

We started Connie class on Monday, October 22nd, and all went well until we got back to the motel and turned on the television.

Present Kennedy was to address the nation later that evening, and we were glued to the TV set as he spoke.

He announced that missile sites had been discovered in Cuba and he was establishing a blockade of Cuba; the United States would regard any missile launched from Cuba as if it were launched from the Soviet Union. Consequently, the U.S. would react with a full-retaliation response against the Soviet Union.

We looked at each other and shook our heads. Eastern Airlines had finally hired us, and after one week of ground school the whole world was about to blow up. We would probably be called up into the military, and there would go our jobs with Eastern. This called for some serious conversation.

We immediately walked across the street and had a few beers at Bryson's Bar.

We continued to study hard while keeping our eyes on the Cuban issue. The media was speculating on what was happening, and we could see convoys of trucks, military equipment, and troops heading south toward Homestead Air Base and Key West daily. This was not looking good.

As the week ended, rumors were that a U-2 had been shot down over Cuba, but there was no confirmation. The press was going crazy, and the world was preparing for war.

We studied as hard as we could under the circumstances that weekend. Monday came and we were back in school for the last week of Connie school.

Monday night the TV sets were ablaze with the news... Khrushchev had announced that the Soviets were removing all ICBMs from Cuba. Apparently, backdoor negotiations were successful, and the crisis was over.

Even though the Cuba crisis was over, we still had our jobs to think about. Flight training on the Connie was to begin in a couple of days.

Boyce Brown was our instructor. He had been a flight engineer, but with the corporate policy to change from the flight engineer system to the second officer system, he remained with the company as a pilot and a second officer instructor.

He was a wonderful instructor. He was patient, well informed, and set up a program that maximized our skills while working on issues that might be foreign to us.

Under Boyce's tutorship we flew through the engineer/flight-training portion of the course, and on November 23rd, Dick and I passed the flight test for flight engineer and pilot on the Lockheed Constellation.

We celebrated with a party at the Hitching Post, a barbeque joint in Hialeah, just across the bridge from Miami Springs, and the next morning we were in the Chevy Impala and on our way to New York City and the Shuttle.

CHAPTER 45
Flying The Shuttle

THE SHUTTLE WAS A STRANGE animal as airline ventures go. The program was established in 1961 between Washington, New York, and Boston with a flight scheduled every two hours. By the time I arrived on the scene in 1962, the flights had increased to hourly.

The idea was radical in so much as every passenger who showed up for a flight was guaranteed a seat. The establishment of standby crews and airplanes ensured this. If the original flight was filled and even one additional passenger showed up before departure time, Eastern would roll out another aircraft and fly that one passenger to his destination. Eastern's publicity department would, of course, alert the press, and we got thousands of dollars of free publicity when that event would occur.

While awaiting my first trip, I bunked in with O'Mara and his roommates as I looked for an apartment for Diane and the family. I returned to the neighborhood of Kew Gardens, where I had lived during my National days. It was handy to all public transportation to the three airports that we were expected to fly out of: Idlewild, LaGuardia, and Newark.

My first assignment was on December 4th, for a standby period.

The Shuttle didn't operate from the regular passenger terminal at LaGuardia Airport. It operated from an old maintenance hangar converted into the Shuttle terminal. Since the mode of payment for a ticket was cash on board the aircraft, there were only two counter spaces used for answering questions from the public. There was a small restaurant and the usual crowd tapes to separate the Boston passengers from the Washington passengers. The hangar terminal was cold in the winter and hot in the summer.

There was a loft area upstairs with offices that housed the administrative personnel and another rather large room that served as the standby facility. There were generally two or three standby flight crews lounging in that room at all times. In one corner, you might see a card game going on, in another someone would be reading, and there seemed to always be a flight attendant knitting. The rest of the standby crewmembers simply watched TV.

The missing person in this group usually was the second officer, the designated flight engineer. His duty was to determine which standby aircraft was assigned to his crew, find it on the ramp, and perform the preflight inspection in preparation for a possible over sale.

As I was to learn, this was not a fun job. The Connies on the shuttle were not the cleanest aircraft around. As a matter of fact, they were the dirtiest and oiliest that I had ever flown. They were workhorses, and didn't get the aesthetical attention that a normal line aircraft might get.

The preflight included a walk-around to check for damage, oil leaks, hydraulic leaks, etc. Then the fun began. The flight engineer would have to drag a heavy ladder, with a crook on the end designed to fit over the leading edge of the wings so that he could climb up and walk on the wing to check the fuel and oil quantity.

On a nice balmy, sunny day, this was not so difficult. But in the winter at LaGuardia Airport, with freezing snow and ice and the wind blowing like a hurricane, it was a different story.

With the information that the captain had given concerning the required fuel, equipped with a long fuel dipstick used to stick the tanks to ensure that the advertised fuel matched the actual fuel on board, a small notepad to record the fuel on board, wearing gloves, earmuffs, and a large overcoat for protection, the plight of the engineer balancing himself on an oily, slippery wing was somewhat less than that of the other crewmembers up in the warm crew lounge.

Once the fuel had been checked, the final act was to check the oil in each engine. That was a balancing act in itself. Each engine had its own oil reservoir located on the engine nacelle between the wing and the engine, just far enough ahead of the leading edge of the wing to make reaching it almost impossible. But not quite impossible. By straddling the nacelle, and extending oneself out forward of the wing, one could barely reach the oil cap, twist it off, determine that the oil quantity was adequate for the flight, and then replace the oil cap. All this and not slip and fall.

The Connie, like most other airliners of its time, consisted of thousands of parts all moving in close concert, causing wonderful things to happen internally which allowed us pilots to operate in a safe manner. Should one of these parts or systems or switches or valves fail to test properly before the flight then the pilot must contact the maintenance department, discuss the problem with the mechanic, and if it is determined that the problem is a safety of flight issue, then the flight must be cancelled.

This is not the case when operating on the Shuttle.

The flight is not cancelled. The captain is simply given another airplane that has just had a preflight accomplished by the standby engineer, loads his passengers on that airplane, and…off he happily flies, safely and on schedule.

The maintenance department then pulls up another airplane, and the lowly standby engineer drags the ladder out, climbs up on the wing of the new airplane, and performs his balancing act a second time.

I can remember doing four preflights in one standby period without flying a trip.

I was lucky on my first standby period. I performed the preflight on our assigned airplane and retired to the crew lounge to await a call to fly if necessary. It came at one o'clock. Captain Kinglsey assembled his crew, and I was soon off to Boston on my first Eastern Airline flight.

Flying on the Shuttle was easy duty, and working the standby shifts gave me plenty of time to apartment hunt.

I found a nice two-bedroom unit at the Curzon Apartments in Kew Gardens. I called Diane and on December 17th, she, Cathy and Tommy flew in.

It wasn't as nice as the place in California. There was no beach and no sister nearby, but it was all that we could afford, and there was a friendly park across the street with shopping handy.

I was pretty good at setting up an apartment by now. We turned on the water and electricity and hooked up the phone. We bought the necessities, including a TV and, in addition, one luxury item, a custom stroller for Tommy.

Crew scheduling was good to me and I had Christmas Eve and Christmas Day off. Santa came Christmas morning, and O'Mara and some of the other pilots stopped by for Christmas brunch.

The New Year began with great promise. The Eastern pilot position was my tenth airline pilot job change in three and a half years. Diane and I had been married for three years and had moved seven times; most moves were across the country. We had never lived together more than three months at any one location. This would be a new experience.

Eastern was hiring pilots every month, and it looked like this job would stick. Although living in Kew Gardens wasn't exactly what we had set our sights on three years earlier, we made the best of it. The neighborhood was nice, the neighbors were friendly, and with a park across the street, we settled in.

I had put in for a transfer to Miami, but as a first-year pilot, I didn't have bidding privileges, so there was nothing to do but to wait it out until my seniority merited a move after one-year of employment.

Life in New York became routine. I would drive to the airport for my daily assignment, either to stand by or to fly, and Diane would load up Tommy in his new pram and she and Cathy would go grocery shopping. That was her only recreation. Money was tight; Eastern was only paying copilots only $375 per month, and that didn't go very far. Ray Davidson, my old ferry pilot buddy, had resigned from North East Airline and joined Eastern. He and his wife, Evelyn, had moved to New York, and we visited them frequently.

It wasn't so bad for me as I got to suit up and fly airplanes three or four times a week. Working on the Shuttle was fun for me. When I went to the airport for a standby session, I never knew what to expect. I might sit all day, not fly, and return home as scheduled. On other days, I would get called out for an extra section and then my schedule would change depending on the needs of the airline.

Once a standby crew was called out, we could end up anywhere in the Shuttle system, including a possible overnight in either Washington or Boston. I was used to working with an irregular schedule, but after about six months I could tell that it was beginning to eat at Diane.

Although she came from an airline environment, her previous experience was with the scheduled end of Eastern Airlines. With few exceptions, such as weather or a mechanical issue, when she went on a trip she could reasonably count on returning within the time published on her assigned schedule. She was having a difficult time with the uncertainty of the Shuttle schedules.

The year, 1963, was slowly passing. I was flying and enjoying the job, but the cramped apartment, limited funds, and my irregular schedule were beginning to take their toll on Diane. Our nerves began to wear thin, and we blamed it on the physical layout of the small apartment. We discussed all the options, including staying where we were for several more years. We both agreed that that was not an option.

Several events were scheduled to take place that would allow us some flexibility.

First, in October I would complete my first year of service, which would give me bidding rights based on seniority, and since Eastern was hiring a number of pilots junior to me, I should be able to bid Miami around the end of the year. Second, I would get a pay raise of a hundred dollars per month beginning with my second year.

Ray Davidson, being slightly senior to me, had just been transferred to Miami, so my transfer should come quickly after my first year had been completed.

We discussed the possibility of a move to Miami in advance of the assumed successful bidding after October. We began to make plans for such a move. Diane perked up right away, and we began to look forward to one final move.

Diane needed a holiday, so she decided to go to Miami for a couple of weeks to scout out the area in anticipation of an eventual move there. She accepted an invitation from her old roommate, Fray Baldridge Bost, and soon she, Cathy, and Tommy were on an Eastern flight southbound.

Hardly a week had passed when Diane called with some good news. There was a very nice duplex for sale in Virginia Gardens, near where we had lived when I was with Riddle Airlines, and according to Diane, it would be ideal for us.

I swapped some trips with O'Mara and was in Miami the next day.

Diane was right, the duplex was perfect.

We had saved a few hundred dollars and with that and a few small loans from some friends, we scraped up enough money for the down payment.

Our credit was approved immediately by a local finance company, Lon Worth Crow, and before we knew it we were landholders and *landlords*.

Whether we were lucky or smart didn't matter. We owned property and our tenants were paying the mortgage payments.

The next issue was furniture.

One of the great things about working for Eastern Airlines in Miami at that time was credit. All you had to do was walk into the Eastern Credit Union and sign your name, and the world was yours.

Within two weeks Diane had the house furnished, including bunk beds for the children. All was made possible by a visit to the Eastern Airlines Credit Union and by the signing of my name.

I closed the apartment in Kew Gardens, packed all our belongings in the old Chevy, except Tommy's carriage, which I sold, and headed for Miami.

I was driving solo this time. No Jim Sink to talk to, no Dick O'Mara to talk flying with, and no Diane and the children to keep me company.

I stopped by High Point to visit Mom and Dad. They were ecstatic about the Eastern job and the new duplex. Dad "almost" promised to fly with me some day on an Eastern flight, a promise he was never to keep.

I left early the next day, with the traditional box lunch prepared by Mom, and headed down the same road that Jim Sink and I had traveled seven years earlier.

The drive to Miami was uneventful, unlike the trip seven years earlier when we had the run-in with the sheriff and the midnight judge in New Smyrna Beach.

In Vero Beach, I grabbed a quick nap at a truck stop and was soon on my way to Virginia Gardens. I arrived around noon to find that Diane, with Fray's help, had practically furnished the duplex and had moved in.

The Stouts came by to welcome us back to South Florida, and so did Bob Jones, who by now had given up his quest for riches at the expense of the casinos in Las Vegas. Carroll Kern, one of the instructors from Kendall Flying School, had gone to work for Eastern, and his wife, Phyllis, had moved into the neighborhood. It was like old homecoming in Miami Springs.

I grabbed a pass and flew back to New York to re-establish myself in the Kew Gardens neighborhood.

There was a notice pinned to the bulletin board in the standby ready room at LaGuardia, advertising furnished rooms in a private residence in Forrest Hills for ten dollars per week. That looked pretty good, and since I didn't relish the thought of sharing a two-bedroom apartment with four pilots, I hopped on the bus to visit it.

The house was located on a quiet residential street. It was large, two stories tall, and was situated on a very large lot surrounded by giant oak trees.

With my last experience in renting a furnished room in a private residence, back in Salt Lake City, still fresh in my mind, I rang the doorbell.

An elderly woman came to the door and offered her hand. "My name is Mrs. Wells," she said, "please come in." She explained that her husband had passed away earlier, and in order to keep the house, she had to rent rooms.

She had three floors: a basement, a first floor, and a second floor. She had a pretty good system. It worked on seniority, just like the airlines. She had finished the basement, and there were four cots aligned down there with one bathroom. That area was for the junior tenants. Up on the first floor were two private bedrooms, and on the second floor was the executive suite—two rooms consisting of a bedroom and a library that opened onto a sun deck shaded by the oak trees. As you gained seniority, you could move up to a more private area.

Mrs. Wells explained the rules of the house. No parties and no loud noises after 10:00 p.m. There was no cooking allowed; however, the kitchen could be used for coffee in the mornings. Rent was due weekly, in advance.

It was perfect.

I signed up immediately and she assigned a cot to me. I remembered that this was not too unlike my first day at the University of North Carolina in the basement of Cobb Dormitory.

I resumed my regular Shuttle schedule, and by swapping a few trips here and there, I managed to visit Diane and the children almost weekly.

The new facility was nice, and more than adequate. I enjoyed visiting with Mother Wells, as the other tenants called her, and we became quite good friends. Her husband had been associated with the tennis facility there at Forrest Hills, and when he died she just couldn't bear to leave the home and especially the area. Renting out to strangers wasn't her first choice, but she allowed that the airline pilots were all gentlemen and it was working out pretty well.

The only issue was that the public transportation was less than desired, especially with winter just around the corner. Fate stepped in and solved that problem quite nicely.

CHAPTER 46

Adventures on Shuttle Standby

ONE OF THE VICES THAT I had developed during my non-sked flying days was enjoying the social aspect of the gambling game of poker.

Out of boredom, as we waited in the standby ready room in LaGuardia, some of the pilots would engage in the "sport." Few of us had any extra money to lose, so the stakes were always low, usually a quarter ante and half pot limit. Some of the pilots were avid poker players; some would play once in a while, while others just refused to play at all. I fell into that middle category. I could take it or leave it. And since I was still struggling financially, I didn't have a lot of money to gamble.

The weather was beginning to turn cold at LaGuardia, and I had just finished the preflight on my assigned Connie. I rushed upstairs to get warm and was immediately hustled into a poker game. I had six more hours of standby duty and the passenger traffic downstairs looked light, indicating that our crew would probably not fly today. I agreed to sit in for a while.

The poker group usually set up a table in the far corner of the room away from the TV set. Someone had borrowed a round banquet table from a nearby supply room, and another borrowed a blanket from one of the Connies. We had a perfect poker table that could seat six players, with Eastern's proud golden eagle logo in the center.

The game was always seven-card stud. The dealer would deal two cards down and one card up. The player with the highest card showing would lead off the betting, and the other players, clockwise, would either fold, call, or raise. Then the fourth card was dealt up, and the betting would continue as before. A fifth card would be dealt up, and betting would continue. A sixth card would be dealt up, with betting continuing, and the seventh card would be dealt down. After the last card was dealt, the remaining players would have four cards showing and three cards down. The final round of betting began with the player with the highest hand showing leading off. The player with the best five cards wins the pot. Often, if a player had four high cards showing, he might bet the limit, hoping that his bluff might cause the other remaining players to fold. He would then win without showing his hole cards. Bluffing was a big part of this game.

As was the usual case, Lady Luck moved around the table without landing on anyone's lap, as the Sinatra song goes. The winning hands moved around the table with no one really showed any signs of a break-the-bank session. It was turning into a routine game, but it was a good way to pass the day.

I had started with fifty dollars and after a couple of hours was up to seventy. A couple of guys had dropped out and were replaced by two other fresh players. One of the new guys suggested that we raise the ante to a dollar. "Since I have been transferred to Atlanta next week, this will be the last time you guys will have a chance to clean me out."

The dollar ante was pretty steep, but after some discussion, we all agreed to the increase. It was getting late and I had made up my mind to contribute only my winnings and quit should my luck turn sour. Another hour went by and we were just exchanging money. No one was gaining on the other players.

And then it happened.

I was dealt a nine of hearts card up, and when I looked at my two down cards, they were also nines. I had three nines.

Now in poker, the catch is, if you are dealt good cards down, you should not let it show in your facial expression—thus the term "poker face." So far, I had a winning hand, but if I raised the bet it would be a dead giveaway. Someone across the table had a king up and bet half the pot, three dollars. I just called, two others called, leaving four of us in the game.

The fourth card didn't help anyone. I was dealt a four of clubs, and the betting slowed down. The guy with the king bet five dollars and everyone called.

The chatter around the table had quieted down considerably. The fifth card was dealt, and a player across the table showed a pair of eights. I showed a pair of fours. That gave me a well-hidden full house, three nines and a pair of fours, almost a sure winner. My mission now was to maximize the pot without running the other players out of this hand.

The pair of eights bet ten dollars, and the other two players folded, leaving just me, with a pair of fours showing, and the bettor, with a pair of eights showing.

I'd better be careful here, I thought. *He could have a pair of eights in the hole, giving him four of a kind.*

"I'll call," I said, after some deliberation. I wasn't that sure of my full house now.

The sixth card came and it didn't help me. Across the table he was showing two pairs; eights and deuces.

He, with much ceremony, counted the pot and bet the maximum, twenty-seven dollars.

I pondered. *If he has four eights, he wins; if he only has a full house, I win.* We still had one more card to go.

The whole room was quiet now. We had an audience, the TV was turned down, and even the flight attendant who was knitting was now watching the action at the poker table.

"I call." The pot was now over a hundred dollars.

The seventh and last card was dealt down. I carefully raised the corner of the card so as to keep it hidden from the gathering crowd.

It was another nine. I had four nines, and even if he had four eights…I'd win.

"Eights bet," the dealer said.

From his actions, I knew that he had four eights, and I wanted him to bet the maximum, but I saw that he was all in. He had no more cash to bet.

"I'll bet half the pot," he said, "but you'll have to take my IOU in the pot."

The room was absolutely silent.

"I don't think that I can do that, what with you leaving for Atlanta in two days. Don't you have anything of value—a watch, or something to bet?" I jokingly suggested. "After all, I'm probably going to call you with cash."

"Okay," he said, confidently, "here's what I can do. I have an airport car that I'm going to sell before I leave New York. It's a 1958 Plymouth and it's worth about a hundred and fifty dollars. I have the title right here in my flight kit."

He reached into his bag and produced a car title. I looked at it and motioned for him to throw it in the pot. He did, announcing, "I'm betting half the pot, fifty-four dollars, which makes me heavy in the pot for about a hundred dollars."

He looked at me to see if I would call.

I hesitated for a few seconds and said, "I'll see your fifty-four dollars and raise you the hundred you have in the pot."

He still didn't get it. There was no way he could beat me even with four eights, but he was blinded by his hand. He never considered that I might have four nines.

"I call," he exclaimed triumphantly. He flipped over his four eights and reached for the pot.

I grabbed his wrist. "Not so fast," I said as I flipped over my four nines.

I raked in the pot along with the car title and calmly asked, "Where are the keys and where did you park MY car?"

All of the Miami pilots were anxious to transfer just as soon as their probation year was up. October came and went and no transfer. The word was that some of the new hires were taking longer to qualify on the Connie, thus delaying our move to Miami. We patiently waited. O'Mara and I would swap trips allowing me to spend more time in Miami, and Diane, Cathy, and I celebrated Tommy's first birthday in Virginia Gardens.

I was in New York on Friday, November 22nd, when the news broke. The first bulletins said that there had been an attempt on the life of President Kennedy in Dallas. When the first word came out, everyone rushed to their TV sets to follow the events. I can remember Walter Cronkite, removing his glasses, trying hard to control his emotions, telling the world that the President had died.

Dick O'Mara and I had dinner that night in a small local restaurant. We were, like everyone else, filled with grief, disbelief, and sorrow for the family and for the country. Dick, being Catholic, was especially distraught and expressed his desire to show his respects by traveling to Washington some time during the next several days to attend the State Funeral.

Being off duty, we agreed to fly down to Washington on Sunday and return on the same day.

We caught the mid-morning Shuttle and arrived at Washington around noon. According to a schedule of events listed in the newspaper, the President's body would be placed in the East Room of the White House on Saturday and moved to the Capitol building to lie in state on Sunday.

We caught a bus and positioned ourselves on Pennsylvania Avenue about midpoint between the White House and the Capitol. The dismal weather of the previous day had improved, and the sun shone brightly as the temperature warmed somewhat.

We waited as the crowd swelled. It was eerily quiet. Thousands of people lined the avenue, and not a sound could be heard.

And then we saw some activity down the avenue toward the White House. The procession had begun to move the President's body to the rotunda of the Capitol building.

The first thing that I saw was the horse-drawn, flag-draped caisson bearing the President's body. Just behind the casket was "Black Jack," a riderless horse representing a fallen warrior; the President's boots were affixed in the stirrups with the toes facing backward.

There were no sounds other than the clacking of Black Jack's hooves and the soft beat of the muffled drums.

It was a scene that remains, to this day, indelibly etched in my memory.

The procession disappeared toward the Capitol. Dick and I looked at each other, said nothing, and headed back to the airport.

There was nothing to say.

On the way to the airport, we heard the report that the accused assassin, Oswald, had been shot and killed in Dallas.

That Dallas was a tough place.

Back in New York I returned to my Shuttle routine. It was mid-December when I received word that my bid for Miami had been honored, and effective January 1, 1964, I would be officially based in Miami.

That was the good news. The bad news was that I must continue to fly out of New York for a few months to cover for some open flying due to expanded schedules. That wasn't too bad, as operating TDY (temporary duty), I received expenses during the time that I was in New York. Additionally, my seniority was improving at Mother Well's boardinghouse, and I had moved into one of the private bedrooms.

Christmas and New Year's came and went, and I welcomed 1964 with great anticipation. Eastern had hired about a hundred pilots, junior to me, and the job looked secure. I had my own bedroom in Forrest Hills, and my "new" car was doing just fine. Diane was happy in Virginia Gardens with the children and her friends, and I got to spend two or three days a week there. The extra expense money came in handy also.

After flying the Connie for over a year, I had fallen in love with her. The Lockheed Constellation, although extremely complex system-wise, was an easy airplane to fly. She was a big, lovable Piper Cub and I looked forward to flying her.

Somebody once said, "If you love your job, you'll never work a day in your life." So true. Flying for Eastern Airlines was like being on holiday, and I looked forward to suiting up and going to work for every assignment.

That wasn't the case with all of the pilots. There were a few who loved to complain. I tried to distance myself from those pilots. To me, Eastern had saved my life. The airline had removed me from the non-skeds, from flying Piper Cubs over the jungles and through the mountains of South America, and, just in time, saved me from going to Vientiane, Laos, and certain disaster. When I heard the complainers complain about the airline, I would surmise that their road to Eastern wasn't as tough as mine or they would appreciate their job more.

And Eastern didn't tolerate chronic complainers either.

I was copilot on a particular scheduled Shuttle flight to Boston. The captain was a local New Yorker who had grown up there, flown in the military, and returned to fly with Eastern, to settle in the area and raise his family.

The second officer, a new hire in his first month, was from Atlanta. He had gone to a flight school, got his ratings quickly, and was hired with very little experience.

The takeoff was uneventful and once we got to cruise, as was customary, the crew might pass the time of day with some idle conversation. We weren't five minutes into the relaxed period when the good ole boy from Atlanta proclaimed, in his best southern drawl, "I'll fly out of New York, but I'm not gonna bring my wife and family up here. I'm not letting my kids go to school with these hoodlums up here."

Oh boy, I thought, *he's just broken the first rule for first-year pilots still on probation. Keep your ears open and your mouth shut.*

I glanced at the captain, who was staring straight ahead. I noted his jaw was clenched and his neck had begun to turn a bit red. He said nothing and neither he nor I encouraged further conversation from our friend in the backseat.

We had a quick turn in Boston for the return trip, and as I was assembling the documents and weather reports for the return flight, I noticed the captain on the company phone. He was emphatic with his gestures, punching his finger at an imaginary target. From what I could hear, it was a one-way conversation with no area for the person on the other end to negotiate.

Nothing was said on the return trip, and upon landing, after deplaning the passengers, we were met by the manager of the Shuttle operation. He met the new hire, took his wings and hat badge, and escorted him through the terminal as far as the front door and formally dismissed him.

I'm not sure that Eastern even gave him a pass back to Atlanta.

Winter was grudgingly giving way to spring, and Mrs. Wells moved me into the executive suite with the library. I welcomed spring from the sun deck, and with the comfort of the security of the job with Eastern, my life was easy.

CHAPTER 47
A Visit by The Easter Bunny...

Really!

It was Easter morning and I had arrived back in Miami the previous day from New York. Diane was dressing Cathy for church. We were still living on limited funds, so an Easter outfit for Cathy wasn't in our budget. Diane had dressed Cathy in her best and brightest dress and put a few colorful ribbons in her hair for the Easter service. As they were about to leave, there was a loud commotion in our front yard.

A car pulled up with the horn blowing. Out jumped a crazy man with an armful of boxes.

"I'm the Easter Bunny," he said, laughing loudly as he came bursting through the front door.

It was Bob Jones.

He had bought Cathy a complete Easter outfit: white patent leather shoes, pink socks with ruffles, a beautiful dress, and to top it all off...an exquisite Easter bonnet.

I'll never know why he did it or how he came upon the outfit. He was worse off financially than we were, and he had a family to support. I do know that there was one happy little girl at the Catholic Church in Virginia Gardens that morning...

And the prettiest.

Do I believe in the Easter bunny? Of course I do...I saw him...*once upon a time.*

CHAPTER 48
Good-Bye, New York City

Hello, Douglas DC-7

I WAS STILL REQUIRED TO fly out of New York in the spring but less and less frequently. I did, however, keep my suite in Forrest Hills, and the car made commuting easier. Eastern was converting their fleet from piston aircraft to turbo prop and pure jet aircraft. The Connies were still the workhorses of the Shuttle, and, with the new hires showing up in New York in numbers, I was finally assigned to the base in Miami. I was assigned to DC-7 school in July.

I said a tearful good-bye to Mrs. Wells, and a gleeful good-bye to New York City. I sold the car and left for Miami.

The ground school portion of the DC-7 course was a snap, and the flight training was fun. My instructor was J. J. Randall—a legend at Eastern, being one of the more senior pilots there.

Once he realized that I had some experience on the DC-7, he began to have some fun with me. We had finished all the prerequisite drills and flying tests, and after a particularly nice performance of an engine-out procedure, he laughed and asked, as we rolled out after landing on three engines, "What would you have done if you had lost two engines?"

I laughed and replied, "Try me and see."

We were both having fun now. We taxied back for another takeoff and roared down the runway, 27 left. I rotated and pulled the aircraft off the ground. We began to climb and I asked for gear up. I felt the thump of the wheels as they nestled in the wheel wells, and that's when Captain Randall cut the number four engine. (In training, the instructor doesn't actually kill an engine; he just retards the throttle to simulate an engine failure.)

I continued to fly the airplane, asked for the proper checklist to be accomplished, and requested the copilot to call the tower and get landing permission.

And then he cut the number three engine. I continued to fly the airplane, give the proper commands, fly the traffic pattern without deviation or missing a call out and turn final approach on two engines. I crossed the "fence", chopped the power on the two remaining engines and made a perfect landing.

Captain Randall laughed, slapped me on the back, and said, "Cooper, you're the only pilot I know that can perform a two-engine-out procedure, make a PA announcement, and drink a cup of coffee, all at the same time."

With my past experience the DC-7 was as comfortable as slipping on a pair of well-worn slippers. Captain Randall signed me off as a first/second officer. I was officially based in Miami and eagerly awaited my first flight assignment.

CHAPTER 49
Bob Jones and Jack Shaw

Entrepreneurs extraordinaire

EASTERN WAS TRANSITIONING FROM PISTON-POWERED aircraft to propjets and pure jets. The propjet-powered Electra was introduced in 1959 followed by the pure jet, the Douglas DC-8 in 1960, and the Boeing 720 in 1961. The last home for the pistons, the DC-7s, and the Connies was the Shuttle, and they would be retired in the mid-sixties.

Consequently, there was very little piston flying out of Miami. After checking out on the DC-7, I was placed on reserve, and for the rest of the year, I flew very little. I was averaging flying about once a month, and hanging around the house all the time began to get tedious.

My old buddy Bob Jones had started a flight school at Opa Locka, a private airport just north of Miami, and he was expanding. How he did this, with no funds what so ever, was nothing short of a miracle. It was a testimonial to his entrepreneurial spirit and, mainly, his salesmanship.

Jones' story began with a chance meeting with a fellow named Al McCurdy. McCurdy, of questionable reputation, ran a small pilot ground school in a local shopping center nearby. His specialty was preparing students for their written pilot exams. He had a reputation for having all the correct answers.

Jones had just returned to Miami from Las Vegas and was figuring out what to do next. He would stop by McCurdy's office from time to time, as McCurdy always knew what the pulse was in the aviation community around Miami.

On one such time, an unsuspecting prospective student wandered in to inquire about flight training. The student had just arrived from England and was quite naive. When it became apparent that the student was prepared to pay in advance for his flight training, both Bob's and McCurdy's interest tweaked.

McCurdy couldn't relieve the student of any money until he had progressed along in flight training to where he needed to pass the written exams. But Bob seized the opportunity and announced to the prospective student that he, Bob Jones, owned a flight school. He explained that it was a small, private tutor type of school and he just happened to have an opening. He allowed that he was busy for the next two days, but if the student would give him his phone number, Jones would call him and set up an appointment.

The student took the bait.

Jones rushed over to Miami Springs, where he quickly rented a small two-room office. Then he ran over to a Hialeah used office furniture company and purchased a few beat-up office desks and some classroom chairs. He finished off his purchases there with a blackboard, some waste cans, and a lamp. Then he was off to a souvenir shop at Pan Am World Airways for some model airplanes and a few posters.

By the next afternoon a local sign painter had logoed and lettered the door and voila!

"GREAT CIRCLE AVIATION" was born.

Bob scattered a few old dog-eared flying magazines around, placed a non-working phone on his desk for appearance's sake, and he was open for business.

The student came in the next day, right on time. Bob enrolled him, relieved him of two thousand dollars as down payment, and set him up for basic ground school.

Now, Bob was no dummy. He was an accomplished aviator and he knew his business when it came to flying. He began teaching the student all the necessary subjects in preparation for his flight training. Only one thing was missing.

An airplane.

Two weeks passed and the student began to question when he would begin to fly. Jones would calm him down, give him more homework, and try to figure out what to do next.

There was an Aeronca Champ airplane, similar to a Piper Cub, available in Waco, Texas. The good news was the price was right, only $2,500. The bad news was, Jones didn't have the $2,500.

Only Jones could pull this off. He explained to the student that it was time to place three thousand dollars in additional funds in advance as the ground school training had eaten up most of his initial deposit. Once that was in place, the flight portion of the course would begin.

The student bit again.

With the three thousand dollars in pocket, Jones purchased two bus tickets to Waco, Texas, and announced to the student that the flight training portion was about to begin…in Waco, with a cross-country training flight to Miami.

When the student protested mildly that he thought he was supposed to learn to take off and land before doing any cross-country training, Jones explained it this way. "You must know how to navigate before you begin to do your solo takeoffs and landings just in case you accidently stray from the traffic pattern."

Only Jones could pull this off.

Before leaving for Waco he rented a small office at Opa Locka Airport, called the sign painter, bought a used desk and a few chairs, and…voila once again!

GREAT CIRCLE AVIATION
Flight Training Division

The trip out and back went well; the student was the only pilot in the world with twenty hours of cross-country training before he had made his first takeoff and landing.

And that's how Great Circle Aviation began. Bob continued to grow the school. McCurdy had built a reputation with his ground school, and he sent Bob a number of flight students. The airlines were beginning to hire pilots as the old World War II pilots were retiring, and the flight school business was about to take off.

I was bored with sitting home, day after day, waiting on Eastern to call me for a DC-7 trip and so it was only natural that I begin to instruct, part time, for Bob.

I began to spend more and more time at the flight school at Opa Locka Airport. The time that I spent flight training was boring, but I could use the extra cash. What really began to arouse my interest was the business end of the school.

I watched Bob Jones, a super salesman, as he would sell a full flight course to a new student. The parents would write a check for five or six thousand dollars, hand it over to Jones without thinking twice, and the young aviator would begin his career the next day. I saw this happen over and over again. I never questioned the accounting end of the business as there always seemed to be plenty of money and Bob never missed a payroll. I was so confident in the future of the company that I even cosigned a note for one new airplane as his fleet grew.

As the school expanded, Bob would take some time off and leave me in charge of the office. Often, I would interview a prospective student, sign him up, and collect the deposit for the advance payment for the course.

I began to spend all of my spare time at Great Circle Aviation, and I would take my uniform to the school in case Eastern called me for a trip. My continued absence from home was becoming a touchy subject. Diane was becoming more and more annoyed with me for spending so much time at Opa Locka Airport.

As 1964 came to an end, I had celebrated my second full year of employment with Eastern, and with several hundred pilots beneath me on the seniority list, I was feeling very comfortable. Eastern was in its transition period from piston aircraft to jets and with very few DC-7s flying out of Miami, and while I awaited my assignment to jet school, I had very little flying assigned to me.

CHAPTER 50
Soloing a Lockheed Constellation

And other Jack Shaw adventures

SPRING OF 1965 CAME AND my status at Eastern remained the same; I was on reserve, they were paying me to stand by, and I was only flying about one trip per month. I was watching the store for Bob Jones at the flight school when a gentleman came in and introduced himself. "I'm Jack Shaw and I heard there's someone around here who can fly a Connie."

"That's me," I answered. "What can I help you with?"

Jack explained that he was starting a cargo airline out of Panama and needed to hire some pilots. I explained that I was employed by Eastern Airlines and would be unable to help him, but that I would keep my eyes open for anyone qualified on the Lockheed Constellation who might be looking for work.

He came by several more times over the next week, and before long we became good friends. His interest in starting an airline stemmed from a friend in Canada who was quite successful in the airline cargo business. So Jack decided that he would venture into the cargo business in a different location. His recent business had been running a bingo hall in Canada where he accumulated some startup money. He had moved down from Canada with his wife and three boys along with his brother and had moved into a house in Miami Springs, six blocks from our duplex.

As he was putting his airline together, we would visit and our families became quite friendly with each other. Jack kept me updated on his progress, and I became fascinated with his drive and enthusiasm for the industry, especially since he had no previous experience.

Jack was a lot like Bob Jones—short on capital but long on salesmanship. He had made a contact in Miami Springs who guaranteed him a load once a week between Panama and an airport in Colombia, South America. With that guarantee in hand, he flew out to Los Angeles and leased a Lockheed 749 Constellation from Allen Paulson, the founder of Gulfstream Aerospace. He managed to scrape up a crew at Santa Monica Airport and ferry the aircraft down to San Jose, Costa Rica, to a maintenance base called COPESA that specialized in maintaining large aircraft. The aircraft had been mothballed for several years and needed some minor work.

Back in Miami, I introduced Jack to Alfred McCurdy, the local ground school operator, who set him up with an out-of-work former Lufthansa pilot who claimed to have a copilot and flight engineer available. They would all meet down in San Jose and fly the aircraft to Panama to set up the flight operations when the maintenance was complete.

The maintenance director for COPESA called Jack and reported that all maintenance had been accomplished, Paulson had paid the bill as previously arranged, and the airplane was ready to be picked up. That's when Jack's problems began. He couldn't find the captain, and the first cargo flight was scheduled in a week.

A day went by and still the captain could not be found. Jack checked with McCurdy, who said that he thought the captain had gone on a trip and was due back in a couple of days.

It was midway through the next day when Jack heard from the captain. He was in Panama, with the copilot, and would meet Jack in San Jose the next day. He asked Jack to find the flight engineer in Miami and send him to meet the crew in San Jose. The flight engineer was nowhere to be found, so Jack came to my house.

He pleaded for me to fly down to San Jose to fly as engineer from San Jose to Panama. It would only be a short trip as Jack's brother, Danny, was to round up the missing engineer and send him to Panama to begin the cargo service.

I declined, using Eastern as an excuse, but Jack would not take no for an answer.

Finally, I agreed to go if I could get a few days off my Eastern flight schedule. I swapped some days off with another DC-7 pilot, got a pass on the local

Costa Rican airline, and met Jack the next morning at Miami Airport for the trip to San Jose.

The whole scene was a disaster from the beginning. The trip down was uneventful, but on arriving in San Jose, Jack said, "By the way, Cooper, did you bring any money?"

"Not really," I said, "I only have two or three dollars. I thought you had the expense money."

"No," he said. "Danny was supposed to meet me at the Miami Airport with some money, but he didn't show up in time. But, he added cheerfully, "I have about three dollars, so between us we have five dollars, and when the captain arrives later today, he'll surely have some money."

I was beginning to learn that Jack was the eternal optimist.

We decided to stay at the airport and wait for the captain to arrive from Panama. His flight was due to arrive at four o'clock in the afternoon.

We met the flight and…no captain.

Jack called his brother, collect, in Miami, who located the captain in Panama, heard all the excuses as to why he didn't show up that afternoon, and swore to be on the next day's flight.

Jack was operating an airline from a pay phone in a foreign country with no money. We had no recourse but to split a sandwich between us, buy two Cokes, and dine in the cockpit of the old Connie. Not only was it to be our restaurant, it was to be our motel room also. Fortunately, the airplane had been a passenger airplane just before Jack had leased it, and although the seats were removed, the curtains were still installed. We ripped a few curtains off the window tracks, made a couple of pallets, and bedded down for the night.

Morning came, and we conducted our toiletries in the terminal restroom, enjoyed some kind of a Spanish pastry with coffee, and settled down to wait for the captain.

There were three flights from Panama, and the captain was on none of them!

Finally, just before dark, the captain confided to Danny in Miami who relayed to Jack in San Jose that he would not be meeting us in Costa Rica. It seems that he and the copilot had gotten into trouble, and there was an issue with the local immigration people. Jack would have to find another crew to fly the airplane to Panama.

I was running out of time, we were running out of money for food, and neither of us had any idea what to do.

Except Jack, the eternal optimist.

"Cooper," he said, as we readied ourselves for another night in the Connie, "you're always telling me what an ace you are, so why don't you just solo the old Connie down to Panama in the morning?"

"Are you crazy?" I exclaimed. "You're not even a pilot, and besides, this airplane requires a three-man crew and, on top of that, I don't think anyone has ever soloed one, so count me out."

As we bedded down on the pallets on the floor in the cold, damp cabin of the Connie, our five dollars was stretched as far as possible, and I began to think. Could one person fly the Connie? I wondered. I had flown the Lockheed Constellation for about two years in New York, and the procedures and systems were still fresh in my mind. All the controls for the engines were back at the engineer's seat, but the prop controls and the throttles were duplicated up front between the captain and copilot's seats.

It might be just possible, I thought, but I quickly discounted the stupid idea and fell asleep.

Jack, the eternal optimist, continued to think that night.

He woke me up at daybreak with "Cooper, I'll give you five hundred dollars to fly this airplane to Panama today."

I'm not sure if it was the money or the challenge, but I agreed.

"Okay, Jack, here's the deal," I explained. "I don't want anyone from COPESA to see this airplane taxi out with only one pilot, so you wait outside until I start the engines, then you pull the wheel chocks and climb up the ladder through the crew door, pull the ladder in after you, and we'll taxi out. You can sit in the copilot's seat, but don't touch anything or say anything," I added. "I'll be too busy to chat."

I went into the Civil Aeronautics office and checked the weather in Panama. It was forecasted to be good, although there was some morning fog there now. I filed a flight plan to depart in one hour and returned to the airplane.

I crawled out on the wings to do a preflight. My mind wandered back to LaGuardia Airport in New York City as I climbed out on the engine nacelles to check the oil. The fuel and oil were sufficient for the short seventy-five-minute flight, the weather was good, and I was ready to go.

I climbed into the captain's seat, went over the checklist, set the parking brakes, and moved back to the flight engineer's seat, which was just behind the copilot's seat, facing the right side of the cockpit and appreciably lower, thus the nickname "the hole."

I shouted out the open door to Jack, "I'm about to start the engines. Stand in front of the airplane until I get all four running; then I'll give you a signal from the captain's window to pull the chocks. Be careful of the propellers, climb in, pull the ladder in after you, and close the door."

The engines started easily enough, with the number three giving a little bit of trouble. After starting all the engines, I moved to the captain's seat, opened the window, and shouted to Jack, "Pull the chocks and be careful."

Soon Jack was on board, the door was closed, and I was ready to taxi.

I called the tower for taxi instructions and taxied from COPESA toward the active runway. So far, so good.

I reached the end of the runway. I taxied far to the side of the taxiway for the preflight engine and systems check. To do this I had to set the parking brakes and move from the captain's seat to the flight engineer's seat, where all of the engine instruments and switches were located. I had a duplicate set of throttles and prop controls up front, but the rest of the levers and switches were located only at the flight engineer's position in the hole.

Back at the engineer's seat, I eased the RPM of each engine up individually to check the magnetos and prop controls while watching over my shoulder to ensure that the brakes were holding and that the aircraft wasn't creeping. All four engines checked out, and the gauges looked okay. Now the fun would begin.

The takeoff would be the tricky part. During the takeoff roll and climbout, the flight engineer is required to monitor the oil and cylinder head temperature. He does that by constantly adjusting the oil cooler doors and the cowl flaps. Today there would be no one back there in the hole to monitor and adjust those oil cooler doors and cowl flaps.

I had thought about this and surmised, based on my experience as a flight engineer after hundreds of takeoffs, that if I adjusted each of the four oil cooler doors and cowl flaps to 50 percent open position before takeoff, and if I reduced the power quickly after takeoff, then I could control the oil and cylinder head temps with acceleration and reduction of power to the engines.

I reviewed the before takeoff checklist while I sat at the engineer's seat, made one last check of the instruments, and moved up to the captain's seat.

"El Coco tower, this is November-4902 Charlie, ready for takeoff," I radioed. "Traffic permitting, I'll need about one minute in position."

"Roger, November-4902 Charlie, taxi into position and hold and let me know when you're ready," the tower answered.

I pulled into position on the runway, set the parking brakes, and jumped back into the hole at the engineer's seat. I toggled the oil cooler doors down to 50 percent, and with the rheostat switches and I set the cowls to 50 percent at the same time. One last check at the engineer's panel and I hopped back up to the captain's seat, buckled my seat belt, set the wing flaps for takeoff position, and called the tower.

"El Coco, November-4902 Charlie is ready for takeoff."

"November-4902 Charlie, you're cleared for takeoff," the tower advised. "After takeoff climb on a heading of zero nine zero degrees and call departure control."

It was a beautiful day, cloudless with no wind at all. If you were ever going to solo a Lockheed Constellation, this would be the day to do it.

And I did.

I eased the power up and heard the engines slowly begin their roar as the propellers bit into the air. I felt the huge airframe begin to move, first slowly; then she accelerated faster. I kept my attention on the centerline of the runway and my eyes on the airspeed but my mind was on the oil temp and cylinder head temps.

The airplane was empty, and being light, she accelerated rapidly down the runway. The airspeed read ninety knots, and I eased the wheel back. She was like a big Piper Cub. With a gentle tug on the control wheel and a turn of the trim wheel, she lifted off. As I noted the rate of climb, I reached over and retracted the landing gear. A thump under the cockpit told me that the wheels had retracted, and I cross-checked the gear lights to confirm my seat-of-the-pants signal. I pulled the power back to climb power. I was well over one thousand feet and only then did I chance a glimpse over my shoulder at the engineer's panel to the oil temp gauges and the cylinder head temp gauges. Number three engine was running a little hotter than the others, so I pulled the power back slightly and soon it was normal.

The 50 percent theory worked fine.

I raised the flaps, set up a normal climb power, and soon I leveled off at 9,500 feet. I set cruise power, surveyed the fuel tank selection, checked the gauges from my vantage point in the captain's seat, and relaxed.

The route took me over Puerto Limón, a small town on the Caribbean side of Costa Rica, and then direct to a radio beacon, Taboga, just southwest of Tocumen Airport, the airport serving Panama.

I cleared out of Costa Rico's airspace and reported my position to Panama Center. They acknowledged and I asked for an update on the weather at Tocumen Airport.

"Roger, November-4902 Charlie," they responded. "The weather at Tocumen is two hundred feet overcast and one-mile visibility."

That was not what I wanted to hear. That was not good for a single-piloted Lockheed Constellation. *Oh well*, I thought. That was just the morning fog and it would burn off before I arrived. I still had another thirty minutes to go.

On the bright side, I did check out the radios, and they seemed to work fine. I pulled out an approach plate, a map that directs you to the proper radio facility and gives you the headings and altitudes for an approach and landing in inclement weather.

I advised Panama Center that I was estimating Taboga radio beacon, a radio fix about eighteen miles southwest of the runway at Tocumen, in eight minutes. They acknowledged, asked me to descend to three thousand feet, and to contact Panama approach control.

"Panama approach, this is November-4902 Charlie passing through six for three thousand feet," I advised.

"Roger November-4902 Charlie, you're cleared for the approach, runway zero three; the ceiling is two hundred feet and the visibility is a mile," the controller advised.

Things began to get a little bit busy then. There was no crew to read the checklist and it must come from memory now. I began to slow the aircraft down to flap speed to prepare for the approach. The Connie was responding great, and I was hoping that I would do as well. I took one last glance back at the gauges at the engineer's desk. All was well there. The oil temps and the cylinder head temps were on the cool side of normal but within the green band of the gauges. I redirected my attention back to the approach as I descended into the clouds. More flaps and slower, I remembered. I was looking for about 120 knots as I passed the radio facility at Taboga. I was right on.

Just to be on the safe side, I reached over and lowered the landing gear early. I felt the familiar bump as they locked down, and the comforting green lights told me that all three wheels were down and locked.

The Man in The Arena...

I crossed the outer marker at 1,700 feet and put the flaps to full down for landing. I could now reduce my speed to around 110 knots and focus on the final challenge of an instrument approach landing.

On a normal approach, with a full crew, one pilot descends by reference to the instruments while the other looks out for the approach lights at the end of the runway. If the non-flying pilot does not see the runway lead-in lights at the prescribed descent altitude, the flying pilot declares a missed approach and executes a go-around.

On this approach, I had no pilot to look out for the lights. I had to be right on the money with the Instrument Landing System. The ILS is an imaginary road comprised of radio beams that give you a gradient from altitude down to the end of the runway and another beam that lets you know if you are left or right of the runway. Those two beams form a sort of cross in a gauge located on the instrument panel....... if you're on the beam.

I had made up my mind to descend to an altitude slightly above two hundred feet, take a quick look, and if I didn't see the lead-in lights at the end of the runway, I would execute a missed approach.

The airplane flew well. I had it on a nice stabilized approach and I felt good about the approach, even with no other crewmembers to assist.

Five hundred feet. I was right on course, right on glide path.

Three hundred feet. *Get ready now.* I was ready to push the throttles forward if I didn't see the lead in lights.

Two hundred fifty feet. *Okay,* I thought, *two more seconds.*

Now, look...

And there they were. A strip of beautiful white approach lights running into the parallel lights indicating the runway.

I took a quick look at the green gear-down lights as I crossed over the fence and chopped the power. She settled down gently at around eighty-five knots with a squeak of the tires when they touched. I rolled down the runway as the aircraft slowed, cleared the runway to a taxiway, and called the ground controller.

I looked over at Jack. He was white and smiling nervously, but he never let on that he was scared.

We parked the aircraft and cleared customs. Jack's brother was waiting for us with expense money, and we proceeded to the El Panama Hilton for a well-deserved meal. And a beer.

That's where we finally met the elusive ex-Lufthansa pilot, Captain McAllister. He was tall, thin, and spoke with a heavy German accent.

We all met in the bar at the El Panama—Jack and I along with Jack's brother Danny and Captain McAllister.

It was late afternoon and the bar was already busy. It was THE place to meet in Panama with its enormous Grand Wurlitzer pipe organ, with one wall filled with three eight-foot by ten-foot windows holding almost every instrument known to man. There were pipes and woodwinds, cymbals and xylophones, banjos and drums, and they were all controlled by three huge, semicircular keyboards with 259 stops. The locals called it El Bombarde, and it was played by the great organ impresario Leroy Lewis from the United States.

We sat in a far corner while Captain McAllister gave us his tale of woe, in broken English, as to how his copilot and flight engineer had jumped ship and we would have to look for two more crewmembers.

Jack looked at me and I knew that I was in trouble. I knew what was coming next. I was scheduled to fly home on Panagra Airlines the next day, and although I still had three days before I was to fly with Eastern, I intended to be on that Panagra flight. I'd had enough fun with Jack Shaw.

Although I protested before he could speak, I suppose it was the offer of another five hundred dollars that caused me to succumb to his salesmanship.

Jack and Danny were both anxious to get the first trip completed. I'm sure that finances entered into it, and additionally, the cargo was stored at the airport and should have been moved two days earlier.

Jack was explaining to the captain that I was an engineer and that he, Jack, could sit in the copilot's seat for the flight.

It was then that the captain protested that he couldn't fly a Constellation without a full crew.

"Of course you can," Jack interjected. "Cooper, here, just soloed the Connie down from San Jose with NO CREW this morning!"

The captain was astounded. In broken English he allowed that I was crazy and that it was impossible. "Nobody in his right mind would attempt that."

The conversation went back and forth, more beer came, and finally, with Jack's persuasion, the captain agreed to the trip with me in the engineer seat and with Jack, once again, in the copilot's seat.

I, foolishly, went along with the scheme. We agreed to do the trip the next afternoon, and Jack left the meeting to find the customer and set it up.

I was exhausted and with a full stomach I slept hard.

Jack and Danny went to the airport early to supervise the loading; Captain McAlister and I followed later in the afternoon. The captain was a man of few words, which was okay with me. He was extremely hard to understand once the conversation moved from familiar aviation terms, so the taxi ride to Tocumen Airport was quiet.

We rendezvoused at the cargo area just as the last boxes were being loaded. Jack and Danny were there with the customer. His name was Pepe Diaz and he was Latin, not very tall, and wore a long raincoat. I thought him to be overly cautious as the previous day's rainy weather had cleared and the forecast was good. But I didn't focus on it as I was interested only in checking the aircraft load for security and to complete a preflight inspection.

Pepe spoke with an extremely thick Spanish accent. Everyone was introduced around, and Jack advised us that Pepe would be accompanying us on the trip to ensure that the off-loading at the destination would go without a hitch. at which time he would pay Jack for the trip.

While I did the preflight, Captain McAllister visited the Civil Aeronautics department to check the weather and file a flight plan. Pepe remained with the cargo. It was late afternoon before we all assembled and prepared for the takeoff.

We closed the doors and took our respective seats in the cockpit, with Pepe seated on the jump seat, a spare seat just behind the engineer's station usually used by observers.

The captain took his seat up front on the left, and Jack moved into the copilot's seat. As a courtesy, I attempted to assist Pepe with his seat belt and was met with some resistance. I was a bit taken aback at the rudeness of the observer, but since I was busy with my own job, I let it pass.

The captain asked for the checklist, and between us we accomplished the required items in preparation for the engine starts. I started the engines. Except for the number three engine, which continued to be a bit pesky, all went well. All the instruments came to life and were normal. The captain made the radio calls to Tocumen ground control, and we were on our way.

The takeoff was normal and we reached our cruising altitude at dusk. I set up cruise power, leaned the engines for best performance, and relaxed. The destination was still an hour away, and my job was simply to monitor the engine instruments and cross-feed the fuel when necessary.

I slid my seat back and remembered that Pepe was behind me on the jump seat. I turned to apologize for crowding him, and that's when I saw why he was wearing a raincoat.

Lying across his lap was a very intimidating sawed-off shotgun.

I froze with fright.

About a hundred things went through my mind instantly. Was Pepe preparing to force us to land and then do us in, or was he just protecting his load? And, by the way, what was the load that required such protection? My mind raced. Was the captain in on this? Was Jack in on some nefarious scheme? Should I do something, or nothing? What could I do?

"Jack," I nodded toward Pepe and in my calmest voice asked, "what's the deal with Pepe and the gun?"

"Oh, that." Jack laughed. "I forgot to tell you about that part of the trip. We're landing at an alternate field where customs will not be involved, and Pepe feels that he must protect us from any banditos that might show up. He's on our side," he added.

"What the hell are we carrying?" I demanded.

"Just cigarettes," he explained, "no dope or anything like that. It's just a scheme to avoid import taxes."

Wonderful, I thought. *Instead of the firing squad we'll only get twenty years if we get caught.*

"Jack," I swallowed hard, "if I ever get back to Miami alive, I'm going to kill you."

"Don't worry, Cooper. We'll only be on the ground for thirty minutes and then we're out of there, back to Panama and on the Panagra flight to Miami before you know it."

The captain pointed out a spot out on the map of Colombia to Pepe. Pepe nodded approval, the captain pulled the power off, and we began a descent into a dark hole next to the Magdalena River in preparation to land at what would turn out to be a grass field. As the captain lined up for the landing, I saw that the runway was dimly lit by gasoline smudge pots. The glow of a small city was visible next to the outline of the river. The captain lowered the gear, set the flaps, and prepared for the landing.

He was good. He was actually better than good. He was excellent and the landing was made expertly. We rolled to a stop, turned, and taxied back to a gaggle of trucks and cut the engines. This was not the captain's first flight in this market.

The Man in The Arena...

I watched in awe at the efficiency of the operation. Cargo trucks backed up just outside the main cabin doors, and wooden chutes were slid up to the two doors of the airplane. The cargo was placed in these troughs, and gravity slid the boxes down to the beds of the trucks. Just as soon as one truck was filled, another backed into position.

Meanwhile, Jack was on the ground at the nose wheel of the airplane collecting the fee for the trip from Pepe. I heard loud voices and as I approached the nose it was apparent that Pepe was holding out on Jack for the whole amount of payment for the trip. The conversation was quite heated. Jack was holding his own, but Pepe was holding the shotgun. They were down to settling the dispute as Jack was pulling Pepe's watch off his arm for final payment when...

My heart stopped!

Someone came up on a bicycle screaming, "Police-eyo, police-eyo" in broken English and pointing frantically toward the road leading from the small nearby town.

The panic that ensued was exceeded only by the confusion.

Pepe grabbed his shotgun, loosed his grip on his watch, and ran toward the workers loading the cargo on the trucks. He was yelling in Spanish, "Rapido... Rapido... Rapido!"

I was the first up the ladder through the crew door, and Jack was a close second.

The captain was running around screaming something incoherently in German, and I was yelling at him to climb up the ladder. He got the message and in a second we were all three in the cockpit.

I hollered for Jack to follow me and help unload while pointing to the captain to get in his seat and prepare to take off.

Jack and I ran to the cabin and began to move, shove, push, and throw the boxes of cigarettes on the chutes for the trucks. As the troughs filled to capacity, we threw the boxes on the ground and kept unloading the airplane.

We only had seconds to work. My heart was pounding but I couldn't stop unloading the cargo.

My last view of Pepe was of him standing between two trucks, shotgun aimed at the workers, screaming something in Spanish.

There were only about fifty boxes remaining, and Jack was working feverishly with a couple of loaders to finish. I ran back to the cockpit and told the captain to set the parking brakes and I'd start the engines.

There was no time for a checklist. I had to do this from memory. I engaged the starter on number four engine and hit the magneto switches. It fired up. I did the same on number three and nothing happened. It wouldn't fire.

Crap!

I let it go and hit the start switch for number two and it started. We had two engines running.

I looked back in the cabin and saw Jack throwing the last boxes out of the cabin door while kicking the two helpers down the chutes to the truck bed.

I shouted to the captain, "Start taxiing, start taxiing, start taxiing!"

"But all the engines are not running," he managed to mumble.

"Start taxiing NOW!" I shouted. "And don't put any lights on. Taxi with number four and two, and I'll get the other two going!"

Jack had thrown the last boxes out of the airplane and was struggling with the two doors when the captain began to taxi on two engines. We were back-taxiing toward the takeoff end of the grass runway.

I got number one engine started and shouted to the captain, "You've got number one running now! Let's go with three engines. PUT THE FLAPS TO TAKEOFF POSITION!" I screamed.

Jack had managed to close the aft cabin door and was working on the forward door when we reached the end of the runway.

I could see the red lights of the police cars as they rounded the perimeter of the airport across the field.

"COME ON, NUMBER THREE," I yelled, pressing the start switch. "C'MON, YOU BASTARD." That engine had given me trouble since I first got in the cockpit of this airplane, and now it just wouldn't fire.

The captain had turned the airplane around on the narrow grass strip and was pointed down the runway. Jack finally got the main cabin door closed and vaulted across me to the copilot's seat.

We could see several police cars at the opposite end of the airport with red lights flashing.

The captain was screaming something in German about the number three engine.

"LET'S GO WITH THREE ENGINES," I yelled. "LET'S GO. USE ONE AND FOUR TO GET ROLLING AND ONCE WE GET SOME RUDDER CONTROL, PUSH UP NUMBER TWO. I'LL KEEP WORKING ON NUMBER THREE!" I was screaming at the top of my voice.

The captain got the message and pushed the two outboard engines up to maximum takeoff power. The airplane began to roll, yawed slightly, but the captain managed to keep her straight with the nose wheel steering. Once we reached about fifty knots speed, he eased the number two engine up to takeoff power. I was standing between the captain and copilot's seat watching the airspeed slowly build. We were empty but having only three engines working, we weren't setting any acceleration speed records. I looked up ahead out of the cockpit windshield and had my third or fourth heart attack of the night.

There were two police cars coming down the runway headed straight for us.

I reached up and switched on the landing lights.

It was a deadly game of chicken AND WE COULDN'T STOP!

The captain had the nose wheel off the ground; the airplane was bouncing along on its main gear but needed about ten more knots to fly when the officers driving the police cars blinked.

They peeled off; one went to the right and the other swerved left. As we broke ground, I could see them pass under our wings, bounding across the rough field.

I reached up and retracted the landing gear while the captain managed to slowly climb the aircraft on three engines.

My attention returned to the number three engine. The speed of the aircraft caused the propeller to windmill—to turn without the starter engaged. I couldn't let it windmill for very long, as the drag would cause major problems.

I shut off the fuel mixture to the number three engine, guessing that it was flooded. I let it rotate for another twenty seconds or so, switched on the magneto switch, and slowly opened up the fuel mixture control. She started up nicely.

"Captain," I said, "you have all four engines."

"*Danke schoen*" was all he said.

"You're welcome." I breathed a sigh of relief.

We landed at Panama within the hour, secured the aircraft, and within another hour we were enjoying the music of Leroy Lewis and his wonderful Grand Wurlitzer pipe organ in the bar at the El Panama hotel.

We had a few beers.

The next day Jack and I were to return to Miami in the afternoon. We lounged around the pool at El Panama, had lunch, and before we knew it we were running late for our Panagra flight.

We packed, dashed to the airport, and ran for the giant green Panagra DC-8. We waved our tickets to the agent and ran up the stairs to the cabin.

I noted our seat assignments on the tickets, 7 C and D, and proceeded back through the cabin to find my seat and relax.

To my surprise, our seats were taken. When I tried to communicate to the persons occupying our seats, I realized that they only spoke Spanish. With hand signals, pointing to the seat assignments on our tickets and motioning for them to vacate our seats, we began to create quite a stir.

The senior flight attendant came to our rescue. I explained, "The airline must have sold the seats twice, and she MUST figure it out."

She examined the two passengers' tickets carefully and admitted that they had every right to be in the disputed seats.

I was beginning to get upset. "I am an airline pilot," I explained, "and I know how airlines work. Panagra must provide us seats."

She asked for our tickets. Time was running out as departure time neared. The passengers were all seated, there were no empty seats, and the attendants were ready to close the door.

She examined our tickets. "Yes, you do have seats 7 C and D on the flight to Miami," she agreed, "but you're on the Buenos Aires flight."

Our embarrassment was exceeded only by our haste to get off the airplane. Luckily, the Miami-bound Panagra flight was at the next gate, and with bags in hand, we ran across the ramp to the Miami plane just as they were closing the door. In two hours Panagra touched down at Miami International Airport.

The next day, in full Eastern Airlines uniform, I checked in at the operations room in preparation for my flight.

"Hello," the captain said, "I'm Captain Fuller."

"It's nice to meet you, sir," I said. "I'm Tom Cooper. I'm your second officer today."

"It's good to meet you. What did you do on your days off?" he asked, casually.

"Nothing special, sir," I replied, "nothing special."

CHAPTER 51

Entrepreneurial "Juices" Discovered

THE SUMMER OF 1965 BROUGHT an event that changed the direction of my life: the demise of Great Circle Aviation.

Eastern, although paying me monthly, continued to under-utilize my services. I continued to spend a lot of time at Opa Locka Airport at Great Circle Aviation.

My main motivation, since early in the 1950s, was to be an airline pilot. Now that I had achieved that goal, and with Eastern using me only on a reserve basis, I felt somewhat lost. I felt that I was drifting, and the only challenge that held my attention was the business side of Great Circle Aviation. I really enjoyed the management side, and as Bob grew his company, he left me in charge more and more. I was happiest sitting behind a desk, scheduling flights, selling flight courses to students, and counseling instructors.

I had just returned from an infrequent flight with Eastern. I hopped in my car and headed north, up Le Jeune Road, to Opa Locka Airport to my part-time job at Great Circle Aviation.

To my surprise, the doors were locked and the company was closed. There were a few students milling around, but no one knew what was going on. The British fellow was there, the first student at Great Circle Aviation, but he knew nothing. I took his phone number and said that if I heard anything I'd let him know.

I drove back to Miami Springs to find Bob Jones, but he was nowhere to be found. He had moved his family from his home on Blue Bird Avenue and disappeared.

I stopped by Al McCurdy's office and he filled me in. It seems that Bob had run short of cash, and although McCurdy had lent him some money, it was not enough to cover some back taxes, Bob's personal expenses, and the ongoing expenses of the flight school. He simply packed up and, with family, left town for parts unknown.

I was devastated. I had enjoyed the diversion from standing by for an Eastern flight assignment, and I enjoyed the bustle of the business side of aviation. Now I had nothing to do but sit at home and sulk.

It was two weeks later that a registered letter arrived from a bank that held the lien on one of Great Circle's aircraft. Since they couldn't find Jones, and since I had guaranteed the loan, they demanded that I pay the note in full. The amount was in excess of sixteen thousand dollars.

That snapped me out of my doldrums and back to reality right quick.

I met with the bank; they formally repossessed the airplane, transferred the title to me, and we set up payments over five years. Even with a generous finance plan, I couldn't afford to sit on the airplane without putting it to use. The payments plus mandatory insurance were too much.

This was the beginning of my business training. Never, EVER co-sign a note without having control over the asset.

I attempted to lease the airplane to several local operators, but there were no takers.

I phoned the British fellow and gave him the information about Bob Jones, and he, too, was depressed at the demise of Great Circle Aviation as he felt some "ownership" of the company.

He was in the final few hours of his professional pilot training when he had a suggestion. "Why don't you let me fly out my time in your airplane, and if I need any instruction, you can give it to me?"

That made perfect sense. We agreed on a price, met at Opa Locka Airport the next day, and he was off on his continued flight training adventure.

He spread the word to his fellow Great Circle students, and I began to receive calls suggesting the same plan for them.

Within a month I had rented an office at the airport, set up a flight schedule, and formed a corporation called AERO TRAINING ASSOCIATES, Inc.

Although I probably didn't realize it then, my life would be changed forever.

The entrepreneurial juices had kicked in and I was hooked on the business end of aviation for life…at, what was to be, the expense of my marriage.

With only one airplane, the flight schedule maxed out quickly. With my golden credit as an airline pilot, I began to acquire additional aircraft, and by the end of 1965, I had a fleet of six trainers and a robust flight school. The airlines had begun to hire pilots, and our roster of students grew rapidly. We advertised very little; most of our students came from word of mouth from other students and from referrals from Al McCurdy, the ground school operator near Miami International Airport.

I continued to be on reserve for Eastern and, as they retired the DC-7s, my flights for them grew less and less frequent. It was just a matter of time until they would assign me to either Lockheed Electra or Boeing 727 school.

That call came January of 1966.

CHAPTER 52

Boeing 727 School

The party's over, a new era begins.

"First Officer Cooper is to report to Boeing 727 first/second officer school January 17, 1966," the note from Eastern read.

The party was over at Eastern Airlines. No more going to Opa Locka Airport daily and running a flight school full time. I realized that I would need some help, as the flight school was growing rapidly and I was the lone proprietor. Luckily, I had two advanced students who had expressed an interest in becoming shareholders and participating in the management of the school.

Lanny Thompson, a Miami policeman, had spare time available on his days off, and Karl Cormey, an Eastern Airlines counter agent, was suited to handle the accounting on his days off. We set up a three-way partnership, and off I went to Eastern Airlines Boeing 727 ground school.

It had been over three years since I had attended a company ground school, and I found it refreshing. Having flown jets six years earlier for Continental Airlines, I found the curriculum simple and the two weeks of ground school relatively easy.

The flight simulator portion of the school was invigorating. Eastern's simulator training department was second to none. The instructors were highly professional, and the flight simulators were state-of-the-art. I remembered, six years earlier, the simulators at Continental, made from cardboard boxes with instruments cut from the flight school manuals and pasted on a makeshift plywood panel.

The Man in The Arena...

The simulators at Eastern accurately depicted any flight situation a pilot might find himself in, and if the student pilot had trouble working his way out of the problem, the instructor could "freeze" the motion of the simulator and discuss the issues with the student. Once the student caught up, the instructor would re-engage the simulator and the flight would continue.

The check out process at Eastern was straightforward. After ground school a check ride was administered by a check airman. If the student passed, he was assigned to a revenue flight to observe a licensed second officer at work. After a predetermined number of hours observing, he was assigned an actual flight with a check airman observing his performance under actual revenue conditions.

I passed all the tests, put in my observer time in the cockpit, and was assigned my first revenue flight as a second officer on the Boeing 727 aircraft.

I checked in at the operations room to meet the check airman who would give me my final approval after observing my performance under actual revenue conditions.

To my surprise, who would show up but my old buddy from Kendall Flying School from ten years earlier, Carroll Kern.

The last time that I was in an airplane with him, I was teaching him to do snap rolls in a Piper Cub over the tomato fields in South Florida.

We passed the time a bit, reminiscing about the good old times at Kendall Flying School, and headed for the airplane.

"Old friends" aside, Carroll was all business in his role as check airman for Eastern Airlines, and I was all business when it came to performing up to the standards I knew Eastern expected of me.

The flight went well. We flew from Miami to JFK, and the flight was uneventful. Carroll showed me a few tricks of the trade, and we took off from JFK back to Miami.

We were crossing over North Carolina, it was dark, and the only illumination was the dim red background instrument lights in the cockpit. Carroll had relaxed behind me seated on the jump seat, and I was keeping watch over the instruments at my second officer panel. Once you get to cruise and set the engine power, there's not much for a second officer to do in a Boeing 727 other than monitor the fuel gauges and watch the pressurization system.

Suddenly there was a loud bang. The airplane shuddered; I felt that it came from the right side. My first inclination was that Carroll had conspired with the captain and they were simulating an emergency situation to see how I would react.

I quickly looked back over my shoulder to see Carroll spring out of the jump seat. He saw my expression, knew what I was thinking, and exclaimed, "Cooper, that's not me; it's the real thing!"

I turned back toward the captain and saw the engine number three gauges unwinding as the fire warning sounded. "Captain, we've just lost number three engine."

"Silence the bell," he commanded to the first officer, and to me he directed, "Essential power, operating engine." It was the normal preliminary steps during such an emergency.

The captain was pretty cool. After the fire alarm was shut off and the electrical busses were powered, he casually directed me to run the engine shut-down checklist and asked the first officer to call the air traffic controller and get us a clearance to Charlotte, the nearest airport to our position.

After we completed the emergency checklist, turned toward Charlotte, and began our descent, Carroll leaned over my shoulder and whispered, "That was pretty good, Cooper. I'm impressed, but not as impressed as I was back at Brown's Airport when you did those snap rolls in a Piper Cub."

Carroll signed me off as a certified second officer, and it was the beginning of a long love affair with the Boeing 727. It was to be the last commercial airliner that I would qualify in, and I would fly the 727 until Eastern shut down in 1991. In twenty-five years, I would accumulate about twenty thousand hours of flying time in that type of aircraft. It replaced the DC-3 as the love of my life.

With the checkout on the Boeing 727, I became a regular line holder and I was given a monthly assignment called a line of flying. This generally would consist of four days of flying and three days off in some type of weekly pattern. Karl and Lanny were doing pretty well at the flight school, but I needed to be there as much as possible, which left me with even less time at home.

My main focus was student recruitment. Lanny worked with the operations of the school and Karl handled the accounting. The sales side of the company was fairly easy. We had a lot of walk-ins; students who had heard of our school from other students and simply stopped in. Being an airline pilot,

I was a self-proclaimed expert on training and the practical side of being an airline pilot, so it was relatively easy to sign up these students.

Another source of students was from Al McCurdy, the ground school operator who had earlier sent his referrals to Great Circle Aviation. McCurdy charged a small "finder's fee" for the students he sent my way. I would pay him 50 percent of the earned commission fee when the student signed up and the balance when that student graduated.

It was Thursday, June 2nd, when I stopped by his ground school in a small shopping center in Virginia Gardens, next to Miami Springs, to settle our account for the previous month. McCurdy, as usual, was on the phone. There was always an air of mystery around him, and today was no different. He was alternately laughing at the person on the other end of the line or yelling about a double-cross by the police. I had heard this story before, and knowing of his constant run-ins with the local authorities, I paid little attention. I was only interested in conducting our business and returning to the flight school.

He was still grumbling, under his breath as I left. I never saw him alive again.

According to the *Miami Herald*, that night he broke into an associate's apartment, where two policemen were waiting with automatic shotguns.

Three blasts from their shotguns, and Alfred McCurdy was out of their hair forever.

And Aero Training Associates, Inc. had lost a good student recruiter.

I had my own ideas as to what really happened to McCurdy, but with two rogue cops patrolling the area with automatic shotguns, I thought it better to keep my opinion to myself. Besides, I had more than I could handle with the flight school and flying full time with Eastern.

The summer dragged on and my workload increased. Lanny had completed his flight courses and had earned the qualifications to fly for the airlines. He was interviewing; it was only a matter of time until he would leave.

Karl came down with a brain tumor that required an operation. It was touch and go with him, and he was expected to be away for an extended period of time.

As fall came, with the school doing well, we had the opportunity to sell. A flight school operator at Tamiami Airport by the name of Tanner came by in November and made us an offer that we accepted.

We split the down payment, held the stock as collateral for the balance, and turned the keys over to Tanner.

That was the last dollar we saw from Mr. Tanner.

In the spring of 1967, we sued Tanner and recovered the assets of Aero Training Associates, Inc.

There was nothing to do but crank up another flight school with the airplanes and equipment. I bought the interests of Lanny and Karl and formed another flight school, Air Florida, Inc.

While setting up the new operation, it was brought to my attention that the Veterans Administration had approved a GI Bill that financed flight courses for veterans.

That was good news. The problem was that for a flight school to qualify, it must have been in business for five years or longer. We had been in existence five days.

I called my old friend Al Burnett, for whom I had instructed, part time, several years earlier. He still owned and operated a small, one-airplane flight school, and he had been in business for over five years. We agreed to merge. It was a terrific marriage. We immediately qualified for the GI Bill, and Al came into my company as general manager. He was a full-time manager, well qualified, and it relieved me to fly for Eastern with no daily responsibilities for the flight school.

It was around then that the differences between Diane and me became too much for either of us. I had spent entirely too much time with my aviation entrepreneurial adventures, and she, understandably, had had enough. Our spats became major battles, and arguments ended in mutual silent treatments for weeks.

I moved out.

I shared a friend's apartment. He was Ray Orchard, an old Riddle Airline acquaintance, who lived about ten blocks away. Cathy and Tommy were both in school, and I wanted to live close by.

Air Florida was an instant success. Al Burnett brought his twin-engine trainer, and with the aircraft salvaged from the ATA lawsuit, we had a sizable fleet. The VA business was excellent, and soon our schedule filled up and we had to acquire additional aircraft. We ended the year with ten single-engine aircraft, two twin-engine aircraft, and a link trainer. We were a full-fledged training center.

We soared into 1968 flying high. We were flying so high that we caught the attention of another entrepreneur in Miami, Stuart Greenfield.

Stuart had resurrected a small, pre-SEC public company called Meter Maid Industries. He had acquired a chain of laundries the previous year and, through an invitation by our mutual banker, he approached us to buy.

The Meter Maid stock was sold over the counter, and Stuart was a great salesman. He painted a rosy picture of the future of his company, and by mid-year he convinced us to sell to him for stock.

I was ready to slow down somewhat. The ATA debacle had been exhausting, and with the success that we were enjoying at Air Florida, it was taking up too much time.

I began to realize that I really enjoyed creating and building companies, not running them.

The acquisition was complete; Allen Burnett stayed on as general manager, Stuart moved his offices into the flight school, and after a short period, I left the company.

The stock that we received was "lettered," which meant that we couldn't trade or sell it publicly for a predetermined time, so I put it in my desk drawer at home and became a full-time airline pilot.

Tommy and Cathy were growing fast, and it was time for separate bedrooms. I purchased a home in the Bird section of Miami Springs, and Diane and the children moved in. It was a nice home, near the duplex, on a small lake, and Tommy and Cathy had their own bedrooms.

I moved into the duplex and settled down to fly the line with Eastern.

That lasted about six months. The flying was great but the days off were boring. I was tiring of playing golf with Jack Shaw, although his stories of his adventures with his cargo airline in South America were interesting. There was just something missing.

I began to miss the excitement of a business. I missed the challenges of business; the hustle and bustle of a working operation and the anticipation of the future.

I didn't miss it enough to start another flight school. There were too many moving parts there, and I had learned my lesson, but good. No flight school for me.

So it was back to the golf course with Jack Shaw and fly the airline with Eastern.

CHAPTER 53

My Short Career as An Ophthalmologist

It was about that time that Diane decided Tommy needed an eye operation. He was born with a "lazy" eye. When he looked straight ahead, both eyes were normal, but when he looked left or right, one eye was slow to react. We thought it would correct itself, but after six years it became apparent that an operation was necessary.

Diane, being a nurse, took charge. She found the best doctor, the best facility, and we set up an appointment to discuss the procedure.

I lasted about one minute into the technical discussion concerning the details of the operation. I graciously turned the conversation over to Diane, remembering my episode in El Paso when I passed out assisting the doctor who was sewing up Cathy's cheek. This medical stuff just wasn't for me.

The appointed day came for the operation. Diane, Tommy, and I went down to the hospital for the operation. Tommy was the bravest of us all and seemed to enjoy all the attention. Diane was understandably nervous, and I, well, I was a basket case. The big airline pilot was just a miserable basket case.

Diane had a final conversation with the doctor while I stood a safe distance away to avoid passing out, and soon Tommy disappeared into the operating area while Diane and I stood by in the waiting room.

I was up and then down. I was sitting and then pacing. Finally, probably to Diane's relief, I left.

I suppose that my conscience was hurting me because I hadn't taken more of a lead in the pre-operation discussions, so there was only one thing to do.

Go buy toys.

I dashed down to the local Sears store, rushed to the sporting department, and bought practically everything I could carry: balls, bats, gloves, footballs, basketballs, and any other thing that I could find.

My conscience was already feeling better.

Now, to get back to the hospital before Tommy got out of the operating room!

I arrived just in time. The nurses, Diane, Tommy, and I arrived at the recovery room at about the same time.

The nurses were amused and Diane doubled over in laughter. She knew of my conscience issue. I placed all the sports equipment around the bed for Tommy's awakening.

One eye was covered with bandages, but with the good eye, when he woke, he saw all the stuff around his bed. He smiled broadly, and the toys set him on the road to recovery.

The operation was a success. Diane credited it to the skill of the doctors and staff, and I suppose there's some truth in that, but I like to think that the sports stuff played the major part of it.

CHAPTER 54
Airline Owner

This airline management stuff is easy.

IT WAS IN LATE 1969 when I received a phone call from the owner of AAT Airlines. He had met Jack Shaw, tried to sell Jack the airline, but Jack wasn't interested. Jack gave him my number, so he called and asked to talk to me about buying the airline. I told him that I wasn't in a financial position to acquire anything. But he insisted, so we met.

I knew of the airline. I had flown for American Air Taxi nine years earlier. A few years later someone bought the air taxi out of a bankruptcy situation, changed the name to AAT Airlines, invested a fortune in new airplanes and equipment, and began to fly around the state as a commuter airline. Eventually they ran out of money and shut down. There were two remaining employees who convinced the absentee investor to invest in a smaller version. He put some money in the company, took it out of bankruptcy, bought a small Beechcraft Twin Bonanza, and with the two last employees began scheduled service between Miami and Key West.

The financier lived in Philadelphia and grew tired of his absentee role. He was also tired of continually being asked for operating funds to keep the airline afloat.

He gave me the sales pitch. He offered the airline to me for ten thousand dollars, and I would take over the payments of the Twin bonanza.

I graciously declined, explaining that I was not in a financial position to purchase anything at this time, much less an airline.

I left the meeting and forgot about AAT Airlines. A week later he called again and we met. He reduced the price to five thousand, but even that was too steep for me at that time.

Again, we parted and I didn't hear from him for about two weeks.

I was at the duplex one Friday evening when the phone rang. It was the owner.

"Cooper," he said, "if you can get out here to the airport before my Eastern flight departs for Philadelphia, I'll give you this damn airline."

And that's how I got into the airline business.

I met him at the Eastern gate for the Philadelphia flight, he signed the stock certificates over to me, and I agreed to take over the payments for the airplane. He signed a bill of sale for the airplane, we drew up a contract on a napkin in which he agreed to pay all debts up to midnight that night, and I owned an airline.

What could be easier than owning an airline? I thought as I drove back home. After all, hadn't I been an airline pilot for over twelve years, and didn't all pilots know that management was a cushy job? All you had to do was buy an airplane, hire a pilot, put some fuel in, and you were there. Passengers would magically show up, pay you for a ticket, and that was that. What could be easier?

I was about to discover the truth about airline management. I had just enrolled in airline management 101 at the school of hard knocks.

It was Saturday morning. I drove to the airport to survey my acquisition. I parked in the lot at the terminal and walked inside toward my new airline's counter. I knew where it was. It was located about midpoint in the terminal, with a small office just behind the counter. It was in a very convenient location and when I saw the sign on the wall behind the counter, AAT Airlines, my chest swelled with pride.

"My own airline," I breathed aloud. Now I had to meet my two employees. No one was at the counter, so surely they would be in the office, I thought.

I stepped over the baggage scales at the counter and tried the door to the office. It was unlocked.

The office looked like a hand grenade had exploded inside. Drawers were dumped, papers were strewn everywhere, and anything of value was gone.

I walked over to the window that opened to the ramp below and saw, to my disbelief, my new airplane parked, one engine feathered, meaning previously shut down in flight, and a pool of oil beneath it indicating an engine failure.

Welcome to the airline business.

I heard a rustling of papers behind me and turned to meet an agent from the next-door airline. I introduced myself as the new owner of AAT Airlines.

He just chuckled and said, "Good luck."

Then he gave me the gruesome details.

Airport gossip was that the couple running the airline was an "item." She was the ticket agent and he was the pilot/mechanic. My airline neighbor related that they spent only enough on the airplane to barely keep it flying, and any money left at the end of the day, after fuel expenses, went "away."

When they heard that a local person had purchased the airline, they cleaned out the petty cash and ran.

I had bought an airline with no pilots, no mechanics, no staff, and a twin-engine airplane with one failed engine.

My first thought was to determine the problem with the airplane. Following close behind that was to find a pilot.

I called one of my former flight instructors at the flight school, Ron Bird. I knew that he had been looking for a job as an airline pilot, and he might just fill the bill.

He was elated at the call. When I explained that I needed a mechanic, he volunteered to check with his neighbor, an aviation mechanic, to see if he was available.

They showed up about an hour later, and I sent the mechanic down to the ramp to attend to the broken airplane.

Ron and I began to clean up the mess and determine if anything was left of any value. There were drawers filled with scraps of paper, manuals in disarray, a checkbook, which looked as if it had never been balanced, a loose-leaf notebook labeled "Reservations," and some blank ticket stock.

We found the aircraft flight manual, the manual published by the manufacturer describing all the systems of the airplane, and a training manual. We had just finished cleaning up the office and the counter when the mechanic came and exclaimed, "The aircraft is okay. It was just a loose oil line. It's fixed and ready for a test hop."

The Man in the Arena...

I looked at Ron and he looked at me. "I've never seen the inside of a Queen Air, much less flown one," he admitted.

I tossed him the airplane flight manual and laughed. "Me neither, let's go. You have a passenger flight tomorrow."

We stumbled through the preflight checklist, finally got the engines running and the radios on, and called ground control. We were cleared to taxi to the runway with me reading the procedures from the flight manual to Ron.

With a clearance to take off, we roared down the runway. Once airborne we headed out over the Everglades for some practice maneuvers. We ended up down at Tamiami Airport for some touch-and-go landings and then headed back to Miami International Airport.

"You're good to go," I told him. "You just passed your check ride, and you have a revenue flight tomorrow morning at 8:30."

I briefed him on airline PA announcements expected of the captain, and he did well. I alerted him that when he began his announcements with "Hello, folks, I'm Captain Bird," he could expect some tittering.

There was a uniform shop in the terminal, so we bought him a couple of airline shirts with epaulets and a black tie, and now he was a real airline pilot.

We all showed up early next morning. I was in shirt and tie, Captain Bird was decked out in his airline outfit, including tie and epaulets, and the mechanic was in pressed work clothes. I brought a coffeemaker, cups, and all the fixings, along with three copies of the *Miami Herald*. We were going to be a "customer service" airline.

The first customer showed up. I was nervous. He looked around and asked, "Is this AAT?"

"Yes, sir," I replied, "and you are?" I questioned as I reviewed the passenger reservation list.

"Jackson, Al Jackson," he replied. "Where's Angie?"

I assumed that he was referring to the previous employee. "She's no longer with the company," I said. "I'm the new owner and you'll be seeing some new faces around here."

I sensed that Mr. Al Jackson was not accepting the new ownership as readily as I would have liked. I suppose he, like most folks, initially rebelled at change.

He presented his ticket, the last leg of a prepaid round trip, and I had no choice but to accept it and make him feel welcome. My first passenger was a freebee.

"Sir," I said, "can I offer you a cup of coffee?"

"Well…yes," he said with some hesitancy, like it was a trick. It *was* a trick. I wanted to trick passengers into seeing that this was going to be a new airline with a new culture.

"And," I added, "perhaps you would enjoy this *Miami Herald* to take with you on your flight. The flight departs at 8:30 from gate number three. Please be there ten minutes prior to departure time."

I hadn't won him over yet, but I could tell that I was making progress.

The next two customers arrived. They were cash customers, and at $22.20 per round trip, I was beginning to like this airline business.

The reaction was almost the same. It seems that Angie had done a pretty good job with the customers at the counter. I wonder what they would have thought had they known that she and her significant other had been skimming from the maintenance fund to line their own pockets.

I met the passengers at the gate and escorted them out to the airplane. There was Captain Bird, dressed resplendently in his airline outfit, waiting at attention at the aircraft door, and the mechanic was wiping down the engine cowlings, looking extremely efficient, and safe. That was when I knew that I had them. The passengers were smiling, comfortable, and confident with this new image, and I knew they would return. Better than that, they would tell others.

I assisted the passengers on board, Captain Bird took his seat, and as I closed the door, I heard him begin his speech. "Ladies and gentlemen, welcome aboard. I'm Captain Bird…" and sure enough there was some giggling from the passengers.

The mechanic took his place in front of the aircraft, and on Captain Bird's signal, he gave the all-clear-to-start wiggle of his finger.

My first flight taxied out. I waited on the ramp as the airplane took off and I watched it turn southbound toward Key West.

We were a real airline.

I needed a counter agent quickly. Like tomorrow. I rummaged through some old applications and reviewed some recent ones. There was a young man's application that caught my eye. He was local, well educated, with some airline courses at a local college. I called him and he came right over. That was a good sign. We talked for a while, agreed on a salary and what the job might entail, and he started work the next day.

Then the phone rang. It was a customer. The office phone was also the reservations phone. I scrambled for the reservation book and booked my first customer. That brought up another issue. Who answered the reservation phone when it was not attended? I solved that by contracting with a telephone answering company in Miami Springs, and voila, we had twenty-four-hour reservations.

Next problem was a second pilot. I knew that after about four days of flying back and forth to Key West that Captain Bird's tail feathers would be dragging.

A quick review of the applications and I found the name of a promising young pilot, Arthur Morris. I called "Art," who showed up within the hour.

He was a clean-cut young man of medium height and good credentials, and after a short conversation I hired him as our number two pilot. His training consisted of sitting at a small desk in the corner, reading the flight manual, riding with Captain Bird, and taking a check ride with me.

He was qualified by Thursday, just as Captain Bird's tail feathers were beginning to drag.

But there was a lot of work to do. The deeper I got into the airline's interworking, the more I realized what I didn't know.

I remembered Vic Carmichael, an older gentleman I had met a year earlier. He was a retired airline executive, so I decided to call him and pick his brain. We met later in the week and he seemed eager to help.

He was a wealth of information, and he required no salary. He mentioned that if we were successful he might be rewarded with some stock in the company. I saw no problem in that.

I was pretty good with pilot and mechanic stuff, scheduling and all, but when it came to the financial end of the business, I was lost. Vic was excellent at that. He taught me to work out cash flows and how to figure how much it cost to operate an airplane per hour. The cost was more than just fuel and pilots; there was cost of the airplane and reserves for engine and propeller replacement and a thousand other things that I had not considered.

I began to realize that managing an airline wasn't such a cushy business after all. The deeper I got into the managing of AAT Airlines, the more I respected the folks who were running Eastern Airlines.

I entered 1970 feeling pretty good. My seniority with Eastern had grown so much that I could pick and choose which flights I wanted to fly. I usually picked lines of flying—a monthly sequence of flights that Eastern published from which the pilots would bid on—that flew two days on and three days off. I had lots of time to spend with the airline.

Although AAT Airlines was doing okay, we were underfunded. I had no cash to invest and Vic was not in a position to financially help either. Our passenger loads were growing slowly, but with the competition—National Airlines with daily Boeing 727s and Southeast Airlines with F-27s—we could not interest any investors.

In the spring of 1970, we leased a Cessna 402, a sexy-looking nine-passenger airplane, and placed the Twin Bonanza on standby and charter basis. Art Morris had a friend, Don Jaycocks, who we hired as our third pilot. The charter business picked up and we leased maintenance space on the northwest corner of Miami International Airport and hired a full-time mechanic.

The airline continued to do well. We weren't awash in cash, but we paid the bills and the passenger loads continued to grow slowly.

In the summer, I sold the Twin Bonanza and leased a Cessna 402B. The Cessna 402B differed from the 402 in so much as it had a longer nose, giving it more baggage capability. The 402B became our frontline aircraft with the 402 being our standby/charter aircraft.

The year passed quickly. Tommy and Cathy were in school, and Diane had moved from the large house on Ibis to a three-bedroom home closer to their school in the older section of Miami Springs.

It was around this time that Diane called me with some news concerning Tommy.

He had decided to become an ice hockey player.

"Fine," I said, "call me when Bass Lake in Miami Springs freezes over."

"No, he's serious," she explained. "Jack Shaw's boys joined an ice hockey league and they've asked him to play. A new ice hockey arena just opened up on Thirty-sixth Street across from the Jai Alai Fronton, and the owner has formed a league for juniors."

Jack's boys, being from Canada, had been skating since they were born. They were experts and Tommy had never been on a pair of skates in his life.

We were both terrified that he would injure himself, but Jack assured us that with the equipment they had, he would be safe.

Tommy was excited about the team, so we grudgingly agreed.

As it turned out, Tommy was the youngest player on the team, and he was also the smallest.

The day for "uniform assignment" came, and we took Tommy down to the ice rink.

Unfortunately, all the uniforms, padding, helmets, and equipment were sized for kids in their teens.

Jack's boys were already there and suited up. They were resplendent in their red and gold pads, glistening red helmets, and flashing skates. Already they were on the ice, dashing around, skating at breakneck speeds around the rink. They would brake to a stop, spraying ice on nearby awed onlookers, and then pirouette, changing directions on a dime, and skate away at speeds one could not duplicate on a motorcycle. It was awesome...and as parents...terrifying. I looked at Diane and she looked at me and we instantly knew that we had made a terrible mistake. Tommy would not survive this adventure.

But...it was too late to turn back now.

We picked up his equipment and, with Jack's help and with copious amounts of duct tape, we "suited" him up. It was about the funniest thing you could imagine. We didn't dare laugh.

He looked like a big red and gold ball...with a red helmet balanced on top...and two wobbly skates attached to the bottom. Two short arms with gloved hands protruded from either side of the "ball," and with them he held the lethal hockey stick.

He was so proud. We were so scared.

Well, there were only a few practice sessions before the first game, and Tommy, although he desperately tried to keep up with the other older kids, just needed more time to practice. But it was not to be. The league, two teams, was to start, and practice or no practice, the games must go on.

The first game was scheduled, and Diane and I were there early for the suiting-up ordeal.

"Tighten up that pad, loosen that strap, here, give me some duct tape for this sock, it keeps falling down and wrapping around his skates, hey, Jack, how does this shin pad fit," we all fumbled as we dressed him. "Hurry, hurry," Tommy would say, "the rest of the team is already out on the ice." We were in no hurry to witness our son's demise at the hands of these "crazed" Canadians.

Finally, when we could delay no longer, we cinched up the last strap and pushed him out on the ice for his certain final period. We retreated to the small bleachers erected for the fans and families, took our seats, and literally covered our faces with our hands, peeking through our fingers to watch the spectacle. Neither of us had ever seen a hockey match, and we knew nothing of what to expect.

Jack Shaw and his wife Pat were laughing their heads off at us.

The game was about to begin. The players were skating about, moving their hockey sticks menacingly about, all except one; Tommy was using his as the third leg of his balancing tripod.

The referee, puck in hand, whistle in mouth, skated about and neared the center of the rink. The time we dreaded had come.

"Face off."

The referee dropped the puck between the centers of each team and the game was on. There was an immediate clashing of hockey sticks in the center of the arena, and almost instantly, one center slapped the puck toward the north end of the rink.

All the players dashed in that direction and the battle for the goal began. The players banged into each other, tripped each other, swung their hockey sticks at each other, and, from my vantage point, the mission was to kill the other team's players, not get the puck into the net goal.

But my fears of Tommy being hurt were dispelled.

He was still near the center of the arena, trying to make his skates work as he headed toward the action at about two feet per hour.

He skated so hard.

Skate, skate, skate.

But those darn skates just didn't work for him like they did for the older boys. He hadn't quite mastered the art of turning one skate sideways and pushing off that skate and gliding on the front skate. His best form of propulsion was by using his hockey stick as a paddle and "canoeing" along.

About the time he finally neared the action on the north end, the puck was slapped back across the rink to the south end and all the other players dashed in that direction.

The puck went whizzing past him; the other players followed the puck and left him all alone at the north end.

Slowly, carefully, so as not to fall, he turned and started toward the action.

Skating as hard as he could to enter the fray…at about two feet per hour.

Skate, skate, skate.

The Man in The Arena...

He was so serious, so intent to get into the action, but to our relief, it was not to be.

This went on for the whole game. Tommy was 180 degrees away from danger at all times, and much to our delight, he became the darling of the team as the fans began to cheer more for Tommy's progress up and down the rink than they did for the older boy's scoring exploits.

Mercifully, it was a short season. One of the older boys got injured, and that was the end of the season of "the great ice hockey adventure."

Tommy hung up his hockey equipment, and we waited for the fall season for something more civilized…football.

It was early fall when an interesting fellow came to visit. I was in the office at the airport when he came in, unannounced, and introduced himself.

He was not too tall in stature, about five foot four, with *brown* hair. He also wore a *brown* suit, *brown* shirt, *brown* tie, *brown* belt, and *brown* shoes and socks.

"Hello," he said, "I'm Arch Brown."

"I'd never have guessed," I said, laughing. "What can I do for you, Mr. Brown?"

"Call me Arch," he said, "and it's not what you can do for me; it's what I can do for *you*."

Oh boy, I thought. *Here comes a sales pitch. Whatever he's selling, I'm not buying.*

Well, I was wrong, about the buying part. Arch was a public relations person and a one-man company. He went on and on about why I needed to hire him, and finally, when he finished and I explained that my budget did not include funds for a PR firm, he made me an offer I couldn't resist. He'd work for expenses and almost no salary for a while to prove that he could improve my passenger loads.

We finally agreed that I would pay him a flat fee of fifty dollars per week plus his expenses and review his progress in six months.

Now, Arch Brown was a special character. He lived off the fat of the land. I don't think he ever spent a dime on food. He ate at receptions, invited lunches, free breakfasts, condominium openings, and wherever else there was a free meal.

The first thing he did after I hired him was order ID cards printed with corporate titles. He also ordered calling cards. This was a good idea, and it opened up a new area of free lunches for him. Public relation people were notorious for being invited to airline receptions, and his new position opened many new doors for him for freebies.

His new calling card offered three phone numbers: a business number, a day number, and a night number. I thought that to be rather curious until I learned that at his apartment in Coconut Grove, he could plug, and unplug, his phone to a neighbor's phone jack in the basement garage. One of his neighbors worked a night shift and one worked during the day. He would simply plug his phone into the appropriate neighbor's jack based on the time of day.

Once he invited me to his home office to sign some papers. I noted that the apartment was not well lit. I inquired as to why it was so dim in there, and to my amazement he admitted that he had a long extension cord passing out through his sliding doors to a neighbor's outside socket. If he used too much electricity, he was afraid that he would blow a fuse there.

Good ole Arch, always thinking of others.

In the '60s and '70s, the State of Florida required that all vehicles be inspected, and that inspection would be evidenced by a sticker in the front left corner of the windshield of the car. Arch solved that expense by gluing a small palm frond across that corner of his windshield.

But, business wise, Arch was very creative. He gave all the red caps at the front of the terminal his card and told them that if they brought a customer, non-pre-ticketed, to our counter, he would give them a dollar. Then he visited all the local airport hotels and distributed our newly printed brochures and made the same offer to the bellhops. He also gave the hotel bellhops pass privileges on AAT Airlines to Key West.

He had stickers with our name, phone numbers, flight schedules, and charter info printed and stuck them near all the pay phones in the terminal.

That's when I got a visit from the airport manager. He had received complaints from the other charter companies and airlines and indicated that the stickers should be removed immediately.

I issued a recall and Arch, reluctantly, removed all of the stickers. While he was at the phones, however, he did take a razor blade and surgically remove all Key West scheduled airline service info and charter info from the yellow pages at each pay phone…except ours.

With the two streamlined commuter airliners, we ended the year in good shape. Our systems were working, reservations were building, Arch Brown's PR programs were selling seats, and we looked forward to the

New Year with great anticipation. My Eastern seniority was growing, and it wouldn't be long until I could expect to be promoted to captain.

The news in early spring of 1971 was good. As a matter of fact, it was wonderful.

National Airlines announced that they were pulling their B-727s out of Key West immediately.

Our reservation phone lines began to light up. We couldn't handle all the business. I had gone to seven days a week service earlier, and now we increased our weekday service from three round trips to four daily.

The airline was cooking. We were in the airline clearing house, all our schedules were listed worldwide in the Official Airline Guide, and we had interline ticketing and baggage agreements with all major airlines. I had set up operation manuals for the station agents, pilots, and mechanics, and we had established credit with most suppliers.

Vic called for a meeting.

He said that we needed capital; we needed a capital infusion as opposed to a loan, and he explained that there might be people out there who would buy stock in the company now that National was out of the picture.

Vic's word was gospel to me. I trusted him implicitly.

He further said that he knew a person from the Turks and Caicos Islands who might be interested.

He said it was time to begin to act like a big airline, and that he would take a bigger part in that transition.

I was busy looking for a larger airplane that we could afford, and I left the big airline stuff up to Vic.

I found a sixteen-seat de Havilland Heron available for lease. This model aircraft was originally designed for the queen of England to be the safest airplane built. It had four engines and could actually fly with only one engine operating. This particular aircraft was being used as an executive aircraft in Canada and the company operating it ceased operation. It was available immediately. I just didn't have the down payment for the lease.

I met with Vic and he agreed to introduce me to the person who might be interested in investing in AAT Airlines.

His name was C. Edward Poynter. I never trusted men who started their names with their first initial, but I let it go in this case as I trusted Vic's judgment.

We met for a while and Vic suggested that C. or C. Edward or Edward—I never knew how to address those people whose initials begin their names—might want to invest in the airline. He was not the principal investor, but he might want to put five thousand in the company as an investment in stock, and later, his friend in Turks and Caicos Islands might invest. He suggested that he, Vic, and I might like to discuss it later and get back to C. or Edward.

I agreed and returned my attention to the acquisition of the four-engine de Havilland.

It was several days later when Vic and I met. He took on a serious air and pulled out his pen and began to jot down his capitalization plan.

"Here's what I think we should do," he said in his quiet and serious voice. "As of now, we have one hundred shares authorized, and you own all of them."

"Yes," I said.

"Let's increase the total authorized shares to a thousand. We'll reissue three hundred to you representing 30 percent of the company, give me 25 percent for my sweat equity, take the five thousand dollars from Poynter, and give him 15 percent. We'll form a board of directors with the three of us, and after the de Havilland arrives, if we need additional capital we'll have 30 percent available for sale."

He continued, "You and I will always have 55 percent of the company, and control, even if we sold the additional 30 percent."

I didn't give it much thought. The math looked good, with Vic and me owning 55 percent of the company, we would always be in control, so I approved. I gave Vic the phone number of an Eastern copilot I had flown with who was a part-time corporate lawyer, and ask that he call the lawyer and set it up. Meanwhile, I would continue with the acquisition of the de Havilland and the training involved.

It was done.

I brought the airplane down from Canada and hired two more pilots, Captain Bill Gonzales and Captain Hector Villamar. Both had come to the United States ten years earlier from Cuba and they had heavy airplane experience.

The training went well and we set up Wednesday, May 19th, for the inaugural flight to Key West.

Arch Brown was in his glory. We had put him in charge of the flight attendant program. He hired two young women and outfitted them in orange "hot pants." He claimed, and I believed him to be accurate, that we were the first airline in the U.S. to sport hot pants on flight attendants.

The Man in The Arena...

For the first flight, he hired a professional model for all the photo shots with the officials at Key West. Her additional chore was to take care of our FAA check airman, Mr. Chuck Smith, who was riding along to approve the airplane over the new routes. As I recall, she did that well. Chuck and I had many laughs over that years later. It might have been his crowning moment as a FAA agent.

The flight went well. Our news was splashed all over the front page of the *Key West Citizen,* and we made the *Miami Herald* also. Arch was really good at getting "free stuff."

The de Havilland was performing well. It was widely accepted by the customers and it was very reliable. We kept the two Cessnas as backup aircraft and for charters.

The charter operation continued to grow. We flew all over the Southeast, Florida, and the Caribbean.

I guess the most interesting charter we did was for NASA in July.

I received a call from NASA, Cape Kennedy, on the afternoon of Saturday, July 24th. The caller had a sense of urgency in his voice when he asked me if I had an aircraft and pilot available. He had called several local operators around the Cape and no one could accommodate his request.

"Yes, sir," I said, as we never said no to a customer. "What can I help you with?"

I was floored when he told me.

He explained that they—NASA—had a moon shot scheduled for Monday morning. It was Apollo 15, it was to land on the moon, and it carried the first LRV, a lunar roving vehicle, a moon buggy he called it, named, I suppose, after the local dune buggies.

All was on schedule until a flaw was discovered in the batteries that were to be used to power the vehicle and transmit communications back to Earth. The replacement batteries were in St. Louis, Missouri, and he needed them at the Cape, NOW!

I looked at my watch. I looked at the calendar. I looked at a giant wall map, calculated quickly in my head, and exclaimed, "We can do it, sir. We can be at the Cape with your cargo by midnight Sunday."

"Hold on," he said. "Let me call my boss."

He came back on in two minutes. "Can you make it six hours earlier?"

"Let me check again," I responded.

I checked the distance; it was about twelve hundred miles from Miami to St Louis and from St Louis to the Cape it was about a thousand.

I calculated again, with two pilots flying directly and minimum stops for fuel only.

"Yes, we can do it," I guaranteed. "You must have the cargo ready with a fuel truck, hundred octane, in St Louis, ready for a quick turn."

"Will do," he said, and we exchanged phone numbers. I began to set up the trip. It was almost dark and I figured we must leave by midnight to make it.

I called Hector Villamar and Bill Gonzales with orders to "get out here as quick as you can with a small overnight bag. I'll tell you about the trip when you get here. By the way," I added, "stop by Royal Castle and pick up a dozen hamburgers to go."

The mechanic was still on duty, so I had him preflight the aircraft and monitor the fueling operation.

I dumped all the cash out of the petty cash fund and pulled the emergency money from the small safe under my desk. *That should be enough for the fuel and any landing fees*, I thought.

Hector and Bill showed up at about the same time, and I briefed them on the trip. They were to stop for fuel only once outbound and once inbound, and when they stopped for gas, they were to call me and I would advise NASA of their progress.

Any delays and we were cautioned that the NASA mission would be scrubbed.

They were as excited as I was, and after filing their flight plan, they were ready to go. They had all the info for the St. Louis pickup. At 11:00 p.m. they taxied out. They were "can do" pilots and I knew that I could rely on them to get the mission done.

They did a great job. They arrived at the Cape an hour earlier than promised and retrieved the batteries. Hector and Bill were treated like astronauts, and Apollo 15 launched on schedule Monday morning at 9:34. I received a nice call, after the launch, complimenting us on our cargo trip.

It was a round trip to St. Louis for the two pilots and the Cessna 402. The batteries were not so lucky.

They're still on the moon.

I was basking in the glow of success of the airline when Vic called for another meeting. He advised me that Poynter's buddy was ready to invest and that he thought we might consider it in order to prepare for the next step, a larger aircraft.

I relied on Vic's judgment on matters such as this and asked him to set up a meeting. He suggested that he contact the lawyer and set up a board meeting to approve the sale of some stock to Poynter's friend, Mr. A. Douglas Russell. I frowned at the mention of another person who began his name with an initial. Vic thought that 20 percent for twenty thousand was doable.

I agreed. We set up a date for a stockholder and director meeting in mid-September at the attorney's office.

I showed up at the appointed time, and the other four attendees were already there. There was the attorney, Vic, Poynter and I representing the full board, and A. Douglas Russell was there as an observer. The attorney slid the agenda across the conference table to me. I quickly reviewed it; opening remarks, review of recent history, financial report, issue of additional stock for new investor, and approval of slate of directors and officers.

I glanced over to Vic, he nodded approval, and I opened the meeting.

I gave an overview of the airline; the successes with the new, larger airplane and the increase in passenger loads due to the departure of National Airlines from the market. I briefed the group on the new offices that we had just moved into at the northwest corner of the airport, the new receptionist and the advanced reservation system I had just devised and set up.

Vic gave the treasurer's report, and when we reached the agenda item concerning the stock for the new investor, Poynter made a motion to increase the authorized shares up from a thousand to one hundred thousand. That motion was seconded by Vic, and I approved, knowing that my percentage of the company would increase accordingly. Pointer made a motion that his 150 shares, representing 15 percent of the company, should be increased to fifteen thousand. That motion also was seconded by Vic and approved by the three of us. Pointer made a third motion to increase Vic's shares from 250 up to twenty-five thousand. It, too, was approved unanimously.

I didn't realize it but at that moment, I gave away control of the airline. Vic and Poynter owned 40 percent and I owned less than one-third of a percent.

I waited for Poynter to make the motion for the increase of my stock prorated up to the hundred-thousand-share level.

The room was quiet.

The attorney broke the silence. "The next item on the agenda is the approval of the slate of directors and officers," he said as he slid a sheet of paper across the table to Poynter.

I was confused. Surely there was a mistake. This was orchestrated so smoothly that Poynter just forgot to make the motion for my stock increase.

I looked around, and then again at the agenda, trying to make some sense of this, when Poynter spoke. "Do I hear a motion to approve the new list of officers and board members?"

I glanced over. My name was not listed.

"I…make such a motion…." I could hardly hear Vic's comments. His head was bowed and he never looked up.

"I second," I heard Poynter exclaim.

"Hey, just a minute." I half stood from my chair. "What's going on here?"

I looked around the conference table. Russell was at the far end, examining his fingernails; The attorney, at my left, sat expressionless; Poynter had slid his chair back as if to remove himself from my immediate proximity; and Vic, my trusted friend Vic, sat, staring down at some imaginary data on the pad in front of him. He never looked up.

And then I got it. The company that I had built had just been stolen. Stolen just as sure as if the thieves at the table had worn bandannas and brandished pistols.

To create a scene now would give them too much satisfaction. My head was spinning. I stood up, closed my notebook, and retreated for the door.

As I left I glanced back, one more time, and saw Vic, still intently examining his note pad. He never made eye contact with me and I never saw him again.

I drove back to the new offices in a daze. This couldn't be…but it was. I could do nothing; after all, I seconded the motion for my execution.

I arrived at my office just as a van pulled out of the driveway. It read "Hialeah Lock and Key."

Margaret, the new receptionist, was in tears. "Here's a new key, Mr. Cooper," she sobbed. "They'll probably fire me next."

I cleaned my desk, retrieved a few pictures off the wall, and left for the safety and serenity of my duplex.

That night Arch Brown, Margaret, and the pilots came by. No one understood why this happened, and they all volunteered to quit in protest, but I suggested that they all stay. I knew the company needed pilots and the pilots needed the job, and I also knew that Arch and Margaret would not be around long.

I was correct on all accounts.

I had lost an airline, but I had learned some valuable lessons.

The School of Hard Knocks offered a tough curriculum, and I had passed Airline Management 101 with flying colors.

CHAPTER 55

Back to College

Embry Riddle Aeronautical University at thirty-four years of age

THE DULL PAIN OF THE AAT Airlines experience slowly subsided as I fled to the bosom of "Mother" Eastern. Flying full time kept me busy, but there were still those days off between flights. That issue was solved by Eastern.

I was checking my company mailbox prior to a flight when I discovered a brochure published jointly by Eastern and Embry Riddle School of Aeronautics. Embry Riddle, in conjunction with a local college, Barry College, was offering college courses culminating in a degree for business persons.

The student would enroll in the courses required, attend all classes that his personal job would allow, and for the courses missed, the student could purchase a tape recording of the missed classes to keep current.

And, best of all, if you worked for Eastern, the company would pay for the courses.

I enrolled. My previous courses at the University of North Carolina plus credits given for my Eastern experience placed me halfway through my junior year, and I could expect to graduate in about two years.

It had been seventeen years since I had driven down to Chapel Hill to enroll in UNC, but I had the same sensations as I drove up to Miami Shores, a small town just north of Miami to process into Barry College. My selected field was aviation, and I was working toward a Bachelor of Science degree in Aviation Management.

The courses offered were surprisingly appropriate. There was Aviation Law, Aviation Accounting, and some courses on personnel management. With the filler courses of art, history, etc., I felt good about the program.

Plus, in the back of my mind, I remembered that I had promised Mom I would someday finish college.

The experience at Barry College went well. The tape recording system worked perfectly, and I could stay current by listening to the recordings on my airline layovers. And, just like at UNC, I began to form some friendships with fellow classmates with like goals.

One such classmate was Vernon Green.

Vernon was an Eastern mechanic and a serious student. He lived near the Miami International Airport, close to Miami Springs, so we studied together and sometimes carpooled. We became best friends, a friendship that lasts to this day.

College kept my mind off the unfortunate experience of AAT Airline, and I continued the program throughout 1972.

In March of 1973, I received notice from Eastern that my number had come up for captain of the Boeing 727. I completed the captain's course and was promoted in May of that year.

I continued my college courses and in December of 1973, I graduated from Embry Riddle Aeronautical University with my parents proudly looking on at the ceremony at Barry College.

In 1973, I was introduced to a tall, pretty young lady by the name of Jerrie James. I didn't expect the relationship to last very long.

I was wrong; we were married a year later in December 1974.

When I graduated from Embry Riddle, Vernon, who had no previous college and needed two additional years to graduate, lost interest and dropped out. He had resigned from Eastern and decided that he wanted to start his own air charter company. He convinced me to help him, and in return he would give me 50 percent of the stock. I had no interest in a charter airline, but with college behind me, I needed a diversion other than golf. So I agreed.

CHAPTER 56
Another Airline Venture

I'm a slow learner.

WE INCORPORATED THE COMPANY UNDER the name of Air Miami, certified it with the FAA quickly, purchased an aero commander, and set up shop on 36th Street at Miami International Airport.

Vernon was the operator and I paid little attention other than when he needed some advice.

I did watch, out of curiosity, the progress of AAT Airlines. In early 1974 they changed their name to Air Sunshine and purchased larger aircraft. Their fortunes were further enhanced in late 1975 when Southeast Airlines, their only competitor in the Miami/Key West market ceased operations.

That whetted my appetite for the business again, and in June of 1976, I convinced Vernon to apply to the Florida State Public Service Commission, the Florida agency that governed the intra-state air routes, for permission to operate between Miami and Key West.

The application was met with fierce resistance, especially since one of the new owners of Air Sunshine was a popular politician from Key West.

The PSC was comprised of three members. We hired an attorney, James Curasi, who had previously been an aide for one of the members, Paula Hawkins. He filed our application and we waited for an answer.

The PSC set up a public hearing in Key West in August 1976. It was scheduled for one day, but it lasted for three with no end in sight. The local owners of Air Sunshine, formerly ATA Airlines, were determined to keep us out, and they put up a terrific fight.

A second meeting was set up a month later, and when that meeting finally came to a close, there was nothing to do but wait. We had put up a good fight, established an argument for competition on the route, and produced data to back up our contention.

A month later the results came down from Tallahassee.

Denied!

We were crushed. Especially Vernon. He had devoted a lot of time and energy to this project and, not having the Eastern salary to back him up, he just couldn't survive on the meager profits, if any, of the small air charter company.

Fortunately, he had begun to develop a second company; an airplane washing company that was becoming quite profitable. He explained that before a large aircraft can move into a major maintenance check, it must be cleaned and all the oil and dirt removed. He had developed an environmentally safe wash facility at the airport and was enjoying an active list of customers.

Since he needed more time to develop his airplane washing company, he offered his shares of Air Miami to me for a reasonable price, and we consummated the deal.

With the entrepreneur juices flowing again, I moved the offices into the back bedroom of the duplex and began to look for additional charter business, other than just walk-in traffic at the terminal.

The casino in Freeport, Grand Bahamas, was beginning to boom, and I made contact with one of the promoters in Ft. Lauderdale. We struck a deal. I purchased a sixteen-seat de Havilland Heron, the same as the old AAT airplane, and began to operate gambling junkets to Freeport.

I leased some ramp space from Mr. Gene Harris on the north side of Miami International Airport and set up a maintenance base and began the junket operation.

It wasn't really that lucrative, and given the prices we were charging, it was more trouble than it was worth. After a year of operating gambling junkets, I was ready to sell the Heron and operate one small Aero Commander when my landlord, Mr. Gene Harris, approached me with a business proposal.

He had acquired a company called Shawnee Airlines in the fall of 1977 that possessed a permit to operate scheduled air service into the Bahama Islands. He suggested that we operate that permit under the Air Miami certificate and split the profits.

I wasn't familiar with the Bahama Islands. I had traveled there only three times before: once to South Bimini, later a fishing trip with some buddies from South Florida and a third time with Jerrie, to Alice Town in Bimini.

CHAPTER 57
Remembering The Bahamas

Bimini and Chub Cay

MY TRIP TO SOUTH BIMINI had been interesting. I was due for a check ride on the B-727, and I wanted to escape from the distractions of Miami in order to study. I struck up a conversation with an Eastern reservations clerk who suggested that I visit South Bimini.

There was a resort there called the Sunshine Inn, formerly the home of Colonel Mackey, the founder and previous owner of Mackey Airlines. He had sold that airline to Eastern in 1967, and since the inn was part of the deal, Eastern found itself running a resort in the Bahamas.

I grabbed a pass and off I went to South Bimini. The flight was on an Eastern Convair and took only about fifteen minutes. A van from the hotel picked me up, and within five minutes I was checking in at the Sunshine Inn.

It was beautiful…isolated…and I was the only guest there. It was perfect for my studies, but I couldn't help but think how much this project was costing Eastern.

The grounds were beautiful. The original house was built on a point overlooking the Atlantic and had been converted into the main reception and dining area. There was an additional two-storied building constructed for more rooms, and a marina rounded out a marvelous setting.

The chef was outstanding; he introduced me to the island delicacy; Bahamian lobster and conch chowder along with Bimini bread. The bartender was outstanding also; he introduced me to the "Bahama Mama".

A beautiful white sand beach was within walking distance, and that's where I found myself the next morning.

I had established a study practice over the past several years that I felt would best prepare me for any check ride. I would divide the study periods into sections: aircraft systems, procedures, limitations, emergencies, and finally Federal Air Regulations and company procedures. I would take one day per subject, and the last couple of days I would spend reviewing all the items I had studied.

The solitary beach was completely deserted—perfect for the final review that I gave myself. I found a nice stick and, starting at one end of the beach and in the sand, I scratched out everything that I had studied in preparation for my recurrent exam. The results of my review went on for hundreds of yards along the beach.

I had all sorts of hieroglyphics etched out across the sandy beach. There were hydraulic systems, fuel systems, air-conditioning systems, and a myriad of numbers representing pressures, temperatures, speeds, and limitations.

I'm sure that if someone had happened along this deserted beach, they would have thought it had been invaded by Martians.

Alas, my handiwork was erased each night by the incoming tide, and I was met the next morning with a clean slate on which to work.

By the end of the day, I had established the subjects where I was weak, and upon correcting those items, I felt comfortably prepared for the upcoming check ride.

The local staff was very friendly, especially when they found out that I was an Eastern pilot. I suppose they thought I was a partial owner. They visited with me and filled me in on all the folklore surrounding South Bimini.

It seems that Ponce de Leon visited South Bimini and discovered the fountain of youth. The staff confirmed that it was somewhere on South Bimini, only no one had found it since ole Ponce left town.

The other tale was of the Chickcharnies—two-foot-tall elves with penetrating red eyes. They are harmless, but it is said that they hide behind the trees, and if you leave your lunch unguarded, they will pilfer it and you will not be able to find it. They are very quick. When one creeps up behind you, you must turn very quickly in order to see it.

Later that night, after a few Bahama Mamas, I saw several.

The other curious thing about South Bimini was the fact that no native would spend the night there. The people who worked there all lived in Alice Town, on North Bimini, and commuted daily by boat. I think that practice is a holdover from the '20s and '30s when South Bimini was a major drop-off point for smugglers supplying liquor to Florida during prohibition. The bootleggers kept the local citizenry terrified of spending the night on South Bimini, where they kept the bulk of the goods warehoused until the smaller boats could come over from Miami and collect their order. It is said that Al Capone was a visitor there a number of times, setting up his supply chain of spirits.

Back in Miami I aced the check ride, thanks, in part, to the solitude of the beach at South Bimini.

The second time I visited the Bahamas was on a fishing expedition with several pals in 1970. One member of the group had a friend who had a cottage on Chub Cay, an island about fifty miles northwest of Nassau. We agreed to stop at Alice Town, North Bimini, and fish for a couple of days, then proceed on to the cottage on Chub Cay, again fish for a few days, and finally proceed to Nassau before returning home.

On the day of departure, the weather was good, and we made landfall at Bimini in only about four hours. The marinas at Alice Town are all on the east side of the island, and to get to them one must head directly toward South Bimini and navigate the tricky sandbars hidden just off shore. That's made easy by two large poles positioned on shore, painted red, which the captain can line up on to ensure he is maneuvering across the deepest part of the sand banks. After traversing the sand banks, you must turn north and hug the coast of South Bimini until you find the deeper waters of the harbor on the east side of Alice Town.

After crossing the sandbar, as we paralleled the beach at South Bimini, I remembered the time I spent there, three years earlier, studying for my B-727 check ride and remembering all the local stories the staff shared with me on that trip. I wondered if the local lore now included some mysterious writings obviously left etched on the beach by an itinerant UFO with a message from outer space.

We tied up at Brown's Hotel and went directly to the bar.

We learned that sandwiches were always readily available there, and we relaxed over a few beers of the local variety, Kalik, pronounced, "Click," while the sandwiches were being prepared.

That evening we discovered a great restaurant nearby. It was nothing more than an oversized shack divided into two rooms. The first room was a bar, and the back room, overlooking the harbor, was the dining area. The outside was painted solid red with a lion painted on the façade. Naturally the name was the "Red Lion." The food was terrific, with the ribs being the best I had ever tasted. The Kalik was good too, and cold.

We had every intention of fishing the next day, but the weather had other ideas. A storm blew up and we were grounded.

With nothing to do, we explored the small town with its two main streets: Queen's Highway along the coast line on the west side of town, and King's Highway paralleling the east side of town along the harbor.

Being a rather small island, the exploring took only an hour, and after a few beers at the End of the World bar down near Chalks seaplane ramp, we found ourselves back at Brown's Hotel and bar for the duration of the day.

It was time well spent. We met the owner, a stately old gentleman by the name of Harcourt Brown. He was about as close to being the patriarch of the town as anyone. He owned the hotel, the power plant, and the freighter that supplied the town weekly with fresh food from Miami.

We also learned the local game of ring toss. It consisted of a string with a metal ring tied to one end and the other fastened to the ceiling. The game was to pull the ring back to a spot next to the player's ear, and then release it. It would then fall in a downward arc toward the opposing wall and would, if released correctly, snag itself on a hook on the wall.

After a few Kaliks, money would eventually be wagered on one's ability at this skillful bar game. We learned, very soon (but not soon enough) not to bet the local populace at this game. We were "high school" players and they were "Olympians."

The next day the other guys went fishing, but I stayed and hung around the bar. I became friends with Mr. Brown, who spent a lot of time with me relating the interesting stories of early Bimini. He had been a close friend of Hemingway and he was very generous with his stories of Hemingway's exploits: the fishing, the boxing, the drinking…and other.

Later that day another legend walked in with a small entourage. I recognized him immediately.

It was Adam Clayton Powell.

The phrase "bigger than life" was written for him. When he entered the room, he owned it. Handsome, tall, and with an infectious laugh, he dominated the surroundings. He and his group grabbed a small round table in the corner, ordered a round of drinks for everyone in the bar, and played dominos for the rest of the afternoon.

Mr. Brown told me later that Powell was the only "local" who lived on South Bimini. He had a small cottage in a development started by Colonel Mackey called Port Royal, but he spent most of his days in Alice Town or fishing. Mr. Brown said that he was spending much more time in Bimini since he had some ethics issues in the House of Representatives in Washington.

At various times during the day, Harcourt's sons would stop by. He introduced me to Julian, Ossie, and Neville. They ran his enterprises around Alice Town. Ossie seemed to be the friendliest, and we spent some time together that afternoon at the bar.

My friends returned with several dolphins, not the flipper type but the mahi-mahi.

Mr. Brown arranged for a local woman to come by and cook for us, and we dined in splendor at the bar in Brown's Hotel.

The next morning, we headed out for Chub Cay. Upon leaving Bimini you must sail south to Gun Cay, a small island next to Cat Cay, about five miles south of Alice Town. There is a cut there, between the two small islands, with deep water allowing you to enter a waterway that leads eastward toward Chub Cay.

The water depth is quite shallow across the Bahama Banks and, given the clarity of the water, you can get the illusion that you are about to run aground. With good weather, it's a nice crossing and such was this day.

Six hours later we were pulling into the dock at Chub Cay. We needed fuel and directions to the cottage where we were to meet up with our friend's acquaintance.

As the attendant began to pump our gas we asked him for directions and he knew immediately of the cottage. He directed us to head about two miles east, and when we reached the end of Chub Cay, we'd turn north between Chub and another island called Bird Cay. He cautioned us, "Don't get too near the next island along there. It's a private island called Whale Cay, and it's owned by a crazy lady. She'll shoot anyone who gets near it."

Well, okay, I thought, *more of this local folklore*, so we finished fueling and set out on our way. Luckily, we didn't encounter the crazy lady and soon forgot the warning.

Years later I happened onto a book by Kate Sommerscale called *The Queen of Whale Cay*. The dock master was right. She was quite eccentric and WOULD shoot you if you ventured too close to her empire.

Her name was Joe Carstair—a tomboy who dressed like a man. She had been an ambulance driver in the First World War, and after the war she owned and operated a taxi and chaperone service in London until her mother died and left her a sizable inheritance from the Standard Oil Company.

She purchased Whale Cay in the mid-thirties for forty thousand dollars and set up her own small country. She built a mansion, a church, a cannery, an airport, and she paved miles of roads throughout the island. She allowed no one on the property without an invite.

She entertained lavishly with such guests as the Duke and Duchess of Windsor and famous entertainers such as Tallulah Bankhead, Greta Garbo, Marlene Dietrich, and others.

She sold the island in 1975 and moved to Miami and then, due to ill health, she moved to Naples, Florida, where she died in 1993.

My only other exposure to the Bahamas was on a mini-vacation to Alice Town on North Bimini in the summer of 1973. Al Burnett, my old partner in the flight school, and I decided to take our girlfriends to Bimini for a short fishing trip. Jerrie had some time off from her job, and my Eastern schedule was open also. So off we went in our forty-two-foot boat.

The trip over had its usual moments, but we managed to make it safely and docked at the Big Game Fishing Club, operated by the Bacardi family. After tying up the boat, we strolled down King's Highway to the Red Lion for dinner. As usual, the lobster and ribs were delicious, and we relaxed over a few beers while we decided what to do next.

I remembered that there was an old, historically significant hotel called The Compleat Anglers that had a small, quaint bar, so I decided to take the group down there for a nightcap.

It was only a few hundred yards south of the Red Lion, and we were there in a second. As we walked under the red archway that led to a walkway to the front steps leading to the reception area, I sensed that there was something different. Although it was early, only about eight o'clock, the lights were out and the place was dark.

I climbed up two steps toward the front door and was halted in my tracks by a very serious and gruff female voice from behind the screen door.

"What are you doing on my property?" she roared.

I was terrified. "Nothing, ma'am," I nervously replied. "I just wanted to show my friends the bar here and have a drink."

"Well," she continued in the very unwelcoming voice, "this place is closed and you're not welcome."

"I'm terribly sorry to have bothered you," I said as I backed down the steps. "We'll leave now……..And, again, I'm sorry to have bothered you."

As we turned to leave, she asked, in a much more civilized voice, "Where are you from?"

Still slowly moving back toward the street, I explained, "We're from Miami and we're only here for a couple of nights."

"Well, if all you want is a couple of drinks, then come on in," she offered.

We followed her into the front room, the reception area, and as she turned on a few dim lights, I made out the small bar located in the rear of the room. It had never been set up for the public, only as an accommodation for the few renters who might stay there. There were six stools, with the usual bottles of liquor lined up on a shelf behind the bar.

She walked behind the bar. "I'm Helen Duncombe and I own this place… that is, until tomorrow morning. I just sold out to Harcourt Brown. I'm leaving tomorrow on the first Chalks Airline seaplane for Miami and then on to England."

While she talked, she began to place bottle after bottle of liquor on the bar. "Take your choice. I don't want to leave a drop of liquor here when I leave," and she added, "It's on the house."

And thus began a most interesting evening.

Mrs. Duncombe gave us the whole history of the hotel. It was actually the second hotel that she and her husband Henry had owned at Alice Town. The first one burned down in 1935, and she and Henry built the existing hotel on the same spot.

She talked about having lumber and building materials sent over from Miami, but she added, a lot of the timbers in the hotel were scavenged from the beach, having washed up as driftwood.

Henry had been the city commissioner for Alice Town earlier and had died in 1949. She continued to operate the hotel until, well, that night.

She broke out the customer register, and we marveled at the names of famous people who had stayed there. There were politicians, movie stars, and famous athletes. We saw Lucille Ball's name there along with King Farouk, the old Egyptian dictator.

She told us stories about Ernest Hemingway. "He would sleep here," she said, "but he liked to hang out around the bars down at Weechs and Brown's Hotel with the guys." I got the impression that she wasn't too fond of Hemingway as I heard her hiss, under her breath, "He was a hell raiser."

We had visited with Mrs. Duncombe for over two hours. In retrospect, I think that she enjoyed sitting with us as much as we enjoyed her company and stories, and that, maybe, she needed to tell the story to somebody. It was as if she was finishing an era in her life and needed to review, and maybe validate, that period.

Knowing that she was rising early the next day, we politely thanked her for the cocktails and, more importantly, her stories and excused ourselves. She followed us to the door and as I looked back I could see her waving good-bye.

We turned up Queen's Highway toward the Big Game Fishing Club and our boat. I couldn't help but think that we had the honor of being the last guests of The Compleat Anglers Hotel while it was under the ownership of Mrs. Duncombe.

The boys' fishing trip to the Bahamas, the study hall on South Bimini, and the brief visit with Jerrie and Al Burnett to North Bimini were the only exposure I had to the Bahamas. But when Mr. Harris made the offer to operate a scheduled airline there, with visions of exotic beaches, famous personalities, and world-class fishing, I excitedly took it.

We needed an additional airplane and such an operation required additional infrastructure. I found another de Havilland Heron, purchased it, and set up the necessary departments for the scheduled operation.

With all the preparation completed, we started the operation in the spring of 1978.

Our first routes were from Miami to Freeport; Miami to North Eleuthera; and from Miami to Marsh Harbour. It was exciting traveling to these Bahamian destinations and setting up the operational bases. I was surprised at the availability of skilled airline agents available at such remote spots. However, I was quick to learn that most of them had worked for Mackey at one time or another.

The airline service was well received by the local business folks and the customers alike. We had convenient schedules and our loads grew rapidly.

Mr. Harris seemed to be pleased with our progress and didn't interfere with the operation other than stop by my office occasionally to discuss future plans.

CHAPTER 58

CUBA!

Rekindling a love for Cuba after seventeen years

IN EARLY SPRING OF 1978, we were chartered by Mr. Ken Turja, president of Tropicana Tours, to operate a series of charters to transport members of his company from Miami to Havana, Cuba. We knew that President Carter had opened up Cuba for American tourists the previous year. We anticipated charter requests such as this, so we had asked for and received permission from the U.S. State Department and the FAA to operate there.

Other than watching the progress of his charters and collecting the fees, I paid little attention to the political aspects of the trips.

It was only in the summer of 1978, when Ken visited me at my offices, that I began to realize the importance of his business. He explained that his company had been contracted by a cruise ship company to travel to Havana to negotiate landing rights at the harbor in downtown Havana. The negotiations broke down, as Ken explained, because the authorities in Havana didn't think the city was prepared to accept ships full of hundreds of American tourists at that time.

The conversation in Havana came around to the question of the cruise ship company's ability to use smaller ships, but the answer was "no," such smaller ships were not available. That was the end of the negotiations for the cruise ship company.

Ken had noticed that when he chartered the small six-seat aircraft used by Air Miami for his charters, there was a larger sixteen-seat aircraft on the ramp, and he wanted to know if it was available for regular trips to Havana, Cuba.

We talked about it. I looked at the Shawnee schedule and saw where we could move some departures around without doing too much damage to the schedule. I agreed that we could accommodate his request if the Cubans would go along with it.

He came back about a week later with a positive answer. The Cuban government agreed to the use of the sixteen-seat aircraft and allowed us to establish our own schedule.

Ken's company, Tropicana Tours, would be the marketing entity and Shawnee would be the transportation arm. We agreed on a schedule that took passengers from Miami to Havana on Friday mornings and returned them to Miami on the following Monday. The Monday flight took passengers down and returned them on the Friday flight.

I reviewed the program with Mr. Harris, and although he wasn't too enthused with the new flights, he reluctantly agreed. His concerns were twofold: he was concerned with security, knowing the sensitive mood of the local Cuban population concerning travel to Cuba, and he wanted to expand into the Bahamas and was concerned about serving two markets.

Our first flight was on Friday, August 18, 1978. Although there had been some ad hoc charters to Havana since President Carter had lifted the travel ban earlier the previous year, we were the first company to establish regular scheduled charter flights between the two countries since the travel embargo was put in place by President Kennedy in 1963.

The flight went off without a hitch. Airport security was heavy, with guards around our aircraft the entire night before the trip and officers with dogs on site during the loading of the aircraft. That procedure remained in effect throughout the ensuing years.

It had been about twenty years since I had been to Cuba. We landed and taxied up to the passenger terminal on the south side of the Jose Martí International Airport and cleared customs. It was a strange experience. I had expected that with the revolutionary government, security would be extreme, with armed guards everywhere. To my surprise, I saw no guards, and the clearing of customs was routine.

The ride into town tweaked my memory; it was as if nothing had changed. Nothing *had* changed. With the exception of a new hospital recently built near the center of town, the town was practically the same as I remembered.

We stayed at the Riviera Hotel, which had retained some of the splendor that it once exuded just after it was built by gangster Meyer Lansky in 1957. It was a splendid hotel, rising twenty-one floors on the Malecón, a boulevard running along the Gulf of Mexico. Its front entrance was still guarded by a beautiful statue created by the intertwining of a mermaid and a swordfish. Inside, the lobby was spacious with a luxurious lounge, L'Elegante, off to the side across from the now vacant casino.

The hotel had opened in December 1957 with an opening act in the casino staring Ginger Rogers. It was nationalized in 1960.

We were treated royally by the Cuban agency, Cubatur, later to be renamed Havanatur, as we participated in the planned excursion around town and the surrounding countryside in modern air-conditioned busses.

The tour included a visit to Hemingway's farm, museums, walking tours in old Havana, a visit to the beaches east of Havana, and, of course, the best seats at the world-famous nightclub, the Tropicana.

I met the managers who ran Cubatur, Ernesto Marcell, Iraido Cartia, a guide, Dios Dado Ponvert, and a special friend to this day, Tony Vasquez, who managed all the fishing and diving throughout Cuba.

Monday came much too soon, and before we knew it we were loading onto the airplane and headed back to Miami.

There was something about the country—about the people—that stuck with me. I didn't realize it then but I suppose on that trip, I fell in love with Cuba all over again.

Back in Miami the business of running Shawnee Airlines and flying for Eastern Airlines continued. In August of 1978, Congress passed the Deregulation Act, which allowed airlines to operate between any two cities without government approval. This was the end of the PSC control over who flew where in the state of Florida.

That created an area of discord between Mr. Harris and me. His idea was to focus on the Bahamas only, but I saw many opportunities throughout Florida and Cuba also.

We continued to expand in the Bahamas, and in the spring of 1979, we opened Bimini and purchased a thirty-passenger DC-3.

The Bimini opening was a splendid event. It had been a few years since I was there, but when I visited Brown's bar, Mr. Brown recognized me immediately. When he learned that we were going to open a scheduled airline, he offered a small office, complete with phone, in the hotel as our downtown ticket office. Perfect.

Janette Cox, the charming woman who ran the airport coffee shop on South Bimini, volunteered her daughter to be our representative in town.

On opening day, Mr. Brown threw a grand party in honor of the Shawnee opening. The gala affair was held just outside his bar on the patio next to the harbor. Entertainment was provided by the local calypso band and by youngsters jumping off the roof of the bar into the bay.

The party was memorialized by another character we had just met.

Leicester Hemingway, Ernest's brother.

He ran a small twice-monthly newsletter there called *Bimini Out Island News* and he charged twenty-five cents per issue. He featured our opening party with pictures of Jerrie on the front page. I think that he fancied her more than the airline.

The year of 1978 flowed into 1979, with the Bahama business going well and the Havana flights operating smoothly, and I began to look for new areas to fly to. This was met with pushback from my partner, Gene Harris, who remained steadfast in his idea to only concentrate on flights to the Bahamas.

In early 1979, the Cuban government began to allow the Cuban-Americans who had settled in the United States to visit Cuba. When Ken Turja and I heard of this, we were elated. This, we thought, would open up a new avenue for business, and we immediately traveled to Havana to discuss the logistics of the decision.

To our surprise, the Cuban government split the "franchise" and only allowed us to continue to transport U.S. citizens. They gave the authority for the transportation of the Cuban-Americans to a local Cuban-American, Fernando Fuentes.

Although we were disappointed, we continued our flights to accommodate the U.S. citizens, and the program continued to be successful.

The Cuban government was interested in the program also. On a number of occasions, they sent several of the managers of Cubatur to visit the U.S. and participate in trade shows to market their destinations in Cuba.

Jerrie and I enjoyed entertaining our new friends from Cuba: Marcell, Dios Dado, and of course Tony. It was an interesting experience; they had proudly shown us around Cuba, and we, likewise, enjoyed exposing them to our country.

I also entered a dialogue with the "Cuba Desk" in Washington—a section that coordinated any communication relative to interfacing with the Cuban travel project. Its senior manager was Wayne Smith. We communicated during the early days of the program, and later he was based in Havana as the chief of the U.S. Interest Section (USINT). Our initial discussions centered on the transportation of cargo to Cuba on behalf of the USINT.

The Man in The Arena...

A call came in September from the Cuba Desk in Washington requesting a charter to transport Wayne Smith and his wife, Roxy, to Havana to assume the post of chief of the U.S. Interest Section there. He was to replace Lyle Lane, who had been the first chief to occupy the post in Havana after the Jimmy Carter thaw.

I had a few days off from Eastern, so I decided to fly the trip personally and to take Jerrie with me. We agreed on a specific meeting place at the Miami International Airport, at the commuter counter, and a definite time.

For small charters, we operated a six-passenger Aero Commander. It wasn't the most aesthetically pleasing airplane around. As a matter of fact, although it was very safe and reliable, it was desperately in need of a paint job, and one engine had just sprung an oil leak on a previous charter earlier that day. The oil leak had been corrected, but the aircraft was a mess, with oil from the engine down the side of the fuselage and over the tail. With no time to wash it, I jumped in with my wife, Jerrie, at our maintenance facility and taxied over to the terminal.

We hurried up the steps from the ramp to meet the newly assigned chief of the U.S. Interest Section in Havana.

We were looking for a sophisticated gentleman, as one would see in the movies, with pinstripe suit and thin mustache, carrying a polished black official briefcase, with a lady on his arm wearing a black dress with pearls.

We saw no such persons.

We did see, pacing around, a tall, bearded man wearing a rumpled bush jacket accompanied by a woman in slacks sitting, looking distressed, on a large suitcase.

They had arrived from Washington and were searching for a tall, handsome pilot with gold bars on his uniform and a hat emblazoned with "scrambled eggs" flying a shiny silver airplane, perhaps a jet, with gold lettering announcing "Air Miami " on the side.

He saw no such person or airplane.

What he did see, looking through the window at the terminal, was a small, ugly airplane with oil smeared from one side to the other...and no handsomely uniformed pilot.

The meeting area wasn't that spacious, and it didn't take long for us to cautiously approach each other.

"Are you the Air Miami pilot?" Wayne questioned.

"Yes, I am," I answered. "Are you the chief of the U.S. Interest Section?"

We both laughed at the absurdity of the misconceptions, and formally introduced ourselves.

Thus began a friendship that continues to this day.

Instead of a polished briefcase, Wayne and Roxy had two steamer trunks filled with clothes that definitely would not fit into the small aircraft. Luckily, we accommodated a couple of smaller overnight bags, and I sent the larger trunks down the next day on our larger scheduled charter.

The trip went well, and in Havana Wayne invited us to a party at his new residence, the home of the U.S. chief of the Interest Section. It was there that all the ambassadors from around the world stationed in Havana gathered to receive him in his new position.

It was a particularly meaningful experience as, eighteen years earlier, Wayne, a junior officer at the embassy, was the last to leave; he literally shut the lights off as he closed our United States embassy in Havana.

Wayne and I bonded and have enjoyed many great times together. Jerrie and I were invited many times for weekends with the Smiths, and we enjoyed relaxing at the five-acre residence and exploring Havana and the surrounding countryside with them.

It was Friday, September 28, when I got the call from Ken Turja. "Hey, Cooper, I've got a request from Washington for a private charter to Havana on Monday and I think you should fly it personally."

"Okay," I said. "What's the deal?"

"I'll be right over to your office to give you the scoop in person," he said and hung up.

He showed up about an hour later and gave me the details.

"I got a call this morning from the office of Cyrus Vance, the U.S. Secretary of State," he explained. "President Carter is planning on making a speech on Monday night over nationwide TV concerning a report that there is a buildup of Russian troops in Cuba and 'we cannot accept the status quo' will be the topic of the speech."

"Apparently," he continued quietly, "Carter's in trouble with his upcoming election and the Iran hostage situation, and rumor has it that this speech is meant to stir the pot a little to divert attention away from that issue. Additionally, Carter's National Security Council Adviser Brzezinski is hawkish on Cuba and is not one of Fidel's favorite people. Fidel doesn't trust him particularly."

"Vance would like to have someone in Havana to sit with Fidel during the speech to put out any fires before they start," he further explained, "and so they called me and I'm asking you to handle this personally. Take Jerrie and make it look like a short vacation. You already have a room at the Riviera."

"Okay," I said, "sounds like fun, but who am I taking?"

"The gentleman's name is Bill Attwood. He's an old friend of Adlai Stevenson and was a speechwriter and later an ambassador for President Kennedy. I was told that he was negotiating with Fidel on behalf of Kennedy to normalize relations between the two countries when Kennedy was shot in Dallas. The negotiations fell apart after that as LBJ wanted nothing to do with Cuba."

"He's arriving on an Eastern flight from D.C. at 9:30 on Monday morning. I gave him directions to your counter and told him that he should be arriving in Havana at around one o'clock. And," he added, "wear civilian clothes and keep this trip quiet."

This was beginning to sound like the old Riddle Airline days, I thought.

Jerrie was game for the trip, and we were waiting at our counter on Monday morning when Attwood showed up.

He was a dapper gentleman, impeccably dressed, and looked forever more like a real ambassador. We introduced each other and proceeded to the gate and on to the airplane. Both Jerrie and I were infatuated with him and soon we became fast friends.

The weather was good, and the trip was smooth. The view of the upper keys in South Florida is always spectacular and today was no exception. Over Marathon, I turned south toward Varadero Beach radio beacon, and at the midway point between Florida and Cuba, I contacted Havana Control.

The approach went smoothly, and the landing was uneventful. I taxied clear of the runway and contacted ground control, anticipating instructions to taxi to the normal small terminal set aside for the flights from the U.S.

"Turn right and taxi to the terminal on the south side of the field," came the instructions.

"The south side of the field?"

"Yes," the controller said. "The building to the west of the domestic terminal is for diplomats. The ground crew will secure your aircraft there."

We taxied up to the front of the "diplomatic building" and were met with an entourage of official-looking people.

We were escorted into the diplomatic building, where drinks were waiting, as were customs officials. Our passports were stamped and in less than five minutes we were out front of the building, loaded into a nice Town

Car, and headed toward the Riviera Hotel. I don't think I had time to finish my mojito.

We were greeted with the same attention at the front desk at the Riviera. It usually took minutes to check in, but only seconds later we were on the elevator to our rooms.

This flying with Bill Attwood was fun.

He was fun too. He suggested that we meet at five o'clock downstairs for a cocktail, and I reminded him of the lounge, L'Elegante, just off the lobby. We agreed to meet there.

Jerrie and I arrived a few minutes earlier and ordered a couple of daiquiris. The bartender in L'Elegante made the best daiquiris in Havana, with the exception of the Floridita, the old Hemingway hangout, in the old section of Havana.

Mr. Attwood showed up, right on time, and joined us. He ordered club soda with lime and I understood why. We ordered three medianoches—the ham and cheese sandwich that is a mainstay of the Cuban menu.

Pretty soon we dropped all formal titles. It was, Bill, Tom, and Jerrie as we got to know each other. In addition to being a diplomat, Bill was also a writer and he kept us merrily entertained with true-life stories about his tenure as ambassador to Guinea and as our first ambassador to Kenya. His experiences with Stevenson and Kennedy were interesting to hear about, and we were on the edge of our chairs when he talked about his previous meetings with Castro.

At about six thirty he stood up to excuse himself. "I'm invited to a party up on the twentieth floor at seven o'clock. I'm sure that you two would be welcome if you wish to come with me," he offered.

I graciously declined, knowing his mission, and we bade each other good-bye as he left. "We'll leave anytime tomorrow," I advised. "Just call us at our room when you're ready."

Jerrie and I sat back down to finish our cocktails and decide what to do with our spare time in Havana.

The bar was dark and quiet. There was no one there except the two of us. We were deciding whether to leave or have another daiquiri when the bartender came over and in broken English asked, "You, Cooper?"

I nodded yes and he made a motion that I was wanted on the phone.

I put the receiver to my ear and announced, "Cooper here."

"Hey, Cooper, Attwood tells me that you are down at the bar. Get up here to our party in 2001."

"Who's this?" I asked.

"I'm Dan Rather, and you better get up here before the food is all gone." I was shocked. "Thanks for the invite; we'll be right up!"

The suite was filled with his staff and other official people. He welcomed us, and Attwood introduced us around.

Rather had just interviewed Fidel the day before, Sunday, and that interview had been released earlier that day. He was staying in Havana for another day to see what the reaction was to the speech by Carter.

At exactly eight o'clock, two well-dressed Cuban officials showed up at the door and collected Attwood to escort him to his visit with Fidel.

At nine o'clock Carter came on the radio. Rather's room was well equipped with the finest radio receivers, and we listened intently as the President explained that he could not accept the status quo and that the so-called Russian instructors were really a Soviet combat brigade and would not be tolerated.

The speech lasted less than ten minutes.

The staff and guests gathered around Dan Rather to hear his comments about the speech. Surely such a widely traveled correspondent would interpret the words for us mortals. Surely he would translate what the President had said into simple words for us. Surely he would compare his interview with Fidel, just the day before, with the learned words of our president and we would all be better for having been exposed to such a vast storehouse of wisdom from one of the most respected newscasters in the world.

"Dan," we all asked, almost in unison, "what do you think?"

"He took too long to say nothing" was Dan's matter-of-fact reply. And then he added, "Can someone tune in the Monday night football game? The Patriots are playing the Packers and I don't want to miss it."

The next day Attwood called us at noon and advised that he was ready to depart. His visit with Fidel lasted until the early hours of the morning, and he had slept in.

We had the same escort back to the airport; the same attention at the diplomatic reception area, and after a non-eventful takeoff, we arrived back into Miami in the early afternoon.

We shook hands outside of U.S. Customs offices, and as Attwood turned to go, he paused and said, "Let's keep this little trip between just us three, okay?"

And we did...until now.

As 1979 came to a close, Shawnee Airlines with both its scheduled flights to the Bahamas and its Cuba flights was doing well.

The partnership with Gene Harris wasn't. We had different philosophies concerning the direction of the company, and in early 1980 we decided to split the companies, with Harris taking the Shawnee division with its scheduled flights to the Bahamas, and I would take the Air Miami division and its Cuba flights.

I moved Air Miami from his facility to some recently vacated Pan Am hangars, continued the weekly charters to Havana, and began to work on other opportunities in the charter area.

Shawnee closed three months later.

The year of 1980 was slowly slipping by with nothing much happening with Air Miami. The Cuban operation was a regular source of revenue, but the business was not increasing as much as I hoped it would.

In late summer my old friend Jim Curasi, the attorney for Air Miami in the Miami to Key West route case with the Public Service Commission, called.

He had been hired by Air Florida as vice president of legal affairs and asked me if I would like for Air Miami to become an Air Florida Commuter operating in and around Florida and the Bahamas.

Air Florida had become a major player in the airline industry, having grown from a new entrant in the intrastate business—flying throughout Florida, operating a few older propjets—to a large interstate airline flying to numerous major cities along the East Coast of the U.S. It was formed in 1971, and in order to expand within the state, they had acquired my old airline, AAT Airlines, newly named Air Sunshine, in 1978.

Ed Acker, former CEO of Braniff International Airlines, became the CEO of Air Florida in 1975, and with his aggressive leadership and knowledgeable background, the company was growing by leaps and bounds.

Of course, I said, "Yes."

It was agreed that we would acquire turbo-prop aircraft for the new commuter service. I would continue to operate to Cuba in our older de Havilland Herons and the DC-3.

I had financed a few small aircraft with a bank in Fond du Lac, Wisconsin, earlier and had formed a bond with one of the owners, Steven Stone. He, like me, had a real affection for aviation, and with his bank's help we acquired three new twenty-three passenger Casa Aircraft, produced in Spain. To help with the transition expenses, Steven and his brother bought into the company, with the funds going into the treasury as working capital.

Our contract with Air Florida was that they would dictate where we flew and what the ticket prices would be, and they would simply pay us by the trip segment.

In October we became an Air Florida Commuter with the three brand-new Casa propjet aircraft, all painted in the Air Florida paint livery; white aircraft with blue and green stripes down the side of the fuselage and up the tail.

Heaven!

What could be easier? All we had to do was keep the pilots trained, keep the aircraft maintained, fly the schedule that Air Florida dictated, and... count our money.

That lasted about six months.

In the spring of 1981, I received a call from Ed Acker's secretary. "Mr. Acker would like to meet with you at your earliest convenience."

A meeting with Mr. Acker, CEO of Air Florida, could only mean one thing. Given our superb on-time performance and the professionalism with which we operated, this could only mean a compliment for our company, and an opportunity for expansion was about to be offered.

Wrong!

I was ushered into his office by the secretary and was met with a friendly handshake by Mr. Acker as he asked me to sit down.

"You fellows over at Air Miami have been doing a great job for us," he began.

I was ready for the big pitch for us to expand into more cities, perhaps with the new generation of small thirty-seat jets that were coming onto the market for commuters.

As my chest swelled proudly, he continued. "I have been examining the financial arrangement that we have with your company, and I am proposing an amendment to the contract."

"Okay." I readied myself for the big offer for expansion.

"As you know," he continued, "we are paying you by the segment. I am proposing that we commence paying you by the revenue per passenger you are flying minus a fee for reservations and other miscellaneous services that we are affording your company. We will, of course, still establish schedules and set fare rates."

My heart sank. My swelled chest collapsed as I realized what he was saying. He was proposing that we get paid per passenger flown. That meant the financial risk would transfer to us even though Air Florida would dictate schedules and fare structure. Some of our routes were revenue positive but some of them were losers.

"But, Mr. Acker, we have a five-year contract that guarantees the current arrangement, and it will stand up in a court of law," I blustered.

"Yes," he said, barely looking up from his notepad, "but if you examine the small print, you will find a thirty-day exit clause for us, and by the time you sue us, we will have a replacement commuter airline in place. And," he continued quite calmly, "how long can you last with no revenue stream?"

I had just received my master's degree in airline management.

I had no recourse. With my tail tucked between my legs, I retreated and returned to my office to explain the situation to my partners.

We decided to make the best of a bad situation. After all, we had a major investment in propjet aircraft with no alternative but to fly for Air Florida and hope for the best.

The good routes, the ones that were revenue positive, paid for the poor routes, and we struggled along. Some months we were profitable and some months we lost money. We continuously communicated with the Air Florida scheduling department to adjust the schedules, putting more flights on the good routes and reducing the poorer ones.

After a few months, with some favorable scheduling adjustments, we climbed back into the black and settled down to run the airline under the new arrangement.

And then, on August 5th, came the final blow to the Air Florida arrangement.

President Reagan fired all the air traffic controllers after they refused to return to work after a controllers' strike.

This created havoc in the airline industry.

With only a handful of controllers available, it became necessary for the air traffic control system to reduce its capacity while new controllers were trained. This resulted in a limit of takeoffs and landings at certain large airports. A makeshift system of slot control was implemented which severely limited Air Florida's capacity into and out of Miami and Tampa, our major hubs.

Since Air Florida and the Air Florida commuter, Air Miami, were jointly included in the slot allocations, Air Florida simply took the most advantageous slots used by Air Miami and internally reallocated them to Air Florida.

Our Key West noon flights into Miami were cancelled in favor of Air Florida flights from New York; our Ft. Meyers eight o'clock morning flights into Miami were cancelled in favor of Air Florida flights from Washington, etc.

Our flight system was decimated, and with the decrease in flying, Air Florida was having financial difficulties that resulted in slow pay for the passenger revenue that they collected on our behalf.

Our protests to Air Florida fell on deaf ears. What had begun as a terrific love affair had deteriorated into an adversarial relationship. We were in a graveyard spiral financially, with no future in the Air Florida arrangement.

I met with my partners and we decided on a bold move. We decided to exercise the thirty-day exit clause with Air Florida and become an independent airline.

On November 1st, we unveiled our new airline, North American Airlines. We finished the year in pretty good shape, with our advanced passenger bookings growing and the Cuban charter operation continuing to produce some positive revenue.

It was about that time that my success as an airline entrepreneur caught the attention of Frank Borman, CEO of Eastern Airlines.

I received a call from Eastern's legal department with a demand to meet with their chief counsel at my earliest convenience… Now! His name was William Bell. There were no polite introductions, no small talk. He barely looked up as I walked into his office. "You can sit there." He nodded toward a very uncomfortable wooden chair in front of his desk.

"Captain Cooper," he began in a cold, uncompromising tone. "It has come to Mr. Borman's attention that you are actively competing with Eastern in several markets throughout the state of Florida. I call your attention to the Eastern Airlines Standard Operating Manual where it addresses competing with Eastern, and I am offering you the opportunity to remain an Eastern captain or to remain a competitive airline executive. The choice is yours. You have one week to make up your mind. Thank you," he mumbled curtly as he finished the meeting. He barely rose from his chair and nodded toward the door.

I suppose that I had expected this sooner or later, but at this time, with North American Airlines struggling to stay afloat, I was at wits' end. I made up my mind to inform my partners and try to work things out. I would have to resign. That was for sure. There was no market for a startup airline with marginal chances of success so a sale of the corporation was out of the question. How would they take it? Would they suggest closing the airline? My brain was spinning.

I was getting up my nerve to call one of my partners, Steve Stone, when he called me first.

"Hey, Coop, I've got a proposition for you," he offered in his cheeriest voice. "You're not going to like it, but please listen to me."

"I'm listening," I said.

"My brother and I would like to buy you out," he blurted. "The company is going to need some capital, and we don't think that you are in a financial position to handle a cash infusion on a pro rata basis with us. Now we know that this is your baby and that leaving will be painful, but we feel that this is best for all concerned."

I held my breath. This was too good to be true. "Steve, I agree with you, the company is going to need to be recapitalized in the near future," I remarked. "What's your deal going to look like?"

Steve had figured it all out. We had four Casa aircraft and one DC-3. We used the Casas on the scheduled runs and the DC-3 on the Cuban charters.

"There won't be much cash, but we will transfer the DC-3 over to you, and you can continue the Cuban charter operation with it," he explained.

We had been talking with a small commuter airline, Pompano Airways, in Ft. Lauderdale about a merger. That had fallen through, but I knew I could move the DC-3 over to their certificate and continue the Cuban operation there.

Within two days we had consummated the deal. I was removed from the records of North American Airlines, the Cuban operation had been transferred to Pompano Airways, and I was off the radar at Eastern Airlines.

It REALLY is better to be lucky than good!

The '80s had begun on a high note; Air Miami had become the first commuter for Air Florida, the high-flying startup airline in Miami, Cathy had graduated from high school in '78, and Tommy graduated in '80.

Cathy enrolled at the University of Florida, and Tommy enrolled at Northeast Louisiana State University.

Cathy graduated from U of F in 1982, and Tommy graduated from NELU in 1984. After graduation, he enrolled in Stetson School of Law and graduated from there in December of 1987

Sadly, after a long battle, cancer took Diane in 1983.

After the conversation with attorney Bell at Eastern, I curtailed my interest in commuter airlines and limited my extracurricular aviation activities to only the charter business. This seemed to satisfy Eastern, as they had no interest in Cuba at that time.

The Cuban business was just enough to keep the company profitable, and with only the Americans flying on my DC-3, the business was steady, but not robust.

In April of 1982, politics again played a role in the charter operation.

President Reagan re-imposed the travel embargo between the U.S. and Cuba...for Americans ONLY.

Since the Cuban government had split the passenger franchise between Fuentes and me, with him getting all the Cuban-Americans and me getting only Americans, there was now only a trickle of business for me between the U.S. and Cuba, while the Cuban-American business boomed.

There was no reason to maintain the DC-3 for such little business, so I traded for a ten-seat Cessna 402 and formed a new charter airline, Caribbean Express.

I operated that company out of my garage at Redbird Avenue in Miami Springs with my sole business being an occasional charter to Cuba or the Bahamas. I played with Caribbean Express for about two years, but with the Cuban business reduced to almost nothing, I sold out to devote 100 percent of my time to Eastern.

By the mid '80s I had been with Eastern for over twenty years. Although I had originally flown the Connie and the DC-7 for Eastern, I checked out as pilot on the Boeing 727 in 1966. It soon replaced the DC-3 as the love of my life, and with each flight, I grew fonder of that aircraft.

To fly for Eastern had always been my goal, and I never tired of any flight assignment for her. I liked to say, "I never got suited up for a flight that I wasn't eager to go on." I never got enough of Eastern and the Boeing 727 and I always felt blessed that I had been hired by her.

CHAPTER 59
Boeing 727 Engine Failure

Training pays off

I SUPPOSE THAT THE DOWNSIDE of getting so comfortable in a particular airplane was complacency. The airplane was so easy to fly, the systems so easy to grasp, and the airplane so reliable that it was difficult to prepare for a possible emergency.

In the "old days" of the Connies and DC-7s, when you lined up on the runway and pushed the throttles up for takeoff power, your mind was triggered for a possible failure. The piston engines—re-engineered over and over again by the manufacturers to gain even the slightest increase of power over the original performance planned for the engines—created issues that often resulted in failures of components of those engines. One's reflexes were tensed as emergencies were expected.

But the Boeing 727, with its JT-6 series jet engines, was different. When you lined up for takeoff and pushed the throttles up, just a slight glance at the engine instruments told you that all was okay as you sped down the runway. The beautiful B-727 could lull you into a false sense of security.

The only antidote for that false sense of security was the Eastern Airlines Training Department.

Every six months the captains would be required to attend a check ride period in the flight simulator. An instructor would put the captain through every emergency one could dream of, and he would usually pile on additional emergencies just to complicate things. If things got too complicated and the captain became confused, the simulator could be stopped, "frozen," and the issues could be discussed and corrected. Then the ride would continue.

Four hours in the simulator every six months would usually return a captain to his senses and make him realize that he was in command of a very large, heavy pipe going five hundred miles per hour, filled with about 150 passengers, and "stuff" could happen. These recurrent sessions prepared him for any eventuality.

Such was the case with me on December 6, 1985.

My assigned trip was flight number 975 departing Miami International Airport at 5:30 p.m., arriving two and a half hours later at the Bridgetown Adams Airport serving Barbados in the British West Indies.

I checked in at the dispatch counter located on the ground floor of the Miami terminal and met the other members of the cockpit crew. The first officer and second officer and I had flown together all month, so the preflight briefing was simple. I looked at the dispatch release, gave the second officer the required fuel load, and he excused himself to proceed to the aircraft and do his 'walk-around", pilot jargon for preflight inspection.

I discussed the weather with the first officer, signed the dispatch release, and we proceeded to the aircraft. The first officer went directly to the cockpit while I visited the galley to introduce myself to the senior flight attendant. I relayed the weather report to her—it was to be smooth—and advised her of the flying time, three hours and twelve minutes. We passed the time of day briefly and I asked her to let me know if she had any issues during the flight. I returned to the cockpit to join the first and second officers.

As we were nearing departure time, I asked for the before-starting-engine checklist, and it was completed. The passenger agent stuck his head in the cockpit and advised that all the passengers were on board and that he was ready to close the main passenger door.

The crackle of static in my headset told me that the ground start crew had hooked up and would soon advise me that all the doors were closed and the baggage carts were clear.

"Captain," he said, "we're clear down here and the nose wheel pins are in. You're cleared to start engines when you're ready."

The nose wheel pins are always disconnected when the aircraft is being towed, to prevent damage to the steering apparatus. So with the information that the pins were in, I knew I would be able to taxi under my own power safely.

"We're starting number three," I relayed to him.

I nodded to the first officer, who proceeded to start the engines. Once all the engines were started and all the gauges were normal, I gave him the signal to disconnect.

"Have a nice flight, Captain," he said. "We'll see you tomorrow."

Ground control cleared us via the inner taxiway to runway 27 right.

We continued to perform the appropriate checklists. I listened to the flight attendant make her announcements and noticed that there were only a few aircraft waiting ahead of us for takeoff.

The flight attendant finished her announcements and advised us. All the checklists were completed and the second officer had computed our take-off speeds and posted them on a visible data card on the instrument panel as we waited our turn to take off.

"Eastern 975, you're cleared for takeoff," came the approval from the tower. "Maintain runway heading after takeoff."

"Roger," the first officer replied. "We're on the roll."

I eased the throttles up evenly, and the first officer made the final adjustments.

The engine instruments spun up nicely.

One of the nice things about the new generations of jets was that someone had perceived that at that critical moment of takeoff, when the performance of the engines is critical and the ability to read and interpret the gauges is paramount, all the needles on the gauges should read at a common position. That position was at nine o'clock on the gauges. What a simple idea. Fifteen engine gauges and one only had to glance at the instrument panel and determine that all the engines were operating as desired.

All was normal as we began to accelerate down the runway. The speed was building nicely as we neared our rotate or V-R speed. The first officer called out, "V-R," and I eased the control wheel back slightly and felt the nose rise. A second later he called out "V-2" as the aircraft lifted off and began its climb.

We were barely fifty feet in the air when it happened.

BANG! A loud noise sounded and the aircraft shook. My first impression was that we had hit a vehicle at the end of the runway.

An alarm bell was ringing loudly, and a red fire warning light was flashing over the glare shield of the instrument panel.

The second officer shouted out, "Captain, we've just lost number three engine."

The alarm bell was deafening; the fire warning light added to the urgency of the situation. We were barely a hundred feet above the ground.

"Silence the bell," I commanded, "and essential power." Those are the first two things that the captain of this aircraft does in this situation, or commands to be done. Now that the alarm bell had alerted you of an issue, it was of no further use. So there is a bell silence button on the panel that quiets the noise. The second thing is to ensure that critical electrically operated systems are not depending on the failed engine alternator for their power, thus the "essential power" command.

"I'll fly the airplane," I called out to the first officer, "and you talk over the radio." I nodded to the second officer. "You handle the emergency."

This all happened in a split second.

"Let's agree on the engine," I commanded.

The second officer again said, "Number three, sir."

"Is that what you see," I asked the first officer.

"Yes sir," he replied.

I retarded the number three throttle, and the fire warning light extinguished. "Shut down number three and run the engine failure checklist," I ordered the second officer, "and start dumping fuel. Call the tower and advise them that we have an engine failure and will be returning to the airport. Ask them for the current winds."

By now I had climbed to about five hundred feet. We were extremely heavy, and with only two engines operating, our climb rate was quite low. We were out over the Everglades so terrain clearance was not an issue. I continued to climb and at fifteen hundred feet, I eased the power back on the two operating engines and prepared for a landing back at Miami International Airport.

The tower replied, "The wind is from the west at less than five knots; what are your intentions?"

"Tell them that we're doing a one eighty out here and will land on runway nine right. It's longer and we'll be heavy."

I turned to the second officer. "We'll be landing in about three minutes; start dumping fuel, figure the landing weights, and give me the numbers."

"Yes, sir," he replied. "We'll be over weight for landing."

"That's okay," I replied, "just figure the weight and give me the landing speeds for thirty-degree flaps."

I motioned to the first officer. "Put in the ILS for nine right and identify it."

The tower cleared the area for us and advised, "Captain, the whole airport is yours. Do you need the emergency equipment?"

I nodded yes to the first officer, who relayed it to the tower.

We would be landing with a heavy aircraft, and our over-the-fence speed would be excessive. Since our landing would be at an exceptionally heavy weight and with one engine inoperative, our initial engine reverse capability would be limited to only the center engine. There was a good chance that we might have to use excessive braking on the main wheels, which could result in a brake fire.

It was better to have the fire trucks nearby at landing.

I was turning through a heading of south toward the east and toward the airport when I finally had time to advise the passengers of the situation.

I picked up the public-address microphone. "Ladies and gentlemen, as you might have noticed, we're turning back toward the airport. We've experienced some difficulties with one of our engines, and it will be necessary to return and swap aircraft. We'll be landing in about two minutes. Once on the ground we'll have to transfer your baggage to the new airplane and refuel it. I suggest that you remain near our gate as an Eastern representative will advise you of our new departure time. And by the way," I added, "I expect to see every one of you on the new airplane. As an added treat, I've ordered champagne for all. Flight attendants, prepare the cabin for landing."

As I hung up the PA microphone, I called for the in-range and before-landing checklist and watched the crew accomplish it.

There was no time to relax. The airport was fast approaching, and with the heavy aircraft, slowing to the appropriate speeds took some concentration.

We were now about four miles from the airport, and I made final mental preparation for the landing. "Gear down, and final checklist," I commanded. "Stop the fuel dumping at five hundred feet."

At three hundred feet I asked the first officer for thirty-degree landing flaps and watched the airspeed dissipate to our required over-the-fence speed for landing.

We were hot but the landing was right on the numbers and smooth. I held the nose up and reversed the center engine. This would allow the speed to dissipate aerodynamically without using too much brake pressure.

Out of the corner of my eye, I saw the fire trucks speeding down the taxiway alongside the aircraft.

I let the nose down gently and slowly began to use the number one reverser carefully so as not to create an asymmetrical yawing effect. The speed was now less than one hundred knots, and with minimum braking I brought the aircraft to a stop well short of the end of the runway.

I taxied clear of the runway and parked to await the Eastern ground crews to show up with a tug to tow us to the gate when I heard the young second officer, almost under his breath, whisper excitedly, "Wow, that was just like the simulator!"

There is a postscript to this story. All passengers did show up, Eastern did show up with a second aircraft loaded with four cases of champagne, and we were back in the air in less that an hour...with **ALL** the passengers from the previous flight.

The decade of the '80s, which had begun with so much promise, was coming to an end. The bright spots—Cathy and Tommy graduating from college—were overshadowed by some low periods. My commuter airline, which soared as Air Florida's first commuter, had gone by the wayside, and the Cuba charter business, which was booming going into the '80s, had now, with Reagan's new Cuban policy, had deteriorated into only a few charters a month.

CHAPTER 60
Storm Clouds at Eastern

Labor strife ramps up

AND THEN THERE WAS EASTERN Airlines.
Eastern, which had continued to expand throughout the post-deregulation era, giving me a strong sense of security, was becoming a battlefield between the company and the machinists' union. After a near strike in the beginning of the '80s, the political situation calmed down somewhat. But that was just a temporary lull. The conflict began to heat up again in November 1986 when Colonel Borman, the famous astronaut and Eastern's president and CEO, fed up with the continued aggravation from the machinists' union and its president, Charlie Bryan, sold controlling interest of Eastern to Frank Lorenzo, the chairman of Continental Airlines.

Lorenzo immediately became the chairman of the board and installed Phil Bakes as president. Phil had been chief counsel for the old Civil Aeronautics Board; he had been hired by Lorenzo to be counsel for New York Air and was later named president of Continental.

Lorenzo and Bates had hardly moved in when the Air Line Pilots Association, ALPA, published a forty-six-page document titled, *THE EASTERN PILOT GROUP TAC ATTACK* aimed directly at Lorenzo and his team, Texas Air Corporation.

That was just a shot across the bow. Now the Eastern unions, egged on by their national union affiliations, began their battle in earnest. The honeymoon was really over when Lorenzo moved six Eastern aircraft over to Continental and shortly thereafter spun off the Eastern reservation system to Texas Air Corp. The unions maintained that Lorenzo was moving assets over to the "non-union" Continental in an attempt to break the Eastern unions. Couple that with the fact that, by mergers and acquisitions, Lorenzo now controlled over 20 percent of the commercial traffic in the U.S., and the labor unions began to take serious notice of his advances in the industry.

Lorenzo had proved successful in breaking the unions at Continental. If he could do the same at Eastern, or move all of Eastern's assets over to Continental, then, with his low-budget model, the unions feared that he would have the power to control the cost structure of the entire airline system in the U.S.

The battle heated up as the unions declared war and began an onslaught of propaganda designed to get Lorenzo at any cost. My mailbox was filled with pamphlets, anti-Lorenzo stickers, and vile tape recordings almost daily.

From my standpoint, although I really didn't get involved in the union politics, I had a tendency to side with the company. I suppose it was because I had been so involved with the complexity of managing an airline, though small, that I felt a compassion for management as they battled the normal elements of running a scheduled airline: customer service, safety, weather, maintenance, competition, personnel, regulations, and a hundred other issues. Then, when you pile on the union agitation, well, it could make the situation almost insurmountable.

The machinists were nearing a contract deadline in about a year in March of 1989, and there was a fear that the pilots and the flight attendants would walk out in support of them.

Battle lines were drawn. You were either against Lorenzo or for him. There were rumors of fights in the cockpit. Lifetime friends became enemies and the outlook for a successful outcome was in doubt.

I had a standard speech that I gave to any crewmembers assigned to me. "No union talk in the cockpit. Let's keep it professional. I don't care what your politics are on the outside, but I do care about the safety of our passengers."

"Let's leave the hate at the gate" was my motto.

It did seem to work for me…with one exception.

There was a rabid copilot, Ron Cole. He held a minor position in the pilot's union and he had trouble leaving his hate at the gate.

He was a strong advocate of Max Safety—an imaginary captain dreamed up by the pilots' union as a symbol of a phony safety campaign. If a union sympathizing pilot could dream up any excuse to delay or cancel a flight using some safety excuse, they would.

Stickers depicting Captain Max Safety began to show up on radical pilots' flight kits and suitcases as the war intensified. This I despised. I felt strongly that to advance one's personal agenda at the expense of hiding behind the skirts of safety was the ultimate act of cowardice.

I had flown for Eastern for almost thirty years, and the company had never asked me to fly an airplane that I deemed unsafe. Eastern had set high standards in the airline industry for maintenance advances, and their training was second to none. Safety was paramount with Eastern and to use Max Safety as a union tool galled me.

On December 22, 1987, I was scheduled to fly to Guatemala City when I saw Cole's name on the manifest as my copilot. His union feelings were well documented around the company. He was the ultimate Max Safety advocate. His only goal in life was to delay and/or cancel every Eastern flight that he was assigned to. He scoured over the preflight paperwork looking for any excuse to delay the flight with weather concerns. He examined the flight log, going back to the beginning of the logbook, for any reason to question the previous maintenance actions, hoping to find a safety excuse for a delay. He had a litany of tricks up his sleeve to work from, and I prepared to be tested by Captain Max Safety.

I took a deep breath and mentally vowed to keep it professional and go by the book.

Ron showed up at the operations counter with Max Safety stickers all over his flight kit and suitcase, and as usual, with no hat. It was a thing with him. He sported an afro and, contrary to the company policy manual, refused to wear his airline cap. With his reputation, the captains let him get away with it, especially the captains with union leanings.

"Hi Ron," I said as we shook hands. "Where's your cap?"

"Sorry, Captain." He smiled. "I must have forgotten it in my car."

"Well," I said, "why don't you run back and get it. You know it's company policy to be in uniform, unless you have a doctor's prescription."

"Are you serious?" he sneered.

"I sure am. We don't want to break any company rules, now do we?" I pointed to his Max Safety stickers.

He spun around and disappeared only to reappear about five minutes later, hat in hand.

"It didn't take you very long to go to the parking lot," I mused.

"I remembered that I left it in my company mailbox upstairs," he replied. "I'll see you at the airplane," he shrugged, "if that's all right with you, Captain."

"Sure, go ahead and I'll finish the paperwork."

Poor Ron. I did feel somewhat sorry for him. With the airline cap pulled down on his head and with his afro protruding out over his ears, he looked ever so much like Chuckles the Clown.

After signing off for the fuel load and checking the weather, I proceeded to the aircraft and I went into the passenger cabin to brief the senior flight attendant.

To my dismay, she was almost in tears. "First Officer Cole came back and told me that there were maintenance issues with the emergency escape door, and if we crashed we wouldn't be able to get out."

That was a favorite trick with the union boys. They would check every window on the airplane, and if one were the least bit scratched they would write it up in the maintenance log. This would cause a major delay while the maintenance people, who were in on these little tricks, would amble out, read the logbook, amble back for a ladder and rag, and slowly polish the identified windows. The emergency exits were a prime target for this scam.

I put her mind at ease and had a talk with the maintenance person assigned to this flight. He went right to work, and in a few minutes the window was polished and the logbook signed off by the mechanic.

As I walked back to the cockpit, I took a deep breath. *This is going to be one of those flights*, I thought.

When I reached the cockpit, it was as I expected. Ron was engaging the second officer in his usual discussion concerning what a terrible airline Eastern was and what a terrible person Lorenzo was.

"Okay, Ron, you know what my policy is," I said as I set my flight kit next to my seat. "No politics in the cockpit. Let's make it a good, safe, uneventful flight."

Settling in I performed my preflight activities and asked for the before-starting checklist. We went down the list, the copilot read the commands, and the three of us responded with the appropriate answers associated with our assigned tasks. All seemed routine, the cabin door closed, and the ground crew hooked up and gave us the all-clear to start the engines.

We taxied out to the active runway. After the normal reading of the before takeoff checklists and the flight attendant's signal that she had finished the passenger briefing, I asked Cole to advise the tower that we were ready for takeoff.

"Eastern 943, you are cleared for takeoff." the tower operator replied. "Maintain runway heading."

I rolled out on the runway, aligned the aircraft, and slowly advanced the throttles toward takeoff power.

All seemed normal until I reached takeoff power.

Something didn't feel right.

Although we had achieved the prescribed maximum takeoff power, I felt the throttles hit the forward stops in the throttle quadrant. In over twenty thousand hours of flying the Boeing 727, I had never felt that before. The takeoff power was adequate, but it took full throttle movement to achieve it. I quickly scanned the engine instruments, but all seemed normal.

We sped down the runway.

Cole called out VR and I lifted the aircraft off the runway and began the climb out. The departure and climb out took my attention, but the throttle position versus the power matter continued to pester me.

We established cruise, passed Key West, and the throttle issue still was in the back of my mind. I had never felt the throttles hit the forward throttle stops before on takeoff.

After establishing the cruise settings, I set the autopilot on the selected course and slid my seat back to a more relaxed position, but the nagging issue kept returning. I scanned the instruments and switches on the instrument panel again. All were normal. My vision moved to the overhead panel, filled with switches, lights, and knobs. All looked normal…wait a minute…wait JUST a minute…the wing anti-ice switches.

They were in the WRONG position! They were ON!

I knew in an instant what the problem was and, just as quickly, what caused it.

The wing anti-ice switches are located high and to the right side of the overhead panel in the cockpit, just over the copilot's head. The anti-ice system is to be used only in icing conditions. It is not to be used on takeoff as it can rob the engines of valuable reserve power and produce excessive heat in the related ducts at high power settings.

With the switches activated, hot air is bled from the engines and fed, through ducts, to the leading edges of the wings and other critical surfaces of the aircraft to eliminate ice buildup when flying in precipitation.

There are warning lights associated with these switches. They are not position lights, but "agreement" lights. If the switches are on and the valves do not completely open, then the associated light will not come on; the reverse is true with the switches in the off position.

The Max Safety guys discovered that if they activated these switches during preflight, there was a good chance that the lights would give a false indication, thus causing the captain to require a maintenance person to visually check the valves to ensure proper position. This inspection would usually take up to thirty minutes—that is, if the aircraft were at a base where there were mechanics. At bases where there was no maintenance, the delay could take hours and the flight could be delayed until the next day.

Checking these valves and activating them on preflight was not in the operations manual and was contrary to company policy. *They were only to be checked by maintenance personnel on prescribed inspections, and pilots were not to touch the switches other than activate them when foul weather required anti-icing procedures.*

When responding to the checklist, the first officer's duty is to confirm that the switches are in the "off" position.

"Cole," I exclaimed loudly as I reached for the switches. He beat me to them and immediately switched the switches to the "off" position. He knew exactly what he had done on preflight. In trying to create a problem where none existed, he had inadvertently left the wing anti-ice switches in the wrong or "on" position. We had taken off with the wing anti ice system on, thus robbing the engines of valuable power should we have needed it in an emergency, and also causing excessive hot engine bleed air to course through the wing anti-ice duct work of the airplane, clearly against Boeing engineering and company policy.

Cole immediately lit into me in an attempt to excuse himself for his careless act. "Damn it, Cooper, that was an honest mistake." He was red in the face and completely out of control. He continued screaming, almost at the top of his lungs, "We are watching you, you make mistakes all the time, you take airplanes that no other captains will take, you are a company lackey, and we are watching you."

He showed no signs of letting up.

The second officer hastily vacated the cockpit.

"Cole," I shouted. "Shut up. I know all your tricks. You could have gotten us all killed back there on takeoff if we'd lost an engine. We have an airplane to fly. For the rest of the flight you are not to say one word unless it is to answer the checklist. Now get yourself together and focus on your job, not your politics!"

"You are not to touch anything in this cockpit without advising me first," I instructed. "We'll continue this conversation when we get on the ground back at Miami."

For the rest of the trip the cockpit was deadly silent. Only a low mumbling of the reading of the checklist was audible, and we arrived back at Miami with no further incidents.

I pondered the incident for several days. The Cole thing was not just one pilot; it had festered and was rampant around the airline. It had become almost a game with the union-sympathizing pilots. A game of who can create the most havoc for Eastern and Lorenzo.

Finally, I decided that I had to make a move. I honestly thought that someone was going to get injured or killed.

I made a move that I felt was best for everyone.

I wrote a letter to ALPA, the airline union, outlining the incident and requesting that they do an intervention with Cole; bring him in for counseling and perhaps cool down the general rhetoric which was permeating the pilot group.

I also copied Eastern.

The union went berserk! I got calls from one of the head union guys, Captain Breslin, who requested strongly that I rescind the letter.

I didn't, and Ron Cole was fired.

At least he didn't have to wear his hat now.

Of course, there was an appeal by the pilot's union, ALPA, on behalf of Cole. The usual hearing with a "neutral" arbitrator was held in late 1988, about a year after the incident.

I was grilled like a criminal for three days by the ALPA lawyers, even though I was still a dues-paying union pilot. The result was that Cole was reinstated, without pay, shortly before Eastern went on strike. That incident even further "endeared" me to the union group and put me clearly on the side of the company, and that was just fine with me.

As 1988 rolled in, so did the storm clouds. The unions had declared open war on Lorenzo, and the battle began to reach a fevered pitch. ALPA filled our mailboxes with propaganda, and Eastern responded with newsletters repudiating their claims.

Although I was labeled as a company lackey by many fellow pilots after the Cole affair, I still avoided company and union meetings. Now I regret not attending and being more vocal in those meetings, but at the time I supposed that Eastern would survive, with or without Lorenzo, and that my input was not needed to facilitate a successful outcome. I remained on the sidelines.

That is, until an article appeared in the Miami Herald.

Charles Whited was a respected journalist in the Miami area. His daily column in the local section of the *Herald* was widely read and offered a welcome view of the happenings in the community. In the April 16th issue of the *Herald* he took on Lorenzo with a commentary titled, "Is This Any Way to Run an Airline?" In reading the article, I thought it to be an unfair overview of the issues being debated at the airline, and I felt that it expressed only the union's point of view. He quoted union leaders and union employees and I took exception to his writings.

I answered on April 22nd with what I thought was a fair working man's opinion. I introduced myself as a twenty-five-year pilot with Eastern and pointed out some improvements with the airline since Lorenzo took over.

I chastised Whited for continuing the "Get Lorenzo, even at the expense of Eastern" preached by the unions and fed to the public by the media.

I included a copy of a recent speech by the machinists' union leader, William Winpisinger, whereby he was quoted as saying that he was at "war" with Eastern and that he would continue fighting "even if the battle ultimately causes the company to collapse."

I explained in my letter, "In my twenty-five years at Eastern, the company has been operated as a country club," and I cited examples. I concluded, "Perhaps the company, and especially the unions, need and deserve Frank Lorenzo with his no-nonsense approach to management. I have enjoyed watching the change for the better these past two years."

It took a while before Whited responded…

But he did.

In the June 7th issue of the *Miami Herald* he reprinted most of my letter.

It didn't take long before the union responded.

Now the pilot's union at Eastern published a fancy, glossy monthly newsletter called *CHECKLIST*, which was dedicated almost solely to the distribution of anti-Lorenzo propaganda and to the degradation of management and any employee who did not fall into line with the union's program of "Get Lorenzo at any cost."

They published Whited's reprint of my letter under the title "A SUPER BLOOPER FROM CAPTAIN COOPER." At the end they finished with "Editor's comment: Are we talking about the same Eastern Air Lines...you know, the one here on planet Earth?"

The gloves came off. I responded and in the October 1988 issue of the *CHECKLIST* they published my rebuttal to their comments.

TO THE EDITOR,

Thank you very much for reprinting my letter to the Miami Herald of June 7, 1988, in your recent CHECKLIST publication.

By your act, you have exposed these moderate ideas to far more pilots than I thought possible. As a result, I have received numerous letters and phone calls from pilots and other employees alike expressing their positive support and agreement with those thoughts.

I am confused, however, about your choice of title for the article. By the use of the term "blooper," are you indicating that I erred in my disagreement with the union's militant stand? For surely that is my right. Or did I err in exercising my freedom of expression in writing to the Miami Herald in defense of Eastern airlines, for surely that is my duty; or perhaps I simply erred by signing my name, which requires a certain amount of intestinal fortitude so sadly lacked by you.

Yes, Jerry, in your publication CHECKLIST, you are doing a marvelous job of transforming those unsigned, vile, anti-company thoughts, heretofore found only on the Terminal bathroom walls, into glossy form. The format is improved but the stench lingers.

Sincerely,
Captain Thomas L. Cooper

If there was any doubt before, that letter sealed the deal. I was a company man, and that was all there was to it.

The year 1988 ended with Eastern being a battlefield between the unions and Frank Lorenzo. With the deadline for the machinists' strike looming in March and Lorenzo's concern that the pilots' and flight attendants' unions would honor the picket line, the lines of communication between the company and the pilots became overloaded. My mailbox was filled daily by propaganda from both sides.

Just before the strike deadline, Lorenzo sent out a video by express mail to each pilot's home. It was a final attempt to convince the pilots not to honor the machinists' picket lines by offering them certain guarantees. From my standpoint, it looked pretty good, but the pilots' union management rejected it and formally called on the pilots to honor the picket line.

CHAPTER 61

Strike!

AT MIDNIGHT, MARCH 4, 1989, the machinists went on strike and established picket lines at all major cities served by Eastern.

Most of the pilots honored the picket line.

I didn't.

I was disgusted with the tactics used by the unions over the past three years, and coupled with my respect and love for Eastern; I couldn't do anything to harm her.

I remembered being hired by Eastern twenty-seven years earlier. I remembered driving eastbound from California in my car on that same day that a Pan Am jet departed Los Angeles for the Far East with my seat empty. In hiring me away from the CIA airline in the Far East, Eastern had probably saved my life, and I wasn't about to participate in any movement that would violate her trust in me.

I telegraphed my resignation to ALPA and headed for the airport.

It wasn't about money. It was out of loyalty to Eastern. In a fit of bravado I crossed the picket line at exactly midnight plus one minute.

I was the "Number 1 Scab."

It was chaotic! The street bordering the northern boundary of the Miami airport was jammed with strikers walking with picket signs and driving with horns blaring. There were mechanics, pilots, and flight attendants, all demonstrating loudly and violently. Driving down the street to the operations building was slow but free from intimidation from the demonstrators as it appeared as though I was "one of them."

That changed when I turned toward the gate to enter the Hartley building, the training and operations headquarters located on the north side of the airport on the Eastern property. The Hartley building had been set up as the operations headquarters in preparation for the strike. It was named to honor a true Eastern hero, First Officer James Hartley.

It was in 1970 on a shuttle flight between Washington and Boston when, as first officer on a flight captained by Robert Wilbur, Jr., a hijacker burst into the cockpit and began firing his pistol. Although shot three times and mortally wounded, First Officer Hartley wrestled the gun away from the hijacker before he expired. Captain Wilber, also shot, was able to recover the gun and shoot the hijacker.

The hijacker, wounded, continued to wrestle with Captain Wilber before the captain was able to subdue him with a blow to the head.

Captain Wilbur, gravely wounded, managed to fly the aircraft to a safe landing. He continued to fly for Eastern and later became an instructor and check airman.

These two airmen exemplified just what it meant to be an "Eastern Pilot."

They were, and still are, true Eastern heroes.

As I turned into the alleyway leading into the Hartley Building, police were there to help ensure that the gate was accessible. The last few feet were difficult. Signs banged against my car, ugly faces pressed against the windows, and to stop would have been disastrous. I kept moving and the police did a reasonably good job. In a few seconds, I was inside the gate with only the noise from the outside still ringing in my ears.

On the inside of the operations building, where all the scheduling and planning for the airline flights took place, it was uncomfortably quiet. Most of the operation managers were there: the director of operations, the chief pilot, and all their assistants. There were a few crew schedulers and some pilots and a few instructors lounging around.

The big question on everybody's lips was "Who's going to show up to fly tomorrow?" Eastern had over one thousand flights scheduled, and no one knew how many crewmembers would show up.

Lorenzo was calling, Phil Bakes was calling, the press was calling…but nobody had any answers.

The crew schedulers were the first to realize the depth of the problem.

I was watching them work at their phones. I watched as Bill Funderburk and Buddy Casey, both senior schedulers, frantically called pilots to confirm that they would be available to fly their sequences tomorrow. The pilots were either not answering the phone or answering with foul comments.

Although the schedulers were being insulted, they kept calling crewmembers. When they would get a positive answer, they would enter the data in the computer. But it just wasn't working. One flight might have a captain, but no first or second officer. Another might have a second officer, but no captain or first officer. Most had no crewmembers assigned at all.

I tried to call some pilots, familiar names with whom I had just flown in the last couple of months, but I got the same reception; no answer or the wife would tell me that the pilot was "too sick" to come to the phone.

The scheduling computers were useless. They could not match up crews. I came to the conclusion that it had to be done manually. I suggested that we simply put the names of all the available crewmembers on a yellow pad, just as I had done with my small commuter airline earlier. We set up three columns for each aircraft type—captains, first officers, and second officers—and with a lead pencil and a yellow pad, we scheduled the next day's Eastern Airlines flights.

A few years earlier Eastern had been the second largest airline in the world, and tonight we were scheduling a few pilots with a pencil and yellow pad.

It was early morning. In a few hours, Eastern was due to launch over one thousand flights, and so far we only had about eighty crews identified for the next day's flights. This was taking on the appearance of a disaster.

With nothing left for me to do, I went home to rest for what I knew was to be a stressful and physically exhausting few days. That was an underestimation of what was to come.

Phil Bakes held a press conference and announced that the airline would not shut down and would continue to fly. I'm not sure that he knew the depth of the problem at that time.

After a fitful night's sleep, I dressed in uniform and went to the airport. I had assigned myself a trip for the next day to Barranquilla and Cali Colombia. A decision had been made to focus on the South American routes. Later I learned that that decision was made to keep those routes viable for resale.

My first officer was a relatively new pilot, Bob Baumer, and my second officer was an older, senior captain named Carl Young. Carl had been in the training and flight test department for years and was a qualified second officer. It was a relatively strange experience for him to "fly the line" in the backseat, but we enjoyed each other's company and bonded quickly.

One of the issues that presented itself at the airport was that of the scheduling of flight attendants. Although the flight attendant union officially honored the strike, many of them, when called by crew scheduling, agreed to show up for their flights. It was only when they arrived at the airport and were intimidated by the picketers that they decided not to fly. That would leave a flight with a front-end crew and without a full legal complement of flight attendants.

At the airport there was a mad scramble for flight attendants by the captains. We literally would scout the terminal, looking for uniformed flight attendants, and steal them from a flight that was scheduled to depart later. For a while, flight attendants were scheduled at the terminal on a first come, first served basis.

Our flight to Barranquilla and Cali Colombia went off without incident. A lot had transpired in the last two days, and although I enjoyed the hustle and bustle in the Miami Flight Operations building, I was glad to be back in the air.

We were on the return flight to Miami when Carl Young alerted me that Miami operations department was calling me on the company radio. "Captain Cooper, we need you and your entire crew to deadhead to Boston," they said.

"Okay, fine," I answered. "When?" I expected that we would fly up the next day.

"We show you landing at around 8:15 tonight and we've got you scheduled one hour later on the 9:15 flight to Boston."

In one day, we had developed a "can do" attitude, and it would come in handy over the next two years.

"I don't have any clean clothes, but if you can call my home, my wife can pack my suitcase and my son can bring it out," I suggested.

We hit the gate at 8:18. Tommy showed up with my suitcase at 8:45, and I, along with my crew, was on Eastern's flight 46 bound for Boston at 9:15.

By the time we reached cruising altitude, the sun had disappeared behind the horizon to the west. I was seated alone in a half filled airplane, the cabin lights had been dimmed, and for the first time in two days, I had a chance to ponder the situation.

I realized that a wonderful thing had taken place over the last two days. It wasn't a result of any corporate action or union decree. No, but in two days something had changed within the airline. No longer must I worry if my copilot was a union zealot or if the flight attendant was going to slip something in my coffee as a result of my political opinions. Everyone flying at Eastern Airlines now...wanted to be there. Yes, the company was bleeding cash as a result of the strike, and management was desperately trying to scrape up capital to keep her afloat, but for the flight crews… Heaven.

Even now corporate vultures were circling the crippled carcass in their attempt to scavenge valuable parts. Donald Trump was rumored to be bidding on the Shuttle. He had made an attempt earlier, but at the last minute, he and Lorenzo couldn't make it work. We had heard rumors that American Airlines was looking at the South American routes, and U.S. Air was already bidding on the Philadelphia gates.

The future looked dismal, but tonight…tonight I felt at peace with myself and with my decision to do what I could to help Eastern survive.

What happened next was a wonderful example of employee "ownership" and company spirit that will live with me forever.

The flight attendant, a male purser, came by and, in the dimness of the cabin, asked if I would like dinner.

"Yes," I answered, "if you have enough." I knew that there were some paying passengers on board and I didn't want to short-change them.

"Yes, Captain, there's enough," he said as he disappeared into the darkness forward.

He returned shortly with the usual first-class table setting: tablecloth with the Eastern logo proudly displayed, silverware, and salt and pepper shakers.

I put my seat back tray down, and he spread the tablecloth in preparation for the meal. As he was about to place the silverware down, he discovered that he had inadvertently placed the tablecloth backward, with the Eastern logo displayed upside down.

He quickly turned the tablecloth around and as he spread it out correctly, he remarked, "Just because we're down, it doesn't mean that we will compromise the quality of our service."

There, somewhere between Miami and Boston, in the darkness of the cabin, I lost it.

All of the emotions that I had pent up inside me came out. Hate of the political process that got us to this point, questioning of the corporate decisions, uncertainty of the future, and above all, love of the airline.

The flight attendant came back with my meal. I pretended to be focusing on the patchwork pattern of lights that interrupted the darkness along the coastline of North Carolina outside the window, far below.

He mustn't see me cry.

The Man in The Arena...

We arrived at Boston's Logan Airport at midnight. With it being so late, I surmised that any union activity, if at all, would be scant.

Wrong!

They were rabid. There were hundreds of picketers there to greet us. It was worse than the first night in Miami. Red faces screeching, women spitting on us, and the signs...the signs were crude to the point of being repulsive. The strikers were allowed to be much too close to our path as we scurried to the transportation van. If it were not for the presence of private guards—the sympathetic union police weren't much help to us—we would have been in serious trouble.

Once in the van I discovered that we were in a convoy. There was one open truck in front of us with drawn shotguns and a similar one behind us equally armed.

The motel was an armed camp also with guards inside and out.

I began flying the Shuttle routes the next day on March 7th. It was at a grueling pace. There were so few of us flying, and with the FAA and the union watching, we could not err in our calculations with regard to flying time versus rest time.

It was on the 9th of March, five days after the strike had been declared, that a passenger sent his card up to the cockpit with a note. "Did you know that Eastern declared bankruptcy this morning?"

Later that day, I watched on TV the press conference held by Lorenzo and Bakes. Lorenzo admitted that he was disappointed with the pilot turn-out, and Bakes reiterated the corporate decision to keep flying.

I flew the Shuttle through the 10th, and on the 11th of March I was reassigned to Miami. It was only then, back in Miami, that I realized the seriousness of the situation. Out of approximately four thousand pilots, fewer than three hundred returned to work, and most of them were captains and first officers.

Rumors were flying that Peter Ueberroth, who had tried to buy the airline before the strike, was a principal partner of a group that was meeting with Lorenzo with an offer to buy. And there were others, but by that time I was too busy flying to really follow and understand the corporate maneuvers.

Our crew scheduling department was back up and running as they had a good handle on all of the crew members available to fly. We were putting an average of 110 flights per day in the air, about 10 percent of the pre-strike schedule, but our on-time performance and load factors were good.

I settled back into my old flight sequence to Guatemala City and, with the exception of the picket lines, nothing much changed.

By the end of March Eastern had begun to hire new pilots, and management was pleasantly surprised with the caliber of talent that was available. The union, of course, camped out in front of the motel where we were housing them and made their life miserable.

I stayed out of the melee as much as I could, except for some "exchanges" with some of my old buddies walking the picket line.

It was about that time that the union began to publicly launch an intimidation program against us, the flying pilots. They sent letters, first requesting us to rethink our decision and then, when that didn't work, the letters got ugly. There was even one union representative who stood in front of the TV cameras and, with a folded sheet of paper in his hand, professed to have a list of all of the "scab" pilots, and if we didn't come back across the picket line to the union side, he would soon release the names to the public.

I took personal offense to that, and an idea came to mind. What if we, the flying pilots, took it on ourselves and published our names voluntarily? But, I realized, we had to get a majority of them to agree or the ploy wouldn't be effective.

The question was, would the other 272 flying pilots agree to publish their names along with mine in some publication?

I approached a few of my close acquaintances who were flying and was encouraged with the response I received. The few friends I solicited called their friends and got the same positive response.

The plan looked solid. All were on board and we agreed to publish a full-page ad in the *Miami Herald*, the *New York Times*, and the *Washington Post*.

I visited the marketing department at Eastern with my plan. There were only two caveats. The first was that we, the flying pilots of Eastern, would pay for the ad, and second, I would be the first on the list.

"Well," George Brennan, the director of marketing, said, "we can easily put your name on the top of the list, but are you sure that you fellows really want to pay for this?"

"Absolutely," I proudly proclaimed. "We certainly do."

"Okay," he agreed, "but you know that it will run around ten thousand dollars per newspaper."

The economics of the issue overcame my pride and quickly I rescinded my offer to pay. Brennan got a big laugh out of that, and Eastern went forward with my plan of full disclosure.

The list was published, and proudly 100 percent of the flying pilots signed on. And the union? Well, they were flabbergasted. When asked on TV about the self-disclosure of the list, the union representative was speechless. He mumbled something like "They must be crazy."

We had just taken the sting out of their most threatening weapon.

It was on April 3rd that the company announced that we had sold the Shuttle to Donald Trump. It would take about sixty days to consummate the deal, and the bankruptcy judge would have to approve.

The union kept announcing that a white knight had appeared and that the sale of the company was imminent. It was a ploy to keep the pilots on the picket line. The white knights never materialized. Names like Ueberroth, Pritzker, Ritchey, and a litany of others continued to appear in the newspapers. But nothing happened.

Morale was at a sky-high level at Eastern. The load factors were improving, and the training department was running at full steam. Another seventy pilots were hired, and the first class was nearly complete and ready for line flying.

Another phenomenon was taking place. Some of the striking pilots were beginning to return to work. A few at first, just after the strike, and then the numbers began to increase.

This posed a problem. It was a good problem though. Eastern needed the pilots to return, we all knew that, but some of the members of our nice little club, now called the Day Oners," had some problems. We were proud of our stand on March 4th and we even went so far as to order some lapel pins to identify ourselves as members of that sacred club.

The company had asked me to design something for the jewelry company to produce, and I came up with a modified hat-in-the-ring pin. It was the old Eastern symbol left over from the days of Captain Eddie, the logo adopted by his old squadron in World War I, and I simply removed the hat and inserted the numeral "1."

By the time the jewelry company had the samples made, so many pilots had returned that the company thought that to stratify the ranks of the company wasn't a good idea. The pin plan was scrapped, and I was given the samples for my troubles. After we thought about it for a while, we all agreed with management that the pin wasn't a good idea after all.

One of our most outspoken pilots was Captain Don Davidson. He was Boston based but after the strike he moved to Miami to be near the action. He, too, realized there could be an issue with the returning pilots.

They had been told by the union that if they returned to work before the strike was over, we, the pilots on the inside, would abuse them, chastise them, and the strike-breaking instructors would fail them on check rides, thus placing a black mark on their careers forever.

Nothing was further from the truth.

Davidson came up with an ingenious idea. He proposed to the company that he set up a one-day indoctrination class to introduce the returnees to their fellow pilots, to management, and to Phil Bakes personally. He even hired a psychologist to talk with the class.

I sat in on the first class. It was good, but not terrific. All the right things were said, but there was still a we/them atmosphere when it was all over. I pondered if there would ever be a healing between the two groups. And then I asked Davidson if I could do an experiment with the seating arrangement. The classroom we used was the standard size with long table desks seating four students to a table and the usual podium and blackboard up front. It just wasn't personable.

Before the next class—there was one per week now—I rearranged the tables against the wall, leaving a large walkway down the center, and I removed the podium. Now the facilitators and managers had to mix with the returnees on a one-on-one basis when answering questions and when giving our side of the story.

It worked. Rob Benson, one of our senior managers, was almost a standup comedian and was an instant hit. He got on well with the returnees, brought them out, and the whole class would break up at his antics. Phil Bakes was as personable as any manager I had ever worked with, and his talks with the class were remarkably emotional as he discussed the difficulties of management and his vision of the "New Eastern."

Don Davidson's idea was wonderful and went a long way toward bringing peace within the ranks of the flying pilots. The union heard of the new attempt to create a friendly workplace and labeled it "Davidson's Brainwashing Class."

Eastern had developed a business plan that called for the sell-off of some assets, the Shuttle and some routes, and to become a smaller airline. In May we heard that Pan Am had leased fourteen Boeing 727s, and another company leased two Lockheed 1011s. The company was shrinking, but with the lines of communication open, we received a written briefing daily. We had been warned of that, so the departure of some of the aircraft didn't cause any issues with the employees.

The Man in The Arena...

The strike had been going on now for two months, and no one knew just how long it would last, or if it would ever end.

I was back into the routine of flying to Guatemala and enjoying two days off in between. I did offer my services to the company if they needed me for anything extra, and I, along with my wife, Jerrie, and the other flying families, would occasionally throw parties at the reservations offices to thank those people for helping us out.

CHAPTER 62
Revolution in Guatemala

You've just won the airport, now let's use it.

JUST WHEN I THOUGHT I had settled down to the ho-hum humdrum of scheduled flying, something would crop up and wake me out of my slumber.

From the beginning, it looked like just another routine Eastern flight. I had been flying the Guatemala City trip out of Miami for three years, and except for the occasional weather issue, the trip was always uneventful.

On every flight, the check-in was normal, the preflight was normal, and the trip was normal. The crew always stayed at the Camino Real Hotel in downtown Guatemala City, ate at a local restaurant next door, took the same hotel van back to the airport, and flew back to Miami routinely.

It was May 8, 1989, and this flight began exactly the same way. Fly down, van to the hotel, dinner next door, and up to the room for eight hours' sleep.

My wakeup call came right on time. A quick shower and I was dressed and on the elevator to the first-floor desk to check out.

That's when the trip took a different turn.

The hotel manager intercepted me as I was approaching the checkout desk. "Captain," he said, "it is impossible for you to leave this morning."

I quickly assumed that there was a problem with the bill. Perhaps a crewmember left an open tab at the bar, or could it be that Eastern was late with their payment for our rooms?

"Don't worry," I quickly assured him, "I can work out any issues you might have."

"No, no, señor." He squirmed uncomfortably. "We have a little problem here in our country. You see, we have a small revolution here in Guatemala, so you cannot go. It will be over in two or three days and then you can go."

"Well, if it's in the country, we can go to the airport and just leave," I offered.

"No, no," he protested, "it's here in the city; the revolutionaries have taken over half the city, and the airport is in their half."

"Okay," I said, "we'll go toward the airport, and if we get stopped and the revolutionaries won't let us use their airport, we'll come back to the hotel."

Over his nervous protests I gathered the crew, told them of the plan, they agreed, and we proceeded to the van at the front of the hotel.

The driver wasn't too inclined to accommodate us, but a twenty-dollar bill changed his mind and soon we were loaded and headed toward the airport.

The city was eerily quiet. Where we were used to seeing multitudes of people, there were none. Ours was the only civilian vehicle on the roads that morning.

There were, however, soldiers standing at intervals at various intersections along the early part of our trip and a few military vehicles scurrying around. Strangely, they didn't interfere with us at all.

And then, about halfway to the airport, there was no one. Not one soldier, not one vehicle…nobody.

The van driver stopped and explained in broken English that this was the area between the government troops and the rebels and that he was afraid to proceed any further.

Another twenty-dollar bill and his courage was bolstered. We proceeded.

In five or six blocks, we began to see movement. There were soldiers appearing. The only difference was that they were wearing blue armbands.

The driver nervously pointed and explained, "Revolutionaries."

But they, too, didn't stop us.

Perhaps it was our uniforms. In retrospect, I suppose a van loaded with folks wearing blue uniforms emblazoned with gold stripes could be mistaken by the government soldiers and the revolutionaries alike as friendly generals headed for important negotiations relative to the revolution.

Whatever the reason, we braved the government lines and the revolutionaries' lines and made it to the airport unscathed.

Eastern's airport manager was there—shocked to see us.

"How did you get here from the hotel?" he asked breathlessly.

"We came by van," I answered nonchalantly, with a smile.

"But what are you doing here?"

I was feeling pretty much empowered by now, having penetrated both battle lines of the revolution. "The last time I checked, this was an airport. I left an Eastern Airlines airplane here last night, and I intend to take it to Miami this morning," I replied.

"Ah, but señor," he protested, "we are in the midst of a revolution, and the revolutionaries have captured the airport."

"Fine," I said, "they now have liberated an airport. I have an airplane, so let's use their airport. We must work together if the revolution is to work." I laughed.

All the while, I was walking from the sidewalk in front of the terminal toward the Eastern operations office, listening to the manager's many reasons why we couldn't fly that morning. A few passengers were milling around, and there were a number of blue armband soldiers watching curiously as the scene unfolded.

They didn't bother us, and we didn't bother them.

We arrived at the operations room; no one was there. Usually, a dispatcher was there to go over the weather with us and file a flight plan for the planned flight to Miami.

"See," the manager exclaimed excitedly, "no one is here to file your flight plan, so you cannot go."

"Okay," I said, "but just in case a dispatcher shows up, let's put any Eastern passengers on board and be ready to go."

I was intent on continuing this charade as long as I could. It was not in my character to fail, and so far I was winning.

He begrudgingly collected the twenty or so passengers and placed them on board as the other crewmembers went about their chores in preparation for departure.

I got into the cockpit and dialed in the tower frequency. "Guatemala ground control," I announced, "this is Eastern flight 866."

"Si?" someone answered.

I was getting somewhere. "Is possible, English?"

"Si," he answered. "Un momento."

I waited patiently, not knowing exactly what to do next. We had come too far to turn back now, unless someone showed up with machine guns in the cockpit.

"Yes, Cap-i-tan?" a voice said over the radio.
"Yes, sir," I replied, "we would like to fly to Miami."
"I think it is impossible today. We have a revolution," he explained.
"Yes," I agreed, "and you've taken over the airport."
"Yes," he agreed, proudly.
"Well, we would like to be the first airplane to use your airport."
"I'm not sure…"
"Just let us start our engines while you check with your authorities," I offered.
"Okay," he replied. "I must contact the general, but don't leave this radio."
"Okay." I said as I motioned to the manager to close the passenger door and move the jet way.

I asked the crew, "Are you ready to go to Miami?"

They were.

We had no ground crew, so the manager removed the jetway stairs, ran down, and gave me the all-clear signal. I started the engines.

"You guys finish the checklist," I suggested to the crew, "and I'll keep talking to this fellow in the tower."

"We're taxiing out," I offered, "and we'll hold at the end of the runway until you get permission from the general for our takeoff."

"Si, okay."

I surmised that he was feeling pretty good about running the airport after winning it in the revolution, and now he was controlling a real airliner.

The runway at the Guatemala airport is near the terminal, so the taxi didn't take long. I noticed that the flight attendants had completed the passenger announcements, so there was nothing to do but await the general's approval for takeoff or…

Just go.

I asked the second officer to have the senior flight attendant come up to the cockpit. I quickly briefed her of the situation, and she agreed with the Miami decision.

I looked at the second officer, who nodded. The first officer exclaimed, "I'm with you, skipper, let's go to Miami!"

I was lined up at about a forty-five-degree angle from the direction of the runway. The checklist was complete. I taxied onto the runway. We were lined up on the runway when my friend from the tower called back. "Still unable to contact the general. Can you return to the gate until I can find him?"

I took a deep breath, turned the radio volume down, and eased the throttles up slowly.

I took a quick look at the first officer for his okay.

He smiled and nodded.

I pushed the throttles up to takeoff power. The Boeing responded and down the runway we went. At VR the lightly weighted aircraft leaped off the runway.

We retracted the landing gear and quickly retracted the flaps to achieve max speed as quickly as possible to expedite our departure.

The sky was clear and uncommonly blue as we sped over the tops of the buildings that made up downtown Guatemala City. "Good luck, Guatemala, with your revolution," I said over my shoulder and then asked the first officer to tune in the normal en route radio frequencies to see if anyone else was in the sky this morning.

I suppose that nobody flies on "revolution day" in Guatemala because the airways were empty as we climbed toward our normal cruising altitude.

In a few minutes, we contacted the Mexican controllers. "Mérida control, this is Eastern 866," the first officer called.

"Eastern, say again your number, please," the Mexican controller asked.

"It's Eastern 866, just off Guatemala City en route to Miami," the first officer responded.

After a few seconds Mérida Control came back. "We don't have any record of you in our computer."

I took the mike. "As we left they were having some political issues, so their communication from the airport might be somewhat confused this morning. Can you clear us to Miami while the problem at Guatemala City is straightened out?"

They did clear us to Miami and we proceeded to the Miami International Airport uneventfully. The approach and landing were normal; we taxied to the gate, deplaned the passengers, and along with the crew, I exited the airplane. We had a short layover before our trip was scheduled to continue to San Juan.

I was met by one of my old non-sked buddies who had progressed up the management ladder and was acting as assistant chief pilot at Miami flight operations.

"Tom," he called me over, "where did you just come from?"

"Guatemala City," I nonchalantly replied.

"I got a call from our dispatch department—we have no record of any of our flights departing Guatemala City this morning."

"Well, you do now." I laughed.

"No, seriously, how did you manage to depart Guatemala in the middle of a revolution?" He was trying to be serious, but it just wasn't working.

"Well," I tried to keep a straight face, "I got in the airport van and drove through the government troops, and then we drove through 'no-man's land, and then we drove through the rebel troops to get to the airport. When I arrived there was no dispatch person, but the tower allowed me to taxi to the runway, and once there I decided that in the interest of safety, we should depart this revolution-torn country, so…"

He interrupted me with his finger to my lips. "Cooper, don't say any more. I didn't hear your last comments. I'm going back to my office…you go on your next flight to San Juan…and let's forget that this morning ever happened."

He turned and walked away, his head slowly shaking as he headed up the jetway.

CHAPTER 63
Flying Through The Strike

ON MAY 24TH, THE COMPANY announced that it had hired a total of 452 new pilots. Another landmark was achieved when the first class of twenty newly hired pilots graduated and was feted with a party in the main hangar by employees wishing them well on the line.

The Shuttle sale was made final at the end of May, and the control would be transferred to Trump in about two weeks. The deal put 365 million dollars at Eastern's disposal, but more importantly, it released a number of pilots, who had been staffing the Shuttle, for line flying on the New Eastern system.

There were some very bad days during the strike and some very good days. One of the good days that I remember most was graduation day for the new hires.

That day was special. The company held a ceremony, outstanding in every aspect. Eastern had an auditorium in its headquarters building, and that's where the celebration was held. After the abuse that the new hire pilots had received from the strikers just outside the training headquarters, it was imperative that they be made to feel at home.

The auditorium was darkened with only a faint light illuminating a blue curtain backdrop behind the stage. The scene was completed with a light accentuating a large white Eastern logo. A spotlight shone on the podium. The graduates stood behind, in full uniform, as Phil Bakes welcomed them to our family.

Each was welcomed personally as a scroll representing course completion was formally presented. Each had an opportunity to speak. Some more eloquent than others, but all had words of appreciation for the chance to work for such a fine organization.

The ceremony was closed as all the graduates were standing on stage in full uniform during a stirring rendition of "Wind Beneath My Wings."

It was difficult to find a dry eye in the auditorium as the song ended.

That summer I was approached by several flying pilots and asked if I would be interested in helping to form an organization to help in the communications with the flying pilots. We had over five hundred pilots now, either flying or in school, and even with the daily *Briefing Notes*, published by the company, rumors were flying and the organizers felt that direct communication with the company was necessary to dispel false information.

I agreed to help, but only if the plan did not include any ideas of forming a union. I'd had enough unions to last a lifetime.

There were a series of meetings, and we decided on a name. FLAG, Flight Operations Action Group. We went to Bakes, who blessed the plan while all the time reminding us that even though they were striking, ALPA, the striking pilot union, still officially represented the pilot group.

Letters went out and almost all of the flying pilots agreed that communications was important and that FLAG was a good idea.

A meeting was held and a steering committee established, and I was asked to chair. I agreed, but only if it was a temporary assignment and would terminate at the end of December with an election with full participation of all the flying pilots.

As FLAG began to take shape, the airline was progressing nicely from an operational standpoint. The basic schedule of 110 flights per day was running smoothly, with our on-time performance being tops in the industry. Load factors were increasing as customers began to return and enjoy the benefits of flying on an airline where the employees enjoyed working. The flight-training department began to turn out quality pilots, and the spirit of the entire workforce was buoyed by our collective progress.

On June 8th, control of the Shuttle reverted to Trump.

With the pilots from the Shuttle, we opened up more cities connecting to Atlanta. The business plan was on schedule with the sale of fifteen more aircraft. The downsizing from the total of 250 prestrike aircraft to 157 was right on target.

Although Eastern continued to lose large amounts of money, from an operational standpoint, the airline's progress since March was a tremendous success.

With each day we moved closer to the plan outlined by management of a smaller, more streamlined airline, and the union sensed it. With each report of our success, the union grew more desperate. The acts of vandalism grew. Cars were "keyed" in public parking places with vile remarks. Obscene phone calls were placed to some of the flying pilots' wives, including calls pretending to be from Eastern announcing an air crash resulting in the death of her husband.

In my case, my car was "keyed" twice, advertising that I was a scab. Eastern paid for the paint jobs, and on another occasion, the doors were rendered inoperable when strikers poured super glue in the locks. Almost every obscene magazine was sent to my house, and on one occasion, upon arriving home I discovered the front of the house stickered with obscene signs.

Not all of their harassment tactics worked. One well-thought-out attempt at intimidation backfired. One of our captains owned a small bar and grill in the southern part of Miami. The union decided to picket his establishment and they alerted the media. The press and TV cameras were present to document the act, and the news was broadcast on all local channels.

Once the news was released, the public backlash was such that the bar enjoyed an increase in business and required additional staff to handle the influx. The captain was proud to exclaim that he'd never enjoyed such success and hoped that the union would continue to picket. He could use the free publicity.

By mid-July, we had hired 924 pilots and were well on our way to the goal of 1,700 pilots required to operate the New Eastern with its streamlined business plan.

I was offered a position as check airman and accepted. After I completed the required training, the FAA approved me for the job.

A check airman, although employed by the airline, is a representative of the FAA in approving newly trained pilots for their position with that airline. After a student pilot had completed the required training—ground and simulator—and passed the oral examination and flight check, he was then assigned to me. I was to observe his performance on the line on an actual passenger flight. In this position, I was the last person a new hire had to fly with before he was issued his wings as an Eastern pilot.

Unfortunately, not all made it. Our training department did a great job of weeding out the weaker pilots during the classroom and simulator periods. Check rides were given in detail, testing whether the applicant knew the systems, could perform the maneuvers and operate within the perimeters outlined in the Federal Air Regulations and the Eastern operations manual. My job was to see if the new pilot could put all that together on an actual flight with passenger issues, bad weather, and a million other things that would distract a pilot from safely performing.

After a full evaluation of the applicant and before I would sign my name to his release for actual service he must pass the ultimate litmus test.

Would I place my family in the cabin with this pilot on a dark and stormy night? If the answer was no, then I reluctantly had to give the pilot a "down check." It was probably the toughest thing I had to do with Eastern.

The training department and the check airmen at Eastern were very thorough as evidenced by the fact that there were no accidents during the rebuilding period attributed to lack of training. We were even publicly criticized by the union for having so many failures coming out of our training department, when the truth was we were so strict, it was extremely difficult to reach the bar we had set.

The success that Eastern was enjoying operation-wise was apparent and meant trouble for the pilot's union.

Would-be buyers, at the behest of the union, came and went, but no deal was struck. By the end of July, Eastern's progress with the hiring and training of substitute pilots was well documented, and the bankruptcy judge called for additional negotiations between Lorenzo and the union.

In early fall of 1989, Captain Bavis, the head of the MEC, the union's Master Executive Council at Eastern, began to negotiate in earnest. The sticking point was the number of pilot jobs that were to be available should he call a halt to the sympathy strike. As of the date of the strike, there were approximately four thousand pilots at Eastern. Now, with the replacement pilots reaching over a thousand and pilots who had crossed the picket line reaching over eight hundred, Lorenzo had enough pilots to operate the planned slimmed-down airline and therefore could only offer well less than a thousand jobs should the union pull down the picket lines. It further upset the union that Eastern insisted on protecting the replacement pilots.

The rank and file, influenced by several radical members of the MEC, notably Skip Copeland and his mouthpiece, Ron Cole, voted down the proposal.

In September, Captain Bavis, having lost the confidence of the membership, was replaced as head of the MEC with Copeland.

But the handwriting was on the wall.

By November Eastern had trained over a thousand replacement pilots, and with the eight hundred pilots who had crossed the line, the pilot's union had no choice but to capitulate.

The pilots' union called an end to the pilots' sympathy strike on November 23, 1989 and pulled down their picket lines. The strike had lasted eight and one-half months.

Two days later, the flight attendants' union also called off their sympathy strike. Only the machinists with their intransigent leader, Charley Bryan, remained on strike with Eastern.

The battle with ALPA, the pilots' union, was over, but as I was to learn, the war at Eastern was not. What I thought was the end of the storm was only a lull; we were only in the eye of the hurricane.

Once ALPA called the strike off, hundreds of striking pilots were available for work; only, there were no slots available. Eastern had trained approximately a thousand replacement pilots, and coupled with the two hundred original strike breakers and the six hundred pilots who had subsequently crossed the picket line, all the available pilot positions required by the New Eastern reorganization plan were filled.

The tumultuous year of 1989 ended in high hopes mixed with trepidation. With the pilot and flight attendant strikes settled, the success of the airline seemed assured. Of course we had heard reports, and the company had reported to us that Eastern had been losing enormous amounts of money—some estimated a million dollars a day—but we all assumed that those losses were associated with the strike, and with that over, well, happy days lay ahead.

As we moved into the New Year, the company reported that we were a "2.4 billion-dollar company that provides jobs for twenty thousand employees and serves ninety-three cities with over 830 daily flights."

What was not emphasized was that Eastern had lost approximately nine hundred million dollars in 1989. This coupled with the fact that Continental Airlines was having cash flow problems resulted in Lorenzo having to revamp his post-bankruptcy offer to the creditors at a lower price. At the time of the bankruptcy in March, his offer, which would take Eastern out of bankruptcy, was a repayment of one hundred cents on the dollar to the creditors. Now, in January, he readjusted his offer to fifty cents on the dollar.

The creditors' committee agreed to the plan with a number of conditions, one of which was labor peace.

The Man in The Arena...

With ALPA still representing all the pilots, the ones flying and the ones still on the street, and with Eastern's adamant stand that the replacement pilots would not be displaced, the chance for labor peace was nil.

In March, one year into the strike, with losses still mounting, revenues remaining stagnant, and with the general turndown of the economy, Lorenzo again revised his offer to the creditors. This time he offered twenty-five cents on the dollar. The creditors' committee rejected this offer flat, and the war with the creditors escalated.

This gave me pause to reflect on the whole situation. I still had confidence in Lorenzo and especially Phil Bakes, but I wasn't so sure about the creditors. There were continued rumblings about liquidation that frightened me.

It was about that time I ran into an old FAA friend, Chuck Smith, in Miami Springs. We passed the time of day and in our conversation, he exclaimed, "Hey, Coop, we miss you over at the FAA. When are you going to crank up another airline?"

"No more airlines for me." I laughed. "I've got my hands full now with this Eastern mess."

We said good-bye, but that got me thinking. It wouldn't be a bad idea to have something to fall back on, just in case things didn't go well with the creditors' committee. If Eastern were to fail, I could make a modest living with a one-horse charter operation, and I knew the business well. "Not a bad idea," I surmised.

The next day I pulled all of my old Air Miami flight and operations manuals out of the closet, and with a quick name change, I submitted them along with my application to the FAA for a new airline certificate.

GULFSTREAM INTERNATIONAL AIRLINES was born.

During this time, the late winter of 1989 and early spring of 1990, the flying pilots began to grumble. ALPA continued to promote the return of the displaced pilots, and the replacement pilots were growing nervous. In spite of the company's assurance that they would be protected whether there was a buy-out, merger, or successful reorganization, their concerns were made clear to me as interim chairman of the FLAG group, the pilots' communication vehicle.

CHAPTER 64

From "Number One Scab" to Union Boss

IN FEBRUARY A GROUP OF flying pilots—Steve Glasgow, Don Davidson, Joe Shea, and a few others—approached me with an idea to form a second union with the purpose of decertifying ALPA. They asked me to head up the group.

I thought about their proposition for a few days and decided, as much as I disliked unions, I would agree to join the movement and lead the group under three conditions: that we advised Phil Bakes, that at least 90 percent of the flying pilots agreed to the plan, and that I would only act as chairman until the end of the year and then the rank and file would have a vote on leadership.

In late February I requested a meeting with Phil Bakes. He agreed to visit with me, but he reminded me at the onset of the meeting that ALPA was still the official representative of the pilots and we couldn't discuss anything that resembled negotiations.

I had learned to like and admire Phil Bakes. He was an upfront guy and if he told you something, you could take it to the bank. Yes, he was Frank's mouthpiece at Eastern, but he brought more experience in airline management to the table than almost anyone at Eastern. He had served as general counsel for the Civil Aeronautics Board before Frank Lorenzo hired him away to assist in the organization of New York Air. He later was named president of Continental Airlines and was brought in as Eastern's president when Lorenzo took over Eastern. I trusted him explicitly and valued his advice.

The meeting was short.

"Phil," I proclaimed almost apologetically, "I'm going to start another pilots' union."

He sat back in his chair, looked at me, and smiled. "Captain, are you sure that you want to do this?"

"Somebody has to do it, Phil," I explained. "ALPA must be stopped, and the only way to do it is to have them decertified and replace them with an alternate collective bargaining agent. I have talked with a couple of the American Airline pilots who did it at American. They have been very helpful and supportive."

"Yes, I know," he said, "but you know, ALPA will come after you with all guns blazing. They really went after the five guys at American. I'm familiar with that project."

"Well," I laughed, "they didn't exactly invite me to their Christmas party last year, and I think I can take all they have to dish out. I have so far."

"Okay, Captain, I wish you luck; you'll need it, and I'll watch your progress with great *interest*." He smiled. He emphasized "interest," and I knew what he meant. We were on the same wavelength, and we both knew that I was right.

We shook hands and I left.

Leaving the executive building, my brain was swimming. *What the hell did I just do?* I asked myself. *As bad as I hate unions, now I'm about to start one.*

That's not a fair statement. I didn't hate ALL unions, just ALPA. I believe there's a place for collective bargaining in our culture. It's just that I hated ALPA. They used the pilots of Eastern for an agenda established by ALPA national. They used the pilots of Eastern to get Lorenzo, and so far, they had done a pretty good job of character assassination at the expense of Eastern.

I believed that for Eastern to survive, it must settle with the creditors and come out of bankruptcy or be bought out by another group. Neither of those scenarios could come about without labor peace—and with ALPA negotiating for the two pilot groups, labor peace just would not happen.

We formed the Eastern Pilots Association, called the EPA. They named me as chairman, and we began the process to decertify ALPA. I learned very quickly that the road to decertification was long…bumpy…and expensive.

We did it right. We formed a corporation and hired an accounting firm and a lawyer. We sent out survey forms and 96 percent of the flying pilots signed on. We began to publish a bimonthly newsletter called *The Communicator* and set up a modest monthly fee assessment. Within a month we were up and running.

As well as things were going for EPA, they weren't going so well for Lorenzo. When the creditors rejected Lorenzo's bid for twenty-five cents on the dollar, they also filed a motion for the courts to appoint a trustee to run the airline.

A date was set for April 13th. During the hearing, Lorenzo upped his offer to the creditors to thirty cents on the dollar, but they would not budge. They wanted Lorenzo to go back to his earlier offer of fifty cents on the dollar, or they wanted a trustee.

They finally countered and agreed to accept 37.5 cents, but to sweeten the deal, they demanded stock in Texas Air, the parent company of Continental Airlines, and 19 percent of Eastern.

The meeting went on into the night, and finally, with no agreement, at around ten o'clock in the evening, the judge made his decision.

Lorenzo was out...

And a trustee was appointed. Martin R. Shugrue, Jr.

Two days later, in the executive offices of Eastern at the International Airport in Miami, Phil Bakes submitted his resignation as president of Eastern Airlines, and Shugrue accepted it.

There are some things that stand out, that are indelibly etched in my memory from those troubled times. It was the class Phil Bakes showed. He had been in the courtroom in New York City when the judge issued his edict removing Frank Lorenzo from control of Eastern, and he knew that he, as a symbol of Texas Air Corp, would be next.

Knowing that he was finished at Eastern, when he arrived at his office on the 19th, he took the time to write a letter of thanks to me for a small act of thoughtfulness that I had shown him the week earlier. The thank-you letter was dated April 19, 1990.

It was arguably the last letter he wrote as president of Eastern...other than his resignation.

Lorenzo was out and Shugrue was in.

I scurried down to the FAA offices on 36th Street to check on the progress of my application for the certification of GULFSTREAM INTERNATIONAL AIRLINES.

Two weeks later the sale of Eastern's South American routes was approved. American Airlines would take over at the end of June.

Eastern seemed somewhat empty without Lorenzo. In my first twenty-five years with the airline, I hardly paid any attention to what was going on at "mahogany row." I enjoyed the flying so much that the business side of the company really didn't interest me at all.

Of course I followed the major events of the airline; the changes of presidents from MacIntyre, to Floyd Hall, and then on to Frank Borman. Yes, I watched as the unions fought with the company, but in the end, all seemed to come out all right. We were always settling labor disputes, buying more airplanes, opening new routes, and I was happy just to suit up and fly the line.

But now, after being a part of the small group of working pilots who worked so closely with Eastern's management, I had more of a feeling of ownership, and I suddenly felt somewhat let down. And still the issue of being represented by a union, ALPA, which did not have the flying pilots' interests at heart, continued to be a real concern. Was Shugrue going to negotiate a settlement with ALPA at the expense of the flying pilots, especially the replacement pilots?

That question loomed large and was yet to be determined. There was nothing left to do but carry on and make the best of what lay ahead.

It wasn't long, May 23rd, before Shugrue communicated publicly to the employees.

It began, "To the men and women of Eastern: I have a clear mission at Eastern: to operate—not liquidate—the airline and restore our financial viability."

So far so good.

He went on to talk about "external relationships" and explained his complete separation with Texas Air and the hiring of a new marketing agency.

So far so good.

And then he addressed "internal relationships." He complimented the skill and commitment among all Eastern employee groups and then he stated that a genuine effort to *reassemble all the elements of Eastern will achieve our full potential.* Then came the crushing comment that I was afraid would come:

"We have opened a dialogue with our labor organizations to move that process forward."

The rest of the letter meant nothing. My phone was already ringing.

The flying pilots of Eastern were reading the letter also.

Then came my worst nightmare. I had to begin to act like a union boss. The consensus among the flying pilots was that they did not intend to stand by, fly the line, while new management negotiated away their hard-earned jobs. Even with heavy heart, but as the representative of 96 percent of the flying pilots of Eastern, I knew that I must communicate those feelings to the new president of Eastern, Martin Shugrue.

On May 29th, I sat down and penned a letter to Shugrue, my first communication with the new president. I advised him that "EPA had formally requested that the National Mediation Board conduct a free election to determine who should represent Eastern's pilots for the purposes of collective bargaining."

In my one-and-one-half-page letter, I explained our position and further demanded that he immediately cease and desist from any further meetings, discussions, and/or negotiations with ALPA.

I cautioned him "to continue the charade of negotiating with ALPA would be extremely demoralizing to the flying pilots, and to conclude an agreement would be considered a hostile act."

I ended with, "The 1,775 flying pilots of Eastern are watching your actions with extreme interest," and I signed the letter, "Sincerely, Thomas Cooper, chairman, EASTERN PILOTS ASSOCIATION."

I hated to write that letter, but I had no choice...although ALPA had discontinued the sympathy strike, we were still at war.

Excerpts from my letter were printed in the prestigious aviation periodical *Aviation Week and Space Technology* magazine. We were a force now.

Shugrue, even though there was no direct threat for a work stoppage, understood the situation. The next day, the vice president of flight operations, Tom Button, quoting Shugrue, issued a company bulletin: "There will be no deal with ALPA that causes the loss of any working pilot."

That brought temporary peace, but it didn't last long.

The court kept insisting on meetings between ALPA and Eastern, and I kept insisting to Marty—we were on a first-name basis now—that if he gave in to the union, bad things *could* happen. In the beginning, his meetings with ALPA were public, usually held in Washington. Later they became more clandestine and secret.

Luckily, I had an ally in headquarters. I knew what Marty was doing about as soon as he knew. When secret meetings were to be held, I knew in advance. Messages were passed on to me by an insider in headquarters using the pseudonym DT. The mole's code name was a takeoff on the Watergate character called Deep Throat. I was Top Cat. It sounds pretty corny now, but in the summer and early fall of 1990, tensions and emotions were running so thick that you could cut them with a knife, and secret alliances were important.

I remember, on one occasion in that period, Marty had agreed in principle over the phone to settle with ALPA, and he was leaving on the afternoon flight at 6:00 bound for Washington to ink the proposed agreement. The information given to me was that "it wasn't going to be good for the replacement pilots." It was late afternoon when DT found me. I rushed to headquarters, insisted on seeing Marty, and confronted him with the news. He appeared to be shocked that I knew of his plan.

"Marty, I know what's going on. If you sign anything with ALPA in Washington, you'll have to come home on a bus, because there won't be an Eastern flight in the air. It's beyond my control now."

It was deathly silent in his office. He thought, for what seemed to be an eternity, and then, with a frown, pushed the intercom button on his phone and instructed his secretary, "Please cancel my reservation on flight 178 to Washington tonight."

I hated myself.

The National Mediation Board, NMB, chaired by Josh Javits, had refused to allow the pilots of Eastern to vote on whether we would have EPA or ALPA represent us. They used as an excuse the fact that there was an issue outstanding concerning whether Continental and Eastern's relationship constituted a "single carrier" situation; whether there should be two seniority lists or a single combined one, and until that was resolved, they would not allow a vote. After dealing with the NMB, I was convinced that they were only an extension of organized labor.

I was now at war with the National Mediation Board, ALPA, and to a certain extent, Shugrue. This union stuff was turning out to be more than I bargained for.

I had no choice but to hunker down and wait until the NMB and Josh Javits decided on the "single carrier" issue.

Two weeks after Shugrue came on board, the sale of the Latin American routes to American Airlines was approved. Although the working people of Eastern had been warned of the impending sale, and even though we were told that, for our survival, we needed the cash generated from the sale, it was a bitter pill to swallow.

I happened to be flying to Panama in June, the last month of Eastern's operation there. We were handing over the entire Latin American division to American on July 1st, and I wasn't too happy about it.

It was June 29th, a couple of days before we were to hand the keys over to American. I was in the cockpit, preparing for the departure from Panama, when an American Airlines employee, an agent, burst into the cockpit and announced quite possessively, "I've got the jump seat."

Well, the jump seat is a sacred item. It's the observer seat in the cockpit just behind the captain. It's used by the FAA to observe the crew's operation or a company flight instructor observation of trainees. After that, it's used at the captain's discretion. Even if assigned by the company, even with the FAA, the proper protocol is for the assignee to introduce himself, show some identification, and address the captain, "Sir, I'm so-and-so, and I would like to sit on your jump seat with your permission."

I swallowed but overlooked his brashness and motioned for the second officer to help him with the seat belt. He brushed off the offer to help with another comment while chuckling. "At American they teach us how to buckle our own seat belts."

I had just about had it with this rude character when, finally settled in his seat, he exclaimed proudly, "Well, in a couple of days we'll take over this operation and then we'll show the this whole area down here just how to run an airline."

I'd had enough. I snapped off my seat belt, slowly turned around, and in a very calm, surprisingly calm voice, addressed the crude American Airline employee. "Young man, please vacate *MY* jump seat, vacate *MY* cockpit, and vacate *MY* airplane, and I might suggest that American Airlines teach you some manners before they teach Eastern how to run an airline."

We taxied out with one less passenger. I hate to admit it but, somewhere down deep inside, I felt a little better about the sale.

As summer wore on, a veritable parade of would-be purchasers courted Shugrue.

There was talk about a deal with JAL, Japanese Air Line, but that fizzled. There was a possible merger between Pan Am and Eastern. It fell through. There was a buy-out proposed by Al Checchi, president of North West Airlines. It was more of a liquidation with all the "good parts" going to Checchi. The creditors killed that. Even Carl Icahn, TWA's chief, stopped by to see if he could bargain for anything.

The Man in The Arena...

In all of the would-be transactions, labor peace was the pacing item. Without that, no one would put any money up for the ongoing operation.

It was late July, and this began to wear on me. I discussed the issue with the steering committee of EPA. "Are we becoming part of the problem instead of part of the solution?" we asked ourselves. I labored over the issue for some time with no resolution. Were we all so gung-ho for the Day Oners, the Cross Overs, and the Replacement Pilots, that our rationale was tainted? Had we become so immoveable in our position that we were blinded to the fact that our original purpose was to save Eastern?

In the Lorenzo days and before the EPA organization, I felt comfortable visiting with Bakes and discussing issues. But now he was gone. Even my old comrade in arms, Don Davidson, had been given the post as vice president of Operations and was not available. There was no one to turn to.

With the exception of Bob Tyler. Bob was a line pilot at the time of the strike, but he displayed such a talent for communication that he was quickly given a post in the company as director of Pilot Relations. We had become good friends and I valued his judgment greatly. He also kept his fingers on the pulse of the corporate side of the furthering adventures of Eastern, so I called him for counsel.

He suggested that we meet off campus and, at his suggestion, we met just off 36th Street, at the Miami Springs Golf Course in a wooded area adjacent to the second fairway.

It was like a secure picnic, with Bob supplying the blanket, food, and drink. He always had a flair for the dramatic.

Under a very large oak tree, I explained my frustrations to him.

He understood completely. He confessed that this same conversation had been going on at headquarters, and there were no solutions to be had there either. He suggested that our conversation be confidential and confessed the grave financial position that the company was in.

"If the employees found out the truth," he whispered, "there would be a panic, and I'm not sure we could keep enough folks around to keep the airline flying. You're in the driver's seat, Cooper. It's imperative that you hold the line with the flying pilots and wait out the NMB until this single-carrier issue is settled. Once you're allowed to have an election, we're sure that your EPA will win. That will be the end of ALPA, and the labor peace that is required by investors will materialize. Then potential investors with real money will come out of the woodwork, and we will emerge from bankruptcy and be on our way."

"What about the machinists?" I asked.

"They've all been replaced, and besides, they're tired and will settle quickly once the pilot issue is over."

"I'm okay until the end of the year," I agreed, "and then, we're having an election to see just who will run the EPA. I'm not running."

We finished lunch, said good-bye, and I pondered our conversation. The message was loud and clear. Keep the pressure on Shugrue not to settle with ALPA, and the company would keep the doors open for investors once EPA was the pilots' union of record.

The airline had reached its post-strike planned level and was running very well operation-wise. The issue was that the business-class passengers were not returning as fast as management would like. Marty had revamped the first-class program by adding larger upgraded seats to the first-class section of our airplanes to entice more of the higher revenue passengers. As a result, load factors began to increase, and it was just a matter of time until the plan produced an increase in revenue. Shugrue's plan was beginning to work.

And then, from out of nowhere on August 2, Iraq invaded Kuwait.

The price of fuel for Eastern doubled and erased any benefit that the company enjoyed from the success of Shugrue's plan.

Given the information that Tyler shared with me, it didn't look good.

In August the FAA approved my application for an Air Carrier Certification for Gulfstream International Airlines. With the Eastern situation requiring all of my time, I hired one charter pilot, rented a small two-room office on 36th Street, and let him run the one airplane charter operation. I just needed to keep the certification alive in case the worst happened at Eastern.

After the pilots and the flight attendants called off their strike, there was no one left to man the picket lines except the machinists. Their ranks were thinning also and when I went to the airport for my usual flights, there were fewer and fewer strikers on the picket lines.

I actually began to feel sorry for them. After all, they were my neighbors, and the chance of them returning to Eastern was slim. The little tyrant Charlie Bryan was enjoying a nice salary while these poor souls were literally existing on food stamps.

The animosity I had felt toward the machinists was waning, and I suppose that was the reason for my strange impulsive behavior one night in November.

First, I must go back a few months as a prelude to the story.

Earlier in the strike, Eastern management decided to design a new pilot's uniform in order to differentiate between the strikers and the flying pilots and also to, perhaps, lift our spirits somewhat. Whatever the reason, we had to visit the Field Shop, a uniform supply business on 36th Street, and get fitted up.

With the new uniform coming soon, I examined my old worn flight kit and decided that with a new uniform I needed a new flight kit. I gave the order and soon the uniform and flight kit showed up. I had ordered my name to be embossed in gold on the flight kit. This was normal and when I picked up the kit, there it was, lettered in gold: Captain T. L. Cooper, and under my name, Eastern Airlines.

Perfect.

Except, in addition and probably as a private joke as I was well acquainted with the shop owner, he included a nametag that read on one side, CREW, and on the other, NO. I SCAB.

I thought that to be the funniest thing I'd ever seen, and instead of storing it somewhere out of sight, I kept it fastened to my flight kit, in full view, as a red badge of courage.

So, back to that dark cold night in November. It was an uncommonly chilly night as I parked my car in the parking lot adjacent to concourse B at the Miami International Airport and walked toward the lower level to enter the Eastern operations area.

It was the first flight of my sequence that month. As I walked past an area that was under construction, I noticed that the machinist pickets had built a bonfire and were huddled around it keeping warm.

They saw me as I passed near their fire and began the usual chants, "Scab! Scab! Scab!" They were a pitiful lot, unshaven, wearing worn-out Eastern mechanics uniforms and faded anti-Lorenzo T-shirts—the ones with Lorenzo's name in a circle with a bar diagonally across it. How could you not have compassion for such an assemblage?

For some reason I stopped, turned, and took a few steps toward the group huddled around the fire and demanded, "Who called me a scab?"

The chanting stopped. The whole group became silent. They had never, in the year and a half of striking, had anything like that happen. They had never been challenged.

Finally, one of the strikers, apparently the unwitting leader, moved cautiously toward me, almost hesitantly, and exclaimed while pointing toward his chest, "I did," as if to say, "What of it?"

"Well," I said bravely, "I'll be passing by here every Monday and Thursday night all month, and I expect you fellows to address me by my correct title," and I pointed to my flight kit…

"I'm known as the Number One SCAB."

They began to hoot and to holler. And then they began to laugh and point at my nametag and, almost in unison, call out as I departed, "Number One Scab…Number One Scab…Number One Scab…" That moment was probably the high point of their striking career, and I'm sure they enjoyed it as much as I did.

I believe that on that cold November night, we came as close to bonding as two adversarial groups ever could.

For the rest of the month, every Monday and Thursday night, I passed that way to the jeers, hoots, and laughter of "Number One Scab…Number One Scab…Number One Scab!"

And in honor of their resolve, I would salute and tip my hat.

At the end of November, the bankruptcy judge gave Shugrue, over the objections of the creditors, 135 million dollars. He had argued that with those funds he could weather the storms of fuel escalating cost, bad publicity around the press articles concerning imminent shutdown, and the general downturn of the economy.

Jerrie and I held a Christmas party for the loyalists at our home in Miami Springs in mid-December and invited Shugrue.

He came.

In our backyard, by the pool, he gave an impassioned speech outlining all the good things that were happening. The 135-million-dollar advance would see us through the rough spell, and the future looked good.

I sincerely believe that he meant every word.

EPA published its Merry Christmas *COMMUNICATOR* issue shortly thereafter, and I did the editorial. Little did I know at the time, it was to be Eastern's eulogy.

The Man in The Arena...

MERRY CHRISTMAS, EASTERN

How nice it is to say that one more time! How many times have they counted you out, Old Girl? How many times have you proven them wrong? I've long since stopped counting. You continue to amaze me with your resiliency and your grit.

So, during this holiday season in particular, I'd like to thank you for all you've done for me over the last thirty years... Let's see, you bought my family a nice home, you sent my two children through college, and come to think of it, you even paid my way through also. Daily bread...well, one look at my waistline and it's easy to see you've fed me quite well too. Oh, I almost forgot all those "grown-up" toys...the airplanes, boats, fast cars, and on...and on...and on...

I'm ashamed to admit that in thirty years I don't think I have ever taken the time to really thank you. Perhaps I've been too busy complaining about being drafted on New Years' Eve or having to fly on Super Bowl Sunday, or having to spend a twelve-hour layover at a hotel that <u>didn't</u> have a heated swimming pool. While I pestered you with a thousand petty complaints, you always treated me with dignity, and you never missed a paycheck.

Christmas is a time to remember family and old friends. Well, Dear Friend, you are a treasured member of the Cooper family and I'm happy to be able to say again, "Merry Christmas, Happy New Year, and Thanks."

Captain Tom Cooper

The Christmas season came and with it came the traditional Eastern company holiday party. Most of the employees from the Miami area came, and we celebrated another year and rejoiced at the good news that Eastern would be around for another year.

Some of the former striking pilots came with families. Eastern had recalled about fifty, and there was hand-shaking and even hugs as both sides pledged to do whatever it took to make Eastern successful.

It was a joyful time but it wasn't real.

Management had already begun to formulate plans for liquidation. It was just a matter of when.

The United Nations, led by the United States, commenced Desert Storm to liberate Kuwait on January 16, 1991.

Two days later, Friday, January 18, at midnight, Eastern folded its wings.

CHAPTER 65

Eastern Airlines Ceases Operations

I HAD GOTTEN A CONFIDENTIAL call from Captain Don Davidson on Wednesday the 16th.

"Cooper," he said quietly, "we're going to shut down Friday night, and I know that you're not scheduled for a flight until next week, but if you want to take one more flight, I can put you on one of our last."

"Don," I replied in shock, "I don't think I'm up to it. I don't think I can manage. My last flight was on the thirteenth. Let's just let it go at that. Thanks for the heads-up."

"It's not public yet, so keep it quiet," he added.

"Okay," I said as I hung up.

I was too tired to weep.

Friday, as I left my home to drive to the flight operations building, the Hartley Building, I got a call from the newly elected head of our Eastern Pilots Association, Captain Terry Milanette. "Cooper," he said, "I thought you ought to know that today the NMB agreed to give us a vote. It's a shallow victory, but I promise that we'll complete the business you started, and we'll throw ALPA off the property."

"Thanks, Terry, I know you will," I replied, but we both knew that it was too little, too late. The NMB and Javits had done their job. They'd delayed our vote for six months—six months that, had ALPA been voted off the property, perhaps financing would have been available. I'd had my personal opinion concerning Javits and the NMB, and this just proved it to me.

A sad chore now awaited me. To be with Eastern on this, her last day.

I wanted to be there when the airline shut down. It was afternoon, but the building, normally busy at that time of day, was eerily quiet. There were some people there but not as many as usual.

They were zombie-like, moving as if in a trance with no apparent purpose other than retrieving their personal belongings and moving toward the door. The tears had been shed yesterday, the day that the announcement had been made, and today was just clean-out day.

I watched the scene with somber curiosity. Upstairs, the operations management area was almost vacant, and the downstairs area, the training facility, was quiet.

The only noise was the muted celebration out on 36th Street by the strikers. With horns blaring, the chants of "We won...we won...we won..." penetrated the walls.

Won what? I kept asking myself? Won *what*?

They would be asking themselves the same question soon.

As it darkened, I began to realize that I was the only one left. It was truly sad.

No one stayed by her bedside while the Old Lady, Eastern, breathed her last breath.

I couldn't leave. I found myself in the office of the vice president of Flight Operations and sat down behind his desk. I propped my feet up and decided to see it through. After all that Eastern had done for me, it was the least I could do.

I would be there, to the end, with Eastern, on her last day.

At midnight, I picked up the phone and recorded the following tape message to the EPA members.

January 18, 1991

Dear Fellow Pilots and Families,

The memory of this day will remain with me forever. It is my sad duty to inform you that tonight, Friday, January 18, 1991, Eastern Airlines will close its doors.

After a valiant struggle against overwhelming odds, the business decision was made to cease operations.

I will not go into the reasons; I will not open old wounds at this time by finger pointing, and I think it inappropriate at this time of grief to attempt to place the blame.

I will, however, ask you to reflect for a moment on the good times at Eastern. Remember her as the airline that, just a few years ago, flew more passengers than any other airline in the free world. Remember her as the "Great Silver Fleet," a pioneer in the industry who spread her silver wings over these United States and commanded the skies so majestically over South America.

What will happen to us, the employees of Eastern? Will she be bought intact by some entrepreneur who will launch her again? Who knows? The futures, our futures, are understandably cloudy now. What is clear, what is absolutely loud and clear is the fact that you, the flying pilots of this airline and your families, supported her with such devotion unexcelled in employee/employer relationships and you… you produced the finest product in the aviation industry. For that, you should be very proud.

Remember, wherever you go, whatever you do, those accomplishments and your splendid professional performance will remain with you and will be your legacy to the aviation industry.

Grieve for her…yes…but when the time for grieving is over, hold up your heads and be proud; proud that you did your best and you did not quit. Carry that with you to whatever your personal future holds.

My best to you and your families.
Captain Tom Cooper

It was a "wake" that I'll never forget.

In contrast, at midnight, Skip Copeland, the radical head of the MEC of ALPA at Eastern, recorded his message to his group.

One single shimmer in my memory: that single moment, March 4th, when I, along with the MEC, made our choice and picked up the phone connected to the strike center and issued the order, 'shut her down'," referring to the decision to strike Eastern.

The sun was peeking over the Eastern Airlines buildings to the east when I found myself walking toward my car. I drove through the gates at Eastern for the last time as I joined 36th Street.

The street was deserted. The only remnants of the previous night's celebration were picket signs strewn along the sidewalks. Their victory celebration was over, and now, for all of us, strikers and non-strikers alike, we must face life without Eastern.

My small, two-room Gulfstream office was only about six blocks down the street. I parked, stumbled up the stairs, opened the door, and found my desk. Exhausted, I laid my head on my desk and slept.

The Eastern chapter of my life was closed.

EASTERN AIR LINES AIRCRAFT THAT I FLEW

Lockhead Constellation, My first EAL airplane

Douglas DC-7B, The second EAL plane that I flew

Boeing B-727, The third and last EAL plane that I flew

AIR CHARTER AIRCRAFT THAT I OPERATED

De Havilland Heron landing at Ocean Reef Resort

Perhaps the first hot pants in the industry

My wife, Jerrie James Cooper

When you are an airline pilot, you are either coming or going during the holidays.

But, when you are home, you play golf and drink beer with your pal.

Captain Thomas L. Cooper

JACK SHAW, *the GREAT ENTREPRENEUR*, and the CONNIE CAPER

The cockpit of a Lockheed Constellation

Flight engineer's panel of a Lockheed Constellation

Jack Shaw, the great entrepreneur

The Man in The Arena...

SCENES FROM HAVANA

Residence of the US ambassador in Havana

Me, Wayne Smith, Chief of the US Interest Section, Jerrie and friends at the Bodeguita del Media, Havana, a famous Hemingway hangout.

Jerrie and I.... and Che in Havana, 1978.

Although our two countries quarreled continuously, the folks that I worked with at the Cuban governmental agencies couldn't have been nicer as evidenced by this holiday wish for "happiness and peace around the world".

The Man in The Arena...

STRIKE AT EAL!

The computers couldn't figure it out so we had to schedule the available flight crews with pencil and on a yellow pad. This is the actual flight crew availability on day one of the strike in Miami

The flying pilot's families gave parties to our support divisions That's me and Captain Erwin Korczynski thanking our ticketing personnel for their support.

One hundred percent of the flying pilots announced their intentions to fly in three major newspapers, Miami, New York and Washington.

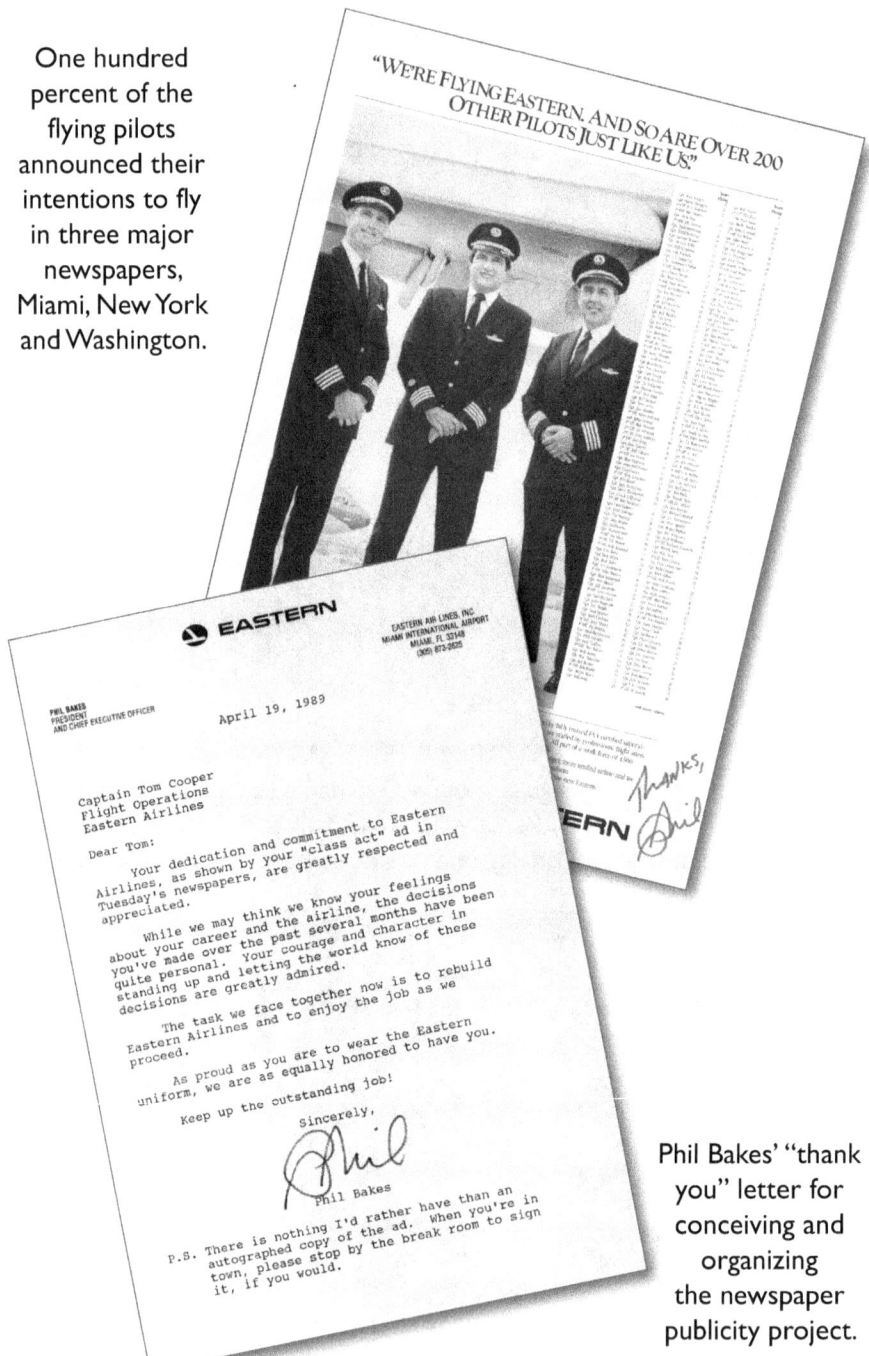

Phil Bakes' "thank you" letter for conceiving and organizing the newspaper publicity project.

AIRLINE TRAINING PAYS OFF

Jet lands safely after engine fails

I was at the controls of the B-727 that experienced an engine failure departing Miami

No one hurt as jet makes fast landing

PLANE / from 1B

the Everglades and dumped the fuel he had just taken on.

"We practice this over and over and over again," Cooper said. "This was just like we practice."

When the plane landed on Runway Nine Right, along the Dolphin Expressway, fire engines and ambulances raced alongside. They had been called as a precaution. They weren't needed, although some passengers seemed a bit shaken.

"I thought it was the end," said Vic Sesto, as he got off the plane with his wife, Shirley.

There were unconfirmed reports of engine parts falling over an area near the airport. Eric Lynch, deputy director of airport operations for Eastern, said that was unlikely. He examined the problem engine right after the plane landed.

"There was no exterior damage," he said. "There were just a couple of fan blades broken, that's all."

Eastern mechanics later said the turbine engine had failed for undetermined reasons. The Boeing 727, the most widely used airplane nationwide, is also rated one of the safest. It can fly with only two of its three engines.

Passengers on the flight were transferred to another 727, where

A shaken Vic Vesto and his wife Shirley disembark after safe landing at Miami International.

they were given free champagne.

PHIL BAKES, A CLASS ACT

EASTERN AIR LINES, INC.
MIAMI INTERNATIONAL AIRPORT
MIAMI, FL 33148
(305) 873-2211

PHIL BAKES
PRESIDENT
AND CHIEF EXECUTIVE OFFICER

April 19, 1990

Captain and Mrs. Tom Cooper
1010 Redbird Avenue
Miami Springs, FL 33166

Dear Jerri and Tom:

I really appreciate your remembering my request for the shirts. What a nice surprise when they showed up on my desk!

Thank you both for your thoughtfulness.

Sincerely,

Phil Bakes

Phil was terminated when the judge replaced Lorenzo with Marty Shugrue on April 19, 1990. This was arguably his last act as president. A thoughtful gentleman, even on his last day at Eastern.

THE MAN IN THE ARENA...

THE END OF AN ERA

A post script to this Eastern chapter. Captain O. B. Bivens pinned this thank you letter to me in December of 1994, almost four years after Eastern folded. He was the Captain who hired me in California 32 years earlier and he remembered and thanked me for "working and trying to save OUR airline".

PART IV
Gulfstream International Airlines

Approach and Landing

CHAPTER 66
Beginning All Over

With nothing

"Wake up, Cooper." I was aroused from my daydream by Fisher. "We're almost there. Is that your airport up ahead?"

I lived in an aero park within the village of Wellington, about fifteen miles west of West Palm Beach. The dark ribbon of asphalt, slicing through the quiet community, identified the runway. "Yes," I answered. "If there are no aircraft in the traffic pattern, you can land straight in."

Stephen made the usual call on the community radio frequency and lined up with the runway.

"After you land, just let the airplane roll out to the other end of the runway," I offered. "I'll show you which taxiway leads to our house."

We taxied up to the house, and Stephen spun the aircraft around on the ramp outside my hangar, in the backyard.

"You're welcome to come in and visit," I said as I opened the door and climbed out on the wing.

"No," he laughed, "I have a business to run now, and I must get back to Sebastian."

"Thanks for the ride," I yelled over the engine noise, "and good luck with your new venture."

He waved good-bye as he closed the door and taxied away.

I waved and he disappeared down the taxiway toward the runway.

As I stood there and watched him depart, I couldn't help but think of how I got to this place in life, especially after the Eastern debacle. A comfortable life with a nice home, on an airport with a hangar in the backyard, two grown kids and six wonderful grandchildren, plus a lovely wife. Top all that with a boat and an airplane, and I marveled at my success.

It had been a long road from that morning in Miami Springs when, exhausted with Eastern's ruinous collapse, I slept at my desk in the small dingy office of Gulfstream International Airlines.

I stood there on the ramp outside my house and remembered how it had been that morning…

A noise outside my office door aroused me. It was the young pilot I had hired to watch over Gulfstream while I was busy with Eastern. He was dressed, as I always insisted, resplendent in a starched white shirt with black tie, gold epaulets, black pants, and polished shoes.

"Oh, excuse me, sir," he said, "I didn't know that you were here."

"It's okay," I responded. "I've had a busy night and I just stopped by for a quick rest."

"Yes," he said sympathetically, "I heard the news, sorry. We have a charter to Walkers Cay and I was just stopping by for some expense money for the landing and customs fees."

I reached into the back of my desk drawer for the petty cash box and counted out two hundred dollars. "There, that should be enough for the Bahamas customs guys," I surmised. "And don't forget to collect the fees from the customers."

At that moment, a transition took place. At exactly ten o'clock in the morning of January 19, 1991, the direction of my whole life changed.

From focusing on Eastern Airlines and its problems, my attention had turned to Gulfstream International Airlines, and I never looked back.

Three days ago my full attention, and my life, was concentrated on fighting with ALPA, arguing with Marty Shugrue, battling with the National Mediation Board, and cajoling 1,775 pilots in an attempt to keep Eastern flying one more day.

Now, I was only concerned that the pilot for Gulfstream would not forget to collect a paltry customs fee from the customers for a Gulfstream charter into the Bahama Islands.

I drove home, showered, dressed, and talked with Jerrie about the events of the past twenty-four hours. "We'll be okay," I lied with a straight face as I feebly tried to assure her of our future, and I headed back to the Gulfstream office without an idea.

The Man in The Arena...

My head was spinning. For the first time in twenty-nine years, I didn't have the Eastern financial safety net. My past aviation ventures were nothing more than hobbies. Whether they were successful mattered not; after all, wasn't Eastern always there to bail me out with a paycheck issued twice a month? Yes, but now, I began to realize I had to get serious.

There was so much to get done. I sat down and took an inventory of what I had to work with. I had paid little attention to Gulfstream since applying to the FAA for a charter certificate a year ago. Once the FAA approved my application and issued a charter license, I routinely requested commuter authority, a license to operate scheduled service, issued by the Department of Transportation. As I was in Washington frequently on union business for the Eastern Pilots Association, I would stop in and check on the progress of the commuter request. It was issued in December, about a month before Eastern shut down, and I simply put it in a drawer for future use.

In the previous summer, I had settled a small lawsuit resulting from the sale of one of my ventures. I had a claim of about thirty thousand dollars, and the company had no way of paying. Their business had failed and they were liquidating. I agreed to accept a run-down, ten-seat Cessna 402B as settlement just to get the aggravation behind me. Having no money or time, I paid little attention to the airplane. As my application moved through the FAA process, I began to slowly pick at it. I had some friends in the maintenance business and, from time to time, I would contract with them to do small jobs on the airplane to gradually upgrade it.

I had the engines gone over and inspected by an engine mechanic I knew. The airframe was in good shape with the exception of the interior and paint. Luckily, I knew a wonderful mechanic, Jim Barrows, who did interiors. In his spare time, he reupholstered the seats and replaced the carpets and headliner.

As 1990 drew to a close and during a lull in my many battles at Eastern, I, along with another friend, went to the airport and repainted the aircraft. Well, we didn't repaint the whole airplane; we washed it and redid the stripes using masking tape and a paintbrush. I painted a big "GA" on the tail and we were in business.

N-200 UV was the queen of the fleet...and the only aircraft we had.

In late 1990, I had hired a young pilot and mostly forgot about the Gulfstream project as the Eastern situation was heating up.

I had applied to the Bahamian government, in the fall, for a permit to operate scheduled flights into three cities on Andros Island in the Bahamas.

I selected those destinations because there was no air service between Andros and Florida. Knowing that the Bahamian government was highly selective of airlines flying into their country, I surmised that my chances were better in Andros than anywhere else in the Bahamas. With the Eastern issues taking up most of my time, I paid almost no attention to that submission.

So, that's where I found myself on January 19, 1991. The inventory took little time.

I had no money… The Eastern retirement fund that I had paid into for twenty-nine years was mainly illiquid, and what little cash there was had been tied up in the courts with distribution issues. My only assets were a small, run-down airplane and a license to operate a scheduled airline. That was about it.

A few days went by. The charter business produced a little cash but hardly enough to keep the doors open. I became totally dependent on my old friend the American Express card as I began to put a plan in place for survival.

It was a few days after Eastern shut down that Don Davidson, the vice president of operations at Eastern, called me for a favor. It seemed that there was one last B-727 left in Ft. Lauderdale, and he needed it ferried down to Miami. I agreed and later that day, he sent a van to transport me, to pick it up.

It was a routine operation. The skeleton operations staff at Ft. Lauderdale had gathered all the paperwork for me, and I headed out to the aircraft to do a quick inspection. All looked okay and I took my seat and asked for the checklist to be read. We accomplished it and started the engines. The first officer asked Ft. Lauderdale tower for taxi clearance, and we were given instructions to proceed to runway 9 left.

I began my taxi away from the gate and noticed a Delta jet had just landed. As he rolled out and pulled off the runway just ahead of me, the ground controller instructed me, "Hold your position, Eastern, and let the Delta pass in front of you to his gate." It was the proper thing to do.

I began to slow to a stop when I heard the Delta captain interject, "No, we'll wait right here for Eastern to taxi out."

"Okay," the controller agreed. "Eastern, continue your taxi to runway 9 left."

I continued to taxi and picked up the mike. "Thanks, Captain," I said.

"Good luck, Captain," he replied. I thought I caught a note of sympathy in his voice.

We both knew. We both knew that his career would continue, but mine was over and he simply wanted to let me know that he understood. And cared.

Although for years, we, the pilots of Eastern and Delta, had been fierce competitors, we were still members of that great aviation fraternity. That unmistakable family of flyers that, although sometimes difficult to understand and explain, is real.

As I passed by the Delta Boeing 767 jet, I couldn't help but see, proudly inscribed on the nose, "THE SPIRIT OF DELTA." It was the very airplane that the Delta employees had contributed thirty million dollars for its purchase from Boeing to donate to the company!

What a fitting end to my career, I thought. I'm on my last flight for Eastern, a company shut down due to labor strife, and there is a Delta pilot who will enjoy a full career with a company whose labor relations are demonstrated by the gift of a Boeing 767 by its employees.

How ironic.

CHAPTER 67

Cap Haitien

First Route

TIME WAS NOT ON MY side. I needed to do something quick, but with almost no funds, I had to be very careful. I had learned in my previous airline ventures that one small step in the wrong direction could be disastrous.

I had watched a small company, Lynx Airline, operating out of Fort Lauderdale to Cap Haitien, Haiti, with interest. There was a large community of Haitians living in Miami, and I knew, from my Eastern experience, that there was a booming business between Miami and Port Au Prince, the capital city of Haiti. Since Pan Am and several other carriers were operating to Port Au Prince, it was obvious that I wouldn't stand a chance in that market, but---to Cap Haitien from Miami, with no other airline in that market, there just might be enough business for a small airline.

I called the only hotel in Cap Haitien and talked to the manager. He enthusiastically endorsed my plan and invited me down to look at the airport and his hotel.

The next day, January 25, I found myself in the Cessna on my way to Cap Haitien.

Cap Haitien was the second largest city in Haiti. It had a large population but a small airport—not large enough to accommodate large aircraft, but it was ideal for a small aircraft such as mine. It was six hundred miles southeast of Miami, about the limit of the flying range of my aircraft, but with careful load planning, it was possible.

The flight was uneventful and the hotel manager picked me up at the airport right on time. As we drove into town, he began to pepper me with questions. How long have you been in operation? How many aircraft do you have? How large are they? Where do you fly now?

My answers did not leave him with a great deal of confidence in my proposed operation, or me. I was truthful and used my past experiences as an airline operator and airline pilot to help bolster his support, and it worked.

He was on the team and all went well until, at dinner, he asked me what I was going to charge for a ticket to Miami.

I hadn't even thought about that. I asked him what the going rate was, and he shared with me the price that the Fort Lauderdale airline was charging: $150 dollars per round trip.

"That sounds fair to me. That's what we will charge," I said with confidence.

And then he asked me the strangest question. "Will you accept gourdes?"

"I don't know," I answered. "I'm not sure about that." I had visions of Haitians lined up in front of my counter with baskets of gourdes, visions of large Haitian ladies with giant bundles of gourdes on their heads to trade for tickets on Gulfstream to Miami.

He saw my hesitancy. "Well, Pan Am takes them in Port Au Prince."

"Okay," I replied, "if Pan Am takes them, then I'll take them."

I went to sleep that night racking my brain as to how I was going to convert tons of gourdes into U.S. currency. I felt reasonably sure that the fuelers in Miami would *NOT* take them.

It was only the next day, when I was checking out of the hotel, that I discovered what a gourde was when the desk clerk asked me, "Are you paying with dollars or gourdes?" She explained that "gourdes" was the name of the currency in Haiti.

I flew home relieved of a problem I never had and with the firm conviction that there was a good passenger market to be had in Cap Haitien.

Back in Miami, I went to work. I confidently set up a flight schedule to begin in little over two weeks, February 15th, with three flights weekly: Monday, Wednesday, and Saturday.

I called the local Haitian radio station and began some advertising. The next thing I knew Arnold, a relative of the radio station manager, who presented himself as a marketing expert, visited me.

Not having any funds for employees, I agreed to give him a commission on each ticket he sold. I now had a marketing department and I was off and running. All I needed was a counter at Miami International Airport.

That should be easy.

Wrong!

The landside manager, the ogre who rented counter space at Miami International Airport, wasn't the least bit interested in renting counter space to a one-horse airline flying eight-passenger airplanes three times a week to Haiti. He allowed that he would put me in line for a spot when one might come available.

I reminded him that Eastern had just gone out of business, and there *might* be something down there. He reminded me of where the door to his office was and ushered me out.

"I'll call *you*," he said.

Hmm, I thought. *This could be a problem.*

Arnold was selling tickets and the first flights were filling up. I went back to the airport to try to convince the ogre to provide space for me.

He wouldn't even see me. "Mr. Cooper," his secretary explained, "the manager is busy and cannot see you. Please try again next week."

Disheartened, I walked through the terminal and while strolling thru the terminal I had a most unusual idea. I discovered that a lot of the South American airlines that flew into Miami International Airport did not operate daily. There might be an airline that flew on Mondays, Wednesdays, and Saturdays, and another that flew on Sundays, Tuesdays, and Fridays, and so on.

Since security was almost nil in 1991, the solution to my problem was simple. I would "borrow" a counter of an airline that wasn't flying on a day that I was scheduled to fly. When selling the ticket, Arnold would advise the customer as to which counter to visit.

I equipped Arnold with a portable counter sign, and he would show up at a counter not being used that day. He would arrive about one hour before flight time and, acting as counter agent, check in the seven or eight passengers. He would give them boarding passes, send them to the airline gate, then rush ahead of them, help the pilot load the bags, and act as the gate agent for the boarding. Once the baggage doors were closed and the passengers were onboard, he would dash around to the front of the aircraft, give the okay to start engines to the captain, and salute the airplane off to Haiti. Of course, he was dressed in proper airline counter personnel attire with shirt and tie along with a prominently displayed homemade Gulfstream ID badge, and he looked *very* official.

This turned out to work unbelievably well.

I was looking forward to February 15th. Eastern would have been shut down for less than a month and I would be running a real airline.

The only downside was, there just wasn't enough money to support a one-destination airline. I needed additional destinations.

And then the first of many miracles happened.

On January 29th, I received a letter from the Bahamian government approving my application into Andros Island. The three small cities that I could serve were Nicholl's Town, on the north end of the island, Fresh Creek, near the middle, and Congo Town, on the southeast side.

Great news. All I needed now were two additional aircraft and operating capital.

I remembered that I had received a call from an aircraft leasing company back in November. They had seen, in a government publication, that Gulfstream International Airlines had been awarded a certificate to operate scheduled airline service, and they assumed, wrongly, that I would need additional Cessna aircraft. With the Eastern situation heating up, nothing could be further from the truth. I took down the number and said that I would call if the need for additional aircraft ever arose.

That time was now, so I called the number and got a partner of MCC Leasing Company, Mr. Bill Buckland, on the phone.

I asked about the two Cessna aircraft he had advertised in November, and he said they were still available. He had taken them in on trade, they were surplus to his needs, and he appeared to be anxious to lease them.

His salesman was scheduled to show up in three days, February 4th.

I had no money and no ideas.

And then a second miracle happened.

CHAPTER 68

Resurrecting Aerial Transit Airline

My EAL buddies to the rescue

AERIAL TRANSIT AIRLINE, A LOCAL cargo company, was shut down by the FAA for maintenance irregularities. The partner of that airline happened to be an old friend of mine. Charles Lawson. He lived in Miami Springs, and we played tennis from time to time. We had bonded as he watched Eastern collapse through my eyes, and as I began to build Gulfstream, we would cry on each other's shoulders as we each met the difficulties of the day-to-day operation of our airlines.

Aerial Transit Airline was an all-cargo airline, utilizing four DC-6s, large four-engine piston airplanes converted for cargo. His partner handled the maintenance, and Charlie handled the operations and sales side of the business. His partner had become ill months earlier, and consequently, the maintenance records began to suffer. It was at a surprise inspection by the FAA that the deficiencies became evident, and Charlie's license was suspended until the problems could be fixed.

His partner had been admitted to the hospital for a heart bypass and Charlie was at his wits' end as to how to get his airline back in the air. A merger with Gulfstream made no sense at all, and I couldn't abandon my operation and expect it to run by itself.

We continued to explore possibilities. I needed money, he needed expertise.

Charlie came up with an ingenious plan to solve both problems.

The Man in The Arena...

He offered me free office space in his building on the airport, free aircraft parking spots, a maintenance office, and a loan of ten thousand dollars if I would move in, take over the task of resurrecting his maintenance department, and help him recover his operating authority from the FAA.

We shook hands and on February 1st Gulfstream International Airlines moved into the Aerial Transit Airline facilities at Miami International Airport.

The Gulfstream offices were upstairs, overlooking the airport, and they were extremely small. There were three offices, each twelve by twelve feet and a closet that measured eight by twelve. The rooms had been used for storage, but with a little cleaning and paint, they did just fine. I took the office overlooking the airport, assigned the outer office for reception, and the third was vacant, to be used later for a part-time bookkeeper. The fourth room remained a broom closet, to be used for storage.

To recertify Aerial Transit Airlines, I called in some old friends from my Eastern days: Steve Joffrion, Keri Johnson, and Irwin Korczynski. Steve and Keri were assigned to redo the operations and maintenance manuals, and Irwin took on the task of cleaning up the facility. I would oversee the physical refurbishing of the four aircraft.

We collectively set up a work schedule of twelve hours a day; 7 a.m. until 7 p.m.

I had borrowed Charlie's partner's office for the scheduled meeting with the MCC Leasing Company sales agent. I placed a nice temporary sign on the door that read "T. L. Cooper, President."

I had learned a lot from Bob Jones back at Great Circle Aviation.

The salesman from MCC Leasing showed up on Monday, February 4th, and Charlie's secretary walked him into my borrowed office overlooking the runways at Miami International Airport.

Impressive!

We struck a deal.

He would deliver the first aircraft immediately and the second in a month. There would be no payments due until the aircraft were certified by the FAA and approved for use, and the lease payments would be applied, 100 percent, toward the purchase price if I ever decided to purchase them.

I had my hands full. The Aerial Transit project was enough for ten men, and I still had to watch and build Gulfstream International Airlines. In preparation for the Andros route, I brought in several Eastern pilots for the new runs. They were first officers I had flown with during the Eastern days, and I knew them to be highly skilled, motivated, and eager to work.

Jim Taylor, Richard Falcon, and Mark Reichard would be—then and for a number of years—the backbone of my pilot staff. Jim would act as chief pilot, Richard would become our director of training, and Mark, with a mechanic's license in addition to his pilot's license, would rotate between the maintenance and the operations department, as needed.

I had started the Cap Haitien route on February 15th and by the end of February, it was working out pretty well. The passenger loads were building, but I was having trouble converting the gourdes that we collected in Cap Haitien into U.S. dollars.

Arnold came up with a great solution. He would take brown paper bags full of gourdes to the Miami airport, go to the Pan Am counter, and stand in line as if he were a customer; there, he would offer a liberal exchange rate of gourdes for dollars to passengers going to Port Au Prince. I, of course, gave him a commission on each transaction. He was pretty aggressive and a huge help during this period.

The first MCC Leasing aircraft arrived on February 18th and we immediately put it into service on the Cap Haitien route as it was newer, its range was better, and it could carry more weight.

I was putting the finishing touches on the Andros schedule for March 15th when an old friend from the Eastern crew scheduling department, Bill Funderburk, stopped by to say hello. He had heard I could use some help and thought he might be of some service.

"That's nice, Bill," I said, "but my budget just won't let me hire anyone else at this time."

"Oh," he said with his slow southern drawl, "I'm not doing anything anyhow, so why don't I just come in and see if there's anything I can do. I don't want any pay. I'll be in tomorrow morning."

He showed up and I put him on the payroll at five dollars an hour. He became one of my most trusted and valuable employees and remained so until he retired.

"What can I do to help?" he asked as he sat down across from me.

"Well," I answered, "other than lack of money, I'm having trouble leasing counter space at the airport. The landside manager won't give me the time of day."

"Hmm." He thought for a minute. "I know one of the managers over there. Give me a copy of your flight schedules and I'll see what I can do."

He departed, but I had little hope.

I was so busy that I didn't give it much thought. Irwin was in the middle of cleaning up the hangar and warehouse. He had trucked two dumpsters of junk out and was cleaning the floor in preparation for paint. Keri and Steve were rewriting the manuals, and I was on top of the maintenance crews, pushing for completion of the first Aerial Transit aircraft that we were readying for inspection by the FAA. We were shooting for March 18th and time was running out.

All the while I was watching the Haitian operation with one eye and the bank account with the other. The Haitian operation was going okay; the bank account wasn't.

Funderburk came back after lunch and with a broad smile announced, "Well, that's settled."

"What's settled?" I asked. I had forgotten where he went.

"The counter issue," he said. "You've got a great counter plus a small office in the rear, overlooking the ramp, and it's between USAir and Bahamasair. Let's go look."

We drove to the terminal and Bill proudly showed me his acquisition. "One of the managers around here owed me a favor," he said, "and this is it."

It was perfect.

"Oh yes," he added, "if I were you, I'd steer clear of the landside manager for a while. They were on to your scheme but just let you go for a while 'cause they figured you'd go broke soon." He laughed. "It was a source of harmless amusement for them."

Bill was willing to do anything, so I put him to work as "Vice President, Systems Station Manager" with headquarters at the Miami terminal in his new office. He hopped down to Cap Haitien to inspect that station, made some refinements, set up strict reporting, and on the way back, he stopped at the three cities in Andros and listed what we needed to commence operations there.

My policy was, never, ever buy a new piece of furniture, and Bill bought into that. We located several used office furniture shops and outfitted all of our stations at a fraction of the cost of new furniture. He delivered all the paraphernalia to the Andros stations, connected the phone systems, and we were ready to commence service on March 15th.

I was juggling Aerial Transit and Gulfstream. With the help of my Eastern friends, I was making good progress. We were scheduled with the FAA for a "show and tell" for the recertification of Aerial Transit on March 18th, and we were looking good for that date. The second aircraft from MCC Leasing arrived on the 12th, and on March 15th, right on schedule, we opened the three stations on Andros Island.

The day for the recertification of Aerial Transit, March 18th, came, and the representatives from the FAA showed up as scheduled.

It was quite a show.

I had refurbished an old unused room in Aerial Transit. I painted the walls, put in carpet, and outfitted it with six long desks, each seating three persons. We decorated the walls with Pan Am posters, installed a whiteboard on the front wall, and built a podium. In the front of the podium was the logo of Aerial Transit.

The hangar was totally renovated with broken windows replaced, walls painted, and the floor painted gray with yellow stripes outlining where various pieces of equipment were placed. Out on the ramp was the one airplane we had concentrated on. It stood proudly, glistening in the sun, with its new paint job and AERIAL TRANSIT lettered along its fuselage.

Jokingly, the FAA representatives allowed they had come to the wrong facility.

Charlie Lawson made a speech and turned the floor over to me. I introduced the ex-Eastern men who had done the cleanup and rewritten the maintenance manuals and operational procedures. I reviewed their credentials, their background and areas of responsibility at Eastern, and then each one took to the pedestal and explained what they did for the upgrade.

The FAA representatives were visibly impressed. They took copies of the manuals, and in three days we received the good news that Aerial Transit was back in the air.

In two days, the first flight of the new Aerial Transit took off for Cancun, Mexico, filled with cargo. The whole company turned out to the car parking lot, next to the runway, to watch the scene. We watched with anxious anticipation as the giant four-engine airplane, filled with cargo, taxied out to the end of the runway in preparation for takeoff.

We could tell that the captain was checking all the engines as we could hear them rev up, each individually, and soon he taxied into position on runway 9 left for takeoff.

There is something magic about the old "round" engines when the throttles are pushed up to takeoff power. The slow acceleration of power as the props bite into the air, the noise of the engines as the orchestration of a thousand parts crescendo into the music of a thundering mechanical orchestra sends a thrill up your spine.

So it was that day.

We saw the props begin to increase in RPMs before we heard the engines begin their roar. And then it came, the low rumble of the engines as the captain eased the throttles toward takeoff power. The old DC-6 began to roll as the engine noise reached its peak. The DC-6 was picking up speed as it passed the parking lot where we all stood in anticipation. The engines were howling, the aircraft was gaining speed, we were holding our breath, and, as the aircraft lifted off the runway at the far end of the airport, with clenched fists thrust skyward, we all gave out a collective yell. "Hooray!"

We watched as she climbed slowly eastward and then began a slow turn southwest toward Cancun. The plane disappeared in the haze over the horizon and we all returned to work. There were three more DC-6s to repair, cargo to sort out, and marketing to arrange for the new Aerial Transit.

Charlie had his "new" airline and I had a small, three-airplane commuter airline to run.

Within the week, Charlie proposed a deal that I should buy his partner's half of the company. I reminded him of my dire financial situation but he was insistent and began to work on a financial arrangement between him, his partner, and me.

I wasn't completely sold on the idea, as I would have to close Gulfstream. Aside from the fact that I had no money to operate with, Gulfstream was doing pretty well. We were beginning to look like a real airline.

We had free rent, three airplanes, six pilots, all highly experienced from Eastern, two mechanics, and two office personnel. We were employing six Bahamians and two Haitians.

I had purchased access in an airline reservations computer system, and our flights were now available to travel agents worldwide for ticketing. I had signed contracts with most major airlines for ticket and baggage agreements which allowed our tickets to be sold by other airlines. That agreement allowed a major airline, for example, United, to sell a ticket in Chicago all the way to Cap Haitien, collect the fare, and write the ticket on their ticket stock. The customer would arrive into Miami, come to our gate, present the Miami-Cap Haitian portion of his United ticket, and fly on Gulfstream to Haiti. I would receive my portion of the fare on the tenth of the next month from the Airlines Clearing House. This was a good deal but a double-edged sword as I was to learn soon.

I continued to scrape for working capital. We watched every cent and Arnold spent a lot of time at the Pan Am ticket counter trading gourdes for dollars.

As we began to fly into the Bahamas, I envisioned an expansion into some of the more densely populated islands. I had discussed with my wife, Jerrie, the possibility of refinancing our home for the necessary funds. The equity that we had built up, about fifty thousand dollars, was our only asset, and it would be quite a leap of faith to squander that by investing in a one-horse commuter airline, especially one run by an ex-airline pilot. Ex-airline pilots were notorious for getting involved in airplane ventures and failing. And so far, Gulfstream had shown no assurances of offering a different outcome.

I had visited several local banks, but I received no encouragement. I continued to scrape by with cash ticket sales and gourdes, but I was literally on a day-to-day existence.

With the vision of the beautiful DC-6 climbing majestically toward Cancun, filled with valuable cargo, and clouded by the reality of my eight-passenger Cessna headed toward Cap Haitien with four or five passengers, I was inclined to accept Charlie's proposal.

We agreed in principle, and the agreement had gone to the lawyers for final contract when, on May 1st, I was called into Charlie's office for a meeting.

His partner was there and he looked serious. "Cooper," he said, "you've done a great job getting this airline recertified, but something has come up. We have a cash offer for the whole airline. I'm recovering from open-heart surgery, and Charles is ready to retire. We want to sell the whole thing, but we want you to approve the deal. Your piece of the contract is that you'll receive free rent for two years in your same space."

I felt relieved. I couldn't agree soon enough. Instantly, a mental load was lifted and now I could concentrate on Gulfstream. With the free rent for two years, and if I could secure a loan against my house, I might just make it.

It was not to be.

CHAPTER 69

Sabotage!

THE PHONE RANG AT MY home. It was three o'clock in the morning, and Charlie was on the other end. "Cooper, we better get out to the airport," he exclaimed. "There's been some kind of an accident, and it's with your Cessnas."

We met at the airport in ten minutes.

There were police cars everywhere on the ramp. Lights were flashing and fire trucks were circling. In the confusion, we found the officer in charge and introduced ourselves as the owners. He led us out to an area on the west side of the ramp where all the activity was, and there I saw the mess.

In the glow of the spotlights, two of my Cessnas lay in a crumpled heap. I couldn't believe it. I stared in shock.

The officer in-charge took me aside and explained. "Someone entered the cockpit of one of the small airplanes, started it up, and jumped out, sending the airplane caroming across the ramp, striking other aircraft."

In the dim light, we traced the path of the aircraft. It had bounced off another Cessna, destroying one wing of the parked plane. It then proceeded across the ramp, where it struck a grounded DC-6, knocking the tail off the runaway Cessna. It then proceeded, tailless, toward the runway. As it jumped a ditch, one wheel became stuck, and the airplane proceeded to spin around until someone from the fire department managed to bravely catch the wing, swing up, and reach inside the cockpit to retard the throttles.

We walked inside the office building to Charlie's office. The officer filled out the necessary forms and said that someone would be by the next day to conduct an investigation.

It was approaching five o'clock in the morning. Charlie left for his house, and I remained in my office, to decide what to do. With almost no money, my options were few. My brain was spinning. My head was telling me to shut down the operation and prepare to head to the Orient, where most of my strike-breaking friends had found work flying for non-union airlines in Asia.

My heart kept telling me to stay, take stock of what was left, and keep going. And my body was just telling me that I was tired.

One more day. I decided to stay at least one more day. It was an important decision, and I would revert to that philosophy a number of times in the next fifteen years.

I washed my face, went up the stairs to my office, once again reviewed what I had to work with, and set up plan B.

I had no time to dwell on who did this deplorable thing. That would come later. I had to use every available minute to establish continuity in my company, maintain a somewhat similar schedule, and above all, as in poker when dealt a bad hand, never let 'em see you sweat.

I looked at the current flight schedule. I had been operating a two-airplane schedule with three airplanes. I now had only one airplane.

I called Jim Taylor, the young Eastern pilot whom I had named as chief pilot. "Jim," I tried to sound casual, "we've had a little bit of sabotage out here on the ramp. Two of our aircraft have been damaged. Can you call the other pilots to come out at around nine o'clock for a meeting to discuss a makeshift schedule until we can have them repaired?"

I answered some quick questions and hung up. I returned to the problem at hand, and with yellow pad in hand I studied the flight schedule.

Okay, I thought, *this can be done. We're doing three flights a week to Cap Haitien. I'll cut that back to two. That frees up some flying into the three cities in Andros.*

By combining some cities in Andros, I decided, I could still serve all three with the existing schedule but with one-stop service; however, that left me with no spare aircraft. My brain was kicking in. I'd set up a night shift for maintenance until the two damaged aircraft were repaired.

I was on my third cup of coffee when my office door swung open and in came the owner of the airline that was my chief competitor to the Bahamas, Airways International. His name was Izad Djahanshahi, but everyone called him Johan.

He was a handsome Iranian who had worked for me as a mechanic ten years earlier in one of my previous charter companies. After that he had worked around the airport at various jobs until he managed to scrape together enough money to rent a small charter aircraft. He was extremely industrious and, against all odds, he grew his company into a sizable commuter airline into the Bahamas.

He was a jovial character with the good looks of a young Omar Sharif.

He came in laughing. "Cooper, I finally put you out of business."

"I suspected that it was you," I joked. "The police are down at your hangar now."

Only good friends could joke in this situation. We laughed and had a cup of coffee, and he reminded me of a time when, working with me, one of our aircraft had a mechanical problem and the pilot landed at an old abandoned airport in the Everglades swamps. While driving out to fix the airplane, the car radio happened to play an old song by Jerry Lee Lewis, "Let's Put It Back Together Again."

We laughed and tried our best to remember the words, but at six o'clock in the morning, they just didn't seem to come out right.

"Okay, Cooper," he began, "I just looked at the mess you've got down there on the ramp, and I can straighten it out for you. I can take the tail off the aircraft with the damaged wing, install it on the aircraft that was in the ditch, and get that airplane back in the air in about ten days. The other one," he went on, "will need a new wing and tail, and I think that I can find those parts and have that aircraft in the air in about a month. I've got a full maintenance staff, and we can use the spare work.

"You're short one airplane," he continued, "and I have a spare aircraft. You can just pay me when you fly it. It can be your spare."

"That's great, Johan, but I honestly have to tell you that I've applied to the Bahamian government for four more destinations in the islands that you serve," I confessed.

"I already knew that, Cooper," he said. "I'd rather have you as my competition out there than someone I don't know. Between the two of us, we can keep the others out."

We shook hands and later that week, after approval by the insurance company, he towed the two aircraft over to his maintenance facility, and his mechanics began work on them.

Later that day, the detective stopped by to talk about the accident. I explained to him that the maintenance company next door had hired some Eastern mechanics that had been harassing my pilots through the fence that separated our two companies. I didn't come out and directly accuse them, but my guess, and his, was that this had to do with my past union activities.

When he learned that we were an international airline, he breathed a sigh of relief. "This is a case for the FBI," he exclaimed. "I'll have one of the Feds call you later today from the local office."

The next day, two agents from the FBI showed up and interviewed me. I told them the same story, about the union, and the rowdies next door.

They went next door and interviewed the mechanics. They never solved the case, but we never were harassed by the next-door rabble-rousers again.

My guess is that they got the message.

Charlie sold Aerial Transit on May 17th to Dan Worth, who had two partners: Lonnie Hawkins and Mark Ottosen.

Dan was an absentee owner with residence in California, so Lonnie Hawkins and Mark Ottosen were the on-site managers.

Mark was a young man, very sharp, but Lonnie Hawkins seemed strange. I couldn't put my finger on it, but he seemed a bit phony. Although he claimed to be an ex-POW from Vietnam, and he had pictures dressed in Air Force blues hung on his office wall, he just didn't seem real.

Once, at dinner at our house, Jerrie placed a large plate of rice on the table. Lonnie jumped up, covered his eyes, and insisted that she remove it instantly, as that was all he had eaten for three years in prison in Vietnam.

Jerrie was in tears.

After several similar instances, Dan and Mark decided to do some research and discovered that Lonnie was a fake. He'd never been in the service, and his Air Force pictures were doctored Civil Air Patrol photos taken in California.

Lonnie departed Miami the next day.

CHAPTER 70

Expansion

Routes awarded into the Bahamas, but no aircraft

ON JUNE 2ND, I RECEIVED word that we had been issued licenses to fly into North Eleuthera, Treasure Cay, Marsh Harbour, and Governor's Harbour in the Bahamas.

That was good news and bad news.

The routes to these four locations were coveted, but with no money and only one airplane flying, it would be a stretch to commence service in the summer when the passenger loads were high. I needed those extra routes to survive. I *had* to operate them, but fast.

I visited all the banks again, gave them my projections, and waited for a positive answer.

To further compound my situation, if I were to begin in mid-July, I needed to advertise my trips in the Official Airline Guide. The OAG is the publication that places your flight schedule before every travel agent in the world. I had to file my schedules in order to begin to book passengers.

Did I dare gamble that the repairs on the two damaged aircraft would be completed in a timely manner? Could I acquire two additional aircraft prior to July 15th? I remembered the plaque on the chief pilot's wall at Eastern: "Not only do I believe in miracles, I rely on them."

I placed the schedules in the Official Airline Guide and went to work.

MCC Leasing had offered two Piper Chieftains to me for lease, but being a different make and model, they would not work. I had heard of two Cessna 402 Cs in Nevada and had previously tried to lease them but my financial situation prevented the deal from closing.

In a conversation with MCC Leasing, I discovered that they were in the process of leasing a larger aircraft to that same airline in Las Vegas. I began to think this out. MCC was stuck with two aircraft in Texas, and the Las Vegas airline was stuck with two Cessnas.

I called Bill Buckland. "Bill," I explained, "why don't you swap your two Pipers in Texas for the two Cessnas in Las Vegas? You're in the middle of a deal with the Las Vegas outfit; you can make that part of this deal, and I'll take the two Cessnas."

"It looks doable," he said, "but you'll have to pay the first month's rental up front."

"I'm okay with that," I answered confidently.

"I'll let you know in a couple of days," he said.

"One more thing, Bill, I've got them scheduled on July fifteenth."

I heard him mumble, "Christ," as he hung up.

I began to work on the necessary funds for the two aircraft. I needed seven thousand dollars for lease payments and another two or three thousand for initial station expenses.

The days turned into weeks. I revisited all the banks, but to no avail. There was just no money available when you mentioned that you were a small airline.

I wasn't about to give up, but July was coming fast. MCC Leasing worked out their part of the deal and sent me lease agreements for the two aircraft. I stared at them on my desk. If I signed, I would have to come up with seven thousand dollars. I had been trying to conserve as much as possible, but I had accumulated very little. There was always something in this business to soak up any surplus dough; a radio would fail, a part was needed, etc.

I was pushing the time limit to receive the aircraft and have them approved by the FAA for commuter service.

And then my expected miracle happened.

It was Thursday, June 6th, when I received a call from Vic Johnson.

"Hi, Cooper," he said cheerily. "I'm sending you three copilots for your Monday class."

I didn't remember anyone by the name of Vic Johnson, and I informed him that we didn't hire copilots. "Hell," I exclaimed, "we don't even have money to pay our captains."

And then he reminded me that I had talked earlier that month over lunch with him and an old friend from Daytona Beach. It seemed that Vic and his partner, Bill Veiga, ran a flight school and in the course of the meal, they complained that at their flight school, when the students finished the commercial course, that was the end of their training. They laughed and said they awarded the students their pilot certificates and sent them packing down the road and were sure they could sell more courses to them if they had something to sell.

I laughed and volunteered. "Why don't you send them down here? I have a vacant copilot seat. With nine passenger seats or less, we don't need a copilot. We can dress them up as a copilot, put them in the right seat, and charge them by the hour and they can log the flight time," I said jokingly and promptly forgot the conversation.

"They'll be at your facility Monday morning at eight o'clock, ready for ground school," he proclaimed.

"I don't know, Vic, I'm not sure that we can accommodate them that quickly."

"They'll each have a check for four thousand dollars for you, representing prepaid two hundred hours of copilot time in your Cessnas."

"*We'll be ready,*" I quickly told him and hung up.

I waited for Jim Taylor, our chief pilot, to finish his day's flight sequence and asked the mechanic to send him up to see me.

"Jim," I said, trying to appear serious, "I have a little project for you."

He started laughing. He knew that when I asked him to do a little project, it was going to be more than little, and most times impossible.

I explained the deal and finished with, "Plus, Jim, it will be a great marketing tool as we'll be the only small airline with copilots, not to mention the safety aspect; another set of eyes in the cockpit and another body to help the captains load the aircraft."

"When is this project supposed to begin?" he asked.

"Monday."

"Christ," he said, shaking his head.

"Let's get Funderburk over here and decide how to set up the classroom," I said. "You get in touch with Richard Falcon and set him up as the instructor, and see if you can see our FAA Principle Operations Inspector and advise him as to what we are doing. You'll have to set up a meeting to have our first officer training curriculum approved by him."

"But we don't have a first officer training curriculum," he explained.

"I know," I replied, "that's the rest of the little project. And, oh yes," I added, "I forgot to tell you, we're going to start the Abacos and Eleuthera, four new stations, on July fifteenth. Bring in three of your flying buddies from

Eastern for the pilot class; we'll need a few captains for the new runs. Have them show up on Tuesday at 8:00 a.m."

Funderburk showed up wearing a smile. He'd already been briefed by Taylor. "Okay, let's get going, what do you need?"

"I need to convert the broom closet into a classroom to accommodate six students for a Monday class," I said.

"Let's go look," he said.

We looked. It was a dismal little eight-by-twelve room. The only saving grace was that it had a large window overlooking the airport.

Bill went straight to work. He got the mechanics to help clean the closet. He found three fold-up tables with six chairs at one of our favorite used office supply stores, and we borrowed the pedestal, whiteboard, and Pan Am posters from Aerial Transit.

That's really all that I expected, but when I came out on Sunday to review for the class on Monday, I was pleasantly surprised to see the room sparkling. Bill had painted the room, installed some surplus carpet, and framed the Pan Am posters with wooden trim. It looked very professional.

Jim visited with the FAA and got their okay for the project and made an appointment for Tuesday to submit his curriculum for the first officer class.

The three much-anticipated students showed up right on time Monday morning. There were two young men and one woman. They were in their early twenties, and they were dressed horribly.

Richard Falcon, who was never seen without starched shirt and pressed uniform, rolled his eyes as he introduced me to the class. He knew that I was a stickler when it came to dress code. I had watched some of the pilots at Eastern attend classroom periods dressed like they were going to the beach. Some would even show up in cut-offs and flip-flops. If the instructor would take exception and question them about their attire, the answer always was "See my union boss." I just wasn't going to have that here. Pilots would be in uniform when in ground school and in the public eye, and ground personnel, even me and any future office staff would be dressed in shirt and tie.

"Ladies and gentlemen, this is Captain Cooper; he's the president and owner of Gulfstream International Airlines, and he would like to say a few words to you."

I welcomed them and explained that they were joining an elite family, most of whom were former Eastern employees. I explained that they represented all of us when they were in the public's eye. I further explained my uniform policy: black shoes, black pants, black tie, and white short-sleeve shirt with epaulets, two gold bars for students, three for first officers, and four for captains plus an airline cap. They would be expected to be in uniform tomorrow for ground school and for any other official gathering where they represented this company in front of the public.

"Captain Falcon," I instructed, "please take these students to the Field Shop, our uniform supplier, for outfitting. And take the men by the barbershop for haircuts."

"Yes, sir." He smiled as he led them down the steps.

I half expected the students to ask for their money back after *that* speech, but I had already sent the checks to the bank with Funderburk. Just in case.

Tuesday morning went better. It went excellent! The ex-Eastern pilots showed up in uniform—Jim had warned them in advance—and the students came in full dress. Captain Falcon issued the gold bars for the epaulets, and class began.

Jim met with the FAA on Tuesday and the curriculum was approved.

We were beginning to look like an airline, more and more.

I busied myself with the preparation for the opening of four stations. It was quite a challenge, but with Funderburks help, we progressed along pretty well. I signed the contract for the two new aircraft, and Jim Taylor arranged to have our pilots pick them up. Johan produced one of the damaged aircraft on schedule, and suddenly our fleet numbered five aircraft, counting the damaged one.

On July 15th we opened all four new stations, and business was brisk from the start.

In looking from the outside, we were progressing along fantastically well. The Cap Haitien routes were producing about 150 passengers per month, and the Andros stations added another 200. With the Eleuthera and Abaco destinations kicking in, we suddenly jumped from 325 passengers in May to 753 in July. We were serving nine stations with five aircraft, all painted in our livery. They looked impressive at the gate at the airport, especially with smartly dressed pilots doing their preflight inspections in full view of the passengers.

But I knew, based on previous experience, the successes that we were experiencing in the summer would soon fade in the fall. The Bahamian business historically dropped by about 50 percent in September and October, and fall was just around the corner.

I needed a Florida destination to take up the anticipated slack. I had noted that in April, USAir Express had ceased operation between Orlando and Vero Beach. I contacted the airport manager at Vero Beach, and he shared their passenger load data with me. It looked pretty good for a small aircraft like ours. The gossip was that they didn't stop for economic reasons; the route was operated because one of their officials lived in Vero Beach and kept that route open for personal reasons. An engine failure on their lone turboprop aircraft assigned there finally caused the shutdown.

I traveled to Vero Beach, leased the only counter space at their small terminal, flew over to Orlando, and contracted with Comair, the Delta Commuter, to handle us there. In record time, we established a one-airplane route and opened operations between the two cities on August 12, 1991 with seven flights daily. We were the toast of the town, the saviors filling the spot that the previous commuter had vacated, and the passenger loads picked up rapidly. By the time the fall passenger drought hit the Bahamas, our total system loads had leveled out, and we survived our first seasonal crisis.

But the financial issue was real and lived with me like wearing a wet five-hundred-pound overcoat. Although our passenger loads were picking up nicely, we were up to over 1,400 passengers in November, our cash flow was dismal. I tried everything. If a long-distance phone call was necessary, I called the party during their lunch hour in hopes that they wouldn't be in and would have to return my call on their nickel.

We couldn't afford a copy machine, so every morning at the terminal, when Bill Funderburk prepared the customs forms for the U.S. and Bahamian authorities, he would visit, alternately, one of seven neighboring airlines with the same story in his slow southern drawl. "Hey, buddy, my copy machine is on the blink—can I run off a few copies on yours?" He was always welcome due to his charming personality, and he was always generous to the other airlines when they requested passes to our popular vacation spots.

It was mid-1992 before we could afford our own copy machine.

Our major problem now was the double-edged sword of the Interline Ticketing and Baggage agreements that we had signed with the major airlines. Although it generated fantastic numbers of passengers, and we couldn't live without those agreements, when those passengers showed up at our counter, we only collected a ticket stub that said that they had paid the originating airline company for passage on our airline.

We packaged these ticket stubs monthly, separated them by airline, and submitted them to the Airlines Clearing House for payment. If we flew a passenger who had purchased his ticket from United Airlines on the first day of the month, we would fly that customer and would not receive our remittance for that ticket until the middle of the next month, six weeks later.

I tried all the banks, but to no avail. The conversations went something like this.

"Look at this." I would show them my ledger sheets representing monies due me from the Airlines Clearing House. "See, United owes me twenty-eight thousand, Delta owes me twenty-one thousand, and American owes me eighteen. The clearing house will pay me in two weeks; can't you loan me at least half of that?"

The loan officers would frown, look knowingly at the ledger sheet, and ask the same question: "What if the airline goes broke?"

"I don't think that United, Delta, or American airlines will go broke."

Their answer was always the same. "That's what we thought about Eastern." And they would stand up, shake my hand, and nod to the door. The meeting was over.

It was near the end of November, and I was near wits' end. It was like watching a train wreck in slow motion. The passenger loads were setting records weekly, our operation was excellent, the Avtar folks, Vic and Bill, were sending three or four copilots a month, but the burden of waiting for the Airline Clearing House to remit cash was killing me. I was continually overdrawn at the bank, and my credit card was maxed out.

I couldn't give up now. We'd come too far. I decided to make one last attempt to refinance our home. Jerrie was on board, so I hit every bank and waited for an answer.

It came a week later from a most unlikely source—the small branch bank at the airport where we had an account for night deposits. They agreed to loan me sixty thousand dollars against my home value. I had a mortgage of ten thousand remaining that must be paid to allow the bank to secure a first mortgage. The closing was set for two weeks hence.

This was going to be close. Bills were piling up faster than I could scrape up money to pay them, and I had a payroll due in one week.

This was the same frustration that I had felt last year at about the same time. Eastern was recovering from the depths of the strike, the future looked good, but with the labor unrest still tainting her image, real or not, no one would lend her money to survive.

I was counting the days till the bank closing, sitting exasperated at my desk, when Funderburk walked in.

I had written the payroll checks and had asked a few trusted pilots to hold theirs for a few days. Having gone through the Eastern debacle only a year earlier, they understandably were concerned, and some went to Bill, the wise old man as he was beginning to be known, for advice.

"What's up, Tom?" He smiled. He knew damn well what was up.

With my best *never let 'em see you sweat* face I said, "Oh, we're just a little light in the pot this week. We'll get over this hump in a week when the clearing house check arrives. Plus, I've just signed for a loan on my house, and it'll come through in a couple of weeks and then we'll be awash in money."

He knew I was lying. I had a stack of payroll checks on my desk that I couldn't distribute, and if I held them back, well, it could be over, not to mention the fuel bill due in two days.

He was carrying a large brown paper sack when he came in. I assumed that it was his lunch. He put the bag on my desk and pushed it across to me.

How nice, I thought, *I'm financially doomed and Bill is sharing his lunch with me.*

"Empty it out." He laughed again.

I turned the bag upside down and suddenly my desk was covered with money. Tens, twenties, and hundreds.

"Don't bother to count it," he said. "There's twenty thousand there. It's a loan for as long as you need it."

"Bill, this is a lifesaver," I gushed. "Are you sure you can spare it, and don't we need to sign some papers to secure this loan?"

"Nope," he drawled, "your handshake is all I need," and he stood up to leave.

As we shook hands he turned. "Oh, by the way, one more thing."

This is it, I thought, *he'll want a piece of the company; here it comes.*

He continued, "Don't tell anyone where you got this money from or every one in the whole company will want a loan," and he disappeared out the door.

In October the largest commuter to the Bahamas, Aero Coach, succumbed to the dreaded fall malaise, ran out of money, and folded. That provided for a windfall of business and opened the door to two new stations. We commenced serving Rock Sound and Georgetown in December.

We finished the year by flying over two thousand passengers in December, up from 160 passengers the previous February, our first full month. We had a small Christmas party in our upstairs modest offices and gave thanks, not for being successful, but for surviving.

CHAPTER 71

Secretary vs. Receptionist?

An angel interviews

It had been a rough year. Beginning with the Eastern shutdown, the struggle for survival had been financially, physically, and emotionally exhaustive. The days were long, mostly twelve to fourteen hours, and there was no time off. An occasional Sunday morning game of tennis with Charlie was my recreational limit, and that happened infrequently.

We had no funds for staff, so almost all of the routine office jobs fell to me. There was the accounting with the complex task of handling the Airlines Clearing House on the income side and the delicate balancing of the payables on the expense side, a juggling act in itself. Jim Taylor's wife came in periodically to produce the payroll.

All the required reports to the various government agencies took time, and the filings with the FAA were demanding. Maintenance records were required as, on the Cessna, there were approximately forty separate parts that had to be tracked for "time limited" exchange. In the scheduled airline business, one cannot wait until a part fails. The FAA assigns each part a life expectancy based on either flying hours, calendar days, or number of landings. Once that limit is reached, the part, although working perfectly, must be removed for overhaul and replaced. Each part is given a card that must be updated after each day's flight. It's a demanding job and requires accurate recordkeeping. I did that in the evenings after each flight.

It was beginning to be more than I could handle. We had come a long way in eleven months from one flight to Cap Haitien three times a week to where we were at year's end; thirty-five flights daily to twelve destinations. I needed some help in the office.

I had learned that if you advertise for a receptionist rather than a secretary, you could expect to pay a lower hourly rate. So that's what I did. In the first week of January 1992, I placed an ad in the *Miami Herald* for a receptionist for the airline. "Call for an appointment and apply in person," it read.

December had been a great month. With the home loan coming through and the additional cash generated from the Aero Coach departure, we were doing pretty well cash wise. We weren't exactly swimming in money, but I could relax and think about the future. I realized that I had been so immersed in the physical work, I hadn't had a lot of time to just sit and think. Now I had to focus on this constant cash crisis, and I couldn't do that if I was preoccupied with all the clerical duties. And I had to solve the Airlines Clearing House cash flow problem.

I prepared for the upcoming interviews.

They called.

And they came.

None of the applicants could even answer the phone correctly, and none had any business experience, even as a receptionist.

There had been a vast array of interviewees through my office during the first week of interviews. They had worn miniskirts, way too short, jeans, way too tight, and hairdos that would scare the bravest. One young woman popped her gum throughout the interview, and one fearless young woman, who claimed to be a typist, burst into tears when I pushed my typewriter over in front of her.

It was Wednesday, the 15th of January, when a woman called for an interview. She had previously been with Pan Am and wished to see me about the job, if it was still available. I assumed that she was a temp and had worked with Pan Am for a few weeks during their recent shutdown. I prejudged her and mentally classed her with the other pathetic applicants.

Aerial Transit's secretary gave her directions to my office. "You go out the back door, over there, turn left, walk through the warehouse, and you'll find some steps. Mr. Cooper's office is at the top of the steps. I'll tell him to look for you."

The secretary called me. "Tom, a nice lady is coming up to interview. I like her. Hire her." We'd had a few laughs at the expense of some of the previous applicants that she had sent up. I thought she might be being facetious.

I turned around as the woman entered my office door. "Hello," she said cheerily. "No one was outside, so I just came on in. I'm Betty Lerner."

She was perfect! She was older than the average women who had interviewed, but appeared to be a bit younger than I was. She was immaculately dressed, with hair coifed perfectly. She was elegant without being snobbish. I felt somewhat intimidated by her as I nodded toward a chair.

"Yes," I said awkwardly, trying to make a small joke. "That's why I'm hiring."

She smiled, made herself comfortable across from my desk, and waited for the interview to begin.

"Well," I fumbled, "you said that you were with Pan Am. I'm sorry to see that it folded. I had the same experience with Eastern last year. How many years did you work there?"

'Twenty-four," she calmly replied.

Christ, I thought, she just spent twenty-four years with Pan Am and she's up here in this crappy little office interviewing for a job with an airline that flies eight-passenger aircraft. This'll be a short interview. She's probably already looking for a way to exit without embarrassing me or her.

I made more small talk about the airline industry in general and I became more comfortable. She asked a few questions about the company—how it started, where we flew, and what type of aircraft we operated.

And then I realized that she was interviewing me! How could I possibly hire someone smarter than I was?

She politely asked more questions. "Just what position, other than receptionist, do you think that I can help your company with? What would be my job scope?"

That put me on the spot. I hadn't thought much about *job scope*. That was a big airline term.

"Well, er, let's see, there's typing, a whole lot of typing. Can you type?"

"Yes, I'm an expert typist," she answered confidently.

I wasn't about to push the typewriter across the desk for *her*.

"And I talk fast; can you write fast if I dictate?"

"I take shorthand."

I felt that I was failing my end of the interview. I was completely outclassed.

I truly liked her at the onset, but I just couldn't see her climbing those steps, in the warehouse, daily. She was too classy, and even if I did offer her the job and she accepted, she probably wouldn't stay with us for long. And she was overqualified for what I was prepared to pay anyway, so that settled that.

"There's a lot more stuff to do around here." I recovered a bit. "There's accounting, government reports, maintenance records, and millions of other things." I was bubbling over with information now and caught myself hoping that she would take the job. I wanted to break the bad news about the proposed salary, but I just couldn't bring myself to do it. I think it was a fear of rejection. I really wanted this woman to join the company and I knew that she would reject me politely and leave when she heard the salary.

She broke the awkward silence. "I like your company and I'm prepared to begin work tomorrow morning at 8:30 if you offer me the job."

"Wow!" I exclaimed. "I mean, we haven't talked about salary yet. I can only offer you eight fifty an hour." I was geared up for the rejection speech or at least the, *I can't live on that salary* speech.

"That's fine." She stood up and moved over to shake my hand. "We have a deal. I'll see you tomorrow morning."

Hallelujah! My heart yelled. I'd just passed the interview.

As we walked the short few steps to my door, I couldn't help but ask, "Mrs. Lerner, you can make more money by staying home and collecting unemployment than working for me; why would you do this?"

"I have to work," she said, with quiet reserve. "I have to work."

As she disappeared down the stairs, her last comment rang clear in my head, and it still does today.

"I have to work."

She didn't say "I have to work because I need the money" and she didn't say "I have to work because my husband wants me out of the house."

No!

She said, "I have to work," because it was part of her DNA. It was her character; her disposition. She possessed an inner strength so sadly lacking now by many in our society today: the need to be productive and contribute.

To give instead of just "take."

I was in the office the next morning, and Betty showed up at exactly 8:30 for work—just like she would do for the next twenty-three years—as my right hand.

And my left hand, also.

CHAPTER 72

Undercapitalized & Understaffed

Full speed ahead

IT HAD BEEN ALMOST A year to the day since Eastern had shut down. With a few dollars in the bank, Betty handling the calls and taking on more and more of the day-to-day clerical responsibilities, I had time to reflect on the past year and do some planning for 1992.

The three Eastern pilots, working nobly for five dollars an hour, who had helped resurrect Aerial Transit for Charlie had moved on when he sold. Keri Johnson joined Captain Don Davidson in Washington as they certified a new airline to connect Washington with Johannesburg, South Africa. Irwin Korczynski got a job as captain in Asia, and Steve Joffrion went to work for another Eastern pilot startup, Ross Fischer's new charter airline, Miami Air, operating B-727s.

Gulfstream's progress over the past year had been nothing less than miraculous. There had been some highs and some extreme lows, but we had survived to fight one more day. The staff, mostly ex-Eastern people, was excellent, all taking enormous pay cuts just to work and all giving 150 percent daily.

As I looked to the future, I could see some issues that must be solved.

There was one more year to enjoy free rent, and although we were already bursting at the seams in the small facility, I had to stay in the present location due to financial restraints.

The Airlines Clearing House cash flow problem had to be solved. We couldn't continue to fly passengers and wait for a month for payment.

And there was the September and October Bahamian malaise, although the Vero Beach to Orlando route was doing quite well, and those passengers would help us out as they did the previous fall. To add to my cash flow problems, in the near future there would be some engine overhauls that I must deal with at approximately $25,000 each.

And I needed one more Cessna for a spare. I had noticed that to keep the aircraft flying, I was spending too much on maintenance overtime. An additional aircraft would lessen the load on our maintenance department and add another level of efficiency to our operation. I made a note to check with the finance companies that had been funding the aircraft for the now-defunct Aero Coach and see if there were any surplus aircraft remaining.

And expansion. I decided to control temptation and hold off any further expansion until I had the cash flow issue solved. Our current routes, thirteen cities, needed further development, and I needed to massage and tweak some of the schedules that we were now operating. We had reached a point where, with careful management, we could be profitable, and it was time to level off and streamline the operation.

That turned out to be a fortuitous decision. Although I didn't know it then, I would need some breathing room as, in the airline business, one can expect the unexpected to happen.

Betty hit the ground running. Funderburk found some more carpet remnants, and soon Betty's reception room and my office had new broadloom. It cost pennies but it made a world of difference. With a used bookshelf, a few pictures, a map, and Betty's businesslike approach to her position, the front reception room took on a new air; we all walked a little bit taller in our humble surroundings. We purchased one of them "newfangled" fax machines, and Bill Funderburk found a used van for use on the airport ramp. We were cooking.

I went to work on the Airlines Clearing House cash flow issue.

The banks were of no use, so I began to look for a factoring company, which is simply a company that advances money to another company based on a specific receivable. It's basically a short-term loan, for a month generally, and the receivable must be from a strong company that is likely to pay.

I approached several companies but when I said the word *airline*, I was shown the door. The airlines, after Air Florida, Eastern, and Pan Am folded, were toxic.

Even though we were having a gangbuster winter season with high load factors, my ticket income was all tied up in the clearing house. My big creditors were Delta, American, North West, and United. My accounts receivables were running around $100,000, but I just couldn't touch it.

Around the beginning of March, I visited a small factoring office, J & D Financial, in North Miami Beach. I sat down with the owner, Mr. Jack Carmel, and explained the whole thing to him. He grasped the situation quickly and agreed to help out. At a very high interest rate.

First, I had to assign my clearing house account to him. Then, as I collected tickets, and on a weekly basis, I would bring them up to him, and he would advance 60 percent of the gross funds to me. For this, he would charge me 18 percent per contract representing a full month of tickets. When the clearing house paid him, he would remit the balance to me, less his commission.

It was onerous, but it was all that I could do. No one would lend a cent to a small airline. This would relieve us of the graveyard spiral that we were in financially, but with the high interest rates that he was charging, we were still in a slow descent.

But it would let me survive one day more.

I got a call in late February from the airport manager in Vero Beach. I was sure that he was going to compliment me on the super service that we were providing the community; the excellent on-time performance with seven flights daily, clean aircraft, and loads growing weekly.

Wrong.

"Cooper," he said, "you guys are doing a great job, but I'm going to have to ask you to move from your counter."

"May I ask why?" I already knew the answer; another airline was coming in.

"Well," he hesitated, "there's a new carrier that's applied to fly in here, Florida Gulf. They're flying large turbo props, and you know how our folks like them turbo props, so we need your counter."

I knew the answer to this question before I asked. "Where do you have us moving to?"

"Well," he sounded really pained, "there's a small desk that one of the rent-a-car companies abandoned across the terminal, and I guess that you can use it."

I had already made up my mind to close the station about fifteen seconds earlier, but I wanted to make him squirm. "I suppose that when my passengers check in with bags that you'll provide someone to carry the bags across the terminal and place them on the ramp so we can load them?"

"Well," he was hating this, "I don't think that the city commissioners will approve of any additional manpower at the airport."

This charade was a waste of time for both of us. "Bill, I'll be moving out. There's not enough business there for two carriers to Orlando. I'll be out in a week."

"Well, that's sure neighborly of you. Will I see you up here on the last day?"

"Nope," and I hung up.

I brought Jim Taylor in and explained that we were pulling out of Vero Beach and why. He was a bit depressed. He wasn't used to retreating, at least during the last year, but when I told him that we'd put that aircraft in service March 1st into the Abacos, where we needed more seats, he perked up. He set up the last round of flights at Vero Beach and implemented the new schedule into Treasure Cay and Marsh Harbour. That gave him room to hire an old friend of ours, the son of Captain Don Davidson, Sr., Don Jr. as a new captain.

It was around the beginning of March that we got bad news from High Point. Mother was ill and it didn't look good. She had survived a serious operation ten years earlier and had bounced back. She wasn't a complainer, she was strong, and I just couldn't conceive of her in declining health. I tried hard not to believe it.

Bill Funderburk got me a pass on USAir, and I visited the doctor in High Point. The prognosis was bad. She had pancreatic cancer and it was advanced.

She would require full-time attention. Jerrie and I worked out a schedule; she would spend a week up there and then I would spend a week. Bill Funderburk talked to the local USAir station manager, who gave us unlimited passes between Miami and Greensboro. We began the schedule in April and set ourselves up for a long siege.

I set up a mini-office in the dining room in our home in High Point with nothing but a fax machine and a dedicated phone line. Betty and I developed a form whereby she could send me all the pertinent data on a daily basis, and we were in business.

The operation had become a lot easier with the ending of the Vero Beach to Orlando run. Leaving that run was a blessing in disguise as the redeployment of that designated aircraft to the Bahamas created an increase in passengers and gave us additional reserve aircraft capability. The only issue that kept cropping up was an immigration issue at the Miami airport with the Cap Haitien flights.

From time to time a passenger would show up in Miami with improper documents. The culprits would use counterfeit passports, fake visas, and any other method to get on the aircraft. They were quite clever. In some instances, after a passenger would show legitimate credentials at the counter and move toward the aircraft, the credentials would mysteriously be handed off to a ramp worker who would then pass them back to a passenger standing in line who would resubmit them as his own. For each passenger that arrived at the Miami airport without proper credentials, we were fined by the U.S. Customs office.

We continued to work with the authorities in Haiti, but they weren't much help. I even hired a retired immigration official to ride on some of the trips, but that was too expensive in the long run. We continued to work to solve the problem as Jerrie and I continued to commute to High Point.

I settled into a routine. One week in High Point and one week at the office in Miami. The operation was running smoothly, but the cost of factoring my accounts receivable still caused cash flow problems, although not as severe as earlier.

The summer in High Point was delightful, but sad. Our home sat on an elevated lot, and with the windows open, the breeze cooled the rooms wonderfully well. The smell of the trees in the wooded area next door gave off a pleasant aroma, and to sit on the back porch with Mother was fetchingly sweet.

We talked more that summer than we had ever talked before. She told me about the old relatives I never knew: her grandpa who, when digging a well, injured his leg and died of blood poisoning. And of her grandmother, Tancy, who lived on the edge of town on Stanton Street. She was a real pioneer woman who gardened and did her own washing until the day she died.

Mom even remembered the donation of her red party dress for the wind sock at Fraley Field and we laughed about that. The airport had long since been plowed under and replaced with warehouses, but the memory of that old wind sock still was fresh in our minds.

She had loved to work in the yard, sweep the walkway, rake leaves, and trim the shrubbery. Even after she was completely bedridden she would say to me, "Tommy, I'll bet the front walk needs to be swept."

"Yes ma'am," and I'd go out and sweep the walkway.

Her situation worsened and it became necessary to have hospice come in—first on a limited basis, but as the summer wore on, more regularly. And my mother's spirits were always lifted by the neighborhood ladies. They were constant companions, stopping in daily for short visits, catching Mom up on all the gossip in the area and at church.

Betty, Jim Taylor, Bill Funderburk, Mark Reichard, and Richard Falcon did a wonderful job keeping the airline running during this period. Betty ran the office, Jim managed the flight schedules, Bill controlled the stations, Mark watched the maintenance, and Falcon ran the ground and flight school division with the first officer program.

I would arrive on alternate Mondays, and Betty would have my desk stacked neatly with "attention Cooper" items. It seemed that by the time I got caught up with her list, and met with the others on the team, it was time to return to High Point.

I was at my desk in May when a visitor stopped by unannounced. He represented the Beechcraft Company and after some small talk, he asked me if I would be interested in purchasing some Beechcraft C-99s.

The C-99 was a popular propjet commuter aircraft with fifteen seats and a baggage capacity sufficient to carry all the passenger's bags.

"I'm sorry, sir, but you've wasted your time," I said. "We can't even afford the Cessnas that we have leased, much less larger aircraft."

The conversation went on for a few more minutes, and he excused himself and left, I supposed, for good.

My attention was quickly directed elsewhere, and the meeting disappeared from my mind almost immediately. I was busy balancing the accounts payables against the accounts receivables and packing up for my trip to High Point.

A very bright spot in our operation was the nicely developing Avtar First Officer Program.

Bill and Vic continued to send first officer students, and the word was getting out about the value of the program. Gulfstream was flying over nine hundred hours per month, and at that rate we could graduate a first officer in about three months, most of them with five to six hundred flight hours.

The first three students who started in the previous June class had graduated in November and were immediately hired by a large commuter airline; they were now flying commuter prop-jets. The next class of four first officers followed a month later, and they also were hired quickly. With those successes, word got out in the industry, and the supply of first officer applicants grew. Not only did the supply grow, the demand for graduates grew also. Word of the quality of the students who graduated was spreading throughout the industry among the larger commuter airlines.

When our graduates showed up for ground school at their new airline, they were always dressed neatly with shirt and tie. Their study habits were excellent, and they passed their check rides with flying colors. On the flight line, they were professional and drew high praise from their fellow captains.

They had all been screened at Gulfstream, and once in the program, if they didn't take it seriously, they were terminated. Those terminated were given a generous pro-rate of their tuition and sent home.

Of course, as the success of the program spread, word of it came to the attention of the pilots' union, and there was an unofficial campaign to discredit it.

The unions were too late. The program was such a success that their maligning slander fell on deaf ears. After all, it was good for all concerned; for the student, it gave great training and experience at an affordable price; for the company, it put cash in the till; and for the passengers, it gave a sense of confidence. After all, we were the only small eight-passenger airline that used copilots. The passengers loved it.

The students received top-flight instruction, thanks to the professionalism of Captain Richard Falcon in the training department and the monitoring of the first officers on the line by Captain Jim Taylor.

By late summer, Mother required full-time help, and we brought in an attendant. She was an angel and with the daily visits by hospice, I had plenty of time in the solitude of High Point to review the past year and a half and plan for the future.

The dreaded September and October Bahamas malaise was looming in the not-too-distant future, and we didn't have the Vero Beach route to act as filler.

I suppose I was basking in the sunshine of success. Even though money was scarce, the loads were triple what they were the year before, but I was still nervous. I began watching the advance fall passenger bookings and I could see a storm coming.

There *was* a storm coming, but it wasn't the September and October Bahamas malaise.

It was Hurricane Andrew!

CHAPTER 73

Hurricane Andrew

IT WAS SUNDAY, AUGUST 16TH, and Jerrie and I were in High Point with Mother when the word of a tropical storm began to hit the news. The storm had not fully developed, but I began to watch it and track it. By Wednesday, August 19th, it had a name and had begun to intensify.

I continued to track it. It was drawing a bead on South Florida and growing.

With the attendant staying with Mother, I felt comfortable enough to head to Miami to secure our home and the airline. Jerrie and I hopped on USAir and came to Miami on Friday the 21st.

By Saturday, the 22nd, the storm had set a course for North Eleuthera, and winds were approaching 150 miles per hour. Tommy and I boarded up the house, and I went to the airport to activate our hurricane plan.

I ceased all flight schedules, grounded all the aircraft in Miami, and asked for volunteer pilots to prepare for evacuation. I selected the senior pilot of the twelve volunteer crewmembers as team leader, issued him cash along with my credit card, and we began to decide on an evacuation destination. Northbound was the best option, as it gave us some escape choices in case the hurricane changed directions. We found an airport in central Florida that could accommodate six Cessnas, and as Andrew struck North Eleuthera at around 4:00 p.m., we launched, en masse.

It wasn't much fun, but it sure was pretty to see my six Cessnas, all in the same Gulfstream International Airlines livery, taxi out and take off in a fifteen-second interval trail formation.

We wrapped the typewriters and fax machine in plastic, taped the windows, and went home to wait.

The winds woke me at around 4:00 a.m. I took a look outside and all seemed normal for a fifty- to sixty-knot wind, so I went back to bed. The morning light woke me for a second time. Jerrie and Tommy were already up with candles as the electricity was out, as expected, but there were no trees down on our property, so I wasn't alarmed.

Our first indication of a major problem was Tommy's report. He and a buddy went on a scouting expedition and came back with a report of serious tree and building damage.

Around noon, the wind had died down sufficiently, so I decided to drive to the airport, check the damage there, and call the aircraft back to re-establish the flying schedule.

I could get no further than a block away due to uprooted trees and downed telephone lines. I retraced my way back home with nothing to do but wait it out.

Around 4:00 p.m., Tommy came home with a fist full of money. He and his buddy had set up a quick business with a chainsaw, cleaning driveways and alleys. They had run out of gas and he was eyeing my car's gas tank.

The answer was "No!"

The day went slowly. The only bright spot was that the phones came on in the afternoon. I made contact with the fleet's team leader and told him to stay put, but keep in contact with the crews and have them on ready alert for an a.m. departure to Miami.

The Miami airport was closed with the exception of emergency flights; no commercial flights were allowed to operate.

Nightfall came, the day had passed, and I had done nothing toward resuming operations. Not having electricity or TV, we knew nothing of the extent of the damage caused by the hurricane.

Jerrie's friend, Roberta Watt, and an old Eastern flying buddy, Gene Massung, lived in a community about ten miles north of us. They had electricity and invited us to spend the night with them. We accepted, and once we found our way to their apartment and looked at the television broadcasts, the extent of the damage became painfully clear.

This hurricane had dealt a major blow to the South Florida community, and spotty reports from the Bahamas indicated the same there.

We returned home on Wednesday, the 26th. I made it to the airport late that day as it had opened earlier. I recalled the aircraft and they began to show up at dusk. The whole staff was there, with harrowing personal tales of the hurricane. Betty, Bill, Jim, Mark, and I began to pick up the pieces and to plan for the next day's operation.

Communication with the Bahamas was almost nil—we had to rely on TV segments from Nassau—so I put together a plan.

The Cap Haitien flight would depart on time Friday. We would dispatch one aircraft to Abaco to visit Treasure Cay and Marsh Harbour. A second aircraft would head toward Eleuthera to review the damage at North Eleuthera, Governor's Harbour, and Rock Sound; and a third would go to the three airports in Andros.

The reports that the pilots brought back were stories of complete devastation. Especially in North Eleuthera, where whole towns were wiped out. North Eleuthera, our busiest destination, had taken a direct hit.

Our company had taken a direct hit also. We had been shut down for five days, and our advanced bookings had dropped by 75 percent. The Bahamas malaise that I had dreaded was here, and the next two months would be dismal.

But that wasn't the worst news. I received a call from High Point with the news that Mother wasn't expected to last through the week.

I left Bill and Betty in charge, and Jerrie and I headed for High Point. Thank goodness for USAir. They had been wonderful during this personal trial, and I will always have a soft spot in my heart for them. I gave Funderburk authority to comply with any pass requests that their employees might ever have.

We were there on Saturday, August 29th, when Mother passed away. She was surrounded at bedside by her family, her loyal attendant, and the neighborhood ladies who had been so attentive to her in her last days.

The debacle in Miami was farthest from my mind as I attended to all the protocol surrounding the death of Mother: the funeral service, the immediate bills, the lawyer, and the meager estate dealings.

We held Mother's service, shipped most of her furniture and personal effects to our home in Miami, and gave the rest to neighbors and relatives. I placed her home and her small rental house, our old home across the street, with a real estate broker and headed back to Miami.

It was September 15th when we arrived back in Miami. Tommy had watched our home and Gulfstream's staff had kept the airline running. The passenger loads were dismal. About the only thing we had to lift our spirits was the satisfaction that we got from the humanitarian loads of bottled water and blue tarps that we carried over to our Bahamian stations in our near empty airplanes.

We would normally cut schedules back for September and October, but in the aftermath of Hurricane Andrew, we had to cut back even more. To make things even worse, any profits that we might have made in the spring and summer were eaten away with the high interest rate that we were paying the factoring company for advancing funds against airline accounts receivable.

We finished the month of September with almost no money. The bank account was dry, the credit card was maxed out, and there was almost no revenue from the extremely low passenger loads. The only bright spot was the revenue from the first officer program. Vic and Bill continued to recruit students, and we continued to hold a first officer's class every second Monday of the month.

With Betty's help, I devised a plan for survival, a plan to get us through one more day until mid-November, when during the Thanksgiving Day holidays, based on historical experience, our loads should pick up considerably.

We recorded all the bills of our creditors in a loose-leaf notebook along with the total of our accounts payable to each. Betty would then remind me when a payment was due to each, and I would call and advise them that I wouldn't be able to pay the entire amount due. I would, however, pay a portion and catch the balance when the season began in the winter.

It was remarkable just how well that worked. Most creditors understood the problem and were helpful. They appreciated the fact that, instead of just ignoring them, I took the time to explain. They went along with the delayed payment plan and continued their services to Gulfstream.

The money continued to flow out at an alarming pace. I feared that I had grown the airline at a rate too fast with too little capital to ensure against emergencies. The hurricane, coupled with the low season in the Bahamas, might be more than we could handle with our daily cash flow.

I literally drove to work each day wondering if we could survive another day.

Although money was scarce I insisted that we would not cut corners in the maintenance department or the training department. I had seen that happen in small commuters, sometimes with disastrous results, and I refused to let it happen here. We were operating a small commuter airline under similar rules as the major airlines, and we could not compromise our standards. Our aircraft were all standardized now with the same paint scheme and logo livery. Our pilots were all dressed smartly and projected an image of professionalism in front of the public. And, with a spare airplane, our maintenance department provided our crews with safe aircraft to ensure reliable schedules.

But in September and October, that wasn't good enough.

We ended September with a total of 936 passengers, a drop from the August total of 2,416. Although I had cut our flying down to 621 hours in September from a total of 934 in August, the reduction was not sufficient to compensate for the low loads.

October 1992 began with no hope for the continuation of the airline. Only a miracle would save us now.

CHAPTER 74

Faith, Hope, and...Beechcraft

OUR MIRACLE CAME ON OCTOBER 5th.

The Beechcraft salesman showed up unexpectedly. Betty showed him into my office, and I burst out laughing. "Surely you're not here again to sell me aircraft?" I joked.

He pulled his chair closer to the front of my desk, pulled out a one-page letter of agreement, pushed it over to me, and explained, "Cooper, this is a deal that you can't afford to turn down."

I didn't even look at it. I pushed it back with a headshake. "I'm worried about making this week's payroll, not to mention paying the fuel bill Friday, and you're trying to sell me an airplane."

"Three airplanes," he corrected me.

I laughed even louder.

"Here's the deal," he continued. "We'll sell you three Beechcraft 99s, give you a signing bonus of seventy-five thousand dollars each, plus allow you two hundred thousand in parts credit, and you give us twenty-five thousand for each aircraft as a down payment."

He continued to ramble on about Beechcraft Finance Company financing the whole deal, monthly payments, delivery dates, and paint schemes, but I had locked on the part about the cash transaction of the proposal, and I heard nothing more. I wasn't an accountant, but I could figure out, pretty quickly, that at the end of the day, when we signed the contract and exchanged checks, I would have $150,000 in the bank.

Done!

That would give me "one day more," plus.

I signed the letter of intent and we agreed to close the transaction on October 19th in Wichita, Kansas, at the Beechcraft headquarters.

I called a meeting that afternoon with all of my supervisory personnel to share the story of our proposed quantum leap into the wonderful world of turbo-prop aircraft.

After the shock of my pronouncement, the questions began. What's the range of the B-99s? Where are we going to fly these aircraft? Will the Avtar first officers be eligible candidates for the right seat? Where are we going to park the aircraft and work on them? We're cramped now with six Cessnas! When does the first one come? Are we going to sell the Cessnas?

I had asked myself all of those questions, plus more, but I didn't have any answers yet. The big question was, where could we move? I had been looking at the calendar as the months passed by. We were nearing the end of 1992, and our two years of free rent were about to come to an end. With our critical financial situation, I had not been seriously looking for a larger maintenance and office area. Now I had to get busy.

The certification process with the FAA, when changing from one type of aircraft to another, is no easy thing. It is especially challenging when the jump is from a single-pilot, eight-passenger, piston-driven plane up to a propjet aircraft that requires a first officer and carries fifteen people. All the manuals must be rewritten to accommodate the changes in the flight operations and maintenance departments along with the training manuals.

Jim Taylor, Mark Reichard, Don Davidson, Jr., and Richard Falcon did a wonderful job rewriting the manuals and presenting their changes to the FAA for approval. Betty's typing and organizational skills were called upon to the maximum, and the transitional manuals were approved in record time.

I closed the transaction in Wichita and set up the first training class for November 2nd.

With the demise of Pan Am, their wonderfully exotic office building on 36th Street, nicknamed the Taj Mahal, became available. The port authority, after trying to rent the entire facility to one entity, decided to parcel it out. We took six offices and moved in on November 13th. A small building also became available next to Rich Airlines, also on 36th Street, and we rented that along with ramp space to accommodate our newly expanded fleet of six Cessnas and three Beechcraft.

In the brief period of four weeks, we had transitioned from a mentally depressed, small, undercapitalized commuter on the verge of financial collapse into a busy, viable scheduled prop-jet airline with a better than even chance for success.

The acquisition of the Beechcraft aircraft was clearly the turning point for Gulfstream. It not only put some much-needed cash into the company, but it gave us a higher level of prestige in the local aviation community.

When in Wichita, after the closing, the salesman drove me to the airport for my return to Miami. I had to ask a question. "Why, with all the other small commuters in the U.S. that you could have made a similar deal with, did you come to me?"

He smiled and what he said made me very proud of Gulfstream.

"Cooper, we did look at a lot of other companies, but we kept coming back to Gulfstream. We visited the airport and we liked what we saw. We saw all your airplanes painted alike, the counter and personnel were very professional, and finally, we bought tickets to ride on one of your flights. Your crews were very professional in their flying skills, their attire, and in their people skills with the customers. We were greatly impressed with your all-around professionalism, and we felt comfortable having you represent our product in this area."

That was a very positive endorsement of my philosophy concerning professionalism and professional attire while in the public view. It was no small thing that I had tried to impart, and it was no small thing as to how my staff and employees had bought into it.

With the hustle and bustle of certifying a new aircraft and moving into new maintenance and administrative offices subsiding, somewhat, I began to ponder what I was going to do with three new aircraft. The bookings were picking up and November looked good. The cash that the Beechcraft deal put in the till was a lifesaver, but if I couldn't figure out how to effectively use the additional aircraft, I would be in worse shape than I was before I made the deal.

The C-99's range wasn't sufficient to allow me to schedule it to Cap Haitien, and with the exception of a couple of Bahama destinations, the passenger loads would not support larger aircraft there. The deadline was nearing for placing the flight schedules in the Official Airline Guide, and I was still massaging the schedule.

It was November the 16th. Betty's call over the interphone heralded the next miracle.

"It's a Mr. Edward St. George," she announced, "from Freeport in the Bahamas. He would like to speak to you."

I had heard of Mr. St. George. He was an icon in the Bahamas, having immigrated there originally in 1956. He was a native of Malta, where he escaped during WW II to England to study as a lawyer.

In 1979, he, along with a partner, gained control of the Grand Bahamas Port Authority, which owned the airport. With the advent of several large hotels and casinos in Freeport, it became apparent that the success of the new community and the success of the airport depended on reliable air transportation.

Apparently, they weren't receiving that, and thus the call to me.

"Mr. Cooper," he went right to the point in his polished British accent, "I hear from around the Family Islands that you run a pretty good airline. I wonder if you would be interested in operating into Freeport."

Freeport was a jewel. There had been a downturn in business recently, and some of the larger airlines had pulled out, leaving a terrific void for a small airline like mine. I knew instantly that the Beechcraft C-99 with fifteen seats would be perfect for that route.

"Yes, sir," I replied, trying to disguise my enthusiasm. "We certainly would, but I don't have that authority to fly there from the Bahamian government, which, based on my experience, could take months to come through."

"I can work that out from this end." He chuckled. "If you got the authority tomorrow, when could you start service?"

Glancing up at the training schedule posted on the wall in my office, I confidently said, "Thirty days."

"I'll have your authority in the mail today," he said. "How about Ft. Lauderdale also?"

"I can do that in mid-February." My head spun.

"Thank you, Mr. Cooper, and when you come to Freeport, please see Mr. Albert Miller at the airport. He's my partner and he'll fix you up with whatever you need there."

"Thank you, Mr. St. George," I stammered.

"No, thank you, Mr. Cooper," he said, "and good luck."

Three days later, the Bahamian authority to operate the routes came in the mail.

I had begun to work on the Freeport schedules when an old friend from my earlier Cuban adventures called.

It was Tuesday, the 8th of December, and the caller was Wayne Smith, the former Chief of the U.S. Interest Section in Havana. He needed to fly to Cuba and asked if I would fly the trip myself. We had done a similar trip earlier, so I agreed immediately and asked, "What's the mission this time?"

"I've set up a meeting for some scholars and politicians to meet with Castro, and I need to visit with him to clear up some loose ends," he explained. "And, oh yes, I'm taking George McGovern with me."

I wasn't very politically oriented; it took me a few seconds to search my mind and remember the name George McGovern.

"Is he the guy who ran for President?" I asked.

"That's the one," he said, "and you'll like him; he's an old aviator like you."

We set up a time, Thursday morning the 10th, and I met them at the Miami Airport Terminal. I took an immediate liking to McGovern.

The trip was pretty exciting. We were met at the airport in Havana, whisked through customs at the protocol terminal while having cocktails, and before we knew it, we were on our way to a private governmental residence in the Miramar section west of Havana where we would spend the night.

While Wayne and McGovern visited with Castro, the Cubans gave me a fine tour of the city. Later that night, when Wayne and McGovern returned, we spent a lovely evening under the stars by the pool reflecting on the day's activities. It seems that Wayne's political group wanted to visit some dissidents, and that didn't fit into the local agenda.

Wayne and the senator agreed that Castro was very friendly but unbending. The planned trip would be called off when Wayne returned home.

Over dinner at the residence, Wayne insisted that McGovern share his wartime experiences with me. I was surprised to learn that he had been a B-24 pilot during the war and had been awarded several medals, including the Distinguished Flying Cross for saving his crew and aircraft after two engines had been shot out on a bombing mission over Germany.

Upon returning to Miami the next day, we shook hands and I watched as he and Wayne ran to catch the connecting flight to Washington.

I hoped that I would see them again.

I began to advertise the Miami to Freeport flights effective December 16, 1992 and the Ft. Lauderdale to Freeport flights effective February 12, 1993. The advanced bookings went wild. The first C-99 arrived November 20th, and the certification came soon after, on December 4th.

The Freeport flights began on December 16th and were an instant success. We were lucky to hire Ms. Jennie Newman as the station manager.

She took over on day one and never let up. She ran the Freeport station with an iron fist, and her employees, along with her customers, all fell in love with her.

We ended 1992 on an absolute high. We were operating six Cessnas and two Beechcraft C-99s with a third one on the way in February. We were serving twelve cities and employed 120 professionals. We set a passenger boarding record of 2,768 passengers in December, and the bookings for 1993 were soaring.

Ninety days earlier, we were on the brink of destruction, and as we ended December, we were sitting on top of the world.

Now I had to tackle the factoring cash flow problem and figure out how to beat the seasonal Bahamas malaise issue coming up in September and October. With our new turboprops, we would now be attractive to a major airline to partner with as a commuter. I had to begin to work on that program also.

While exploring every avenue for working capital, I kept one eye on additional destination opportunities within our immediate area.

We opened the Ft. Lauderdale to Freeport route right on schedule in February of 1994 with outstanding success. Once in the Ft. Lauderdale market, I noted that there was no air service between Ft. Lauderdale and Nassau. Nassau was the crown jewel of potential business, with an ever-expanding local population coupled with the expanding tourist attractions.

A quick call to Edward St. George in Freeport, and I received a license to operate from Nassau to any point in Florida within the week.

On April 16th, we dropped the Miami to Cap Haitien route due to continued problems associated with managing the customs regulations. We commenced service between Ft. Lauderdale and Nassau with three trips daily and between Miami and Nassau with one trip daily.

The company was growing and doing well. Two years earlier, in May, we had flown 325 passengers, and in May of this year, we would fly over 6,600 passengers. At that level, I could call a halt to any further expansion plans and focus on the cash flow issues and the expected drop in passengers in the fall.

Nothing could deter me from focusing on that mission.

Until Betty rang me on the interphone. It was April 20th. "There's a Mr. Frank Lorenzo on the phone for you," she said.

CHAPTER 75
Frank Lorenzo Calls

Will the Eastern wound never heal?

"Hum," I thought out loud. "I wonder what Frank Lorenzo wants. Other than a thoughtful Christmas card, I haven't heard from him in over two years."

I hesitated for a second before I picked up the receiver. "Mr. Lorenzo?"

"Oh, hi, Tom," he answered, "and please call me Frank."

He asked how my wife was doing, and we talked a bit about my airline. He again thanked me for my stand against the unions at Eastern, and we passed a few more minutes with small talk.

And then he spoke frankly concerning the purpose of his call.

He was developing a new low-cost airline to operate out of Baltimore and was preparing his fitness application to present to the Department of Transportation in Washington for a license to operate.

He anticipated resistance from the unions representing the pilots and machinists, and he wondered if I would be willing to testify, on his behalf, as an expert witness.

He wasn't the least bit pushy and said he'd understand if I didn't feel comfortable with it. He cautioned me that the unions might retaliate in some way against Gulfstream for revenge.

I agreed with him on his last assertion and asked if I could think about it overnight and get back to him.

"Sure," he replied. "I look forward to hearing from you. Say hello to Jerrie."

The Man in The Arena...

The rest of the day went by slowly. As hard as I tried to concentrate on the airline, my mind kept returning to the conversation with Lorenzo.

I had bought into his style of management. I really believed that the unions were wrong at Eastern and that they were the root cause of the problems. We had problems before Lorenzo. Even the gentleman astronaut Borman couldn't get along with them.

That reminded me of a time, once, when Borman visited the cockpit on one of my flights and was relating a Lorenzo story. It seems that Lorenzo was purchasing some DC-9 aircraft from Eastern. Borman laughed as he remembered, "Lorenzo doesn't start negotiating until after the contract is signed."

I had heard all the stories, the claims that he was stripping all the assets from Eastern. Maybe so, but I remembered an old saying, "A company gets the management that it deserves." Eastern, all of us, deserved Lorenzo and his no-nonsense attitude toward the business.

But then was then and now was now. Was I about to jeopardize my airline to stick up for Lorenzo? Although I had no proof, I was pretty sure that some strikers had vandalized my company aircraft the year before by destroying two-thirds of my fleet, almost shutting me down. What could I expect now? This would put me on a nationwide stage as ally of the most hated man in aviation. This would surely open old wounds.

On the other hand, just as I believed then, I still believed in the mission to save Eastern by continuing to work and later to oust the pilots' union. If I backed down now, I would admit that the effort, although Eastern would eventually shut down, was in vain. If I didn't stand up for Frank now, I wasn't being true to my cause.

I went to sleep thinking about it and awoke the next morning thinking about it. A new issue came to mind. It wasn't just about me; I now had over a hundred employees to think about. Could the union retaliate to the point of shutting us down?

I went through the morning routine at the office. I sat at the morning staff meeting, but my mind wasn't there. There were a few delayed flights, a maintenance issue, and some of the usual gossip. Soon the staff was excused and I was alone in my office.

It was approaching 11:00 when I made up my mind. It was a matter of principle. "I wasn't a coward in '89 and I'm not a coward now," I resolved to myself.

"Betty," I asked over the intercom, "get me Lorenzo."

"Hi Frank, I'm on board," I announced with some bravado.

"Great," he said. "I'll let the lawyers know in Washington, and they'll get in touch with you. And, Tom," he said, "you don't know what this means to me."

I felt pretty good about it too.

The law firm Beckman, Kirstein and Murphy called, and a Mr. Robert Beckman briefed me on my expected participation. I would submit my testimony in writing and appear in person at the hearing in Washington.

The trial was set for the last week of June, and I was set to testify on Tuesday the 28th, at 9:30 a.m. Later, in a letter, Beckman advised that I would probably be cross-examined by the attorneys representing ALPA, the IAM, and the public counsel representing the Department of Transportation. "You should not be on the stand for more than two hours," the letter said, "and, oh yes, there will be TV cameras there as well!"

I was there on the appointed date and observed the venue. The courtroom was of medium size, with the judge's podium centered at the front and the witness chair positioned to his left. There was a row of tables and chairs in front of the judge's bench shaped in the form of a U. The representatives from the DOT were on the immediate left occupying three chairs; the ALPA representatives occupied half of that row and half of the center row. The representatives of the IAM union filled the balance of the chairs on the center and half of the chairs on the right. Lorenzo's key personnel and his attorneys occupied the remaining five chairs on the right-hand side.

And it was hot. There was no air-conditioning and the temperature was well into the mid-nineties.

I mused to myself as I looked around at the participants. *This doesn't look like a fair fight.* The DOT had only three people seated, Lorenzo only had five, but ALPA and the IAM, collectively, had about thirty.

I watched the proceedings with great interest. The trial seemed to be taking on the appearance of a kangaroo court. Lorenzo was treated quite rudely, not only by the ALPA and the IAM lawyers, but by the judge as well. At one point, Lorenzo was admonished abusively by the judge for removing his jacket despite the heat. Through all this, I felt that Lorenzo handled himself in a mannerly and professional fashion.

My turn came to testify and, although I was prepared for the worst, the attorneys seemed to let me off easy. After being sworn in, the DOT attorney passed on any cross-examination, and the ALPA and IAM attorneys had me on the stand for less than thirty minutes.

The hearing lasted for two days before we were dismissed to await the judge's verdict. I was happy to leave Washington that hot summer, and on the

The Man in The Arena...

flight home I had time to review the last couple of days' activities. I was sure that I hadn't heard the last from the pilots' and machinists' unions, but there was nothing I could do but wait and see. I was anxious to return to Miami and to the day-to-day running of the airline. I had much to do.

It would be September before the judge would render his opinion. As I suspected, he ruled against Lorenzo in favor of the unions.

Frank had lost his bid to return to the air in his newly formed airline, but I had won. I had won, in principle, by standing by the firmness of my convictions, and I had validated my old feelings concerning my stand at Eastern. It was now time to go back to work and move my airline forward.

The Lorenzo episode soon faded from my memory.

But not from the union's.

August was a banner month. We flew an all-time record of 9,280 passengers that month, up from 1,173 in August of the previous year. We acquired our fourth C-99 and prepared to open the Key West to Miami route. This would be our first domestic route since the Vero Beach debacle and would help reduce the liability of the Bahamian fall malaise, the curse of every September and October.

CHAPTER 76
Expansion to Key West

"WOW, I've always wanted one of these coconut heads!"

I FLEW TO KEY WEST in late August to contract with the airport manager for counter and ramp space for our planned expansion.

In 1993, the terminal in Key West was neat, but small. It was an open-air structure with the airline counters directly across from the open entranceways located alongside the street. As you entered the terminal to the right was a small souvenir shop, and further down the hall to the right was a restaurant. The counter space was limited to only five positions with limited office space behind them. The ramp area was spacious and could handle additional transient aircraft.

The issue was counter space. All the spots were rented.

The airport manager appeared to be sympathetic but had no solution. I began to have the same feelings that I had felt two years earlier at the Miami airport. The airport manager simply had no space and little time to discuss any alternative. His attitude was, "Why waste time worrying about this issue because Gulfstream will go broke soon anyway. And besides, we have enough airlines in here now."

We walked around the small terminal, and finally he directed me to the outside sidewalk.

To my absolute horror, he suggested that we could set up a fold-up stand and card table and greet our customers there, on the sidewalk. When I questioned him about rain, he simply shrugged his shoulders and headed inside and murmured, "That's my only solution." It was a classic take-it-or-leave-it attitude.

I followed him inside and noticed a small area, off to the right, next to the souvenir shop, about ten feet by fifteen feet. "What about this area?" I suggested. "We can build a counter, check passengers in, and carry the bags through the walkway across the terminal to the ramp for loading."

"Oh boy," he exclaimed, "that will block the side view of the souvenir shop, and the lady who owns it would never approve."

"And if she were to approve, can I have the spot?"

"I don't see why not," he answered, "but she's a tough cookie. She'll never allow it."

"I'll give it a try," I said as I turned toward the souvenir shop door.

I walked in and saw the clerk, an elderly woman, seated behind the counter. She looked up as I entered but said nothing. I guessed that she was the proprietor, but I didn't engage her in conversation…yet.

I began to shop. Let's see, here were some nice postcards, and over here, a small crate of plastic oranges, and there's a banner announcing the advent of the "Conch Republic." As I shopped and began to collect a few items, I noted from the corner of my eye that her interest in me began to increase somewhat.

The more I selected, the greater her interest.

Finally, she came around from behind the counter and asked, "Can I help you?"

"Well," I said remorsefully, "I've got some kids at home, and I must take them some souvenirs from Key West as I probably won't be this way again."

I picked up a few more trinkets and placed them on the counter.

"Wow," I exclaimed, "I've always wanted one of these coconut heads, and this one is really neat with Key West painted on it."

I now had a sizable stack of trinkets and paraphernalia stacked on her counter, and I had her attention.

"Why won't you be visiting us again?" she asked.

"Oh," I said, "I own a small airline and I am down here to rent counter space, but the airport manager says that there's no room for us here."

It was too early to set the hook yet.

"That's too bad," she said with a frown. "Surely there's something we can do."

I caught the word "we." Now she was my ally.

"Oh look," I said, "here's a CD that I've looked all over for." I stacked two CDs by a local musician on the counter. "No," I continued, "we've looked all over the terminal, and there's nothing available."

She stuck her head out of the door, reviewed the counter space, and nodded her head in agreement as she returned to her spot behind the counter and began to tally up my purchases.

It was time to set the hook.

"The only suitable space is right here, next to your shop, and I know that the airport manager would never allow me to build a small counter there."

"I wouldn't be so sure of that," she exclaimed confidently. "I know him very well. You just let me handle him."

"You're kidding," I said admiringly. "You must have a lot of pull around here."

She handed me a bill for seventy-five dollars and fifty cents and said, "Watch the shop for a minute, and don't worry, I'll be right back."

She dashed out of her shop and headed for the stairwell that led to the airport manager's office.

She was back in less than two minutes with a broad grin on her face. "He agreed to let you have the spot," she announced proudly. "I told you not to worry."

The Key West counter problem was solved, I thought as I flew home triumphantly, but I now had another problem. What the hell was I going to do with a coconut head and a small crate of plastic oranges?

CHAPTER 77

Further Expansion and Capital from An Unlikely Source

WE OPENED KEY WEST ON schedule, and I was pleased with the passenger loads and advanced bookings. This market would go a long way toward leveling off the September and October dip in Bahamian passengers.

Additionally, I was beginning to develop a scheduling philosophy that centered around the fact that most of our Bahama passengers flew on Friday, Saturday, and Sunday with lesser loads on Thursday and Monday. Tuesdays and Wednesdays were dismal. By establishing routes in the Florida area, I could capitalize on the businessman market that was active mainly during the week, Monday through Friday. By redeploying my aircraft into the Florida market during the weekdays and focusing on the Bahamian routes during the weekends, I could maximize the utilization of my aircraft fleet and level off my passenger loads over a seven-day period.

I began to look for other city pairs in the state of Florida.

We were becoming successful, even though we were continuously short on working capital. And it wasn't all about me. The staff at Gulfstream was doing a bang-up job. Betty was running the office professionally to a level far and beyond what I had envisioned when I started the airline. She commanded respect, not by bullying but by giving off a degree of quiet sophistication, reflecting the image that all respected.

Captain Jim Taylor ran the flight operations and set an example on the flight line, and all the pilots looked up to him. Captain Mark Reichard was our utility infielder who would tackle any challenge I gave him. Captain Richard Falcon administered the flight training department with such dignity and professionalism that his reputation spread throughout the industry. We were delighted when he was awarded the prestigious award from the FAA as Top Aviation Trainer of the year in 1993.

In November, we received our fifth Beechcraft C-99 and immediately placed it into service in the Ft. Lauderdale market, flying to Marsh Harbour, Treasure Cay, and North Eleuthera.

In December, we hit two milestones in our company. We exceeded ten thousand passengers for the first time by flying 11,671 customers in one month.

And the other significant happening was the leasing of our own hangar at the airport. We rented an old hangar from the Miami Port Authority that had previously been utilized by Pan Am. It was historically significant, as it was the first building that Pan Am erected at the airport. It had originally been constructed in Key West in 1927, and one year later, when Pan Am moved its operation to Miami, it was disassembled and transported to Miami, where it was reassembled on its present site.

Over the past several years, it had been used primarily as a storage building, being too small to accommodate modern jets, and it had fallen into a terrible state of disrepair.

To me, it was beautiful. Even on a limited budget, I vowed to clean and fix it up. There were walls to be repaired, doors to be hung, bathrooms to be reactivated, fans to be hung, and a plethora of other areas to be upgraded. I brought in a small neighborhood renovation company for the job and placed them on a limited budget. In retrospect, it was one of the smartest things I ever did. The repair company was excellent; the work was done on time, and the finished product was something to be proud of.

But the best thing was that one of the workers decided to come to work for us permanently. His name was John Spargo, a man for all seasons. There was nothing he couldn't do; carpentry work, welding, electrical repairs, painting. And he tackled each and every job as if it were a personal challenge. He became a most valued employee and a trusted member of the Gulfstream family.

The maintenance department took on a new air. Up until now, all maintenance had been done outside at the mercy of the weather. We had purchased a surplus canopy on wheels that protected the mechanics somewhat,

The Man in The Arena...

but with the South Florida rainstorms that are prevalent and violent, it did little good. We lost many mechanic man-hours during those storms.

With our name, GULFSTREAM, painted proudly on the front of the façade of the hangar, the mechanics walked a little bit taller, and production improved tremendously.

We finished 1993, our third year of operation, with some highs; our gross sales topped six million, we flew eighty-four thousand passengers—up from sixteen thousand just two years earlier—and we were now operating thirty-four flights daily, utilizing five Beechcraft 99s and seven Cessnas.

We still had not figured out how to relieve ourselves from the onerous 18 percent factoring cost, and we still had not negotiated a commuter arrangement with a major airline.

Christmas came about two weeks late in 1993. It was mid-January of 1994, when talking to an old acquaintance, I was lamenting the woes of the factoring arrangement and how it was strangling us. He suggested that I call a newly formed company in Nashville, Tennessee, called Sirrom Capital. According to him, it was a small venture capital lending company, and my company would fit into their profile nicely.

What could I lose? I asked myself. *I've ruined my welcome with all the lending agencies in Florida, and Tennessee is nice in the winter. I might as well give it a try. Besides, perhaps they haven't heard of the Air Florida, Pan Am, and Eastern collapses.*

"Betty," I asked on the intercom, "see if you can find a Sirrom Capital in Nashville, Tennessee, and get someone on the phone for me."

Barely seconds later she buzzed me back. "I have a Mr. Miller on the phone for you."

"Hello, Mr. Miller," I said, "I'm Tom Cooper and I was told that you ran a company that lent money to small businesses."

"Hello there, Tom," he replied in a thick southern drawl. "Yes we do. Where are y'all located and what's your bid-ness?"

"I'm in Miami, Florida, and I run an airline," I said, expecting him to hang up immediately.

"What's your gross annually?"

"We're estimating to do ten to twelve million this year," I proudly proclaimed.

"Well, okay, let's talk. Can you come up here to my office?" he queried.

"Yes, sir," I replied.

"I'm in a hurry now; have your secretary call mine and set up a time. I'll see you then," and he hung up.

"That was the strangest 'no' I have ever received," I thought aloud. "He wants me to fly to Nashville so he can say no in person. But, what the hell, I've got nowhere else to go for money, so I might as well give it a shot."

"Betty, call Mr. Miller's secretary and set up a meeting, and see if you can get me a pass to Nashville."

A week later I arrived at the Nashville airport and took a taxi to the offices of Sirrom Capital. It sounded like a "Far Easterner" name, and I was half expecting to see some strange people wearing robes and such when I arrived. I was surprised to meet a very attractive young woman who said that she was expecting me and would I sit down and she'd bring me a cup of coffee as Mr. Miller was on a long-distance call and would be a few minutes. She also explained that the name Sirrom Capital was not taken from the Far East but was simply a reversal of the family name that funded the company, Morris.

The few minutes turned into thirty and thirty turned into forty-five minutes. I began to look at my watch. I had a return flight scheduled later that day as I had surmised that it wouldn't take Mr. Miller long to say no, and I could return to Miami without the expense of a motel.

Two cups of coffee later, he called through the door and asked me to come in.

"I'm running a little late today, so tell me 'bout your company, what you do, where you fly, and leave me any info that you might have brought with you," he hurriedly drawled.

I quickly went through my story; the rags to riches one without the riches, as I watched him cram my material into his briefcase and stand up in preparation to leave.

I had been in his office less than five minutes and was already getting the brush-off.

As I stood up to leave, I noticed on his bookshelf a baseball cap with UNC on it. "I see your hat there; did you go to UNC?" I asked.

He stopped for a minute. "Yeah, I did, for some advanced studies. How do you know UNC?"

"I went there in fifty-four, fifty-five, and fifty-six," I offered.

"That's great. It's a great school. Why didn't you finish?"

"Well, I wanted to get on with my flying career, so I quit and moved to Florida. I did finish college later," I added, not wanting him to think that I was a quitter.

"Okay, that's great," he said as he bolted out the door. "I'll get back to you later." And just like that, he was gone.

"Shall I call you a cab?" the secretary asked.

"Please," I replied as I packed my briefcase.

I was back in Miami behind my desk before dark. That was the strangest day I had spent in a long time, and the strangest rejection, I thought. *Oh well, I have a million things to do, and thinking about Sirrom Capital will be a waste of time.*

The good thing about rejection in this business is that you don't have to brood over it for long. There are always a million more productive things to occupy your mind, and that's exactly what I had going for me the next day.

An opportunity arose a week earlier that I had to take advantage of. Beechcraft was beginning to receive, on trade-in, some Beechcraft 1900 type of aircraft. These aircraft were a stretched version of the Beechcraft C-99, with the exception that they were faster, had nineteen seats, and were pressurized. The arrangement that Beechcraft offered me was favorable, and I agreed to accept two aircraft with options for more as I sold my Cessnas.

A few days later as I was preparing for the acceptance of the new aircraft, Betty interrupted my thoughts with, "Tom, Mr. George Miller's on the phone for you."

Great, I thought. *At least he has the courtesy to phone me to say 'no'.*

"Cooper, how's the airline bid-ness today?" he asked in his best southern drawl.

"Great," I replied, not knowing what to expect next.

"Listen," he said, "I like your bid-ness, and anybody from UNC must be okay, so if you can get back up here to Nashville and sign some papers at 8 percent interest, I'll lend you a million dollars."

"Mr. Miller," I stammered, "I'm speechless."

"Well, don't be, and get your ass up here and sign these papers before I change my mind." He laughed. "They'll be on my secretary's desk waiting for your signature, and, oh yeah," he added, "have your secretary tell my secretary what your bank wire transfer information is. Good luck." He hung up.

The next day I was in Nashville in front of his secretary's desk, and the next day he wired one million dollars to Gulfstream's account in Miami.

The 8 percent interest was high, but it was a heck of a lot better than the 18 percent I was paying Jack Carmel. We were forecasting around twelve million dollars gross this year, and with the saving of 10 percent with the new loan, I was a hundred and twenty thousand dollars ahead. Although it took a lion's share of the million-dollar loan to purchase my position with J & D Financial back, it was worth it to be relieved of the 18 percent interest contract.

We prepared for the new type of aircraft; the first one arrived in late January. It was certified quickly and soon operating on revenue flights. A second one was due in a month, and I began to look for other routes where it would be productive.

A committee had approached me from Cayman Brac, a small island south of Cuba. It was east of Grand Cayman and had no air service other than a small air taxi between its airport and Grand Cayman. The projected passenger load data they presented looked good, and the only drawback was the fact that there was no fuel at the airport. The nearest fuel was at Grand Cayman, but they guaranteed that, if I would start service, they would install a fuel farm there.

CHAPTER 78

Senator George Mcgovern

Fellow aviator, gentleman, and pal

IT WAS IN MARCH WHEN I received a call from George McGovern.

"Hi Tom," he reintroduced himself in his slow mid-western drawl. "This is George McGovern. Are you ready to go to Cuba again?"

"Hello, Senator, I sure am. When do you want to go?"

He gave me the dates and we set up the rendezvous point at the terminal at the Miami airport. Again, I was flying, and it was the same drill in Havana; soon we found ourselves in the same protocol house where we had stayed with Wayne Smith earlier.

A server met us at the front door with a gigantic tray of libations—every cocktail one could think of, just for two people. When I asked later about the custom, the server said that his instructions, and he pointed his finger upward indicating upstairs politically, were that the guests must not wait one second for their cocktail.

McGovern left immediately for his meeting with Castro. I declined the offer of the city tour and relaxed by the pool in the backyard.

It was several hours before McGovern returned. He joined me by the pool and we began to chat about the events of the day. He said that he was on an unofficial assignment from Washington. He offered little more information than that, and I didn't press the issue.

We continued to talk as dusk turned into darkness. Dinner was served and later we returned to the pool and continued our discussion.

He was a marvelous storyteller. It was like walking through history as it unfolded when he relived stories of his past forays into politics.

"Bill Clinton, our president," he began. "You know, Tom, I gave him his first job in politics."

I was on the edge of my chair as he told the story of how a young man, tall with a bushy head of hair, named Bill Clinton, interviewed for the job as manager of the McGovern presidential campaign for the state of Arkansas.

"I was so impressed," he mused with a smile, "that I offered him a much bigger job, the job of managing my campaign in Texas!" He was chuckling now. "And you know what happened then? He agreed to the job, and as he turned to leave, he asked me for a favor. 'I'll need an assistant,' he explained. 'There's a very intelligent girl I'd like to hire; her name is Hillary Rodham.'"

As he said the girl's name, he laughed out loud.

We both did.

There were stories about George Bush, stories about Jack Kennedy and Nixon. He never would say a bad thing about Nixon, in spite of the Watergate thing. But that was McGovern. I never heard him say anything bad about anyone.

The evening grew late, but he seemed to want to stay up and talk. Perhaps it was a combination of the damp, dank evening in a secluded section of Havana coupled with generous offerings of Havana Club rum, the seven-year-old stuff. Or perhaps he just needed someone to talk with.

His conversation turned somber. He began to relate stories about his daughter, Terry. He talked about her disease, alcoholism. He talked about her challenges, her successes in fighting the illness, and her lapses into complete failure. He stopped short of taking the blame, but I could tell that there was some guilt there, even though he and his wife, Eleanor, had done all that was humanly possible for her. In the darkness, he became emotional and wiped a tear from his cheek.

He regained his composure and ended the conversation upbeat. "We've just moved her back to Madison, where she wants to be. We set her up in an apartment, and so far she's doing fine. Eleanor and I pray for her every night."

"George," I whispered, "it's late. I have to fly you home tomorrow. I must get some sleep. I'll see you in the morning."

I left him there alone. I wish I hadn't.

It was a scant nine months later when they found Terry in a back alley in Madison, curled up, frozen, in a snow bank.

CHAPTER 79

Cayman Brac and Other Ventures

Well, it looked good on paper.

WE STARTED CAYMAN BRAC IN April and the loads were good. But we had to limit seats to accommodate round trip fuel on the southbound flights, which rendered the route a loser. We continued to fly, but there was no sign of a fuel farm being built. When I would inquire as to when the fuel would be available, I got the same answer. *It's in the works. It will come soon.* I began to watch that route closely; if no fuel showed up soon, I would discontinue the service.

Meanwhile, in our search for more Florida markets, we opened the St. Petersburg, Clearwater airport to Miami route. It was doing well and we needed additional seats to accommodate the demand. There were more Beechcraft 1900s and C-99s available, so I visited Beechcraft and ordered more. By the end of the year, I would have eight Beechcraft C-99s and five 1900s.

I began to talk to an old friend at United Airlines, Tony Gattone, the manager of their Code Share Alliances. I had watched the United Express commuter airline that was operating in Florida pull out, and I felt that United might be susceptible to negotiations with Gulfstream to replace it.

A phone conversation turned into an invite to United's headquarters in Chicago and further conversations concerning a "commuter" relationship. I envisioned my aircraft flying the Florida and Bahamas skies with UNITED EXPRESS boldly displayed on their fuselages.

The negotiations were going along smoothly, and we were about to set the date for the joint announcement when I received a phone call from another high official at United.

"Cooper, this is a phone conversation that we never had," she began. "You guys are doing a terrific job down there, and there's nothing more I would like to do than to sign a commuter agreement with you, but..."

"But what?" I asked, dumbfounded.

"It's just that our pilot union found out about the deal, and, well, you're well known in the industry; your Eastern reputation precedes you. Mind you, I'm not passing judgment, it's just that, and I'm quoting their spokesman, if United signs a commuter agreement with you, blood will run in the hallways at United."

My last conversation with Lorenzo flashed back in my mind. *The bastards will never forget.*

"Okay." I breathed deeply, collected myself, and asked, "Where do we go from here?"

"Here's what we can do. I've talked it over with everyone up here," she continued. "We can do a code share arrangement. It's the same as a commuter agreement except that you can't put United's name on the side of your airplane. Your flights will show up in the computers as United Airlines flights, and you can advertise as a United Airlines code share partner."

My fantasies of flying with United Express on the side of my airplanes flew out of the window, but the code share agreement was better than nothing, so I agreed to proceed.

In May, we signed a United Code Share Agreement. Tony Gattone came to Miami and presided over a huge party at the airport with guest dignitaries from all of our stations attending.

We were *somebody* now.

With a solid code share agreement in place with a major airline, and the factoring issue solved, there was nothing to do but to run the airline and not do anything stupid.

That was easier said than done.

This business has no plateaus on which one can rest. There are always opportunities to seize and pitfalls to avoid. Both come with little warning. You must operate full speed ahead but constantly look behind to see what's gaining on you.

After five months of flying half-full aircraft to Cayman Brac, we pulled the plug and left that market. That became my modus operandi for the next several years. With very little passenger data between some of the smaller cities that we might choose to fly, we simply would set up a schedule, try it for a while, and if it paid off, as Key West had, we'd stay. If it didn't, well, we'd pull out of the market, give notice to the community, explain to them why we were leaving, and leave.

Aircraft-wise, my goal was simple: standardize my fleet with the newer Beechcraft 1900s. That meant selling the Cessna 402s and the Beechcraft C-99s. I would sell the Cessnas next year, and they would disappear rapidly. As for the C-99s, they would go, as I bargained for the 1900s from Beechcraft, at a much slower pace.

In keeping with my policy of testing the market to determine its profitability, we opened Miami to Daytona Beach, Miami to Marathon, and Miami to Gainesville.

In November, we were awarded an Essential Air Service route between Atlanta and Anniston, Georgia. The EAS routes are subsidized by the government and, if bid correctly, ensured profitability. We opened up a station in Anniston and contracted with another airline in Atlanta to handle us there.

We ended 1994 riding high. In December, we broke all single-month records by flying 22,500 passengers. Our total passenger count for the year was 194,000, and our gross sales topped twelve million dollars.

Surely now we were out of the woods financially. Was the roller-coaster ride over? Were we stable, and could we only expect slow growth without the deep downturns that we had experienced in the first four years of our existence?

Maybe. But only if I didn't do anything stupid.

We moved to the front of the Taj Mahal, the old Pan Am office building in the spring, and I enjoyed a wonderful office previously occupied by a senior Pan Am executive. It had paneled walls with a built-in bookcase behind my desk. There was a full map of the world on one wall and a hideaway whiteboard on the other. There was room for a conference table, and the windows overlooked a reflecting pool adjacent to 36th Street.

Betty was almost in tears when I assigned her an office. She exclaimed, "I've been in the airline business for over twenty-five years, and I've never had my own office."

We opened up West Palm Beach with a route to Tampa, and it was an instant success. We followed that with connections to Tallahassee; that, too, proved to be a good route.

In late summer, there was a remarkable addition to the Gulfstream family.

I had mentioned to Tony Gattone, of United Airlines, that if he ever retired from United, I'd like him to consider coming to work for us. I had mentioned it half-jokingly, but in August I received a call from him saying that he was considering retiring, and if my offer were still good, he'd be willing to join us.

I jumped at the opportunity. In August, Tony joined our firm as senior vice president of marketing and sales. His credentials were outstanding. He had been with United for thirty-eight years in many capacities, mostly managing their alliance programs. With Gulfstream, he would focus on the relationships with other airlines and work on route expansions.

He was extremely talented in the marketing of our product. Soon we were in all the newspapers. We became the official airline of the Special Olympics and the Miss Florida Contest, and, with Tony's promotional ability, I was soon the toast of the town in the state with newspapers regaling my accomplishments and of the airline's miraculous growth in four short years.

Somewhere during late fall, I made a major mistake. I began to believe my press clippings.

It didn't happen all at once, but over time, I began to believe that anything I did would work out. Yes, the small cities we tried to serve might fail, but that was part of the grand overall plan and I was okay with it.

Our passenger load factors were good, even great in some instances, so when a leasing company executive representing the Shorts 360 aircraft, a thirty-six-seat propjet, approached me, I took the bait and agreed to a lease of five of those aircraft.

The Anniston to Atlanta route should have been profitable due to the government subsidy, but with only one aircraft up in Georgia, the reliability factor suffered. To support that route, with no backup aircraft, we spent a lot of money transporting parts using our only remaining Cessna for overnight maintenance support. Even with the government subsidy, it was a loser.

I had two choices: shut down the Anniston operation, or expand to include several other rather large cities in the southeast and move four aircraft to that area and set up a division there.

The answer was simple. In keeping with our philosophy of pulling out of markets that were not profitable, I should have cancelled the route. But, with all of my super successes that I kept reading about, I chose to expand into Mobile, New Orleans, Montgomery, and Columbus. We would connect to Atlanta and to our Tampa hub, and sit back and enjoy an expected success in these markets.

We opened these new markets in October to great fanfare in the press. "See, I told you so," I told myself. I was still believing my press clippings.

While watching the great southeast expansion, I managed to certify the new larger aircraft. This was quite a chore. There were a lot of additional items to attend to. The FAA certification required that we operate under a different set of rules called FAR 121, the same rules that the larger airlines worked under. Our dispatchers needed to be licensed, and we had to set up a new division within our company for the management of flight attendants. My staff did a remarkable job, led by Captain Jim Taylor and Captain Don Davidson, Jr.

On October 1, we began service in the Shorts 360 thirty-six-seat turboprop, with service from Miami to Key West, Tampa, and Orlando.

Thanks to the efforts of Tony Gattone, the new aircraft sported paint jobs depicting palm trees and dolphins. He had contracted with Sandals Resorts in Nassau and the Grand Bahama Company in Freeport to advertise those destinations on the side of our aircraft. They paid for the original paint job and also a monthly fee for advertising. Tony got Gulfstream nationwide publicity coverage with that scheme.

With the disaster that was developing with the southeastern routes not fully manifesting themselves, as I still believed my press clippings, another issue had slowly developed over the past several years.

CHAPTER 80

Aviation Insurance

Simply complex

ONE OF OUR LARGEST EXPENSES was insurance, and with the advent of more and more aircraft, our insurance costs were rising at an alarming rate.

The way insurance works, at least in the airline business, is that an airline company hires an agency to negotiate on its behalf in arranging for the total insurance package with the underwriters. An underwriter is actually the company that insures you. The airline signs a contract with the agency—an "Agency of Record Letter—" that allows only that agency to bargain with the underwriters.

When an airline grows to a level whereby one underwriter cannot or will not insure the whole airline, then the agency approaches a number of other underwriters, and each one usually takes a portion to complete the total insurance package.

I had been using a small agency in Atlanta ever since I was a one-airplane airline carrier, and over the past four years, the agency had gradually increased my rates according to my growing fleet size. Over the years, when cash was low, the agency would allow me to delay payments over an extended three-month period. This was convenient for cash flow purposes, and I was prepared to continue that arrangement into March of 1996.

I was shocked when I received a letter from that insurance agency alerting me that I should expect a total insurance bill for 1996 of approximately 1.4 million dollars.

I had been attending the Regional Airline Association conventions for the past two years and had made some friends in the industry. We shared experiences and I discovered that, for my fleet size, I was being grossly overcharged. In talking to other airline presidents, I realized my estimated cost should be $700,000 to $800,000.

I decided to hold a "beauty contest." In the industry that's what they call a series of meetings between the airline and insurance agencies, whereby the airlines determine who they will hire to represent them with underwriters.

Time was running out for me. Gulfstream's policy was due for renewal in mid-December, and it was already early December. My current outstanding balance to the agency was approximately $200,000, which I expected to pay in the first quarter of 1996, with our mutual understanding.

A meeting was set with an agency called Sedgwick. Their representative, Mr. Kevin Life, arrived for the meeting and immediately pointed out that I shouldn't be paying more than $800,000, if that. If I signed the Agency of Record Letter with him, we could immediately fly to London and Paris and put a new package together for a major savings for the company.

I immediately liked Kevin, and although I really hated to leave my current agency, for half a million dollars, I had no choice. I didn't have the $200,000 to pay off the current liability with that agency, but I would be able to pay it off under the existing gentleman's agreement that we had made a handshake on. It would be paid by the end of March '96.

And, after all, the owner of that agency would understand, I rationalized. Hadn't we been doing business for the past five years? I was sure he'd want what was best for the company.

With that happy thought in mind, I signed the Agency of Record Letter with Sedgwick. Betty got me a pass on British Airways to London, and Kevin set up a series of meetings with the underwriters there. In a couple of days we were strapped inside a British Airways 747 on our way to London.

The Mayfair Hotel was wonderful. It was a throwback to the early days of the century. The days when tea was served in the lobby in the afternoon, and cigars were allowed in the bar in the evenings.

It was my first visit to London and I immediately fell in love with her. We dined around the corner at Langdon's, recovered from jet lag with a few martinis, and went to bed early in preparation for our round of meetings the next day.

As I fell asleep, I felt comfortable that, with all our successes, growth rate, professional reports, and newspaper clippings, we would be received with open arms, and the insurance underwriters would clamor for our business.

I slept soundly.

It would be three nights before I slept restfully again.

With black suit, to look businesslike, and red tie to look powerful, I met Kevin in the lobby and off we went to our first meeting.

We were ushered into a small meeting room and offered coffee. Before long a representative presented himself and asked Kevin to come outside for a chat.

It was about fifteen minutes before Kevin returned. He had a piece of paper in his hand—a telex from my former insurance agent—and it was crushing. Although I figured that he wouldn't be pleased at losing me as a customer, I didn't think he would stoop to this.

The telex was addressed to every underwriter in London and read, *You will probably be visited by a Mr. Thomas Cooper, President of Gulfstream International Airlines, to petition you to underwrite his insurance policy. Please be advised that Mr. Cooper owes this agency approximately $200,000 and has made no offer to pay before his policy ends on December 16th and we have no hope to recover if your company allows renewals through Sedgwick Agency.*

I gave the representative my side of the story, but I got the answer that I half expected. "Sorry, but we'll have to get back to you."

It was the same at the next meeting, and the next, and the next. It was beginning to look hopeless.

It was noon on Wednesday, December 13th, and I had until Friday at midnight to get this mess sorted out or else I'd have to shut the airline down due to lack of insurance.

Kevin had a lunch meeting set up with an underwriting company named British Aviation Insurance Group, BAIG, in their offices. A pleasant gentleman whom Kevin knew well met us. His name was Rod Dampier and he was their senior underwriter. He was a big deal. He was small in stature, but had the air of a giant. He graciously introduced us around the table to his colleagues, and we began our defense, as we knew that they had received the telex.

We had embarked on this trip with the thought that we would be positively recounting the successes and progress we had made, but we found ourselves spending our time defending the reason for the change of agency.

The lunch went okay, and we finally got to the part of the conversation concerning reliability, safety, and professionalism of the airline. That part of the conversation, though stuffy, was going well when one of the associates asked me, "Mr. Cooper, what do you plan to do if you can't get your insurance renewed?"

I had no idea how to answer the question. I had vaguely begun to plan an orderly shutdown of the operation, but I certainly wasn't going to outline that plan here.

From somewhere in the back of my mind—and being surrounded by men with that wonderful British accent—I remembered a line from a popular British sitcom called *Black Adder* that I had watched and of which I was a large fan.

"I have a cunning plan," I said confidently.

The associate laughed out loud. "That sounds exactly like Baldrick in the *Black Adder*."

We both laughed as I explained that the *Black Adder* was my favorite TV show back in the States and that my second favorite was *Keeping up Appearances*. Everyone was getting into the game now. Another executive across the table chimed in, "It's Bouquet, not Bucket," imitating the star of the show with her classic denial of her name.

Luckily, I was a fan of almost every British sitcom, and we all began to reminisce about our favorite shows. "Don't forget, 'Are you being served,'" I added, which unleashed another round of guffaws as some of the favorite lines were remembered around the table.

I could see that Rod was enjoying the comedic respite, but his time was short. He took one look at his watch, smiled, and indicated that he must depart.

Kevin made one last plea for our case, and Rod finished the meeting with a surprise announcement.

"We'll take the same percent of the policy that you have with us now with one caveat," he said, "that you promise to pay the existing bill to your old company during the time frame that you promised."

"I promise," I agreed as everyone rose to leave. "And thank you very much."

Kevin broke in with one last request, knowing Rod Dampier's reputation in the insurance community. "Rod," he pleaded, "will you make some calls for us?"

"I will." He shook hands and turned and disappeared down the hallway.

Could it be that I was saved by the British sitcoms? I'm sure of it.

The meetings in the afternoon went better than the morning meetings, thanks to Rod's calls, and our policy was beginning to fill up. Kevin made some calls to the underwriters who had not been too receptive earlier in the day, and they all came around, some not as high a percentage as we had hoped, but we were nearing our goal in London.

I spent a restless night as I prepared for the next day's activity. We had a few meetings with the London underwriters set for the morning and then we were scheduled to take the "Chunnel" to Paris, the high-speed train that travels under the English Channel.

We were reasonably successful with the morning meetings and soon were on the train to Paris. We expected the same reception in Paris and were prepared for it. What we were not prepared for was a major transportation strike.

We arrived at the Gare du Nord train station at dusk and walked outside to hail a taxi.

No luck. The city was gridlocked.

Kevin was familiar with the town, so we grabbed our bags and started walking toward the bed-and-breakfast he had rented for the night. We had an early day ahead of us and who knew what problems we would face, not only from the telex but also from the transportation strike?

With Paris literally shut down by the strike, it would be impossible to meet our schedules, even if the underwriters were there. Kevin got on the phone and, with the cooperation of some of the underwriters, partially solved the problem.

We would walk to the International Grand Hotel near the Opera House, and they would meet us there in the lobby. The only mode of transportation remaining in Paris was personal motor scooters and bicycles, and the underwriters would use those to meet us.

To further compound matters, Paris was suffering through a record-setting cold spell and the weather was miserable. Our pre-set meetings in the hotel lobby were delayed; some cancelled at the last minute.

We weren't as well received in Paris as in London. I suppose Rod's influence wasn't as effective here. We did achieve some agreements from sympathetic underwriters, but not enough to fill our policy. By Kevin's count, we had about 96 percent, with no more underwriters to visit.

Time was running out. I began to panic. We were in Paris, it was ungodly cold, and we needed to get back to London to revisit the markets in hopes of loosening up another 4 percent to fill our policy. We had a three o'clock reservation on the Chunnel. It was two o'clock in the afternoon when we began our walk to Gare du Nord train station.

It was cold and snowing. The streets were crowded, and my suitcase was heavy. We pushed on to make our three o'clock train.

We arrived at 2:45.

The trains were not running due to the strike.

We were done.

It was three o'clock in the afternoon in Paris. It was nine o'clock in the morning in Miami. I had fifteen hours left to either figure something out or shut the airline down.

We ducked into a bar inside the train station, and while Kevin made some calls, I called my chief operating officer and gave him the story. "Go to the airport and quietly set up a shutdown scenario for midnight. We'll talk in a few hours."

At that moment, a terrific explosion shook the windows. "What was that?" the COO exclaimed.

"I think the strikers just blew up a train, but don't worry," I assured him. "It didn't damage the bar." Humor was helpful at a time like this. "I'll call you in a couple of hours."

Kevin was feverishly making calls, but to no avail. While he made his calls, I watched the action on the tracks. From time to time a train would depart, apparently operated by British crews. We decided that we must get to London at all cost, so we headed to the holding area to attempt to wedge onto any London train.

With Kevin running interference and me following closely behind, we managed to work ourselves onto a train bound for London.

It was 8:00 p.m. in Paris and we would arrive in London at 9:20 local time in the evening. That would be 4:20 in the afternoon in Miami. I had set a time limit to commence operation shutdown for 5:00 p.m. Miami time and left word that I would give the command from London.

The plan was simple. Since we would have no insurance after midnight, it was necessary to return all the aircraft to Miami before then. If we gave the order to shut down the operation at five o'clock, we would have time to muster the crews and head toward Miami with enough time for the ferry flights.

This was a disaster. I was in a tunnel 250 feet under the English Channel while my company was being shut down in Miami. I was silent. Kevin was silent.

The few cocktails on board the Chunnel didn't dull the pain as the train began its deceleration into London's St. Pancras station.

It was 7:20 p.m. local time and in Miami it was 4:20 in the afternoon, forty minutes till doomsday.

We left the train and headed toward the nearest pay phone. I got there first and was resolved to call Miami and pull the plug on the airline, but Kevin, the eternal optimist, asked to use it first, "Just in case my office in New York came up with anything."

His conversation became animated. I couldn't make out what was going on until he turned, and with a huge grin and a fist pump thrust into the air exclaimed, "They got it done in New York!"

I called Miami operations. I got the chief operating officer on the phone, and the line was dead silent. He didn't want to hear what he was afraid he was going to hear.

"Call off operation shutdown," I said matter-of-factly. "We just got our insurance renewed."

When we finally got to our quarters in Sedgwick's private townhouse, we found that there were no bars open at that hour from which to celebrate. Kevin, ever resourceful, knew of a gentleman's club nearby where, for an initiation fee, we could join and enjoy some cocktails.

Kevin failed to mention that there were also ladies there for entertainment.

"No, ma'am," I said. "Just bring me a double martini. I've had enough fun for one night."

My last thought, as I lay exhausted in the bed, was, *will this roller-coaster ride never end?*

Two weeks later, we celebrated a banner year, having flown over 360,000 passengers and exceeded twenty-two million dollars in gross revenues.

CHAPTER 81

Five Years

*The company has survived and so has
the union grudge.*

The year 1996 began with great promise, and I was to be on a terrific ego trip.

Aviation International News, a well-respected worldwide publication, selected me as one of the "1995 Top Ten Newsmakers."

Their premise was that airline pilots make lousy businessmen, especially in the aviation industry, and the magazine featured me as an exception. They ran a flattering article with a review of Gulfstream's history and what our plans were for the future. I had to order all my hats a size larger.

My forecasts and prognostications were not always on target.

Tony Gattone came to me with a proposal. "I call it Sun-Pac," he explained with a proud smile. "We'll package ten round trips between any two city pairs on our system, plus, we'll throw in three additional round trips as a bonus. They'll be interchangeable between customers, and we'll offer 'Mileage Plus', United Airlines miles. It'll sell like hot cakes to businessmen and folks who have their boats in the Bahamas for the summer."

"Okay," I humored him, "we'll see how it goes." I immediately discarded the program and forgot about it completely.

Six months later, Tony stopped by my office and asked if I had been watching the Sun-Pac sales lately.

"I know that the reservations department has sold a few," I said, "but I can't say I have watched the numbers that closely."

"We just topped half a million dollars in sales, and it's growing," he crowed as he turned and left my office.

I resolved to pay more attention to Tony's ideas in the future.

It was in the spring that my son, Tommy, joined the firm. He had graduated from Stetson School of Law a few years earlier and had worked briefly as a junior member at a law firm. It wasn't his cup of tea, so he rebelled and joined the fast food chain of Chili's, not as a lawyer, but as a waiter. When I questioned that career move, he shrugged his shoulders and said, "I make more money at Chili's." I couldn't argue with that.

I assigned him an office and gave him the directions to the nearest used office furniture store. He set up shop and was an instant success, both in offering his legal services to our more than five hundred employees and, as he liked to say, "keeping Dad out of jail."

In April, the old ALPA pilot union curse reared its ugly head again.

In the airline industry, during that time, it was a common courtesy for airlines to exchange jump seat privileges—the use of the observer seat in the cockpit to other pilots employed by other legitimate airlines. Gulfstream had become a major regional airline, and as such, its pilots enjoyed jump seat privileges on all the other carriers.

Gulfstream now had over a hundred pilots, and the supply of local ex-Eastern pilots had long since been depleted. We now employed pilots from all over the United States, and consequently, on vacations and extended days off, they would understandably travel to their hometown, taking advantage of the mutual jump seat arrangement between airlines.

I was visited, one afternoon, by one of my captains. He was highly upset as he had been denied jump seat privilege on a United Airlines flight. It wasn't so much that he had been denied, it was the way the captain of the flight treated him.

As a former captain for a major airline, I knew the sensitivity surrounding the use of the jump seat. I had established a short course for my pilots during their indoctrination ground school that taught the proper protocol. The pilots would approach the flight captain and produce their ID badge, introduce themselves, and ask politely, "Sir, may I occupy your jump seat today?"

This pilot went through the usual protocol, and when he offered his ID to the captain, he was surprised at the insults that spewed from his mouth.

"You work for that scab Cooper?" he exclaimed rudely. "Nobody who works for that lowlife will ever fly in my cockpit! Now kindly leave my cockpit and don't ever let me see you around here again!"

My pilot related that the captain was still ranting and raving as he ran for the safety of the terminal.

"I'll fix that," I vowed to my pilot. "I'll get back to you shortly."

I was upset, but I knew exactly what to do. The last thing I wanted to do was to call United Airlines in Chicago and upset our new code share relationship. I could handle this locally.

I asked Betty to send out an email to all stations. "Effective immediately, no United Airlines pilot will be allowed jump seat privileges on any Gulfstream flight," and I sat back and waited for the call I was sure that I was going to get.

Gulfstream, over the last two years, had established itself as the major link between Orlando and Miami with eight flights daily, far more than anyone else. We literally operated a shuttle from 7:00 a.m. till 10:00 p.m.

I had observed that there were a number of United Airlines pilots using the jump seat procedure on our service to commute from their homes in Orlando to their base in Miami for their scheduled flight assignments. It was not unusual to have several United pilots on one flight, and we always welcomed them with courtesy.

It was the next morning when the first call came—from our station manager in Miami, who had a major problem at the gate. The first United pilot had shown up for his jump seat flight home to Orlando, and he was denied boarding. I could hear him yelling at our manager and I asked to speak to him.

I was very calm. "Hi Captain, I'm Tom Cooper, the owner of Gulfstream. How can I help you?"

"I've been commuting for a year on this flight, and all of a sudden I've been denied boarding," he nearly shouted. "I'm going to report this to my chief pilot, and you guys will hear from him!"

Boy, he was upset.

"Well, maybe that's a good idea," I agreed calmly with him. "Your captains have started denying our pilots the jump seat on your flights, and I'm sorry, but I have to reply in kind. Now, Captain," I added apologetically, "I'm going to allow you on the flight, as I know it's important that you get home to your family, but you're the last jump seat that I am going to authorize, so I'd appreciate it if you would spread the word to your fellow pilots so as to avoid further embarrassment at our gates in the future."

It wasn't five minutes until Betty buzzed me. "Tom, I have the chief pilot for United Airlines in Miami asking for you."

It was about the nicest phone call that I had ever received. "Captain Cooper," he purred, "thanks for taking my call."

"Yes, sir," I answered, "and what can I help you with, Captain?" We were now speaking captain to captain.

"I understand that we had a little misunderstanding at your gate this morning," he began, cautiously selecting his words. "I'm sure that you and I can work this out. Can you share with me just what prompted this change in your policy toward us?"

I gave him the story and the flight number and the date of our pilot's denied jump seat.

The United chief pilot asked for a few seconds; I heard him punching at his desktop computer. "Oh yes," he acknowledged. "That captain is rather a, shall we say, hothead, and this is not the first time I've gotten stories about him."

"I understand, sir."

"What can I do to make this right and return to our old policies?"

"Well, Captain," I replied, "I suppose the ball is in your court. You could send out a memo to all stations and to your pilots clarifying United's jump seat policy with Gulfstream. I can give a copy to each of my pilots just in case one of your captains might have missed your memo."

"I can and will do that, and can you do the same?"

"I'll be glad to," I agreed. "And one more thing, " I added, "please send a copy of your letter to the pilots' union chief and copy me at the bottom."

I wanted the union chief, and the rogue pilot, to know that I had a copy.

He laughed knowingly. "Done," he said.

The great jump seat caper was over with no casualties, except maybe the rude captain's rogue jump seat policy toward Gulfstream's pilots.

CHAPTER 82
Tea with Tom

And the Florida Panthers' great rat saga

I STARTED A PROGRAM IN the summer of '96 called "Tea with Tom." We had grown to over five hundred employees, and I feared that I was becoming too distant from the rank-and-file members of our company.

I would reserve a private room at a local restaurant for lunch. We would invite one member from each department: flight operations, maintenance, stations, administrations, records, accounting, and a representative from the Bahamas, along with one of my fellow executives.

We would be seated around a long table with the guest executive at the far end from me. The only formal aspect of the meeting was at the beginning, when I would ask each to give a brief bio of themselves. After that, the lunch became an informal discussion of anything that the guests wanted to talk about.

The lunch was a wonderful place to dispel rumors and to emphasize management's dedication to, not only the company, but to the individual employees. Those positive ideas would be taken back to the various departments and, with the airline's grapevine rumor mill, spread like wildfire.

On more than one occasion, I received reports from guests returning to their departments bragging with comments like, "Well, I had lunch with the 'ole man' yesterday. He told me some stuff that…"

The lunch was personal, but the message spread companywide.

"Tea with Tom" was a semi-formal lunch, but it wasn't the only social gathering we had at Gulfstream. There developed, quite by accident, another meeting that was held every Friday evening with my managers, called, "Get

Tanked with Tom." We didn't really get tanked, but one of the wives labeled it such, and the name stuck. I kept an ample supply of Cuban rum on hand—Havana Club—and we put it to good use at that function.

Just as management shared our innermost secrets with the employees at Tea with Tom, I learned more about the company at Get Tanked with Tom from my managers than I sometimes cared to know. After a few shots of rum, my managers would loosen up, and the gossip and the stories were sometimes wild.

We were all loosened up a bit one night in particular, and we were all getting excited about the Miami hockey team, the Panthers. They were barely three years old and suddenly they were in the running for the Stanley Cup playoffs. They had won the first round by defeating the Boston Bruins and the second round by beating the Philadelphia Flyers. The whole town was excited and, at the Friday night Get Tanked with Tom social, we were no exception.

To add to the excitement, the mascot for the Panthers was a rat. It seems that earlier in the season, a rat had run across the Panthers' locker room floor, and, unfortunately for the rat, one of the players dispatched him with his hockey stick against the wall, resulting in his untimely death. Later in the game, that player scored two goals, and the legend began. Fans began to bring rubber rats to the games in increasing numbers, and with the Panthers' success in the playoffs, the plastic rat was the most popular souvenir sale item in Miami.

I got caught up in the excitement of the playoffs, the rat, and the prospects of the Panthers reaching the Stanley Cup finals. In a bit of alcohol-induced bravado, I exclaimed, "If the Panthers reach the Stanley Cup finals, I'll personally paint a rat on the side of one of our aircraft!"

I had forgotten that I had made that vow until, when the Panthers defeated the Pittsburg Penguins a week later and the big news splashed across the front page of the *Miami Herald*…PANTHERS ADVANCE TO THE STANLEY CUP PLAYOFFS!

Unfortunately for me, one of my senior executives had a girlfriend who worked for a local TV station. He had relayed my misguided bluster to her, and she in turn, told her manager, and now they were on their way to our hangar to film my proposed artwork.

There was no backing out now.

"Betty," I screamed. "Help! I need a picture of a rat and some black paint and some paintbrushes."

She dispatched someone to the local hardware for some black paint and the smallest paintbrush they could find. We began to look for a picture of a rat. We had no luck until she found a small, one-inch picture of a rat in her dictionary.

"Good enough," I said. I grabbed a copy from the copy machine and headed for the hangar.

We had just received a newly leased aircraft that had not yet been painted, and luckily, it was in the hangar. I pulled a work stand over to the airplane and began to size up the drawing area.

The paint and the TV crews arrived at about the same time, and before I knew it, I was painting a big, fat black rat on the side of our new airplane.

The red eyes made it look fierce, and to polish off the work of art, I inscribed in large letters, "GO PANTHERS" on the side of the fuselage!

The report was carried on the TV channel, the newspapers picked it up, and someone said it was on ESPN. I suppose that was so because we got calls from all across the country.

The artwork, whose genesis was at a Get Tanked with Tom gathering, gained Gulfstream and the artist great fame, but unfortunately, it did nothing for the Panthers…they lost the playoffs to the Colorado Avalanche the next week.

CHAPTER 83

The Highs and Lows Continue

"Our chief pilot goes with Sir Freddy.

As celebrated as I had become, in the airline business, there is always something that can bring you back to earth, and quickly. My come-back-to-earth moment came, not in a moment, but over a six-month period.

The southeast expansion had not gone well. Try as we might—discounted tickets, juggling schedules, and increased advertising—nothing worked. The customers we had projected stayed away in droves. The losses were killing us and there was nothing I could do but swallow my pride and pull the plug.

The great Mr. Top Ten in 1995 and the Michelangelo of the aviation industry tucked his tail like a whipped dog and retreated to Florida.

Where he belonged.

As miserable as I was, Tony Gattone was soaring. He had us recognized around the state at every function, and his Sun-Pac sales were breaking records every month. We gained great prestige by sponsoring the Special Olympics, and the Miss Florida Contest spread our name statewide through the TV coverage.

The State of Florida traditionally contracted with major airlines for state-sponsored travel for employees on state business. Tony became aware of this and went immediately to Tallahassee, our state capital, to petition for the contract. To my surprise and delight, he came home with it, and the results immediately impacted our loads, especially on the routes between Tallahassee, Tampa, and Miami.

As luck would have it, the additional aircraft that we retrieved from the disastrous venture into the southeast came in handy as we increased our schedules over the busiest routes, and the additional flying absorbed the surplus aircraft.

The money we lost in the southeast venture we could make back, but there were some losses that hurt. This particular loss began with Betty buzzing me, "Tom, there's a Sir Freddy Laker on the phone for you."

Sir Freddy Laker, the British aviation icon, and I had recently become friends in a most peculiar way. My wife and I had been visiting Georgetown in the Bahamas for a regatta sailing competition when I accidently met him at the bar at the Peace and Plenty Resort. We hit it off pretty well as we passed the time of day over a gin and tonic. When he left, he invited Jerrie and me for cocktails, and to meet his wife on his yacht, *Lady Jacqueline*, later that afternoon.

We arrived at the appointed time. He met us on the gangplank and invited us in.

"Dear, this is Mr. and Mrs. Cooper," he introduced us graciously to his wife with his very proper English dialect. "And," he motioned with a nod, "this is my wife Jacqueline."

Surprisingly, Jacqueline rushed over, gave me a big hug, and we both began to laugh. I had known her earlier as Jackie Harvey, when she had been a flight attendant with Eastern before she had met Sir Freddy. We had flown together many times and were on a first-name basis. The coincidence was one of those "small-world" moments.

From that moment on, Sir Freddy and I bonded. We exchanged war stories, but my rag to riches commuter stories couldn't stand up to his big airline tales. Even so, he always recognized me publicly at any meeting or convention that we found ourselves attending, and he would always have me stand and he would acknowledge my achievements.

What could Sir Freddy want? I thought as I picked up the phone.

"Good afternoon, Tom," he said in his very identifiable British accent.

"Hi, Sir Freddy," I said. "What can I help you with?"

"This is a terrible call, but I am forced to make it," he said quite distressed. "As you know, I've started a new airline between Ft. Lauderdale and London, and we're hiring some pilots."

"Yes, Sir Freddy, I'm aware of that."

"Well, we have an application from one of your employees. This is painful, but I have to inquire of you if it's okay if we hire him as a pilot. If you have the slightest objection, I'll just reject him, no damage done," he added.

"No, Sir Freddy, we lose pilots all the time. I take great satisfaction in seeing my pilots move up the aviation ladder, and a move to your organization would make me very proud," I said.

"That's a great relief," he said as he breathed a sigh.

"May I ask who the pilot is?"

"It's a chap that's been with you for quite some time." I could hear him fumbling through some papers. "A Mr. Taylor, James Taylor."

My heart sank. Jim Taylor, my most senior pilot and the chief pilot to boot. We had been through thick and thin together, and he was my most reliable pilot. I could snuff this now, with one word to Sir Freddy, but that wouldn't be fair to Jim.

"That's great, Sir Freddy, he's a good man and a better pilot," I said with some enthusiasm. "He's a good family man, and I know his wife will be pleased to see him move up."

There were a few more seconds of small talk, and he excused himself and rang off.

Two days later, Jim came in with a long face and gave me the bad news.

I never let on that I already knew.

CHAPTER 84
Continental Connection

But the ups and downs continue

IN LATE '96, A SMALL Florida commuter by the name of GP Express, with a commuter relationship with Continental Airlines, ceased operations. They had moved into the Florida market a year earlier, but their route system was too spread out, resulting in the carrier declaring bankruptcy and closing down.

I perceived a void in the Florida area for connecting flights with Continental Airlines, so I called them in late winter. As the year ended, we had begun serious talks toward the establishment of Gulfstream as their connection in Florida and the Bahamas.

Miami International Airport came out with their 1996 statistics, and Gulfstream had moved into second place in terms of airplane movements, takeoffs, and landings, right after the combination of American Airlines and American Eagle. We'd come a long way in five years, when we had to "borrow" an unused counter from some unsuspecting South American airline three times a week.

In spite of my miscalculations in the southeast routes, we ended the year in pretty good shape.

Systemwide, we had an average of 120 flights departing daily, and we grossed forty-five million dollars for the year. Our fleet at the year's end consisted of sixteen Beechcraft 1900s and five Short 360s.

As we welcomed 1997, I was still looking for a closer relationship, and the Continental negotiations were moving along quite well. To my absolute delight we signed a marketing agreement in late January as a "Continental Connection" and began to prepare for that operation to commence in April.

Continental Airlines had been the doormat of scheduled airlines for the past decade. Although it had been a leader in the industry years earlier, under the leadership of Bob Six, recently it had deteriorated to the position of absolute last place in airline standings. That was before Gordon Bethune took over as president and chief operating officer in 1994. Losing over fifty million dollars a year and on the verge of filing for bankruptcy for the third time in the last ten years, the airline was turned around in record time by Gordon, with his communication and organizational skills. Within a couple of years, it was the darling of the industry.

Continental was flying high, and I was excited to hitch Gulfstream onto their rising star.

Over the past year we had streamlined our schedule by trimming some of the non-producing cities. We had established satellite flight crew bases in Key West, Tampa, and West Palm Beach. In some of our larger markets, we were practically running hourly shuttle service. Our reliability was excellent, and that was reflected in the additional customers we were boarding.

In June, I received a shocking visit from Vic and Bill, the two men who ran Avtar. "We're leaving South Florida. We're broke and there are some dissatisfied students who are threatening to sue us, so we're closing up," they chimed in together.

"Betty," I called out, "get Tommy in here quick."

This was a serious problem. We had extended credit to Avtar for some students who were about halfway through their course, and now Avtar wouldn't be paying for the balance of their training. Also, there was a class due to begin in about a week, and all those students had paid Avtar in advance.

"We're leaving right now," they said, sliding the keys over to me, "so if you need anything from our office you'd better get it now. The manager of the building has orders to evict us tomorrow."

I looked at Tommy and he looked at me. My mind was racing. We had to be careful not to appear to be taking over Avtar. We had heard that they were using other airline companies for the same program, and the rumor mill had it that the other airlines were not as sophisticated as Gulfstream. There was a lot of dissatisfaction out there with the other programs, and there would be liabilities going forward.

I knew that I wanted to keep the program, but to keep it in house. Further, I knew that Avtar had bought several townhouses in Miami Springs and Key West to house their students. We had to maintain those residences. The only other asset was their phone number. They had advertised worldwide in all the popular magazines. As a result, phone calls representing potential students would continue to come in.

Tommy worked out a quick agreement to have the apartments assigned to a separate corporation. We gave Bill and Vic three hundred dollars for the rights to the phone number, and they said good-bye.

We quickly formed a separate corporation, Gulfstream Training Academy, leased a small office on 36th Street, and had the phones transferred there. A quick visit to the used office furniture shop, and we were in business.

"Who's going to run this thing, Dad?" Tommy asked.

"You are, of course," I replied.

Actually, he organized the company pretty well. He hired one salesperson and kept an eye on the school as it grew.

I knew that if we interrupted the current students for nonpayment, the publicity would be devastating. So we continued their training, uninterrupted, and welcomed the new class, although we never got paid a cent for their training.

No one ever missed Avtar, no one ever knew the story, and no one ever saw me sweat.

The one nagging issue that began to eat at me was the practicality of the Shorts 360 aircraft. Yes, it carried more people, but it was slow and, being unpressurized, it couldn't operate above ten thousand feet, unlike the smaller, faster Beechcraft 1900, which could operate at twenty-five thousand feet.

Customer dissatisfaction grew, as the pilots couldn't fly over the summer thunderstorms in Florida. The pilots, under my instructions, were not allowed to penetrate heavy areas of bad weather. This resulted in long delays or additional flying time added to the flights as the crews circumnavigated around storm areas.

In preparation for the Continental Connection launch, I made a decision to begin to return the Shorts to the lessor. It was my intent to standardize the fleet with Beechcraft 1900s as soon as possible.

At first the return discussions went well. The lessor had customers for two aircraft, and we began to return the Shorts on schedule; the first one went in April and the second in May. We agreed to revisit the return issue and keep three Shorts until, at least, spring of '98.

The Continental Connection launch went well, and we began to enjoy, almost immediately, increased passenger loads. One issue that we had not planned on was the interruption in cash flow. Under the new agreement, Continental collected all the tickets and cash and remitted to us after the clearing house settled with them.

As we worked through this, Continental would later advance us money interest free if we experienced serious cash flow difficulties. It was a five-million-dollar problem, and some of our creditors had to simply wait for payment. Most understood, but some didn't.

The Shorts 360 lessor didn't. Although we explained the shortfall we were temporarily experiencing, they refused to cooperate and wait for two weeks for full payment.

It was a Sunday night in mid-August when I got the call from dispatch. "Mr. Cooper, someone stole all three of our Shorts tonight!"

I knew right away what the answer was. The lessor had repossessed the remaining three Shorts.

"I'll be right out," I said and I headed for my car.

Along with the embarrassment of having three aircraft repossessed, the issue now was passenger inconvenience.

I was pretty good at reacting to impossible situations, and as I drove to the airport, I remembered six years earlier when I made the same drive after the sabotage of two-thirds of our fleet. This would be easier, and I was happy to be rid of the last three Shorts.

The brutal truth was that if the lessor had simply asked for the aircraft back, I could have saved him a lot of trouble. I was told later that the customer who took the first two aircraft suddenly needed the other three immediately, thus the subterfuge.

The head of the scheduling department was already there when I arrived. We put our reserve aircraft into service, combined a few flights, alerted the crews to the schedule change, and when the sun came up Monday morning, Gulfstream had the appearance of normality.

We still needed to replace the missing three aircraft. I remembered that an old friend, Doug Voss, the president of Great Lakes Aviation, a similar commuter airline, had some surplus 1900s available. A quick call to him and there were three Beechcraft 1900s en route to Miami by noon. They were in excellent shape, and by Thursday we were flying 100 percent of our original schedule, and with a fully standardized fleet of Beechcraft 1900 aircraft.

The roller-coaster ride continued, but the peaks were not so high and the valleys not so low.

Surely, 1998 would be better with no drama and no surprises.

I was a slow learner.

The first five months of '98 were routine. I was lulled into a false sense of security as everything was going smoothly. And then I had an interesting dinner with my insurance agent, Kevin Life.

"Cooper," he said as we enjoyed a couple of martinis, "I've got a deal for you. I've got a client in Ft. Lauderdale that owns an airline, and he's in trouble with it. He's an absentee manager, and I think he'll sell. It's Paradise Island Airlines."

I knew what Paradise Island Airlines was. It was a "one trick" pony show operating only between Ft. Lauderdale and Paradise Island, a resort just across the harbor from Nassau. They operated four large four-engine turboprop aircraft with the capacity of fifty passengers each, and the airline had a terrible reputation.

I protested and allowed that Gulfstream was doing well now, the money was sufficient to keep the stomach ulcers away, and the Continental arrangement was great. I didn't want to upset the apple cart.

He argued for a while and gave up with, "Okay, but if you change your mind, here's Bobby Fessler's phone number," and he slid a calling card across the table to me.

I went to sleep that night thinking about the deal. Kevin was quite persuasive. Paradise Island Airlines did have some assets: a hangar at the Ft. Lauderdale airport, good route authority, and the four de Havilland Dash 7 aircraft that carried fifty passengers each.

I called Fessler the next day and set up an appointment. There's nothing wrong with just talking, right?

Wrong!

Within a month we had consummated a deal, and on July first we took over the management of Paradise Island Airlines. It was a decision that was to change the whole trajectory of my life.

Once I got involved in the operation, it was apparent to me that the scheduling person at Paradise Island Airlines was asking too much from the lumbering Dash 7s. They were designed to be STOL aircraft, not speed demons. The very acronym STOL stands for "Short Takeoff and Landing" aircraft. They had scheduled the flying time between Ft. Lauderdale and Paradise

Island far too short, and they had not allowed enough time at the gates for the ground crews to properly fuel and service the aircraft between legs.

Consequently, by the second round trip at 10:00 a.m., the airline was already running late, and it continued to operate later as the day went on. Their on-time performance was around 25 percent. As a result, customer satisfaction was at such a low level that none of the local passengers would book and fly on it, and the loads were atrocious.

The solution was easy. We added fifteen minutes to every flight leg and thirty minutes to each time that the aircraft was on the ground. We washed and restriped the aircraft, changed the carpets, and kept two aircraft as ready spares in case of a mechanical issue.

It was magic. The airline's schedule reliability jumped to over 96 percent, and the customers began to return. We added three round trips from Miami International Airport and two round trips from Palm Beach.

In a matter of a month, the whole complexion of the airline had changed.

With a "free" hangar in Ft. Lauderdale, we began to make plans to move the entire operation there.

In September, we sadly said good-bye to our Taj Mahal office building and the historic Pan Am hangar and moved into new offices across from the Paradise Island Airlines hangar, soon to be the Gulfstream hangar.

With very little effort, we increased our passenger loads by 25 percent with no appreciable increase in our fixed operating cost.

Kevin Life was correct; it was a good deal.

My luck continued.

I got a call from Cuba. Actually, it wasn't from Cuba, it was from Paris. It was from an old friend, Tony Vasquez, whom I had done business with in Havana in the late seventies. Back then he had been in charge of all fishing and water activities in Cuba, and now he was assigned to Paris as Havanatur's agent in France.

"Cooper." He spoke perfect English with hardly any accent. "Havanatur has a big problem in Havana. Two of the three U.S. agencies flying passengers to Cuba have been stopped by the U.S. government for some sort of violations, and we have people literally sleeping in the terminal trying to get out. I told the managers there that you could help them out."

"I think I can be of some service," I said. "How can I help?"

"We need airplanes now!" he exclaimed. "How soon can you get some aircraft to Havana, and with how many seats?"

"How about tomorrow, three trips at fifty seats each?" I suggested.

"I'll call you right back," and he hung up.

I called Paradise Island dispatch and asked how long it would take to scramble a crew for some Miami to Havana flying. They confirmed that we had crews available and would put them on standby status.

Tony called back within the hour and said, "It's all set." He gave me the name and the phone number of the agency and the manager who gives the landing permits in Cuba, a Mr. Brown, and requested that I give him my proposed schedule for the next week at the rate of three flights per day.

"And, oh yes, they would like you to come down on the first flight to discuss future arrangements. They'll pick you up at the airport," and he hung up.

I called one of my senior staff members, Pierre Galoppi, who spoke Spanish, and the next morning, at 8:00, we found ourselves taxiing out of the gate at Miami airport bound for Havana.

And just like that, we were back in business in Cuba.

I set up three round trips per day. The Customs and Immigrations department along with the Miami airport authority were very cooperative and gave me a designated gate and provided all security personnel to operate the operation.

With no hope in sight for the other two companies to resume operation any time soon, we felt good about the long-term business opportunities. In November, the Cuban authorities gave us authority to operate a leased Boeing 727 over the route, and we began that service on November 14th.

In November, we moved the training academy, Gulfstream's first officer program, to Ft. Lauderdale. We leased a facility at the nearby Ft. Lauderdale Executive Airport that had been recently abandoned by a major flight school. It was ideal for our purposes. Nestled behind a stand of stately palm trees, it measured nineteen thousand square feet, stood two stories tall, and with our newly designed logo proudly displayed on the façade, GULFSTREAM INTERNATIONAL AIRLINES WORLD TRAINING CENTER, it was very impressive.

On the second floor were thirty-five dormitory rooms that could accommodate seventy students, an exercise room, laundry facilities, and a canteen.

The first floor was perfect. There were three classrooms, two simulator bays, and six general administration offices. In the impressive reception area with vaulted ceiling hung a six-foot-wingspan model of the *Spirit of St. Louis*, Lindbergh's plane, which I had reclaimed from a wrecking crew that was refurbishing a restaurant at the Houston International Airport.

The academy, now under our control, was a success beyond our wildest imagination. The classes were filled three months in advance, and large commuter and major airlines alike were hiring our graduates, without exception, just as soon as they graduated.

As much as I would like to take the credit for the success of the first officer program and Gulfstream Training Academy, I cannot. From its inception, the chance meeting with the two flight school operators, through its growth, a lion's share of the credit goes to the staff and instructors. At all times, they maintained an air of professionalism that permeated the school and reflected well in the caliber of students we graduated.

Probably one of the more prominent aspects of the school was the semi-formal lunch held monthly for the new students. I had been holding it for several years, and it was nice—nothing outstanding, just nice.

And then one day, into my office walked a fully uniformed Continental Airlines captain. Our first officer lunch was about to change.

"Hello," he said, holding out his hand, "I'm Captain Rick Swanson. My son is enrolled in your first officer program and…"

Here we go, I thought as we shook hands. *He's gonna put the arm on me for a courtesy discount with that fellow captain stuff.*

"And," he continued as he sat down, "I just wanted to compliment you on your fine school."

I almost fell out of my chair. By now, in this business, I was conditioned only to hear complaints.

He continued with glowing accolades about the academy and finished with a request.

"I understand that you have a monthly lunch for new hire students, and I would like to participate in that program, if it's okay with you." He continued hurriedly, "I'll fly in at my own expense monthly if you approve my presentation."

I was dumbfounded at his generosity and accepted immediately.

As it turned out, his program was wonderful.

I had held the luncheon at a local hotel ever since the beginning of the first officer program, and it had evolved into quite a spectacle. The average class was sixteen to eighteen students, and they would all attend lunch in full airline uniform.

The tables were arranged, in the private dining room, in U shape with the students seated on either side of the U. I was seated along with the Vice President of Operations Captain Mike Vaughn and another randomly selected key company officer at the head of the U.

I would make a short speech and then ask each student to stand, give us his name, his background, and perhaps share his or her ambitions in the aviation business with the guests. The formal aspect of the lunch set the tone of professionalism and was well received by the students.

But when Captain Swanson came on board, the program took on an even greater air of professionalism.

Standing in front of the class, in full airline uniform, he was the epitome of their dreams and aspirations. His lecture, augmented with a meaningful PowerPoint presentation and coupled with his sensitive talk of the responsibilities of an airline captain, held the students and me spellbound.

Captain Swanson's apparent professionalism in the cockpit and the strong Christian influence in his personal life radiated out in his presentation, and even though I was privileged to observe it numerous times, I never tired of it.

And I always felt, as I left the lunch, that I was a better man for having heard him.

Captain Swanson never asked for a penny, not even for expenses. His only reward, I suppose—no, I *know*—was having the satisfaction of knowing that he had, in some way, helped a young person along in their chosen field of aviation....and their life.

He was one in a million, and I don't think I ever met anyone in this business as selfless and caring as Captain Swanson.

To top off the year, I was awarded the Edward V. Rickenbacker award by the Greater Miami Aviation Association for "Leadership in the Aviation Industry which has Contributed to the Economic Growth of South Florida."

As 1998 ended, the company was hitting on all eight cylinders.

The airline, with its two major airline code sharing partners, Continental and United, was going fantastic; Paradise Island Airlines was paying off like a slot machine; the Cuba charter operation had turned profitable; and the flight academy was booming.

Going into 1999, I kept telling myself, "Don't do anything stupid!"

That lasted for about a month.

It was February 10th. I was packing my briefcase to head to Havana for a meeting with Havanatur when the door to my office opened and in walked an old friend, Bill Jones, the president of Chalk's Airline, along with another gentleman.

We exchanged hellos and he introduced me to his friend, a lawyer, and explained that Chalk's had just declared bankruptcy and they needed some cash to make payroll.

It was their intention to remain in business, and once they were over this little hump, they would emerge from bankruptcy. The lawyer assured me that by advancing them money today, I would be the owner at that time. They needed $50,000 to make it through the week.

I was rushing to make my flight to Havana out of Miami, but the idea of owning Chalk's Airline, the oldest scheduled airline in the world, fascinated me. I also had visions of a seaplane route between downtown Miami into the Havana harbor.

I quickly agreed to advance them the money, and as I headed out of the door, I gave Betty instructions to cut them a check, give Tommy the fax number of the Nacional Hotel in Havana, create a short contract, have it signed by Bill, and get it to me in Havana. I would sign it there and fax it back. At that time she could release the check.

I arrived at the Nacional Hotel four hours later, and the fax was waiting for me at the desk. I signed it, faxed the signed copy back to Betty, and she released the check.

Chalk's made payroll and I was debtor in possession of Chalk's Airline.

Three days later I returned to Ft. Lauderdale to inspect my new toy.

Earlier in the year I had named Leo Krupilis as director of maintenance. He was working for Paradise Island Airlines when I acquired the company, and I had observed his attitude and professionalism. We had just lost our director of maintenance, so I put Leo in charge of that division of Gulfstream.

His resume had shown that he had worked for Chalk's earlier, so I called him to go with me to visit their operation.

"You did what?" He laughed as he came into my office.

I explained that I had bailed them out and that we would be running the place until it came out of bankruptcy and then we would own it.

"You must be crazy," he exclaimed. "Their maintenance is crap, their airplanes are crap, and the attitude of their employees is crap."

"Oh, Leo," I said, "it can't be that bad. Come on, let's go over and have a look."

He laughed again and away we went to the Chalk's operation located on the north side of Ft. Lauderdale airport.

Leo was right. He was more than right.

The hangar was a mess. The mechanics, only two, looked like they had just come out from under a bridge somewhere, and the parts department consisted of an old derelict airframe from which the mechanics would cannibalize parts, if they were lucky.

They had two seaplanes that were operational. One was flying and one was on the ramp in front of the hangar.

"Let's go look at that airplane," I suggested to Leo.

We walked out to the lone seaplane on the ramp, and I began to inspect it. I saw some bubbling under the paint on the side of the fuselage, and I suspected some minor corrosion. I scratched it lightly with my fingernail.

To my shock, my finger went through the side of the airplane.

"Leo," I shouted as he ran from the other side of the airplane, "I'm grounding the fleet immediately."

He laughed out loud. "I told you so."

"If you think that's funny," I said with a smile, "laugh at this. You're now in charge of this maintenance operation." As I headed back toward the hangar, I added, "Get some of your guys over here to clean this mess up, and give the two mechanics some expense money and send them to JCPenney's for a set of blue work clothes."

I went back to my office, called Bill Jones over, and gave him the new deal.

"Bill," I said, "you are still in charge, but you have to do it my way. Leo will be the temporary manager of the maintenance department. I've grounded the fleet and substituted our land-type aircraft, the Beechcraft 1900, over the routes. They can use the airport on South Bimini, and I have discontinued service to Walker's Cay. Move your passengers over from the seaplane base in Miami to Miami International terminal and use our counter and gates.

"We'll concentrate on inspecting and returning one seaplane to service for the time being. Once we get that one back up, we'll begin to work on the second," I added.

We didn't miss a beat. Our schedules were up and running the next morning, and within a few weeks, with reliable schedules and a more professional operation, the Chalk's Airline program would be another jewel in the Gulfstream crown.

But it wasn't to be. We were too successful. Within a few months we totally refurbished the two seaplanes, put them back into service, streamlined the schedule, and the airline was turning a profit.

When the airline emerged from bankruptcy in August, the lawyer's promise that we would certainly be the eventual owner did not materialize. We were outbid by a fellow Eastern pilot, Jim Confalone, on the courthouse steps for ownership of the airline. I was disappointed, but I should not have been.

It turned out to be the luckiest day of my life. Unfortunately, on December 19, 2005, on takeoff from the Miami Seaplane Base, a wing separated from the fuselage of one of their aircraft, resulting in a horrible crash—and that was the end of Chalk's Airline.

The loss of Chalk's wasn't the only disappointment I suffered that year.

In July, I was summoned to the office of Butch Kersner, the son of the owner of Atlantis, the resort on Paradise Island that owned the airport we used.

It was there that he gave me the bad news that they were going to close the airport and build condos and a golf course. All my reasoning fell on deaf ears, and I was given a date in August for the last flight.

I had no recourse but to redeploy the large, slow, four-engine STOL aircraft to the Nassau International airport until I could figure out what to do with them. What we had turned into a virtual gold mine was suddenly transposed into a giant liability in the shape of four unusable aircraft.

Almost simultaneously, in late August we were approached by TWA to open a base in San Juan and be their code-share partner there. From San Juan, they proposed that we connect to St. Maartin, St. Croix, St. Thomas, St. Kitts, and Tortola.

I looked at the proposal, studied the passenger load history in all the markets, and against my firm convictions that my expansion days were over, I agreed.

After all, what could go wrong? There were ample passengers, there was only one competitive airline, American Eagle, and we were promised the old abandoned Prinair hangar by the port authority located nearby across from the terminal. This would be easy. We'd just put our schedules in the Official Airline Guide, transfer six aircraft down there, and sit back and count our money.

Continental wasn't too happy about the deal, but in the end, they went along with it.

We opened those routes on Monday, November 1, 1999.

It was a gala affair. All the dignitaries were there from the islands that we were going to serve. The TWA big shots were there and so was I, with golden scissors about four feet long, to cut the ribbon.

There was one guest that was late to the party…

Hurricane Lenny.

She was two weeks late, but she made her presence known by forcing a shutdown of the airline for three days.

To add to our woes, the port authority couldn't work out the Prinair hangar lease, and we were forced to operate out of a nearby airport, causing the added expense of ferrying the aircraft across the harbor to that maintenance base nightly.

This operation was going to require more attention than I bargained for.

My attention was redirected from San Juan to Houston by a communication from Continental Airlines.

We had become a big part of Continental's program in Florida and the Bahamas. So big, in fact, that they approached me with an offer to purchase an interest in the airline.

They would buy 28 percent of the stock, extend our marketing agreement up to ten years, and place two of their representatives on the board. The funds for the stock would be used to reduce all the debt of the company and repurchase any stock that I had distributed as I had given some shares to valuable fellow workers. Continental would arrange for the purchase of twenty-five Beechcraft 1900 D model aircraft and lease them back to Continental Express until we were ready for them. I would net out zero dollars personally for my shares, but I would keep control of the company. It was now profitable, operating twenty-five state-of-the-art aircraft, and it would be debt free.

We completed the transaction in December, and I was happy to have such a formidable partner.

Another thing happened in December. Jerrie and I moved into our dream house. We moved to Wellington, a small community about ten miles west of West Palm Beach, located on a small private airfield. Jerrie got a new spacious kitchen, and I got an airplane hangar in the backyard.

A fair deal!

A neighbor stopped by to welcome Jerrie into the neighborhood. "We have a Cessna 172. Do you have an airplane?" she asked.

"Yes," Jerrie replied, "we have twenty-five."

For the next six years, until I sold Gulfstream, I commuted in a small aircraft each weekday. I would depart at 8:15 in the morning to arrive at 8:45 at the Gulfstream hangar in Ft. Lauderdale in time for the 9:00 operations meeting. In the evenings I would depart the hangar at around 6:00 p.m. for the short flight home.

Some of our neighbors would set their watches by my schedule, and on occasion when I wouldn't fly, they would call to see if I was ill. I got to know the air traffic controllers by name, and my aircraft number, N-951TC,

November 951 Tango Charlie, was often welcomed with friendly comments when I announced my position along the short route.

In reflecting on the year, I couldn't complain. The jury was still out on the San Juan expansion, but I surmised I could fix that with some attention to the scheduling, and the Continental transaction was a big deal.

We welcomed in the new century with high hopes. The Continental arrangement was going okay. They were still suspicious about the San Juan hub, as was I, but our domestic and Bahamas connecting flights were beneficial to them as we continued to work out the transition from our 1900 B and C aircraft to their more modern 1900 D models.

We were still licking our wounds from the closing of the Paradise Island airport, but the Miami, Ft. Lauderdale to Nassau passenger loads had picked up somewhat, so the expected impact wasn't that severe.

The Cuba and the flight school businesses were doing nicely, and overall, we were in pretty good shape as we went into the next century.

As our relationship with Continental continued to blossom, I had the good fortune to become friends with its chairman, Gordon Bethune. In a conversation at the Wings Club in New York, knowing that I was operating charters to Cuba, he expressed a desire to visit Havana.

I agreed to set up a trip, and in May we spent four days in Havana. He was fascinated with the area, loved the people, and saw some real possibilities for Continental in that market in the future. Seeing his interest in that market, I began to see what I could do for Continental, as I was currently chartering jets from other companies to fly there.

We developed a friendship during that trip that continues. When I returned to Miami, I began to work on an idea that I had for Continental and the Cuban charter market.

As friendly as my personal relationship became with Bethune, our corporate relationship slowly soured with Continental. I suppose it began with the San Juan, TWA episode. Additionally, on several occasions, they recommended that I hire personnel to fill vacancies that came available with people from their organization. This began to create issues with our chain of command; the new employees were loyal to Continental, and often the lines of communication bypassed me. Often suggestions concerning schedule changes were made, to the advantage of Continental and not necessarily to ours and if I didn't agree, they would insist.

On the bright side, we received our first D model Beechcraft in September, and the laborious task of converting from our older models to the newer, more sophisticated models began.

The Cuba operation continued to work well, and I found myself visiting Havana more frequently to meet with Havanatur.

The Hemingway house on the outskirts of Havana was in a state of disrepair, and a group out of Boston began, with the agreement of the U.S. and Cuban governments, to restore it. Gulfstream partnered with them by donating free transportation, both for passengers and cargo, to Cuba for the duration of the renovation process.

The year ended and my resolve was to try to get along with Continental better and improve the relationship.

As the year 2000 ended, I began to take a serious look at the San Juan hub. In spite of all that we did—new schedules, discount fares, and massive advertising—nothing worked. In researching the market prior to embarking on the project, we had assured ourselves that there was ample passenger traffic to ensure profitability, and we entered the area with full confidence.

What we didn't foresee was the element of competition. After a better than expected opening and high advanced passenger bookings, our loads suddenly dropped dramatically toward the middle of the year.

It didn't take us long to figure it out. American Eagle was bracketing our scheduled trips with flights before and flights after our scheduled flights. When we changed ours, they changed theirs.

As the year ended, we made the painful decision to abandon the market. American Eagle was just too strong with deeper pockets.

Back home again, we concentrated on Florida and the Bahamas and enjoyed a period of operational stabilization. With the flight academy and the Cuban operation doing well, we settled down to run a no-drama airline.

What could go wrong?

September began and we had our usual anxieties about the normal decrease in business in the Bahamas.

As was my custom now, I flew down to the Ft. Lauderdale airport in my small Beechcraft, landed, and climbed the steps to the morning operations meeting.

It was September 11, 2001.

CHAPTER 85

Disaster

The 9-11 survival story

JUST AS I WAS SITTING down for the ops meeting in the hangar, someone came in and reported that an airplane had flown into one of the World Trade Center towers in New York City. With sympathy for the pilot, we discounted the report as some private pilot getting lost, and we continued our meeting.

It was a quick meeting and within fifteen minutes I was in my car and driving the two miles to my office on Griffin Road, next to the airport.

I turned on the radio and heard the broadcast of a second aircraft flying into the adjacent building. *Surely, they must be confused,* I thought. Two aircraft hitting two buildings in downtown New York?

I parked the car and rode the elevator to my office and quickly turned on the TV. The announcers were speculating about two aircraft, and as that news began to sink in, there was another bulletin that interrupted the news, concerning Washington, D.C.

"A third aircraft, an airliner, had flown into the Pentagon in Washington" and it was afire.

"Betty, get dispatch on the phone for me," I shouted.

Pete Taggart was our Vice President, Manager of Flight Control. "Pete, have you heard the news?" I asked.

"Yes," he said.

I immediately ordered, "Pete, stop all flights that are still on the ground, and for the flights en route, order them to land at the nearest Gulfstream base."

Thus began one of the most bizarre periods of my life.

With the TV blaring news, some accurate, some speculative, and some just plain rumors, I began to make plans. It was obvious to me that the U.S. was under some kind of attack, but from where, and by whom?

My staff gathered around the TV in my office, and without knowing any of the facts, we were clueless as to a plan. The one thing I was sure of was that I didn't want any of our planes in the air.

Shortly thereafter, a fourth airplane was reported down in Pennsylvania, and we got a call from the FAA to ground all aircraft.

I had beaten them to it by thirty minutes.

I scheduled a staff emergency meeting for every three hours until further notice, and I cancelled the Cuba flights. Roy Cantor, our vice president of customer service, made arrangements for accommodating the inconvenienced passengers and grounded crews.

Throughout the day bulletins and orders were being passed back and forth to and from the FAA. Their team would arrive the next morning.

We finished the day just as confused as we were at 10:00 a.m.

The FAA team showed up the next morning with no additional information other than we were on "indefinite lockdown."

The second day dragged on with no notice from the FAA as to when we would be allowed back in the air. We established schedules only to cancel them when the curfew was not lifted.

The third day after the attack, Thursday, September 13th, the FAA allowed certain airports to open, and a few of the larger airlines, on a selected basis, went back in the air. The smaller commuters were limited as smaller airports were still closed, and so we waited.

On Friday the 14th, we were allowed to operate some flights into Nassau, and on Saturday we were released to operate any schedules that we had pre-registered with the FAA.

Realizing the financial repercussions from this malicious attack and with the clear understanding that even though airports would open and we would be allowed to fly, I surmised that the passengers would stay away in droves, I began to plan for the financial disaster that surely lay ahead.

I had to shove the horrible stories of the attack from my head as I began to shrink my airline.

I worked all day Saturday, and on Sunday I released, to the staff, "Operation Survival".

I would reduce the fleet from twenty-five aircraft to fifteen, plus one spare. I had trimmed the schedule down for that number of aircraft, and I gave the dispatch department the new schedule to implement. I cut all departments and issued furlough letters. Managers' salaries were cut by 25 percent, and the pilots were given the option of reducing their flight hours by 30 percent or some would have to be furloughed.

When the sun rose on Monday morning, we were a new airline. We were 40 percent smaller and the loads were even smaller.

Just as the acts of terrorism displayed the depths to which the evilest amongst us can stoop, it also brought out the best from others. While there were volumes of stories written of the heroics of our citizens, there were reports of acts of friendship and support from our many international friends that boosted our spirits.

The *Miami Herald* reported in its issue of Saturday, September 15th, a report from Cuba. Fidel Castro condemned the attack, and the Cuban government issued an official government statement: "The government of our country rejects and condemns with full force the attacks against the mentioned installations and expresses its sincerest condolences to the American people for the painful and unjustifiable loss of human life."

While we were slowly digging our way out of the 9/11 mess, I proposed my "Continental Jets to Cuba" plan to Bethune.

There were now five agencies, like Gulfstream, that were flying charters to Cuba. The Clinton administration had relaxed the restrictions for travel, and the passenger loads had grown to a level that would support the additional companies.

We all used different airlines for our airplanes. Each charter agency was allowed to fly only on certain days by Havanatur. We would pick an airline that might have surplus aircraft available that day and on an on going basis.

It was a patchwork operation. The Monday flight would go out of airline A's counter and gate, and the Tuesday flight would go out of airline B's counter and gate, and so on. It was confusing to the passengers and very impractical.

In addition, it was not uncommon for a charter airline company to remove its airplane from the Miami area to more productive flights elsewhere, resulting in the agency having to scramble to get their flights covered with an alternate carrier.

Since Bethune had mentioned that he had an interest in getting involved with the Cuban market, I approached him with the following: "If you can assign a dedicated aircraft to the Cuban market, at a competitive price, I think I can convince Havanatur to work out schedules with my competitors for enough business for three flights per day for the week."

He agreed, gave me a very competitive price, and I went to Havanatur with the plan.

I had become good friends with the new manager of Havanatur, Tony Diaz. I approached him with the plan, and he was ecstatic. He knew immediately what it would mean for the program. All the flights would operate out of the same counter and gate in Miami and give the impression that it was a "Continental" operation. It would be good for the customer, good for Havanatur, and good for the two countries.

"But, Cooper," he said, "how can we get the other companies to cooperate with the plan? They will think it's a Cooper/Gulfstream program and they won't buy into it."

"If I can get four of the five companies to buy in, will you support it?"

"Sure." He smiled as I left his office.

I had another chat with Bethune, asked him to shave a few bucks off the original offer, and with the new price in hand, I called a meeting with my competitors. We met at the Holiday Inn in Coral Gables. Just to make sure it didn't appear that it was a Cooper/Gulfstream operation, I asked Continental to provide a couple of representatives and they did.

The meeting went okay but was not met with much enthusiasm until I gave them Bethune's pricing schedule.

Four of the five companies agreed, and we were in business.

We set up schedules and Havanatur was the final authority as to which agencies would be issued landing permits and on which day. We commenced the Continental Airlines jet flights in November 2001.

With the memories of 9/11 still vivid in my mind, I said good-bye to 2001. The airline was still taking a beating passenger-wise, and the enrollments at the academy were down due to the adverse publicity around airlines in general. The only bright spot on our horizon was the Cuban operation with the Continental involvement.

I looked forward to a better 2002.

There was sad news in January when I heard, from Havana, that an old acquaintance, Gregorio Fuentes, had passed away. Gregorio had been Ernest Hemingway's boat captain for many years and was said to be one of the inspirations for Santiago, the fisherman in *The Old Man and the Sea*. A dear friend, a taxi driver in Havana named Salvador Soto, had introduced me to him.

It was a hot afternoon in Havana and Soto had offered to take me to a small fishing village, Cojimar, a few miles to the east for a beer and lunch. I had a few hours to spend, so I accepted his suggestion and off we went.

The road east of Havana passed through a tunnel, under the harbor, past Morro Castle and out along a pleasant tree-lined boulevard toward the village.

"I want to introduce you to a friend of mine," he said as he drove. "He was Hemingway's captain, and he can be found at a restaurant called La Terraza. It was the restaurant mentioned in *The Old Man and the Sea*, and I am sure that Gregorio will be there," he added. "He's about ninety-five years old, but he comes down to the restaurant every day."

Once we left the tree-lined boulevard, the road became narrower, and soon we crested a small hill. There, below us, lay a charming panorama of small houses nestled along side the left side of the road with the harbor stretching out to the sea to our right. At the far end, an ancient fort rose as if still guarding the small bay.

Down the hill and on the right, Soto maneuvered his taxi into a tight parking spot next to the restaurant and invited me to follow him in.

With Soto leading the way, we passed the bar and walked to the restaurant area in the rear. There I saw the "Old Man" seated at a table with some friends.

Soto introduced me, and the old man invited me to sit down with a nod toward an empty chair across from him. Of course, I bought everyone a beer, and soon, with Soto translating, I was one of the gang.

The old man regaled me with stories of his fishing days with Hemingway and, just as exciting, some of their nights.

At one point I asked him what he attributed his long life to, and he replied,

"Whik-ky."

"Whisky." I laughed. "You like rum?"

"No," he exclaimed. "Whik-ky, whik-ky... Scotch!"

The time came, too soon, when we had to say good-bye to the old man. Soto took my photograph with him, and I slipped him a twenty-dollar bill.

Soto had one more local sight for me to see, and soon we were driving down the narrow main street that borders the bay headed toward the fort.

Near the fort is a monument dedicated to Hemingway. It is said that a year after he died, all the poor fishermen in the community, in honor of Hemingway's memory, collected all their brass fishing paraphernalia—anchors, props, and anything else that could be used for a statue—and gave the collection to the famous sculptor Fernando Boada Martín who used it to create the bust that is the focal point of the monument. It is a beautiful spot and is almost sacred to the local population.

It would not be the last time that I would see the "Old Man." Even when he became too infirm to make the short walk down the hill to La Terraza, he would welcome me at his home, show me the old rod and reel that Hemingway had given him, and again, setting on his front porch, regale me with his stories.

CHAPTER 86

Lunch with Fidel

IT WAS SHORTLY AFTER I learned of Gregorio's death that I received a phone call from Havana. Bethune had expressed an interest in meeting Castro, so I let it be known that I, too, would like to visit him.

The call came from Luis Molina. I had first met him when he was assigned to the Cuban Interest Section in Washington, D.C. We had become friends when he was there, and our friendship continued after he was transferred back to Havana as the United States Specialist, Minsterio de Relaciones Exteriores.

It was all set. Gordon, his young son, and his chief operating officer at Continental, along with my son and I, would be welcome for lunch with Fidel.

Luis suggested that if we wished to have lunch with the President, we should make ourselves available during the week of January 21 and, once we were in Havana, a schedule would be set for sometime during that week.

We arrived in Havana and checked into our hotel, the Melia Cohiba. The Cohiba was built in 1994 and is one block from the famous boulevard called Malecon that winds along the oceanfront and separates Havana from the sea.

It is a modern hotel with over four hundred rooms sporting all the modern conveniences found in any five-star hotel: pool, multiple restaurants, bars, and breakfast with strolling violins.

Luis did his best to entertain us while we whiled away our time waiting for the call. We visited all the places of interest: Hemingway's farm, the Revolution Museum, the Aviation Museum, old Havana, and, of course, all the bars made famous by Hemingway.

It was Wednesday morning when we received the call. We were in the old section of Havana, visiting an ancient convent, when Luis' cell phone rang.

"The President will receive us for lunch at one o'clock today." He smiled.

We rushed back to the hotel to change clothes and, as arranged with Luis, departed the hotel at 12:30 for lunch.

We hopped into the car provided by Luis and turned west on the Malecon, which passes through a tunnel under the Almendares River and turns into Fifth Avenue as it enters the neighborhood of Miramar.

We passed the old Havana Yacht Club, rounded a roundabout, and headed south. As we passed the Palco Hotel, the car slowed down and turned in to a driveway leading to a rather large building, set back in some trees, fronted by a covered portico. The car stopped and Luis got out and spoke to a doorman. He motioned for us to get out of the car.

Could this be where we were to have lunch with the country's president? There was no security, only a doorman. We followed Luis through the front door and were met by a couple of gentlemen who gave us a quick once-over. Assured that we were only carrying cameras, they nodded toward the elevator in the lobby.

Led by Luis, I was the last one in the elevator. We all rode up to the floor where we were to meet the President. There were no security personnel in the elevator, only Luis as our guide.

The elevator stopped, the door opened, and I stepped out, not knowing what to expect.

I looked to my right, and there, framed in a doorway with the lights from a window behind him highlighting his silhouette, was Fidel Castro.

It was a bigger-than-life moment. He was dressed in his familiar green military fatigues with no medals or decorations other than the small insignias on his epaulettes. He wore a military-type belt, about three inches wide, cinched around his midriff, and he looked, forever more, like someone hired from central casting.

He waved us all into a reception room where there were cocktails waiting.

The room was very attractive, with wooden walls prominently decorated with a six-foot, modernistic painting depicting a Cuban farm scene.

Although Castro speaks very good English, he had an interpreter at his side. She was excellent, and to speak through her was like talking directly to him.

Luis introduced each of us to him, with a short biography, and after a round of mojitos and about fifteen minutes of small talk, Castro invited us to an adjoining room where we were to have lunch.

He was the perfect host. As the meal was served, Castro asked me, "How do you like the wine?"

"Well, Mr. President, I'm not a connoisseur of wine, but it tastes very good," I offered.

"It's very expensive, but it's not my favorite." He motioned to the server to bring his favorite. It came and he proudly offered me a glass of his favorite wine. "How do you like *that wine?*" he asked with pride.

I was prepared for him to claim that it cost hundreds of dollars per bottle. "I like it very much," I said. "I like it better than the first bottle." I added in expected agreement.

He laughed aloud and joyfully exclaimed, "It's from Chile, and it's only $3.95 a bottle." I noted that the name was Santa Emma. We all laughed and that seemed to break the ice. He began to entertain us with stories, expound on facts, and amaze us with his apparent photographic memory.

When the topic of aviation came up, Gordon asked him about his private jet, and he reminded us that it was an older Russian model.

Bethune questioned him about the safety of an older aircraft and said that he should be flying around in a modern aircraft. Gordon laughed and reminded him that he was a former executive of Boeing and that he could get him a good deal on a 737. Castro simply chuckled and said, "Cuba can't afford such a luxury."

"But, Mr. President, if your fellow countrymen knew of the danger of flying an old aircraft, they would surely vote to purchase a new aircraft for you," Gordon said, half in jest.

Castro laughed again and closed the subject with, "I'd veto it."

The conversation covered a wide range of topics. It went from the wine industry; Cuba had tried to grow grapes but to no avail in this climate, so they were resigned to total import, to the aerial spraying of mosquitoes in Cuba. We'd seen some agriculture type of aircraft spraying over Havana earlier.

When that subject came up, we got a fifteen-minute lecture concerning the habits of the mosquito in the Caribbean, their mating habits, and how they could migrate, or in some species, not migrate.

Bethune was seated directly across from Castro, next to me, when Fidel asked him a question concerning his former military career.

"You're a big strapping man. Were you ever in the military?" he asked.

"Yes sir," Gordon answered, not knowing where this conversation was headed. "I enlisted in the Navy when I was seventeen as a seaman but, over time, when I retired, I had earned a commission as lieutenant."

"Well," Castro grinned and pointed to the Commander in Chief's insignia on his epaulettes, "you've done a lot better than me. I've been in this outfit for almost forty-five years, and I haven't received *one* promotion!"

That brought the house down. There were guffaws of laughter around the table, and Castro was extremely pleased with his joke.

The lunch went on and the conversations continued. At one point, Castro looked at me and asked how I liked the side dish that was just served.

It looked like spaghetti. I looked at Tommy, who shrugged, and we tried it. It wasn't bad, but it wasn't spaghetti.

"The container says that they are baby eels," Castro offered. "But I discovered something about them that's strange. If you look closely, you will see that they have no eyes. They are fake," he proudly confessed. "They come from Spain and they are made from synthetic matter."

And with a snap of his finger, he ordered his valet to bring me a tin of the fake baby eels as a souvenir. That can still remains in my library.

Castro was a master host. He made each of us feel comfortable as he moved the conversation around the table. He looked at Tommy, seated across the table, and asked him what he did.

"I'm an attorney and I work for my father," he answered.

"You be careful", he cautioned with a wry grin. "That's how I got started."

Again, the guests roared and it became apparent that our time with him was nearing an end. We retired to the original reception room for after-lunch cocktails and photos, and soon it was time to leave.

He ordered one of his compatriots to be sure that we were each given a box of Cohiba cigars, his best, and with a handshake all around, charming to the end, Fidel Castro bid us a safe journey home and we departed.

It was probably the fastest three hours I have ever spent…and the most surreal.

To share lunch with someone who represented the opposite side of the political spectrum, contrary to everything I had been taught; to share cocktails with someone who expounds on the horizontally opposed political views from that which I believe in, and to spend three hours with someone so despised by the Cuban community in my country, and understandably so, and to thoroughly enjoy the afternoon left me strangely confused.

There had been no discussions of politics, no debates about religion, just a few guys sitting around the table, telling stories and laughing at jokes.

I think if we did more of that as a country, we'd all get along better, and the world would be a better place.

CHAPTER 87
Winding Down

*Unwinding the Continental arrangement,
saying good-bye to an old friend, and health issues*

As we moved into 2002, the repercussions of 9/11 were still with us, and were compounding my issues with Continental. Due to reduced passenger demand, they had, understandably, reduced their schedules and offered fewer flights into Florida. They also understood that Gulfstream would need some capital to survive through the buildup period following the drastic drop in passengers as a consequence of the attack in New York.

With the capital advance loans came help in the management area of our airline. To enhance Gulfstream's feed to them, they began to influence our scheduling department by scheduling all of our flights to meet with theirs. This caused severe problems with our regular customers, the business passengers who relied on us to transport them from point to point within the state, and for our vacationers to the Bahamas.

It was a lose-lose situation for us. If we didn't schedule in accordance with Continental's wishes, then the cash advances would stop. When we did use their schedules, our loads dropped precipitously, causing severe losses.

Although our loads were gradually improving, the relationship with Continental wasn't.

However, as our relationship with Continental continued to fester, the Cuban business began to pick up.

In September, there was a major trade fair in Havana. After forty years of a trade embargo, Washington eased some of the restrictions on food and medicine and allowed companies in the U.S. to sell to Cubans.

In an effort to display their goods, 280 companies representing thirty-three states participated in a giant agricultural exhibition held in Havana. The company that sponsored the trade show contracted with Gulfstream to furnish the transportation for the participants.

It was quite a challenge, as there were more than six hundred representatives booked to travel. We rose to the occasion, and the travel portion of the event took place without incident. I suppose our most famous guest was Jessie Ventura, former professional wrestler and governor of Minnesota, representing his state's products.

Companies represented were, among others, Cargill, Con Agra Foods, Tyson Foods, Wrigley Chewing Gum, and Sarah Lee Cakes.

The participants were charmed by Castro's frequent appearances and his interest in the food products. He even fed the two cleverly named baby bisons, Louise and Clark, from a baby bottle, to the delight of the crowd.

The Americans sold approximately 90 million dollars' worth of food, and the expo was a rousing success.

As successful as our participation was with the Cuban Food Expo, our differences with Continental became intolerable. We finally settled our differences in late 2002 with a compromise. I would purchase the 28 percent of our Gulfstream stock back, and they would cease any further subsidies to Gulfstream.

We regained control of the flight scheduling and set up a new schedule effective in early 2003. I terminated several employees and began to look around for someone with a keen knowledge of regional airline business to assist me in the planning.

I had met Dave Hackett when I testified before the CAB on behalf of Frank Lorenzo in his unsuccessful attempt to create a new airline. I had found him to be extremely knowledgeable in all areas of the aviation industry, and he was very likable. He had joined Continental after graduation from the University of Houston in 1985 as a financial analyst. He was quickly promoted to senior financial analyst and continued to rise in the hierarchy of Continental, acting as the director of financial planning until his departure in 1991.

We had stayed in touch over the last eight years. When I became aware that he was available, I contacted him and proposed that he join Gulfstream. He agreed and we set the date of his employment for February of 2003.

The business of running Gulfstream had settled down to a routine. With the advent of the arrival of Dave Hackett, it became even easier. I named him president, and I remained chief executive officer and board chairman. Tommy became more involved in the business end of the airline, and Betty was the glue that held the whole thing together.

The highs were not as high and the lows continued to smooth out. All the divisions were working efficiently, due to the people heading them, and the company was, at last, comfortably profitable.

While the company was doing well and we had recovered from the ravages of 9/11, there was a personal tragedy unfolding.

My dear friend Charlie Lawson was having health issues, and the symptoms appeared to be getting worse. I finally convinced him to visit Mayo Clinic in Jacksonville for a complete physical examination.

I flew him up in my small twin-engine Beechcraft and waited while he went through the paces. Since he was single and had no family, when the doctor prepared to brief him on the results of his tests, Charlie asked that Jerrie and I be there.

We were a somber group, but I was sure that Mayo could fix him right up. After all, wasn't Charlie the healthiest person around? Didn't he go on bicycle rides of over forty miles with his cycle group? And didn't he play tennis and golf regularly? This would be easy for Mayo to fix.

But it wasn't to be.

The doctor gave us the brutal truth. Charlie only had a short time to live.

The doctor continued to talk, but I heard very little. He said something about chemo, and something about an intestinal splice, but he always came back to the same solution.

No hope.

I was in shock and I noticed tears streaming down Jerrie's face. I excused myself and ushered her out to the waiting room to wait for Charlie.

While waiting in the lobby I penned a few lines that I later used in the airline's quarterly *In-flight* magazine. It was due to go to press shortly, and I wanted to remember Charlie, and his courage.

WELCOME ABOARD!

The deadline for this letter has come and gone, and the editors are screaming. Nothing, however, could be further from my mind right now than talking to you about new routes, fancy airplanes, and modern aviation innovations. I am sitting in the waiting room of Mayo Clinic after just witnessing a dear friend and fellow aviator being told that he has terminal colon cancer, and that his options are limited to procedures and medication that will only help his quality of life until his time comes.

While Charlie dresses I will wait for him here in the lobby as my mind rushes through a myriad of emotions... Confusion... Why Charlie, a man so apparently healthy? Anger...why didn't I insist, even force him to get the dreaded checkup as I do? Sympathy, forget that! Charlie wouldn't tolerate that even in his terminal condition. Charlie will come out shortly, bravely make a few jokes about his malady, and I will chuckle, hopefully just as brave, and we'll return to Miami. Charlie will do what the strong do in these conditions, and I'll try to be supportive.

As helpless as I feel now, one thought comes to mind. That is of you, the Gulfstream customer. A brochure here says that two out of three of us can be cured, if diagnosed in time. I'm told that over a quarter million customers will read this magazine. If just one of you reading this is diagnosed timely and survives this dreaded disease, then perhaps Charlie's desperate situation will serve some useful purpose.

So please have a checkup...for yourself, for your loved ones, and for all of us here at Gulfstream... We want to have you as a customer for a long time.

Thomas L. Cooper
President & CEO
Gulfstream International Airlines.

EDITOR'S NOTE: Charlie passed away four weeks after this writing.

The success of the airline did little to ease the pain of Charlie's passing, but the daily challenges of the commuter airline tended to provide a therapeutic diversion from the anguish of his death.

While Dave and I were exploring the feasibility of a larger aircraft to increase flights in the heavier-traveled markets, a competitive airline, serving some cities in northern Florida, ceased operations. They sold us five of their Beechcraft 1900 D-type aircraft, and we grew, overnight, by 15 percent by connecting Tampa with Pensacola and Panama City.

While our entire operation was going smoothly, I was watching the political events surrounding Cuba very closely. George Bush was nearing the end of his first term, and he began courting the anti-Castro population in Florida to secure their sympathies and their votes for his next run as president.

I had watched the ups and downs, over the past thirty years, in the Cuban market. Without fail, when the Republicans held the office of the presidency, the embargo restrictions were strictly enforced, and when the Democrats were in office, the policy was more lax.

Bush was going to have a run for his money with public sentiment for the Iraq war waning, and it was apparent that he was going to make a policy move in Cuba to enhance his vote share in Florida, a swing state in the upcoming election.

Our Cuban operation was going nicely, with the Continental charter deal operating smoothly, but I wasn't comfortable with the gossip on the street.

It happened in October.

Bush announced a tightening of the embargo, restricting the people-to-people programs for American-born citizens, and he severely limited the Cuban-Americans' ability to travel back to Cuba to visit their families.

The competitive agencies selling tickets to Cuba quickly announced that they were cutting back to almost no flights and, as a consequence, Continental's charter business dropped to a point whereby they couldn't afford to place a designated jet at our disposal.

I was the only agency that owned an airline, and I made the decision to operate a daily flight in spite of the precipitous drop in demand.

I happened to be in Havana when Bush made the announcement. I was at the airport with some members of Havanatur when we were besieged by reporters from the Cuban TV channel.

I publicly made the announcement on Cuban TV that "even though the business aspects of future flights between the U.S. and Cuba look dim, Gulfstream will guarantee daily flights."

That announcement was well received by the Cuban populace, and for at least one night, I rivaled Fidel as the most popular person in Havana. I was dining at the restaurant in the popular hotel Parque Central and was startled as people stopped by my table to offer thanks. The manager, in a great display of public fanfare, even treated me to dinner.

I kept my promise and Gulfstream kept the thin string of air transportation open between the U.S. and Cuba with daily flights in our nineteen-seat Beechcraft 1900 D aircraft.

At the beginning of 2004, Dave Hackett had forecast that the price of fuel would continue to rise, and the only way we could insulate ourselves from that certain increase was to operate larger aircraft.

We had luck on our side. In early summer, Delta Airlines was offering some thirty-seat Embraer 120-type aircraft for sale. They were anxious to sell, and we took advantage of the situation and purchased six aircraft from them.

The training went well, and by the first of January 2005, we had the first ones on certificate and in scheduled service. The first flight was to Freeport, where a proud station manager, Jenny Newman, met us.

The aircraft fit into our projections perfectly and were an instant success, both from passenger acceptability and profitability. We were named Airline of the Year by the minister of tourism of the Bahamas, and our airline was operating at a highly efficient level.

I had long admired a building complex on Griffin Road, five miles west of our present location. It came on the market, and after a month of negotiations, we bought it and began the renovations for the move. It had ample space for both our main headquarters offices and the flight academy and the transaction would save the corporation over two hundred thousand dollars per year. We moved to the new offices in January of 2006, with our name, GULFSTREAM, along with our logo, GA, proudly displayed in lights on the roof over the fourth floor.

Dave Hackett was a major asset, and as he began to take on more responsibility, I began to look at the calendar. In one year, I would be seventy years old. That was about the time I felt I should retire.

CHAPTER 88

To Retire or Not to Retire?

THERE HAPPENED AN EVENT THAT would whet my appetite to retire even more.

In early October, I made my annual visit to Mayo Clinic in Jacksonville for a routine physical. As always, after all the tests were completed, I met with my personal physician for a debriefing session. Just as we sat down in his office, I received a phone call from my office. "Let me call you back in ten minutes," I said. "This is routine and I'll be out of here soon."

And then I heard the doctor interrupt me as he scanned his computer. "Not so fast there, Tom."

"Oops, I'll call you right back." I blanched as I hung up and turned to the doctor.

He gave me the news. I had shown a high PSA level (prostate specific antigen) indicating early warning for prostate cancer. I would have to come back for more tests, and if my PSA continued to rise, then I'd have to make a decision.

That was an eye opener. When I returned to Ft. Lauderdale, I made up my mind to actively pursue retirement.

Although there were no suitors knocking on my door at this time, it wasn't uncommon for potential buyers to appear out of nowhere.

Enter Tom McFall, right on schedule.

Tom was a principal associate of an investment group named Weatherly Group, LLC. and was a friend of a friend. He was introduced to me in late October, and over lunch he inquired if the company might be for sale.

That seemed to fit into my retirement plans, so I replied, "Of course."

We continued to discuss the possibilities over the next several months, but with the additional activities surrounding the office and flight academy move, I didn't devote that much time to it.

A biopsy on January 8, 2006 brought me back to the negotiating table in earnest. My PSA had continued to elevate, and the biopsy indicated that I had cancer of the prostate.

I sold the company to McFall's group on March 15, 2006 and scheduled my prostate operation for April 28th.

The transaction was relatively simple; they would get the airline, Gulfstream International Airlines, and the flight academy, and I would retain the Cuban operation, Gulfstream Air Charter. I would remain on board for a short period of time during the transition as Chief Executive Officer.

My prostate operation was a success; I was scheduled to be released from Mayo Clinic on May 5th.

While waiting in the lobby for my release, I remembered sitting in the same room while waiting for my dear friend Charlie to appear after being given the bad news that he had terminal colon cancer. I wrote the following letter to the customers to be published in the next Gulfstream *In-flight* magazine.

Dear Customers,

Please allow me to digress from my usual letter concerning Gulfstream's new routes or new aircraft to something a bit more personal. I'll call it "A TALE OF TWO CANCERS."

Two years ago, I wrote to you from the lobby of the MAYO CLINIC in Jacksonville, where I had just witnessed the doctors advise a dear friend that he had only six weeks to live. He had put off having a colonoscopy too long, and the diagnosis, colon cancer, came too late to help him. Within a month he had died.

Today, I am sitting in that same lobby awaiting my final release with a clean bill of health. Six months ago, during my annual routine examination, through a simple blood test, the doctor noticed a rise in my PSA level (prostate-specific antigen), an indication of prostate cancer. After getting my initial panic attack under control, I asked the usual questions, "Are you sure? How far has it spread? And what can I do?"

The doctors at Mayo field these questions daily, and he quickly responded, "No, we're not sure; we don't know if it has spread, and here's what we can do." At his suggestion, we waited two more months for another PSA test. "If it continues to elevate, we'll do a biopsy, and if that proves to be positive, we'll have another planning session," he explained.

The PSA did elevate and the biopsy proved to be positive. To prepare for our planning session, he suggested that I read up on prostate cancer, which I did. I discovered that it's a very common disease and, if discovered soon enough, is completely curable in almost all cases; there are numerous procedures for successful treatment. We decided on radical prostatectomy, which, simply, means remove the prostate surgically.

My operation was on Friday, I was walking on Saturday, and I went home (nearby resort) on Sunday, where I rested until today (seven days later) and I'm now released. A miracle!

But the miracle of modern medicine cannot be accomplished without your help. Early diagnosis is the secret, so as I said in my letter to you two years ago when I implored you to have regular checkups: "Do it for yourself, do it for your family, and do it for Gulfstream...we want to keep you as a customer for a long, long time."

Thank you for flying with us today and enjoy a safe and healthy flight.

Thomas L. Cooper
Founder and CEO
Gulfstream International Airlines, Inc.

In memory of Charlie and with thanks for my successful operation, I established free examinations for all my employees and their families for colon and prostate cancer.

Within a week, I was back in my airplane, commuting between Wellington and Ft. Lauderdale, and at my desk.

This wasn't to be my year. About four months later, I noticed that the vision was blurred in my left eye. After a trip to Bascom Palmer Eye Institute in Miami for an evaluation, once again within six months, I found myself being rolled into the operating room on a gurney with tubes dangling from my arm. I had a "macular hole" in my left eye, which, luckily, could be corrected to about 90 percent of my original vision. The recovery time was ten days, and by October I was back in the office.

George McGovern invited Jerrie and me to the opening of the George and Eleanor McGovern Library on the campus of Dakota Wesleyan University in October. I had recovered sufficiently and we flew out to South Dakota for the gala affair in early October.

George was very gracious and invited us to all the special events, including a special screening of a film of his life, *One Bright Shining Moment; The Forgotten Summer of George McGovern*, a documentary of his grassroots run for the presidency in 1972.

The event was laced with speeches by a number of dignitaries, most notably Senator Bob Dole and former President Bill Clinton. We renewed an old acquaintance with Mike Farrell, who played B.J. Hunnicutt in the TV series *M*A*S*H*. He and I served on the same board of a Washington-based nonprofit research and advocacy group, and we had traveled together to Tegucigalpa, Honduras, earlier on a deforestation fact-finding mission.

Over dinner, McGovern confided in Jerrie and me that he still received requests to run for president. He laughed and admitted with a cheery wink, "I'm too old to *run* for president, but perhaps I could just *stand* for president."

Back in Ft. Lauderdale, my time with Gulfstream was running out. Dave Hackett was doing a fine job as president, and Tom McFall was becoming more involved in the day-to-day decision making. My time at Gulfstream was nearing its end.

Christmas came and went, and somewhere around the middle of January 2007, I walked in and told Betty that I was leaving. "But don't worry," I said, "we'll still work together on the Cuba operation. I'll just work from home."

And that's the way my involvement with Gulfstream International Airlines ended.

The company, with the help of dedicated employees, had grown from literally nothing to a major commuter airline employing over a thousand people, flying over a million passengers a year, and grossing over a hundred million dollars a year.

The Man in The Arena...

I packed a couple of boxes of personal belongings, removed a few pictures off the wall, and walked out.

No fanfare, no champagne, no marching bands or gala party with dancing girls. It had been almost sixteen years to the day since it all began.

I left the same way that I had come in after that lonesome ride down 36th Street leaving the smoldering ashes of Eastern Airlines behind me.

Finally...I was off the roller coaster.

CHAPTER 89

Retired

Almost

FOR ALL PRACTICAL PURPOSES, I was retired. I still had the Cuban operation to manage, but that was more a labor of love than a job. Several years earlier I had opened an office on LeJeune Road, south of Miami International Airport, and a young woman in our accounting department, Mildred Diaz, requested that she be named as manager. She had a good understanding of accounting and was bilingual. She was well qualified and highly motivated for the job.

And she did a great job. She immediately took ownership of the operation, and I was left with only the aircraft scheduling, pricing, and general overseeing of the operation to keep me busy.

Mildred managed the day-to-day operation and coordinated with the Cuban agency, Havanatur, which was responsible for monitoring the flights between the two countries. I worked with our attorney in Washington, Ms. Lonnie Pera, who kept us legal…and screamed at me a lot.

With the Bush administration's policy with Cuba, the passenger loads remained low but steady. The only flux was the bump in passenger loads during the weekends and holidays. I kept my promise to the Cuban people and maintained daily flights by juggling the different aircraft I had at my disposal. On low passenger days, I would use the nineteen-seat Beechcraft, and on heavier traveled days I used the thirty-seat Embraer.

This required quite a bit of swapping of aircraft at the last minute, and the gentleman in charge of issuing landing permits in Cuba, Mr. Roberto

Brown, was very accommodating—as were all of the other managers of the various agencies I worked with in Cuba. They were all very considerate and professional, and I was never asked to do anything that even came close to violating any rule of either country, or that might compromise the trust we had earned for each other.

CHAPTER 90

With George Mcgovern and Wayne Smith in Havana

OVER THE PAST THIRTY YEARS, I had made many friends, both Cuban and American, in my operation of the Cuban flights. Wayne Smith and George McGovern were among my special friends, and when McGovern called to ask if I would fly him and Wayne to Cuba, I of course said, "Yes!" They had accepted an invitation to visit a new school for the training of doctors in Havana, and I jumped at the chance to join them.

"And, oh yes," McGovern added, "can you bring along another pilot so you and I can stay up late and exchange war stories?"

"Sure, Senator," I said, smiling. We'd done this before.

The flight was uneventful. We were housed in a familiar "protocol" house that we had stayed in before. We were made comfortable by the staff, and next morning we were picked up for our visit to the school.

Escuela Latinoamericana de Medicina, the Latin American School of Medicine, is nine miles west of Havana on the coast and housed in the former naval academy overlooking the sea.

We traveled out Fifth Avenue, past the seaside city of Jaimanitas. A few miles further, we passed the famous Hemingway Marina, where Fifth Avenue turns into the Panamericana Highway, and soon, perhaps three miles, we saw the campus.

The driver pointed it out proudly. "It's over there," he said, "ahead and to the right." It was nestled on a peninsula overlooking the sea, with a scenic inlet entering from the sea to the east and opening westbound, creating a beautiful lagoon.

We were met at the administration building by an attractive middle-aged woman who immediately invited us to join her for juice and snacks. We relaxed while she explained the history of the school and its mission.

"The school was established in 1999, with students drawn from the poorest communities and the most disadvantaged families around the world. We offer full scholarships with free room and board, textbooks, and uniforms. We also provide a small expense account of one hundred Cuban pesos monthly. It is the intent that the graduates will return to their impoverished roots for their practice."

We toured the facility; Senator McGovern and Wayne Smith peppered the woman with questions as we walked.

"How many students do you have enrolled?" one would ask.

"How many from the United States?" another would ask.

"Who decides who will be accepted?"

The questions kept coming.

The woman was very patient and answered every question clearly, and in great detail. "We have approximately thirty-five hundred students currently enrolled, with approximately ninety from the U.S. Students are considered based on a lot of things—background, family wealth, area from which they come—and then they are selected by the faculty here and the Cuban Ministry of Public Health."

The tour finished with another round of juice and snacks and a last session of questions.

McGovern's last question was the burning question that I had wanted to ask since the beginning of the tour: "How can you be sure that after a student is trained, he will return to the impoverished area that he came from to practice his medical profession?"

The woman smiled, shrugged her shoulders, and, with a deep breath she almost whispered, "Well, we can't be completely sure, and we realize that some will not return." She hesitated as if to collect a thought. "But we have to try something, don't we?"

"Yes," McGovern said, as a man who had spent most of his adult life trying to erase world hunger. "Yes, we do."

That evening we dined with Ricardo Alarcon, the president of the National Assembly. Alarcon, dressed in his usual starched white guayabera, brought his daughter Maggie with him, and to her delight she met George McGovern.

It was another one of those "small- world " moments.

"Mr. McGovern," she gushed in perfect English with a slight Yankee dialect, "you are my hero!"

"Yes?" McGovern sheepishly replied.

"Yes," she went on, "when Dad was Cuba's ambassador to the UN, I was a teenager living on Long Island with Mom and him, and you ran for president. You were my favorite candidate. I used to put bumper stickers on people's cars at the shopping centers reading, *McGovern for President!*"

We all enjoyed that with a round of laughter. It was a lighter moment of the evening, and I could see that McGovern was extremely pleased.

The conversation turned to "polite" politics, and eventually, after a few scotches, Alarcon asked to be excused.

It was an early evening and I was to learn later that Alarcon's wife, Margarita, was deathly ill. He visited her in the hospital nightly, regardless of any other engagements he might have, governmental or other. Sadly, she would pass away in 2008.

Later that night at the protocol house, the Senator, Wayne Smith, and I relaxed by the pool in the backyard and enjoyed the hospitality of the staff. Rum was the selection of the evening, and in the dimly lit patio we discussed the day's activities.

Later, Wayne shared some stories of his relationship with Fidel when he was Chief of the U.S. Interest Section in Havana, most of which I had read in his book, *The Closest of Enemies*, but coming from the horse's mouth, they were even more interesting.

A few more rums and we prevailed upon McGovern to relate some of his adventures in World War Two. He was always extremely shy about discussing his war stories. Once, at my home in a conversation across the bar in my library, I had asked him why he didn't exploit his experiences as a bomber pilot to promote his candidacy when he ran for president.

"Well, Tom," he quietly explained, "I just didn't think it would help me administer any better."

With his modesty slightly compromised by the rum and the atmosphere of the cool Havana night air, we prevailed, and McGovern thrilled us with the story of a bombing mission over Germany.

We listened in rapt reverence.

The Man in The Arena...

McGovern was a twenty-two-year-old lieutenant, based in San Giovanni, Italy, in command of a giant four-engine B-24, which, along with the B-17, were the workhorses of the Army Air Force.

It was December 20, 1944, and McGovern was assigned to a bombing mission over Pilsen Germany, six hundred miles to the north.

All went well until he was about one hour short of the target. He lost power on his number two engine. He could have turned back, but he chose to secure the engine and continue on toward the target on three engines. About a minute short of the target, his aircraft was struck by flak, ground fire, and the number three engine failed.

He continued on course to the target with only two of the four engines operating and released his bomb load on target before turning toward his home base in Italy. Operating on only two engines, his speed dropped, and to maintain flying speed he was forced to lose altitude. The rest of the formation was pulling away, and he was left alone as a sitting duck for the Luftwaffe fighters.

He managed to navigate, using cloud coverage to his advantage, and escape interception by the German fighters as he worked his way over Yugoslavia to the Adriatic Sea toward his airbase.

Just when it seemed that he might bring the crippled B-24 home, the number three engine burst into flames.

Up ahead was the small island of Vis, in the Adriatic Sea. It had a short emergency landing strip. With the number three engine on fire, he quickly made the decision to try for that island, although the B-24 was far too large an aircraft for the airstrip to accommodate safely.

"I gave the crew the option of bailing out over the island or chancing a landing with me," he said. "You know," he added proudly, "every one of them opted to stay with me."

He landed the aircraft and stopped short of the end of the runway with the number three engine burning, the brakes smoking, and the tires flat.

For that, George McGovern was awarded the Distinguished Flying Cross.

The evening wore on, but no one was tired, and with the omnipresent staff member refilling each empty glass, we continued to enjoy the night.

Wayne reminded McGovern that I, too, was an aviator with some stories to tell, and George insisted that I add to the evening's entertainment by relating one of my adventures.

After shyly declining, but with their insistence, I related the "running out of gas over the jungles of South America" story.

It was met with great expressions of awe and amazement, undoubtedly promoted by the rum, and with a great display of mock surrender, McGovern shook his head, threw up his hands, and declared laughing, "Tom, I give up, you're a bigger bullshit artist than me."

CHAPTER 91
The Cuban Operation

A labor of love

THE CUBAN OPERATION WAS GOING nicely. The passenger loads were low, due to the Bush administration policy, but the company provided a modest profit, and operating between Miami and Havana was interesting, to say the least.

There were six other operators now and we would be called to Havana two or three times a year for a business conference which would usually last two or three days. We discussed any issues with customs or other regulatory agencies, reviewed the passenger history since the previous meetings, and discussed any recent changes in the regulations from either Cuba or the United States.

My second home became the Hotel Nacional in Havana. The sixth floor, the executive floor, was where my room was located, and the bar, the Vista al Gulfo, on the ground floor overlooking the Malecon and the ocean, was my man cave.

The Nacional was, and is, steeped in history, and to visit there is like taking a walk through the past eighty years of the history of Havana. The hotel was built in 1930 and was, at that time, arguably, one of the most luxurious in the world.

The list of notable guests visiting there is impressive.

You can almost see Winston Churchill setting up his easel in the back patio, preparing to paint a seascape with Morro Castle in the background, and over there, it's said, is where Frank Sinatra and Ava Gardner used to enjoy cocktails on their honeymoon. And just around the corner, in the room that was then the casino, you can imagine Santo Trafficante, Meyer Lansky, and Lucky Luciano huddled in deep conversation.

The hotel is just as exciting now as it was in earlier days. Yes, there are newer, more modern, more upscale hotels in Havana today, but where can you stay and, if your senses are keen enough, catch a whiff of Winston Churchill's Romeo y Julieta cigar, or catch a glimpse of Gary Cooper strolling through the lobby, impeccably dressed for a night at the Tropicana?

Nowhere!

To be welcomed to the Nacional by its public relations manager, Yamila Fuster, is indeed a treat. She has an uncanny ability to make each guest feel that they are the only guest in the hotel, and she makes every effort to ensure that you feel perfectly at home there. She is a walking history book and will be delighted to charm you with stories of the hotel and its famous guests.

The manager of the hotel is Antonio Martinez. Tony and I have been friends since he became manager. He was brought in after an abhorrent sabotage of the lobby by an offshore anti-Castro group in 1997. A bomb was exploded, wounding several guests and employees.

Tony always greets me with a hearty handshake and a hug, remembering the time when I had a group of forty of my friends staying there. He desperately needed the rooms on our last night due to an unexpected arrival of a Russian delegation in advance of a Putin visit. He had no choice as he pointed his finger upward, indicating that the word had come down from upstairs, but he accommodated us royally. He ordered for us, in the luxurious Aguiar room, the finest dinner I've ever had in Havana and provided a bus for Varadero Beach, a resort fifty miles east of Havana, where everything—dinner, drinks, shows—was on the house.

The group was impressed and could not have been more pleased.

As the year 2008 began, my semi-retirement was going well. The Cuban program continued to operate at the same level as it had since the Bush administration had curtailed travel to the island, but locally in the U.S., our president's election was just around the corner.

I began to look at the slate of candidates and review the possible nominees, because the results of the election would affect my Cuban operation greatly. Early in the year it looked like the nominee for the Democratic Party would be Hillary Clinton and for the Republicans it would be Mitt Romney.

As the summer wore on, the political picture gradually changed. John McCain began to gather momentum, and that race was neck and neck. On the Democratic side, a little-known senator from Illinois, Barack Obama, was giving Hillary a run for her money.

I continued to watch the races with one eye and the Cuban operation with the other. If the Republicans got in the White House, then I could expect little or no change in the Cuban policy, and the business would continue at the lower level. If the Democrats won the presidential election, then I could expect a surge in the demand for seats.

When Obama was named as the candidate for the Democratic Party in August, followed by McCain being nominated as the candidate for the Republican Party in September, I began to plan for four more years of the same lower level of business between the U.S. and Cuba. McCain would be a shoe-in. After all, how could you expect a black man with the name of Barack Hussein Obama, a name sounding like a Middle Eastern terrorist, to win an election against a bona fide American war hero? No way! I began to plan on business as usual in the Cuban market.

On November 4, 2008, Barack Hussein Obama won the election as President of the United States of America.

The T. L. Cooper School of Political Predictions was cancelled.

With the inauguration of Obama in January of 2009, I began to plan on ramping up the Cuban operation in preparation for the anticipated normal loosening of the Cuban regulations by the White House. That came in September when the White House eased the restrictions on family visits, the ability of Cuban Americans to return to Cuba.

With that easing of the regulations the Cuban business really began to expand. I went from using the smaller aircraft to using jets, as did the other competitive travel agencies, and the Cuban operation grew accordingly.

Mildred was doing a great job at her end, and I began to spend more time in the Miami office. We both were required to attend an increased number of Havanatur meetings in Havana, and during the off days, I spent more time in the local Havana surroundings.

The old section of Havana was a favorite place to hang out. It was bordered by old forts and castles, and one could explore the remnants of the old wall that once encircled the ancient city.

The imprint of Hemingway was everywhere. The Ambos Mundos Hotel, where he lived in room 511 for a while, was my favorite spot to spend a few hours. The lobby bar, with its grand piano, was relaxing, and if you closed your eyes you might imagine Hemingway, khaki pants, loose-fitting shirt, collecting his morning newspaper from the desk counter and strolling across the street for his breakfast, before a marlin fishing trip with his buddies.

Down at the end of Obispo Street was the famous El Floridita Restaurante, where Hemingway would enjoy his Papa Special, a daiquiri with no sugar. A short stroll away, near the Old Cathedral Square, was another Hemingway haunt called La Bodeguita del Medio, where he would order another favorite drink, the mojito.

There is a sign with a quote by Hemingway hanging behind the bar at the Bodeguita: "For my mojito it's La Bodeguita, for my daiquiri, it's El Floridita."

And for dinner, for me, there was only one place in Havana. Overlooking the Plaza de San Francisco de Asis is the Café del Oriente. The restaurant is two floors tall and has been restored to its original seventeenth-century stately beauty. The ground floor houses the bar, lounge, and seating for casual dining, while the second floor is an elaborate venue for formal dining under a marvelous mosaic ceiling of colored glass illuminated by soft indirect lighting. The view across the Plaza is accentuated by soft music featuring the finest musicians in the city.

In the entire world, I have never dined in such a luxurious setting.

Mildred handled the expansion very well. She hired a few extra people for the airport check-in counter and a few more for our reservation department, and the business settled down to a routine operation.

Another business opportunity presented itself in early 2010. A small airport operation in Sebastian, Florida, came up for sale, and I decided to visit it. The city of Sebastian is located about mid-state on the East Coast south of Melbourne. It's a quaint little town, and the minute that I visited it, I was hooked. The company, Sebastian Aero Services, was a small operation consisting of a hangar and a small administration building. It offered aircraft maintenance, fuel, flight instruction, air taxi, and tie-down services. It looked like a good long-term investment with the possibility of some growth in the flight instruction and air taxi business.

I purchased the company in June of 2010 and hired an old friend, Robert Taylor, who had worked for me at Gulfstream Academy as manager. He was ideal for the job as he was a licensed mechanic and commercial pilot with a flight instructor's license. At the level that the business was when we bought it, he would only need to hire a line person for the fueling and a part-time bookkeeper.

We spent a month cleaning and organizing, and I left him to run the Sebastian operation while I returned to the Cuban operation in Miami.

The increase in business in Cuba required me to travel to Havana more frequently. There was an annual function called EXPO International held in the fall, sponsored by Alimport, the Cuban agency responsible for purchasing food and medicine from the U.S.

It is an interesting operation held just outside of Havana near Parque Lenin in a rather elaborate series of pavilions. One such pavilion is designated as the U.S. pavilion, and various purveyors from the U.S. rent booths for the annual weeklong program.

The salespeople would set up their booths, man them with their staff, and wait for a representative from a Cuban agency to stop by and sample their product. Negotiations were held either there or away from the pavilion, and if a deal was struck, then the selling company could ship its product to Cuba. Under the U.S. rules, shipments could not leave a port in the U.S. until full payment was received in a U.S. bank.

We would always share a booth with Havanatur. Mildred would travel to Havana and meet with the women from Havanatur to set up schedules for manning the booth. I would follow a few days later and spend some time there.

The high point for me in the whole operation was a cocktail party that I co-sponsored with Havanatur and Alimport, held either on Wednesday or Thursday of the event week at the end of the day.

I was always elected as the master of ceremonies, and Havanatur would provide a translator. It was a gala affair featuring me, Tony Diaz of Havanatur, and the president of Alimport making speeches, followed by hors d'oeuvres and cocktails. It gave me a good opportunity to meet my customers from the U.S., and I formed some close friendships at those meetings.

Other than watch the Gulfstream International Airline operation at a distance, I hadn't paid much attention to it since I sold out. I was surprised, in December, when I read that it had declared bankruptcy. The news was that the company had run into hard times with the fuel price escalation and couldn't continue without an influx of cash. That didn't materialize, thus the Chapter Eleven.

When I sold the company, there was a small air taxi included in the deal. We had used it for private charters around the state, to the Bahamas, and for an occasional cargo run to Cuba. The fleet in the on-demand air taxi was comprised of two Piper Chieftain nine-seat aircraft, of which I had retained ownership and leased back to the company.

In early 2011, a group of investors out of Chicago purchased Gulfstream International Airlines out of bankruptcy, invested in the basic airline, but had no interest in the air taxi. They did not choose to continue with the lease agreement for the two Piper Chieftains and advised me that they would return them.

I had a choice to make. Park the aircraft and place them up for sale or create another air taxi and return to the airline business. In my discussions with the Chicago group, the future of the small air taxi company came up. They made an offer to sell it to me and I accepted.

Betty Lerner had been doing some work for me in the Cuban operation and had expressed a desire to retire, or at least slow down. The air taxi operation was a perfect opportunity for her to semi-retire, so she came on board with me. It was like old times.

With the Obama administration gradually opening up travel to Cuba and the organizing of the air taxi company, re-named Sun Air, we once again found ourselves totally immersed in the airline business.

The Cuban operation was in full swing, with more and more U.S.-born American citizens traveling there under the newly broadened people-to-people license. There was little time to spend on the air taxi business, and I began to look for a buyer.

The Cuban business had peaked out, and we now were operating between six and ten Boeing 737 flights per week to Havana. We were carrying over four thousand passengers per month average, and with the increase in business, I was required to spend more time in Havana.

CHAPTER 92

Good-Bye, Senator McGovern

IN THE LATE SUMMER OF 2012, I received a phone call from my old friend George McGovern. It was a strange call as the phone rang at about six o'clock on a Sunday morning.

McGovern's speech was even slower than usual and, suspecting that he was in South Dakota, I surmised that it was around four o'clock from where he was calling. The conversation was somewhat rambling, and I guessed that he just wanted to talk to someone. I felt that he was either sedated or his brilliant mind had begun to let him down.

"Tom," he reminded me, "we had some good times in Cuba with Castro, didn't we?"

"We sure did," I lied. I had never been with him in the presence of Fidel.

"And those sailing trips with Jack and Jackie were such fun. Do you remember?"

"Yes, I remember, Senator. They were great fun," I lied again.

He went on for some time, and I got the strangest feeling that he was calling to say good-bye.

He sounded tired and his voice was weak. "Tom, you're one of my best friends in the world. When can we go to Cuba again?" he faintly asked.

"You just call me, Senator, and set the date," I offered, but I knew, again, I was lying.

When he rang off, I had a bad feeling.

It was on a Sunday in October, barely a month later, when I heard the news over the television. George McGovern had died.

It was a sad time for me.

I remembered how we had met on that first trip to Cuba, and all the other trips there. How our friendship had flourished with weekends at my home in South Florida. I owned an old antique airplane, a Fairchild, like the one that he flew for his pilot training in World War II. We would fly that open cockpit plane together. He still had his pilot skills from sixty years earlier.

I remembered sitting at my library bar and listening for hours of his political experiences and hear him quote his favorite phrase, "You must learn to disagree…without being disagreeable."

They say that George McGovern was a leftist because of his stand against the Vietnam War, and a loser because of his defeat in the presidential election of 1972, but I don't remember the senator that way. I remember him as an officer in the Air Force who fought valiantly for his country, a gentleman who spoke his mind and never wavered from his convictions, and a humble man who spent most of his adult life in an attempt to erase world hunger.

I think history will remember him, as I will, a national treasure. . . . and a winner.

CHAPTER 93

Sadly, It was Time to Sell The Cuban Operation

THE CUBAN OPERATION CONTINUED TO do well through 2013, but the air taxi, Sun Air, was becoming more than I could handle. I had certified it as a scheduled commuter air taxi and, with the help of David Hackett, applied for and was awarded some government subsidized routes in Texas and Pennsylvania.

Late that year I agreed to sell Sun Air to Hackett, who took over in January of 2014.

I was watching the Cuban operation closely. Given the Obama administration's continuing to show signs of opening up further, there might be a problem on the horizon. With the restrictions previously placed on air transportation between the U.S. and Cuba, the only air traffic allowed was by charter companies.

There was even talk of reopening the old U.S. embassy there. It had been closed since Kennedy was President, but since the Carter administration, we had maintained a presence in Cuba, utilizing our old building, with a diplomatic post called the United States Interest Section. That entity operated almost the same as an embassy except we didn't fly the flag in front of our building and the officer who would normally be the ambassador was called the Chief of the U.S. Interest Section.

If that happened, then scheduled airlines wouldn't be far behind. If the scheduled airlines began to operate there, it could be curtains for the charter companies.

In the spring, Mildred reported that we were transporting a large number of major airline executives to Havana onboard our charter flights.

The handwriting was on the wall. Obama was coming to the end of his administration, and it was no secret that he wanted to open up Cuba to the extent allowable under the law. The trade and the travel embargos could only be lifted by acts of congress, but the President could, with Executive Orders, go a long way toward normalization.

And allowing major airlines to fly there was one of them.

It was mid-summer, and I was playing golf with one my major customers. Tony Gonzalez and I had been friends for over fifteen years. He and his beautiful wife, Rosa, owned a chain of travel agencies called Va Cuba throughout the Miami and Ft. Lauderdale area. They had been my best customers.

A rain cloud moved overhead, and we scurried for protection into the local clubhouse bar. Over a few beers, Tony looked at me, laughed, and said, "Hey, Cooper, you're getting old. When are you going to sell me your company?"

Thinking he was talking in jest, I replied, "Make me an offer."

He quickly picked up a napkin, scribbled a few numbers on it, signed it, and slid it over to me. "Here's your offer," he said.

I laughed out loud.

He grinned and said, "I'm serious."

While still laughing, I slid the napkin, now wet, over to Hackett, one of our foursome, and said, "What do you think, Hackett?"

Dave, once the right-hand man of Frank Lorenzo, laughed and said, "Well, you know what Frank used to say: the first offer is usually the best."

I signed the napkin and we shook hands and agreed to meet the next week to finalize the details.

It would take three months for all the legal documents and permits to be changed from my name to his. There had to be a sign-off by the U.S. Treasury Department and the Cuban government and a certain transition period while the lawyers met and papered the deal. I made sure that Tony knew there was a good possibility that the big airlines might enter the market between the U.S. and Cuba, but he said he didn't care.

Just before closing there was a dispute within the accounting department's reconciliation, amounting to a difference of $17,000 in the sale price.

We went back and forth, with friendly locker room banter, and after a few beers Tony laughed and exclaimed, "Okay, Cooper, I'll play you a game of golf for the seventeen thousand."

"But, Tony, you know that wouldn't be fair. I can whip you any day of the week at golf," I bragged.

"I'll see you this weekend," he said confidently.

Now Tony and I are not very good golfers. Actually, if we break a hundred on any day, it's a good round. For us to play for anything more than a dollar a hole is ludicrous. But we set a date.

We met the next weekend and it was "game on."

As expected, there was no spectacular play from either of us. Neither player was ever two strokes ahead of the other, and there was a lot of trash talk between us.

We ended the 15th hole even up, and with three holes to play, the game began to get serious. The trash talk quieted somewhat as we tied the 16th and 17th holes.

We were going into the 18th hole tied. We both got off pretty good drives, and Tony's second shot was just short of the green. My second shot landed in the sand trap.

Tony was next to shoot; he hit a good wedge to within fifteen feet from the pin.

I was in trouble.

Sand trap shots are pretty easy when executed properly.

I was next up.

I settled in the sand trap, waggled my feet in the sand until I felt comfortable, sighted again. *Let's see,* I thought, *if I just make a normal three-quarter swing, hit the sand about one inch behind the ball, it should pop up and roll to the pin. No sweat.*

"Okay," I took a deep breath, "now, a good grip, swing easy, and follow through."

I blasted out of the sand trap, erroneously hit the ball squarely, and sent it about a hundred yards over the green.

Tony fell over laughing.

He's still laughing.

I'm still crying.

Tony took over in December; I packed up my stuff and drove home.

After twenty-three years of looking after me, Betty Lerner retired. She was the best! I always said if I ever wanted to start a company, she would be the first person I would hire.

I was left with only one aviation enterprise, Sebastian Aero Services. Robert Taylor had been doing a good job of holding the fort while I decided what I wanted to do with it.

We had discussed a number of options: buy a few more airplanes and build up the flight school division, acquire a larger airplane and focus on the air taxi side, or hire a few more mechanics and increase the maintenance department.

As the year 2015 slowly passed, I still hadn't made a decision.

CHAPTER 94

The Last Aviation Enterprise

Gone

LATE IN THE YEAR, I was approached by Stephen Fisher, owner of an aircraft rental business, who expressed an interest in the company. It suited his plans perfectly, and over the next few months we came to an agreement. In February 2016, he purchased Sebastian Aero Services.

He had picked me up earlier that morning in his Piper Cherokee aircraft, and now, after we had signed all the papers and shook hands, it was time to head back to Wellington.

"Hey, Tom," he said in his strong British accent, "let's fly you back home to Wellington. I've got to get right back up here. I have a business to run."

THE END

Epilogue

I WAITED ON THE RAMP in front of my hangar until Stephen took off.

I could hear him revving up the engine out at the airstrip as he performed his preflight checks.

Soon I heard him apply the takeoff power to the engine, and I knew that momentarily I would see his airplane pass the trees that hid my house from the runway.

He used the runway that headed toward the southeast, and as he passed my house, he made a right turn toward the west, dipped his wing as if to say, "good-bye," and soon he disappeared to the north.

I turned and walked through my aircraft hangar, past my airplane, the ancient Fairchild trainer, and into my library.

I had promised my grandchildren that someday I would sit down and write my memoirs. Now, finally after sixty years, I had no aviation interest as an excuse, so this just might be the time to do it.

But, how do you start a book?

You should have "motivation." Let's see, I suppose a promise to my grandkids is motivation enough.

You should have "purpose." Since a biography is nothing more than a long obituary, that's a good purpose.

But there must be something more. There must be something there that the grandkids can take with them as they prepare for that great roller-coaster ride of life. Something about "striving for excellence." Something about "not being afraid to fail," and something about "even if you do happen to fail, get back up and try again."

But…I am so stupid. The answer is right here on my desk, framed. I have placed this quote on every desk that I have ever worked at, and I have referred to it often. It has invigorated me and often inspired me to make it "just one more day."

Teddy Roosevelt said it better in one page than I did in 627 pages.

"It is not the critic that counts, not the man who points out how the strong man stumbled or where the doer of deeds could have done better.
The credit belongs to the man who is actually in the arena………"

Gulfstream International Airlines first aircraft
"The Queen of the Fleet". *Our only aircraft.*

On the ramp at Miami International Airport, 1994
"What a difference three years *made"*

Captain Jim Taylor. A former co-pilot with me at Eastern and Gulfstream's first chief pilot.

Jim Barrows refurbished the interior of our first aircraft and was a mainstay of our maintenance department as we grew.

With my 1943 PT-26 filming a promotional segment for GIA

The Special Olympics team ready to take off.

KEY WEST WAS NOT ALL WORK

The annual Key West "Fantasy Fest" parade was hard work but someone had to do it.

And of course there was the annual "Miss Hawaiian Sun Tan" contest that Gulfstream was asked to help judge. I always accepted the challenge. That's Roy Cantor, our station manager there, on the far end, assisting me.

The Man in The Arena...

WHAT AN EGO TRIP

1995 Top Ten Newsmakers

Tom Cooper
Gulfstream International Airlines

There is a widely held belief in the airline industry that the era of airlines run by pilots has ended, that the bankers have taken over. But just as the bumblebee has been proven to be aerodynamically incapable of flight, some pilots haven't gotten the word so, like the bumblebee, they keep on flying–and running airlines.

The case in point is Thomas Cooper, founder, president and CEO of Gulfstream International Airlines. Cooper was an Eastern Airlines captain when that airline ceased operations, leaving him and a lot of other people on the beach.

Cooper has been overheard to remark that he had been an airline pilot for many years and then, "Eastern went and I had to get a real job!"

So he formed his own airline. It started slowly with a single Cessna 402B piston twin providing on-demand air-taxi service between the Miami area and Haiti. Then in 1989 the airline received FAA certification as a Part 135 regional carrier and the route structure began to expand into the Bahamas. By the end of 1995 the company served 27 destinations, ranging from New Orleans to Atlanta, throughout Florida and the Bahamas.

A major milestone came in May 1994 when Gulfstream International signed a code-sharing arrangement with United Airlines that has turned the bottom-line ink from red to black.

A gauge of how the company has grown during its relatively short lifespan can be made by charting total passengers boarded each year. In 1992 the total was 23,368. In 1993 the number had more than tripled to 83,799. The 1995 total, according to projections based on the first six months of the year, was expected to reach 330,000.

Gulfstream made headlines last year when it signed on as North American launch customer for an airplane that so far exists only in the form of a flying prototype. The aircraft is the Indonesian IPTN N-250 turboprop. Gulfstream has signed firm orders for four of the 64-seat turboprops and has taken options on another six.

More recently, as of the end of November, Gulfstream received approval to transition from Part 135 to Part 121 operations, a change necessitated by the acquisition of 36-seat Shorts 360s. However, Cooper said, "We have

been operating under many of the more stringent regulations for some time now. Safety has always been our first priority and we will continue to work with FAA and NTSB to identify any and all areas where safety can be enhanced."

Last October the company took delivery of the first of five Shorts 360s and hired its first flight attendant as required by the Part 121 regulations.

At year's end the Gulfstream fleet consisted of 18 Beech 1900s and two Shorts 360s. By July 1 this year, the company expects to have 19 Beech 1900s and five Shorts 360s on line.

Looking ahead, Tom Cooper keeps his eyes open for further under-served markets in his area. For example: Gulfstream is one of the small handful of U.S. airlines that legally flies to and from Cuba. The company provides a weekly charter flight for the U.S. government, carrying people and supplies to and from the U.S. Interests Section in Havana. "We don't make much money on those charters," says Cooper, "but I think it's worthwhile just to maintain a presence there; we may be able to get in on the ground floor when and if Cuba ever opens up for the average American."

In some airlines, going to Part 121 would mean letting go some superannuated pilots who have passed the magic age of 60 but were still legal under Part 135. However, that doesn't apply at Gulfstream; all the pilots are well below 60, with one notable exception–Cooper himself. He isn't totally grounded, though. Last year Cooper went to Norman, Okla. and flew back a reconditioned "like new" Fairchild PT-26 of the type in which hundreds of World War II pilots took their initial instrument training. "I was probably six years old when that airplane was built," he laughed.

He admits he avoids any high-G maneuvers in the old bird; there's a lot of 50- to 60-year-old wood in the wing-fuselage attach points. But the occasional gentle loop or slow roll is just fine. –D.A.

Flattered, but I learned, never believe your press clipings

Captain Thomas L. Cooper

"NO NONSENSE" FLIGHT TRAINING

GULFSTREAM INTERNATIONAL AIRLINES *World Training Center*

Teaching *students not only to be superb pilots
but to be the finest aviators in the industry
by emphasing dress code, discipline and character along with flying skills.*

THE MAN IN THE ARENA...

THE FLORIDA PANTHERS RAT MASCOT CAPER

TV cameras catching me celebrate the Panthers reaching the Stanly Cup playoffs by painting their fan's acclaimed mascot on one of our aircrtaft

The nickname "Cheezer" on the aircraft went viral and we got calls from around the world.

A nice thank you letter from the Panthers management

THE CUBA BUSINESS BLOSSOMS

That's me awarding Sr. Tony Diaz, manager of Havanatur, a trophy which his team won by defeating our "Gulfstream All-stars" in softball in Havana. They gave us a good lesson in not only soft ball but in international relationship. Our players came away with a new perspective on Cuba and its wonderful people.

Dra. Mayda Moline, the Director of Aero Transport and International relations of the Institute of Civil Aeronautics of Cuba and a good friend.

Sr. Roberto Brown, Head of the Departmento Permisos y Planificacion de los Vuelos of CACSA. The Cuban agency tha issues landing permits in Cuba. We've been friends for over forty years.

The Hotel Nacional, My" home" in Havana

Gregorio Fuentes, first mate on the Pilar, Hemingway's boat and said to have been the inspiration of Santiago, hero of Hemingway's novel, "The Old Man and the Sea".

Sr. Salvador Soto. A taxi driver, a writer and my dear friend in Havana

Sr. Tony Vasquez, now retired, was formerly with Havanatur and in charge of all aquatic activities in Cuba including diving and fishing. A special person and a special friend.

My daughter, Cathy (left), relaxing with Wayne Smith's daughter, Melinda, at the Embassy residence in Havana

Captain Thomas L. Cooper

LUNCH WITH FIDEL

My son Tommy and I with Fidel Castro

THE MAN IN THE ARENA...

SENATOR GEORGE MC GOVERN

George McGovern, Wayne Smith, Jerrie and me at our old "watering hole" in Havana, La Bodeguita del Medio in Old Havana.

Senator McGovern preparing for a few turns around the airport pattern in my PT-26. It is the same type that he learned to fly in as a cadet in World War II where he won the Distinguished Flying Cross as captain of a B-24 Liberator.

Relaxing in Havana with my wife, Jerrie and good buddy, Charlie Lawson.

La Bodeguita del Media, a watering hole with a clientele of famous artists and personalities. Note the General Electric logo on the freezer. Has it been there since the bar was opened in 1942? Perhaps, I can't say for sure but I can personally attest to the last 60 years.

THE COOPER FAMILY

The greatest reward a man can receive is the gift of a wonderful family

FRONT ROW, THE GRAND CHILDREN; Ryan, Madilyn and Jacob Cooper. Christopher, Bridgette and Bradley Brunk.

BACK ROW; My son, Tommy and his wife Melissa. My wife, Jerrie and me. My daughter Cathryn Mary and her husband Stephen Brunk

Acknowledgments

- TO MY PARENTS, PAUL and Pearl, who taught me right from wrong by their actions, not shallow words.
- To my teachers at Allen Jay High School who laid the foundation of learning that remains with me today.
- To all my "hangar flying" pals at Fraley Field and especially Mr. John Spencer, the aviation guru who soloed me and to all the others; Dwight Lohr who taught me to laugh, to Pete Dickens who taught me to be an aviator and to Melvin Robinson who taught me how to REALLY fly.
- To Mary Gaffaney, aviatrix extraordinaire, who gave me my first job in aviation.
- To all my buddies during the "maelstrom" years; Dick O'Mara, Bob Jones, Carol Kern, Chuck Hudson and the many others, who marched through that period with me and gave support when I needed it.
- To all the Eastern Airline folks, management and employees alike who loved Her as I did and did what they believed was the right thing to do for Her survival.
- To all the Gulfstream International Airlines employees who, without their skills and professional dedication, the company would not have succeeded.
- To Gary Kozan, neighbor, friend, fellow aviator and serious critic who gave invaluable assistance to the editing of this book.
- And finally; to Betty Lerner, my long time assistant of 23 years, of whom I have often said; "If I ever wanted to start up another company, she would be the first person that I would hire.